Property Loss Adjusting

Property Loss Adjusting

Donna J. Popow, J.D., CPCU, AIC
Director of Curriculum
American Institute for CPCU/Insurance Institute of America

Third Edition

American Institute for Chartered Property Casualty Underwriters/
Insurance Institute of America
720 Providence Road, Malvern, Pennsylvania 19355

Third Edition • Second Printing • March 2004

Library of Congress Control Number: 2003111540
ISBN 0-89463-140-3
Printed in Canada

Foreword

The American Institute for Chartered Property Casualty Underwriters and the Insurance Institute of America are independent, nonprofit organizations serving the educational needs of the risk management, property-casualty, and financial services businesses. The Institutes develop a wide range of curricula, study materials, and examinations in response to the educational needs of various elements of these businesses. The American Institute confers the Chartered Property Casualty Underwriter (CPCU®) professional designation on people who meet its examination, ethics, and experience requirements. The Insurance Institute of America offers associate designations and certificate programs in the following areas:

- Accounting and Finance
- Agent Studies
- Business Writing
- Claims
- Global Risk Management and Insurance
- Information Technology
- Insurance Fundamentals
- Management
- Marine Insurance
- Performance Improvement
- Personal Insurance
- Premium Auditing
- Regulation and Compliance
- Reinsurance
- Risk Management
- Surety Bonds and Crime Insurance
- Surplus Lines
- Underwriting

The American Institute was founded in 1942 through a cooperative effort between property-casualty insurance company executives and insurance professors. Faculty members at The Wharton School of the University of Pennsylvania in Philadelphia led this effort. The CPCU designation arose from the same type of business and academic partnership at Wharton as the Chartered Life Underwriter (CLU) designation did in 1927.

The Insurance Institute of America was founded in 1909 by five educational organizations across the United States. It is the oldest continuously functioning national organization offering educational programs for the property-casualty insurance business. It merged with the American Institute in 1953.

The Insurance Research Council (IRC), founded in 1977, is a division of the Institutes. It is a not-for-profit research organization that examines public policy issues that affect property-casualty insurers and their customers. IRC research reports are distributed widely to insurance-related organizations, public policy authorities, and the media.

The broad knowledge base in property-casualty insurance and financial services created by the Institutes over the years is contained mainly in our textbooks. Although we use electronic technology to enhance our educational materials, communicate with our students, and deliver our examinations, our textbooks are at the heart of our educational activities. They contain the information that you as a student must read, understand, integrate into your existing knowledge, and apply to the tasks you perform as part of your job.

Despite the vast range of subjects and purposes of the more than eighty individual textbook volumes we publish, they all have much in common. First, each book is specifically designed to increase knowledge and develop skills that can improve job performance and help students achieve the educational objectives of the course for which it is assigned. Second, all of the manuscripts for our texts are reviewed widely before publication, by both insurance business practitioners and members of the risk management and insurance academic community. In addition, the revisions of our texts often incorporate improvements that students and course leaders have suggested. We welcome constructive comments that help us to improve the quality of our study materials. Please direct any comments you may have on this text to my personal attention.

We hope what you learn from your study of this text will expand your knowledge, increase your confidence in your skills, and support your career growth. If so, then you and the Institutes will truly be *succeeding together*.

Terrie E. Troxel, Ph.D., CPCU, CLU
President and CEO
American Institute for CPCU
Insurance Institute of America

Preface

This text was written for use in the Insurance Institute of America's Associate in Claims (AIC) designation program. AIC 35, Property Loss Adjusting, is a key element in the Personal Insurance Homeowners path and the Commercial Insurance Property path in attaining the AIC designation.

The first four chapters of this text deal with coverage for property losses. Chapters 1 and 2 discuss property insurance concepts in a general way. Chapter 3 reviews homeowners coverage, and Chapter 4 reviews commercial property coverage under the Building and Personal Property Coverage Form and the related causes of loss forms. The remaining chapters of this text concern specific types of losses:

- Fraudulent losses
- Catastrophic losses
- Residential building and contents losses
- Merchandise losses
- Business income losses
- Inland marine and specialty property losses
- Auto physical damage and contractors' equipment losses

The following reviewers contributed substantially to the accuracy and clarity of this text: John A. Chionchio, Esq., P.E.; Anthony Clark, AIC, RPA; Thomas Curry, Esq.; Elise M. Farnham, CPCU, CPIW; Thomas K. Genett, CPCU; Joseph B. Green, AIC; Fred L. Harlow, AIC; Patrick Jeremy, CPCU, AIC, RPA; Douglas Kent, Esq.; David W. Mandt, CPCU; Tony D. Nix, CPCU, CIFI; William C. Stewart, Jr., CPCU, AIC, RPA; Marcia Sweeney, CPCU, AIC, ARM; Kenneth A. Travers, CFPS, ARM, MBA.

The work of the contributing authors to the second edition of this text carries over to this edition, and the Institutes acknowledges them here: Robert G. Anderson; Tracy A. Bachtell, CPCU, AIC; Linda L. Bean, Esq., CPCU, AIC; Robert A. Bender, CPCU; Michael H. Boyer; Walter E. Gilpin, CPCU, AIC; John A. Haight, CPCU, AIC; James T. Hargrove, Esq.; Susan L. Henn; Timothy R. Keary, CPCU; James J. Markham, CPCU, AIC, AIAF; Frank G. Mastro; and Layne S. Thompson, CPCU.

The Institutes give special thanks to the following organization for contributing photographs used in this text:

National Property & Casualty Claims Research Services, Inc. (NPCCRS), Publisher of the ADR and PDR reports. Phone: (717) 776-3900, Fax: (717) 776-3969, Website: http//www.npccrs.com.

We welcome your comments on this text.

Donna J. Popow

Contributing Author

The American Institute for CPCU, the Insurance Institute of America, and the author of this text acknowledge, with deep appreciation, the work of the following contributing author:

Richard C. Kelly, Esq.

Contents

Chapter 1

Direct Your Learning

Property Insurance: Insurable Interests, Property, Causes of Loss

After learning the subject matter of this chapter, you should be able to:

- Explain the extent and importance of an insurable interest in a given loss situation.
- Explain how the rights of those with insurable interest are protected.
- Describe the differences in insurance coverage for real property, personal property, fixtures, and improvements and betterments.
- Explain the evolution of covered perils.
- Explain the difference in the coverage analysis of a specified-perils policy and a risk of direct physical loss policy.
- Explain how the burden of proof for a specified-perils policy differs from the burden of proof for a risk of direct physical loss policy.
- Describe how definitions and additional coverages affect covered causes of loss in a policy.
- Describe the various perils typically insured under property insurance.
- Explain why various exclusions are included in property policies and what the common exclusions are.
- Explain the concept of concurrent causation and the various approaches used to deal with it.

OUTLINE

Develop Your Perspective

What are the main topics covered in the chapter?

This chapter introduces the concepts of property interests, different types of property, and various causes of loss.

Analyze a property loss.

- Whose interests are protected by a property policy?
- What types of property are covered by a property policy?
- What causes of loss are insured against by a property policy?

Why is it important to know these topics?

To properly adjust a claim under a property policy, a property loss adjuster must understand the various property interests and whether they are insured under a policy. The adjuster must also be able to classify the types of property found at a loss to correctly calculate insurance to value. Finally, the adjuster must be able to properly identify the cause of loss and determine whether the policy covers it.

How can you use this information?

Review a property policy upon assignment of a loss.

- As a property loss adjuster handling a property loss, what policy provisions would you need to review to make a proper adjustment of the loss?

Chapter 1

Property Insurance: Insurable Interests, Property, Causes of Loss

Property losses are featured prominently in the news, with reports detailing cases ranging from mild property damage caused by inclement weather or vandalism to devastating accidents, catastrophes, and natural disasters.

The news does not always show such losses' aftermath, but most of the people whose property is damaged are insured and receive payments for their losses from insurers, often within days. The insurance industry fulfills its promises and obligations to its insureds through the work of property loss adjusters. Property loss adjusting is one of the most gratifying, and one of the most demanding, careers in the property-casualty insurance industry.

Property loss adjusters must have a detailed understanding of insurance policies; a vast knowledge of property values, costs, and repair methods; and at least a working knowledge of accounting and construction methods and materials. Additionally, property loss adjusters must be tactful and sensitive in dealing with insureds who have suffered great stress and anxiety from their losses. Adjusters must also detect and prove fraudulent claims.

This text presents major property loss adjusting principles. Although it does not require a student's prior knowledge of property loss adjusting, the text develops the key concepts to a substantially expert level. The homeowners HO-3 form, 2000 edition, and the commercial property Building and Personal Property Coverage Form (BPP), 2002 edition, from Insurance Services Office, Inc., (ISO) are used in the text as representative policies. Other forms exist, from ISO, from other rating bureaus, and from specific insurers, so a property loss adjuster must learn to review the policy on each loss.

This chapter begins the analysis of property loss adjusting with a general discussion of who and what are covered under property insurance policies. It also discusses related insurance principles as well as policy forms and provisions that grant or limit coverage. Insurance protects people, not property. Although every policy limits its coverage to specific property or types of property, property loss adjusters should focus on who is insured and what the insured's interests are in the property to determine coverage. This is a key part of the property loss adjusting process. Another part of the process concerns the different types of property insured under the policy. Finally, this chapter concludes with a discussion of the various causes of loss and exclusions found in property coverage forms.

INSURABLE INTEREST

Insurable interest
An interest that exists when the insured derives a monetary benefit or advantage by the preservation and continued existence of property or would suffer a monetary loss from its destruction.

Insurable interest in property at the time of a loss is an underlying principle that makes the property insurance system work. It helps to determine who should recover in a loss situation. An **insurable interest** exists when someone derives a monetary benefit or advantage by the property's preservation and continued existence or would suffer a monetary loss from its destruction. In other words, if a person will suffer a financial loss if a piece of property is damaged or destroyed, that person has an insurable interest in that property. Additionally, to recover the loss amount resulting from the property damage, that person must have an insurable interest in the property at the time of loss.

What Are the Purposes of the Insurable Interest Requirement?

The insurable interest requirement in property insurance policies serves three purposes. See the following box.

Three Purposes of Insurable Interest Requirement

1. To indemnify the proper people for the proper amount
2. To prevent wagering on losses
3. To deter people from committing fraud or intentionally causing a loss

Each of these purposes is discussed in the following sections.

Indemnification

Contract of indemnity
A contract under which the insured is entitled to payment only if he or she has suffered a covered loss and then only up to the extent of the financial loss actually suffered.

An insurance policy is a **contract of indemnity.** It is designed to restore an insured who has suffered a loss to the same financial condition as before the loss. A person who has no insurable interest would, by definition, not suffer any financial loss if the property were damaged. Insurable interest is not acquired by simply paying the policy premium. Furthermore, someone who has an insurable interest should recover no more than the value of his or her interest. However, a policy that indemnifies the insured based on current replacement cost allows the insured to collect more than the property's value at the time of the loss. While this technically violates the indemnity concept, the insured does pay a premium to obtain this extra coverage.

Wagering

Preventing wagering is important for legal as well as ethical reasons. Insurance differs from gambling because when a person places a bet, he or she hopes to win more than the amount wagered. Gambling results in one of two possible outcomes: the bettor either loses money or wins money. With insurance, an insured pays the premium, then either has a loss during the policy period or does not. After a loss, the insured receives just enough money from the insurer to pay for the loss, and no more. Insureds should not make a profit from insurance. However, replacement cost coverage can be viewed as a means of profiting from a loss, so adjusters must be vigilant for the potential for fraud when handling losses involving replacement cost coverage. The insurable interest requirement prevents wagering by removing the possibility for gain. If the insured has no loss, the insurance company uses his or her premium to help pay for other policyholders' losses. Even when no loss occurs, the insured pays for, and receives, protection and peace of mind.

Suppose that John could purchase a policy on Richard's house. John has no insurable interest in Richard's house, but he thinks buying a policy might be a good investment because Richard's house might burn down. In this situation, John is wagering his premium in the hope that Richard has a loss. Without the insurable interest requirement, a loss would allow John to collect money on the claim, and John would have no duty to use the money to repair the house. The entire payment would be profit, or winnings on his bet. Without the insurable interest requirement, many people could profit in such a manner from others' losses.

Fraud

The insurable interest doctrine discourages insureds from committing fraud or intentionally causing a loss. In the case of John and Richard, if John had paid premiums on Richard's house for a few years but never had any claims to file, he might start a fire just to make money.

If this scenario seems far-fetched, it is because the insurable interest doctrine makes it rare. The insurable interest requirement, established centuries ago, still works well. Without the insurable interest requirement, such crimes would be common. Yet adjusters must remain alert for potentially fraudulent claims and investigate insurable interest in each loss.

Who Has an Insurable Interest?

An insurable interest is not limited to the property owners. Also, the named insured on a particular policy does not automatically have an insurable interest at the time of the loss. Only four types of interest are considered insurable interests. See the following box.

> **Four Types of Insurable Interests**
>
> People with the following types of interest in property have insurable interests:
>
> 1. Ownership interests
> 2. Occupancy interests
> 3. Custody interests
> 4. Security interests

Ownership Interests

Ownership interests can exist in various forms for both personal and business personal property and for real property.

Personal Ownership

Personal ownership means that the person who owns the property has the right to use it, change it, sell it, rent it, or dispose of it in any way that he or she chooses.

A homeowner often has a home mortgage, but the homeowner's insurable interest is for the property's full value, including equity and the mortgage amount. A homeowner is entitled to purchase enough insurance to protect both equity and debt because, in case of a serious loss, the homeowner would still be personally responsible for repaying the mortgage debt, or balance. Thus, a homeowner has an insurable interest for the portion of the home owned free and clear (equity) and the portion on which the bank has a lien (the mortgage balance).

Property is often owned in some form other than full individual ownership. Other types of ownership include joint owners, tenancy in common, and life tenants.

Joint owners/tenants
Two or more persons each having a full interest in the property. Each tenant has an insurable interest to the full extent of the property value.

Tenancy by the entireties
A type of joint tenancy available only to a husband and wife.

Tenancy in common
The ownership of property, in equal or unequal shares, by two or more joint tenants who lack survivorship rights.

1. *Joint owners*. **Joint owners,** or **joint tenants**, are two or more persons each having a full interest in the property. On the death of any joint tenant, the remaining tenant or tenants continue to have full ownership of the entire property. Each joint tenant has an insurable interest to the full extent of the property value. However, an adjuster making settlement should include all joint tenants on the settlement draft. In the case of a husband and wife, joint tenancy is known as **tenancy by the entireties**.
2. *Tenancy in common*. When two or more persons own a piece of property, but each has a distinct fractional, or percentage, interest, they are a **tenancy in common**. Collectively, these tenants have an insurable interest to the full extent of the property value, but each tenant's interest is limited to his or her respective fractional value. Loss settlement should be made with all members of the tenancy in common collectively.

3. *Life tenants*. Someone entitled to a piece of real property's full use and possession for his or her life is known as a **life tenant**. That person is said to have a **life estate** in the property. Upon the life tenant's death, the full interest in the property passes to someone else. Life tenants may not leave any interest by will to their heirs. Life tenants have a legal duty to preserve the property for the party with the future interest. This legal duty plus the life tenancy itself confer upon life tenants an insurable interest to the full extent of the property value.

Life tenant (life estate)
A person entitled to full use and possession of property for his or her life. Life tenants have an insurable interest to the extent of the full value of the property.

Note that joint tenants, those in a tenancy in common, and life tenants are not tenants under a lease, as described later in this chapter in the section on occupancy interests.

Business Ownership

Businesses also own property, but ownership rights depend on the type of business. The most common types of business ownership are sole proprietorships, partnerships, and corporations.

1. *Sole proprietorship*. In a **sole proprietorship,** one person owns the business's assets and is personally liable for the business's debts.
2. *Partnership*. A **partnership** exists when two or more people voluntarily join in business. They share in both the business's profits and losses. All partnership property is owned in common by the partners, all of whom have an interest in the property. Most states provide a statutory distinction between general and limited partners. General partners' personal assets can be liquidated to pay the partnership's debts. In contrast, limited partners' liability would be limited to the partners' individual investments.
3. *Corporation*. A corporation is a legal entity created for the purpose of conducting business, either for profit or as a nonprofit organization. As legal entities, corporations can own and transfer property, sue, and be sued in their own names. Executive officers, members of the board of directors, other officers, and even stockholders all have a role in the business's operation. A corporation's daily operation is usually managed by the officers, but all other parties stand to gain or lose depending on the business's success.

Sole proprietorship
A form of business in which one person owns the business assets and is personally liable for the business's debts.

Partnership
An agreement in which two or more people voluntarily join in business to share the profits and losses.

The main difference between a corporation and a partnership or a sole proprietorship is the so-called **corporate veil**. This veil insulates the assets of the corporation's owners in case the corporation goes bankrupt. The corporation's owners, the stockholders, are not personally liable for the corporation's debts.

Corporate veil
A doctrine that insulates the assets of the owners of the corporation in case the corporation goes bankrupt. The corporation's owners, the stockholders, are not personally liable for the corporation's debts.

A corporation that owns property is, in many ways, like a private citizen who owns a home. The corporation has the right to sell, change, rent, improve, or dispose of the property as it sees fit. The corporation can also purchase enough insurance to cover its interest in the property.

Limited liability corporation (LLC)
A business entity that insulates its members from creditors and lawsuits brought against the business.

The **limited liability corporation (LLC)** is becoming a more prevalent business entity. Each state has a law that either allows or forbids the formation of a limited liability corporation. The LLC is attractive because it insulates its members from creditors and lawsuits brought against the business while having a partnership's tax advantages. The LLC has the same ability to own, sell, rent, change, or improve property as a regular corporation.

Occupancy Interests

Tenant, or **lessee**
Someone who pays to use, possess, or occupy property belonging to another.

Someone who pays to use, possess, or occupy property belonging to another is a **tenant,** or **lessee**. Tenants usually sign a contract, or lease, for a certain time period. The insurable interest arises out of the property's use value for the time remaining on the lease or rental agreement.

If a tenant signs a lease for twenty years at a rent of $1,000 per month, and the building burns down before the lease is up, the tenant must find another building. The new rent for a comparable building might increase to $2,500 per month. Thus, the tenant bears the risk of losing $1,500 per month if the original lease is terminated.

Tenants who lease buildings for an extended time period often make improvements and betterments to the building. These improvements are at the tenant's (lessee's) expense and, according to most leases, would remain in the building when the tenant leaves. If the improvements are damaged or if the building is damaged and the lease is terminated, the tenant would lose either the money invested in the improvements or the use of those improvements for the remainder of the lease.

For example, suppose XYZ TV, a television retail business, rents space from a landlord. To store and display its TVs, XYZ must install shelves and counters. Interior walls must also be built, and extra electrical outlets must be added. All of these improvements cost $50,000, and XYZ must pay for them. XYZ has signed a ten-year lease and plans on using the building and the improvements for at least that much time. If a fire damages the building, XYZ would have to pay at least $50,000 to rebuild the improvements. If the lease is terminated, XYZ would have to relocate and make improvements in the new premises.

Many lessees sublease all or part of the property to another tenant for a profit. Under these circumstances, the lessee would potentially lose income as a lessor if the building were to become damaged and untenantable. Improvements and betterments are further discussed later in this chapter.

Custody Interests

Custody interests include those of bailees, consignees, common carriers, and trustees.

Bailees

Bailees are people and businesses who take possession of others' property for a specific purpose and for a limited time. Examples include repair shops, cleaners, and printers. A bailee has interest in the property up to the value of the material, labor, storage, or other unpaid charges incurred by the bailor (The bailor is the party who hands over the goods to the bailee. In most, but not all, situations, the bailor is the property owner.). For example, someone who repairs computers might spend time and buy materials fixing a computer for a customer, but a fire might damage the computer before it is returned to the customer. The bailee cannot receive payment for the work because the computer has been damaged. The bailee needs insurance protection for the amount of time and money that he or she invested in the computer. Moreover, the bailee might be legally liable to financially compensate the customer for the computer's full value. Liability for replacing the computer is another interest of the bailee handled by insurance.

Bailee
A party who takes possession of property of others for a specific purpose and for a limited time.

Consignees

A **consignee** is a person or a business holding property owned by someone else for the purpose of selling it. When the sale is made, the consignee earns a percentage of the sale or another fee for this service. If the property is damaged before it can be sold, the consignee loses the fee. This loss represents an insurable interest of the consignee. Furthermore, consignees might be legally liable to the owner for the property's value and should protect themselves against such liability.

Consignee
A person or a business holding property owned by someone else for the purpose of selling it.

Common Carriers

Bus lines, airlines, and other transportation businesses that are required by law to convey passengers and property for a price are called **common carriers**. If property is damaged on a common carrier before it is safely delivered, the carrier might lose its freight charges for services rendered. Additionally, common carriers might be legally liable for damage to property in their possession and must protect themselves against such liability.

Common carriers
Bus lines, airlines, and other types of transportation that are required by law to convey passengers and property for a price.

Trustees, Guardians, Administrators, and Executors

Property or assets belonging to minors or incompetent people are sometimes placed in the care of a trustee, or guardian. This **trustee,** or **guardian,** has the legal title to the property but is responsible that it be used, handled, and transferred solely for the beneficiary's benefit. The trustee or guardian has an insurable interest up to the full extent of the property value because he or she would be required to compensate the trust or estate if the property were damaged. Likewise, administrators and executors of deceased persons' estates have an interest to the full extent of the property value.

Trustee, or **guardian**
Someone who has the legal title to a property but is responsible that it be used, handled, and transferred solely for the benefit of the beneficiary.

Security interest
An interest in property (real or personal) that allows the property to be sold on default to satisfy the debt for which the security interest was given.

Mortgage
An interest in land created by a written document that provides security for the payment of a debt.

Mortgagee
A secured creditor—usually a bank or another financial institution—that made a mortgage loan to a borrower (called the mortgagor) to enable the borrower to purchase real property.

Loss payee
A party entitled to share in whatever loss payment an insured receives.

Lien
A right or claim that provides the lienholder with security for payment of a debt or duty.

Mechanic's lien
A lien granted by law to anyone who repairs a specific piece of property.

Tax lien
A type of lien held by local, state, and federal governments through operation of law in the amount of unpaid taxes and interest.

Judgment lien
A lien, in favor of the holder of a judgment, that attaches to the property of the one who owes the judgment.

Security Interests

Security interests involve those who hold a mortgage or another type of lien on property, such as a mechanics lien or a judgment lien.

Mortgage Interest

A **mortgage** transfers an interest to a mortgagee. The **mortgagee** is the bank, financial institution, or person who lends money to the buyer to finance the purchase of the property. The mortgagee takes the mortgage as security for the loan. The loan's unpaid balance is the extent of the mortgagee's interest. Once recorded on city or county records, mortgages give the mortgagee priority over all other subsequently secured interests and creditors if a foreclosure occurs. A security interest in the mortgagor's personal property is called a chattel mortgage. Mortgagees receive additional protection in property insurance policies. A mortgagee is entitled to make a claim even if the insured's claim is denied.

Loss Payee

A **loss payee** is a person or an entity, other than a mortgagee, who will be paid if a property loss occurs. The loss payee can be named in the declarations or by endorsement. Loss payees are usually owners of equipment leased to the insured, or they are the purchasers/sellers under a contract of sale. They do not receive the additional protection afforded by the policy to mortgagees.

Other Lienholders

Like a mortgage, a **lien** provides the lienholder with security in the event of property foreclosure. The lienholder's interest must be protected before any general creditor can benefit from a foreclosure. Liens can arise out of the operation of the law or because the owner has granted a lien.

The law grants a **mechanic's lien** to anyone who works on or repairs a specific piece of property. Liens can be held on real property (for example, a roofer would have a mechanic's lien on a house on which he or she has worked) or on personal property (an auto mechanic who has worked on an auto would also have a mechanic's lien). The lien is for the value of the work performed. Local, state, and federal governments might have **tax liens** in the amount of unpaid taxes and interest on a property through operation of law. **Judgment liens** arise out of court verdicts. Property owners do not voluntarily incur any of these types of liens; they all exist by operation of law.

A property owner might, however, voluntarily grant a lien on his or her property to borrow money from a lender who insists on such security. A mortgage is this type of lien. Such security liens are also commonly associated with expensive personal property, such as autos and machinery. Often, the party that sells the property provides the financing for the purchase and obtains a **purchase money security interest**. This is a lien with special priority in certain circumstances. The holder of a purchase money security interest would have priority in a foreclosure over subsequent lienholders or general creditors. A second mortgage is a security lien on real property, but with a lower priority in foreclosure than a first mortgage.

Purchase money security interest
A type of security interest that gives the holder priority in foreclosure over subsequent lienholders or general creditors.

General Creditors

Although most liens arise out of credit transactions, a general creditor does not automatically have a lien against any specific property and therefore no insurable interest. Unless the owner has granted a security interest or the creditor has obtained a judgment lien, a general creditor has no interest in any specific property of the debtor.

Who Does Not Have an Insurable Interest?

Before a loss, an insured's rights under an insurance policy cannot be assigned without the insurer's consent. However, after a loss, the insured may assign its right to collect on the claim. The assignee does not have insurable interest in the property. Instead, the assignee has a contractual right to the claim payment. For example, when an owner sells property, the rights or benefits due on a claim but not yet received can be assigned by contract agreement. A homeowner who is selling his or her home with a damaged roof may assign the anticipated claim payment from the insurance company to pay for a new roof. In the sales agreement, the seller gets full value for the house but assigns the policy benefits to the buyer. Therefore, the buyer must rely on the insurance coverage to pay for the roof, which was damaged before the sale took place. The **assignee** did not have an interest in the property at the time of the loss and would have had no claim for the damage, except for the assignment of benefits.

Assignee
The individual or entity to whom property, rights, or interests have been transferred.

How Are the Rights of Those With Insurable Interests Protected?

Insurance policies normally protect the rights of those with insurable interests by listing them as named insureds, mortgagees, or loss payees. Mortgagees have rights under insurance policies separate from the named insureds' rights. Loss payees do not.

Lienholders, assignees, and other security interest holders do not have the same protection as mortgagees. Most policies have no special clauses designed for them, but they can be protected by appearing on the policy as a lienholder, a loss payee, or an additional insured. If named, they should be included on all payments of claims and notified if the policy is canceled.

Those who have an insurable interest are responsible for ensuring that they are appropriately named or qualify for coverage under the proper policies. Those who handle claims should verify the various interests in the property as part of the initial investigation and protect all the interests when payments are made.

Named Insureds

When a policy is purchased to protect certain property, the property owners should be listed on the policy as named insureds. Their interest is primary and provable by the title. The insured or the insured's agent should be especially careful to list the property owners' names on the policy in exactly the same way as they appear on the title to avoid any misunderstanding should a claim arise.

Occupants have several ways to insure their interests. For example, tenants often carry coverage on their personal property only and leave the landlord to cover the building. A common alternative occurs when the owner/landlord requires the tenant to insure the building and to list the owner/landlord as an additional insured. This practice prevents duplicate coverage for the building while still protecting the interests of both owner and tenant.

Special policies are written for bailees and other custodians of property that protect the bailee for legal liability or for the labor and materials invested in the property. The property owner is not protected unless the bailee is legally liable for the loss. In contrast, bailees' customers policies, storekeepers policies, and other similar policies cover the interest of the owner as well as the bailee without regard for the bailee's legal liability. Common carriers have their own types of policies to cover the liability imposed on them by statute. Furthermore, shippers can obtain coverage for their property that is in a carrier's possession.

Trustees who have a long-term responsibility for the care of property are usually named on the policy as named or additional insureds.

The Mortgage Clause

The most common security interest is that of the mortgageholder. A special mortgage clause, which gives the mortgagee rights and duties independent of the named insured, is included in all property policies written for buildings. The BPP has language similar to the mortgage clause of the HO-3 that reads in part as follows:

> 2. If we deny your claim, that denial will not apply to a valid claim of the mortgagee, if the mortgagee:
>   a. Notifies us of any change in ownership, occupancy or substantial change in risk of which the mortgagee is aware;
>   b. Pays any premium due under this policy on demand if you have neglected to pay the premium; and
>   c. Submits a signed, sworn statement of loss within 60 days after receiving notice from us of your failure to do so. Paragraphs **E.** Appraisal, **G.** Suit against us and **I.** Loss Payment under Section 1—Conditions also apply to the mortgagee.
> 3. If we decide to cancel or not to renew this policy, the mortgagee will be notified at least 10 days before the date cancellation or non-renewal takes effect.

4. If we pay the mortgagee for any loss and deny payment to you:
   a. We are subrogated to all the rights of the mortgagee granted under the mortgage on the property; or
   b. At our option, we may pay to the mortgagee the whole principal on the mortgage plus any accrued interest. In this event, we will receive a full assignment and transfer of the mortgage and all securities held as collateral to the mortgage debt.[1]

In summary, a mortgagee is entitled to make a claim even if the insured's claim can be denied. For example, an insured who is guilty of arson for profit could not collect any insurance proceeds. However, the mortgagee can comply with all of the mortgage clause's provisions and collect up to the balance owed on the mortgage loan, even if the claim resulted from arson committed by an insured.

TYPES OF PROPERTY

Property loss adjusters must determine not only who, but also what, is covered under property insurance policies. They must therefore know property characteristics and property-related insurance principles.

Real property is distinguished from **personal property** under both the law and insurance contracts. See the following box.

Real property
Land and anything that is permanently attached to, embedded in, or growing on the land.

Personal property
All property that is not real property.

Real Property and Personal Property

Generally, land and anything attached to land are considered real property. Buildings and all of the construction materials and elements incorporated in and attached to them are real property.

Everything else is personal property:

- Furniture
- Intellectual property (which is not insurable under a property policy), such as copyrights, trademark rights, and other intangibles such as the value of a business's goodwill
- Machinery
- Merchandise
- Personal effects (called tangible personal property)

The distinction between real and personal property is usually obvious. This section discusses the importance of that distinction for adjusters and highlights cases in which that distinction is not as clear.

Distinction Between Real and Personal Property

The distinction between real and personal property is important to insurance adjusters for several reasons, including the following:

- The possibility of overlapping coverages
- The different valuation methods involved
- The effect on coinsurance requirements

Overlapping Coverages

More than one policy might cover a loss. This overlap happens infrequently with real property. Occasionally, an owner or the owner's insurance agent mistakenly causes two policies to be in effect simultaneously, or a mortgage lender might purchase its own policy during a foreclosure in fear that the owner will allow coverage to lapse. Otherwise, overlapping coverage on real property is unusual.

With personal property, overlapping coverage, though hardly the norm, is much more common. Because of its movable nature, personal property can be located anywhere, including away from the real property in which it is usually housed and/or used. In such situations, coverage might be provided by both the owner's policy and the policy covering the real property where the personal property is located when the loss occurs. Overlapping coverage also occurs with improvements and betterments, further detailed later in this chapter. Other situations of potentially overlapping coverage are described in Chapter 12, which discusses inland marine coverages.

Valuation

All insurance policies stipulate how the covered property is to be valued when a loss occurs. Under many policies, valuation methods differ for real and personal property. For example, the ISO HO-3 homeowner policy values real property at replacement cost and personal property at actual cash value. This difference makes the adjustment process substantially different for real and personal property. Chapter 2 discusses valuation.

Coinsurance Requirements

Coinsurance
A clause that requires the insured to bear a portion of every loss unless the insured carries an adequate amount of insurance.

Coinsurance requirements cause the insured to bear a portion of every loss unless adequate insurance has been purchased. The adequacy of the amount of insurance purchased is measured against the value of the property insured. Sometimes the insured property's value does not include personal property; coinsurance compliance is then measured only against the real property's value. In these cases, the adjuster must be able to ignore personal property and its value when testing coinsurance compliance. Policies can have coinsurance requirements ranging from 0 to 100 percent. The most common percentage is 80 percent. For a loss to be paid in full, with 80 percent coinsurance, the amount of insurance purchased must be equal to

80 percent of the property's value at the time of the loss. Coinsurance calculations are shown in Chapter 2.

Fixtures, Trade Fixtures, and Improvements and Betterments

Certain types of property are not clearly real or personal. Such property is discussed below, along with a brief description of how policies treat such property.

The Law of Fixtures

Personal property can become real property by becoming so attached or adapted to real property that it becomes a part of it. In such a case, the property is known as a building fixture. By definition, building fixtures (or just **fixtures**) are part of the real property. All of a building's elements are fixtures, but all construction materials and elements are considered personal property until they are incorporated into a building.

Fixtures
Personal property that becomes real property when attached to, adapted to, or incorporated into a building.

Despite this definition, the term "fixture" is normally applied to a type of property that seems to retain its separate identity. A brick that has been incorporated into a building is legally and technically a fixture but is not normally called by that name. For insurance purposes, the term "fixture" is applied to something that has been added to a building after its original construction, such as a utility sink added by a tenant. A sign on a building might also be considered a fixture.

Some property can be considered as either personal property or fixtures (real property). Drapes, drapery hardware, carpets, shelves, lights, large appliances and machinery, and building ornamentation can be either personal property or fixtures, depending on the circumstances of installation, construction, ownership, and so on.

No single factor determines whether an object is personal property or a fixture, but the three important considerations in making such a determination are (1) attachment, (2) adaptation, and (3) intent. See the following box.

Attachment

Any property's physical attachment to a structure strongly indicates that the property is a fixture and has become part of the real property.

- However, the attachment would have to be more permanent and secure than, for example, a plug connecting an electrical appliance to an outlet.
- A building's rain gutters, which rest on support brackets, are real property, while a picnic table bolted to the ground to prevent it from being stolen or blown over is probably still personal property.

Continued on next page.

Adaptation

Whether an item is especially adapted to the use of the real property is important in distinguishing between real and personal property. See the following example.

- If property is incorporated into the building or structure and defines the building or structure, it becomes part of the building for insurance purposes. The relationship between a tennis court (which is clearly real property) and the net exemplifies this concept.

  Without the net, the tennis court cannot be used appropriately. The net is incorporated into the court and helps to define the structure as a tennis court. It is specially adapted to the real property's use. As such, it is considered a fixture and thus part of the real property.

  Although it is possible to argue that the net is personal property because the net can be moved easily, the net would more likely be considered part of the real property. This is because the net's function as an integral part of the court is probably more important than its ability to be moved.

Intent

Although subjective, the owner's intent might determine whether certain property is a building fixture. See the following example.

- A restaurant owner might select carpets, drapes, and ornamentation to suit her operation. When she moves to a new location, she might intend to move this property. In this type of case, the intent might be sufficient to deem these objects personal property. The intent to move property from one location to another might qualify an item as personal property even though it is bolted to the structure.

Trade Fixtures

Trade fixtures
Property installed in a structure and used in business, such as shelves, cabinets, and display cases, which the tenant has the right to remove at the end of the lease.

Property installed in a structure and used in a business is often referred to as **trade fixtures**. Trade fixtures can include items such as the following:

- Cabinets
- Cases
- Counters
- Display windows
- Racks
- Shelves

This property might or might not be a fixture in the legal sense. For example, property that is attached to the building but intended only for the tenant's (businessowner's) use and that serves the business rather than the building is personal property. The term "trade fixtures" is firmly entrenched in industry usage and is generally synonymous with "personal property" in insurance policies. As long as the adjuster knows the legal difference between legal fixtures and trade fixtures and knows how a policy applies to all types of property, referring to personal property as a "trade fixture" is appropriate.

Improvements and Betterments

Improvements and betterments are changes made by a tenant to a structure to suit the tenant's purposes. In commercial leases, tenants commonly rent bare space in which all interior walls, finishes, and furnishings must be added. All improvements and betterments are fixtures because they are added to the structure after it was constructed. The term "improvements and betterments" exists because in lease and insurance agreements, treating these types of fixtures separately is important.

Improvements and betterments
Changes made to a structure by a tenant to suit the tenant's purposes.

All leases that allow tenants to install improvements and betterments usually provide (1) that the items can or must be removed at the end of the lease or (2) that ownership of the items will transfer to the landlord at the time of installation or at the end of the lease. The lease provisions determine the extent of the tenant's "use" interest in improvements and betterments. The lease specifies how many years of use the tenant has and whether the tenant can renew the lease.

Because the tenant has a use interest in improvements and betterments, insurance policies have specific provisions for covering such property. Coverage might exist under the landlord's policy or the tenant's policy, or both. In any case, the adjuster must understand the nature and extent of the different interests in improvements and betterments.

DETERMINING COVERAGE FOR A CAUSE OF LOSS

To determine coverage for a given loss, property loss adjusters should systematically analyze the applicable policy. Exhibit 1-1 indicates the steps to determine coverage. Although the steps appear sequentially in the exhibit, coverage analysis does not always follow this sequence. Depending on what is being analyzed, adjusters may find themselves moving from definitions to conditions and then to perils and exclusions. The policy drives the analysis. Yet, regardless of the order of the steps, each of these policy sections are included in the analysis. This discussion assumes that coverage verification (meaning that the policy is in force for the date of loss and that the location is covered by the policy) has already occurred.

EXHIBIT 1-1

Steps in Determining Coverage

1. Determine whether the loss is a direct physical loss.
2. Determine whether the loss was caused by a covered cause of loss.
   2a. Review policy definitions for clarification.
3. Determine whether any additional coverages apply to the loss.
4. Determine whether any exclusions apply to the loss.
5. Determine whether all policy conditions have been met.

Determine Whether the Loss Is a Direct Physical Loss

The first step in determining coverage for a particular loss is to review the insuring agreement and determine whether the loss is a direct physical loss. This section of the chapter explains the meaning of this threshold requirement of policy coverage. An adjuster must next determine whether the policy coverage is specified perils or special form. An adjuster must also review the definitions to see whether they expand or limit the coverage. With a special-form policy (formerly known as an "all-risks" policy), the adjuster must determine whether any exclusions apply. With specified-perils coverage, the adjuster must determine whether any of the listed perils cover an insured's loss and then check to ascertain whether any exclusions apply. Additional coverages might provide coverage that is otherwise excluded or not provided by a policy. Finally, compliance with the policy conditions are as significant to determining coverage as is any other part of the policy.

Direct physical loss
A loss that is physical (not just financial) and results immediately from the occurrence.

Property insurance policies (other than those for time element losses) protect against **direct physical loss** only. Any loss that is not a direct physical loss is not covered. This is true under both special-form and specified-perils policies. To be covered, a loss must be *both* a direct loss and a physical loss caused by a covered peril. To further identify a direct physical loss, as well as to clarify the meanings of other insurance policy terms, see the following box.

Identifying a Direct Physical Loss

Policy forms do not define the phrase "direct physical loss." However, policies do define the meanings of many terms in an insurance policy. To determine or clarify a term's meaning, the following four sources should be consulted in order of priority:

1. Definitions listed in the policy
2. Definitions given to the term by previous court decisions
3. Definitions found in dictionaries or other references
4. Meanings from common usage

Because "direct physical loss" is not defined in insurance policy forms, a definition must be found elsewhere. *Black's Law Dictionary* defines "direct loss" as "one resulting immediately and proximately from the occurrence and not remotely from some other consequences or effects thereof."[2] One dictionary definition of "direct" is "marked by absence of an intervening agency, instrumentality, or influence."[3] An example of a direct loss is a store burning down. An indirect loss associated with the fire would be the loss of market resulting from the store's being closed for six months to rebuild.

Direct Loss

All losses must be "direct" (as defined above). Indirect losses, if covered by insurance, are separate from direct losses. The most important type of indirect loss is the loss of use of property. Whenever property is damaged or destroyed, it cannot be used. Property insurance covers only the value of the damaged or destroyed property, not the loss of use of it while it is repaired or replaced. Coverage for loss of use is separate and is discussed in Chapters 3 and 11.

Physical Loss

A loss is "physical" if it involves tangible property's damage, destruction, or disappearance. Nonphysical losses, if covered by insurance, are separate from physical losses. Nonphysical losses include all kinds of *financial* loss, such as loss of value to an inventory caused by changes in fashion or obsolescence, loss of value to a financial investment such as stocks or bonds, loss of income from an interruption in a business's operation, or loss to a business of customers' goodwill. Likewise, embezzlement, swindling, and other forms of financial fraud are not physical losses and would be covered, if at all, only by special fidelity policies.

Evolution of Covered Perils

Because much of the logic of current insurance policy coverage stems from the historical predecessors of today's policies, this section provides a brief overview of what causes of loss were originally covered and how such coverage evolved. In this discussion, the text uses the terms "causes of loss" and "perils" synonymously.

Among the first types of insurance coverage was fire insurance for commercial and private real property. Only building structures were covered for the peril of fire. Lightning coverage was added later, however, because it became extremely difficult, if not impossible, to separate damage caused by lightning from damage caused by the resulting fire. The so-called standard fire policy legislatively mandated in many states protected against fire and lightning. Because of its historic origins, property insurance is still often referred to as fire insurance.

Other perils were gradually added over the years and formed two types of broader coverages called extended coverage and broad-form coverage.

Extended Coverage

In the late 1930s and early 1940s, the Extended Coverage endorsement was developed. It added seven additional perils to the two (fire and lightning) already covered. These additional perils were the following:

- Windstorm
- Hail
- Explosion
- Riot or civil commotion
- Vehicles
- Aircraft
- Smoke

This package of covered perils forms the foundation of the most basic coverages available today.

Broad-Form Coverage

A new form called the Broad Form endorsement added the following covered perils to the Extended Coverage endorsement:

- Vandalism or malicious mischief
- Breakage of glass in a building, storm door, or window
- Falling objects
- Weight of ice, snow, or sleet
- Collapse of buildings
- Damage resulting from a steam or hot water heating system
- Accidental discharge or overflow of water or steam
- Freezing of plumbing, heating, air conditioning systems, or domestic appliances
- Sudden and accidental damage from artificially generated electrical current

The Extended Coverage endorsement and the Broad Form endorsement only covered losses that were caused by the perils specifically listed in the policy. The package of covered perils available under the Broad Form endorsement is very similar to the Broad Form specified-perils policies available today.

Special-Form Coverage

A Special Form endorsement that provided "all-risks" coverage on fixed real property, covering all losses unless specifically excluded in the policy, arose among inland marine underwriters who offered "all-risks" coverage for property in transit or connected with transportation (bridges and tunnels).

This Special Form endorsement and homeowners policies originally insured "against all risks of physical loss to the property," but the current forms insure "against risks of direct physical loss to the property." The word "all" has been eliminated, although the coverage is intended to be essentially the same as that of the previous forms. The word "all" was eliminated because various courts ruled that if an insurance policy covered "all risks," then that is exactly what the policy must do, regardless of exclusionary language. This text uses the term "special form" to refer to policies that insure against risks of direct physical loss. Some insurers may refer to these types of policies as open-perils policies. If the term "all-risks" is used in the text, it means that the policy specifically states that it is all risks, as some inland marine policies do. Adjusters should be cautious about using the term "all-risks" because it might mislead an insured.

Most of the early stock insurance companies that wrote fire coverages belonged to a rating bureau that represented a group of insurers from designated territories. Rating bureaus developed standard policy forms and set the specific coverage rates. The insurance companies had to send copies of their fire policies (dailies) to their specific bureau, where they were reviewed to make sure that the proper premium was charged and that the correct forms were used.

While this system was being used, each peril was separately coded, a loss history was developed for that peril, and a pure premium was established for the peril. Once special forms were used, however, determining the loss history of any specific peril covered by a special form became almost impossible. Eventually, the various local rating bureaus ceased to exist, and in 1971, a single advisory organization, ISO, replaced them. ISO still develops standard forms and calculates and disseminates loss cost information for most types of insurance.

The following coverage comparison chart shows the evolution of the coverage forms with the additions of new covered perils.

Coverage Comparison Chart

Fire Policy	Extended Coverage	Broad Form	Special Form
Fire	Fire	Fire	Risk of direct physical loss unless excluded
Lightning	Lightning	Lightning	
	Explosion	Explosion	
	Windstorm	Windstorm	
	Hail	Hail	
	Smoke	Smoke	
	Vehicles	Vehicles	
	Aircraft	Aircraft	
	Riot	Riot	
	Civil commotion	Civil commotion	
		Vandalism and malicious mischief	
		Sprinkler leakage	
		Sinkhole collapse	
		Volcanic action	
		Falling objects	
		Weight of snow, ice, or sleet	
		Water damage	

Specified-Perils Versus Special-Form Coverage

Coverage is fundamentally different under specified-perils policies and special-form policies. (The terms "specified perils" and "named perils" are used synonymously throughout the text.)

Specified-Perils Coverage

In specified-perils policies, a loss is covered only if the policy identifies the cause of loss (or peril). Both the Basic Form and the Broad Form are specified-perils policies. For example, if the policy states that it provides coverage for fire and lightning, the loss must be caused by either fire or lightning. Any other cause of damage is not covered. When investigating coverage under a specified-perils form, an adjuster must verify an identified peril that caused the loss before paying the loss.

Special-Form Coverage

Special-form policies cover any loss unless the loss is specifically excluded or limited by the policy. Although special-form policies generally have many more exclusions than do specified-perils policies, their coverage is still broader than even the most generous specified-perils policies. Exhibit 1-2 illustrates the application of special-form coverage.

EXHIBIT 1-2

Illustration of Special-Form Coverage

Assume that a building's interior suffers water damage because rain during a windstorm entered through a defective or worn-out roof.

The building's interior damage would be covered under an HO-3 policy because the policy insures the building "against risk of direct physical loss to the property" and the policy has no exclusion for this type of damage. However, because the HO-3 policy provides only specified-perils coverage for contents, water damage to personal property from this same loss would not be covered. The windstorm or hail peril does not cover loss caused by rain unless "the direct force of wind or hail damages the building causing an opening in a roof or wall and the rain . . . enters through this opening."[4] In this case, the roof was already worn and open.

If this same damage occurred to a commercial building having special-form coverage, no exclusion would apply, but a limitation reads,

> We will not pay for loss of or damage to . . . the interior of any building or structure caused by or resulting from rain, snow, sleet, ice, sand or dust, whether driven by wind or not, unless: (1) the building or structure first sustains damage by a Covered Cause of Loss to its roof or walls through which the rain, snow, sleet, ice, sand or dust enters. . . .[5]

Again, because the roof was already worn and gradual wear is excluded, the rain damage would not be covered.

Burden of Proof

Burden of proof
A legal principle that requires a party to establish by evidence the facts necessary to prove that party's case.

An important consequence of the distinction between the specified-perils and the special-form approach is its effect on the burden of proof. A party has the **burden of proof** when it is his or her duty to prove the truth of information that is in dispute. The burden of proof is crucial in doubtful and difficult-to-determine cases.

Specified Perils

An adjuster's approach when investigating a loss depends on the type of coverage provided. When the insured has a specified-perils policy, the insured is obligated to determine which peril applies to the damage to his or her property. Thus, the insured has the burden of proving that one of the specified perils was the cause of the loss. When the insured has the burden of proof and cannot prove what caused the loss, there is no coverage. See the following box for an example.

Burden of Proof: Specified Perils

The HO-3 covers personal property for theft including "loss of property from a known place" when the property has likely been stolen. An insured who reports a piece of jewelry missing must at least prove that the jewelry was likely stolen.

Unless the insured was robbed or there is evidence of burglary at the insured's house, the fact that the jewelry is missing is not, by itself, sufficient to prove theft.

Special Form

Conversely, to avoid paying a claim under a special form, the insurance company must prove, on the basis of a policy exclusion, that the policy does not cover the cause of the damage. Proving that a loss resulted from a cause excluded in the policy is difficult. When the insurer has the burden of proof and cannot prove that an exclusion applies, coverage is afforded for the loss.

Determine Whether the Loss Was Caused by a Covered Cause of Loss

Whether an insurance policy covers a particular loss depends on the specific cause of the loss. Property loss adjusters must therefore investigate the cause of the loss and determine whether it falls within the coverage defined by the policy. This part of the chapter discusses the essential considerations in the definition and investigation of specific causes of loss that are commonly found in property insurance policies.

Fire

Property insurance was created to provide coverage against the peril of fire. The damage and destruction caused by fire are unmistakable. When a fire has caused damage, all damage caused by smoke, water, and firefighting activity is considered to arise out of the fire and is therefore covered.

Fire
The rapid oxidation of combustible material, releasing heat and flame. Without flame, there is no "fire," for insurance purposes.

Insurance Definition of Fire

Fire is the rapid oxidation of combustible material, releasing heat and flame. Without flame, there is no "fire," for insurance purposes. Slower types of oxidation and other chemical reactions might release heat or cause heat buildup. However, heat alone is not considered fire. A scorch on a countertop from a hot pot is not fire damage. No one needs to witness the flame if an expert can attest to its presence or if its presence is obvious from evidence such as charring. In the absence of a flame, damage from heat and smoke is not covered as fire. Smoke, however, is a separately specified peril, and certain types of smoke and heat-related losses might be covered depending on the policy form.

Friendly fire
A fire deliberately created in a place designed to contain fire, such as an oven, a heater, or a fireplace.

Hostile fire
Any fire not created in a place designed to contain fire. Only losses from hostile fires are covered within the fire peril.

Friendly Fire Versus Hostile Fire

The distinction is sometimes made between "friendly fire" and "hostile fire." A **friendly fire** is deliberately created in a place designed to contain fire, such as an oven, a heater, or a fireplace. A **hostile fire** is any other fire. Only losses from hostile fires are covered within the fire peril. This distinction is made primarily with regard to losses from the attendant heat and smoke of friendly fires—they are not covered under the fire peril, although smoke damage is a separate and standard covered peril. Should a friendly fire escape its container, it would become a hostile fire, and any resulting damage would be covered.

Lightning

Lightning is a natural electric discharge in the atmosphere that can cause damage in its flow to the ground.

Types of Lightning Losses

Following are three main types of lightning losses:

1. A direct hit
2. A near miss
3. A ground surge

Direct Hits and Near Misses Lightning damage to a building following a direct hit usually consists of shatter or blast-like damage or resulting fire damage. The blast or shatter damage is obvious at the point of contact. Likewise, fire damage is obvious, although lightning might not have caused the fire.

When hit by lightning, some buildings ignite. Others do not because of differences in the combustibility of materials used in the structure and the extent of grounding afforded by lightning rods and metal roofs. Some engineers have offered the explanation that although all lightning is high-voltage electricity, some bolts are of high amperage (large flow of electricity), but others are of low amperage (small flow of electricity), and that the high amperage electricity causes ignition. These bolts are called "hot" and "cold," respectively. This distinction also explains why lightning can come into a building on power lines without blowing a fuse. Metal roofs offer protection only if the metal is $^{3}/_{16}$ of an inch thick or more, and only if installed so that they are electrically continuous and adequately grounded. Otherwise, they can attract lightning and provide little protection. Near misses do not usually cause physical damage but can disturb electrical equipment's functioning.

Ground Surge The type of lightning loss most difficult for an adjuster to handle is alleged ground surge damage to the wiring of a house, a business property, or an electrical appliance. A ground surge travels through the ground, usually only a few hundred feet, creating a burrow, before entering a building. The only evidence of a lightning strike might be nonfunctioning electrical equipment. Large losses justify an electrical expert's services, but most losses are not large. Weather records might establish that lightning was or was not a possibility in the area when the alleged loss occurred. Under a specified-perils form, the insured has the burden of proof to show that a specified peril caused the damage.

Coverage for Lightning Losses

Lightning losses were originally covered in early insurance forms as a type of loss from fire. Lightning is now a separate peril because it can cause damage separate from that caused by ordinary fire.

If lightning causes a fire, the resulting damage caused by the fire will be covered under the fire peril—if for any reason the damage will not be covered under the lightning peril, such as if the policy has an exclusion for the lightning peril specifically applicable to the type of property damaged.

Damage to wiring, allegedly caused by lightning, might involve various exclusions. Losses sometimes occur when wiring in a building shorts out and a claim is submitted to rewire the building, or at least the wiring that shorted out. The cost of bringing the entire wiring in the building up to code is usually excluded under all policy forms. The cost of repairing wiring that has shorted out might be restricted or excluded by the wear and tear exclusion found in most property forms. However, damage caused by a resulting fire is covered. Most property forms also have an exclusion for any loss resulting from any power failure off the premises.

Explosion

Most explosions are obvious events, yet explosion is difficult to define. An explosion is usually considered to occur if a sudden and violent release of pressure or energy has caused a bursting or breaking and a noise. To be an explosion, the breaking must be caused by the pent-up force of confined air or gases, which finally burst into the open, such as a steam boiler explosion. An explosion does not have to be accompanied by fire.

Non-Explosions

When something breaks by itself, whether or not accompanied by noise, an explosion has not occurred. The sheer weight of grain in a bin might cause the sides of the bin to break. This is not an explosion. However, if a bin is airtight, and the grain ferments, creating heat and gas, the expansion of the gas with its resulting increase in air pressure might cause the bin to explode. Other forces that are not explosions are sonic boom, electric arcing, rupture of water pipes, and rupture or bursting of rotating parts of machinery caused by centrifugal force.

Windstorm

Property insurance policies provide protection against windstorm. They do not specify the wind velocity needed to constitute a windstorm. The definition usually accepted for windstorm is a wind velocity having sufficient force to cause damage. Although wind is not a covered peril, damage from windstorm is usually referred to as wind damage.

A tornado is certainly a windstorm, but so are many storms of much lesser velocity. In doubtful cases, local weather records should be checked, and surrounding property should be checked for damage.

Wind Versus Water Damage

Occasionally, a covered loss, such as a windstorm, occurs, and at the same time, another loss occurs that is not covered, such as a flood. This can happen along the Atlantic and Gulf coasts, where floods frequently accompany hurricanes. The windstorm peril, under both specified-perils and special-form policies, covers the wind damage, but it does not cover the damage caused by flood, surface water, waves, tidal waves, high water, or overflow, whether driven by wind or not.

The flood exclusion is particularly troublesome in the case of beachfront property during hurricanes and other severe windstorms accompanied by high waters. The policy wording is clear as to what is covered and what is excluded. The difficulty arises in trying to segregate the wind damage from the excluded water damage.

In beachfront areas, flood insurance coverage is available only through the National Flood Insurance Program at a price that the property owner often is not willing to pay. In many cases, the losses are disastrous. Therefore, property owners commonly try to collect under windstorm insurance. These cases are challenging to adjust and require considerable investigative and persuasive abilities to resolve satisfactorily.

Hail

Hail is precipitation in the form of small, hard pellets that can cause damage on impact. Icy precipitation, such as sleet or icy snow, is not considered "hail" and is not covered under the hail peril. Damage caused by ice storms, snow, or weight of snow is not covered under the hail peril, but it might be covered by a separately specified peril, as discussed below.

In some parts of the United States, hail can be the size of a golf ball and has been known to cause serious damage to real property. Hail can dent metal mobilehomes and other steel or aluminum structures. In some cases, the dent repairs require reskinning the damaged structure. In other cases, an appearance allowance (a claim settlement based on loss of value caused by appearance, rather than cost to repair, since repair is usually impractical) might be the best type of adjustment.

Smoke

Smoke damage must result from a sudden, accidental cause. The damage cannot result from an accumulation over time. It does not include loss from agricultural smudging or industrial operations.

Smoke damage from a friendly fire is covered if it is sudden and accidental.

Vehicles

Coverage for vehicle damage differs depending upon the policy form. Some policies cover damage to personal and real property. Some policies exclude damage caused by an insured's vehicle. Most policies require physical contact with the vehicle to trigger coverage.

Aircraft

Aircraft includes not only airplanes and helicopters but also self-propelled missiles and spacecraft. This peril includes loss caused by objects falling from aircraft.

Riot or Civil Commotion

The personal insurance specified-perils forms include riot or civil commotion as a peril. However, the forms provide no definition to indicate what the peril includes. Commercial insurance policies give a better description but still do not completely define the terms.

Generally, a riot is defined as a violent breach of the peace by three or more persons assembled together. A riot need not result from conspiracy; it can be spontaneous. Some states' criminal codes require only two people in defining the action as a riot, and others require that there must be as many as five. The rioters' act or acts must be of an unlawful nature. Any loss caused by a rioter is covered regardless of whether the loss is caused by fire, breakage, theft, looting, or vandalism.

Vandalism or Malicious Mischief

Vandalism is the willful or malicious destruction or defacement of public or private property. It is sometimes called malicious mischief.

Vandalism (malicious mischief)
The willful or malicious destruction or defacement of public or private property.

Element of Intent

Damage alone does not indicate vandalism. The insured, in submitting the claim, must be able to show that the damage was *willfully* or *maliciously* caused. Usually, vandalism does not have eyewitnesses; however, intent can be established by circumstantial evidence. Paint spilled on a floor is not conclusive, but the same paint used to write graffiti on floors or walls is evidence of vandalism. A broken window can be accidental, but a pattern of broken windows indicates an intentional act. Other similar damage in a neighborhood, notification to the police, and recurrences of the same type of damage all indicate vandalism.

Damage caused by domestic animals is not covered. Claims are often submitted for carpets damaged by a dog or drapes damaged by cats climbing up them. These losses are not covered. Animals cannot form the intent necessary for vandalism. Additionally, policies have exclusions for damage caused by animals.

Coverage Suspension

Coverage for vandalism and malicious mischief is suspended once a property has been vacant for more than a certain time period. The amount of time varies among policies, with thirty to sixty days being common. A building under construction is generally not regarded as vacant. Vacancy has been interpreted to mean that the building does not contain any contents pertaining to the building's customary occupancy.[6]

Theft

Coverage for theft varies according to the policy form. Theft is generally defined as the fraudulent taking of personal property belonging to another without consent, with the intent to deprive the owner of its value. The contrast between the homeowners and commercial BPP approaches to theft coverage is unmistakable. Homeowners policies provide substantial coverage for theft because it is a major risk for homeowners' personal property. The BPP provides no coverage, or much more limited coverage, by design. To fill this void, the commercial crime coverages provide theft coverage in a commercial setting. Upcoming chapters discuss these differing approaches in greater detail.

Falling Objects

Much of the damage caused by falling objects is covered under the vandalism, windstorm, aircraft, and lightning perils. Any other damage from falling objects is covered only under a special-form policy or a policy in which falling objects is a specified peril. The falling object must make a hole in the structure's exterior for coverage to apply.

Weight of Snow, Ice, or Sleet

Most policy forms cover damage caused by the weight of snow, ice, or sleet that accumulates on the roof of a main dwelling, an appurtenant structure such as a garage, or a commercial building. The peril for weight of snow, ice, or sleet should be considered in connection with the collapse coverage.

Water Damage

Water that damages a structure can come from several different sources. The adjuster must therefore consider how the water entered or flowed into the property.

Often, policies that provide protection against water damage are primarily designed to cover only damage by water escaping from broken pipes and appliances. Generally, all other causes of water damage are excluded.

Seepage

Although not specifically mentioned as an exclusion, water damage resulting from seepage or leakage over time is excluded.

Flood

Both the HO-3 form and the BPP with the Causes of Loss—Special Form exclude water damage caused by "flood, surface water, waves, tides, tidal waves, overflow of any body of water, or their spray, all whether driven by wind or not."[7] In fact, the majority of personal insurance and commercial first-party policy forms excludes these types of water damage. Chapter 6 discusses flood insurance.

Sewer Backup

When sewer systems are unable to carry away extensive runoff and surface water, flood water starts to flow backward through the sewers, causing water and sewage to back up through toilets, sinks, and drains. The water might even be strong enough to lift steel sewer covers off the streets. This floodwater can carry raw sewage, contaminating both buildings and contents.

Water that backs up from sewers or drains is excluded in both the HO-3 and the BPP with the Causes of Loss—Special Form. Insurers differ as to whether water that backs up from a clogged toilet or drainage system *on the insured premises* is, in fact, excluded. Some insurers argue that the water is not backing up out of the sewage system but that the sewage system cannot accept the water that is flowing into it, so the insurer should cover the loss. Other insurers do not cover any water damage caused by water that backs up from a toilet, a sink, an automatic dishwasher, or a sewage system. All insurers exclude any damage resulting from water backing up from a drainage or sewer system because of blockage *off* the premises.

Other Water Damage

Water damage caused by a mudslide or mudflow and damage caused by subterranean water that exerts pressure or seeps or leaks through a building, sidewalk, driveway, foundation, swimming pool, or another structure is excluded under both the personal insurance and commercial special-form policies. These exclusions refer to water *under* the ground surface.

Glass Breakage or Damage

Glass damage is actually a consequence of other perils rather than a peril itself. Nevertheless, some policies list it among covered perils. This, in effect, becomes "all-risks" coverage for glass, except to the extent otherwise restricted. However, glass damage caused by any other specified perils is still covered. That is, glass can be broken or damaged by fires, windstorms, explosions, and other perils. If so, it is covered without regard to the glass-breakage peril. This coverage is important because the glass-breakage peril only applies to glass that is part of the real property (including storm doors and storm windows), and coverage under that peril might have dollar limitations.

Safety Glazing Required by Law

Almost all property forms have an exclusion stating that the insurer will not pay for the added cost of making necessary repairs because of the enforcement of any ordinance or law. However, this provision does not restrict the added cost of replacing glass with safety glazing material if required by law. Building code agencies have changed their requirements for the type of glass that can be used in buildings. Therefore, if an ordinance does not allow the replacement of the glass with glass similar to that which existed at the time of the loss, the added cost might appear to be excluded by the ordinance or law provision. However, both personal and commercial insurance forms have provisions allowing for the replacement of glass with safety glazing material if required by ordinance or law.

Collapse

The older forms included collapse as an insured peril. Current personal and commercial insurance forms now include collapse as an additional coverage.

Covered Causes of Collapse

Collapse coverage is unusual because the insurers agree to pay for collapse of the insured building, or any part of the building, caused by those perils listed in the form. Also covered is collapse caused by hidden decay; hidden insect or vermin damage; weight of people or personal property; weight of rain that collects on a roof; and use of defective materials or methods in construction, remodeling, or renovation if the collapse occurs during construction, remodeling, or renovation.

Generally, special-form policies exclude *damage* caused by hidden decay, hidden insect or vermin damage, or use of defective materials or construction methods. However, *collapse* caused by these perils is covered.

Extent of Collapse

How much of the property must collapse for collapse coverage to apply? Both the HO-3 and the BPP with the Causes of Loss—Broad Form define the extent of **collapse**. According to the policies:

Collapse
An abrupt falling down or caving in of a building or any part of a building with the result that the building or any part of the building cannot be occupied for its intended purpose.

> Collapse means an abrupt falling down or caving in of a building or any part of a building with the result that the building or part of the building cannot be occupied for its intended purpose.[8]

A building in danger of falling down or caving in is not a "collapse." The part of a building left standing after another part has collapsed is not part of the collapse loss. A building that is standing but has evidence of cracking, bulging, sagging, bending, leaning, settling, shrinkage, or expansion is not a collapse.

Volcanic Action Coverage

Volcanic action coverage was added because of the 1980 Mount St. Helens eruption in southwest Washington, which scattered ash over thousands of square miles. It covers damage caused by shock waves, ash, dust, or particulate matter and lava flow. The peril defines any volcanic action occurring within a seven-day period as a single occurrence. The time period is used so that multiple deductibles are not applied.

Role of Definitions

In specified-perils forms, the statements about, and definitions of, the specified-perils are as important in determining what is *not* covered as are the exclusions. Anything not contained within the definition of a specified peril is not part of that peril and is not covered. For example, in the Causes of Loss—Broad Form, vandalism is defined as "willful and malicious damage to, or destruction of, the described property."[9] Any damage not fitting this definition would not be vandalism and would not be covered unless it was contained within some other peril. Another example from the same form is water damage, which is defined in such a way as not to cover some of the most common types of water damage, such as floods or gradual seepage.

Exceptions From Definitions

In addition to explicit statements that define a peril, most of the specified-perils forms include explicit exceptions as part of a definition. For example, the definition of windstorm or hail in the BPP with the Basic Form and Broad Form is almost entirely phrased as an exception to coverage. It reads, "Windstorm or Hail, but not including. . . ." The remainder of this definition of a specified peril concerns what is *not* windstorm or hail.

Determine Whether Additional Coverages Apply

Drafters of insurance policies frequently include a section of coverages called "additional coverages." Certain coverages are distinguished from the rest of the policy for various reasons.

Supplement to Limits

Some additional coverages increase the available limit. For example, the additional coverage for debris removal under the HO-3 provides an additional 5 percent of the underlying limit for debris removal. Debris removal would be covered as part of the underlying loss, but this additional coverage increases the available limit.

New Types of Coverage

Certain additional coverages differ from the main coverages and could not exist at all except as additional coverages. For example, fire department service charges are not direct physical loss to covered property. They might arise out of such direct physical losses, but they are by nature strictly financial obligations. Likewise, the additional coverage for trees and shrubs under the

HO-3 would not exist otherwise because trees and shrubs are not within the underlying coverages for the dwelling, other structures, or personal property.

Reinstatement of Coverage

Some additional coverages are created to reinstate coverage that has otherwise been eliminated by exclusions. This approach clarifies that the only available coverage is that contained in the additional coverage. For example, the HO-3 excludes collapse as a covered peril, except to the extent provided in the additional coverage for collapse.

Determine Whether Any Exclusions Apply

All insurance policies list exclusions, the exposures for which underwriters do not allow coverage. These are found in both specified-perils and special-form coverages. In specified-perils policies, a loss is covered only if it is listed as one of the perils in the insurance agreement. The coverage is specific, and relatively few exclusions apply. However, the perils themselves might also include definitions that limit the coverage or that exclude a certain aspect of the peril. Special-form policies, conversely, have very broad coverage (every loss is covered unless it is listed in the exclusions or limitations), so many exclusions apply. A good rule to remember is that policies with narrow insurance coverage have few exclusions, whereas policies with broad coverage have many exclusions.

Reasons for Exclusions

This section discusses some reasons for exclusions. Remembering the general rationale for exclusions is easier than trying to remember the exact wording of every exclusion in various policy forms.

Uninsurable Loss Exposure

To be insurable, a loss exposure must have an element of predictability, and it should be non-catastrophic. Therefore, exclusions are written to eliminate such exposures as war; nuclear hazards; and, to a certain extent, earthquake and flood. These exposures are generally uninsurable because of the difficulty of spreading risk, the events' unpredictability, and their potential for catastrophic loss.

Gradual Hazards

Other exclusions eliminate gradual, inevitable physical hazards such as the following:

- Wear and tear, smog, rust, mold, and wet or dry rot
- Settling; cracking; shrinking; bulging; or expansion of pavements, patios, foundations, walls, floors, roofs, or ceilings
- Damage by birds, vermin, rodents, insects, or domestic animals

These hazards are considered uninsurable because of their gradual and unavoidable nature.

Moral and Morale Hazard

Some exclusions, such as those for intentional loss and for failure to perform necessary maintenance, reduce moral and morale hazards. **Moral hazard** refers to some people's mindset that leads them to exaggerate, fabricate, or cause losses. **Morale hazard** (or **attitudinal hazard**) is some people's disposition to be less careful because they are insured than they would be if they did not have insurance.

Moral hazard
A condition that increases the likelihood that a person will intentionally cause or exaggerate a loss.

Morale hazard, or **attitudinal hazard**
A condition of carelessness or indifference that increases the frequency or severity of loss.

Specialized Coverages

Exclusions can eliminate coverage that would duplicate other specialized policies that the insured could obtain. Coverage for earthquake, flood, boiler and machinery exposures, and crime exposures, though important to certain insureds, is not needed by most and is therefore excluded in standard policies and made available through specialized policies.

Specific Exclusions

The following section lists specific exclusions common to property policies.

1. *Ordinance or law*. An increase in construction or demolition costs resulting from a local law or ordinance is excluded except as provided by additional coverages or by endorsement. This exclusion can generate significant disagreement during the adjustment process. The term "law" can be broadly interpreted to include government-issued codes, rules, or regulations. An adjuster must check case law in the loss jurisdiction to understand what the term "law" means there.

   From a practical standpoint, this exclusion does not require special enforcement from the governmental body. Simply rebuilding in compliance with the code is sufficient to trigger the provision. An adjuster valuing the loss must complete two estimates to determine what the increased costs are. One estimate would be to rebuild or repair as the building existed before the loss. The other estimate would be to repair or rebuild in compliance with the codes.

   The increased costs associated with this exclusion can appear in several areas. The cost of debris removal can increase if the debris contains hazardous material requiring special disposal procedures. An increase can occur in the length of time it takes to restore the building to pre-loss condition due to the code requirements. Hiring an engineer or an architect to redesign the building to comply with the regulations might be necessary. These costs would result solely from the regulations and would not be covered.

   Despite that fact that this is a common exclusion in property policies, the HO-3 gives limited coverage for increased costs due to ordinance or law.

2. *Earth movement*. Earth movement is defined as earthquake, including shock waves or tremors before or after a volcanic eruption; landslide; mine subsidence; mudflows; and earth sinking, rising, or shifting, whether caused by humans, animals, or nature.

3. *Water damage*. Water damage from flood, surface water, sewer backups, subsurface water, and waterborne material (sewage) is usually excluded.
4. *Power failure*. A power failure to the insured premises from a lightning strike is covered. However, a power failure occurring off the premises is not covered. A covered cause of loss that results from a power failure is covered.
5. *Neglect*. Neglect is defined as the insured's failure to use all reasonable means necessary to preserve and protect property from further damage at and after the time of a loss.
6. *War*. The war exclusion includes undeclared and civil war; warlike actions by a governmental military force; and acts of insurrection, rebellion, revolution, or usurped power.
7. *Nuclear hazard*. This exclusion eliminates coverage for loss or damage from nuclear reaction, radiation, or contamination, regardless of the cause. Ensuing fire damage would be covered.
8. *Governmental action*. Property destruction by an act of government authority is not covered unless the property is destroyed to prevent the spread of a fire that would have otherwise consumed the property.
9. *Exceptions to exclusions*. The phrasing of some of the exclusions in the special form leaves coverage in place rather than excludes it. For example, the Causes of Loss—Special Form contains an exclusion for water damage from freezing pipes "unless (1) You do your best to maintain heat in the building or structure; or (2) You drain the equipment and shut off the water supply if the heat is not maintained."[10] Therefore, an insured who took these steps would be covered for water damage caused by freezing pipes.

Concurrent Causation

Concurrent causation
A single loss caused by two or more perils, acting either simultaneously or in succession.

Both the HO-3 and the Causes of Loss—Special Form begin with the wording that a loss is excluded "regardless of any other cause or event contributing concurrently or in any sequence to the loss."[11] This language was the insurer's attempt to clarify whether a loss caused by concurrent causes would be covered. **Concurrent causation** is defined as a single loss that was caused by two or more perils, occurring simultaneously or in succession. Concurrent causation becomes an issue when one of the perils is a covered peril and the other is not. Much debate over how to handle concurrent causation claims occurred before the introduction of policy language. Even with the policy language change, courts still interpret the policy language differently from one jurisdiction to another. The insurance industry's position is that a loss is excluded if caused by an excluded cause, whether or not that excluded cause is the predominant one.

The courts have used three approaches when considering concurrent causation. See the following box.

Three Concurrent Causation Approaches

1. Efficient cause approach: If the loss is caused by a covered peril and a non-covered peril, the loss is covered if the "dominant," "efficient," "prime," or "moving" cause is a covered peril.
2. Liberal approach: The entire loss is covered as long as one of the causes is a covered cause of loss.
3. Conservative approach: If a covered cause of loss and an excluded cause of loss combine to produce the loss, then the loss is not covered.[12]

Burden of Proof

Another important aspect of concurrent causation is how the burden of proof shifts, depending upon the approach followed and what type of policy is involved. For an "all-risks policy," jurisdictions following the efficient cause approach put the burden of proof on the insurer to prove that the policy excluded the dominant cause. The jurisdictions using the liberal approach and the conservative approach have not fully addressed the issue of burden of proof. If a specified-perils policy is involved, the jurisdictions following the efficient cause approach will require the insured to prove that the covered cause of loss was the dominant cause. The burden then shifts to the insurer to prove that it did not. With a specified-perils policy, a jurisdiction that follows the liberal approach makes the insurer rebut the insured's evidence that the covered cause of loss contributed to the loss, as well as give its own proof that the dominant cause of the loss was excluded. Finally, the conservative approach requires the insured to prove that a covered cause of loss was the dominant cause but then allows the insurer to show that an excluded or non-covered cause contributed to the loss.[13]

Policy Conditions

Property loss adjusters must also examine insurance policy conditions in determining coverage. Conditions explain the rights and duties of the parties to the policy. Chapter 2 discusses specific conditions.

SUMMARY

Property loss adjusting begins with determining who and what a policy insures. The insurable interest requirement must be investigated and resolved. To prevent wagering and fraud, insurers developed the principle of insurable interest. Insurable interest represents the financial harm that one would sustain if a loss occurs. Because insurance policies are contracts of indemnity, they will pay only if the insured has suffered a financial loss.

Insurable interest can be held by the property owner as well as others who might have a financial interest, such as an occupancy interest, a custody interest, or a security interest. Financial interest can be based on a contract, such as in the case of a mortgagee or a loss payee; based on occupancy, such as in the case of a tenant; or based on custody, such as in the case of a motor truck carrier. A security interest can result from a judgment, such as a tax lien or a mechanic's lien. Property can be owned by a single person, by joint owners who each have a full interest, by a tenancy in common with a percentage interest, or by life tenants whose interest ends at death. Property can be owned by a business as a sole proprietorship, a partnership, or a corporation.

Property insurance protects two kinds of property: real and personal. Real property is land and anything attached to it, such as a building. Everything else is personal property. Understanding the distinction between real and personal property is important because coverages might overlap. The valuation of real and personal property differs so that miscategorization could affect coinsurance requirements and policy limits.

The policy makes the insured a coinsurer of the property through a coinsurance clause. If the insured fails to purchase sufficient insurance to meet the coinsurance clause, the insured will be penalized if a loss occurs. Only the value of real property is used in the coinsurance calculation.

Not all property is easily categorized into real and personal property. Some personal property additions become attached or adapted to the real property and become a building fixture. Building fixtures are usually items added to the building after its original construction. A sign might be considered a building fixture. Some items can be considered either fixtures or personal property. Drapes, lights, and carpets may fall into either category depending upon attachment, adaptation, and intent. Adjusters examine these three areas to determine how integrated into the building the item has become and whether the owner intends to take it upon leaving. Insurers consider trade fixtures, such as shelves, cabinets, cases, and racks, to be personal property. A tenant's improvements and betterments are considered a fixture. The tenant's lease specifies whether the improvements and betterments are to be removed or must remain at the lease's expiration.

Reviewing a policy for coverage requires a systematic approach. After an adjuster determines who is insured and what is insured, the next step is to determine if the cause of loss is covered. Property coverage has evolved from the original fire policy to the Extended Coverage Form to the Broad Form, each adding additional covered perils to the policy. The final evolution occurred when the Special Form (formerly the "all-risks" form) was devised to cover direct physical loss unless excluded.

A policy's definitions section does not define "direct physical loss." "Direct" is understood to mean resulting from the occurrence without an intervening agency. "Physical" means tangible property's damage, destruction, or disappearance.

An important consequence of property insurance forms' evolution is the shift in the burden of proof. In a specified-perils policy, the insured is obligated to determine which specified peril caused the loss. In a special-form policy, the burden is on the insurer to show that the loss is not covered because of an exclusion.

A specified-perils policy contains a list of covered perils, such as fire; lightning; windstorm; hail; explosion; riot and civil commotion; vehicles; smoke; vandalism and malicious mischief; theft; falling objects; weight of snow, ice, or sleet; water; glass breakage; collapse; and volcanic action.

A property policy also contains additional coverages, some of which increase the available policy limit and some that grant coverage distinct from the main policy. Others are meant to reinstate, in a limited way, previously excluded coverage.

Both a specified-perils policy and a special-form policy contain a list of exclusions. Exclusions usually concern loss exposures that are considered to be uninsurable because of the difficulty in spreading risk, the events' unpredictability, and their potential for catastrophic loss. They eliminate exposures such as war; nuclear hazard; and, to a certain extent, flood and earthquake. Gradual, inevitable physical hazards such as wear and tear; smog; rust; wet or dry rot; settling, cracking, or sinking of foundations and walls; and damage caused by birds, vermin, rodents, insects, and domestic animals are excluded. Other exclusions are meant to deal with moral and morale hazards, such as the ordinance or law exclusion and the neglect exclusion.

Determining coverage can be difficult when two or more causes of loss occur in a single event. If one of the two causes of loss is not a covered cause of loss, it is often impossible to determine which caused the damage that might be covered under the policy. To prevent such a concurrent causation dilemma, policies such as the HO-3 and the BPP with a specific causes of loss form have language stating that if an excluded cause of loss occurs, the event is excluded regardless of any other cause or event contributing to it. However, courts are still interpreting this language.

Another important aspect of concurrent causation is that the burden of proof shifts depending upon the judicial interpretation given to the concurrent causation language.

Having determined that the property involved in the loss is the subject of the policy and that the cause of loss to the property is covered, a property loss adjuster then determines the amount of the loss and how the policy limits and conditions affect the amount of the loss. Chapter 2 discusses how a loss is valued and how policy limits and conditions can affect the loss.

CHAPTER NOTES

1. Form HO 00 03 05 01, Copyright, Insurance Services Office, Inc., 2000.
2. *Black's Law Dictionary*, 5th ed. (St. Paul, Minn.: West Publishing Co., 1979).
3. *Webster's Ninth New Collegiate Dictionary* (Springfield, Mass.: Merriam Webster, Inc., 1990).
4. Form HO 00 03 05 01, Copyright, Insurance Services Office, Inc., 2000.
5. Form CP 10 30 04 02, Copyright, Insurance Services Office, Inc., 2001.
6. For further information, see *Commercial Property Insurance and Risk Management*, 6th ed., Jerome Trupin and Arthur L. Flitner (Malvern, Pa.: American Institute for CPCU/IIA, 2001), p. 3.43.
7. Form CP 10 30 04 02, Copyright, Insurance Services Office, Inc., 2001.
8. Form CP 10 20 04 02, Copyright, Insurance Services Office, Inc., 2001.
9. Form CP 10 20 04 02, Copyright, Insurance Services Office, Inc., 2001.
10. Form CP 10 30 04 02, Copyright, Insurance Services Office, Inc., 2001.
11. Form CP 10 30 04 02, Copyright, Insurance Services Office, Inc., 2001.
12. Adapted from Steven Cozen, ed., *Insuring Real Property* (New York: Matthew Bender & Co., Inc., 2002), 48.01[6], pp. 48-8 to 48-10, with the permission of Matthew Bender & Company, Inc., a member of the Lexis Nexis Group. All rights reserved.
13. Adapted from Cozen, 48.04[3], pp. 48-76 to 48-78.

Chapter 2

Direct Your Learning

Property Insurance: Valuation, Limits, Conditions

After learning the subject matter of this chapter, you should be able to:

- Explain the difference between replacement cost and actual cash value (ACV).
- Given a loss to a specific piece of property, calculate:
  - ACV
  - Market value
- Explain the application and effect of valued policy laws.
- Explain the repair or replace option and its appropriate use.
- Given a loss, explain the settlement to be made under the following provisions:
  - Stated or agreed value
  - Selling price
  - Original cost
  - Warranty services
  - Pair or set
- Given a loss, calculate an adjustment that includes the following:
  - Policy limits and special limits of liability
  - Deductibles
  - Coinsurance
  - Other insurance
- Given a loss involving other insurance, calculate the settlement using the following:
  - Pro rata share method
  - Payment by equal shares method
- Explain how waiver and estoppel can occur and can be avoided with respect to the insured's duties following a loss.
- Given a proof of loss, determine whether it is properly completed, and if not, explain how and why it should be rejected.
- Explain the purpose and operation of the appraisal procedure.

OUTLINE

Develop Your Perspective

What are the main topics covered in the chapter?

This chapter continues the introduction of basic property loss concepts by discussing how the property insurance policy values property. It also discusses how property valuation can be affected by case law, state laws, regulations, policy limits, policy conditions, and other relevant policy provisions.

Value a property loss.

- Does the policy provide for replacement cost or actual cash value?
- Do case law, state laws, and regulations apply to the loss?
- Do policy limits and deductibles apply to the loss?
- Do other policy provisions and conditions affect the value?

Why is it important to know these topics?

To properly adjust a claim under a property policy, a property loss adjuster must be able to properly value the property involved. The accuracy of the coinsurance calculation depends on accurate valuation. The adequacy of the loss settlement depends on the proper application of policy limits, deductibles, and other relevant policy provisions and conditions, in addition to case law, state laws, and regulations.

How can you use this information?

For a simple property loss, perform the settlement calculations with and without a coinsurance penalty to determine the difference in the amounts.

Chapter 2

Property Insurance: Valuation, Limits, Conditions

After coverage has been determined for a property insurance claim, the insured and the adjuster consider how much is to be paid on the claim. Insureds are concerned about the amount and timing of payment for the loss. Adjusters are also concerned with making a fair, equitable, and timely settlement, based on the insurance contract and the facts of the loss. However, the insured and the adjuster might interpret policies differently, so the adjuster must remain open-minded about legitimate contrary interpretations and should make every effort to reach an amicable agreement with the insured on the loss settlement amount.

Various policy provisions and conditions as well as laws and regulations determine how much recovery an insured may receive from the insurer. See the following box.

Factors Determining an Insured's Recovery Amount

- The property valuation methods described in the policy
    - Case law, state laws, and regulations that affect policy valuation
- Coverage limits within the policy
- Policy deductibles on the claim
- Policy conditions, such as whether the insured must coinsure the loss for failing to carry adequate amounts of insurance
- Policy provisions and conditions, such as the other insurance condition

This chapter presents property valuation and other relevant provisions, policy limits, and policy conditions affecting the amount that an insured recovers for a loss.

PROPERTY VALUATION

All insurance policies specify the valuation basis for lost or damaged property. Insurers can repair or replace lost or damaged property, but they usually make a settlement with money. The insurance policy states, in general terms, how much the property is worth for loss settlement purposes. Property is almost always valued either at replacement cost or at actual cash value (ACV). See the following box.

Property Valuation Methods

- Replacement Cost
  - Usually, the current cost of replacing damaged or destroyed property with property of like kind and quality.
  - Replacement cost is determined by the current cost of the damaged or lost property's functional equivalent.
  - Policy provisions and legal requirements can limit the valuation amount.
- Actual Cash Value (ACV)
  - Usually, replacement cost minus depreciation.
    - Depreciation methods
      - Straight-line depreciation: An item steadily and predictably deteriorates.
      - Accelerated depreciation: An item depreciates rapidly when first purchased and then more slowly.
      - Decelerated depreciation: An item hardly deteriorates until a certain time and then rapidly deteriorates.
    - Depreciation causes
      - Physical wear and tear
      - Age
      - Obsolescence
  - Some courts have ruled that ACV is fair market value.
  - Other courts have a broad evidence rule stating that factors such as economic, technological, or fashion obsolescence—in addition to depreciation and market value—should determine ACV.

Replacement Cost

Replacement cost
The cost of replacing lost or damaged property with new property of like kind and quality at current prices.

Replacement cost is the cost of replacing lost or damaged property with new property of like kind and quality, or its functional equivalent, *at current prices*. Even if property is several years old, or if its replacement cost now exceeds its original purchase price, the insured is entitled to the current cost to replace the property. However, policy provisions and legal requirements can limit valuation.

Like Kind and Quality

Replacement cost can still be determined even if the item of property is no longer manufactured. Sometimes, a particular model or style of an item is no longer made and has, in a strict sense, become irreplaceable. But this does not make the object's value unlimited. If the object can no longer be purchased, the replacement cost for property of **like kind and quality** should be paid. For example, if a particular style of an armchair or appliance with certain features is discontinued, an item of like kind and quality will probably be available, often from the same manufacturer. The original item's replacement cost can be based on the existing model's cost. Settlement on this basis is usually acceptable to the insured, as long as the adjuster does not try to settle on the basis of an inferior object.

Like kind and quality
A method of determining replacement cost valuation using a comparable model or item.

Functional Equivalent

Some policies may be written using a **functional valuation approach** to provide replacement on a **functional equivalent** basis. This type of replacement cost coverage is used on older, more ornate buildings. To insure them for actual replacement cost would be very expensive because of outdated construction methods and materials. Functional equivalent replacement cost provides coverage for the cost to repair or replace using current construction methods and materials. For example, Victorian-style homes have plaster walls and ceilings. The current replacement for such homes' walls and ceilings would be drywall.

Functional valuation approach (functional equivalent)
A valuation method in which the insurer is required to pay no more than the cost to repair or replace the damaged or destroyed property with property that is its functional equivalent.

Functional equivalent coverage can also be purchased for personal property (other than stock). It is particularly useful when old machinery or equipment is to be insured, because it might no longer be available for purchase. Therefore, if damaged beyond repair, such a machine could be replaced by the closest equivalent property available through this coverage.

Limitations on Replacement Cost Recovery

Replacement cost provisions technically violate the principle of indemnity. According to the **principle of indemnity**, insurance policies should only indemnify (compensate) the insured for losses; they should not allow the insured to profit from losses. An insured that has sustained a loss to old, used property and replaces it with new property has indeed profited. For this reason, virtually all replacement cost policies provide replacement cost only after the insured has actually replaced the damaged or destroyed property or when the loss is small. Until insureds have replaced the property, they are entitled to, and receive, only an ACV settlement. A loss settlement condition from the homeowners HO-3 policy illustrates this concept:

Principle of indemnity
The principle that insurance policies should provide a benefit no greater than the loss suffered by an insured.

> We will pay no more than the actual cash value of the damage unless:
>
> (a) actual repair or replacement is complete; or
>
> (b) the cost to repair or replace the damage is both:
>
> (i) less than 5% of the amount of insurance in this policy on the building; and
>
> (ii) less than $2,500.[1]

Thus, computing actual cash value is important, even with policies requiring replacement cost settlement.

Actual Cash Value

Actual cash value (ACV)
A method of determining amounts payable for a property loss; calculated as the replacement cost minus depreciation, market value, or a valuation determined by the broad evidence rule.

Loss settlements based on **actual cash value (ACV)** are common with personal property under homeowners policies and with both personal property and buildings under commercial policies. Although the term "actual cash value" is undoubtedly one of the most important terms in property insurance, no policy defines it. Various explanations of the term exist, and the courts have had a major role in defining it. The many explanations of actual cash value (discussed below) are, however, consistent with one another.

Replacement Cost Minus Depreciation

Most property has its highest value when new. It thereafter loses value, mainly because of age and use. In this context, actual cash value is best expressed as, and is usually determined by, replacement cost minus depreciation. Determining depreciation is more difficult than determining replacement cost. Depreciation represents any loss of value, and numerous factors affect the rate and amount of loss of value.

Straight-line depreciation
A method of determining the loss in value of an asset by depreciating the asset by the same amount each year over the asset's useful life.

One method of calculating depreciation is **straight-line depreciation.** This method measures a piece of property's steady, predictable deterioration. An example of straight-line depreciation is a refrigerator's depreciation over its useful life. If the refrigerator's current cost is $500 and has a useful life of ten years, it will depreciate $50 per year ($500 divided by 10 years). If the refrigerator is three years old at the time of the loss, the depreciation amount is $150 (3 × $50). A graph of the depreciation amount over ten years shows a straight line. See the following box.

Straight-Line Depreciation

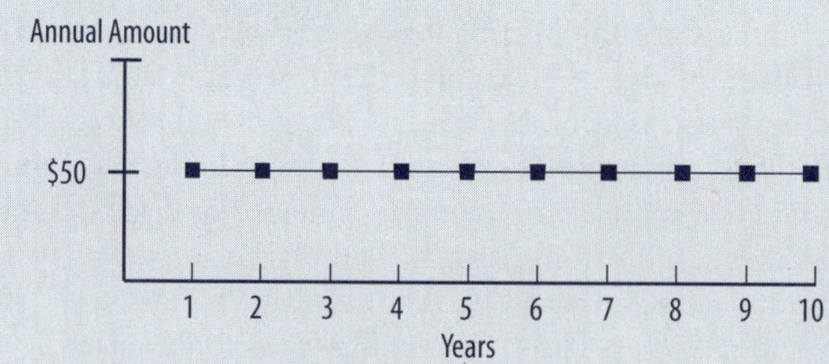

Accelerated depreciation
Depreciation that occurs more rapidly when an item is first purchased and then more slowly in subsequent years.

The **accelerated depreciation** method is used for items that depreciate at a more rapid rate than that indicated by straight-line depreciation. Accelerated depreciation may be applied when an item depreciates rapidly when first purchased and then more slowly in subsequent years. Motor vehicles, electronics, computer equipment, and power tools all depreciate on an accelerated basis. A graph of accelerated depreciation shows a spike in the early years and then a slower rate of depreciation. See the following box.

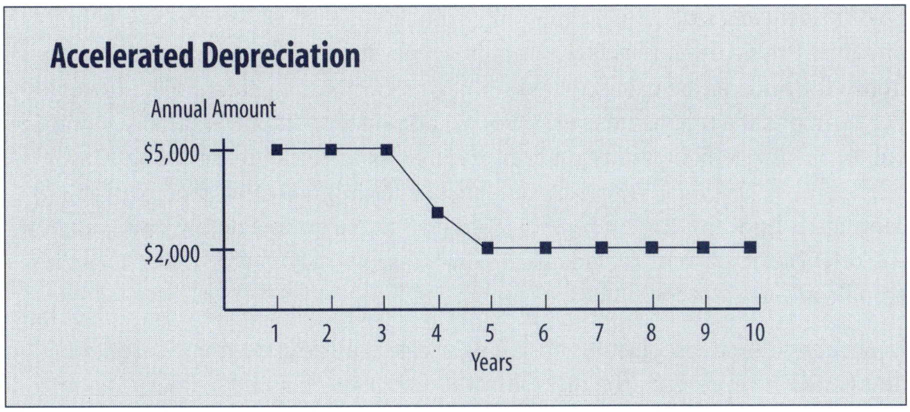

Some items do not depreciate but instead appreciate or gain in value. Other items may depreciate little, if at all, until a given time period has passed and then lose value rapidly. This is called **decelerated depreciation.** Items subject to decelerated depreciation usually have an expiration date and do not depreciate until that date has passed, and then they depreciate rapidly. A graph shows this depreciation as occurring at the end of a calendar's useful life.

Decelerated depreciation
Depreciation that occurs slightly for a given time period and then increases rapidly.

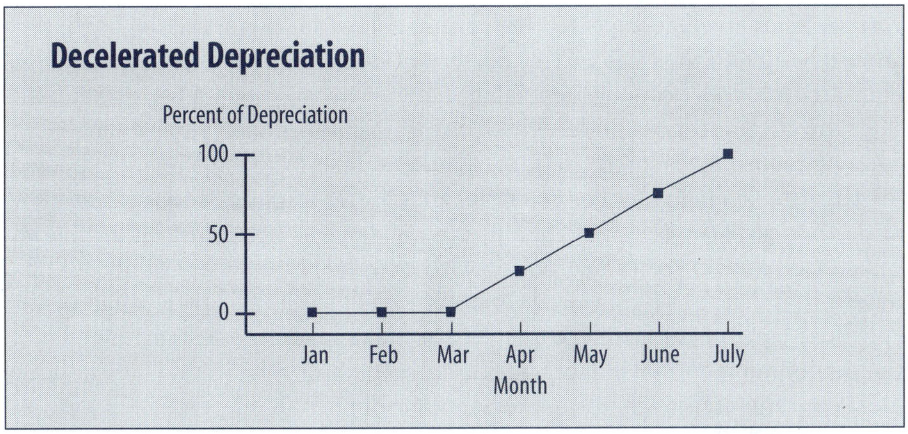

Film, food, medicine, and batteries are examples of items subject to decelerated depreciation. Some items are so new at the time of loss that depreciating them is inappropriate.

Depreciation Causes and Depreciation Calculations

Physical wear and tear causes loss of value, but other factors such as age and obsolescence can result in loss of value and should be identified in computing depreciation.

This section provides specific examples of how actual cash value can be determined according to different causes of loss of value and different types of deterioration.

Physical Wear and Tear Physical wear and tear is the most obvious cause of loss of value. Physical wear and tear usually occurs at a steady rate throughout an item's life and can be calculated as a fixed amount, or a percentage, per year. For example, if a television is expected to last eight years, it would lose 1⁄8 of its value, or 12.5 percent, every year. At five years of age, it will have lost 5⁄8, or 62.5 percent (5 × 12.5 percent), of its value. This amount of depreciation is subtracted from the *current* replacement cost to determine actual cash value. If the television's current replacement cost is $1,000, a five-year-old television's actual cash value is $375 ($1,000 minus $625 depreciation).

In straight-line depreciation, an adjuster can point out to the insured that depreciation represents the amount of use that the insured has already gotten from the property. If the insured had already enjoyed 5⁄8 of the television's expected use, 5⁄8 of the value of a new television should be deducted.

The rate at which a particular item is depreciated depends on what it is and how it is used. For example, clothing depreciates faster than furniture. Also, buildings' structural elements have widely different life spans. A roof might predictably wear out every twenty years, whereas an element of the frame carpentry might last indefinitely.

Most insurance companies publish guides for their adjusters that indicate various items' average expected life. These guides are useful as long as they are used as guidelines only. They present an *average* life for various items, but variation does occur. When using such guides, adjusters must also consider the circumstances under which the particular property has been used. These circumstances might indicate a much longer or much shorter expected life than the average life. For example, an adjuster might reasonably determine that carpeting, under different circumstances, might last either a few years (such as wall-to-wall carpeting with extremely heavy use or abuse) or indefinitely (such as a treasured Oriental carpet subject to little wear and excellent care). Insurance companies also have guidelines established for the maximum amount of depreciation to be taken on an item. Generally, most contents items are not depreciated at more than 50 percent as long as they were still in use at the time of the loss. However, exceptions occur, so adjusters should ask for their company's guidelines on this issue.

Age An object's age usually corresponds closely to its extent of physical wear and tear, but age might be considered as a separate factor affecting depreciation. Age alone, however, should not cause an object to lose a large percentage of its value. If the object is functionally sound, it should retain most of its full value.

Obsolescence
The loss of value caused by changes in technology or fashion.

Obsolescence Although age alone should not disproportionately affect depreciation, obsolescence might cause some objects to lose their value. **Obsolescence** is the loss of value caused by changes in technology or fashion. An object can lose value through obsolescence even though it has incurred no real wear and tear. Additionally, obsolescence can occur suddenly, regardless of an object's age. For example, fashions change overnight. Likewise, advances in technology and reductions in manufacturing costs have quickly rendered items only a year or two old obsolete.

Explaining Depreciation

A common term to use to explain depreciation is betterment. An object's amount of depreciation is identical to the amount of how much better, or more valuable, a new object is compared to the older object. Generally, an insured who receives a new object would be better off than would someone who has an older model of the same object. When the property is insured for actual cash value, the amount of the loss settlement reflects the betterment that would exist were replacement cost values used. Explaining actual cash value as betterment can often help the insured understand why depreciation is calculated and applied against replacement values. Using the term "betterment" is not misleading. Quantitatively, betterment and depreciation are always equal. The term "betterment" expresses a different way of looking at the same situation.

Explanations of actual cash value in terms of betterment and the use already derived from the property can help the insured understand the concept of depreciation. Nevertheless, even after the insured understands the concept, the adjuster and the insured might disagree about how depreciation is applied to a piece of property. The adjuster must carefully listen to the insured's arguments and negotiate in good faith. Although the insured has obvious interests in the matter, the insured is also the party most familiar with the property and the circumstances of its use.

Except when replacement cost cannot be determined, calculating actual cash value as replacement cost minus depreciation is usually appropriate. This approach includes all information that would be considered in any other formulation of actual cash value. Nevertheless, two other approaches to actual cash value are important because of the support they have received from the courts. They are (1) the market value approach and (2) the broad evidence rule.

Market Value

Some courts have ruled that actual cash value means fair market value. An item's **market value** is the amount at which a knowledgeable buyer under no unusual pressure would be willing to buy an item and a knowledgeable seller under no unusual pressure would be willing to sell it. Buying a house is a good example of market value. The house's price will fluctuate depending on the supply and demand in the area. Having a market for an object depends on having a sufficient number of buyers and sellers and a complete flow of information regarding products, prices, and buyers and sellers. For many items, the market is irregular, imperfect, or even nonexistent. These conditions occur when there are not enough potential buyers or sellers or when information is too difficult to obtain. The courts that have criticized the market value approach have invariably done so when the market is not functioning properly. Any time that a commodity becomes controlled by a small number of sellers or

Market value
The amount for which a knowledgeable buyer, under no unusual pressure, would buy and for which a knowledgeable seller, under no unusual pressure, would sell.

a small number of buyers, the market value is artificial and therefore may not be a true indicator of actual value. This has occurred with diamonds, gold, and silver when a limited number of sellers has controlled the amount of the commodity available for sale at any one time (despite vast reserves) to drive up the price. Under such circumstances, the market value approach is inappropriate.

Role of Market Value

Perfectly functioning markets use the information contained in the actual cash value formula of replacement cost minus depreciation. No market would value an object for more than the cost to replace it. A market would also consider the depreciation factors previously discussed. When the market for an object is functioning well, that object's market price accurately reflects the value obtained by using replacement cost minus depreciation. Property loss adjusters should cite market prices as support for, and proof of, depreciation amounts.

Market valuation is particularly useful when an object has no real replacement cost, that is, when no other object of like kind and quality exists, as with antiques, works of art, and other collectibles. Additionally, market valuation can be useful with older buildings made from construction materials and methods that are no longer in use. Some features of older construction add to the property's value, but other features detract from it. A market valuation of the property would include both types of features.

Distinguishing Building and Land Values

Real property's market valuation includes both the land's value and the structure's value. Property insurance policies apply only to the structure, making the land's value irrelevant. Fortunately, eliminating the value of the land from loss calculations is easy. Generally, damage to, or destruction of, the building does not affect the land's value. Therefore, any change in the property's value following a loss must result from changes in the buildings' value. The market value determination of loss to a building can be calculated as follows:

$$\begin{array}{c}\text{Market value of loss}\\ \text{to the building}\end{array} = \begin{array}{c}\text{Market value of entire}\\ \text{property before loss}\end{array} - \begin{array}{c}\text{Market value of entire}\\ \text{property after loss}\end{array}$$

This quantity is likely to equal the cost to repair when a minor portion of a building is damaged.

The above formula applies when the value of the land is *unaffected* by loss to the building. Sometimes, however, the land's value increases following a loss, and sometimes it decreases. When the damaged structure does not make the best use of the property to begin with, its destruction might actually increase the land's value. For example, if an old warehouse is located in an area suitable for an office park or apartment development, the warehouse's destruction might increase the land's value, at least to the extent that demolition costs are reduced. Conversely, the destruction of a building that enjoyed privileged use of the land might reduce the land's value. For example, local building and zoning codes typically exempt properties that existed before the codes were enacted. However, an exempt structure's destruction renders any replacement structure subject to the codes. Because complying with building and zoning codes typically increases construction costs, the land's value might decrease.

Case Law Requirements for Market Value

In some states, most notably California, the courts require the use of market value to determine actual cash value. Except for when replacement cost is indeterminable, the market value approach should yield the same results as the replacement cost minus depreciation approach.

Requiring the use of market value in the absence of a real functioning market can harm the insured by artificially devaluing the property. Most items of personal property immediately and dramatically lose market value when they are taken from the retail store where they were purchased. Soon they have no market value. For example, the market for used clothing is small, compared to the market for new clothing. However, a property loss adjuster cannot maintain that a one-year-old suit bought for $250 and still in good condition has virtually no value, even though it has no true market value. Obviously, the replacement cost minus depreciation value is much fairer to the insured and should be used to evaluate the suit.

The Broad Evidence Rule

The **broad evidence rule** has resulted from court-determined case law and explicitly requires property loss adjusters to consider *all* relevant factors when determining actual cash value. Adjusters should, however, already be considering all relevant factors when determining actual cash value by market value in a well-functioning market or by appropriately applying the replacement cost minus depreciation formula. The broad evidence rule arose when courts stipulated that adjusters must consider more than just depreciation or market value when determining actual cash value. See the following box.

Broad evidence rule
A court ruling explicitly requiring that all relevant factors be considered in determining actual cash value.

Broad Evidence Rule

Factors that must be considered, in addition to depreciation and market value, in calculating actual cash value include the following:

- Replacement cost
- Economic, technological, or fashion obsolescence
- The circumstances of the property's use
- Income that might be derived from the property
- Any other related factors

The broad evidence rule might appear to be the most flexible and complete approach to determining actual cash value. However, both the market value and the replacement cost minus depreciation approaches, when properly understood and applied, can be just as accurate and fair. In effect, all three approaches accommodate the same valuation information.

State-Specific Valued Policy Laws

Valued policy laws
Laws that dictate the amount of money that the insured can expect to receive in settling certain claims.

Valued policy laws dictate the amount of money that the insured can expect in settling certain claims. Some states have adopted such laws to protect insureds after loss. These laws require insurance companies to pay the policy's face amount for a total loss. If a valued policy law applies, a property loss adjuster must offer to settle the loss for the policy's face amount, even if a building was overinsured at the time of loss. In the absence of valued policy laws, an adjuster determines the building's value at the time of loss. If the value is less than the amount of insurance, the settlement will be based on the building's value, not the policy limit.

Valued policy laws were enacted to ensure a fair settlement amount based on the total dollars of coverage on which the insured's premium was based. The theory is that if the insured is paying the premium for $200,000 worth of coverage, then $200,000 should be paid for a total loss.

Application

Valued policy laws usually apply only to a total loss to a building, and not to partial losses. They also apply only to buildings and structures, not to personal property losses. Valued policy laws apply only to certain causes of loss, such as fire, but some states add other causes of loss. Exhibit 2-1 is a sample of a valued policy law.

EXHIBIT 2-1

Sample Valued Policy Law

State of New Hampshire
Title XXXVII
Chapter 407
The Fire Insurance Contract and Suits Thereon

@ 407:11. Policy Value

I. If a building insured for a specified amount, whether under a separate policy or under a policy also covering other buildings, is totally destroyed by fire or lightning without criminal fault on the part of the insured or his assignee, the sum for which such building is insured shall be taken to be the value of the insured's interest therein unless overinsurance thereon was fraudulently obtained.

II. If an insured building is only partially destroyed by fire or lightning, the insured shall be entitled to the actual loss sustained not exceeding the sum insured.

III. Nothing contained in paragraphs I and II of this section shall be construed as prohibiting the use of coinsurance, or agreed amount.

IV. When a building is insured not for a specified amount but under a blanket form with one amount covering 2 or more buildings or one or more buildings and personal property, the provisions of paragraph I of this section shall not apply.

HISTORY: 1885, 93:2. PS 170:5. PL 276:8. RL 326:8. RSA 407:8. 1959, 163:1, eff. Jan. 1, 1960.

Jurisdictions With Valued Policy Laws

Because valued policy laws vary, adjusters must check the law in the jurisdiction where a specific loss occurs. Valued policy laws are in effect in Arkansas; Florida; Georgia; Kansas; Louisiana; Minnesota; Mississippi; Missouri; Montana; Nebraska; New Hampshire; North Dakota; Ohio; South Carolina; South Dakota; Texas; West Virginia; Wisconsin; and, if the insured chooses to pay an additional fee for such coverage, in California.

Incentive for Fraud

Valued policy laws violate the principle of indemnity whenever the coverage exceeds the insured property's value because insureds can emerge after a loss in better financial condition than they were in before the loss. Insurers are deeply concerned about the increased potential for fraud whenever valued policy laws are in effect. Under such laws, for example, an insured might have greater financial incentive to commit arson. To counteract this possibility, insurers must be careful not to overinsure.

SETTLEMENT PROVISIONS

Most claims are settled for cash. In some claims, the insurer has the repairs performed by a contractor or repairer or replaces lost or destroyed property. This option to repair or replace the property is contained in virtually all property insurance policies, and it is strictly the *insurer's* option. The insured cannot insist that the insurer repair or replace property.

Repair or Replace Option

Because insurers reserve the option under many policies to repair, rebuild, or replace the property with other property of like kind and quality, insurance companies have for many years worked with camera dealers, furriers, jewelers, and similar merchants and often offer to replace property for insureds. The volume of business they do with these stores enables them to obtain discounts. For certain types of property, such as cameras, insurers can replace items with used equipment of like kind and quality. In addition to merchants, many large replacement service companies serve the insurance industry and stock most items of personal property. The higher the markup on an item, such as jewelry, and the more frequent the type of loss for the insurer, the greater the likelihood that the insurer will elect to replace the property through one of these services.

Insurers exercise the repair or replace option when (1) settling the claim using this method is less expensive or (2) the insured is suspected of trying to profit from the claim. The first condition might exist when the insurer has standing arrangements with wholesale suppliers to replace items of lost property. The insurer might be able to obtain attractive prices because of volume and because it can deal on the wholesale level.

The repair or replace option makes the insured's profiting from a loss very difficult. Insureds who falsify or stage a claim are usually interested in cash. Even if a falsified claim has been submitted, the repair or replace option limits the insurer's exposure on the loss.

Other Loss Settlement Provisions

The two standard loss settlement alternatives are (1) settlement for cash, at replacement cost or actual cash value, and (2) repair or replacement of the property. Other settlement provisions, described below, apply to special cases.

Stated or Agreed Value

A stated value settlement provision requires the insurer to pay a previously agreed-on amount for a total property loss. This provision is not the same as the valued policy laws, which are legislatively imposed. Instead, the stated, or agreed, amount is determined by agreement between the insured and the insurer. This approach is very common with property floaters (which are usually inland marine policies or endorsements) because they are designed to cover a specific piece or type of property. A stated value settlement is also preferable when determining the replacement cost or actual cash value of an object is difficult, as with a piece of fine art.

Selling Price

A manufacturer or retailer can endorse its policy to be covered for the selling price of its inventory. Normally, the inventory would be insured for replacement cost or actual cash value (which, for current unused stock, might be equivalent). Selling price includes the normal business markup above replacement cost. Chapter 10 further addresses the valuation of stocks of merchandise.

Original Cost

An item's original cost is usually irrelevant for claim-settling purposes. However, one exception occurs during loss settlement on a tenant's improvements and betterments. These losses are sometimes settled based on the unused amount of the original cost of the improvements or betterments. For example, a tenant who has spent $25,000 on improvements to a property on which he or she had a ten-year lease would enjoy $2,500 worth of use every year (the improvements become the landlord's property at the end of the lease). If the property were destroyed in year seven, the tenant would lose three years' worth of use of the improvements. This loss is calculated as 3 × $2,500 = $7,500. The dollar value of loss of use is based on the original cost of the improvements, prorated over the life of the lease.

Warranty Services

Similar to the replacement service is a newer service that provides warranties for repaired property. Generally, insurers replace warranties for machinery in a factory, for example, that has been damaged and is considered repairable. Manufacturers are rarely required to continue the original warranty of such damaged items, so insureds have reasonable concerns about the sufficiency of repair. The insurer's warranty service continues the manufacturer's original warranty on the machinery after the repair is complete. This service allows the insurance company to save the cost of a new machine and helps the insured to get back in business faster than if it had to order new machinery. The insurance company might pay a large premium for the warranty, but it will realize a savings on the entire adjustment.

Pair or Set Clause

The **pair or set clause** in policy forms is a traditional concept in property adjustments. This clause states that the insurer has the option (1) to repair or replace any part of a pair or set to restore it to its value before the loss *or* (2) to pay the difference between the property's actual cash value before and after the loss. Often, the value of property is severely diminished when a part of a set is damaged or lost. If the jacket of a suit is damaged, the adjuster will unlikely be able to locate a matching jacket. If one of four three-year-old pairs of drapes in a dining room is damaged, a match could be unlikely to make. However, if a creamer in a silver tea set is damaged, it might be a stock item that is easily replaceable, and the adjuster should invoke the pair and set clause. Replacing the damaged item would restore full pre-loss value to the set. Adjusters should not consider a pair or set a total loss simply because a portion is damaged. They must investigate possibilities of restoring the pair or set to its pre-loss condition by replacing the damaged or lost item.

Pair or set clause
A clause that indicates how values will be established when part of a pair or set is lost, damaged, or destroyed.

RECOVERY LIMITATIONS

Most insurance property coverages have specified limits of what can be paid for a claim. These limits are usually actual dollar amounts. Other limits are based on specific policy provisions that limit recoverable amounts. For example, the cost to repair or replace damaged property is usually expressed as a limitation on the insurer's liability.

Policy Limits

Policy limits
The maximum that can be paid on the claim, regardless of the actual value of the property damaged.

Virtually all property coverages carry a policy limit. **Policy limits** are also referred to as "amount of insurance," "limit of insurance," or "limit of liability." Policy limits are normally the maximum that can be paid on the claim, regardless of the actual value of the property damaged. For example, assume that the policy limit for Coverage A—Dwelling in a homeowners policy is $150,000 and that the home suffers a total loss from a fire. Because of the limit of liability, or policy limit, the most that could be paid to the insured for the claim for the home is $150,000, even if rebuilding the home would cost $155,000.

Policy limits are normally inviolable, with some exceptions. Some policies can have an endorsement or provisions that provide for payment of the full cost to replace the structure or the contents, even if payment exceeds the policy limit, assuming that certain conditions are met. An Insurance Services Office, Inc., (ISO) homeowners policy can have an endorsement called Additional Limits of Liability for Coverages A, B, C, and D, which increases the limits when there is a total loss to the dwelling and the limit shown in the declarations is insufficient to replace the dwelling. It applies, if the insured has maintained a Coverage A limit equal to 100 percent of the dwelling's full replacement cost as determined by the insurer. Other policies may have an endorsement that guarantees replacement cost.

These endorsements can be important in catastrophe situations. For example, the costs to replace buildings may skyrocket because of the demand for competent contractors and a limited supply of construction materials.

Special Limits of Liability

Special limits of liability
Internal dollar limits on certain specified classes of property that apply regardless of the overall policy limit.

Many insurance policies carry internal dollar limits on certain specified classes of property. In the homeowners policies, these are called **special limits of liability**. Commercial property policies also have internal policy limits. These limits can be found in several sections in the commercial policies, including Coverage Extensions and Limits of Insurance.

Deductibles

Deductibles are included in most property insurance claims, whether personal or commercial. One important purpose of a deductible is that it requires the insured to share in the loss. By sharing in the loss, the insured has added incentive to prevent and to minimize losses. Deductibles also eliminate the insurer's obligation for small losses, those below the deductible amount. The insurer benefits because it does not have the administrative costs of small claims. The insured simultaneously benefits by having lower premiums.

Buying coverage for small losses is generally a poor decision for the insured. Because of the insurer's overhead costs of handling small claims, a much smaller percentage of the insured's premium dollar can be expected to be paid out in claims. The insured can save the premium expense of low levels of coverage and absorb the losses through the deductible. Most insureds should select the highest deductible that they can comfortably afford. As deductibles increase, premiums decrease.

Straight Deductibles

Homeowners policies typically have a deductible in the amount of $100, $200, or $250. Most homeowners policies have a **straight deductible**, which means that if a $100 deductible is selected, that would be the deductible whether there is a claim for windstorm, theft, fire, or any other covered cause of loss.

Straight deductible
A dollar amount that the insured must pay toward a covered loss regardless of the cause of loss.

Split Deductibles

An adjuster might occasionally encounter a **split deductible**. For example, a policy might carry a $250 theft deductible and a $100 deductible on all other covered losses. A higher deductible on theft gives the insured a greater incentive to guard against it. Additionally, the insurer is spared the economic impracticality of investigating small claims. Many questionable claims are alleged thefts. Conducting a thorough fraud investigation in such cases is not warranted unless substantial values are involved.

Split deductible
A deductible that applies one deductible for most causes of loss but a different, higher deductible for other specified causes of loss.

Deductibles on Commercial Policies

Commercial property policies commonly have a standard $250 deductible. With an adjustment in premium, the $250 deductible can be raised or lowered. Frequently, the deductible is raised to $500, $1,000, or $5,000.

No Deductible

Some specific coverages do not have a deductible. In commercial coverage, no deductible applies to the fire department service charge. The homeowners policy deductible does not apply to the fire department service charge or to the credit card, fund transfer card, forgery, and counterfeit money coverages. These claims are generally small, and their coverage limits are restrictive.

Absorbing a Deductible

To **absorb a deductible** means to apply the deductible to the actual loss before applying any coverage limits. A deductible can sometimes be absorbed in the property loss settlement. If the loss exceeds the coverage limit by at least the deductible amount, then the insured could collect the full coverage limit without further application of a deductible. See the following box for examples that illustrate this principle:

Absorb a deductible
To apply the deductible to the actual loss before applying any coverage limits.

Absorbing a Deductible

Example 1. Jane Rogers has a homeowners HO-3 form with a $100 deductible and a special limit of liability for cash in the amount of $200. A theft occurs at her residence. The following are stolen:

Television	$220	(ACV)
Cash	350	
VCR	250	(ACV)
Total loss	$820	

The total actual loss that Jane sustained is $820. Because of the special limit of liability for cash, $820 cannot be paid on the claim. The adjusted loss is as follows:

Television	$220	(ACV)
Cash	200	
VCR	250	(ACV)
Total loss	$670	

Jane has suffered a $150 uninsured loss of cash ($350 stolen minus $200 for the coverage limit), which cannot be paid under the insurance policy. Because she has already shared in the loss, no deductible would be applied. She should be paid $670 for her claim. Her $100 deductible is absorbed by the excess $150 cash loss.

Example 2. The Carr family has an HO-3 policy with a $250 deductible and a $1,000 special limit on jewelry. A theft occurs, and the following are stolen:

Diamond necklace	$1,200	(ACV)
Camera	300	(ACV)
Rifle	500	(ACV)
Stereo	1,200	(ACV)
Total loss	$3,200	

The total loss suffered by the Carr family on this claim is $3,200. According to policy provisions, the following should be paid on their claim:

Diamond necklace	$1,000	(special limit)
Camera	300	(ACV)
Rifle	500	(ACV)
Stereo	1,200	(ACV)
Total loss	$3,000	

The Carrs have an excess loss of $200 ($1,200 loss minus $1,000 coverage) on the jewelry. However, they carry a $250 deductible. The $200 excess loss allows $200 of the deductible to be absorbed because this is the insured's share of the loss. The remaining $50 of the deductible must be subtracted from the $3,000 subtotal above. The Carr family should be paid $3,000 minus $50, or $2,950, for their claim.

The principle of absorbing a deductible applies to both commercial property and homeowners coverage. Whenever a claim exceeds the policy limits, the excess loss can be applied to the deductible to absorb part or all of the deductible. To absorb all of the deductible in a claim, the excess loss amount must exceed or equal the deductible amount.

Absorbing deductibles is common in insurance, although the practice is never specifically stated in an insurance policy. Most property loss adjusters regard the practice as part of the correct claim-adjustment process because the policy usually states that the deductible is to be applied to the loss, not to the policy limit. The only justification for handling the deductible otherwise would be if a policy clearly stated that the deductible was to be applied to the *covered* loss, rather than to the loss itself. Such a policy would never pay the full amount of its stated coverage limits.

Coinsurance

Coinsurance is a condition of the property insurance policy that can affect the recovery amount. Insurers include coinsurance clauses in their policies to encourage insureds to carry adequate insurance. The coinsurance clause requires the insured to carry an amount of insurance equal to or greater than a specified percentage of the property's total insured value. An insured who does so is considered adequately insured for a partial loss. For example, in a policy with an 80 percent coinsurance requirement for buildings, the insured must have an amount of insurance equal to or greater than 80 percent of a building's replacement cost to be considered adequately insured. The replacement cost is determined using the policy valuation provisions.

Coinsurance Examples

Jones Hardware Store has a policy with $90,000 coverage on the structure and an 80 percent coinsurance requirement. A partial loss to the building occurs. At the time of the loss, the structure's replacement cost was $100,000. Jones met its coinsurance requirement by having more than the required minimum $80,000 (80 percent of $100,000) coverage. For a partial loss to the structure, Jones has adequate insurance, so the property loss adjuster will pay the full adjusted loss. If Jones Hardware had not met the coinsurance clause requirement, Jones would be paid only a portion of the adjusted loss.

Assume that Jones Hardware had carried only $60,000 worth of coverage on the structure to save premium, because more premium is charged for higher levels of coverage. With an 80 percent coinsurance requirement, Jones is inadequately insured. The minimum amount of insurance required is 80 percent × $100,000 (the property's replacement cost), or $80,000. If Jones were to suffer a loss under this set of circumstances, the amount paid would be calculated as follows:

$$\text{Amount paid} = \frac{\text{Amount of insurance carried}}{\text{Amount of insurance required}} \times \text{Amount of loss}.$$

The following is the shorthand version of this formula:

$$\text{Amount paid} = \frac{\text{Did}}{\text{Should}} \times \text{Loss.}$$

If Jones Hardware has a $10,000 windstorm loss:

$$\frac{\$60{,}000 \text{ (Amount carried)}}{\$80{,}000 \text{ (Amount required)}} \times \$10{,}000 \text{ (Loss amount)} = \$7{,}500 \text{ (Amount paid)}$$

> **Adjuster Tip**
>
> A common error when performing this coinsurance calculation is to use the wrong number in the "amount required." The amount required is not 100 percent of the replacement cost but is the coinsurance percentage amount stated in the policy, or 80 percent in this example. Therefore, the amount required is 80 percent of the replacement cost.

Because of inadequate insurance, Jones Hardware must partially insure the loss, forgoing the benefit of the insurer's paying all of the loss. Therefore, Jones Hardware and the insurer are coinsurers.

Application of Deductibles With Coinsurance

Deductibles must still be applied even when the insured bears a coinsurance penalty. The insured benefits by applying the deductible to the loss first, then applying the coinsurance penalty. In the second Jones Hardware example, this would work as follows:

Deductible Applied First

$$\$10{,}000 \text{ loss} - \$100 \text{ deductible} = \$9{,}900.$$

$$\frac{\$60{,}000}{\$80{,}000} \times \$9{,}900 = \$7{,}425.$$

Coinsurance Applied First

$$\frac{\$60{,}000}{\$80{,}000} \times \$10{,}000 \text{ loss} = \$7{,}500.$$

$$\$7{,}500 - \$100 \text{ deductible} = \$7{,}400.$$

The first method should be used unless the policy indicates that the deductible takes effect *after* the coinsurance clause has been applied. The second method is prescribed in most commercial policies.

> **Adjuster Tip**
>
> Review the coinsurance provision and the deductible provision of the policy form involved in the loss to ensure the correct application of the deductible.

Determining Values for Coinsurance Purposes

When determining whether coinsurance requirements are met, adjusters must determine the insured value of *all* property, both damaged and undamaged. This effort can seem unwarranted for small losses. Fortunately, several sources of information can aid adjusters.

Replacement cost guides and services are available in both printed and computerized form. These enable the adjuster to quickly approximate structures' replacement cost based on square footage, use, and construction method. An insured's records of inventory can usually be accepted as an accurate approximation of the inventory's value.

With small losses, the adjuster might be satisfied to see that the insured has *apparently* complied with coinsurance requirements, rather than to precisely determine compliance. In such cases, any coinsurance penalty would be a small percentage of the loss.

POLICY CONDITIONS

As in any other contract, the conditions are an integral part of the insurance contract. **Conditions** are qualifying agreements that state who is to do what, as well as when and how it is to be done, for the contract to become effective. Conditions explain the rights and duties of the parties to the contract. The following discussion focuses on conditions found in most property policies.

Conditions
Qualifying agreements stating the duties that each party must fulfill for the contract to be valid.

Other Insurance

In property insurance, more than one insurance policy sometimes covers a loss. Such a situation is usually referred to as overlapping coverage. Overlapping coverages might exist for part of a claim or even for the entire claim. Overlapping coverage usually occurs inadvertently. For example, an insured might forget to cancel an existing policy after a new one has been acquired. Coverage for property covered under a specific floater might also exist under general policies, such as the HO-3 or the Building and Personal Property Coverage Form (BPP). Sometimes, a mortgage company and a property owner separately insure the owner's property. However, these situations are uncommon. Another possibility is that the insured has intentionally obtained multiple coverages, which strongly indicates attempted fraud. Adjusters should thoroughly investigate these situations.

In investigating a claim, an adjuster should identify overlapping coverages. The first place to check is with the insured. The adjuster should ask the insured whether more than one policy covers the loss. If other insurance is inadvertently involved, most insureds will report it. If the adjuster believes that the insured is not being honest, the adjuster must investigate further. The adjuster can contact others associated with the claim (such as contractors or—as another example—a jewelry appraiser and employees of the retail store where a piece of jewelry was purchased) to question whether another insurance company has contacted them about the same claim. If so, overlapping coverages are likely.

A claim investigation might reveal other indicators that lead the adjuster to suspect other insurance. One indicator would be if the insured's property were grossly underinsured by one policy. Another indicator might be if the insured incorrectly indicates which agent or broker is servicing the policy. For example, the insured might indicate an agent not associated with the adjuster's company. If these indicators appear, the adjuster should investigate the case to determine what other insurance might be involved.

If the property loss adjuster discovers other insurance, he or she should review the policy's other insurance conditions. These conditions usually deal with overlapping coverages through primary/excess insurance or proportional (pro rata share) insurance.

Primary/Excess

Primary coverage (for other insurance purposes)
A policy that pays for covered losses before other applicable policies until its own limits are exhausted

Insurance policies might indicate that one coverage is primary. **Primary coverage** means that the claim will be paid from that policy first until the limits are exhausted. Excess coverage pays the amount over the primary coverage.

For example, Sharon Mitchell has property insured under two policies. Policy A, with a $6,000 limit, states that it is primary coverage; Policy B, which has a $10,000 limit, states that it is excess. Sharon has a $10,000 loss covered by both policies. Policy A will pay its $6,000 policy limit of coverage; Policy B will then pay the $4,000 amount of the loss over $6,000.

Types of Excess Insurance

Excess-of-other-insurance
Insurance that pays an amount over the primary layer of coverage.

Excess insurance, in this context, means insurance that is excess over other valid and collectible insurance. An **excess-of-other-insurance clause** is distinct from a true excess policy. A true excess policy covers losses only over some large deductible amount, usually in the six- or seven-figure range, and does not cover smaller losses, regardless of whether they are covered elsewhere. A policy with an excess-of-other-insurance clause is a primary policy, which pays only after the coverage of other primary policies is exhausted.

Policies Presumed Primary

Few insurance policies explicitly state that their coverage is primary. Therefore, the general rule is that coverage is primary unless the policy states otherwise. Without an "other insurance" condition indicating that the coverage is excess or pro rata, the property loss adjuster should treat existing coverage as primary. If one policy states that it is pro rata and the other policy states that it is excess, the excess clause is effective and the pro rata policy becomes primary.

Deductibles

Adjusters must also apply primary/excess deductibles. With primary/excess coverage, the excess coverage can occasionally pay the difference in the deductibles. See the following box.

Deductibles Example

Suppose that ABC Insurance Company's policy states that its coverage is excess and has a $100 deductible. XYZ Insurance Company's policy does not have the other insurance condition, and its policy has a $250 deductible. For a loss, XYZ's coverage would be primary, and its obligation would be to pay the adjusted claim minus the $250 deductible. ABC's obligation would be to pay the difference in the deductibles, $250 minus $100, or $150. ABC would be obligated to pay only the difference in the deductibles when, as in this example, ABC's deductible is smaller than XYZ's. If XYZ has a smaller or an equal deductible, ABC would have no obligation to pay any part of the claim.

Proportional (Pro Rata) Share Method

A common method of dealing with overlapping coverages is **proportional** or **pro rata share**. With this method, insurers contribute to the loss payment in the proportion to which they contribute to the total amount of coverage purchased. See the following box.

Proportional (pro rata) share
An approach to other insurance by which the insurers contribute to the loss payment in the proportion to which they contribute to the total amount of coverage purchased (their limits of liability).

Proportional (Pro Rata) Share Method Examples

- Suppose that Insurance Company A has a policy with $40,000 coverage and that Insurance Company B has a policy on the same property with $60,000 coverage. The insured suffers a covered loss of $10,000. Insurance Company A would owe

  $$\frac{\$40{,}000 \text{ (Insurance Company A's amount of coverage)}}{\$100{,}000 \text{ (Total amount of coverage: } \$40{,}000 + \$60{,}000)}$$

  or

  40%, 4/10, or .40 of the loss

  $40\% \times \$10{,}000 = \$4{,}000.$

  Insurance Company B would owe

  $$\frac{\$60{,}000 \text{ (Insurance Company B's amount of coverage)}}{\$100{,}000 \text{ (Total amount of coverage: } \$40{,}000 + \$60{,}000)}$$

  or

  60%, 6/10, or .60 of the loss

  $60\% \times \$10{,}000 = \$6{,}000.$

  The combined payment of the companies equals the total payable claim of $10,000. The insured would not collect more than the amount of the loss.

- Suppose that Mark and Cindy Wilkinson are insured by two homeowners insurance policies. Both policies have other insurance conditions indicating that losses must be adjusted using the proportional share method. The Wilkinsons have $75,000

Continued on next page.

worth of coverage with Company C and $25,000 worth of coverage with Company D. Both insurance policies cover a $12,000 claim.

Company C owes

$$\left(\frac{\$75{,}000}{\$100{,}000}\right) \times \$12{,}000 = \$9{,}000$$

Company D owes

$$\left(\frac{\$25{,}000}{\$100{,}000}\right) \times \$12{,}000 = \$3{,}000$$

This method is traditionally called payment by policy limits.

Other Proportional Sharing

Two other less common methods of proration are (1) payment by equal shares and (2) payment by amounts payable. These methods apply only when the other insurance clause indicates.

Payment by equal shares
An approach to other insurance by which the loss is paid equally by both policies until one policy is exhausted; then the other policy alone pays.

Payment by Equal Shares Under **payment by equal shares**, the loss is paid equally by both policies until one policy is exhausted; then the other policy alone pays. Consider the Wilkinsons' coverage for losses of $40,000 and $60,000. The $40,000 loss would be shared equally ($20,000 each) by Company C and Company D. On a $60,000 loss, the two companies would equally share the loss up to $50,000 ($25,000 for each), at which point Company D's coverage would be exhausted. Company C would then pay the remaining $10,000 of the loss.

Payment by amounts payable
An approach to other insurance by which each insurer pays a portion of the loss equal to the amount that one insurer would separately pay, divided by the total of the separate amounts payable by all insurers.

Payment by Amounts Payable When the **payment by amounts payable** approach to other insurance is used, each insurer pays a portion of the loss equal to the amount that one insurer would separately pay, divided by the total of the separate amounts payable. Using the example of the Wilkinsons, Company C and Company D would share the loss in the following proportions:

Amount Company C would pay separately is $40,000.

$$\frac{\$40{,}000}{\$40{,}000 + \$25{,}000} \times \$40{,}000 = \$24{,}615$$

Amount Company D would pay separately is $25,000.

$$\frac{\$25{,}000}{\$40{,}000 + \$25{,}000} \times \$40{,}000 = \$15{,}385$$

Total: $\$24{,}615 + \$15{,}385 = \$40{,}000.$

When both insurers fully cover the loss, this method results in an equal split.

Prorating Deductibles

In addition to loss payment, policy deductibles are proportionally split in cases of overlapping coverage. If Company C has ¾ of the coverage, it would subtract

¾ of the deductible amount from its claim payment. Company D would subtract ¼ of the deductible amount when it carries ¼ of the total coverage.

The deductible application follows the straight proportional method unless the two companies have different deductible amounts. See the following box.

Prorating Deductible Example

Suppose that the insured has a policy with Company X with a \$100 deductible and a policy with Company Y on the same property with a \$250 deductible. Both policies have other insurance conditions calling for a proportional share settlement. The Company X policy has \$10,000 of coverage; the Company Y policy has \$90,000 of coverage. Now assume that the insured sustains a \$10,000 covered loss.

Begin the calculations by subtracting the largest deductible from the loss. Company Y has the \$250 deductible, so the loss payable is \$10,000 – \$250 = \$9,750. This loss is the common loss shared by both companies. The loss is apportioned between them as follows:

Company X $$\frac{\$10{,}000}{\$100{,}000} \times \$10{,}000 = \$1{,}000.$$

Company Y $$\frac{\$90{,}000}{\$100{,}000} \times \$10{,}000 = \$9{,}000.$$

The two companies would then calculate a proportional share of the common deductible. The common deductible is the smallest deductible amount that the two companies share. In this case, the common deductible would be \$100; both companies have a deductible of at least this amount. The adjuster would apply the proportional share computation as earlier computed.

Company X's deductible would be as follows:

$$\frac{\$10{,}000 \text{ (Company X's coverage)}}{\$100{,}000 \text{ (Total coverage: } \$90{,}000 + \$10{,}000)} = 10\%.$$

or

1/10, or .10

10% of the common \$100 deductible = \$10.

Company Y's deductible would be as follows:

$$\frac{\$90{,}000 \text{ (Company Y's coverage)}}{\$100{,}000 \text{ (Total coverage: } \$90{,}000 + \$10{,}000)} = 90\%.$$

or

9/10, or .90

90% of the common \$100 deductible = \$90.

Continued on next page.

In addition to Company Y's proportional share of the common deductible, Company Y would also subtract the additional unshared deductible amount from the loss. The additional deductible amount for Company Y would be as follows:

$250 (Company Y's total deductible) – $100 (common deductible) = $150.

Company Y would then have a total deductible applicable to the claim of $240 ($90 + $150).

Company X would apply a $10 deductible to its claim payment. The insured would be subject to the total deductible of $100, an amount equal to the smallest deductible on any policy. Note that the $150 difference in Company Y's deductible calculation is still not accounted for. This $150 difference is added into the claim payment made by Company X. Company X pays this portion of Company Y's deductible because it is an insured loss under Company X's policy. By doing this, the insured is only charged the larger of the two deductibles ($250) for the loss, while the $250 deductible is apportioned between the two companies. The loss payment calculation would then look like this:

Co. Y: $10,000 x 90% = $9,000 – $240 (deductible) = $8,760.

Co. X: $10,000 x 10% = $1,000 – $10 (deductible) = $990 + $150.
(the difference between the two deductibles) = $1,140.

Total loss payment to the insured: $8,760. + $1,140 = $9,900.

Despite these examples, applying the proportional share method to two different deductibles is uncommon.

Both Stated To Be Excess

Two insurance policies applying to the same claim sometimes contain the other insurance condition stating that their coverage is excess. In that case, the coverage reverts to a proportional share method of contribution.

Disagreements Over Other Insurance

Sometimes, insurers disagree about their obligations for payment when overlapping coverage exists. Three approaches can be used to resolve these differences:

1. Compromise
2. Application of the Guiding Principles
3. Resolution in court

Compromise

The most common approach is to reach a compromise agreement between the two insurers. Adjusters must attempt to make the insured whole while negotiating this compromise. One means of accomplishing this would be for each insurer to pay the amount that it believes it owes and half of the amount in dispute. The insured would then be satisfied, and the insurers could then attempt to resolve their differences through continued negotiation and arbitration.

Guiding Principles

Another approach to resolve overlapping coverage problems is to apply the Guiding Principles. Excerpts of the first-party property Guiding Principles appear in the Appendix to this chapter. Please note in the Foreword that these principles apply to all coverages except overlapping boiler and machinery coverage. The **Guiding Principles** were established by industry-wide associations in the 1960s to resolve conflicts among multiple insurers covering the same loss. Companies had to be signatories to the agreement in order for the Guiding Principles to be binding on them. Although many companies are no longer signatories to the Guiding Principles, many adjusters still use them as a way to resolve overlapping coverage problems.

Guiding Principles
A set of industry-agreed-upon principles designed to resolve situations of overlapping coverage.

Application of Guiding Principles

The Guiding Principles apply when the other insurance clauses are contradictory or when other insurance clauses do not exist. The Guiding Principles operate only when more than one policy covers a loss and when the policies' other insurance clauses do not resolve how to apply the respective coverages.

Priority of Policies

The Guiding Principles indicate when policies are primary to or excess over one another. They also provide a method of proration for policies that are neither primary nor excess to one another. The listings of policy priority, as primary or excess, are set forth for two different situations: (1) when the policies cover the same property and same interest—for example, two homeowners policies covering the same insured and same home and (2) when the policies cover the same property but different interests—for example, a homeowners policy and a dry cleaners policy that each covers the homeowners' clothes if destroyed at the cleaners.

In establishing priority, the Guiding Principles make policies that cover more specifically described property, at more specifically described locations, primary over more general policies. Paragraph 1 of the Guiding Principles, applicable to policies covering the same property and the same interest, lists policy priorities in subparagraphs 1.A through 1.F.

When policies have the same priority level, proration depends on subparagraph 1.G and general condition 2 of the Guiding Principles. Proration does not depend on the limits of insurance, but on the amounts payable method previously described.

Court Resolution

When all else fails, the only remaining approach to resolve disputes between companies is to file a lawsuit and to have a court determine the outcome. This is usually the case when large amounts of money are involved. Unfortunately, resorting to the courts for a resolution can be a highly uncertain option because adjusters can never be sure of what a court will decide. Courts have inconsistently addressed overlapping coverage.

Insured's Duties After Loss

The insured's duties after a loss are explicitly stated in a policy's provisions. Adjusters must proceed carefully, however, because waiver and estoppel can affect the insured's duties.

Waiver and Estoppel

Waiver
The intentional or voluntary relinquishment of a known right.

Estoppel
A legal principle that prevents a party from enforcing a present claimed position because it is inconsistent with that party's past conduct.

Nonwaiver agreement
An agreement by which the insurer and insured agree that the insurer's investigation of a claim does not waive any of the insurer's rights or the insured's rights.

Reservation of rights letter
A letter that the insurer sends to the insured reserving the right to enforce all policy provisions and conditions regardless of what action the insurer takes to investigate or defend the claim.

Proof of loss
A document that is the insured's sworn description of the details of the loss, property values, and interests in the property.

Waiver involves voluntarily and intentionally relinquishing a known contractual right. **Estoppel** prohibits a party to a contract from enforcing certain conditions of the contract because that party's behavior or words caused a breach of contract. Estoppel results when one party's behavior or words cause another party to rely detrimentally on that behavior or those words. Estoppel prevents one party from enforcing contract conditions. Adjusters often waive the need for a proof of loss on small property losses. For example, estoppel occurs when an adjuster tells an insured to throw out a damaged carpet before it is inspected. The adjuster is estopped from denying the claim for the coverage because it is not available for inspection.

If the insurer wishes to invoke any condition in the policy, the insurer or adjuster must advise the insured by either a **nonwaiver agreement** or a **reservation of rights letter**. These documents are discussed in greater detail in Chapter 6. Either one of these instruments preserves the insurer's rights to invoke a condition at a later time. The adjuster must be alert to coverage problems in a loss adjustment and must protect the insurer's interest with a nonwaiver agreement or reservation of rights letter whenever the possibility of waiver exists.

Proof of Loss

The **proof of loss** is a document describing the details of the loss, property values, and interests in the property for which the insured is making a claim under the policy. The insurer usually provides the insured with the proof of loss form. In some states, insurers are required to provide the form. In other states, no particular form is required, as long as all necessary information is included.

Proof of Loss Requirement

To be meaningful, the proof of loss should be required early in the adjustment process. The proof of loss is a powerful adjusting tool that commits the insured under oath to a specific set of facts.

Some insurers require a proof of loss at the end of the adjustment process. By that time, however, the adjuster has presumably agreed on the settlement, and the proof of loss accomplishes little, except to document the claim file. For routine or small claims, many insurers intentionally (or by inaction) waive the proof of loss requirement, which can facilitate the adjustment process. Many insurers simply disregard the proof of loss requirement on most losses and enforce the requirement only by exception. Others invoke the proof of loss requirement on losses such as total losses, questionable losses, or losses over a certain dollar figure. Some insurers invoke the requirement on all losses. Adjusters must know the requirements of the insurance company or companies for which they are handling claims so as not to waive rights under the policy.

Changes in or Waiver of Proof of Loss

If the insured wishes to change a proof of loss or file an amended proof of loss, the adjuster will consider these alterations after he or she thoroughly reviews the situation with the insurer's management. Any agreement considering a change or amended proof of loss might serve as a waiver by the insurer should it later want to deny a claim based on the original proof of loss. Courts freely permit changes to proofs of loss to correct honest errors.

Rejection of Proof of Loss

After the insurer has invoked the proof of loss requirement and the insured has filed the proof of loss, the insurer must, within a designated time set by either the policy, state insurance code, or case law, make a decision. The insurer can choose one of the following actions:

1. Accept the proof of loss as submitted
2. Reject the proof of loss, using specific language as to why it is not acceptable, and give the insured an opportunity to refile a corrected proof of loss
3. Reject the proof of loss, giving specific reasons for the rejection, and allow the insured to make the next move without any further direction

Timeliness If the proof of loss is rejected for any reason, the rejection must be timely. Promptly rejecting the proof of loss protects the insurer in policies with language stating that payment will be made within a certain time after receiving proof of loss. Therefore, if the insurer does not reject a proof of loss immediately, the insurer might be compelled to pay even if the proof is believed to be deficient. After an insurer receives the proof of loss, state insurance codes allow a time period either to pay the claim or to reject the proof. In any case, an adjuster must check the state statutes or state-mandated insurance policy provisions or forms before rejecting a proof of loss.

Specification of Reasons If the proof of loss is rejected, it must be rejected for specific reasons, and with the consent of the insurer's management. Typical reasons for a rejection are as follows:

1. The proof of loss does not contain sufficient documentation to support the amount claimed.
2. The proof of loss was incomplete on its face.
3. The proof of loss was not filed within the time required by the policy.

Examination Under Oath

Examination under oath (EUO)
The sworn oral statement of the insured that enables the insurer to obtain the insured's account of a loss and explanation of documents submitted as proof of the loss.

Examination under oath (EUO) can be valuable to the insurer when arson is suspected, committed either by the insured or by collusion with an insured; when fraud is suspected; or when the adjuster has been unable to obtain information regarding how a loss occurred. Although it generates some expense, the savings gained can often offset the costs. Examinations under oath enable the insurer to obtain sufficient documentation from the insured either to support or refute the claim. Comparing the oral testimony from an examination to records supplied by the insured is also an ideal way to support or refute a claim.

Any question about the purpose and validity of the examination under oath has been answered by the United States Supreme Court in the case of Claflin v. Commonwealth Insurance Company:

> The object of the provisions in the policy of insurance requiring the insured to submit himself to an examination under oath, to be reduced to writing, was to enable the company to possess itself of all knowledge, and all information, as to the other sources and means of knowledge, in regards to the facts, material to their rights, to enable them to decide upon their obligations, and to protect them against false claims. A false answer as to any matter of fact material to the inquiry, knowingly and willfully made, with intent to deceive the insurer, would be fraudulent. If it accomplished its results, it would be a fraud effective; if it failed, it would be a fraud attempted. And if the matter were material and the statement false, to the knowledge of the party making it, and willfully made, the intention to deceive the insurer would be necessarily implied for the law presumes every man to intend the natural consequences of his acts.[2]

According to this statement, the EUO gives the insurer a means to determine whether it will deny or provide coverage on a claim. Chapter 6 provides a complete discussion of the EUO.

The Appraisal Provision

Almost all property insurance policies have a condition providing a method for resolving differences between parties. The appraisal provision is used in most property policies. Any party that wants to preserve its rights must adhere to this provision.

Purpose of Appraisal

The appraisal provision provides a means to resolve disputes regarding value without one party having to sue another. The provision has no role in resolving any questions of coverage or policy language interpretation. The provision's language is clear on that point. For instance, if the damaged property will be repaired and not replaced, one of the factors that can create differences concerning the loss amount is the repair method. The repair method, as well as the extent of repair, affects the repair's cost, which, in turn, affects the amount of loss. Many contractors or engineers consider tearing down sections of a building and rebuilding less expensive than repairing the structure as it stands. The appraisal provision can be invoked when the insured, insurer, and appraiser differ about repair methods and the amount of loss.

Nothing in the appraisal clause provides for resolving any other disagreements between the parties. (Such disagreements are discussed elsewhere throughout this text.) Generally, coverage questions are not resolved through the appraisal process. Courts vary in their decisions, but the provision is intended to determine only the amount of loss. When what may or may not be covered in a loss is questioned, the parties involved must pursue avenues other than the appraisal provision.

Demand for Appraisal

The appraisal provision uses the word "demand," which means that if either party makes a demand, the other has no choice but to submit to the appraisal. If the insurer sends a letter to the insured "demanding" an appraisal, the insured cannot refuse. To do so would be considered a violation of a policy condition, and the insurer could deny the claim based on that violation. However, an insurer that denies coverage altogether waives its right to appraisal.

Some states have amendatory endorsements that have made the appraisal process voluntary or non-binding, or have completely removed it from the policy. Adjusters should check the rules of the jurisdiction before invoking the appraisal clause.

Appraisers' and Umpire's Qualifications The appraisal provision addresses the appraisers' qualifications in terms of competence and economic interest, as well as the selection of an umpire.

Appraisers' Competence The appraisal provision states that each party will choose a *competent* appraiser within a specific time frame. Either party could plausibly question an appraisal award if the other party chooses an incompetent appraiser. If a dispute arises about the amount of loss on an extensive fire claim and the insured selects a friend who is an unlicensed carpenter as the appraiser, the insurer might have a reasonable basis to challenge the appraiser's competence and to contest the selection of that appraiser.

If one of the appraisal parties objects to the competency of the opposition's appraiser and that party continues to retain that appraiser until the appraisal is completed, the other party could contest the appraisal award through the courts. To avoid this possibility, each party to the appraisal must select an appraiser carefully.

Appraisers' Interest Another area that should be considered is the appraiser's interest in the outcome of the appraisal. An appraiser with a strong conflict of interest should never be selected. In some policies, the appraisal provision states that the appraisers named by the parties must be disinterested. An example of an appraiser who is not disinterested is a contractor who was chosen by the insured but who had already agreed to perform the repairs on the insured's property. An insured's employee is another example.

The insurer should also be careful to choose a disinterested appraiser. This does not mean that the insurer and the appraiser have never dealt with each other in the past—only that the appraiser not be economically dependent on the insurer. All dealings between an adjuster and an appraiser should be professional. An adjuster should never select an appraiser because of personal favors. If the particular policy's language states that the appraiser must be disinterested, the insurer should name a disinterested appraiser to avoid jeopardizing its position or waiving its rights.

Umpire Selection The appraisal provision states that the two appraisers should choose the umpire. This is usually accomplished without a problem, and the appraisal can proceed. When no agreement on the umpire can be reached, the selection goes to a court having jurisdiction over the dispute for resolution.

The Appraisal Process

The procedure required by the appraisal clause is not overly detailed, allowing some flexibility for the appraisers. A formal hearing is not required to complete an appraisal.

Separate Appraisals The policy stipulates that each appraiser "separately set the amount of loss." The appraisers should go to the loss site, review the damage, and provide their own figures on what they determine to be the amount of loss. Different appraisers will probably select different repair techniques and will determine different costs. However, following their reviews, the two appraisers should try to agree on the scope of the damage—whether property should be repaired or replaced and its quantity (dimensions and amount) and quality. Separate appraisals act as competitive bids in keeping costs in line. Nevertheless, two appraisers commonly work together to resolve the scope of the damage.

Umpire's Role Appraisers often disagree considerably about the amount of loss. The appraisal provision indicates procedures for handling such cases. Most policies contain language that requires the appraisers to submit their differences to an umpire. In this case, the appraisers submit only differing figures. According to some policies, the appraisers submit all of their figures on the amount of damage for the umpire to consider. The adjuster must carefully read the policy before proceeding with the appraisal process.

Appraisal Decision Generally, in the appraisal provision, any agreement between two of the three parties sets the amount of loss. This language might differ in other policies, but it usually states that if *any* two agree, whether it is two appraisers or the umpire and one of the appraisers, then the appraisal is set and completed.

Challenges to the Decision Once an appraisal has been set, it is binding on all parties. This is not to say that an appraisal cannot be challenged, but usually only fraud, collusion, and mistake of law are valid grounds to challenge and perhaps overturn an appraisal. Sometimes, a challenge is based on the contention that the appraiser was incompetent or that coverage issues were involved. In most cases, if the appraisers and the umpire are properly selected, the award stands.

Expenses The final consideration in the appraisal relates to costs and expenses. The provision requires each of the parties to the appraisal to bear their own appraiser's costs. The parties equally share the umpire's cost and expenses.

Waiver and Estoppel The adjuster should advise the insured throughout the adjustment of any condition that the insurer might invoke. The adjuster's action or lack of action could waive the insurer's rights to invoke that condition later. If an appraisal is being considered and the decision is made to invoke it, the insurer must advise the insured in a demand letter using exact policy language. The insurer must then follow all rules of the appraisal promptly and professionally. Any violation of the rules in the appraisal provision might result in an estoppel against the insurer to enforce the provision.

For example, if the insurer demands an appraisal and the insured properly names its appraiser within the twenty-day limit, but the insurer does not name its appraiser in the time allowed, the insured could refuse the appraisal because of the insurer's violation of the condition.

Precondition to Lawsuit Because the appraisal provision is one of the policy conditions, this provision's requirement must be observed before a lawsuit can be filed. For instance, assume that the amount of loss is disputed and that the insurer demands an appraisal. However, the insured refuses appraisal and proceeds to file a lawsuit for contractual damage against the insurer. Each state has different laws, and courts typically differ in their findings, but the policy conditions must generally be complied with before a lawsuit is filed. In this example, the insured would lose. Alternatively, if the insurer denies coverage, the insurer will be deemed to have waived the appraisal right. An insured could initiate suit immediately after a coverage denial.

The Adjuster's Role in the Appraisal Process The appraisal provision is not used often, but when it is used, the adjuster must be prepared to follow the procedure through to a conclusion. The adjuster must also be thoroughly familiar with how the procedure operates, ensuring that it is followed according to the policy and that the appraisal conforms to the insurance code of the state in which it is being conducted.

Sometimes, the appraisers or the adjuster might testify. If an appraisal involves a large loss, the insured and insurer will usually be represented by counsel and will have their own appraisers. In such cases, the umpire can receive testimony from the appraisers, the attorneys, and the adjuster. The adjuster's knowledge of the procedure and the expectations of each party to the appraisal help the process to move smoothly.

SUMMARY

Determining who and what are insured is the initial issue that faces an adjuster on every claim. Having confirmed that the insured and the property are covered for the loss, the property loss adjuster must next concentrate on the recovery amount. The recovery amount depends on several factors:

1. Policy valuation of property involved in the loss (which could be affected by case law, state laws, and regulations)
2. Policy coverage limits
3. Policy deductibles
4. Policy conditions, such as the coinsurance penalty if required
5. Potential of other insurance applying to the loss

Real and personal property are usually valued at replacement cost or actual cash value. Replacement cost is the cost of replacing the damaged property with new property of like kind and quality, at current prices. Because replacement cost provisions provide new property for old property, they violate the principle of indemnity.

Actual cash value (ACV) has been defined in many ways. A commonly used definition is replacement cost minus depreciation. Depreciation can be straight-line, accelerated, or decelerated. Some items will not depreciate at all but instead will appreciate over time. The amount of depreciation taken is based on physical wear and tear, age, and obsolescence. Some courts have held that ACV means market value. Market value is often described as what a willing buyer would pay to obtain an item from a willing seller. Market value can be useful for unique items or for older buildings that contain materials and construction no longer in use. When determining a building's market value, the land's value must be eliminated from the calculation.

Some courts have determined that depreciation and market value are not sufficient to ascertain actual cash value. These jurisdictions adhere to a broad evidence rule stating that many factors, such as economic, technological, or fashion obsolescence, should be considered in determining ACV.

Some states have valued policy laws. These laws require the insurer to pay the face amount of the policy if a total loss occurs. These laws apply only to buildings and structures, not to personal property. Like replacement cost coverage, valued policy laws violate the principle of indemnity.

Insurers have the option to repair or replace damaged property or to pay the cash value. Some property policies have an agreed value that is an amount that the insured and the insurer have agreed will be paid if a loss occurs. Policies for manufacturers or retailers often have an endorsement that values the stock and inventory at selling price.

Policy limits are the maximum amount payable on a loss. However, homeowners policies can have endorsements that provide for payment of the full cost to replace the dwelling even if the loss exceeds the policy limit.

Property policies also contain internal limits or special limits for specified classes of property, such as money, jewelry, and precious metals.

Property policies contain deductibles. The application of the deductible amount is specified by the policy. Most policies apply the deductible to the loss and then apply the policy limit. This practice is called absorbing the deductible.

Property policies contain a coinsurance provision that encourages insureds to purchase adequate insurance. The provision requires the insured to carry an amount of insurance equal to or greater than the specified percentage of the property's total value. If the insured fails to do so, the amount recoverable under the policy is reduced. The calculation for coinsurance is usually expressed as:

$$\text{Amount to be paid} = \frac{\text{Did}}{\text{Should}} \times \text{Loss.}$$

Unless the policy states otherwise, the deductible is taken from the loss before the coinsurance calculation is made. For the purposes of the coinsurance calculation, the amount required is the value of all property, damaged and undamaged, multiplied by the coinsurance percentage. On small losses, it is usually sufficient to show that the insured has apparently complied with the coinsurance provision.

Policy conditions also affect the amount recoverable under the policy. If more than one policy or coverage applies to the loss, the other insurance provision must be used to determine how the loss will be paid. Most policies are primary, meaning that they will pay first. Some policies specifically state that they are excess of other insurance, meaning that they pay after the primary policy coverage has been depleted. Other policies may state that they pay on a pro rata basis with other policies.

When overlapping coverage exists and the insurers disagree over the amounts they must pay, there are three ways to resolve the dispute. One is by compromise and arbitration. The second option is to apply the Guiding Principles to the situation. The Guiding Principles provide a means of ascertaining policy priority without resorting to a lawsuit. Although many insurers are no longer signatories to the Guiding Principles, adjusters still rely on them as the basis for an amicable resolution. If agreement cannot be reached, the third way to deal with a dispute is to file a lawsuit and seek judicial resolution.

The policy outlines certain duties of the insured and the insurer after a loss has occurred. The adjuster must be aware of these duties so that waiver and estoppel do not occur. Waiver is the voluntary relinquishing of a right. In small property losses, adjusters often waive the need for a proof of loss. Estoppel occurs when one party's behavior or words cause the other party to detrimentally rely on those words or behavior.

One of the conditions that the insured must comply with after a loss is the submission of a proof of loss. The proof of loss details the circumstance of the loss, the property values, and the interests in the property. Once the proof of loss is submitted, the insurer must respond to it within a time period that is designated by the policy, state insurance code, or case law. The insurer can accept the proof of loss or can reject it. If it is rejected, the rejection must be timely and must state the reasons for the rejection.

Another duty of the insured after a loss is to cooperate with the investigation of the loss. The insurer can demand that the insured be examined under oath. This procedure is often used when fraud is suspected or a question exists concerning the coverage for the loss. The examination under oath (EUO) enables the insurer to obtain information to support or refute the claim.

If the insured and the insurer disagree as to the value of the loss or damage, the policy has an appraisal provision that will resolve the dispute. Appraisal must be attempted before the filing of any lawsuit. Either the insured or the insurer can invoke the appraisal provision. It is usually a binding decision on all parties, but some states have made it voluntary or non-binding or have eliminated the language completely from the policy.

Both the insured and the insurer each pick a competent appraiser. Competent is interpreted to mean someone with property damage expertise as well as someone who has no interest in the final outcome. The two appraisers appoint a third person to act as umpire. The appraisal process can be as formal or informal as the umpire desires. Each side is responsible for the expense of their chosen appraiser, and both sides split the cost of the umpire. Any agreement between two of the three parties sets the amount of the loss.

Having learned the basic concepts of property insurance, a property loss adjuster applies these concepts to an actual loss under a property policy. Chapter 3 acquaints the adjuster with the specific coverages provided by the ISO HO-3 Homeowners Policy. Chapter 4 discusses coverage in commercial property forms.

CHAPTER NOTES

1. Form HO 00 03 05 01, Copyright, Insurance Services Office, Inc., 2001.
2. Claflin v. Commonwealth Insurance Company, 110 U.S. 81, 3 S.Ct. 507 (1884).

Appendix

The Guiding Principles

FOREWORD

Under practices predating these Guiding Principles, where an overlap in coverage existed between or among policies in the casualty, fire or inland marine classifications of insurance, each such classification participated as a group in the adjustment (subject to extent of available insurance and limiting conditions) without regard to the number of policies involved under each classification.

With the advent of multiple-line policies[1] which cross and re-cross jurisdictional lines, the Associations recommending these Guiding Principles have concluded that, excepting overlap between boiler-machinery policies with any other classification of insurance, it is no longer practical to group policies by "segments" of the industry; rather that each policy should contribute as an individual policy unless it be concurrent[2] with another policy or policies, in which instance such group of concurrent policies should contribute as if it were a single policy, subject to the Specific Principles and General Conditions contained herein.

However, retention of the classification concept is necessary to determine under which of the Principles certain overlaps are apportioned; namely, casualty, fidelity,[3] fire, inland marine; casualty-casualty, fire-fire, inland-inland. For this purpose, and not to determine concurrent policies, the component coverages found in multiple-line policies should be identified on the basis of their traditional underwriting classification, i.e., the burglary and theft coverages of homeowners policies are casualty; the all-risk personal property coverage found in certain homeowners policies is inland marine.

GUIDING PRINCIPLES FOR OVERLAPPING INSURANCE COVERAGES (SUPERSEDING ALL GUIDING PRINCIPLES OF PRIOR DATE)

The Purpose

WHEREAS from time to time disputes arise in the adjustment and apportionment of losses and claims because of overlapping coverages, which disputes require litigation or arbitration, and

WHEREAS the occurrence of such disputes is against the interests of the insuring public and the companies, and

WHEREAS it is desirable to lay down certain Principles for the elimination of these disputes,

THEREFORE BE IT RESOLVED that the Association of Casualty and Surety Companies, the Inland Marine Underwriters Association, the National Automobile Underwriters Association, the National Board of Fire Underwriters, the National Bureau of Casualty Underwriters and the Surety Association of America recommend to their respective members and subscribers their concurrence in adopting the following Guiding Principles, effective as to losses and claims, other than losses and claims involving retrospective[4] rated policies, occurring on and after November 1, 1963.

Note: When retrospective rated boiler-machinery—fire policies overlap, these Guiding Principles do apply.

The Plan

These Principles provide for the equitable distribution of available insurance. As among insurance companies, the "other insurance" clause(s) which is (are) contained in a policy(ies) of insurance, and which may include an excess provision,[5] shall be set aside and be inoperative to the extent that it is (they are) in conflict with the purpose of these Principles. Otherwise, these Principles will not change coverage or other conditions under any policy(ies) of insurance.

Further, the application of these Principles shall in no event operate to reduce recovery to the insured below that which would have been obtained under any policy or policies covering the risk.

Part I

The Procedure

Dealing with first-party property losses and claims, except those situations more specifically provided for in Part II (Specific Principles—casualty-casualty, fire-fire and inland-inland) and the General Conditions.

General Principles

1. Insurance covering same property and same interest:
   A. Insurance covering a specifically described article or object, whether or not for an express amount, at a designated location[6] shall be primary to any other insurance. (See Notes 1 and 2 below)
   B. Insurance covering a specifically described article or object, whether or not for an express amount, without designation of location shall be excess as to 1-A but primary as to any other insurance. (See Notes 1 and 2 below)
   C. Insurance covering a specifically described group or class of related articles or objects, whether or not for an express amount, at a designated location shall be excess as to 1-A and 1-B but primary as to any other insurance. (See Notes 1 and 2 below)
   D. Insurance covering a specifically described group or class of related articles or objects, whether or not for an express amount, without designation of location shall be excess as to 1-A, 1-B and 1-C but primary as to any other insurance. (See Notes 1 and 2 below)
   E. Insurance covering at a designated location and not specific as to an article or object or as to group or class of related articles or objects shall be excess as to 1-A, 1-B, 1-C and 1-D but primary as to any other insurance. (See Notes 1 and 2 below)
   F. Insurance without designation of location and not specific as to an article or object or as to group or class of related articles or objects shall be excess to 1-A, 1-B, 1-C, 1-D and 1-E.

      However, as between insurances without designation of location and not specific as to an article or object or as to group or class of related articles or objects, the policy for the more limited purpose[7] (other than peril) to which the insurance applies shall be primary. (See Notes 1 and 2 below)
   G. Two or more policies providing coverage as set forth in 1-A through 1-F, respectively, shall be contributing. Contribution shall be as follows:
      (1) Whether or not deductibles are involved, contribution shall be on the basis of the Limit of Liability Rule[8] except that, in the event there is an area of common coverage under two or more

policies and separate coverage under any one or more such policies, the policy or policies affording separate coverage shall respond first to that loss it alone covers and the remainder of its limit of liability shall contribute to the common loss on the basis of the Limit of Liability Rule.

(a) When one of the policies is subject to a deductible, the amount of loss in excess of the deductible will be considered as the common loss. The policy(ies) without a deductible shall first respond to the loss which it alone covers to the extent of its limit of liability, thereafter the remainder of its limit of liability will contribute with the other insurance to the common loss on the basis of the Limit of Liability Rule.

(b) When two deductibles are involved, the amount of loss in excess of the higher deductible will be considered as the common loss. The differential between the higher and lower deductible shall be assessed to the limit of liability of the policy(ies) subject to the lower deductible. The remainder of its limit of liability will contribute with the insurance subject to the higher deductible to the common loss on the basis of the Limit of Liability Rule. Where there are more than two deductibles, the same procedure shall apply. (See Notes 1 and 2 below)

Note 1. In overlapping situations involving boiler-machinery policies, classifications 1-C, 1-D, 1-E and 1-F shall not consider other insurance primary. Therefore, losses will be apportioned in accordance with General Principle 1-G.

Insurance effected on a specifically described article or object as defined in General Principles 1-A and 1-B shall be primary to the boiler-machinery policy. However, a building is not construed in overlapping situations involving boiler-machinery policies as a specifically described "article" or "object."

Note 2. In overlapping situations involving burglary policies the term "article" or "object," wherever used in these Principles, is not construed to include buildings or structures.

2. Insurance covering same property and different interests:

   A. Bailee's customers insurance shall be primary to other insurance effected by the same named bailee-insured. (See General Condition 8)

   B. Insurance secured by a custodian covering property belonging to others shall be primary to any other insurance. Where there is more than one custodian, the insurance of the custodian in possession of the property shall be primary. (See General Condition 8)

   Note: Bankers and brokers blanket bonds, and fidelity, burglary, theft and jewelers block insurance providing coverage on property "held by the insured in any capacity whether or not the insured is liable for the loss thereof," or with equivalent verbiage, are not construed as insurance covering "different interests" and are not bailee's customers insurance or insurance secured by a custodian covering property belonging to others.

Exceptions: General Principle (2-B) shall not apply:

(1) when the custodian's insurance is afforded under a policy provision containing the words "property for which the insured is liable," ". . .may be liable," ". . .is legally liable," or equivalent verbiage;

Note: For the purpose of these Guiding Principles the above verbiage is construed to provide liability coverage.

(2) when the owner and custodian of the property have stipulated otherwise by written agreement prior to the loss.

C. Contents policies insuring at the place of the loss and covering "employees'," "partners'" or "executives'" personal property, except in 2-B-(1) above, shall be primary to any off-premises coverage available under the employee's insurance. However, insurance covering a specifically described article or object, whether or not for an express amount, shall be primary.

D. Coverage for property "used" or "worn" by the insured, for property of servants or guests, and insurance afforded by the "physical damage to property" coverage, shall be primary to any available insurance in the name of the owner of the involved property, except insurance covering a specifically described article or object, whether or not for an express amount, shall be primary.

E. Installment-Sales or Deferred-Payment Merchandise Insurance:

(1) Evidence of insurance issued by a vendor to a vendee under the provisions of a dual-interest policy specifically or generally describing the article or articles and their values individually or in total as invoiced under a conditional-sales contract shall be deemed to be insurance on specifically described property.

(a) Above-described insurance shall be primary when overlapping with other contents policy(ies).

(b) Above-described insurance shall contribute on the basis of the Limit of Liability Rule when overlapping with insurance expressly describing an article(s) or object(s) whether or not an express amount of insurance applies to each such article(s) or object(s).

(2) When no such evidence of insurance has been issued, the dual-interest policy shall be deemed to be blanket floating insurance.

(a) Above-described insurance shall be excess to other contents insurance in those cases where loss occurs at the location shown in the contents policy.

(b) Above-described insurance shall contribute on the basis of the Limit of Liability Rule when overlapping with a floater policy. It is to be noted that the ten percent (10%) optional extension of the fire policy is floater coverage.

General Conditions

As to General Principles 1 and 2, and any additional Principles or amendments as may hereafter be adopted, it is AGREED that:

1. To provide the greatest recovery to the insured, the insurance declared to be excess or non-contributing under the governing Principle shall not include, in applying any coinsurance, average, or distribution clause(s) contained in any policy(ies), the value or loss on property covered under the insurance declared to be primary. However, it shall include any excess value not covered by the primary insurance and the loss unrecoverable under the primary insurance.

   When a coinsurance (not reduced rate contribution or average) clause is present in any or all policies, it shall be applied as if it were a reduced rate contribution or reduced rate average clause. However, if by this procedure the insured collects less than he would collect under the terms of the coinsurance clause, the coinsurance clause shall be applied as such.

2. "Contribution," unless otherwise as specified in General Principle 1-G, shall be on the basis of the applicable limit of liability under each respective policy or group of concurrent policies as though no other insurance existed, and the limit separately determined under each policy or group of concurrent policies shall be the smallest of the following:

   (a) the amount of insurance,

   (b) the amount of loss, or

   (c) the amount payable after applying any policy limitation(s).

   The limits so determined of all policies or groups of concurrent policies herein declared contributing shall be added and, if the total amount exceeds the whole loss, each policy or group of concurrent policies shall pay such proportion of the loss as its limit bears to the sum of all the limits, but if the sum of the limits of liability is less than the whole loss, then each policy or group of concurrent policies shall pay its limit of liability. The determined liability of a group of concurrent policies shall be apportioned pro rata among the policies of the group.

3. Insurance covering property both scheduled and blanket, or both specific as to location and floating, shall be deemed to insure each item or portion separately, and the loss shall be apportioned in accordance with the Principle applying to each item or portion declared to be separately insured.

   In applying such Condition:

   A. Extensions of coverage in the name of the same insured, whether optional, those creating additional insurance, or based upon a percentage of the principal building or contents policy(ies), whether "permitted" or not, and without reference to inception date, shall be considered as excess to any specific coverage applying to the involved property. However, in the absence of specific insurance, the extensions shall be considered as:

(1) Blanket insurance for on-premises losses.

Examples:

Private structures.

Rental value.

Additional living expenses.

Improvements and betterments.

Replacement cost coverage.

Debris removal.

(2) Floater insurance for off-premises losses.

Examples:

Contents while "elsewhere."

Property removed for preservation from damage caused by the perils insured against.

Livestock, farm and dairy produce while "elsewhere."

4. When the owner of a building is also the owner of the contents of the building and any overlapping coverage exists involving items of building equipment and fixtures essentially in the nature of real property, the building policy(ies) shall be primary.

Examples: Covered under building policy(ies).

Antennae and Towers—TV, detached—not affixed[9] to the building or to an outbuilding

Porandas—demountable screened enclosures.

Readily removable equipment and fixtures that are included in the realty mortgage.

Wall-to-wall carpeting only when included in the realty mortgage.

Note: The building policy(ies) shall include, whether in position or stored on the premises, storm doors, storm sash, shades, blinds, wire screens, screen doors and awnings.

5. When the owner of a building is also the owner of the contents of the building and any overlapping coverage exists involving items of building equipment and fixtures essentially in the nature of personal property, the contents policy(ies) shall be primary, except when such items are included in the realty mortgage, in which event the policy(ies) covering building shall be primary.

Examples: Covered under contents policy(ies).

Antennae and Towers—TV, affixed[10] to the building or to an outbuilding.

Fuel.

Laundering machines whether or not attached to the realty.

Portable air-conditioning and ventilating units.

Refrigerators.

Stoves.

Wall-to-wall carpeting when not included in the realty mortgage.

6. Tenant's improvements and betterments insurance shall be primary to building insurance when the insured is owner and occupant of a co-operative apartment. However, the tenant's insurance shall first be made available to the loss on his own property and to property not otherwise insured.
7. The Principle specifically providing the basis of apportionment shall prevail over any Principle more general in scope.
8. Where a bailee's policy(ies) covers his own property, as well as property of others, the bailee's policy(ies) shall first be made available to the loss on the bailee's own property and to property not otherwise insured. Such claim or claims will be adjusted subject to all policy conditions affecting the adjustment, except that value and loss of otherwise insured property shall be deleted from the adjustment.

   A second statement of loss should then be prepared by the adjuster including all values and loss covered by the terms of the bailee's policy(ies) as written to determine the maximum liability under the policy.

   Distribution should then be made

   (a) to the loss on the bailee's own property and to the loss on otherwise uninsured interests,

   (b) to the otherwise insured interests for the difference, if any, up to the maximum liability under the bailee's insurance.

   While right of action under subrogation is retained by the bailors' insurers, the inclusion of the bailee insurer's name in any action against the bailee is contrary to the intent of these Principles.

   Claim filed by other insurers with the bailee insurers after payment or advance to owners shall be recognized to the same extent as if directly presented by the owner through the bailee in order to fulfill the purpose of these Principles, except where the bailee insurer may have certain facts in connection with a specific claim that justify reimbursement in a sum less than the amount paid by the bailor insurer.
9. Differences of opinion respecting the application or effect of these Principles shall be submitted for arbitration in the manner determined by the participating Associations. Payments of loss, or advances under loan agreements, or otherwise, shall be without prejudice to the rights of the insurers under these Principles.

Definitions of Insurance Terms for the Purpose of These Guiding Principles

AFFIXED—A television aerial or antenna is affixed to a building or outbuilding when the weight of the antenna is borne principally by the building.

BLANKET—(Casualty)—When a policy covers at a specified location and any number of other unspecified or non-scheduled locations as well, it is said to be "blanket."

(Fire and Inland Marine)—When a single amount of insurance covers several unrelated items, the policy is said to be written blanket.

Example

One amount of insurance covering two or more buildings or a building and its contents.

CONCURRENT POLICIES—Concurrent policies are those insuring the same interest and the identical property involved in the loss or claim, which divide the risk of a specific major hazard between or among policies or companies, even though policy dates and amounts vary and certain policies contain reduced rate contribution, average, coinsurance, or deductible clauses, while others do not.

Examples

Two or more standard fire policies.

Two or more contractors installment floaters.

Two or more furriers customers policies.

Two or more mercantile theft policies.

A policy(ies) providing coverage under more than one underwriting classification; i.e., casualty—fidelity—fire—inland marine or multiple-line, shall not be considered concurrent to policy(ies) limited to one classification.

Examples

A standard fire policy and a homeowners or MIC.

A boiler-machinery and a fire policy.

A special multi-peril motel policy and a mercantile theft policy.

EXCESS PROVISION—A provision in a policy which stipulates that the policy is liable only after other applicable insurance, covering the risk, has been exhausted—not to be confused with "pure excess" insurance. However, depositors forgery insurance which by its policy terms is primary to employee dishonesty coverage shall remain so.

FLOATER POLICY (FLOATING)—A policy under the terms of which protection follows movable property, covering it wherever it may be.

Example

A policy on tourist's baggage.

LIMIT OF LIABILITY RULE—As described in General Condition 2.

LIMITED PURPOSE—A policy(ies) is said to be for a more limited purpose when it is designed to provide coverage for a specific exposure as contrary to one which includes that exposure and other exposures as well.

Example

A trip transit policy is a more limited purpose policy than a household furniture policy with off-premises coverage.

LOCATION—A site specifically defined in the policy.

OVERLAPPING—When two or more types of insurance cover the same risk, the insurance is said to be "overlapping."

RETROSPECTIVE RATING—A plan under which the final premium for a risk is adjusted on the basis of its own loss experience during the policy period.

Appendix Notes

1. Wherever the term *policy* is used, it shall be construed to include fidelity bonds, certificates or certifications of insurance.
2. See Definitions.
3. Fidelity wherever used in these Guiding Principles shall not include surety or public official statutory or qualifying bonds.
4. See Definitions.
5. See Definitions.
6. See Definitions.
7. See Definitions.
8. See General Condition 2.
9. See Definitions.
10. See Definitions.

Chapter 3

Direct Your Learning

Homeowners Policies

After learning the subject matter of this chapter, you should be able to:

- Describe the various parties and interests that may be insured under a homeowners policy.
- With respect to an HO-3, explain what is covered and what is excluded under:
  - Coverage A
  - Coverage B
  - Coverage C
  - Coverage D
  - Property subject to special limits of liability
  - Debris removal
  - Ordinance or law
- Describe the insured's duties after a loss under an HO-3.
- Describe the loss settlement provision for Coverages A, B, and C of an HO-3.
- Adjust a loss according to the terms of a specific homeowners policy involved.

OUTLINE

Homeowners Forms

The HO-3

Summary

Develop Your Perspective

What are the main topics covered in the chapter?

This chapter describes the coverage provided by the HO-3 policy. It applies these coverage provisions to claim scenarios.

Examine the HO-3 form used by your company or a company that you represent.

- How does the HO-3 differ from other homeowners policy forms?

Why is it important to know these topics?

Most homeowners and tenants have insurance coverage for their buildings and the personal property contained inside. Knowing which coverages are provided by a specific homeowners policy enables the property loss adjuster to correctly adjust a loss.

Review an HO-3 loss in your office.

- Determine who is the named insured.
- Determine whether the loss results from a covered cause of loss.
- Determine the amount of loss payable under the policy.

How can you use this information?

If you are assigned a loss under a homeowners policy, you must review the applicable policy provisions and apply them to the facts of the loss to determine whether the loss is covered and (if covered) how much can be paid.

Chapter 3

Homeowners Policies

Those who own their home, have a mortgage, or rent an apartment can purchase insurance to protect their financial interests in the residence. Homeowners policies can cover the building and the personal property within it, along with other structures on the premises.[1] A homeowners policy can also reimburse insureds for additional living expenses, for fair rental value, and for loss of use. Insurance Services Office, Inc., (ISO) and the American Association of Insurance Services (AAIS), as well as many insurers, have extensive homeowners products to meet homeowners' needs.

Chapters 1 and 2 introduce the basic concepts that an adjuster must understand to determine coverage and adjust a loss. This chapter focuses on the ISO HO-3 Homeowners Policy, 2000 edition, and applies these concepts to the specific terms of the policy. The HO-3 is the basis for this chapter because it provides the broadest average and is widely used.

HOMEOWNERS FORMS

ISO produces six types of homeowners forms:

HO-2	HO-5
HO-3	HO-6
HO-4	HO-8

All of these forms except the HO-4 and the HO-8 provide replacement cost coverage on the insured building. (The HO-1, which provided limited specified-perils coverage, has been withdrawn from today's market.) The HO-8 is specifically designed to allow for loss settlements on a "functionally equivalent" basis. This means that the loss is paid on the basis of repair cost or actual cash value using current construction methods and materials rather than true replacement cost. The HO-4, designed for tenants, essentially covers only personal property and does not cover the building. The HO-6, designed for condominium owners, primarily covers personal property but also covers the building exposures faced by these owners. All of the ISO forms cover personal property at actual cash value (ACV), unless a replacement cost endorsement is added.

The HO-2, HO-4, and HO-6 cover a broad range of perils. The HO-8 is a named-perils policy. The HO-3 insures against risks of direct physical loss to the building and other structures, subject to certain exclusions, but covers personal property only for the broad-form perils. The HO-5 provides the broadest coverage of any standard unendorsed homeowners form. It insures the building, other structures, and personal property for risk of direct physical loss unless otherwise excluded. All of the HO forms include liability and property coverages.

THE HO-3

The HO-3 begins with a general insuring agreement followed by a section of definitions, a deductible provision, and Section I—Property Coverages for the dwelling, other structures, personal property, additional coverages, and loss of use. It continues with Section I—Perils Insured Against for the dwelling, other structures, and personal property, followed by Section I—Exclusions and Section I— Conditions. Section II—Liability Coverages and Exclusions appear next, along with Section II—Additional Coverages and Conditions. The policy concludes with conditions applicable to both Sections I and II. An adjuster must review all parts of the policy to determine whether it covers a loss.

Suppose that a detached garage has burned down and that the insured submits a claim for business property that was in the garage, in addition to the building damage. To determine coverage, the adjuster must examine Coverage B—Other Structures and Coverage C—Personal Property of the Section I—Property Coverages. The adjuster should review the perils insured against and the exclusions. Reviewing the definition of "business" property in the definitions section is necessary. If debris removal is involved in the loss, reviewing the Additional Coverages would also be necessary. Then the adjuster must review the Section I conditions and the conditions applicable to both Sections I and II before concluding the loss adjustment.

Adjuster Tip

Adjusters who regularly handle the same type of claim tend to rely on memory for coverage analysis. However, a better approach is to use a systematic method, as Chapters 1 and 2 discuss, for coverage analysis and to use it on every loss. Misapplying coverage based on memory is possible. Moreover, if a property loss adjuster must testify in court as to how he or she conducted coverage analysis, it is far better to say that the policy form was reviewed systematically than to say that his or her memory was relied upon.

Who Is Insured?

Analysis of the HO-3 Section I coverages begins with who is insured under the policy. Who is insured is not as obvious as it might seem. Although an insured named on the policy is considered a "named insured," others qualify as insureds by their relationship to the person who is named. See the following box.

Who Is Insured?

Four key points about who is **insured** are as follows:

1. Only those whose names appear on the declarations page are called "named insureds."
2. Others might qualify as "insureds" if they meet the criteria stated in the policy's definitions section.
3. Mortgagees and lienholders must be named on the declarations page to protect their interests.
4. A person who claims to have an insurable interest and wishes to file a claim must be named on the policy or qualify as an "insured" by definition. Otherwise, he or she has no rights under the policy, and that person's interest might not be protected.

The adjuster must also be aware of the distinction between (1) "you" (the named insured) and (2) "an insured" (which includes, but is not limited to, the named insured).[2] The HO-3 definitions state that "you" and "your" refer to the "named insured" shown in the declarations and the spouse if he or she resides in the same household. "An insured," "the insured," or "any insured" includes not only the named insured but also any other person so defined as an "insured" in the Definitions section. Homeowners form HO-3, Section I—Conditions, Paragraph A states the following:

> **A. Insurable Interest and Limit of Liability.**
>
> Even if more than one person has an insurable interest in the property covered, we will not be liable in any one loss:
>
> 1. To an "insured" for more than the amount of such "insured's" interest at the time of loss; or
> 2. For more than the applicable limit of liability.[3]

Insurable interests are also important in another part of the adjustment, as reflected in the following excerpts from conditions B and K:

> **B. Duties After Loss.**
>
> In case of a loss to covered property . . . these duties must be performed either by you, an "insured" seeking coverage or a representative of either.
>
> 8. Send to us, within 60 days after our request, your signed, sworn proof of loss, which sets forth, to the best of your knowledge and belief: . . .
>
>   (B) The interest of all "insureds" and all others in the property involved and all liens on the property . . . .[4]
>
> **K. Mortgage Clause.**
>
> 1. If a mortgagee is named in this policy, any loss payable under Coverage A or B will be paid to the mortgagee and you, as interests appear.[5]

When making payments under the policy, an adjuster must remember these two conditions to protect the various interests.

Coverage is available for all who qualify as insureds as well as mortgagees and lienholders, and an insured's personal property is covered anywhere in the world. Likewise, exclusions apply to every insured. For example, the intentional loss exclusion extends to "any loss arising out of any act an 'insured' commits or conspires to commit with the intent to cause a loss."[6]

The Named Insured

The homeowners declarations page specifies the named insured and lists a mailing address. HO-3 policies are designed to cover owner-occupied dwellings. The person or persons named as insureds should be occupants with a valid insurable interest in the covered property. However, the legal owner is not always an occupant, as in the case of trustees, executors, and landlords. The owners should appear on the declarations page with a complete mailing address.

The address listed is usually the address of the residence premises insured. If, however, the mailing address differs from the insured premises address, the mailing address should be included in the space for the insured address. This is because the adjuster will send correspondence to the insured at the mailing address, not to the address of the insured location, if the two are different.

Mortgageholders' names and addresses should also appear on the declarations page if they have an interest in the home. Most dwellings are secured by a mortgage from a financial organization. These organizations require the owners of the real property to have an insurance policy to protect the bank's financial interest. The HO-3 policy provides this type of coverage for residential property.

Loss Payees

Loss payees might also be named on the declarations page or added to the policy by endorsement.

Additional Insureds

Additional insureds might be parents or other persons who lent money to the insured to buy the home. An additional insured could also be a person who sells a home on contract and continues to have a financial interest in it. These persons might not be legal owners and might not hold a mortgage, but they can be listed on the policy to protect their interests.

Spouses

In the homeowners HO-3 form, the introductory paragraph in the Definitions section reads as follows:

> In this policy, "you" and "your" refer to the "named insured" shown in the declarations and the spouse if a resident of the same household.[7]

The usual meaning of "spouse" is "one's wife or husband." But what about common-law spouses or couples who live together without being married? Are they covered without being named on the declarations page?

The answers vary depending on a state's laws. In some states, a certain number of years must pass before a couple can be considered spouses under common law. In other states, the fact that a couple lives together with mutual agreement to be spouses might constitute a common-law marriage.

A couple's best option is to put both names on the policy as named insureds. This step protects both people's property. If this is not done, the property claim adjuster must review the state's law on the matter to determine whether a common-law spouse would qualify as an insured without being named on the policy.

The unnamed spouse is insured only if he or she is a resident of the "same household." A separated married couple might still be married, but when one of the spouses moves out of the home, that spouse is removed from coverage. This situation is a further reason to list both names of a couple on the policy as "named insureds."

The Innocent Coinsured

The denial of coverage to an insured when another insured has independently committed an intentional act that causes the loss or an act of fraud is frequently challenged. The most common situation involves a spousal relationship that is in the process of dissolution by a divorce. If one spouse commits arson by setting fire to the insured dwelling, can the other innocent spouse collect under the policy? Such an issue can arise with a partnership, joint venture, corporation, trustee, or member of the household.

Insurers intend not to grant coverage to any insured when another insured has caused the loss or committed fraud. Changes in policy language regarding the definition of "insured" and the use of the phrase "an insured" are meant to clarify this position. However, many states have case law or statutory law that grant coverage to an innocent coinsured. The case law has focused on the policy language, the nature of the ownership, and public policy. When property is jointly owned, the courts are less likely to grant coverage to the innocent coinsured. In a spousal relationship, the ownership can usually be severed based on each spouse's having a 50 percent ownership in real property.[8] State statutes have focused more on public policy issues. The Special Provisions Endorsement for the state of Georgia (HO 01 10 10 01) deals with the innocent coinsured issue in a narrow factual setting. If the loss arises out of an intentional act of family violence, the intentional act exclusion will not be applied to the innocent coinsured.

Other Insureds

"Insured" is defined in the homeowners HO-3 form as follows:

> "Insured" means you and residents of your household who are:
>
> 1. your relatives, or
> 2. other persons under the age of 21 and in the care of any person named above.[9]

This definition expands the list of those who qualify as insureds to include residents, relatives, and minors in an insured's care.

Because no specific length of time is required for one to be considered a resident, many difficult coverage questions can arise. For example, suppose Glenn Edwards, the insured named on the policy, has a nineteen-year-old brother from another state who stays with Glenn for nine months while he goes to college in Glenn's hometown. Is Glenn's brother a resident of Glenn's household? As another example, suppose that John Hill's divorced daughter and four-year-old granddaughter move in until the daughter can find a job and a new place to live. Are they residents?

No easy solutions apply to every set of circumstances. Case law varies by state, so adjusters should consult an individual state's laws and previous court decisions. Generally, however, a person is not required to stay in a dwelling permanently to establish residency. See the following box.

Residency

The following are some of the criteria that courts have used to determine residency:

1. Intent to stay at a residence for a long or an indefinite period of time
2. No other residency in any nearby location
3. Official records, such as federal and state tax returns, employment forms, and mail, showing the person as a resident of the insured premises

Relatives

To be an insured, generally a person must be both a resident *and* a relative. A relative is a person connected with another by blood or marriage. Of course, immediate family members are relatives. Others related by blood, such as aunts, uncles, grandparents, cousins, and nephews, are included as relatives. But what about in-laws, stepparents, stepbrothers and sisters, and distant members of the extended family?

Each case must be examined according to the laws in each jurisdiction. However, because courts have interpreted the term "relative" to mean related by blood or marriage, anyone who can show that he or she is related to the insured by either blood or marriage, regardless of how distant, might be considered a relative.

Others Under the Age of Twenty-One

Other persons under the age of twenty-one who are cared for by an insured are also insureds. If a foster child or another minor who does not qualify as a relative is staying with and is in the care of an insured, then that person would be an insured.

Students

A full-time student who was a resident of the insured household before attending school is an insured as long as the student is under the age of twenty-four, a relative of the named insured, or under the age of twenty-one and in the care of the named insured or relatives who are residents of the household.

The Named Insured's Duties

The differences between types of insureds are important when a loss occurs and a claim is presented. Section I—Conditions of the HO-3 policy states that specified duties must be performed by the named insured, an insured seeking coverage, or a representative of either.

Both the adjuster and the named insured, the insured making claim, or a designated representative, must realize that these duties are included in the insurance contract for good reasons. Failure by the named insured, an insured making claim, or the designated representative to comply can result in the claim's denial by the insurer. Compliance results in adjustment and payment of the claim, as stated in the loss payment condition: "We will adjust all losses with you. We will pay you unless some other person is named in the policy or is legally entitled to receive payment."[10]

The Mortgagee's Rights

Sometimes the mortgage clause can cause unique obstacles for the property claim adjuster. Suppose ABC Bank and Trust Co. is named on the declarations page as a mortgagee on Glenn's home, and suppose Glenn has a roof damage claim on his home. The adjustment is made, and the draft is made payable to Glenn Edwards and ABC Bank and Trust. Assume then that Glenn calls the adjuster to try to have the draft reissued without the mortgagee named on it. Glenn might say,

- "The work is completed, and the roofer needs the money right away."
- "I can't get the repairs done without the money. ABC is out of state. If we send the draft to ABC, it will cause a delay, and my roof will leak before it is repaired."
- "I pay the premium, not the mortgage company. Why should ABC have anything to do with the claim payment?"

The adjuster might feel pressured to remove the mortgagee from the draft. However, the mortgagee has an important interest in the home, and that interest is protected by a special clause, which reads in part:

> If a mortgagee is named in this policy, any loss payable under Coverage A or B will be paid to the mortgagee and you, as interests appear.[11]

If the adjuster removes the mortgagee's name from the draft without proper authorization from the mortgagee, the insurer might be required to make a second payment to the mortgagee for the full amount of the first draft.

Insurers and mortgage companies sometimes can reach agreements that allow the insurers to remove the mortgagee from drafts that pay small claims below a specified amount. Usually, losses under $1,000 or $2,000 fall into this category. Without such an agreement, the mortgagee should not be omitted from any payments for building losses.

What Is Insured?

The homeowners policy was developed to cover the kinds of property that most people own in connection with the home they live in. Property claim adjusters should carefully review the policy form applicable to each loss so as not to misstate the coverage to the insured.

Coverage A—Dwelling

Coverage A in the Property Coverages section of the HO-3 provides coverage for the following:

> a. The dwelling on the "residence premises" shown in the Declarations, including structures attached to the dwelling; and
>
> b. Materials and supplies located on or next to the "residence premises" used to construct, alter or repair the dwelling or other structures on the "residence premises."
>
> We do not cover land, including land on which the dwelling is located.[12]

Residence premises is defined in the policy as follows:

> a. the one family dwelling where you reside;
>
> b. the two, three or four family dwelling where you reside in at least one of the family units; or
>
> c. that part of any other building where you reside;
>
> and which is shown as the "residence premises" in the declarations.
>
> "Residence premises" also includes other structures and grounds at that location.[13]

Coverage A would include a garage that is attached to the house, a patio cover, a porch, and any other structures that are attached to or are a part of the dwelling. The amount of insurance shown on the declarations page is the limit for all of these structures combined. Additionally, if a homeowner is planning to remodel or repair a home and has some lumber, shingles, sheetrock, or other materials stored on the property for use in this remodeling, those materials and supplies would be included in Coverage A.

"Residence Premises" and "Insured Location"

The distinction between "residence premises" and "insured location" is worth noting. "Residence premises" does not include as many places as "insured location," and both terms are used in the homeowners policy. See the following box.

Insured Location

"Insured location" includes the "residence premises" and also includes the following:

- The part of other premises, other structures, and grounds that the insured uses as a residence, that are shown in the declarations, or that the insured acquires during the policy period for use as a residence premises
- Any premises used in connection with the residence premises or newly acquired residence premises
- Any part of a premises (1) not owned by an insured or (2) where an insured is temporarily residing
- Vacant land, other than farmland, owned by or rented to an insured
- Land owned by or rented to an insured on which a one-, two-, three-, or four-family dwelling is being built as a residence for an insured
- Individual family cemetery plots or burial vaults of an insured
- Any part of a premises occasionally rented to an insured for other than business use

Coverage B—Other Structures

ISO homeowners policies refer to Coverage B as **Other Structures**. Other policies might call this coverage "appurtenant structures" or "dwelling extensions." Regardless of how the coverage is labeled, its purpose is to give coverage for man-made structures that are not attached to the dwelling. The policy reads as follows:

> We cover other structures on the "residence premises" set apart from the dwelling by clear space. This includes structures connected to the dwelling by only a fence, utility line, or similar connection.[14]

Other Structures (HO-Coverage B) (Also known as appurtenant structures or dwelling extensions)
Coverage for man-made structures that are separated from the dwelling by a clear space or are connected to the dwelling by a fence, a wall, a wire, or another form of connection but not otherwise attached.

Other structures would include fences, freestanding mailboxes, gazebos, light poles, outdoor fireplaces, sheds, swimming pools, and any other structures that are a permanent part of the real estate. Land, including land on which other structures are located, is specifically excluded.

For coverage to apply under this section, three conditions must exist:

1. The structure must be separated from the dwelling. Carports, breezeways, garages, or other such buildings attached to the dwelling would have to be included in Coverage A. If only a fence or utility wire connects the structure to the dwelling, then the structure will be considered to be detached.
2. The structure cannot be one from which any business is conducted or that is used to store business property. However, the structure is covered if it contains business property solely owned by an insured or a tenant of the dwelling as long as the property does not include gaseous or liquid fuel other than that in the fuel tank of a vehicle or craft parked in the structure. ("Craft" refers to watercraft, aircraft, and hovercraft.)

3. The structure cannot be rented to anyone except a tenant of the dwelling unless used solely as a private garage.

The exclusions set forth in paragraphs 2 and 3 exist because business or rental exposures should not be covered under a homeowners policy.

"Business" is defined as a full-time, a part-time, or an occasional trade, profession, or occupation or any other activity engaged in for money or compensation, except for volunteer activities involving no compensation beyond payment of expenses, the mutual exchange of home day-care services, or the rendering of home day-care services for a relative. Also excepted are business activities in which any insured received more than $2,000 in total compensation for the twelve months before the policy's inception date. Thus, an insured who operates a print shop or an auto repair business in his or her detached garage would have no coverage for the garage under the HO-3, unless the business earned less than $2,000 during the year preceding the policy year. A structure containing business property will be covered if the business property is solely owned by an insured or a tenant of the dwelling, provided that the business property does not include gaseous or liquid fuel—except for fuel in the tank of a vehicle or craft parked or stored in the structure. For example, coverage will apply to the detached garage of a music teacher who stores sheet music and music stands there.

The amount of insurance available for structures under Coverage B is limited to 10 percent of the Coverage A amount. Therefore, if the dwelling is insured for $85,000, there will be $8,500 coverage for all of the detached buildings and structures. If an insured owns two sheds and has a fence surrounding the premises, the limit of insurance for Coverage B would probably not be sufficient. Additional coverage is usually available by endorsement for an additional premium.

For example, suppose that Glenn has $100,000 coverage on his dwelling and a tornado comes through town, causing the following damages:

Damage to the dwelling	$35,000
Cost to rebuild the fence	3,000
Cost to replace storage shed	8,000
Cost to repair children's playhouse	2,000

Glenn claims all of the damages, totaling $48,000. He expects to be paid the full amount because he has over $100,000 in coverage. However, Glenn's limit for Coverage B is $10,000, and the fence, shed, and playhouse are all Coverage B structures. He has more than sufficient coverage under Coverage A to cover the damage to his house, but he cannot use the unused coverage of Coverage A to make up the deficiency under Coverage B. He would receive only $45,000 for his claim: $10,000 under Coverage B and $35,000 under Coverage A. The same principle holds true if the damage to the dwelling is greater than the policy limit. The 10 percent limit for Coverage B has no application to any other coverage and cannot be used or added to any other coverage.

A question might exist as to whether swing sets, small aluminum sheds, doghouses, and other similar items are covered under Coverage B or whether they are personal property covered under Coverage C. If these structures are permanently attached to the land, they should probably be considered under Coverage B. If the swing set is cemented into the ground, or if the shed is anchored or mounted onto a slab of concrete with the insured's intention of leaving it on the premises, they will be considered other structures. A doghouse that sits on the ground, play equipment, and other similar property that is movable and not permanently affixed to the ground should be insured as personal property.

Coverage C—Personal Property

Personal property, or "unscheduled personal property," as it is sometimes called, is legally defined as everything other than real estate that is the subject of ownership. Some policies use the term "contents" to describe personal property, but personal property includes more than a home's contents. Essentially, any property of any kind that is not real estate is personal property. Still, the distinction is not so clear-cut as to eliminate all coverage questions.

Appliances can pose difficult questions. Is a dishwasher real property or personal property? How about a microwave, built-in range, and refrigerator? Generally, if the appliance is built into the counter or cabinetry in such a way as to leave a hole or to deface the building if it is removed, it would be considered part of the building and covered under Coverage A. Therefore, built-in dishwashers, ranges, and other appliances that are a permanent part of the kitchen counters and cabinets are generally covered under Coverage A. Furnaces, water heaters, water softeners, and central air conditioning units are also covered under Coverage A because they are part of the home's plumbing or heating system.

Conversely, free-standing refrigerators, free-standing stoves or ranges, microwave ovens that sit on a counter, and washers and dryers that are only connected to the building by hoses, exhaust vents, or an electrical cord plugged into a wall socket are personal property, and Coverage C should cover these items.

For example, for purposes of loss valuation, the HO-3 policy states, in part:

> Loss Settlement. Covered property losses are settled as follows:
>
> a. Personal property;
>
> b. Awnings, carpeting, household appliances, outdoor antennas and outdoor equipment, whether or not attached to buildings;
>
> c. Structures that are not buildings; and
>
> d. Grave markers including mausoleums;
>
> at actual cash value at the time of loss but not more than the amount required to repair or replace[15]

This clause relieves the adjuster from determining whether items such as awnings, carpeting, household appliances, outdoor antennas, and outdoor equipment are personal property or real property for valuation purposes.

Unscheduled Coverage

The personal property coverage on the HO-3 does not require a schedule. The limit of insurance shown on the declarations is a lump-sum amount, usually 50 percent of the Coverage A limit. This amount is not tied to any particular items of personal property, so it is used for all the Coverage C property until the amount is exhausted. The intent is to make the coverage flexible enough to cover the property of the insureds as they obtain, replace, discard, or trade their property throughout the policy period. Nothing need be listed with the insurer, and nothing need be changed as the insured buys new items. Even the amount of the policy limit is automatically increased or decreased when the limit for Coverage A is increased or decreased. If the 50 percent of the Coverage A limit is inadequate, the insured can obtain higher Coverage C limits by requesting that an increased amount be shown on the declarations page. An additional premium is charged for this.

Geographic Scope of Coverage C

This coverage is worldwide. The policy reads in part, "We cover personal property owned or used by an 'insured' while it is anywhere in the world."[16] Property owned by the insured is therefore covered wherever the insured is on vacation, in an automobile, or traveling in a foreign country.

Property Used by Insured

Nonowned personal property, that is, property merely used by an insured, is given the same coverage as owned personal property: coverage applies anywhere in the world. This is *not* liability coverage for property owned by others. For example, if Glenn has borrowed Sue's snow skis for a trip to Switzerland, these skis, along with all of Glenn's personal property, would be covered for the perils named later in Glenn's homeowners policy. This coverage eliminates the need for Sue to file a claim under her HO-3 if the skis are stolen or damaged while Glenn is using them. Glenn's coverage would apply regardless of whether Glenn is at fault for the loss.

Property of Others

The rest of Coverage C reads as follows:

> After a loss and at your request, we will cover personal property owned by:
>
> a. Others, while the property is on the part of the "residence premises" occupied by an "insured"; or
>
> b. A guest or a "residence employee", while the property is in any residence occupied by an "insured"[17]

An insured would need to request coverage for property of others and guests because the policy belongs to the insured. An insured must initiate all of the claims under that policy. If the skis were the only item stolen from Glenn, he might decide not to file a claim under his own policy but let Sue make a claim under her own HO-3. Sue might not like that idea and might try to file a claim under Glenn's policy, but Glenn's policy would provide no coverage unless Glenn requested it.

Unless it is used by the insured, property of others, guests, and residence employees is covered only while it is on an insured's premises. Note the subtle differences between the wording in clauses a. and b. above. Property of "others" must be on the part of the residence premises occupied by an insured. This means that a boarder or tenant who lives in a separate part of the home not occupied by the insured does not have coverage. Property of "guests or residence employees" is covered as long as the property is in any residence occupied by an insured. The property is covered anywhere on those premises. This coverage is logical because guests or employees would probably have some room or quarters inside the home that they, rather than the insured, temporarily occupy.

There might appear to be an inconsistency in the coverage for property of others. One clause says that any property used by the insured is covered anywhere in the world. The next paragraph says that property of others is covered only when it is in the insured's premises. The term *used* is the key. Many items that belong to other people and that the insured does not use might be in the insured's premises. Friends or relatives often lend or leave property at an insured's home, but the insured might not be using the property. In short, if the insured is using the property, it is covered as if he or she owned it. If it is not being used, the coverage is more restrictive.

Other Residences

The following paragraph addresses property at other residences.

> Our limit of liability for personal property usually located at an "insured's" residence, other than the "residence premises," is 10 percent of the limit of liability for Coverage C or $1,000, whichever is greater.[18]

Many insureds own second homes, cabins, vacation homes, or other premises. The HO-3 policy is designed to prevent an insured from buying one policy that simultaneously covers property at several different locations. Normally, each separate residence should have its own policy. But if for some reason a separate residence is uninsured, some limited coverage is available under the insured's HO-3. The limit is $1,000 or 10 percent of the Coverage C limit, whichever is greater.

This limitation does not apply to a newly acquired principal residence for thirty days after the insured begins to move into the new residence. When a person buys a new home and starts to move personal property, he or she might temporarily have large amounts of property at both locations. The insured does not need to buy duplicate coverage at both residences just to overcome the 10 percent limitation, as long as he or she transfers the policy or applies for a new one for the new residence within thirty days.

Special Limits of Liability

Despite the overall limit of coverage for personal property under Coverage C, certain types of personal property are subject to special internal limits. This is because these types of personal property present a risk that the underwriter does not want to assume, are insured elsewhere, or represent high values that the underwriter does not want to insure for full value.

The HO-3 policy specifies that the following special limits of liability are not in addition to the Coverage C limits. The specified amounts are the *only* amounts of coverage available for the types of property in each category and are included within the Coverage C limits. Insureds who need more coverage than the amount specified in any area should consider a personal articles policy or an endorsement to the homeowners policy. Most of the special limits in the homeowners policies can be changed by endorsement, which has an additional premium. Exhibit 3-1 is a list of the property subject to special limits of liability by category and some examples of the kind of property in each category:

EXHIBIT 3-1

Property Subject to Special Limits of Liability

- *Category 1: $200 on money, bank notes, bullion, gold other than goldware, silver other than silverware, platinum other than platinumware, coins, medals, scrip, stored value cards, and smart cards.*
    - Money is legal tender, cash currency commonly accepted as the medium of exchange in any country.
    - Bank notes are issued by a bank and circulated like money. A note is payable to any bearer on demand.
    - Bullion is a bar or solid mass of gold or silver not in the form of coins.
    - Gold other than goldware, silver other than silverware, and platinum other than platinumware includes any form of those precious metals not included in the bullion definition above, such as gold dust or nuggets, or pieces of refined gold that are not jewelry or tableware. Because goldware, silverware, and platinumware have a separate limit for a greater amount, these items are not included.
    - Coins are metals formed or minted into metal money, authorized by a government with appropriate markings for use as legal tender. Rare or collectible coins are also in this category. The value of any of these coins is normally the greatest of one of the following: (1) the coin's face value, (2) the coin's metal value if melted down, or (3) the coin's market value as a collectible, subject to the $200 special limit.

- Medals includes medals of commendation or awards for outstanding service or performance. Examples include medals won in the military or in athletic contests.
- Fundraisers often use scrip. It is sold for a percentage of the redeemable value, with the difference being donated by a retailer.
- Stored value cards are cards that can be loaded with a value that can be spent, like a prepaid phone card.
- Smart cards have an embedded chip in them, used to store personal or medical information.

- *Category 2: $1,500 on securities, accounts, deeds, evidences of debt, letters of credit, notes other than bank notes, manuscripts, personal records, passports, tickets, and stamps.*
    - Securities include stocks, bonds, notes, or other documents that represent a share in a company or a debt owed by a company.
    - Accounts are statements showing debits or credits, including accounts receivable.
    - Deeds are documents transferring title to real property.
    - Evidence of debt is the paper showing the debt of one to another, such as a promissory note.
    - A letter of credit is a written request authorizing one person to pay money or extend credit to another on the credit of the writer.[19]
    - Notes other than bank notes are a two-party financial instrument that identify who is entitled to negotiate the note. The names appear on the note, and no one else can or should be able to cash the note.
    - Manuscripts are an author's work product—an original, rough, unpublished book or other document.
    - Passports allow the bearer to travel internationally. A passport is issued by the country of which the holder is a citizen. Documentation is required to prove citizenship.
    - Tickets entitle the bearer to passage on various modes of transportation or to entry to or participation in events. Included are tickets to travel on airlines, trains, buses, or any other type of common carrier. Also included are tickets for events such as games, concerts, the theater, or even a lottery.
    - Stamps include postage stamps of all types and stamp collections. Stamp collections are valued similarly to coin collections, according to the stamp's face value or market value as a collectible, up to the special limit amount. Food stamps and cash value coupons are also included.

The $1,500 limit applies regardless of whether the media on which the material appears are computer media or paper records, and the limit includes the cost to research and replace lost information.

Continued on next page.

The limit of liability for the items in Category 1 is lower than the limit for the items in Category 2 for the following reasons:

1. Cash and most of the items in Category 1 are readily transferable. Anyone who possesses cash, coins, or gold can spend it.
2. Securities, accounts, and evidences of debt are merely papers that, when executed properly, are converted into money. Because they are not easily negotiable, and because even the rightful owner might have difficulty or delays in cashing these papers, the limit of insurance can be higher.
3. Names and records are kept on the items in the second category. If securities are stolen, they can often be voided, making them worthless; then new documents can be reissued to the rightful owners. Duplicates of some documents and accounts are also available. The owner could have some of these items stolen but would not suffer any financial loss because of steps taken to replace or void them.

- *Category 3: $1,500 for watercraft of all types, including their trailers, furnishings, equipment, and outboard engines or motors.* Insureds owning small fishing boats or canoes might find $1,500 in coverage sufficient and not need a separate boatowners policy. However, the trailers, equipment, motors, and furnishings are all included in the $1,500 limit, so the watercraft would have to be small. Watercraft includes any vessel that travels on the water and that can carry people. Jet skis, windsurfers, sailboards, and other similar craft are considered watercraft and would be subject to the limitation.
- *Category 4: $1,500 on trailers or semitrailers not used with watercraft of all types.* This limit includes utility trailers, camping trailers, travel trailers, horse trailers, trailers to haul recreational vehicles, and any other trailer that is not self-propelled and is pulled behind another vehicle.
- *Category 5: $1,500 for loss by theft of jewelry, watches, furs, and precious and semiprecious stones.*
    - Jewelry is defined as objects of precious metal often set with gems and worn for personal adornment, including rings, earrings, bracelets, necklaces, and even belt buckles.
    - Watches are subject to this limit, regardless of whether the watch works, is an antique, or has special sentimental value.
    - Furs are generally considered to be pelts of animals used to make, trim, or line wearing apparel. Coats, collars, wraps, and stoles are some of the forms in which furs appear. Animal furs and hides that are hung on the walls or laid on floors as decorations are not usually included in this limit because they are not worn as apparel.
    - Precious and semiprecious stones are grouped together because they are often used to make jewelry. They have intrinsic value even if they are not part of a setting, but their value can be greatly enhanced with a quality setting. Diamonds, rubies, sapphires, and emeralds are considered to be precious stones.

Semiprecious stones include opal, jade, onyx, coral, lapis, topaz, citrine, aquamarine, garnet, and amethyst. The line between precious and semiprecious is not clearly defined. Some rare opals or jade of extremely high quality or large size are very valuable. However, determining whether a particular stone is precious or semiprecious is not necessary because both are subject to the same $1,500 limit.

- *Category 6: $2,500 for theft of firearms and related equipment.* A firearm is a weapon that uses gunpowder to discharge shots. The size or caliber can vary, but the shell must be propelled by an explosion. Related equipment includes items such as telescopic sights, gun cases, and ammunition. Toy guns, bows and arrows, lasers, darts, and knives are not under this limitation.
- *Category 7: $2,500 for loss by theft of silverware, silver-plated ware, goldware, gold-plated ware, platinumware, platinum-plated ware, and pewterware. This includes flatware, hollowware, tea sets, and trays and trophies made of or including silver, gold, or pewter.* These types of tableware are very valuable because they are often antiques or ornate. They might be family heirlooms, or they might contain many ounces of gold or silver. Thieves melt tableware and sell the metal for a fraction of its value.
- *Category 8: $2,500 on property, on the residence premises, used primarily for business purposes.* Many policies have much less coverage than $2,500 for business property. Some do not differentiate between business property on or off the premises.
- *Category 9: $500 on property, away from the residence premises, used primarily for business purposes.* This limit does not apply to electronic apparatus and other property described in Categories 10 and 11.
- *Category 10: $1,500 for loss to electronic apparatus and accessories while in or upon a motor vehicle, but only if the apparatus is equipped to be operated by power from the motor vehicle's electrical system while still capable of being operated by other power sources.* Electronic apparatus includes accessories, antennas, tapes, wires, records, discs, and other media that can be used with electronic apparatus.
- *Category 11: $1,500 for loss to electronic apparatus and accessories used primarily for business while away from the residence premises and not in a motor vehicle.* The apparatus must run off the power from the motor vehicle and be able to operate using other power sources. This limitation pertains to equipment, such as a two-way radio, that is carried to a job site and can be run off the power from the vehicle. Accessories are the same as those mentioned in Category 10.

Some of the limits apply only to theft losses (Categories 5, 6, and 7); therefore, if these classes of property suffer some other type of covered loss, such as fire, the special limit does not apply to the claim. If a gun, for example, is burned in a fire at the insured's residence premises, the insured could be paid its full actual cash value, even if it exceeds the $2,500 limit applicable to the gun theft. These limit amounts vary by insurance company and by policy.

Scheduled Personal Property Endorsement

Coverage for personal property can be increased by specifically scheduling items on this endorsement or on a personal articles policy (often referred to as a personal articles floater because the items are movable in nature). Commonly scheduled items are jewelry, furs, cameras, and fine arts. The endorsement provides broader coverage and fewer exclusions than the HO-3 policy.

Coverage D—Loss of Use

When a home is damaged to the point that it is unusable, the insured loses more than just the cost to repair or replace the damaged property. A home's loss of use value can also be serious and costly. Coverage D in the policy covers these losses and pays the expenses necessary to allow the insureds to maintain their normal standard of living until they can return to the home.

Coverage D applies only if the damage results from a loss that is covered under Section I of the policy. A family with a flood-damaged dwelling might also have damage that would require it to move elsewhere, but flood is *not* a covered cause of loss under the HO-3; therefore, Coverage D would *not* apply.

Coverage D is automatically provided at a limit that is 20 percent of the Coverage A limit and applies in addition to the Coverage A limit. Simply changing the amount appearing on the declarations page can increase the Coverage D limit. No endorsement is required to increase the Coverage D limit, but an additional premium is charged.

Three coverages are grouped under Coverage D:

Additional living expense (ALE) Coverage for the cost of any necessary increase in living expenses incurred by an insured who has suffered a covered loss that makes the residence not fit to live in.

1. *Additional living expense (ALE)*. If a family must live elsewhere until its dwelling is repaired, it may need **additional living expense (ALE)** coverage. Coverage D pays for any necessary *increase* in living expenses required to maintain the household's normal standard of living. A claim representative might help the individual or family relocate to a temporary residence that is similar to the insured residence. The rent for the temporary residence would be an increase in expenses that would be covered by Coverage D. If the family relocates temporarily to a hotel (which might be reasonable if the repairs could be completed in a few weeks), eating at restaurants would cost more than the family's normal groceries. This difference between a reasonable cost of eating out and the family's normal food costs would also be covered by Coverage D. Note that Coverage D does not cover *all* living expenses while the insured is unable to live in the insured dwelling. Instead, it covers only the *necessary and increased* expenses caused by the temporary relocation; in other words, only the *difference between* the insured's normal living expenses and the higher expenses due to the relocation is covered.

   The insured property need not be uninhabitable to trigger an ALE loss. Suppose that a kitchen fire occurred and that the kitchen was unusable while the rest of the house was still habitable. The increase in meal expenses, above what the insured would normally have incurred, would be an ALE claim.

Expenses must be incurred, but that does not necessarily mean money spent. An obligation to pay, which can either be legal or moral, is sufficient to trigger coverage. The best example of this would be an insured's gift to a friend who has allowed the insured to stay in the friend's home free of charge during the restoration period. Naturally, the gift would have to be a reasonable one under the circumstances.

Necessary increase in expenses is the additional expense above and beyond what normally would have been spent. These expenses can be for the increased cost of food, housing, utilities, laundry expenses, and transportation, even the boarding of pets. It does not include items such as clothing, equipment, or appliances. These would more properly be covered under Coverage C.

Payment is made for the shortest time required to repair the dwelling or to permanently relocate the household.

The ALE loss is limited by the time required to repair or replace the damaged dwelling or that portion of the dwelling, using due diligence and dispatch. It can also be limited by the time needed to settle into new, permanent quarters. The ALE claim is not limited by the policy's expiration. If the period of restoration extends past the policy's expiration date, the expenses can still be claimed as additional living expenses.

2. *Fair rental value*. If part of the residence is rented to others and a covered loss makes that part of the residence unfit to live in, the insurer will reimburse the insured for the lost rental value, or **fair rental value,** (minus expenses that do not continue) until repairs are made.

   For example, an HO-3 might be used to insure a duplex where the insured lives in one half and rents the other half. A fire that damages the rented portion of the duplex could make it unfit to live in until repairs are made. While the repairs are being made, Coverage D provides coverage for the lost rent minus expenses that do not continue.

   Assume that the lost rent's fair value is $500 per month and that the insured had been paying an average of $100 per month for heating and water expenses that would not continue during the repair period. If the reasonable time to repair the duplex were three months, the insured would be compensated under Coverage D as follows:

$500 per month lost rent × 3 months	$1,500
$100 noncontinuing monthly expenses × 3 months	−300
Total payment	$1,200

   Note that fair rental value coverage applies even to units not currently rented to a tenant as long as the unit is held for rental.

Fair rental value
The rental value of insured property that is made uninhabitable by a loss, whether or not the property was rented at the time of loss.

3. *Loss of use due to civil authority*. Occasionally, civil authorities prohibit property owners from using their residence premises because neighboring property is damaged, even though an insured's own property might be undamaged. For example, a forest fire threatening an area could cause civil authorities to evacuate a neighborhood that has not yet been damaged. Coverage D reimburses the insured for both additional living

expenses and fair rental value (as previously described) for no more than two weeks for the loss of use due to civil authority.

For this coverage to apply, the threat to the property must come from a peril insured against by the HO-3. Flooding that causes the authorities to order an evacuation would not create a loss covered by Coverage D, because flood is not a covered peril.

Property Not Insured

Some kinds of property are either uninsurable or are better insured by other types of policies. The HO-3 excludes coverage for these types of property, listed in Exhibit 3-2. The insured can benefit from these exclusions because duplicate coverages are avoided, and premiums are charged only for what is needed by typical homeowners around the country.

EXHIBIT 3-2

Property Not Insured by the HO-3

- *Articles separately described and specifically insured, regardless of the limit for which they are insured, in this or other insurance.* Examples of separately insured property include boats, autos, and property named on personal articles policies or inland marine policies. Only one policy should cover any one piece of property. This exclusion allows the policy that is more specific to provide the coverage. If two homeowners policies are in force at the time of loss, the claim will be handled according to the other insurance provisions of each policy.
- *Animals, birds, or fish.* Placing a value on pets would be difficult, in part because of the emotional attachment between some people and their pets. Coverage for these animals is better obtained from specialty companies that deal in life and health insurance for pets.
- *Motor vehicles, including their accessories, equipment, parts, and electronic apparatus and accessories designed to be operated solely by power from the motor vehicle's electrical system.* All homeowners policies exclude coverage for self-propelled land or amphibious vehicles. This means any vehicle propelled by a motor that moves on land or water, including automobiles, motorcycles, four-wheelers and off-road vehicles, recreational vehicles, and mopeds.

  Not only is the vehicle itself excluded, but also excluded are its equipment and accessories. Parts, tires, jacks, and seats are all excluded because an auto policy should cover them. Some insureds who let their auto coverage lapse look to their homeowners policy for coverage. The property loss adjuster must explain that anything that is a part of the vehicle, or an accessory, has no HO-3 coverage.

  However, assume that an insured goes to a parts store and buys spare parts or accessories for his or her car. If a loss occurs before they are installed on the vehicle, the parts would not yet be considered to be part of the car and could be covered as personal property. The exclusion is limited to equipment or accessories in or upon the vehicle.

Riding lawnmowers and other tractors used to service the property and motorized wheelchairs would also be excluded but for an exception in the last part of paragraph 3:

> We do cover "motor vehicles" not required to be registered for use on public roads or property which are:
>
> a. Used solely to service an "insured's" residence; or
>
> b. Designed to assist the handicapped[20]

A source of difficulty for adjusters and insureds alike is the exclusion regarding sound equipment for vehicles. It applies to the following:

> Electronic apparatus and accessories designed to be operated solely by power from the electrical system of the "motor vehicle". Accessories include antennas, tapes, wires, records, discs or other media that can be used with any apparatus described above.[21]

This exclusion applies only when the property is in or on the vehicle. Essentially, this exclusion means that stereos, radios, citizens' band radios (CBs), tape players, compact disc players, and video players are not covered, nor are the tapes or discs if they are in or on the car. Problems arise when insureds discover that their auto policy might not cover the tapes, either. Some car stereos are built to be removed easily to avoid theft and vandalism. The only sound equipment that would be covered under the HO-3 policy if stolen from a car is a portable stereo or radio that runs on batteries or AC power and just happens to be in the car at the time of loss.

- *Aircraft and parts, whether or not attached to the aircraft.* Most insureds do not own aircraft. Those who do must buy coverage through another policy. A model plane or a hobby plane that runs on remote control and does not carry people would be covered.
- *Hovercraft and parts.* Self-propelled motorized ground effect vehicles and their parts are specifically excluded.
- *Property of roomers, boarders, and other tenants.* People who pay rent and live in part of the insured's home should buy a renter's policy for their personal property. Coverage C does not apply to tenants because they are not guests, and their property is not on the part of the premises occupied by an insured.

  A roomer or boarder who is related to an insured would have coverage because of an exception to the exclusion and because resident relatives are considered insureds.
- *Property in an apartment regularly rented or held for rental to others by an insured.* Personal property that the insured owns and puts in a rental unit, such as couches, chairs, and tables, is excluded because these items should be insured under the rental dwelling policy. This exclusion does not exclude property that the insureds rent for their own use. It does, however, exclude property that the insureds rent to other people. The additional coverage for landlord's furnishings reinstates some coverage for this property.
- *Property rented or held for rental to others off the residence premises.* This exclusion is very similar to the one that precedes it. The only difference is that this exclusion

Continued on next page.

removes coverage for property rented off-premises, and the preceding exclusion deals with property in an insured apartment only.

- *Business data.* This exclusion applies to business data whether on paper records or electronic media. Personal accounts and the cost of blank computer tapes and discs are covered, as are prerecorded computer programs available on the retail market. The policy excludes business data for two reasons. First, the policy is supposed to be a personal insurance policy for nonbusiness exposures. Second, reconstructing these records would be time-consuming and costly.
- *Credit cards; electronic fund transfer cards; or access devices used solely for deposit, withdrawal, or funds transfer.* Except for the coverage provided by the Additional Coverages section, Coverage C does not apply to losses arising from unauthorized use of a credit or fund transfer card or for access devices used solely for deposit, withdrawal, or transfer of funds. The reference to unspecified access devices recognizes that computers, cell phones, and other electronic devices are now frequently used to transfer funds from one account to another. (The coverage provided by the Additional Coverages is discussed next in the text.) The coverage is detailed and specific. The purpose of the exclusion in this section is to remove coverage for any other potential losses relating to credit cards, electronic fund transfer devices, and access devices falling outside the additional coverage.
- *Water or steam.* Water and steam are not covered property. The homeowners policy provides no property coverage for the cost of replacing water in a damaged swimming pool that must be drained and replaced, and it does not provide coverage for the cost of water, billed by a utility company, that escapes from a burst pipe.

Additional Coverages

Additional coverages are provided separately because they do not belong strictly to any one of Coverages A through D. They have a section of their own for the following four reasons:

1. They might involve Coverages A, B, and C simultaneously. For example, the Additional Coverages for debris removal, reasonable repairs, or property removed might apply to any of the underlying coverages.
2. They might not fit into any of the underlying coverages. For example, the coverage for trees, shrubs, and other plants; for fire department service charges; and for loss assessment are truly separate and additional.
3. They might give back some parts of coverages that have been carefully excluded in other parts of the policy. The credit card and collapse coverages are designed for this purpose.
4. Some of the additional coverages exist because they provide an additional amount of insurance above the regular policy limits. Also, in some cases, the deductible does not apply to claims under the Additional Coverages.

Before any additional coverage can apply, the adjuster must determine whether the property that has been damaged is covered property and whether the peril causing the loss is a covered peril.

Debris Removal

The cost to demolish and remove debris is usually included in contractors' bids to repair buildings. These amounts are usually paid as part of the building or contents loss, without the need to involve any additional coverage. However, when the policy limits are reached or exceeded for any of the coverages, and extra money is needed to remove the debris, an additional 5 percent is available for each coverage. The example in the following box illustrates such a case.

Debris Removal Additional Coverage Example

Coverage	Limits
A	$100,000
B	10,000
C	70,000

Damages are as follows:

Coverage A damage	$100,000	
	$4,000	Cost to remove debris
Coverage B damage	$ 20,000	
	$1,000	Cost to remove debris
Coverage C damage	$68,000	
	$3,000	Cost to remove debris

Total amounts payable per coverage:

Coverage A	$104,000	(Policy limits plus cost to remove debris)
Coverage B	$10,500	(Policy limits plus 5 percent)
Coverage C	$71,000	(Cost of damage plus debris)

The additional coverage for debris removal applies only to the debris from covered property damaged by an insured peril.

This additional coverage also provides up to $1,000 to remove from the residence premises an insured's trees felled by wind or the weight of ice, snow, or sleet. The same additional coverage applies to remove from the residence premises a neighbor's trees felled by any of the Coverage C perils. In both cases, coverage applies only when the trees damage a covered structure or when no damage occurs to a covered structure but the trees block a driveway on the residence premises or block a ramp or fixture used by a handicapped person to gain access to the premises. Additionally, the $1,000 limit applies to the entire loss, not to each tree. No more than $500 will be paid for the removal of any one tree.

> **ADJUSTER TIP**
>
> Tree removal can be a hotly contested issue. If a tree has fallen on the covered dwelling or another structure and caused damage, then it must be removed so that any damage can be repaired. Some insurers include the removal cost as part of the cost of repairing the damaged structure. Other insurers apply a more strict policy interpretation and cover the tree-removal costs under this additional coverage.

Reasonable Repairs

Reasonable repairs
Temporary repairs to prevent further damage to the property. The amount spent should bear a reasonable relationship to the value of the property.

It is in the best interest of all parties that the insured take necessary steps to prevent further damage after a loss, even if the adjuster has not yet inspected the loss and authorized the temporary repairs. Indeed, the policy conditions require the insured to protect covered property and make **reasonable repairs**. The insurer will pay the cost of these repairs as long as the damage was caused by an insured peril. The only limitation is that the cost be "reasonable." That is, the amounts spent should bear a reasonable relationship to the property's value. The policy limits are not increased for this coverage.

Trees, Shrubs, and Other Plants or Lawns

Trees, shrubs, and other plants or lawns are neither structures nor personal property. Consequently, they would have no coverage except for this additional coverage. The coverage provided is specific and includes only the following perils:

- Fire or lightning
- Explosion
- Riot or civil commotion
- Aircraft
- Vehicles not owned or operated by a resident of the residence premises
- Vandalism or malicious mischief
- Theft

The coverage for all trees and plants is limited to 5 percent of the limit of liability for the dwelling. There is a $500 per-tree or per-plant limit. This coverage is not meant to include trees grown for business and does not increase any of the other policy limits.

Fire Department Service Charge

Rural areas and small fire departments sometimes enter into contractual agreements that allow homeowners to call on the fire department in case of a fire. The homeowner is then charged for the fire department's service. If such an agreement is made, the insurer will pay up to $500 for the service as long as the property is not located within the city limits or jurisdiction of the fire department that is making the charge. No deductible applies to this coverage. The charge must be incurred to save or protect covered property from an insured peril.

Property Removed

This section provides coverage for direct physical loss from any cause to personal property while it is being removed from premises endangered by a peril insured against for up to thirty days. Removal might save the insured's property from further loss and reduce the potential claims against the insurer.

The personal property already has named-perils coverage anywhere in the world, but under the Property Removed coverage, any direct loss from any cause is covered for thirty days. The coverage does not raise the limits, and a deductible applies.

Credit Card, Electronic Fund Transfer Card, or Access Device; Forgery; and Counterfeit Money

Credit card companies provide instructions for the rightful owner to prevent unauthorized use of a lost or stolen credit card. If the owner calls the card company immediately so that the card can be voided, the card thief will probably be unable to charge anything on the card. If the unauthorized user already has charged or is still able to charge items on the card, the card company will usually not require the rightful owner to be responsible for more than $50.

The HO-3 provides up to $500 coverage for the insured's legal obligation to pay for the theft or unauthorized use of credit cards or fund transfer cards in the insured's name. This coverage extends only to the insured's legal obligation. It is not intended to indemnify any merchant or credit card issuer harmed by the unauthorized use. No coverage applies if the card is used as follows:

1. By a resident of the insured's household
2. By a person who has been entrusted with the card
3. If the insured has not complied with all terms and conditions under which the card is issued
4. If an insured's business use or dishonesty has resulted in a loss

In addition to coverage for credit cards, electronic fund transfer cards, or access devices, coverage also applies to the following:

1. Loss to an insured caused by forgery or alteration of any check or negotiable instrument
2. Loss to an insured through acceptance in good faith of counterfeit United States or Canadian paper currency

Finally, a lawsuit might be brought against the insured by a card company or bank that believes that the insured still owes money after a forgery or unauthorized use of a card. The final portion of this coverage is actually liability coverage for defense costs associated with such proceedings.

Loss Assessment

Homeowners who are members of a homeowners association are sometimes assessed for repairs to association property, such as a clubhouse, tennis courts, or pools. Under this coverage, the insurer will pay these assessments up to $1,000 if the following conditions are met:

1. The assessment is made because of a direct loss to property that all the members own collectively.
2. The loss is caused by a peril insured against under Coverage A other than earthquake and volcanic tremors.
3. The insured is an owner or a tenant of the residence premises.
4. A governmental body does not charge the assessment against the insured.
5. The loss assessment is charged during the policy period.

If the loss assessment must come as a result of a peril insured against, one might wonder why the association does not submit the claim to its insurance company. Many associations have significant deductibles in an effort to save premiums. An association with a $5,000 or $10,000 deductible might have to assess its members even if it does file a claim with its insurer. Another reason for the association to assess its members is that it might have a bad loss history and does not want to file smaller claims with the insurer for fear of cancellation. A third reason might be that the association has had a bad loss year and its aggregate limit of liability has been exhausted, so the insurer can make no more payments.

Adjusters must be aware that assessments are often for routine maintenance of the property, such as painting a fence, replacing an old roof, or fixing the parking lot. These assessments are not covered under the loss assessment coverage because they do not result from a direct loss caused by an insured peril. Furthermore, if just a few of the association members are assessed, there is no loss assessment coverage. The assessment must be made against all of the members for property owned collectively.

Collapse

Collapse is explicitly defined to mean an abrupt falling down or caving in of a building or any part of a building so that it cannot be occupied for its intended purposes. The costs of repairing a building that is still standing or one that is in danger of collapsing do not qualify for payment under this additional coverage.

The additional coverage for collapse extends to direct physical loss to covered property involving collapse of a building or part of a building, as long as it is caused by one or more of the following:

- One of the Coverage C perils insured against
- Hidden decay, unless known to an insured before the collapse

- Hidden insect or vermin damage, unless known to an insured before the collapse
- Weight of contents, equipment, animals, or people
- Weight of rain that collects on a roof
- Use of defective materials or methods, only if the collapse occurs during the course of construction, remodeling, or renovation

The decay, the insect damage, and the vermin damage themselves are not covered. Only a collapse resulting from such conditions is covered. Weight of snow and ice is not mentioned here because it is already covered as one of the named perils for Coverage C that pertain to collapse.

The policy excludes losses to awnings, fences, patios, decks, pavements, swimming pools, underground pipes, flues, drain, cesspools, septic tanks, foundations, retaining walls, bulkheads, piers, wharves, or docks, unless the loss directly results from collapse of a building or any part of a building. Settling, cracking, shrinking, bulging, and expansion are specifically excluded.

Glass or Safety Glazing Material

Coverage is provided for the breakage of glass or safety glazing material (safety glass, etc.) and for the damage caused by that breakage. Coverage is excluded if the dwelling has been vacant for more than sixty days before the loss.

Landlord's Furnishings

The additional coverage for landlord's furnishings adds back some coverage otherwise eliminated by the exclusion for property in an apartment regularly rented to others. The additional coverage is limited in three ways: (1) it extends only to appliances, carpeting, and other household furnishings; (2) it is limited to $2,500; and (3) it does not cover theft. Other than the limitation for theft, this additional coverage applies to the same perils as does Coverage C.

Ordinance or Law

Following a loss, insureds are often required by a local building ordinance or law to upgrade their property with building designs or methods that are more expensive than replacement of the property's original features. Property insurance policies generally exclude this increased cost. The HO-3 excludes loss caused by "ordinance or law requiring or regulating the construction, demolition, remodeling, renovation, or repair of property, including removal of any resulting debris."[22] Even apart from such an exclusion, insurance policies need only pay for like kind and quality materials and construction methods.

The additional coverage for ordinance or law reinstates a limited amount of coverage otherwise eliminated by the above exclusion. This additional coverage provides up to 10 percent of the Coverage A limit for increased costs caused by enforcement of an ordinance or a law that regulates the repair of a damaged structure or requires the demolition or remodeling of the undamaged portion of such a structure. The additional coverage might also be used for removal of debris that results from enforcement of the ordinance.

Grave Markers

Grave markers do not clearly qualify as either personal property or real property that would be covered elsewhere in the HO-3 policy, so they are treated as an additional coverage. For loss caused by the Coverage C perils, including vandalism, $5,000 in coverage applies to grave markers and mausoleums on or away from the residence premises. Although the policy does not specify whose grave markers are covered, they would presumably be those in which the insured has an insurable interest.

Section I—Perils Insured And Excluded

Section I—Perils Insured Against has the following divisions:

- Coverage A—Dwelling and Coverage B—Other Structures
- Coverage C—Personal Property

Each division describes the covered perils that might damage or destroy the covered property. To determine whether windstorm, fire, or water damage is an insured peril, one would look in this segment of the policy.

No covered perils are listed in this section for Coverage D—Loss of Use or for the additional coverages, because Coverage D and three of the additional coverages apply only when other covered losses occur. The remaining additional coverages individually describe when coverage applies.

Perils Insured Against for Coverages A and B: Direct Physical Loss

This section begins with the following broad statement:

> We insure against risk of direct physical loss to property described in Coverages A and B.[23]

Insured Perils for Coverage A—Dwelling and Coverage B—Other Structures are grouped together because the items insured under these two coverages include real property items with similar loss exposures. The approach to describing the perils insured against for Coverages A and B is known as special-form coverage. Coverage is provided for direct physical loss to property unless the loss is caused by a peril specifically excluded by the policy or the policy specifically limits the amount of coverage.

Perils Excluded

The excluded perils for Coverages A and B are described under the following headings:

- *Collapse*. Although collapse is excluded as a *cause* of loss, coverage for collapse that *results* from another cause is provided under a Section I additional coverage, as explained earlier.

- *Freezing of a plumbing, heating, air conditioning or automatic fire-protective sprinkler system, or a household appliance*. Freezing can cause pipes and hoses to burst or leak, causing extensive damage. If the insured fails to take reasonable precautions against freezing, such as keeping the heat on or shutting the water off and draining the system, coverage will be excluded for any resulting damage.
- *Freezing, thawing, pressure or weight of water or ice*. Damage to external property (such as fences, pavements, patios, decks, swimming pools, foundations, piers, and docks) caused by freezing, thawing, and the pressure of water or ice is excluded.
- *Theft of construction materials*. Building materials and supplies for a home under construction are valuable and are attractive to thieves. Theft of these items is excluded until the dwelling is finished and occupied.
- *Vandalism and malicious mischief to vacant dwellings*. Vacant dwellings are targets for vandalism. Coverage for vandalism, including ensuing losses such as a fire, is excluded for dwellings that have been vacant for more than sixty consecutive days.
- *Mold, fungus, or wet rot*. Mold has recently received renewed public attention as a property and health threat, becoming the focus of an increasing number of property insurance claims. Coverage for loss by mold, fungus, or wet rot is excluded unless the mold, fungus, or rotting is hidden and results from an accidental leak of water or steam from plumbing, heating, or air conditioning systems or household appliances or from a storm drain or water, steam, or sewer pipes off of the residence premises. Sump pumps, roof drains, and the like do not qualify as plumbing systems or household appliances in this context.

  When checking water damage around an automatic dishwasher or sink, or damage in or around a bathroom, the adjuster must establish the moisture source. The adjuster determines whether a pipe broke, and, if so, how long the water was flowing, or whether the damage was merely caused by a slowly dripping pipe, an improperly installed shower door, or a drain pipe. The adjuster can usually establish how long the water was leaking by the type of damage. If there is wet rot, then the water would certainly have been present for a long time, and the exclusion would apply.

  The adjuster can also take the insured's statement in an effort to establish the water source. The adjuster may ask the insured what caused him or her to identify a leakage problem and what he or she did to correct it. If such damage occurs in a rental property, a similar statement can be taken from the tenant or the property manager. So if the insured has taken precautions to maintain heat in the building, but for some reason beyond the insured's control the heat is disrupted, then the preceding exclusion would not apply. For example, assume that the insured arranges with a local oil supplier to fill the oil tank of his or her vacation home, and through a mistake on the supplier's part, the oil is delivered to the insured's next-door neighbor. The oil in the insured's tank would then be used up, the furnace would shut off, the pipes would freeze and break, and water would start flowing again when the temperature rose. Extensive water damage could then occur, but the loss would be covered.

- *Natural deterioration*. Dwellings naturally age and deteriorate over time. They require maintenance to keep them in good shape and prevent serious damage. Losses caused by age and natural deterioration are called "maintenance losses" and are not covered. The policy specifically excludes the following: wear and tear, marring, deterioration, mechanical breakdown, latent defect, inherent vice, or any quality in property that causes it to damage or destroy itself. Also excluded are smog, rust, other corrosion, and dry rot.
- *Smoke from agricultural smudging or industrial operations*. Damage resulting from smoke caused by agricultural smudging or industrial operations is excluded from coverage. Agricultural smudging intentionally creates a dense smoke to prevent plants from frost.
- *Pollutants*. The policy excludes coverage for damage caused by pollutants, whether they are solid, liquid, gaseous, or thermal. An exception is made if the pollutants are released or escape as the result of any of the perils insured under Coverage C, discussed later in this chapter. The following cases are examples of excluded and covered pollution losses:
    - Because a worker opened the wrong valve at a chemical plant, chemicals were accidentally released into the air and damaged the siding of an insured's home. This pollution loss is excluded by the HO-3 because a worker's error is not a peril insured under Coverage C.
    - Because of a chemical plant explosion (a peril insured under Coverage C), chemicals were accidentally released into the air and damaged the insured's home siding. The HO-3 would cover the resulting damage to the insured's siding.
- *Settling of the dwelling*. Losses resulting from the settling, shrinking, bulging, or expansion of foundations, footings, patios, pavements, bulkheads, and the building structure are excluded from coverage.
- *Animals*. As mentioned earlier, the HO-3 does not cover damage *to* animals, because they are not covered property. The HO-3 also excludes damage caused *by* animals that an insured owns or keeps, or by birds, vermin, rodents, or insects. For example, damage caused by a pet that rips a carpet would not be covered. Likewise, damage caused by a squirrel (a rodent) that enters a dwelling and builds a nest in the wall would not be covered. However, the policy does cover a loss caused by a deer (not owned by the insured and not on the list of excluded animals) that breaks through the large glass door of the dwelling and causes damage to the wall-to-wall carpet.

Exception to Excluded Perils: Water Damage Coverage

Unless the loss is otherwise excluded, the HO-3 covers water damage to buildings or other structures resulting from an accidental discharge or overflow of water or steam. The water or steam must come from a plumbing, heating, air conditioning, or sprinkler system; from a household appliance on the residence premises; or from a storm drain, steam, or sewer pipe off the residence premises. Coverage is provided for damage caused by the water and for the cost of tearing out and replacing any part of the building or other structure necessary to make repairs. However, the loss to the damaged system or appliance is not covered.

Therefore, the insurance adjuster must determine both (1) the cost of removing the wall or flooring to uncover the area where the water is leaking and (2) the cost to repair the area and paint the wall to match the surrounding area. The actual cost of replacing the worn-out plumbing system or appliance is not covered. The coverage's intent is to pay for the damage resulting from the worn-out or defective plumbing or appliance, not the replacement or repair of the appliance or plumbing itself.

The following examples demonstrate how this exception applies:

- If a water line inside a wall ruptures and causes flooding in the basement, coverage will be provided for the resulting water damage and the cost to tear out the wall and repair the damage. The insurer will not pay for replacing or repairing the pipe itself.
- If a dishwasher suddenly leaks water and damages the kitchen floor, coverage will be provided to tear out the damaged floor and repair the damage. The insurer will not pay for repairs to the dishwasher itself.

If a water line under a paved driveway breaks and the escaping water damages a building on the premises, coverage will be provided for the cost to (1) repair the damage to the building, (2) break through the driveway to access the plumbing break, and (3) repair the damaged area of the driveway. The insurer will not pay for replacing or repairing the pipe itself.

Ensuing Losses Covered

Ensuing losses not specifically excluded by the HO-3 are covered. An **ensuing loss** is caused by a subsequent peril that occurs after, or as a result of, the initial peril. For example, settling of foundations is excluded, but if a settling foundation causes a water pipe to break, damaging the basement, the ensuing water damage would be covered.

Ensuing loss
A loss caused by a subsequent peril that occurs after, or as a result of, the initial peril.

Perils Insured Against for Coverage C

Coverage C applies to personal property. The perils covered for Coverage C—Personal Property differ significantly from the special-form coverage previously described for Coverages A and B.

Named Perils

Named perils, to which Coverage C applies, are listed and described in the policy. Only losses caused by those listed perils are covered. Therefore, coverage for personal property under the HO-3 is not as broad as coverage for dwellings and other structures. For example, an insured who accidentally spilled bleach on wall-to-wall carpeting (part of the building, covered under Coverage A) would be compensated for the loss because that peril is not excluded under Coverage A. However, if the spilled bleach also ruined the couch and coffee table (Coverage C—Personal Property items), no coverage would apply for these items because spilled bleach is *not* one of the named perils for Coverage C.

Named Perils Covered

The named perils for which coverage is provided for personal property items under Coverage C are listed below. Some examples are provided for those perils for which coverage is qualified.

1. *Fire or lightning.* Chapter 1 discusses these perils.
2. *Windstorm or hail.* Damage to personal property caused by rain, snow, sleet, sand, or dust is covered only if wind (including hurricane and tornado) or hail first damages the building and causes an opening in a roof or wall through which the rain, snow, sleet, sand, or dust enters. For example, there would be no coverage if water damaged a sofa, television, and stereo because rain came through a window that was left open. However, if windstorm or hail first damaged the building by breaking a window, by tearing shingles off the roof, or by causing a tree to fall and break through the roof, the resulting water damage to the sofa and other personal property would be covered.

   Coverage for windstorm or hail damage to watercraft, their trailers, furnishings, and equipment is provided only while these items are inside a fully enclosed building. Windstorm or hail damage is not covered unless the building is first damaged.
3. *Explosion.* Explosion means a rapid chemical reaction with the production of noise, heat, and the violent expansion of gases. An explosion sometimes occurs as a result of natural gas accumulation in a dwelling.
4. *Riot or civil commotion.* Chapter 1 describes this peril.
5. *Aircraft.* This peril includes damage from self-propelled missiles as well as spacecraft. It does not require physical contact with the aircraft, so damage from a sonic boom is covered.
6. *Vehicles.* Damage to personal property in the back seat of a car involved in an auto accident would be covered, as would damage to a bicycle backed over by a garbage truck or even by the insured's own vehicle. No distinction is made based on who owns or operates the vehicle that causes the damage.
7. *Smoke.* Sudden and accidental smoke damage to personal property is covered. Soot, fumes, or vapors from a boiler or furnace are included as smoke for purposes of this peril. Loss caused by smoke from agricultural smudging or industrial operations is excluded.
8. *Vandalism or malicious mischief.* Vandalism or malicious mischief is covered as long as the premises have not been vacant more than sixty consecutive days immediately before the loss.

9. *Theft*. Theft includes losses of personal property resulting from burglary, robbery or "mysterious disappearance," which is the loss of property that has disappeared from its last known location if it is likely that the property has been stolen. Coverage applies if the circumstantial evidence is strong enough to establish that theft is the cause of the loss.

   The following types of theft are excluded for personal property:

   - Theft coverage is excluded if the theft is committed by an insured. Because the definition of insured includes resident relatives and people under the age of twenty-one in the insured's care, theft of covered property by a teenager who lives in the household, for example, is not covered.
   - Theft from a building under construction and theft of construction materials are not covered under Coverage C. (Building materials can also be covered property under Coverage A, but a specific theft exclusion, mentioned earlier, also precludes such theft coverage.)
   - Theft from that part of the insured premises rented to someone other than another insured is not covered. For example, if the named insured rents a room to an unrelated college student, the student's belongings would not be covered if they were stolen.
   - Theft of personal property from another residence that the insured owns, rents, or occupies is not covered unless the insured is temporarily living there. For example, theft of property at an insured's vacation home at the beach is not covered when the insured is not occupying it. However, the insured's property stolen from a hotel room while the insured is staying there on vacation would be covered.
   - Theft of property belonging to an insured who is a student at a residence away from home (such as a college dormitory room) is not covered if the student has not been in the room for more than sixty days. For example, if the insured's twenty-one-year-old daughter left her own furniture and stereo in her unoccupied dorm room over the summer, she would not have coverage for theft of her belongings occurring seventy-five days after she left the dorm. However, if she returned to live in the room on the seventieth day, her coverage would resume.
   - Theft is excluded for watercraft, including its furnishings and equipment, away from the residence premises (such as a boat at a dock or boat landing).
   - Theft of trailers, semi-trailers, and campers that occurs away from the residence premises is excluded.

10. *Falling objects*. Coverage is provided for losses to personal property if a falling object breaks through the dwelling's roof or wall and damages the contents. For example, coverage would be provided for damage to a dining room table crushed beneath a tree that has first broken through the roof. Coverage would *not* be provided for damage to a table if a chandelier dropped onto the table, because no falling object penetrated the building.

11. *Weight of ice, snow, or sleet.* Coverage applies only to damage to property contained in a building.
12. *Accidental discharge or overflow of water or steam.* Personal property is covered if it is damaged by water or steam that is accidentally released by a plumbing system, a heating system, an air conditioning system, or a fire sprinkler system or a household appliance. For example, furniture damaged as a result of overflow from a dishwasher or clothes washer is covered. However, damage caused by mold, fungus, or wet rot is not covered unless it is hidden by walls, ceilings, or floors. Damage by water from a sump pump or roof drain is not covered.
13. *Sudden and accidental tearing apart, cracking, burning, or bulging.* Personal property is covered if damaged by water or steam released from a hot water heating system, an air conditioning system, or an automatic fire protective sprinkler system. For example, personal property damaged by a ruptured water heater is covered.
14. *Freezing.* Damage to personal property resulting from the freezing of a plumbing system, a heating system, an air conditioning system, or a fire-protective sprinkler system or of a household appliance is covered as long as the insured has taken reasonable precautions to maintain the heat or shut off and drain the system or appliances.
15. *Sudden and accidental damage from artificially generated electrical current.* This peril does not include loss to tubes, transistors, or electronic components or circuitry of appliances, computers, or home entertainment equipment. It would, for example, cover loss to a window air conditioner's compressor resulting from a power surge or a brownout.
16. *Volcanic eruption.* This peril does not include loss caused by earthquake or tremors. Damage caused by airborne shock waves and ash, for example, is covered. However, coverage for debris removal, found in the additional coverages section of the HO-3 form, includes the reasonable expenses for the removal of ash, dust, or particles from a volcanic eruption that has caused direct loss to a building or property contained in a building.

Section I—Exclusions

Some perils are excluded for both buildings and personal property covered under Section I. The list of these exclusions begins with the following statement:

> We do not insure for loss caused directly or indirectly by any of the following. Such loss is excluded regardless of any other cause or event contributing concurrently or in any sequence to the loss. These exclusions apply whether or not the loss event results in widespread damage or affects a substantial area.[24]

This statement, combined with the exclusions that follow, is intended to address a difficult issue in special-form insurance coverage. Because a special-form policy does not preclude a loss unless the cause of loss is specifically excluded, questions can arise when two or more perils, simultaneously or in sequence, combine to cause a loss, and one peril is covered while the other is excluded. This is known as concurrent causation. For example, assume that vandals blow up a dam, releasing surface water that causes damage to downstream property. Vandalism and explosion are covered perils, but flood is an excluded peril, as explained later. Without this provision, the damage might be considered a covered vandalism or explosion loss. However, the policy language clarifies that any flood loss is excluded, even if another peril is associated with it. Although one normally thinks of floods as covering many square miles, this provision would also clearly apply to water escaping from a pond on the insured's own property.

Perils Excluded Under Section I

The following are excluded perils under Section I.

- *Ordinance or law*. Other than the coverage that is provided in the additional coverages section of the policy, loss that results from the enforcement of an ordinance or a law is excluded.
- *Earth movement*. Earthquake and other types of earth movement, such as landslides, mudslides, mudflows, mine subsidences, and sinkholes are excluded perils. However, damage caused by an ensuing fire or explosion is covered. For example, an earthquake ruptures a gas line in a house. The gas then ignites, and the house is burned. The damage caused by the earthquake is excluded, but the fire damage is covered.
- *Water damage*. The water damage exclusion eliminates coverage for losses caused by flood, surface water, waves, and water or water-borne material such as sewage that backs up through sewers and drains. However, ensuing losses from fire, explosion, or theft resulting from water damage are covered. Assume, for example, that a homeowner must evacuate a flooded home. Thieves subsequently enter the home and steal several items of property. The theft would be covered.
- *Power failure*. An insured who loses electrical power or utility service because of a problem away from the residence premises is not covered for the resulting damage. However, a loss is covered if power is interrupted by an insured peril occurring on the premises. These examples help to illustrate this exclusion:
    - A storm causes power lines to break ten miles from the insured's home. The loss of electrical power causes the food in the insured's freezer to thaw and spoil. Coverage for this loss is excluded because the power failure occurred off the residence premises.
    - A transformer at a power station trips during a storm, and the resulting power surge causes a fire in a toaster oven on the residence premises. The resulting fire damage is covered.
- *Neglect*. An insured is expected to use all reasonable means to protect property at the time of a loss and after a loss occurs. No coverage exists for losses resulting from the insured's failure to provide this protection.

The insurer agrees to pay the cost of reasonable repairs under an additional coverage.

- *War*. Property losses resulting from war, including the discharge of nuclear weapons, are excluded.
- *Nuclear hazard*. Property losses that occur because of a nuclear hazard are excluded. A nuclear hazard is defined in the Section I—Conditions portion of the policy as any nuclear reaction, radiation, or contamination.
- *Intentional loss*. The policy defines "intentional loss" to mean any loss arising out of any act that an insured commits or conspires to commit with the intent to cause a loss. The policy states that no insured can recover, not even those who did not commit or conspire to commit the act that caused the loss. This situation has been referred to as the "innocent coinsured" issue and was discussed at length in the beginning of this chapter. Because the law varies on this topic, an adjuster may want to seek legal counsel before denying a loss to an innocent coinsured.
- *Governmental action*. Property described in Coverages A, B, and C is not covered against the destruction, confiscation, or seizure by order of any governmental or public authority. For example, if law enforcement officials seize an insured's personal computer to search for files that might be related to a crime, the insured may not successfully submit a theft claim on the computer.

The next three exclusions apply only to Coverage A—Dwelling and Coverage B—Other Structures. The policy excludes losses from these perils, but any ensuing loss is covered as long as the policy does not preclude coverage for that ensuing loss. Examples of covered ensuing losses are provided.

- *Weather conditions*. Weather is an excluded peril if it contributes to any of the previously excluded perils. Therefore, torrential rain that causes a mudslide is not a covered peril, because earth movement (mudslide) is an excluded peril. However, if the weight of rainwater collected after a heavy downpour on a roof causes the roof to collapse, coverage would be provided because collapse caused by the weight of rain on a roof is covered as an additional coverage.
- *Acts or decisions*. Acts or decisions of other people, organizations, or governmental bodies that cause property damage are not covered. This exclusion is similar to the exclusion for governmental action, but this exclusion is not preceded by the concurrent loss language. Therefore, an unexcluded ensuing loss is covered.[25] If an agency or organization responsible for the public water supply failed to provide water pressure to fire hydrants, and a home was destroyed because firefighters could not get water to extinguish a fire, the fire damage would be covered.
- *Faulty workmanship*. Damage resulting from faulty construction, planning, or materials is excluded. The exclusions specifically listed are faulty planning, zoning, surveying, design specifications, workmanship, construction, renovation, materials, and maintenance. Thus, if an insured's house floods from rainwater because faulty surveying led to a drainage

problem, no coverage will be provided. However, if faulty construction of a chimney in the insured's house results in an ensuing fire, the damage caused by the fire will be covered.

Insured's Duties After Loss

The insured's duties after a loss are explicitly stated in the policy provisions in the Conditions section. For a summarized list of an insured's typical duties after a loss, see the following box.

Insured's Duties After a Loss

- Give prompt notice to insurer or insured's agent.
- Notify police in the event of a theft.
- For a loss involving a credit card, an electronic fund transfer card, or an access device, notify the appropriate card or access company.
- Protect property from further damage. If necessary, make reasonable repairs and keep records of repairs and expenses.
- Cooperate with the insurer in the claim investigation.
- Prepare complete inventory of damaged personal property.
- Make the damaged property available for inspection.
- Provide insurer with documents as requested.
- Submit to an examination under oath.
- Submit a signed, sworn proof of loss to the insurer.

Adjusters must carefully review these conditions because waiver and estoppel, as Chapter 2 explains, can affect the insured's duties.

This set of conditions begins with the statement, "In case of a loss to covered property, we have no duty to provide coverage under this policy if the failure to comply with the following duties is prejudicial to us."[26] A showing of prejudice to an insurer tends to be very fact-specific as well as jurisdiction-specific. As an example, if the insured disposes of all of the damaged property before the insurer inspects it, it might be said that the insurer's right to inspect the loss has been prejudiced. But before an adjuster attempts to deny a loss in such a situation, it may be best to consult with counsel to see whether it is likely that the insurer will prevail if the denial is contested.

Prompt Notice

Following a loss, the insured must give prompt notice to the insurer or to the insured's agent. The HO-3 policy's prompt notice clause does not require written notice, only that notice be given in some form. Other types of policies may require written notice of loss. Also, the time period for giving notice is not specified; it is required to only be prompt. The insured is held to a standard of what is reasonable notice under the circumstances. Notice to the agent is notice to the insurer, so if the insured reports the claim to the agent, proper notice has been given.

Notice to Police

The insured must notify the police after suffering a loss by theft. The police might be able to trace and recover the stolen property and arrest the thief. This policy requirement might also deter fraudulent claims, because in most states, submitting a false police report is a felony. In some areas, police reports are a matter of public record and can be obtained by the property loss adjuster. This condition also benefits the insurance company, which can notify the police of its interest in any recovered property that the company might have already paid for in the form of settlement with the insured.

Notice to Credit Card Company

The insured must also notify the credit card company, the fund transfer card company, or the access device company if the loss involves credit, fund transfer, or access device coverage. This provision's purpose is to restrict the insured's liability for charges or withdrawals made with the insured's credit card, fund transfer card, or access device by an unauthorized person.

Protection of Property

The insured must protect the damaged property from further damage. The insured is responsible for making reasonable and necessary repairs to protect covered property from additional damage. After a fire, boarding up the property, obtaining temporary electrical service, or renting portable heaters to prevent freezing might be necessary. For water damage, shutting off the water and removing wet carpets might be necessary. Although the policy indicates that the insured is responsible for protecting property, the policy does provide coverage for the expense of doing so. The Additional Coverages section of the HO-3 states that "we will pay the reasonable cost incurred by you for necessary measures taken solely to protect covered property that is damaged by a peril insured against from further damage."[27] The insured must keep an accurate record of repair expenses, according to Section 1—Conditions, B.4.b. Without documentation, the insured will have no basis for a claim for reimbursement. Furthermore, this provision states that the repairs must be both reasonable and necessary.

Cooperation With the Insurer

The insured has a duty to cooperate with the insurer in the claim investigation. As obvious as this sounds, not all insureds are cooperative. They may be intentionally uncooperative, or they may simply be too busy to cooperate. Whatever the reason, a failure to cooperate can be grounds for a claim denial. However, it is recommended that a denial for lack of cooperation be carefully reviewed by management and counsel before being sent.

Inventory of Damaged Personal Property

The insured must prepare an inventory of damaged personal property showing the quantity, description, actual cash value, and amount of the loss and attach all bills, receipts, and related documents to support that inventory. Because damaged personal property is either damaged or destroyed or has disappeared, the insured must inventory this property. The inventory must describe the property, list its quantity and actual value, and list the amount that the insured is claiming for the loss.

Along with the inventory, the insured must provide records to substantiate the amount claimed and must present bills, receipts, and related documents of sale. If the insured does not have bills or receipts, then photos, warranty cards, or instruction manuals usually suffice. The insured must be able to prove both ownership and value of the items listed. The insured must prove the loss; the insurer need not disprove that an item was damaged or lost. This becomes extremely important for extensive damage or a substantial theft loss. Make this request tactfully, acknowledging that the insured might have experienced a traumatic incident in the loss. It is usually a good idea for the adjuster to submit a written request for this information.

Showing Damaged Property

As often as the insurer reasonably requires, the insured must show the damaged property. The insured must allow the insurance company to inspect the damaged property to verify the circumstances and amount of loss. The company is entitled to more than one inspection; in fact, the company might need several inspections to complete its investigation. The insured should be reminded in such cases that the policy states that the property is to be shown as often as the insurer reasonably requires.

Records

The insured must provide the insurer with the records and documents that it requests and permit the insurer to copy them. This records provision allows the insurer to obtain any of the insured's records that substantiate the claim. Records can include documents such as bank records, employment records, driving records, and income tax records. Submitting income tax records is controversial. The adjuster should check applicable state court decisions on this matter. This provision can be extremely important because obtaining the insured's records helps the adjuster to prepare for the taking of an examination under oath.

Examination Under Oath

The insured must submit to questions under oath and sign and swear to them. Chapter 2 discusses this provision, and it is developed more fully in

Chapter 6. Although examination under oath (EUO) is frequently used when fraud is suspected, it can also be a useful tool in ascertaining the facts of a loss or establishing the extent of the damages.

Proof of Loss

Among the insured's duties in the event of loss under the HO-3 is the following requirement:

> Send to us, within 60 days after our request, your signed, sworn proof of loss which sets forth, to the best of your knowledge and belief:
>
> (1) The time and cause of loss;
>
> (2) The interests of all "insureds," and all others in the property involved and all liens on the property;
>
> (3) Other insurance which may cover the loss;
>
> (4) Changes in title or occupancy of the property during the term of the policy;
>
> (5) Specifications of damaged buildings and detailed repair estimates;
>
> (6) The inventory of damaged personal property described in 6.e. above;
>
> (7) Receipts for additional living expenses incurred and records that support the fair rental value loss; and
>
> (8) Evidence or affidavit that supports a claim under E.6. Credit Card, Fund Transfer Card or Access Device, Forgery and Counterfeit Money under Section I—Property Coverages, stating the amount and cause of loss.[28]

Time for Submitting Proof of Loss

In the HO-3 policy, the proof of loss is due within sixty days after the insurer makes the request. The time for filing a proof of loss differs by policy. Many policies state that the insured must file a sworn statement in proof of loss within sixty days of the date of loss. In the HO-3 policy, the time for filing the proof of loss could be considerably longer than in other policies. For example, an adjuster handling a claim under an HO-3 policy might continue to investigate for forty days after the date of loss and then advise the insured of the proof of loss condition. In that case, the insured would have up to 100 days from the date of loss to meet the demand. Courts do not require strict compliance with filing deadlines when the insured has a good excuse for delay. However, the insurer is usually compelled by state unfair claim practices acts to respond to a proof of loss, by accepting or rejecting the Proof of Loss form, within a specific time period. In many states, that time frame is fifteen days. Check the individual state regulations when handling claims involving a proof of loss.

Time and Cause

The time and cause of loss provision requires that the insured advise the insurer about the time and cause of the loss. Both can be important in the decision to deny or pay a claim. An investigation could show that the facts do not support the time and cause reported by the insured. When the insured swears to these statements in the proof of loss or in an EUO and the facts prove otherwise, the insured might be committing material misrepresentation, giving the insurer cause to deny the claim.

Interests

The interests provision requires the insured to specify all parties who have any financial interest in the property. These parties are typically mortgagees, chattel interest holders, or lienholders.

Other Insurance

The other insurance provision is important to the insurer. If other insurance applies to the property, the loss settlement will generally be prorated between the insurers. If the insured states that no other insurance covers the property and an investigation determines otherwise, the insurer must consider the possibility that the insured withheld the information to defraud the insurer by collecting more than once for the same loss.

Changes in Title or Occupancy

The change in title or occupancy provision is also important to the insurer. If the insured has sold the property, the proof of loss must record the sale because the insured's insurable interest in the property would be in question.

Determining change in occupancy is also important. A change in occupancy could result in an increase in hazard, which might create a coverage question. Assume, for example, that an insured who has a homeowners policy and lives in the property converts the property into a four-unit apartment. If a fire occurs, the insurer could probably deny coverage.

Specifications and Estimates

The specifications and estimates provision requires the insured to document proof of damages and damage costs. This provision is especially important for a total loss. Determining how a house was built and the quality of materials after the house has been destroyed by fire or hurricane is difficult. The insured is required to specify what was in a house and how it was built and to estimate the costs to repair or rebuild the dwelling.

Inventory

The inventory provision of the proof of loss requirement relates to provision B.6. and B.8.f. of the Duties After Loss condition. With damage or a total loss, the insured must provide an inventory of the damaged personal property. The property loss adjuster has no way of knowing what personal property was damaged or the personal property's age, condition, or value.

Documentation of Loss of Use

The additional living expense (ALE) provision requires that the insured keep receipts for all expenses incurred. The insured must prove incurred expenses by submitting receipts with the proof of loss.

The second portion of this section is proof of "fair rental value loss." The insured could show canceled checks obtained from the tenant or produce the rental agreement, if one were in effect, to prove that the room was being rented for a certain amount or held for rental.

Proof of Credit Card Forgery

The final provision under the proof of loss requirement is related to a credit card, forgery, or counterfeit money claim. The insured must provide proof of loss by a bank statement, affidavit, or some other form of evidence supporting both the cause of loss and the amount of damage claimed. With illegal credit card use, proof might come from the credit card company, showing the signature on a credit card receipt of someone other than the insured. In the case of forgery or counterfeit money, the insured might get proof from a bank.

Appraisal Provision

The HO-3 uses the appraisal process when the insured and the insurer cannot agree on the amount of the loss. Some jurisdictions have expanded the authority of the appraisal process, so it is wise to check the case law in the jurisdiction of the loss. The parties must select impartial and competent appraisers within twenty days of the written demand for appraisal. They must agree on an umpire within fifteen days after the appraisers are selected; otherwise, the court of record will make the appointment.

Loss Settlement

Having established that the loss or damage is covered under the policy, the adjuster must determine how the loss settlement will be calculated. Section I—Conditions establishes how the amount that will be paid for property after a loss will be determined. There are two settlement methods: one method is established for Coverage A—Dwelling or Coverage B—Other Structures, and the other method is established for Coverage C—Personal Property.

Replacement Cost Under the HO-3 for Coverages A and B

Buildings and other structures are insured for replacement cost under the HO-3, provided that the insured has a limit of insurance that is at least 80 percent of the structure's full replacement cost. An insured with a sufficient limit will receive the cost to repair or replace the damage to the structure, subject to the policy limit.

An insured with a limit of insurance less than 80 percent of the structure's full replacement cost will receive a loss settlement based on the greater of actual cash value or a portion of the full replacement cost, with loss sharing similar to coinsurance. This is not strictly a coinsurance requirement because the insured can always receive at least actual cash value.

The amount payable for a building loss might be one of three amounts: (1) the replacement cost, (2) the actual cash value, or (3) an amount between these two numbers. It all depends on how the limit of insurance compares to the replacement cost value of the damaged building at the time of the loss.

The methods for determining the loss settlement for a building are as follows:

1. *If the limit of insurance is 80 percent or more of the replacement cost:* The insurer will pay for the replacement cost of the damage up to the limit of coverage.
2. *If the limit of insurance is less than 80 percent of the replacement cost:* The insurer will pay the *greater* of (1) the ACV of the damage or (2) the proportion of the cost to repair or replace the damage that the limit of insurance bears to 80 percent of the replacement cost. This second method is sometimes easier to understand as a formula:

$$\text{Loss payment} = \frac{\text{Limit of insurance}}{80\% \times \text{Replacement cost}} \times \text{Replacement cost of the loss.}$$

The following box provides examples of how the loss settlement for a dwelling would be determined. (These simple examples ignore any deductible that might apply.)

Loss Settlement: Dwelling

Example 1. Dwelling limit equals or exceeds 80 percent of the replacement cost:
An insured has a home with a $200,000 replacement cost and an HO-3 with a Coverage A limit of $180,000. Lightning strikes the central air conditioning unit and destroys it beyond repair. The unit has a replacement cost of $5,000 and is five years old.

The dwelling is insured for more than 80 percent of the replacement cost ($180,000 is 90 percent of $200,000).

Loss payment: The insured would receive $5,000 to replace the unit.

Example 2. Dwelling limit is less than 80 percent of the replacement cost:
If this same insured has an HO-3 with a Coverage A limit of $100,000 (50 percent of the replacement cost), the insured's coverage would be below the 80 percent replacement cost requirement, and the second loss settlement method would be used. The insured would then receive the *greater* of the following:

- The air conditioner's ACV is calculated by using the $5,000 replacement cost minus depreciation. If a central air conditioner has a useful life of ten years and is now five years old, this air conditioner depreciates by 50 percent. The ACV equals $2,500.
- The payment developed by the formula is as follows:

$$\frac{\$100{,}000}{80\% \times \$200{,}000} \times \$5{,}000 = \$3{,}125.$$

Loss payment: The insured would receive the greater amount of $3,125.

Except for small losses (generally under $2,500), the insurer will not pay more than the actual cash value until repairs are actually completed. An insured who has not decided whether to rebuild can initially seek loss settlement on an ACV basis and has up to 180 days after the loss to tell the insurer that he or she intends to complete the repairs and make settlement on a replacement cost basis.

The insured is not required to rebuild a damaged or destroyed building on the same location. However, if the building is rebuilt on different premises, the insurer will pay no more than it would pay if the building were repaired or replaced at the original premises.

Regardless of the method used to determine the loss settlement amount, the limit of coverage shown on the declarations page is the maximum amount that will be paid for any loss.

Coverage C and Miscellaneous Items

Losses to personal property listed under Coverage C, as well as awnings, carpeting, appliances, antennas, outdoor equipment, structures that are not buildings, and grave markers or mausoleums, are settled at the *lesser* of the following:

- Actual cash value at the time of the loss
- The amount required to repair or replace the items

For example, a property loss adjuster working with an insured who has a damaged microwave oven as the result of a kitchen fire might first determine the microwave's ACV. This valuation can be determined by checking to see what a new microwave would cost and then subtracting a percentage of that value based on depreciation. A microwave's depreciation is largely determined by age and also by the circumstances of its use. For example, if a new microwave costs $200, but the damaged one was five years old, the adjuster might calculate that the damaged microwave depreciated 50 percent (appliances are sometimes estimated to have a useful life of ten years). The microwave's ACV would then be $200 × 0.50, or $100. If the property loss adjuster then determined that it would cost $300 to repair the microwave, the representative would settle the loss for the lesser amount of $100.

Loss to a Pair or Set

Often, items that are in pairs or sets are more valuable together than the items' value individually. Because of the increased value of pairs or sets, a policy provision establishes the amount that an insurer will pay if an item that is part of a pair or set is damaged or lost.

Deductible

Following the definitions, the policy begins with a statement that the insurer will pay only property losses that exceed the deductible amount shown in the declarations. The deductible that appears on the declarations page is a specific amount to be deducted from payment for a loss covered under Section I. The most common deductible amounts are $250 and $500. They apply to all perils insured against under Section I of the policy. Many insurers in catastrophe-prone areas also use special higher deductible amounts that apply to specified perils.

Questions arise as to how to apply the deductible when adjusting a loss involving items covered by the policy's special limits provisions. As a general rule, the deductible is taken from the overall loss, and then the specific limits are applied. See the following box.

Deductible Example

Coverage C's limit is $100,000, with a $500 deductible on the policy. The insured has $5,000 worth of jewelry stolen along with other personal property valued at $5,000. The policy has a $1,500 limit on jewelry, so the deductible is applied to the difference between the jewelry loss ($5,000) and the limit ($1,500). The $3,500 of remaining loss would absorb the $500 deductible. Payment would be $1,500 for the jewelry loss and $5,000 for the other property.

SUMMARY

The homeowners policy can be used to protect the insured's interest in a dwelling, an apartment, or a condominium. Various HO forms and editions offer differing coverage levels. The ISO HO-3 is one commonly used form.

The HO-3 insures buildings and other structures for risk of direct physical loss. It provides coverage for loss or damage to personal property but only from specified perils. The HO-3 also provides coverage for additional living expenses and loss of use of the premises.

Upon receiving a loss, the property loss adjuster must determine who is insured under the policy and what any insured's insurable interest is in the property. A mortgagee or a loss payee may also be covered by the policy. The adjuster must ensure that the named insured has complied with his or her duties before and after a loss has occurred.

The adjuster must also determine what is insured under the policy. The HO-3 makes an important distinction between residence premises and insured location. Other structures such as a pool or a shed are covered by the policy. Personal property, subject to a set of internal sublimits and specified perils, is also covered. Because of the various additional coverages within the HO-3, the adjuster must carefully allocate the various parts of the loss to the correct coverage because an incorrect apportionment will affect policy limits.

The adjuster must investigate the cause of the loss and then determine whether the policy covers it or whether exclusions apply. The issue of concurrent causation may appear in this part of the analysis.

Finally, if the loss is found to be a covered loss, the adjuster must determine the amount to be paid. The HO-3 provides replacement cost coverage for the dwelling and other structures and actual cash value coverage for personal property. The loss is subject to coinsurance as well as internal sublimits for certain types of personal property and a deductible.

CHAPTER NOTES

1. For additional treatment of this topic, see Eric A. Wiening, George E. Rejda, Constance M. Luthardt, and Cheryl L. Ferguson, *Personal Insurance* (Malvern, Pa.: American Institute for CPCU/IIA, 2002).
2. For further information, see Eric Wiening, *Foundations of Risk Management and Insurance* (Malvern, Pa.: American Institute for CPCU/IIA, 2002), p. 12.7.
3. Form HO 00 03 05 01, Copyright, Insurance Services Office, Inc., 2000.
4. Form HO 00 03 05 01, Copyright, Insurance Services Office, Inc., 2000.
5. Form HO 00 03 05 01, Copyright, Insurance Services Office, Inc., 2000.
6. Form HO 00 03 05 01, Copyright, Insurance Services Office, Inc., 2000.
7. Form HO 00 03 05 01, Copyright, Insurance Services Office, Inc., 2000.
8. Adapted from e-mail authored by Michael P. Griffin, training specialist, Liberty Regional Agency Markets, Keene, N.H.
9. Form HO 00 03 05 01, Copyright, Insurance Services Office, Inc., 2000.
10. Form HO 00 03 05 01, Copyright, Insurance Services Office, Inc., 2000.
11. Form HO 00 03 05 01, Copyright, Insurance Services Office, Inc., 2000.
12. Form HO 00 03 05 01, Copyright, Insurance Services Office, Inc., 2000.
13. Form HO 00 03 05 01, Copyright, Insurance Services Office, Inc., 2000.
14. Form HO 00 03 05 01, Copyright, Insurance Services Office, Inc., 2000.
15. Form HO 00 03 05 01, Copyright, Insurance Services Office, Inc., 2000.
16. Form HO 00 03 05 01, Copyright, Insurance Services Office, Inc., 2000.
17. Form HO 00 03 05 01, Copyright, Insurance Services Office, Inc., 2000.
18. Form HO 00 03 05 01, Copyright, Insurance Services Office, Inc., 2000.
19. *Black's Law Dictionary*, 5th ed. (St. Paul, Minn.: West Publishing Co., 1979), p. 813.
20. Form HO 00 03 05 01, Copyright, Insurance Services Office, Inc., 2000.
21. Form HO 00 03 05 01, Copyright, Insurance Services Office, Inc., 2000.
22. Form HO 00 03 05 01, Copyright, Insurance Services Office, Inc., 2000.
23. Form HO 00 03 05 01, Copyright, Insurance Services Office, Inc., 2000.
24. Form HO 00 03 05 01, Copyright, Insurance Services Office, Inc., 2000.
25. Diane W. Richardson, *Homeowners Coverage Guide: Interpretation and Analysis*, 2nd ed. (Cincinnati, Ohio: *The National Underwriter*, 2002).
26. Form HO 00 03 05 01, Copyright, Insurance Services Office, Inc., 2000.
27. Form HO 00 03 05 01, Copyright, Insurance Services Office, Inc., 2000.
28. Form HO 00 03 05 01, Copyright, Insurance Services Office, Inc., 2000.

Chapter 4

Direct Your Learning

Commercial Property Policies

After learning the subject matter of this chapter, you should be able to:

- Describe the various parties, interests, and types of property that may be insured under the Building and Personal Property Coverage Form (BPP), and apply this knowledge to claim situations.
- Distinguish between the Basic Form, Broad Form, and Special Form in terms of covered property, covered causes of loss, exclusions, and additional coverages, and apply these coverages to claim situations.
- Describe the various additional coverages and coverage extensions in the BPP, and apply them to claim situations.
- Apply policy conditions and loss settlement conditions to a loss.
- Describe the purpose of the Difference in Conditions Policy.

OUTLINE

Develop Your Perspective

What are the main topics covered in the chapter?

This chapter describes the coverage provided by the Building and Personal Property Coverage Form (BPP) and the various causes of loss forms that can be attached to the BPP. It also discusses endorsements often added to the BPP and the use of the Difference in Conditions Policy (DIC) to fill gaps in coverage.

Examine a commercial property coverage form used by your company or a company that you represent.

- Is this a coverage form other than the BPP?
- How does your coverage form differ from the BPP?

Why is it important to know these topics?

Almost every commercial insured is covered by a commercial property policy. Knowing which coverages are provided by the BPP and which are not will enable the property loss adjuster to correctly adjust a loss.

Review a commercial property loss in your office.

- Determine who and what are insured.
- Determine if a covered cause of loss applies.
- Determine the amount of loss payable under the policy.

How can you use this information?

If you are assigned a commercial property loss, you must review the applicable policy provisions and apply them to the facts of the loss to determine whether the loss is covered and, if covered, how much would be payable.

Chapter 4

Commercial Property Policies

Commercial property policies vary according to the type of business and the type of property to be insured. This variety makes adjusting commercial property losses interesting and challenging.

A commercial property loss can involve damage to the structure itself, damage to the structure's contents, loss of business income, debris removal, salvage, and subrogation. While the adjustment of these losses often requires the adjuster to use experts for many aspects of a loss, such as evaluating salvage potential or calculating the business income loss, the policy analysis used in the adjustment is the same as that described in Chapters 1 and 2. This chapter applies the basic concepts that Chapters 1 and 2 discuss to the specific policy language of the BPP and the three causes of loss forms usually associated with the BPP.

Commercial property coverage is often provided as part of a commercial package policy. The package might contain property coverage, liability coverage, and other types of coverages, depending on the insured's needs. Some insureds may qualify for coverage under businessowners policies (BOPs) that provide both property and liability coverage in a package similar to a homeowners policy. The commercial property coverage forms discussed in this chapter are the Building and Personal Property Coverage Form (BPP) from Insurance Services Office, Inc., (ISO) and the Difference in Conditions Policy (DIC).

BUILDING AND PERSONAL PROPERTY COVERAGE FORM

The BPP policy consists of a declarations page, common policy conditions, commercial property conditions, the building and personal property coverage form, and one of three possible causes of loss forms as well as endorsements.

Declarations Page

A property loss adjuster should first examine the declarations page when reviewing coverage for a commercial property loss. Exhibit 4-1 is a sample declarations page. A declarations page contains the following information:

1. The insured parties
2. The insured property locations
3. The type of coverage provided for each location and the applicable limits

EXHIBIT 4-1

COMMERCIAL PROPERTY
CP DS 00 10 00

COMMERCIAL PROPERTY COVERAGE PART DECLARATIONS PAGE

POLICY NO. A12345 EFFECTIVE DATE 07 / 15 / XX "X" If Supplemental Declarations Is Attached

NAMED INSURED JAC Enterprises

DESCRIPTION OF PREMISES

Prem. No.	Bldg. No.	Location, Construction And Occupancy
	1	123 Market Street, Anytown, PA

COVERAGES PROVIDED Insurance At The Described Premises Applies Only For Coverages For Which A Limit Of Insurance Is Shown

Prem. No.	Bldg. No.	Coverage	Limit Of Insurance	Covered Causes Of Loss	Coinsurance*	Rates
	1	Building	$1,000,000	Special	80%	

*If Extra Expense Coverage, Limits On Loss Payment

OPTIONAL COVERAGES Applicable Only When Entries Are Made In The Schedule Below

Prem.	Bldg.	Agreed Value			Replacement Cost (X)		
No.	No.	Expiration Date	Cov.	Amount	Building	Pers. Prop.	Including "Stock"

Inflation Guard (%) Bldg.	Pers. Prop.	*Monthly Limit Of Indemnity (Fraction)	Maximum Period Of Indemnity (X)	*Extended Period Of Indemnity (Days)

*Applies to Business Income Only

MORTGAGEHOLDERS

Prem. No.	Bldg. No.	Mortgageholder Name And Mailing Address

DEDUCTIBLE

$500. Exceptions:

FORMS APPLICABLE

To All Coverages:

To Specific Premises/Coverages:

Prem. No.	Bldg. No.	Coverages	Form Number

CP DS 00 10 00 Page 1 of 1

4. The mortgagees, if any
5. The deductible amounts
6. A list of coverage forms and endorsements applicable to the policy
7. Any coinsurance percentages that apply
8. Any optional coverages

Who Is Insured?

Determining who is insured under a commercial policy is not as complicated as it can be under a homeowners policy. The standard BPP does not even include a definition of "insured."

The Named Insured

Commercial coverage presents no questions of residency or relatives. The policy declarations page simply leaves a space for the named insured and the insured's mailing address. The paragraph at the beginning of the BPP coverage form reads as follows:

> Throughout this policy the words "you" and "your" refer to the Named Insured shown in the Declarations. The words "we," "us," and "our" refer to the Company providing this insurance.[1]

If the insured is a sole proprietorship and the name on the declarations page is Walter Johnson's Barber Shop, for example, Walter Johnson would be the named insured, and his business would be covered. Customers, employees, and Walter's family members would not be insureds.

The same rule applies for partnerships. If Jerry Johnson and Tom Peterson form a partnership and put the name of Johnson & Peterson Investments on their policy, they would be the named insureds. The property belonging to the partnership would be considered "your business property," and the duties specified in the conditions section would have to be performed by "you," meaning Jerry and Tom.

Corporate Named Insureds

If the name that appears on the policy is that of a corporation, such as Watson Video, Inc., the insured would be the corporation. In this case, "you" in the policy refers to the corporation. A corporation is a legal entity, and it has most of the same legal powers as those of an individual. The corporation designates an officer, a director, or some other person with authority to deal with the adjuster if a loss occurs. Otherwise, the loss adjustment is the same as that involving a sole proprietor. The corporate officers must ensure that the policy duties are performed. Payment is made to the corporation.

A corporate named insured's duties in the event of a loss are the same as those of a sole proprietorship or a partnership. These duties are substantially similar to the duties outlined in the homeowners policy, which Chapter 3 discusses. See the following box.

Duties of Named Insured in the Event of a Loss Under the BPP

- Notify the police if a law has been broken.
- Give the insurer prompt notice, including a description of the property involved.
- Describe how, when, and where the loss occurred.
- Protect property from further damage, and keep a record of expenses incurred.
- Prepare a complete inventory of damaged property.
- Permit the insurer to inspect.
- Submit to examination under oath (EUO).
- Submit a signed, sworn proof of loss to the insurer.
- Cooperate with the insurer in the claim investigation.

Other Interested Parties

Mortgageholders are protected by a mortgage clause similar to the one in the homeowners policy. Lienholders, vendors, suppliers, loss payees, and others who have an insurable interest in the property of a business can be added to the policy as additional insureds, loss payees, or lienholders. Their names would appear on the declarations page.

Lender's Rights

Large commercial property risks often have mortgages on their property. They might also have borrowed money to purchase equipment, or they might lease much of their equipment. They might also sell equipment to others. The mortgageholder, the owner of leased or rented equipment, and the purchaser of the insured's equipment could all be protected from loss by the Loss Payable Provisions endorsement, if it is added to the policy. If an additional insured, loss payee, or mortgageholder is listed on the policy, the adjuster must include such a party on any claim payment involving that party's property.

Mortgageholders Provision

The Mortgageholders provision is found in the Additional Coverages section of the BPP. The provision covers the mortgageholders' interest in the buildings and structures (real property), as their interest may appear. "As their interest may appear" is a phrase not defined in the policy. It generally refers to the amount due and owing on the debt, appearing on the lender's books and records or on the debt instrument, at the time of the loss.

The mortgageholder can recover for a loss even if the insured's claim is denied because of the insured's acts or failure to comply with the policy conditions, such as filing a proof of loss. To collect, the mortgageholder must pay any premium due; file a proof of loss; and notify the insurer of any change in property ownership, change in use, or change in occupancy.

Usually a single claim payment is made, showing both the insured and the mortgageholder in the payee portion of the check or draft. Situations might arise in which the insured or the mortgageholder wants a separate check. Property loss adjusters should consult with their claim manager before agreeing to issue separate payments.

Loss Payable Provisions

The Loss Payable Provisions Endorsement is used to protect the interests of banks and lenders that have a security interest in personal property. It also protects owners of leased or rented equipment as well as the insured's interests in property sold but not yet delivered. The endorsement has three options. See the following box.

> **Loss Payable Provisions Endorsement Options**
>
> 1. Loss payable
> 2. Lender's loss payable
> 3. Contract of sale

Loss Payable If the insured has requested that a loss payee be added to the policy, the adjuster must adjust the loss with the insured and make the claim payment payable to the insured and the loss payee as their interest may appear. The same advisory made concerning separate checks for mortgageholders applies here.

Lender's Loss Payable The lender's interest must be evidenced by a written contract, such as a rental agreement, a lease agreement, or a bill of lading. Payment is made to the lenders in order of precedence and as their interests may appear. Under this option, the lender's interest would be protected if the insured's claim is denied because of an insured's act or failure to comply with the policy terms and conditions. In this situation, the lender must satisfy the same criteria as the mortgageholder does under the Mortgageholders provision to collect on the claim.

Contract of Sale This option of the Loss Payable Provisions Endorsement is not used frequently. It might be used when the insured is selling property over a period of time. A third party might enter into a contract to buy a business, but rather than going to a bank and getting a mortgage and completing the sale in a single transaction, that party works out a deal with the insured owner of the property to pay the owner over a period of time while the owner continues to operate the business until the third party completes the sale and takes complete control. At any point during that contract until the final payment, both parties have an insurable interest in the property.

This relationship differs from that of mortgagor and mortgagee and therefore must be addressed in a loss payable clause, thus the need for endorsement.

The buyer (who has yet to gain legal ownership interest through title because the contract's terms have not been fulfilled) would be the loss payee to the extent of his or her interest in the contract, and the seller (who has yet to surrender legal ownership through title) would be the named insured who still has a definite interest.

Without the endorsement, the buyer would not be a party to the insurance contract and would have no way to protect his or her interest except through a separate insurance agreement or policy.

Insurable Interest

The commercial property conditions that apply to building and personal property coverage also address the insurable interest requirement. In the BPP coverage form, condition 4, Loss Payment, reads in part as follows:

> d. We will not pay you more than your financial interest in the Covered Property.
>
> e. We may adjust losses with the owners of lost or damaged property if other than you. If we pay the owners, such payments will satisfy your claims against us for the owners' property. We will not pay the owners more than their financial interest in the Covered Property.[2]

The Additional Conditions section of the BPP, paragraph 32, which treats mortgageholders, states the following in reference to insurable interest:

> b. We will pay for covered loss of or damage to buildings or structures to each mortgageholder shown in the Declarations in their order of precedence, as interests may appear.[3]

What Is Insured?

Regardless of which causes of loss form is attached, the BPP covers only direct physical loss. The property is covered only at the premises described in the declarations page and only if a limit of insurance appears next to that type of property.

Building Coverage

An insured who owns the building but does not occupy it or have any business property on the premises would probably elect to insure only the building. Refer back to Exhibit 4-1. Notice that only the term "building" is listed in the "Coverage" column in the space left for "Coverages Provided." Next to that is a limit of insurance. Because the insured in this example neither occupies nor keeps property on these premises, no other property with corresponding limits of insurance is listed.

A tenant who leases the building and has business property inside can choose to buy personal property coverage only. The only time that a company would need all of the coverages available under a BPP is when it is the owner-occupant or a tenant with an agreement to carry insurance on the building for the owner's protection.

Those who select building coverage must describe the building that they wish to insure in the declarations. This is usually done with a street address, but it can also be a plot map description or some other type of description, as long as it makes the property identifiable. That building or structure is covered along with the following:

(1) Completed additions;

(2) Fixtures, including outdoor fixtures;

(3) Permanently installed:

  (a) Machinery and

  (b) Equipment;

(4) Personal property owned by you that is used to maintain or service the building or structure or its premises, including:

  (a) Fire extinguishing equipment;

  (b) Outdoor furniture;

  (c) Floor coverings; and

  (d) Appliances used for refrigerating, ventilating, cooking, dishwashing, or laundering;

(5) If not covered by other insurance:

  (a) Additions under construction, alterations and repairs to the building or structure;

  (b) Materials, equipment, supplies and temporary structures, on or within 100 feet of the described premises, used for making additions, alterations or repairs to the building or structure.[4]

Anything attached to the building becomes part of the building. Fixtures, machinery, or equipment attached to the building receives building coverage.

Item (4) in this list, coverage for personal property under the building coverage, might be surprising. It is included because an insured who buys only building coverage should not have to pay extra for personal property coverage just to cover the maintenance equipment and items used to service the building. Items (4)(a) through (4)(d) are covered as part of the building as long as the insured owns them and uses them to maintain or service the property.

Materials and supplies used in the building's construction are sometimes covered under a builders' risk policy or by the contractor. For this reason, they are covered by the BPP only if no other policy provides coverage.

Business Personal Property

For those with business personal property to insure, the coverage Your Business Personal Property covers various property that must be in the building described in the declarations or within 100 feet of the premises. An option is available to purchase coverage that would apply if the property were more than 100 feet from the premises.

The policy lists seven kinds of property covered:

1. Furniture and fixtures;
2. Machinery and equipment;
3. "Stock";
4. All other personal property owned by you and used in your business;
5. Labor, materials or services furnished or arranged by you on personal property of others;
6. Your use interest as tenant in improvements and betterments. Improvements and betterments are fixtures, alterations, installations or additions:
   (a) Made a part of the building or structure you occupy but do not own; and
   (b) You acquired or made at your expense but cannot legally remove.
7. Leased personal property for which you have a contractual responsibility to insure, unless otherwise provided for under Personal Property of Others.[5]

With items 1. and 2. above, some fixtures, machinery, and equipment are covered under building coverage and under personal property coverage. The BPP is designed to be flexible. A tenant who primarily needs personal property coverage can get coverage for certain trade fixtures without having to buy building coverage.

Stock is the property that a business has available for sale, raw materials, and in-process or finished goods.

Item 4. is a catch-all category for anything that is not included in the first three categories. The policy's intention is to start with coverage for all property in the building, provided that it is used in the business. Coverage for some items is excluded in the Property Not Covered section.

Item 5. above introduces coverage for the value of the insured's work on the property of others. When a businessperson takes in someone else's property to repair or work on, that person has an insurable interest in the property even though someone else owns it. The intent of this part of the policy is to cover the value of the materials and labor used to fix or repair the property.

The improvements and betterments coverage described in item 6. comes under the heading of personal property even though the improvements, by definition, are made a part of the building. Lessees generally want to buy only personal property coverage. They can protect their investment in their improvements to the building with this coverage.

Because a business may not own all of the personal property used in its operations, item 7. provides coverage for leased equipment when the insured is contractually obligated to obtain insurance.

Personal Property of Others

The BPP also covers personal property of others under the following conditions:

1. In your care, custody or control; and
2. Located in or on the building described in the Declarations or in the open (or in a vehicle) within 100 feet of the described premises.[6]

Many businesses take in customers' property to repair it, consign it, or clean it. This practice is a bailment, and the insured business is the bailee. If the property were damaged while on the insured's premises, the insured would usually want its insurance company to cover the damages to preserve a favorable relationship with customers. Essentially, the property of others is covered and handled in the same way as the insured's own property. All other policy provisions apply, including the deductible. This coverage is not liability coverage.

The insurer is not required to settle separately with each of the different customers whose property might be damaged. The adjustment and payment for the personal property of others may be made to the insured for the owner's account. The following box provides an example of typical property coverage needs. Also see Exhibit 4-2, which shows a sample declarations page based on this example.

Property Coverage Example

ABC Furniture Store is a retail store specializing in high-quality furniture, most of which is made in a factory located at the same address, but 200 feet from the retail store. ABC owns the building that houses its retail operation, but ABC leases the factory building from Landlord Company.

The BPP declarations page makes identifying the coverages that apply to each building easy. Each building can be insured under the same policy, but the insured and the adjuster must pay careful attention to building numbers and policy limits for each coverage.

Building #1 is the retail store. Because ABC owns it, ABC purchases building coverage, and the limit of insurance is listed as $400,000. All of the inventory and furniture in Building #1 must be insured, so the declarations page shows $300,000 for business personal property. No limit of insurance is shown for personal property of others because all property of others is worked on, or stored in, the factory.

ABC does not need any building coverage on the factory because Landlord Company is responsible for that coverage. Still, valuable furniture is being built in this building, and the building houses expensive machinery and equipment. To handle these exposures, ABC purchases $600,000 worth of coverage on the business personal property for Building #2. It also purchases $50,000 worth of personal property coverage for personal property of others in Building #2.

EXHIBIT 4-2

COMMERCIAL PROPERTY
CP DS 00 10 00

COMMERCIAL PROPERTY COVERAGE PART DECLARATIONS PAGE

POLICY NO. XA98765 **EFFECTIVE DATE** 7 / 15 / XX **"X" If Supplemental Declarations Is Attached**

NAMED INSURED ABC Furniture Store

DESCRIPTION OF PREMISES

Prem. No.	Bldg. No.	Location, Construction And Occupancy
	1	520 Retail Avenue, Anytown
	2	520A Retail Avenue, Anytown

COVERAGES PROVIDED Insurance At The Described Premises Applies Only For Coverages For Which A Limit Of Insurance Is Shown

Prem. No.	Bldg. No.	Coverage	Limit Of Insurance	Covered Causes Of Loss	Coinsurance*	Rates
	1	Building	$400,000	Special	80%	
		& Pers. Prop.	$300,000			
	2	Pers. Prop.	$600,000	Special	80%	
		Pers. Prop. Others	$ 50,000			

*If Extra Expense Coverage, Limits On Loss Payment

OPTIONAL COVERAGES Applicable Only When Entries Are Made In The Schedule Below

Prem.	Bldg.	Agreed Value			Replacement Cost (X)		
No.	No.	Expiration Date	Cov.	Amount	Building	Pers. Prop.	Including "Stock"

Inflation Guard (%)		*Monthly Limit Of Indemnity (Fraction)	Maximum Period Of Indemnity (X)	*Extended Period Of Indemnity (Days)
Bldg.	Pers. Prop.			

*Applies to Business Income Only

MORTGAGEHOLDERS

Prem. No.	Bldg. No.	Mortgageholder Name And Mailing Address

DEDUCTIBLE

$500. Exceptions:

FORMS APPLICABLE

To All Coverages:

To Specific Premises/Coverages:

Prem. No.	Bldg. No.	Coverages	Form Number

CP DS 00 10 00 Page 1 of 1

Property Not Covered

As with the HO-3, some types of property are not insurable or are better insured under another policy. The following categories of property are not covered in the BPP (policy language appears in italics):

a. *Accounts, bills, currency, deeds, food stamps, or other evidences of debt, money, notes or securities.* Some companies keep large amounts of money and securities at their business location, and others keep very little. By excluding such property from the basic policy, insureds who require coverage for such financial items can purchase separate coverage for it.

b. *Animals, unless owned by others and boarded by you, or if owned by you, only as "stock" while inside of buildings.* Pet stores that sell animals have coverage because animals are their merchandise. A retail store's owner who allows his dog on the premises at night to deter burglars has no coverage for the watchdog.

c. *Automobiles held for sale.* Car dealers must buy special coverage for their inventory from another type of policy.

d. *Bridges, roadways, walks, patios or other paved surfaces.* This item extends the types of property not covered beyond personal property.

e. *Contraband, or property in the course of illegal transportation or trade.* This property is uninsurable by any policy.

f. *The cost of excavations, grading, backfilling or filling.* Insurance policies normally do not cover land and land's preparation below the surface of the ground.

g. *Foundations of buildings, structures, machinery or boilers if their foundations are below:*

   (1) The lowest basement floor; or

   (2) The surface of the ground, if there is no basement.

h. *Land (including land on which the property is located), water, growing crops or lawns.* Companies in the landscaping or nursery business must buy special insurance.

i. *Personal property while airborne or waterborne.*

j. *Bulkheads, pilings, piers, wharves, or docks.*

k. *Property that is covered under another coverage form of this or any other policy in which it is more specifically described, except for the excess of the amount due (whether you can collect on it or not) from that other insurance.* This parallels the HO-3 exclusion for items with more specific coverage. The purpose is the same: to avoid duplicate coverage and allow the policy that schedules the property to be primary.

l. *Retaining walls that are not part of the building described in the Declarations.*

m. *Underground pipes, flues or drains.*

n. *The cost to research, replace or restore the information on valuable papers and records, including those which exist on electronic or magnetic media, except as provided in the Coverage Extensions*. All valuable papers coverage is removed here. Some is restored under the coverage extensions.

o. *Vehicles or self-propelled machines (including aircraft or watercraft) that:*

   (1) Are licensed for use on public roads; or

   (2) Are operated principally away from the described premises;

   This paragraph does not apply to:

   (a) Vehicles or self-propelled machines or autos you manufacture, process or warehouse;

   (b) Vehicles or self-propelled machines, other than autos, you hold for sale; or

   (c) Rowboats or canoes out of water at the described premises. The BPP is simply not designed to insure vehicles except nonlicensed vehicles used in the business and on the premises. A forklift is covered, as are lawnmowers, carts, other such vehicles, and small boats.

   (d) Trailers, but only to the extent provided for in the coverage extension for non-owned detached trailers.

p. *The following property while outside of buildings:*

   (1) Grain, hay, straw or other crops. These items are perishable and susceptible to damage by the weather.

   (2) Fences, radio or television antennas, (including satellite dishes) and their lead-in wiring, masts or towers, signs (other than signs attached to buildings), trees, shrubs, or plants, (other than "stock") all except as provided in the Coverage Extensions. Some of the property excluded in this section is restored in the coverage extensions.

Commercial Property Coverages: Causes of Loss Forms

Under the BPP coverage forms, one form states the general coverage provisions. To this form must be added one of the causes of loss forms to complete the policy. The causes of loss forms provide specific types of coverage. The Building and Personal Property Coverage Form reads:

> We will pay for direct physical loss of or damage to Covered Property at the premises described in the Declarations caused by or resulting from any Covered Cause of Loss.[7]

Under "Covered Causes of Loss," the BPP coverage specifies on the declarations page the selection of the Basic, Broad, or Special causes of loss form. The Causes of Loss—Basic Form and the Causes of Loss—Broad Form are specified-perils forms, which means that they have a list of covered causes of loss as well as a list of exclusions. The Causes of Loss—Special Form insures against direct physical loss except for causes specifically excluded or limited. Understanding the Causes of Loss—Basic Form, even though it is not widely used, provides the foundation for the Broad Form and the Special Form.

Basic Form: Covered Causes of Loss

The Basic Form provides coverage for eleven perils. Because earlier chapters discuss many of these perils, this section mentions only differences and distinctions of this policy.

Covered Causes of Loss

The following are the Basic Form causes of loss:

1. *Fire*.
2. *Lightning*.
3. *Explosion*. This peril covers explosion, including the explosion of gases or fuel within the furnace or any fire vessel or within the flues or passages through which the gases of combustion pass. It does not include loss or damage by the following:
    a. Rupture, bursting, or operation of pressure-relief devices
    b. Rupture or bursting due to expansion or swelling of the contents of any building or structure, caused by or resulting from water

    Pressure-relief devices are on many types of pressurized systems such as hot water heaters, boilers, and turbines. Although the devices' purpose is to release pressure when it builds up to a specified point, depending upon the device, this venting can actually be explosive in nature. Loss caused by such devices' rupture or bursting is not covered.

    Explosion losses could be accidental or deliberate. When the explosion is obviously not accidental, the adjuster should investigate the insured's activities prior to the explosion to determine whether the insured caused the loss or whether a third party's actions might have caused it.
4. *Windstorm or hail*.
5. *Smoke*.
6. *Aircraft or vehicles*. The Causes of Loss—Basic Form and the Causes of Loss—Broad Form define the aircraft or vehicles peril to include only losses caused by physical contact of an aircraft, a spacecraft, a self-propelled missile, a vehicle, or an object thrown up by a vehicle with the described property or with the building or structure containing the described property. This cause of loss includes loss or damage by objects falling from aircraft.[8]
7. *Riot or civil commotion*. This peril covers acts of striking employees as well as theft that might occur during a riot or civil commotion.
8. *Vandalism*. Adjusters may have to distinguish between damage caused during a theft and damage caused by vandalism if both have occurred in the same incident. Note the BPP language, which states that coverage exists for damage caused by the breaking in and exiting of burglars. The Causes of Loss—Basic Form and the Causes of Loss—Broad Form define vandalism as "willful and malicious damage to, or destruction of, the described property."[9] Therefore, although the Basic Form covers damage caused by a break-in, it does not cover theft.

Other situations can give rise to a claim for vandalism damage. The property loss adjuster distinguishes between a true vandalism claim and damage that results from a tenant's abuse of the property.

- Vandalism versus tenant abuse. Sometimes, landlords submit losses for alleged "vandalism" caused by prior tenants in an effort to have their insurers pay for repairs to the property before future sale or rental to another tenant. The adjuster's first notice of the loss is usually from the insured or the insured's agent to advise, after the fact, that a tenant who was either evicted or who left without notice vandalized the insured's property. These cases typically involve a tenant who leaves without paying all of the past-due rent.

Tenant abuse claims
Demands that landlords make to insurers for payment for loss caused by renters who damaged the rental property through carelessness or neglect.

Tenant abuse claims are demands by landlords for payments for loss caused by renters. Most are for damage resulting from poor maintenance or sloppy housekeeping. No amount of neglect or sloppiness, no matter how severe, amounts to vandalism. Thus, unless the damage gives the appearance of being a deliberate act, such as holes punched in the walls or sinks pulled away from the walls, the damage is probably the result of an excluded cause of loss.

Vandalism by a current or former tenant might be a covered cause of loss. There is no exclusion for a tenant's acts. Vandalism by a tenant is covered just as is vandalism by an outsider.

9. *Sprinkler leakage*. The peril of sprinkler leakage is included in both the Causes of Loss—Basic Form and the Causes of Loss—Broad Form:

> Sprinkler Leakage, meaning leakage or discharge of any substance from an Automatic Sprinkler System, including collapse of a tank that is part of the system.
>
> If the building or structure containing the Automatic Sprinkler System is Covered Property, we will also pay the cost to:
>
> a. Repair or replace damaged parts of the Automatic Sprinkler System if the damage:
>   (1) Results in sprinkler leakage; or
>   (2) Is directly caused by freezing.
>
> b. Tear out and replace any part of the building or structure to repair damage to the Automatic Sprinkler System that has resulted in sprinkler leakage.
>
> Automatic Sprinkler System means:
>
> (1) Any automatic fire protective or extinguishing system, including connected:
>   (a) Sprinklers and discharge nozzles;
>   (b) Ducts, pipes, valves and fittings;
>   (c) Tanks, their component parts and supports; and
>   (d) Pumps and private fire protection mains.
>
> (2) When supplied from an automatic fire protective system:
>   (a) Non-automatic fire protective systems; and
>   (b) Hydrants, standpipes and outlets.[10]

The sprinkler leakage peril contains an extensive explanation as to how it is to be applied.

10. *Sinkhole collapse*. Sinkhole collapse has recently been added to the BPP—Causes of Loss—Basic Form and the Causes of Loss—Broad Form. The policy reads as follows:

    Sinkhole Collapse, meaning loss or damage caused by the sudden sinking or collapse of land into underground empty spaces created by the action of water on limestone or dolomite. This cause of loss does not include:

    a. The cost of filling sinkholes; or

    b. Sinking or collapse of land into man-made underground cavities.[11]

    This is a significant addition to the Causes of Loss—Basic Form because the Basic Form does not have the additional coverage for collapse provided by the Broad Form and the Special Form.

    Coverage for the sinkhole collapse peril applies to loss or damage to covered property only, which would include the building, as described in the declarations, as well as completed additions. According to the BPP, covered property does not include land (including land on which the property is located), growing crops, or lawns. The sinkhole collapse coverage does not apply to collapse caused by mines or mining activity.

11. *Volcanic action*. The peril of volcanic action has also been added to the Causes of Loss—Basic Form and the Causes of Loss—Broad Form:

    Volcanic Action, meaning direct loss or damage resulting from the eruption of a volcano when the loss or damage is caused by:

    a. Airborne volcanic blast or airborne shock waves;

    b. Ash, dust or particulate matter; or

    c. Lava flow.[12]

    - Time Limit. Most forms put a one-week time limit on coverage for volcanic eruption (as well as for earthquakes). The following is the limit in the BPP forms: "All volcanic eruptions that occur within any 168-hour period will constitute a single occurrence."[13]
    - Volcanic Action Versus Volcanic Eruption. The rationale for covering volcanic action but not volcanic eruption is to exclude earthquake-like ground tremors and shocks. The insured is covered for damage caused by airborne volcanic blasts, airborne shock waves, ash, dust, particulate matter, or lava flow, as well as resulting damage caused by fire.

Basic Form Exclusions

Section B—Exclusions begins with the statement that the insurer will not pay for loss of damage caused directly or indirectly by any of the eight listed exclusions. It states that such loss or damage is excluded regardless of any other cause that contributes concurrently or in any sequence to the loss. The excluded causes of loss are as follows:

1. *Ordinance or law*. As previously discussed, the policy does not cover costs associated with bringing a structure up to code.

2. *Earth movement.* All forms of earth movement are excluded except for the sinkhole collapse found in the Covered Causes of Loss list in the Basic Form. Volcanic eruption, explosion, and effusion are also excluded.
3. *Government action.* Destruction of property by order of governmental authority is not covered unless a fire that would be a covered cause of loss occurs and destruction of property is ordered to prevent the spread of that fire.
4. *Nuclear hazard.*
5. *Utility services.* The exclusion for utility services applies when an off-premises power source fails and service to the insured premises is interrupted. Failure of service includes blackouts and brownouts. The exclusion applies regardless of the cause of the power interruption. If damage from a covered cause of loss results, the damage from the covered cause of loss will be covered.
6. *War.* War, military action, and warlike action must be initiated by a government or sovereign. War does not have to be declared for this exclusion to apply.
7. *Water.* The exclusion for water includes flood; surface water; waves; tides; tidal waves; overflow of any body of water; mudslide; mudflow; water that backs up or overflows from a sewer, drain, or sump; or water that seeps through foundations, walls, floors, basements, paved surfaces, doors, windows, or other openings.
8. *Fungus, wet rot, dry rot, and bacteria.* The policy has added a new exclusion in response to the growing number of mold damage claims. The exclusion applies to the presence, growth, proliferation, spread, or activity of fungus, wet or dry rot, or bacteria. It does not apply if the fungus, wet or dry rot, or bacteria result from fire or lightning. It states that there is limited coverage in the Additional Coverage section for loss or damage caused by a peril other than fire or lightning.

Basic Form: Additional Exclusions

The policy continues with a list of additional exclusions as well as special exclusions that apply only to business interruption coverage. Chapter 11 discusses business income coverage and exclusions. The additional exclusions are as follows:

1. *Artificially generated electric current.* Generally, this refers to power surges and electrical arcing that cause damage to electrical devices and appliances. If a fire ensues, the loss by fire will be covered.
2. *Rupture or bursting of water pipes (other than automatic sprinkler systems).* This is not covered unless caused by a covered cause of loss.
3. *Leakage or discharge of water or steam from any part of a system or appliance containing water or steam, unless the system or appliance is damaged by a covered cause of loss.* There is no coverage for loss or damage caused by or resulting from continuous or repeated seepage or leakage of water or the presence or condensation of humidity, moisture, or vapor that occurs over a period of fourteen days or more.

4. *Explosion of steam boiler, steam pipes, steam engines, or steam turbines owned, leased, or operated under the insured's control.* Coverage for this type of loss is usually found in an equipment breakdown policy, or a boiler and machinery policy, which Chapter 12 discusses.
5. *Mechanical breakdown, including rupture or bursting caused by centrifugal force.* An example would be a turbine that loses a blade, and then the cowling bursts. This type of loss is also usually insured on a boiler and machinery policy.
6. *Neglect.* The insured has an obligation to use reasonable efforts to save and preserve the insured property from further damage at the time of loss and after a loss has occurred.

Basic Form: Additional Coverages

As mentioned, the Basic Form provides limited additional coverage for fungus, wet rot, dry rot, and bacteria. For the Additional Coverage section to apply, the loss must result from one of the following causes and occur during the policy period and only if all reasonable means to save and preserve the property were taken:

1. A covered cause of loss other than fire or lightning
2. Flood, if the Flood Coverage Endorsement applies to the affected premises

The section defines the phrase "loss or damage" to mean direct physical loss or damage to covered property caused by fungus, wet or dry rot, or bacteria, including the removal of same; the cost to tear out and replace any part of the building as needed to gain access to the fungus, wet or dry rot, or bacteria; and the cost of testing after removal, repair, replacement, or restoration is completed provided that there is reason to believe that the fungus, wet or dry rot, or bacteria are still present.

This additional coverage for fungus, wet rot, dry rot, and bacteria is limited to $15,000. Regardless of the number of claims, this limit is the most that will be paid for the total of all loss or damage arising out of all occurrences of covered causes of loss (other than fire or lightning) and flood that occur in a twelve-month period. This additional coverage does not increase the applicable limit of insurance on any covered property.

Broad Form: Covered Causes of Loss

The Broad Form expands the Basic Form list of covered causes of loss by three.

Additional Covered Perils

The three added causes of loss are (1) falling objects; (2) weight of snow, ice, or sleet; and (3) water damage.

1. *Falling objects.* If an object falls on the insured building, the damage will be covered. This does not apply to personal property in the open or to the building's interior unless the roof or outside wall is first damaged by a falling object.

2. *Weight of snow, ice, or sleet.* Damage to the building from the weight of snow, ice, or sleet is covered. An example is the accumulation of ice and snow in the gutters that causes them to pull away from the building. This also does not cover damage to personal property outside of the building. Personal property inside the building is covered if the building sustains damage that allows the snow, ice, or sleet to enter.

3. *Water damage.* This refers to the accidental discharge or leakage of water or steam as the direct result of the breaking apart or cracking of a plumbing system, a heating system, an air conditioning system, or another system or appliance located on the insured premises and containing water or steam. It does not include discharge or leakage from an automatic sprinkler system; a sump; or related equipment and parts, including overflow due to sump pump failure or excessive volume of water or from roof drains, gutters, downspouts, or similar fixtures or equipment. The cost to repair any defect that caused the loss or damage is not covered. Loss or damage caused by or resulting from continuous or repeated seepage or leakage of water or the presence or condensation of humidity, moisture, or vapor that occurs over a period of fourteen days or more is not covered. Loss or damage caused by or resulting from freezing is not covered unless the insured has tried to maintain heat in the building or structure or has drained the equipment and shut off the water supply if the heat is not maintained.

   If a water damage loss is covered and the building or structure containing the system or appliance is covered property, the cost to tear out and replace any part of the building or structure to repair damage to the system or appliance from which the water or steam escapes will be covered. However, the cost to repair any defect that caused the loss or damage will not be covered.

Broad Form: Exclusions

This section starts with the provision that the insurer will not pay for loss or damage caused by the listed exclusions. Such loss or damage is excluded regardless of any other cause or event that contributes concurrently or in any sequence to the loss. The list of exclusions is the same as in the Basic Form: ordinance or law; earth movement; governmental action; nuclear hazard; utility services; war, military action, and warlike action; water; and fungus, wet rot, dry rot, and bacteria. The difference between the Basic Form exclusions and the Broad Form exclusions can be found in the exclusions outlined in the Additional Exclusions section. While the Basic Form has six additional exclusions in this section, the Broad Form only has four: (1) artificially generated electrical current, (2) explosion of steam boilers, (3) mechanical breakdown, and (4) neglect. The wording of these four exclusions is the same in both the Basic Form and the Broad Form.

The Broad Form also has the Special Exclusions that apply only when specific coverage forms for business income, leasehold interest, and legal liability have been added to the policy.

Broad Form: Additional Coverages

In the Broad Form, the additional coverage for collapse is added. The provision is quite extensive in its discussion of what collapse means and what coverage is to be provided. This was done in an attempt to avoid various judicial interpretations of collapse. However, in the event of a collapse claim in which there is doubt as to whether this provision applies, it is best to seek the advice of legal counsel to determine what the current judicial interpretation is. Also note that sections apply to the insured building and that sections apply to insured personal property.

C. Additional Coverage—Collapse

The term Covered Cause of Loss includes the Collapse Additional Coverage as described and limited in **1.** through **5.** below.

1. With respect to buildings:
   a. Collapse means an abrupt falling down or caving in of a building or any part of a building with the result that the building or part of the building cannot be occupied for its intended purpose;
   b. A building or any part of a building that is in danger of falling down or caving in is not considered to be in a state of collapse;
   c. A part of a building that is standing is not considered to be in a state of collapse even if it has separated from another part of the building;
   d. A building that is standing or any part of a building that is standing is not considered to be in a state of collapse even if it shows evidence of cracking, bulging, sagging, bending, leaning, settling, shrinkage or expansion.
2. We will pay for direct physical loss or damage to Covered Property, caused by collapse of a building or any part of a building that is insured under this Coverage Form or that contains Covered Property insured under this Coverage Form, if the collapse is caused by one or more of the following:
   a. Fire; lightning; explosion; windstorm or hail; smoke; aircraft or vehicles; riot or civil commotion; vandalism; leakage from fire extinguishing equipment; sinkhole collapse; volcanic action; breakage of building glass; falling objects; weight of snow, ice, or sleet; water damage, meaning accidental discharge or leakage of water or steam as the direct result of the breaking apart or cracking of a plumbing, heating, air conditioning or other system or appliance (other than a sump system including its related equipment and parts), that is located on the described premises and contains water or steam; all only as insured against in this Coverage part;
   b. Decay that is hidden from view, unless the presence of such decay is known to an insured prior to collapse;
   c. Insect or vermin damage that is hidden from view, unless the presence of such damage is known to the insured prior to collapse;
   d. Weight of people or personal property;
   e. Weight of rain that collects on a roof;

f. Use of defective material or methods in construction, remodeling, or renovation if collapse occurs during the course of the construction, remodeling, or renovation. However, if the collapse occurs after construction, remodeling, or renovation is complete and is caused in part by a cause of loss listed in **2.a.** through **2.e.,** we will pay for the loss or damage even if use of defective material or methods, in construction, remodeling, or renovation, contributes to the collapse.

The criteria set forth in **1.a.** through **1.d.** do not limit the coverage otherwise provided under this Causes of Loss Form for the causes of loss listed in **2.a.**

3. With respect to the following property:

   a. Outdoor radio or television antennas (including satellite dishes) and their lead-in wiring, masts or towers;

   b. Awnings, gutter and downspouts;

   c. Yard fixtures;

   d. Outdoor swimming pools;

   e. Fences;

   f. Piers, wharves and docks;

   g. Beach or diving platforms or appurtenances;

   h. Retaining walls; and

   i. Walks, roadways and other paved surfaces;

   If the collapse is caused by a cause of loss listed in **2.b.** through **2.f.** we will pay for loss or damage to that property only if:

   a. Such loss or damage is a direct result of the collapse of a building insured under this Coverage Form; and

   b. The property is Covered Property under this Coverage Form.

4. If personal property abruptly falls down or caves in and such collapse is not the result of collapse of the building, we will pay for loss or damage to Covered Property caused by such collapse of personal property only if:

   a. The collapse was caused by a Cause of Loss listed in **2.a.** through **2.f.** above;

   b. The personal property which collapses is inside a building; and

   c. The property which collapses is not of a kind listed in **3.** above, regardless of whether that kind of property is considered personal property or real property.

   The coverage stated in this Paragraph **4.** does not apply to personal property if marring and/or scratching is the only damage to that personal property caused by the collapse.

   Collapse of personal property does not mean cracking, bulging, sagging, bending, leaning, settling, shrinkage or expansion.

5. This Additional Coverage, Collapse, will not increase the Limits of Insurance provided in this Coverage Part.[14]

The other additional coverage added is D. *Additional Coverage—Limited Coverage for "Fungus", Wet Rot, Dry Rot and Bacteria*. This is the same provision as in the Basic Form.

Causes of Loss—Special Form

The Special Form provides coverage on an open-perils basis, which means that it insures against risks of direct physical loss except for those causes specifically excluded or limited in the form. **Open perils** refers to a policy that provides such coverage. Despite the Broad Form's name, the Special Form provides the broadest coverage available. In terms of the forms' names and evolution, the Basic Form came first and provided the building blocks for all forms that follow. Next came the Broad Form, so named because it provided broader coverage than the Basic Form. Years later, the Special Form was created to provide even greater coverage to the insured.

Open perils
A type of policy that provides coverage against risks of direct physical loss except for those specifically excluded or limited by the policy.

Exclusions

Because the Special Form is an open-perils form, it does not list the covered causes of loss in it. Instead, it has extensive lists of exclusions and limitations. The exclusions start with the same eight exclusions as the Basic Form and the Broad Form: ordinance or law; earth movement; governmental action; nuclear hazard; utility services; war, military action, and warlike action; water; and fungus, wet rot, dry rot, and bacteria.

The additional exclusions start with artificially generated electrical current but differ after that (policy language in the following list of exclusions appears in italics).

- *2.b. Delay, loss of use or loss of market*. Simply stated, the policy does not cover the consequential financial loss associated with the physical loss or damage to the property.
- *2.c. Smoke, vapor or gas from agricultural smudging or industrial operations*. This same exclusion is found in the HO-3 policy.

The next exclusion, 2.d., has seven subparts to it, each dealing with a different but often related cause of loss.

- *2.d.(1) Wear and tear*. This is intended to eliminate losses that occur over time through normal use.
- *2.d.(2) Rust, or other corrosion, deterioration, hidden or latent defect or any quality in property that causes it to damage or destroy itself*. In this exclusion, "*latent defect*" means a defect that is present but has not yet made itself known and is not easily detectable. The most obvious example of such a quality can be found in wood, particularly wood that is in storage. Wood warps when exposed to extreme heat. Wood has moisture in it, and if the moisture starts to dry out the cells within the wood, it starts to collapse, causing it to warp in that direction. Wood swells when exposed to extreme humidity, thereby causing a bedroom closet door, for example, to stick during a rainy season.

- *2.d.(3) Smog.* Smog specifically refers to a combination of fog and smoke, usually produced through the accumulation of industrial or chemical discharges and pollutants. It also refers to accumulated gases that are trapped in an atmosphere as a result of humidity or other natural conditions. Therefore, automobile emissions trapped in the valleys of Los Angeles, for example, lead to a condition of smog. A loss by smog would specifically be the resultant dirt, grime, or residue that would either discolor or possibly damage a surface more severely depending on the components of the chemicals in the smog.
- *2.d.(4) Settling, cracking, shrinking or expansion.*
- *2.d.(5) Nesting or infestation or discharge or release of waste products or secretions, by insects, birds, rodents or other animals.* A memorable example of this situation is a claim that was submitted by a property owner for honey that was seeping through the walls into the building. The walls had been infested with honeybees whose hive became filled with honey, and when the interior got warm enough, the honey started to run.
- *2.d.(6) Mechanical breakdown, including rupture or bursting caused by centrifugal force. But if mechanical breakdown results in elevator collision, we will pay for the loss or damage caused by that elevator collision.*
- *2.d.(7) The following causes of loss to personal property.*

  (a) Dampness or dryness of atmosphere;

  (b) Changes in or extremes of temperature; or

  (c) Marring or scratching.

  But if an excluded cause of loss that is listed in 2.d.(1) through (7) results in a "specified cause of loss" or building glass breakage, we will pay for the loss or damage caused by that "specified cause of loss" or building glass breakage.
- *2.e. Explosion of steam boilers, steam pipes, steam engines or steam turbines owned or leased by you, or operated under your control. But if explosion of steam boilers, steam pipes, steam engines or steam turbines results in fire or combustion explosion, we will pay for the loss or damage caused by that fire or combustion explosion. We will also pay for loss or damage caused by or resulting from the explosion of gases or fuel within the furnace of any fired vessel or within the flues or passages through which the gases of combustion pass.*
- *2.f. Continuous or repeated seepage or leakage of water, or the presence or condensation of humidity, moisture or vapor, that occurs over a period of 14 days or more.*
- *2.g. Water, other liquids, powder or molten material that leaks or flows from plumbing, heating, air conditioning or other equipment (except fire protective systems) caused by or resulting from freezing, unless:*

  (1) You do your best to maintain heat in the building or structure; or

  (2) You drain the equipment and shut off the supply if the heat is not maintained.
- *2.h. Dishonest or criminal act by you, any of your partners, members, officers, managers, employees (including leased employees), directors, trustees, authorized*

representatives or anyone to whom you entrust the property for any purpose:

(1) Acting alone or in collusion with others; or

(2) Whether or not occurring during the hours of employment.

This exclusion does not apply to acts of destruction by your employees (including leased employees); but theft by employees (including leased employees) is not covered. An insured with this type of exposure would obtain crime coverage that will be discussed in a later chapter.

- *2.i. Voluntary parting with any property by you or anyone else to whom you have entrusted the property if induced to do so by any fraudulent scheme, trick, device or false pretense.*
- *2.j. Rain, snow, ice or sleet to personal property in the open.*
- *2.k. Collapse, except as provided below in the Additional Coverage for Collapse. But if collapse results in a Covered Cause of Loss at the described premises, we will pay for the loss or damage caused by that Covered Cause of Loss.*
- *2.l. Discharge, dispersal, seepage, migration, release or escape of "pollutants" unless the discharge, dispersal, seepage, migration, release or escape is itself caused by any of the "specified causes of loss". But if the discharge, dispersal, seepage, migration, release or escape of "pollutants" results in a "specified cause of loss" we will pay for the loss or damage caused by that "specified cause of loss".* This exclusion does not apply to damage to glass caused by chemicals applied to the glass. This exclusion limits pollutant cleanup and removal coverage to "sudden and accidental" occurrences caused by specified causes of loss. The phrase "Specified Causes of Loss" is defined in the form under the Definitions section.

> 2.m. Neglect of an insured to use all reasonable means to save and preserve the property from further damage at and after the time of the loss.[15]

Subpart 3 continues with the list of exclusions. If an excluded cause of loss listed in 3.a. to 3.c. results in a covered cause of loss, the insurer will pay for the loss or damage caused by the covered cause of loss. These exclusions are as follows:

> 3.a. Weather conditions.
>
> 3.b. Acts or decisions, including the failure to act or decide, of any person, group organization or governmental body.
>
> 3.c. Faulty, inadequate or defective:
>
> (1) Planning, zoning, development, surveying, siting;
>
> (2) Design, specifications, workmanship, repair, construction, renovation, remodeling, grading compaction;
>
> (3) Materials used in repair, construction, renovation or remodeling; or
>
> (4) Maintenance;
>
> of part or all of any property on or off the described premises.[16]

The Causes of Loss—Special Form also includes the same special exclusions as seen in the Basic Form and the Broad Form.

Limitations

The Causes of Loss—Special Form continues to modify what perils and property are covered by using a set of "Limitations."

C. Limitations

The following limitations apply to all policy forms and endorsements, unless otherwise stated.

1. We will not pay for loss of or damage to property, as described and limited in this section. In addition, we will not pay for any loss that is a consequence of loss or damage as described and limited in this section.
   a. Steam boilers, steam pipes, steam engines or steam turbines caused by or resulting from any condition or event inside such equipment. But we will pay for loss of or damage to such equipment caused by or resulting from an explosion of gases or fuel within the furnace of any fired vessel or within the flues or passages through which the gases of combustion pass.
   b. Hot water boilers or other water heating equipment caused by or resulting from any condition or event inside such boilers or equipment, other than an explosion.
   c. The interior of any building or structure, or to personal property in the building or structure, caused by or resulting from rain, snow, sleet, ice, sand or dust, whether driven by wind or not, unless:
      (1) The building or structure first sustains damage by a Covered Cause of Loss to its roof or walls through which the rain, snow, sleet, ice, sand or dust enters; or
      (2) The loss or damage is caused by or results from thawing of snow, sleet or ice on the building or structure.
   d. Building materials and supplies not attached as part of the building or structure, caused by or resulting from theft.

      However, this limitation does not apply to:
      (1) Building materials and supplies held for sale by you, unless they are insured under the Builders Risk Coverage Form; or
      (2) Business Income coverage or Extra Expense coverage.
   e. Property that is missing, where the only evidence of the loss or damage is a shortage disclosed on taking inventory, or other instances where there is no physical evidence to show what happened to the property.
   f. Property that has been transferred to a person or to a place outside the described premises on the basis of unauthorized instructions.
2. We will not pay for loss of or damage to the following types of property unless caused by the "specified causes of loss" or building glass breakage:
   a. Animals, and then only if they are killed or their destruction is made necessary.
   b. Fragile articles such as statuary, marbles, chinaware and porcelains, if broken. This restriction does not apply to:
      (1) Glass; or

(2) Containers of property held for sale.

c. Builders' machinery, tools and equipment owned by you or entrusted to you, provided such property is Covered Property.

However, this limitation does not apply:

(1) If the property is located on or within 100 feet of the described premises, unless the premises is insured under the Builders Risk Coverage Form; or

(2) To Business Income coverage or to Extra Expense coverage.[17]

The policy then specifies those categories of property that are subject to a special limit.

3. The special limit shown for each category, a. through d., is the total limit for loss of or damage to all property in that category. The special limit applies to any one occurrence of theft, regardless of the types or number of articles that are lost or damaged in that occurrence. The special limits are:

a. $2,500 for furs, fur garments and garments trimmed with fur.

b. $2,500 for jewelry, watches, watch movements, jewels, pearls, precious and semi-precious stones, bullion, gold, silver, platinum and other precious alloys or metals. This limit does not apply to jewelry and watches worth $100 or less per item.

c. $2,500 for patterns, dies, molds and forms.

d. $250 for stamps, tickets, including lottery tickets held for sale, and letters of credit.

These special limits are part of, not in addition to, the Limit of Insurance applicable to the Covered Property.

This limitation, C.3., does not apply to Business Income coverage or to Extra Expense coverage.

4. We will not pay the cost to repair any defect to a system or appliance from which water, other liquid, powder or molten material escapes. But we will pay the cost to repair or replace damaged parts of fire extinguishing equipment if the damage:

a. Results in discharge of any substance from an automatic fire protection system; or

b. Is directly caused by freezing.

However, this limitation does not apply to Business Income coverage or to Extra Expense coverage.[18]

Because the coverage under the Special Form is so broad, it is necessary to restrict the coverage through these various limitations. Many of the limitations look familiar because they pertain to causes of loss found in the Basic Form and the Broad Form. One example is the section dealing with steam boilers, pipes, engines, and turbines. The Basic Form and the Broad Form have an exclusion for explosion of steam boilers, pipes, engines, and turbines. In the Special Form, this appears as a limitation because by its very nature, the Special Form provides broader coverage. Likewise, the special limits on furs, jewelry, and tickets appear similar to those in the HO-3.

The Causes of Loss—Special Form provides the first instance of theft coverage in the BPP. It provides theft coverage but excludes "the dishonest or criminal act by you . . . your employees . . . or anyone to whom you entrust the property for any purpose."[19] The Causes of Loss—Basic Form and the Causes of Loss—Broad Form (specified perils) do not include theft among the perils they cover, although, as previously noted, looting by rioters is covered under the riot peril. The vandalism peril under these forms states that no coverage is provided for loss or damage "caused by or resulting from theft, except for building damage caused by the breaking in or exiting of burglars."[20] Chapter 12 discusses comprehensive theft coverage for businesses.

Additional Coverages: Collapse and Fungus

Just as the Broad Form had additional coverages for collapse and fungus, so does the Special Form. The Special Form's language mirrors that of the Broad Form.

Additional Coverage Extensions

The Special Form provides limited coverage for the insured's personal property while in transit. The loss must be caused by one of the enumerated causes of loss, and it is subject to a maximum limit of $5,000. The insured with a substantial exposure to personal property while in transit is better served by purchasing an inland marine policy. Chapter 12 discusses these types of policies.

Additional Coverages

The BPP form has additional coverages that apply regardless of which causes of loss form is attached to the policy. Some of these coverages are the same as HO-3 coverages, so they will only be summarized here.

Debris Removal

Debris removal
Coverage that pays for removal of debris of covered property damaged by an insured peril.

Debris removal coverage pays the expense of removing debris of covered property from the premises after a covered loss. The expenses must be reported to the insurer within 180 days of the date of loss. This coverage does not apply to the expense associated with extracting pollutants or removing, restoring, or replacing polluted land or water. The most that can be paid for the direct loss plus debris removal is the limit of liability selected for the location. If the total amount of debris removal expense plus the amount of the direct physical loss exceeds the policy limit, then this section will provide for an additional $10,000 in coverage.

Preservation of Property

Removal coverage
Coverage for loss to property being removed from a loss scene; also covers property while stored at a temporary location for up to thirty days.

This coverage pays for any direct physical loss or damage to covered property that occurs while moving the property from the premises or while temporarily stored at another location to preserve it from a covered cause of loss. That property is covered at the temporary storage location, but only for thirty days. This coverage is often called **removal coverage.**

Fire Department Service Charge

When an insured is obligated by contract or local ordinance to pay for fire department charges, coverage up to a limit of $1,000 is provided.

Pollutant Cleanup and Removal

Whenever a covered cause of loss causes the "discharge, dispersal, seepage, migration, release, or escape" of pollutants, an additional coverage is available to pay for the extraction of such pollutants from land or water at the described premises. Such cleanup expenses must be reported to the insurer within 180 days of when the covered loss occurs. This coverage is limited to $10,000 per twelve-month period of the policy and is not available to test or monitor for pollution, except during extraction of the pollutants.

Increased Cost of Construction

This additional coverage only applies to buildings insured for replacement cost. It provides $10,000 or 5 percent of limit of insurance, whichever is less, to pay for increased costs incurred to comply with the enforcement of an ordinance or a law in the course of repairing or rebuilding the premises. It does not cover increased costs resulting from an ordinance or a law that the insured failed to comply with before the loss. It does not pay for costs associated with pollution cleanup, testing, or monitoring.

Coverage Extensions

The six extensions in this section are provided at no extra charge or premium, as long as the insured adheres to a coinsurance percentage of 80 percent or more. Unless otherwise noted, the property must be located in or on the insured premises, in the open, or in a vehicle that is within 100 feet of the premises.

Newly Acquired or Constructed Property

This extension's purpose is to immediately give limited, temporary coverage to the insured for new business property or buildings that are built or acquired during the policy period.

Structures

New buildings while in the course of construction on the described premises are covered. If a new building that is located off the premises is acquired, it must be used as a warehouse or in a manner similar to that of the described building. The limit of insurance for either of these situations is $250,000 for each additional building.

Personal Property

For business personal property, the extension applies to property acquired by the insured at any location other than fairs, trade shows, and exhibitions. The limit for newly acquired personal property is not more than $100,000 at each new location.

This coverage does not apply to personal property of others that is temporarily in the insured's possession in the course of work or in the course of manufacturing or wholesaling activities. The coverage for these newly acquired properties terminates (1) when the policy expires, (2) thirty days after the insured acquires the property or begins construction, or (3) when the insured reports values to the insurer for new policies to be written. The insurer charges the appropriate back premium for the newly acquired property once it receives notice of the acquisition.

Personal Effects and Property of Others

Many people take personal items from home to the workplace. Coats, purses, glasses, pictures, and other similar items might not be used in the business, but people have such items with them while at work. The insured and their employees, partners, and officers are covered by an extension that grants the same coverage as for business personal property, except that these personal effects are *not* covered for theft, and the limit of liability is $2,500 at each premises. Additionally, this coverage extension applies to the personal property in the insured's care, custody, or control. This coverage might seem unusually broad, but it is optional. The coverage extension states, "You may extend the insurance that applies to Your Business Personal Property to apply to. . . . " If others' personal property is damaged, the adjustment and the payment will be made for the owner's account.

Valuable Papers and Records—Cost of Research

If information on paper or electronic media is lost or damaged and duplicates are not available, this extension will pay up to $2,500 for the cost to research, replace, or restore the lost information. The records and papers themselves would be covered under business property. This extension restores some limited amount of coverage excluded in the Property Not Covered section. Increasing the amount of this coverage is possible.

Property Off-Premises

Businesses often send property to another location for various reasons. The off-premises extension gives the insured a $10,000 coverage limit for non-stock property that is temporarily at a location that the insured does not own, lease, or operate; is in storage at a leased location (as long as the lease was executed during the policy period); or is at a fair, trade show, or exhibition. The extension does not apply to property if it is located at the following:

- In or on a vehicle
- In the care, custody, or control of a salesperson of the insured, unless at a fair, trade show, or exhibition

Outdoor Property

This extension covers outdoor fences, radio and television antennas (including satellite dishes), signs (other than those attached to buildings), trees, shrubs, and plants (other than stock)—including debris removal expenses—for loss resulting from fire, lightning, explosion, riot or civil commotion, or aircraft. The amount of the coverage extension is $1,000 for any one occurrence and $250 for any one tree or shrub, up to the $1,000 per occurrence limit. The Property Not Covered section excludes fences, radio and television antennas, signs, trees, shrubs, and plants. This provision restores coverage for these items, but only if the loss is caused by one of the specified causes of loss.

Nonowned Detached Trailers

Many businesses use trailers as offices or for storage. To be covered under this extension, the trailer must be used in the insured's business and be in the insured's care, custody, and control at the insured premises. The insured must also have a contractual obligation to pay for any loss or damage to the trailer. The limit of this extension is $5,000. It is excess over any other insurance coverage on the trailer. If the trailer is attached to any motor vehicle or motor conveyance or is in the process of being hitched or unhitched, it will not be covered under this extension.

Common Policy Conditions

The following six Common Policy Conditions may affect the handling of a claim:

1. Cancellation
2. Changes
3. Examination of books and records
4. Inspections and surveys
5. Premiums
6. Transfer of your rights and duties under the policy

At first glance, all of these conditions might not appear to affect a claim. However, each can have claim implications.

Cancellation

Only the first named insured, whether an individual or a corporation, shown in the declarations can cancel the policy. Likewise, any notice of cancellation from the insurer must be mailed or delivered to the first named insured.

It is possible for an insurer to improperly cancel a policy. It is also possible for someone other than the named insured to request a cancellation. This can arise because of some internal business dispute. However, if this request does not come from a party authorized to speak as the named insured, the request for cancellation would be invalid and the coverage would remain in place.

Changes

Only the first named insured, with the insurer's consent, can change the policy.

Examination of Books and Records

The insurer has the right to examine the insured's books and records as they relate to the policy. This condition can be most helpful if the insurer suspects fraud.

Inspections and Surveys

This condition applies to both loss control inspections and loss inspections. Depending upon the nature of the loss, it can be helpful to the property loss adjuster to inspect the entire premises, not just the area where the loss or damage occurred. A more complete inspection of the premises can reveal overall housekeeping conditions, the use and occupancy of the location, and the condition of alarms and sprinklers. It may also expose possible fraud.

Premiums

The first named insured is responsible for the payment of all premiums. Admittedly, it is not necessary for the premium to be paid for coverage to be bound on a risk. However, nonpayment of the premium or even late payment of the premium can hint at financial difficulties that may affect the adjustment process.

Transfer of Your Rights and Duties Under This Policy

The insured's rights and duties cannot be transferred without the insurer's written consent, except in the case of death of an individual named insured. Although this condition does not usually arise in the context of a commercial property claim, it sometimes becomes an issue. The most likely scenario is that the property is being sold and the new buyer mistakenly believes that the existing property insurance will continue to provide coverage. It will not do so unless the insurer agrees to the transfer in writing. However, the proceeds or payment of a claim can be assigned or transferred to a third party without the insurer's consent.

Commercial Property Conditions

These conditions appear on a separate form and apply to all the coverage forms included in the policy. They can be superceded by a condition contained in a specific coverage form. These conditions can become very important in the adjustment of a loss in which fraud is suspected or other insurance is involved.

Concealment, Misrepresentation, or Fraud

Fraud committed by the insured at any time, relating to the coverage, voids the policy. Additionally, intentional concealment and/or misrepresentation of a material fact by any insured, at any time, can void the policy. Concealment and misrepresentation can occur during the application for insurance. If concealment or misrepresentation of a material fact by the insured is found, the adjuster must determine whether the insured knew that the information was false. The adjuster must also determine whether the information was material to the underwriting process. In other words, if the true facts were known, would the underwriter have declined the risk or written it at significantly different terms? One additional consideration is whether the policy has a mortgagee listed in it. The mortgagee is not usually penalized for the insured's fraud, misrepresentation, or concealment, as long as the mortgagee is unaware of these actions when they occur.

Because of the various legal interpretations on the issue of material misrepresentation, any suspicion of fraud, concealment, or misrepresentation is usually thoroughly reviewed by counsel (and others, depending on an insurer's procedures) before being acted upon.

Control of Property

This condition specifies that the acts of others who are not under the insured's direction or control will not affect coverage. As an example, suppose that the insured is a tenant in a strip mall. The insured premises and the property next door share a common exit to the back alley. The owner of the next-door property leaves the back door open one night, and vandals come in and set fire to the building. That act of negligence would not be imputed to the insured.

The second part of this condition states that a breach of any condition at any one or more locations does not affect coverage for locations where the breach does not exist. Suppose that the policy has multiple locations listed and that an 80 percent coinsurance requirement applies to all of the locations. The insured suffers a loss at location A and is found to be in compliance with the 80 percent coinsurance clause. At the same time, it is discovered that the location next door (location B), which did not have a loss, is only insured to 70 percent of its value. This breach of the condition at location B would not affect the loss adjustment at location A.

Insurance Under Two or More Coverages

This condition states that if two or more parts of one policy apply to the loss, the insured can recover only the actual amount of loss or damage. It essentially means that the insured cannot collect twice for the same loss.

Legal Action Against the Insurer

For an insured to sue his or her insurer, the insured must comply with all of the policy terms and the lawsuit must be brought within two years of the date that the loss or damage occurred. This condition is often invoked when the insured files suit before participating in the appraisal process.

Liberalization

Any policy revision that broadens the coverage (without charging additional premium) will apply to the policy as long as the revision occurs within forty-five days before the policy's inception or it occurs during the policy's term.

No Benefit to Bailee

Simply stated, this policy does not cover the bailee's liability for the insured's property while it is in the bailee's possession.

Other Insurance

The "other insurance" calculations that Chapter 2 discusses apply to this condition.

Policy Period, Coverage Territory

A policy period normally begins at 12:01 A.M. Standard Time at the property location on the effective date on the declarations page. For policies with multiple locations in different time zones, the policy may actually specify that the policy becomes effective at 12:01 A.M. in a specific time zone. If the policy does not specify a time zone, then the inception would be 12:01 A.M. in the time zone in which each listed property is located.

Transfer of Rights Against Others to Insurer

This condition authorizes an insurer to subrogate against a responsible party, to the extent that the insurer has made a payment. The insured can waive the right of subrogation if it is done in writing and the agreement pre-dates the loss. Adjusters routinely find this in lease agreements and service contracts.

Loss Conditions

The BPP loss conditions are similar to those found in the homeowners policy. There is a provision for appraisal as well as an outline of the insured's duties after a loss. Two provisions concern physical property after a loss has occurred: the Abandonment clause prohibits the insured from abandoning the property to the insurance company, and the Recovered Property provision details how recovered property will be handled.

The Loss Payment provision is also similar to that of the homeowners policy. It outlines the insurer's option to repair, replace, or pay the value of the property.

Vacancy

The BPP has a Vacancy provision that is very specific. An owned building is vacant unless 31 percent of total square footage is rented or used by the owner to conduct customary operations.

If the insured is a tenant, the premises must contain sufficient business personal property to conduct normal operations; otherwise, it will be considered vacant. A building is not vacant if under construction or renovation.

If the insured premises has been vacant for sixty or more days, there will be no coverage for vandalism, building glass breakage, water damage, theft or attempted theft, or sprinkler leakage (unless it was protected from freezing). If a loss caused by a different covered cause of loss occurs, the loss settlement will be reduced by 15 percent.

Limits of Insurance

The amount payable for any one occurrence is listed in the Limit of Insurance section of the declarations. Similar to the homeowners policy, sublimits are listed in this condition as well as elsewhere in the policy. This provision also states that the coverage extensions and the additional coverages for fire department service charge, pollutant cleanup, and debris removal are all in addition to the limits of insurance. Payments made for the preservation of property are within the Limit of Insurance. Increased cost of construction is an additional insurance subject to the limits within that provision.

Deductible

The coverage form explains in great detail how deductibles are to be applied. This explanation is necessary because the commercial property policy can have several different deductibles listed in it. It is possible that each location on the policy may have a different deductible. Some perils, such as windstorm, hail, or theft, can have specific deductibles associated with them.

The deductible is applied per occurrence. If one occurrence causes loss at several locations insured on the policy, only the largest applicable deductible is used.

Loss Payment

The policy provides the insurer with four settlement options. See the following box.

BPP Loss Payment Options

1. Pay the value of lost or damaged property.
2. Pay the cost of repairing or replacing.
3. Take the property at the agreed or appraised value.
4. Repair, rebuild, or replace with like kind and quality.

The policy also specifies that the insurer must advise the insured as to which option it will exercise within thirty days of receipt of a proof of loss.

Any payment made for the loss or damage to the property will usually be on an actual cash value (ACV) basis. If the loss is less than $2,500 and all additional conditions and coinsurance are complied with, the loss will be valued at replacement cost. Awnings, floor coverings, appliances, outdoor equipment, and furniture will still be paid on an ACV basis.

Stock that is sold but not delivered is based on selling price less discounts and expenses incurred. Otherwise, it is paid at ACV.

Glass will be replaced with safety glazing if required by law.

Tenants betterments and improvements are paid at ACV, if they are repaired or replaced promptly. If the insured does not repair or replace them promptly, the loss will be paid on a proportional basis. The proportion is calculated by taking the original cost of the improvement and multiplying it by the number of days from the date of loss to the end of the lease or to the end of the renewal option period. This number is then divided by the number of days from the date that the improvement was installed to the end of the lease or renewal option period. This figure is the amount that will then be paid.

Suppose that the tenant operates a shop with a one-year lease running from January 1 to December 31, and he or she has a one-year renewal option. On February 1, the tenant installs shelving at a cost of $1,500. On August 4, a fire occurs and destroys the business. The insured closes his or her shop and does not reopen. The loss would be calculated in the following way:

$$\$1{,}500 \times 150 \text{ (days left to end of lease)} = \$225{,}000.00.$$
$$\$225{,}000 \div 334 \text{ (number of days from installation to end of lease)} = \$673.65.$$

If the insured has a renewal option, as in this example, the calculation changes:

$$\$1{,}500 \times (150 + 365) = \$772{,}500.00.$$
$$\$772{,}500 \div (334 + 365) = \$1{,}105.15.$$

The extra year of the renewal option is added in to this calculation because the insured would have had the benefit of his or her improvement had he or she renewed the lease at the option date.

Valuable papers are paid at the cost of the blank media and the labor involved to transcribe or copy from duplicates. Prepackaged software is not included in this valuation.

The BPP Coinsurance Provision

The BPP has different coinsurance percentages based on how much premium the insured is willing to pay and the underwriting standards of the insurance company that wrote the policy. Most companies have minimum acceptable coinsurance requirements, often 80 percent. In commercial insurance, policies are commonly written with 90 or 100 percent coinsurance requirements. The coinsurance clause in commercial policies can apply not only to buildings or dwellings (as in the homeowners policy) but also to business personal property coverage. Some special commercial endorsements contain coinsurance clauses—for example, sign endorsements.

The required amount of insurance should be based on the covered property's actual cash value whenever ACV is the standard for loss settlement. If replacement cost coverage has been purchased, then the required amount of insurance will be based on the property's replacement cost value.

ACV is usually the settlement standard for both buildings and personal property under commercial coverages. In the BPP form, the policy includes examples of coinsurance computations. These examples are useful when a property loss adjuster must explain coinsurance to an insured. The adjuster can refer the insured directly to the policy for a clear explanation. The following is an excerpt from the BPP:

1. Coinsurance

   If a Coinsurance percentage is shown in the Declarations, the following condition applies.

   a. We will not pay the full amount of any loss if the value of Covered Property at the time of loss times the Coinsurance percentage shown for it in the Declarations is greater than the Limit of Insurance for the Property.

      Instead, we will determine the most we will pay using the following steps:

      (1) Multiply the value of Covered Property at the time of loss by the Coinsurance percentage;

      (2) Divide the Limit of Insurance of the property by the figure determined in step (1);

      (3) Multiply the total amount of the covered loss, before the application of any deductible, by the figure determined in step (2); and

      (4) Subtract the deductible from the figure determined in step (3).

      We will pay the amount determined in step (4) or the limit of insurance, whichever is less. For the remainder, you will either have to rely on other insurance or absorb the loss yourself.

   Example No. 1 (Underinsurance)

   When:

The value of the property is	$250,000
The coinsurance percentage for it is	80%
The limit of insurance for it is	$100,000
The deductible is	$250
The amount of loss is	$40,000

   Step (1): $250,000 × 80% = $200,000 (the minimum amount of insurance to meet your coinsurance requirements).

   Step (2): $100,000 ÷ $200,000 = .50.

   Step (3): $40,000 × .50 = $20,000.

   Step (4): $20,000 – $250 = $19,750.

   We will pay no more than $19,750. The remaining $20,250 is not covered.[21]

If the adjuster determines that the insured has insurance adequate to meet or exceed the minimum required by the coinsurance percentage, computing steps 2 and 3 would be unnecessary. For example, assume that Margaret Allen has a commercial building insured for $450,000. The building's value at the time of the loss is $500,000. Margaret's policy has a 90 percent coinsurance requirement. Multiplying $500,000 × 90 percent shows that Margaret has met her coinsurance requirement. The adjuster must only subtract the deductible from the amount of loss.

Optional Coverages If Purchased

The BPP gives insureds several options regarding loss settlement. The insured can purchase the Agreed Value option, the Inflation Guard option, or the Replacement Cost option. The selected option will be noted on the declarations page under "Optional Coverage."

Agreed Value

Under the Agreed Value option, the insurer and the insured determine the maximum amount that will be paid in the event of a total loss. The coinsurance provision is eliminated, so if the agreed value and the policy limit are the same, the loss will be covered 100 percent.

Inflation Guard

The Inflation Guard option automatically increases the limit of insurance by a percentage rate (shown on declarations) on an annual basis. It is calculated by using the number of days since the policy inception, or the number of days since the last policy change affecting the limit of insurance, divided by 365. So if the loss occurs on the 146th day of the policy period, the calculation would look like this:

Limit of insurance	$100,000
Annual percentage increase	× 8%
	$8,000
Multiplied by the number of days	× 146 days
	$1,168,000

$1,168,000 ÷ 365 = $3,200.

Replacement Cost

The Replacement Cost option can be purchased for building and business personal property. Stock can be covered for replacement cost by selecting that option and listing it on the declarations page. Personal property of others, contents of a residence, manuscripts, and works of art are not covered for replacement cost. The insurer will not pay replacement cost on a loss until the lost or damaged property is actually repaired or replaced as soon as reasonably possible after the loss. The insured can accept an ACV settlement and has up to 180 days after the date of loss to give notice to the insurer that the insured wishes to make claim for replacement cost. A tenant's improvements and betterments are not considered personal property of others, so they would be eligible for replacement cost coverage under this provision. If an improvement or a betterment is not repaired or replaced within a reasonable time after the loss, the value will be calculated as a portion of the original cost, using the same formula as was outlined in the "Loss Payment" section of this chapter.

Extension of Replacement Cost to Personal Property of Others

If this option is selected on the declarations page, this extension will delete the exclusion of personal property of others from the Replacement Cost provision. There are limitations, however. If an item belonging to someone else is subject to a written contract, such as a lease, and that contract stipulates what the insured's liability is for loss or damage, then the item's value will be based on the amount of liability under the contract. However, this value cannot exceed the lesser of the replacement cost or the limit of insurance. Suppose that the insured leases a machine and the lease states that the machine is worth $10,000. The policy limit chosen for the replacement cost of personal property is $50,000. When the loss occurs, the machine's replacement value is $7,500. The insured would recover only $7,500 because it is the lesser of the amounts.

Insured's Duties After Loss

The insured's duties after a loss are explicitly stated in the Conditions section of the policy. The duties are essentially the same as the duties outlined in the HO-3, which Chapter 3 discusses. Only the following distinctions need to be highlighted.

Proof of Loss

The Proof of Loss condition in the BPP is phrased differently than in the HO-3 policy, but both request basically the same information. The HO-3 policy specifies what is to be included with the proof of loss. The BPP simply requires the statement to contain "the information we request. . . . " This means that the insurer must specifically list those items that it wants included with the proof of loss. It also means that information requested will vary by claim and by company. The BPP also specifies that the insurer will provide the forms.

Samples for Testing

Under the BPP, the insured must allow the insurer to take samples of damaged and undamaged property for inspection, testing, and analysis. This provision is not found in the HO-3. It is included in the BPP because of the likelihood of loss involving stock and inventory.

Imagine a refrigerated warehouse that holds premium ice cream. A fire in one part of the warehouse occurs. The power to the warehouse is knocked out and not restored for three days. The insured claims that all of the ice cream in the warehouse had melted and refroze, causing ice crystals to develop in the ice cream. The insured claims that the ice cream no longer meets its high-quality standards and makes a claim for damage to all of the ice cream in the warehouse. In such a situation, the property loss adjuster should ensure that various portions of the ice cream inventory are sampled and tested to determine if damage actually occurred and, if so, to what extent. The ice cream also must be checked to determine whether it can be sold as salvage. It is very important in losses involving large amounts of stock and inventory that this sampling be allowed to take place. If sampling and testing were not allowed, many items that are superficially contaminated or damaged might be claimed as a total loss.

Examination Under Oath

The Examination Under Oath requirement of the BPP appears last in the list of duties in the event of loss. This condition specifies that any insured can be examined and that the examination can occur while the insured is not in the presence of any other insured. It also states that the examination might extend to any matter related to the insurance, as well as the claim. Thus, an insured can be interrogated about the circumstances under which the insurance was purchased, including any possible misrepresentations at the time of application or changes in the coverage before the loss. Finally, this provision requires an insured to sign his or her answers. An insured's failure or refusal to sign is a failure to comply with this policy condition.

ENDORSEMENTS TO THE BPP

The BPP can be endorsed to include coverage for ordinance or law, business interruption, flood, and earthquake. These endorsements help tailor the policy to the insured's specific needs.

Ordinance or Law

The Ordinance or Law endorsement provides three types of coverages:

1. Coverage A covers the reduction in value of the undamaged portion of the building that must be demolished to comply with an ordinance or a law. It can either be on an ACV or a replacement cost basis. If the coverage is written as replacement cost, then the policy pays the lowest of the following amounts:
   a. Amount the insured actually spends
   b. The limit of insurance applicable to the building

   No separate amount of insurance must be shown for Coverage A. It becomes part of the building coverage.
2. Coverage B covers the cost to demolish the undamaged portion of the structure and remove its debris. A separate amount of insurance must

be shown for this coverage. The coinsurance provision does apply to this coverage.

3. Coverage C covers the increased cost to repair, reconstruct, or remodel undamaged portions of the property to conform with the minimum requirements of an ordinance or a law. If this option is selected, replacement cost must also be selected. A separate limit of insurance must be indicated on the declarations page, and coinsurance does apply. Coverage C will also apply to the increased cost of repairing or reconstructing excavations; grades; backfilling; foundations; pilings; and underground pipes, flues, and drains.

None of the three coverages will pay for any costs incurred because of an ordinance or a law that requires a response to, or an assessment of, the effects of pollutants. Nor will they pay for any loss stemming from an ordinance or a law that the insured failed to comply with, if the compliance was required before the loss.

Business Income Loss

The BPP does not include any coverage for business income losses. The Business Income Coverage Form is available for this purpose and can be made part of the commercial package for an additional premium. Chapter 11 addresses this topic.

Flood

Some property insurers endorse flood coverage onto a commercial property policy. It can be written to be added as a covered peril for damage to the structure and contents, for business income loss, and for ordinance or law coverage. Usually the flood endorsement has a limit of insurance that is lower than the regular policy limit. Even with this limit, most property insurers are reluctant to include flood coverage on property policies because of the potential for catastrophic loss. An alternative means of coverage is to obtain flood insurance from the National Flood Insurance Program (NFIP), which is run by the federal government. The NFIP policy for commercial property covers up to a maximum of $500,000 on buildings and $500,000 on contents. Chapter 6 more fully discusses NFIP policies.

Earthquake and Volcanic Eruption

The endorsements available for earthquake and volcanic eruption are a prime example of coverage that most insureds do not need, which is why they are not included in the regular policy but are available by endorsement. Two ISO forms are designed to add earthquake and volcanic eruption as covered perils under a commercial property policy. They typically provide a million or two million dollars in coverage. Neither endorsement defines "earthquake," but the endorsements do state that all earthquakes and shocks occurring within a 168-hour period are considered a single quake. This same time period applies to volcanic eruption. Volcanic eruption is defined in the endorsements as the eruption, explosion, or effusion of a volcano. The difference between the two endorsements concerns coinsurance. One endorsement, CP 10 40, is subject to the coinsurance clause already contained in the property policy that it is attached to. The other endorsement, CP 10 45, is not subject to coinsurance and thus can be written with its own sublimit that may be lower than the policy limit for other covered perils.

DIFFERENCE IN CONDITIONS POLICIES

Difference in conditions (DIC) insurance
Policies designed to bridge coverage gaps in ordinary insurance policies; covers additional perils such as earthquake and flood.

Difference in conditions (DIC) insurance is written to supplement commercial property policies. The DIC reduces the chance of an uninsured loss by covering additional perils and by filling coverage gaps in the ordinary property forms. DIC policies are generally written on an "all-risks" basis, but most policies exclude damage caused by fire and the perils of the extended coverages, as well as certain other perils.

The DIC policy intentionally uses "all-risks" coverage to address those exposures not covered in the basic property forms. For example, earthquake and flood are excluded in the basic property forms but are the most important exposures covered by the DIC policy. They are covered either because of the coverage's "all-risks" nature or because flood and earthquake are named as perils under a nonstandard form or manuscript form. DIC coverage is primarily used by risk managers as flood and earthquake coverage.

Standardized DIC forms do not meet the needs of most insureds and insurers. Consequently, insurers provide their own nonstandard DIC forms. If the nonstandard forms provided by insurers do not meet the requirements of a large insured corporation, the corporation's risk manager might manuscript a policy or form to cover that business's unique exposures. Because of these policies' nonstandard nature, adjusters handling DIC losses cannot assume they understand the coverage until they carefully read the policy in question.

DIC policies are usually written in one of the following ways:

1. "All-risks" coverage with exclusions for the perils that the standard property policy form covers;
2. Specified-perils coverage; or
3. An excess property form that provides additional limits of insurance for causes of loss that are limited on the standard property policy.

Because the DIC is usually written without a coinsurance clause, obtaining coverage for the partial value of the property is possible. This allows the insured to protect only those items that are truly exposed to the peril, such as the lower floor of a building that would normally flood.

When handling a loss under a DIC policy, the property loss adjuster must read and understand the policy. The adjuster should confirm that there is no coinsurance requirement. Pay careful attention to the covered perils' definitions as well as the exclusions' wording. Some policies cover all property, but others cover only buildings. Some policies are written on an ACV basis, but others are written for replacement cost. Even though DIC forms provide "all-risks" coverage, they contain exclusions for certain property similar to those in the BPP. DIC policies generally exclude currency, money, deeds, evidences of debt, notes, securities, jewelry, gems or precious stones, furs, fine arts, crops, watercraft, aircraft, motorized vehicles licensed for highway use, and animals and birds.

Some DIC policies contain the exclusions found in most "all-risks" forms. These exclusions include, but might not be limited to, wear and tear, deterioration, dampness of atmosphere, smog, shrinkage, evaporation, and wet and dry rot. Employee infidelity is also not covered because this coverage is generally available under a fidelity form. Mysterious disappearance and unexplained loss or shortages are also excluded.

DIC policies can be written as an excess policy, although most are not. When written as an excess policy, they are structured so that they do not duplicate the standard policy's coverage. However, unless the DIC language mirrors the standard policy form's language, a duplication of coverage might occur. Because of this possibility, it is recommended that the adjuster examine the "other insurance" clause in the DIC and in the standard form to see how they will interact with one another.

SUMMARY

The BPP is a flexible commercial property policy. It can be used to cover just a building, just business personal property, or both. The BPP is available in three causes of loss forms. The Basic Form provides coverage for fire, lightning, explosion, windstorm and hail, smoke, aircraft or vehicles, riot or civil commotion, vandalism, sprinkler leakage, sinkhole collapse, and volcanic action. The Broad Form extends this list of covered perils by adding falling objects; weight of snow, ice, or sleet; and water damage. The Special Form provides the broadest coverage available by covering risks of direct physical loss unless excluded by the policy.

The BPP allows the insured to select what type of valuation applies. The policy can be written with agreed value coverage, actual cash value coverage, inflation guard coverage, replacement cost coverage, or a combination of these options.

The BPP can be further tailored to the insured's needs by adding endorsements to it. Ordinance or law coverage can be added to cover the increased repair or replacement costs resulting from an ordinance or a law. Business income coverage can be obtained by adding the Business Income Coverage Form to the policy. It is possible to endorse flood and earthquake and volcanic action as covered perils. However, many insurers are reluctant to do so because of the potential for catastrophic loss. A DIC policy can be used to supplement commercial property insurance to reduce the chance of an insured loss. A DIC policy can cover additional perils or fill coverage gaps in the insured's other insurance. The National Flood Insurance Program provides an alternative means for flood insurance.

This chapter and Chapter 3 discuss coverage. Chapter 5 examines the loss adjustment process and what steps are needed to adequately adjust a loss. Chapter 6 discusses how the cause of loss determines what investigative techniques are needed.

CHAPTER NOTES

1. Building and Personal Property Coverage Form CP 00 10 04 02, Copyright, Insurance Services Office, Inc., 2001.
2. Building and Personal Property Coverage Form CP 00 10 04 02, Copyright, Insurance Services Office, Inc., 2001.
3. Building and Personal Property Coverage Form CP 00 10 04 02, Copyright, Insurance Services Office, Inc., 2001.
4. Building and Personal Property Coverage Form CP 00 10 04 02, Copyright, Insurance Services Office, Inc., 2001.
5. Building and Personal Property Coverage Form CP 00 10 04 02, Copyright, Insurance Services Office, Inc., 2001.
6. Building and Personal Property Coverage Form CP 00 10 04 02, Copyright, Insurance Services Office, Inc., 2001.
7. Building and Personal Property Coverage Form CP 00 10 04 02, Copyright, Insurance Services Office, Inc., 2001.
8. Causes of Loss—Basic Form CP 10 10 04 02, Copyright, Insurance Services Office, Inc., 2001.
9. Causes of Loss—Basic Form CP 10 10 04 02 and Broad Form CP 10 20 04 02, Copyright, Insurance Services Office, Inc., 2001.
10. Causes of Loss—Basic Form CP 10 10 04 02, Copyright, Insurance Services Office, Inc., 2001.
11. Causes of Loss—Basic Form CP 10 10 04 02, Copyright, Insurance Services Office, Inc., 2001.
12. Causes of Loss—Basic Form CP 10 10 04 02, Copyright, Insurance Services Office, Inc., 2001.
13. Causes of Loss—Basic Form CP 10 10 04 02, Copyright, Insurance Services Office, Inc., 2001.
14. Causes of Loss—Broad Form CP 10 20 04 02, Copyright, Insurance Services Office, Inc., 2001.
15. Causes of Loss—Special Form CP 10 30 04 02, Copyright, Insurance Services Office, Inc., 2001.
16. Causes of Loss—Special Form CP 10 30 04 02, Copyright, Insurance Services Office, Inc., 2001.
17. Causes of Loss—Special Form CP 10 30 04 02, Copyright, Insurance Services Office, Inc., 2001.

18. Causes of Loss—Special Form CP 10 30 04 02, Copyright, Insurance Services Office, Inc., 2001.
19. Causes of Loss—Special Form CP 10 30 04 02, Copyright, Insurance Services Office, Inc., 2001.
20. Causes of Loss—Special Form CP 10 30 04 02, Copyright, Insurance Services Office, Inc., 2001.
21. Building and Personal Property Coverage Form CP 00 10 04 02, Copyright, Insurance Services Office, Inc., 2001.

Chapter 5

Direct Your Learning

Loss Adjustment Process

After learning the subject matter of this chapter, you should be able to:

- Describe and explain the steps in the loss adjustment process after a loss notice is received.
- Describe public adjusters' role in the adjustment process.
- Explain how to verify losses through the use of the following:
    - Statements
    - Documentation, such as books, records, or photographs
- Describe the uses of various experts in a given claim situation.
- Identify the potential for subrogation in a given claim, and explain how experts and arbitration would facilitate recovery.
- Describe how to issue claim payments to account for all interests.
- Describe a denial letter's contents.

OUTLINE

Develop Your Perspective

What are the main topics covered in the chapter?

The loss adjustment process has six main steps:

1. Acknowledging receipt of the insured's report of loss and assigning an adjuster
2. Verifying coverage
3. Initiating contact with the insured
4. Investigating the facts
5. Determining the cause of loss and extent of loss
6. Concluding the loss adjustment

This chapter discusses these steps and some issues that an adjuster may face while completing these steps.

As you read this chapter, consider how your company handles each of these steps.

Why is it important to know these topics?

Often, meeting with the property loss adjuster is the only face-to-face discussion that the insured has with the insurer. The property loss adjuster should be prepared to handle the loss in a manner that is efficient and results in a fair and equitable outcome. This helps to retain the insured as a customer and helps to protect the adjuster from bad-faith allegations.

How can you use this information?

This chapter provides a foundation for handling property losses. Following the same basic steps in handling every property loss reinforces good claim-handling practices.

Chapter 5

Loss Adjustment Process

A property loss adjuster follows the same loss adjustment process regardless of the coverage involved in the loss. The adjuster follows six steps to resolve a property claim. See the following box.

> **Loss Adjustment Process**
>
> 1. Acknowledging receipt of the insured's report of loss and assigning the loss to an adjuster
> 2. Verifying coverage
> 3. Initiating contact with the insured
> 4. Investigating the facts
> 5. Determining the cause of loss and the extent of loss to insured property
> 6. Concluding the loss adjustment.

Adjusters must properly investigate, document, and report their activities and claim settlements. Specific loss adjustment procedures for various types of losses are discussed in Chapter 6. Estimating, a key aspect of documenting a property damage loss, is treated at length in Chapters 8 and 9. Property loss adjusters can expect public adjusters, contractors, service providers, and certain experts to be involved in adjusting many claims. After a loss adjustment is complete, the adjuster must conscientiously pursue the insurer's right of recovery against any responsible third party and report the claim settlement properly and adequately. In addition to conducting the loss adjustment process, adjusters must be able to deny claims and deal with reinsurance, depending on the details of a claim.

REPORTING LOSSES TO THE INSURER

When a loss occurs, several steps must be taken before the insurer can begin the adjustment process. Normally, the insured notifies the agent or broker of the loss or contacts the insurer directly. An agent or a broker notes some basic information about the loss, such as the date it occurred, its location and type, the extent of damage, and any other special details. With this information and additional information from his or her files, the agent or broker completes a loss notice such as the one shown in Exhibit 5-1 and electronically submits the loss to the insurer. The completed loss notice form states details of the loss; the coverage that applies, including the insurer, the policy number, the policy's effective dates, the amounts of coverage, and the deductibles or coinsurance; and the form numbers and edition dates. Mortgagees or loss payees are also listed on the loss notice form. The agent/broker may also advise the insured about emergency repairs as well as assign an adjuster to inspect the loss. If the insured calls the insurer directly to report a loss, the insurer will obtain the same information that an agent or a broker would obtain.

STEPS IN THE ADJUSTMENT PROCESS

After the loss notice is received, the insurer begins the loss adjustment process. The insurer's claim department assigns the claim to an adjuster. The adjuster acknowledges the assignment and initiates contact with the insured.

Step 1: Acknowledgment and Assignment to an Adjuster

After the agent reports a loss to the insurer, a claim department manager or supervisor decides which adjuster will handle the claim and assigns that adjuster. For an independent adjuster, the insurer often calls the adjuster with the assignment, giving the adjuster the information on the property loss notice along with any other relevant policy data or special handling instructions. Most insurers follow up with written confirmation of the assignment, and they send the independent adjuster any claim documents that they have received or special policy forms involved. Both the staff adjuster and the independent adjuster need to review the policy to ensure that neither adjuster inadvertently commits waiver or estoppel. Upon receipt of the assignment, the adjuster assigned must promptly call the insured. During this telephone conversation, the adjuster questions the insured to learn essential facts about the loss and the extent of damage. The adjuster might have to direct the insured to protect the property from further damage, such as instructing the insured to board up windows following a serious loss. The adjuster can also make an appointment to inspect the loss site or advise the insured of who will be out to inspect the loss.

Adjuster Licensing

Most, but not all, adjusters handle losses within a specific geographic area. Some adjusters handle losses on a global basis. Adjusters handling only a specific geographic territory in the United States should be familiar with the adjuster licensing laws of those states. Noncompliance with these laws can result in fines levied against the insurer. These laws may apply to the insurer's staff adjuster, to independent adjusters, or to public adjusters, depending upon the state. If an independent adjuster is hired to handle a loss on the staff property loss adjuster's behalf, the independent adjuster

EXHIBIT 5-1

ACORD Property Loss Notice

ACORD™ PROPERTY LOSS NOTICE

DATE (MM/DD/YYYY): 8/1/0X

PRODUCER: PAUL PROCTOR, PLAINFIELD, OH
PHONE (A/C, No, Ext): INS AGENCY TEL # 3
CODE: 39542 SUB CODE:
AGENCY CUSTOMER ID:

MISCELLANEOUS INFO (Site & location code): 215 555-2100
DATE OF LOSS AND TIME: 7/29/0X — AM: X / PM
PREVIOUSLY REPORTED: YES / NO: X

POLICY TYPE	COMPANY AND POLICY NUMBER	NAIC CODE	POLICY DATES
PROP/HOME	CO: IIA POL: HO 1894370	39542	EFF: 6/16/0X EXP: 6/16/0Y
FLOOD	CO: POL:		EFF: EXP:
WIND	CO: POL:		EFF: EXP:

INSURED

NAME AND ADDRESS OF INSURED: LEONARD HILLMAN, 156 SIXTH AVENUE, PLAINFIELD, OH 48740
DATE OF BIRTH:
SOC SEC # OR FEIN:
RESIDENCE PHONE (A/C, No): 215 555-8181
BUSINESS PHONE (A/C, No, Ext): 215 555-5000
NAME AND ADDRESS OF SPOUSE (IF APPLICABLE):
DATE OF BIRTH:
SOC SEC # OR FEIN:

CONTACT

CONTACT INSURED:
NAME AND ADDRESS OF INSURED: JULIA HILLMAN
RESIDENCE PHONE (A/C, No): 215 555-8181
BUSINESS PHONE (A/C, No, Ext):
WHERE TO CONTACT: HOME
WHEN TO CONTACT: ANYTIME

LOSS

LOCATION OF LOSS:
POLICE OR FIRE DEPT TO WHICH REPORTED:
KIND OF LOSS: FIRE / LIGHTNING / FLOOD / OTHER (explain) / THEFT / HAIL: X / WIND: X
PROBABLE AMOUNT ENTIRE LOSS: $5,000
DESCRIPTION OF LOSS & DAMAGE (Use separate sheet, if necessary): WIND AND HAIL SERIOUSLY DAMAGED ROOF AND BLEW SHINGLES OFF. CONTENTS INSIDE ALSO DAMAGED.

POLICY INFORMATION

MORTGAGEE: PLAINFIELD FEDERAL SAVINGS AND LOAN ASSOCIATION
NO MORTGAGEE

HOMEOWNER POLICIES SECTION 1 ONLY (Complete for coverages A, B, C, D & additional coverages. For Homeowners Section II Liability Losses, use ACORD 3.)

A. DWELLING	B. OTHER STRUCTURES	C. PERSONAL PROPERTY	D. LOSS OF USE	DEDUCTIBLES	DESCRIBE ADDITIONAL COVERAGES PROVIDED
$90,000	$9,000	$45,000	$18,000	$100	

COVERAGE A. EXCLUDES WIND
SUBJECT TO FORMS (Insert form numbers and edition dates, special deductibles): HO-3 INFLATION GUARD

FIRE, ALLIED LINES & MULTI-PERIL POLICIES (Complete only those items involved in loss)

ITEM	SUBJECT OF INSURANCE	AMOUNT	% COINS	DEDUCTIBLE	COVERAGE AND/OR DESCRIPTION OF PROPERTY INSURED
	BLDG / CNTS				
	BLDG / CNTS				
	BLDG / CNTS				

SUBJECT TO FORMS (Insert form numbers and edition dates, special deductibles):

FLOOD POLICY: BUILDING: DEDUCTIBLE: CONTENTS: DEDUCTIBLE: ZONE: PRE FIRM / POST FIRM; DIFF IN ELEV; FORM TYPE: GENERAL / DWELLING / CONDO

WIND POLICY: BUILDING: DEDUCTIBLE: CONTENTS: ZONE: FORM TYPE: GENERAL / DWELLING / CONDO

REMARKS/OTHER INSURANCE (List companies, policy numbers, coverages & policy amounts)/NY ONLY: PREVIOUS ADDRESS OF INSURED & WIFE'S MAIDEN NAME: NO OTHER INSURANCE.

CAT #: FICO #: ADJUSTER ASSIGNED: ADJUSTER #: DATE ASSIGNED:

REPORTED BY: LEONARD HILLMAN
REPORTED TO: ANN ADAMS
SIGNATURE OF INSURED:
SIGNATURE OF PRODUCER: *Paul Proctor*

ACORD 1 (2002/01) NOTE: IMPORTANT STATE INFORMATION ON REVERSE SIDE must provide proof of a valid license if one is required in that state. Many insurers have centralized the responsibility for regulatory compliance, so it may not be necessary to have proof of a valid adjuster license in every claim file. Adjusters should check with their manager to determine what the insurer's policy is regarding adjuster licensing. Also, most adjuster licensing laws exempt catastrophe adjusters.

Step 2: Coverage Verification

Usually, a property loss adjuster is able to quickly verify that a policy is in force. However, if the actual paper policy is required to thoroughly review the forms and endorsements, the adjuster may need additional time to obtain the policy and perform the review. The adjuster usually accomplishes the policy review before contacting the insured and inspecting the loss, but this may not always be the case. If the coverage verification and review cannot be completed before contacting the insured, the adjuster must take care not to say or do anything that might waive any policy defenses.

The following box lists some of the questions that an adjuster should have in mind when reviewing a policy.

Key Questions When Verifying Coverage

After receiving a loss notice, an adjuster reviews the policy and determines the answers to the following questions:

- Does the loss fall within the policy's effective dates?
- Who is the insured in the policy?
- What is insured in the policy?
- What caused the loss, and is that cause of loss covered by the policy?
- Do any exclusions apply to the loss?
- How is the loss to be valued?
- Is the amount of recovery limited by the policy?

The adjuster should read the applicable policy forms carefully, mindful of obvious coverage questions. For example, is a theft claim being filed under a named-perils policy that does not include theft? Is the insured a tenant who is claiming building damage under a personal property form? The adjuster should examine limitations and exclusions. Perhaps an insured homeowner has just reported a theft of $5,000 cash during a break-in, but a review of the standard HO-3 reveals a $200 limit on money. A nonwaiver agreement might be necessary if policy violations are known, such as late reporting or discarding of the damaged property before inspection.

Verifying coverage, the adjuster sometimes must consult with an expert to determine issues such as cause of loss. Perhaps an extensive computer network broke down shortly after a thunderstorm, and the adjuster must determine whether it was damaged by lightning or suffered a coincidental mechanical breakdown. The typical adjuster may not have the expertise to make such determinations, but an expert can expedite the adjustment process. If an expert is needed, the adjuster should schedule the first meeting with the insured so that the expert can attend.

An adjuster's final consideration before going to the loss site should be the information that the insurer will expect in the adjuster's reports and how such information will be gathered. The preparation time spent before the meeting allows the adjuster to establish credibility. That time will not be wasted—the preparation ultimately speeds the adjustment process to the benefit of all concerned.

Step 3: Contact With the Insured

After receiving the claim assignment and reviewing the initial loss report and policy, the adjuster should contact the insured and make an appointment to meet at the loss location, either on the same day or within the next few days. During this initial contact, the adjuster should get information about the extent of the loss and how the loss occurred. The adjuster will then be able to make some preliminary decisions about the need for outside vendors, such as a restoration company, to assist with the loss adjustment. During this initial contact, the adjuster may also learn that the insured has retained a public adjuster. The first trip to the loss site, together with the first meeting with the insured, sets the tone for the adjustment. The adjuster should listen to the insured. The insured probably considers the loss a major disruption; he or she might never have made a claim under the policy before. The adjuster might be the first representative of the insurer that the insured has met, and the insured might be apprehensive about what will occur during the adjustment of his or her claim.

Initial Visit

Most insureds do not understand their coverage thoroughly. The adjuster must explain the policy and its meaning in relation to the loss.

Perhaps the most important information that the adjuster must convey is any possible policy violation, exclusion, or limitation that might affect coverage. The adjuster must be honest. Withholding this type of information might be construed as a breach of the adjuster's duty to deal fairly. Furthermore, because the adjuster is acting as an agent of the insurer, the insurer is liable for any of the adjuster's unfair acts or practices. At the initial meeting, the adjuster should explain the adjustment process and do the following:

1. Explain what inspection, appraisal, and investigation the adjuster will be conducting.

2. Tell the insured what is required to protect the property and to present the claim.
3. Supply the insured with blank inventory forms, a blank proof of loss form, and any necessary written instructions.
4. Note potential coverage questions or policy limitation or exclusions, and obtain a nonwaiver agreement (when necessary). Be prepared to tell the insured what additional investigation is needed to resolve potential coverage issues.
5. Explain the time involved to process and conclude the claim.
6. Assist the insured in protecting the property by arranging for board-up, storage, and restoration and cleaning firms (when appropriate).
7. Be prepared to make emergency advance payments to the insured for clothing, living expenses, food, or other expenses, and obtain an appropriate receipt for the payment when the circumstances support such a payment.
8. Assist the insured by arranging for temporary housing (when necessary).

The insurer's adjuster must ensure that requests for documentation and the need for compliance with policy conditions are communicated to the insured in writing. This is a good policy to follow whether a public adjuster is involved or not.

Public Adjusters

Public adjusters
Persons who help insureds present claims to insurers for a fee.

Public adjusters are active in some states and metropolitan areas. They help insureds present claims to insurers for a fee. Although some claims lead to disputes between public adjusters and insurer-employed adjusters, the goal of both is the proper adjustment of the insured's claim.

Public Adjusters' Role

Public adjusters are most often involved in presenting fire claims to insurers, but they also handle property claims caused by flood, water, wind, burglary, and theft. The fee for their services is typically 10 to 15 percent of the amount paid under the policy.

Public adjusters perform many of the duties required of insureds in presenting and documenting claims. They analyze the scene and prepare a scope of the loss and damages, prepare inventories, and obtain repair or reconstruction estimates in connection with personal property and structure losses. They also assist insureds in documenting and presenting claims for loss of earnings, business interruption, and loss of rent. Finally, they are involved in settlement negotiations and sometimes act as appraisers when differences arise regarding the amount recoverable in accordance with policy conditions. Because of public adjusters' knowledge of property policies and experience in claims, they can help insureds by doing the following:

1. Presenting claims in an organized manner, which may expedite settlement

2. Compiling and documenting claims to fulfill the insured's obligations under the policy and to allow the insured to focus on other tasks
3. Reassuring the insured that the claim settlement is fair

Because most states require public adjusters to be licensed, they meet certain minimum qualifications based on experience and education. Most public adjusters have worked as property adjusters for one or more insurers. They generally have extensive knowledge of property policies and insurers' claim procedures. Many public adjusting firms belong to the National Association of Public Insurance Adjusters (NAPIA). The association was founded in 1951 and seeks to establish ethical and professional standards for representing insureds before insurers.

Dealing With Public Adjusters

Public adjusters can help or hinder efficient claim processing, depending on the adjuster or public adjusting firm with whom the insurer is dealing and the claim's circumstances. Problems with public adjusters are usually related to how public adjusters procure business from insureds and the manner in which they evaluate and present claims for insureds.

Public adjusters may obtain business by monitoring police and fire calls and appearing on the scene immediately after a loss. Unfortunately, some public adjusters take advantage of the insured's vulnerable position by stating or implying that the claim-handling process is highly technical and legalistic. They might also cause the insured to distrust the insurer by indicating that a fair settlement cannot be reached unless a public adjuster is retained. The insured's resulting anxiety might cause him or her to hire a public adjuster. Most insurance company adjusters proceed in good faith and do not treat insureds in an overly legalistic or unfair manner.

Public adjusters are usually paid a percentage of the amount paid to the insured by the insurer. This fee arrangement may encourage some public adjusters to overstate or exaggerate, and in some cases to misrepresent, the extent and/or amount of loss to increase the amount of recovery. For example, disputes might occur over the cost to repair or replace structures. Public adjusters also may submit bids from contractors who routinely work with them, which can make reaching an agreement on scope and price more difficult.

During the claim adjustment, some public adjusters resist or delay the submission of documentation, books and records, and inventories, and object to other requests to which the insurer is entitled under the policy. Such public adjusters must be reminded that compliance with all policy conditions is a prerequisite to payment. Public adjusters might also appear at examinations under oath to try to object to questions posed to the insureds by claim personnel and the insurer's attorneys even though they have no contractual or other legal right to do so.

Claims involving public adjusters should be handled no differently than if an insurer-employed adjuster were dealing directly with the insured, meaning expediently and professionally.

Step 4: Investigation

Following the preliminary interview and discussions, the adjuster investigates, inspects, and appraises the loss. Good investigation is the basis of every claim settlement. Property loss adjusters are responsible for determining what investigation is appropriate in individual claims. The adjuster receives direction from his or her company's claim-handling guidelines and supervisor as to how much investigation is appropriate. The adjuster's goal is to investigate enough to make the appropriate decision. A loss's dollar value does not necessarily indicate the amount of investigation needed to arrive at a decision. Every investigation should determine the facts about what caused the loss, how coverage applies, and what the amount of the loss is. The insured's duties following loss and statements from the insured and witnesses are key tools in the property loss adjuster's investigation.

The Insured's Duties

Almost all of the insured's duties in the event of loss, as described in the property coverage forms, are designed to aid the adjuster's investigation. According to the insurance policy, the insured must prove (1) that a loss is covered by the policy, (2) the amount of the loss, and (3) that the insured has complied with all duties and conditions specified in the policy. After a loss, the insured's duties are the essential conditions of the insurance policy. Property loss adjusters should review those duties with the insured to remind the insured of what is expected. Nevertheless, insurers and claim adjusters aim to provide good service to their customers, especially after a loss. Unless they suspect fraud or lack of coverage for the loss, adjusters should work with insureds to accomplish the insured's duties. Review of these duties also helps the adjuster to organize his or her own investigation and specify what is needed from the insured.

Statements of the Insured and Witnesses

The insured's statement is often waived in connection with smaller or uncomplicated claims; the facts of a loss are typically clear, and coverage applies. In larger or more complicated losses, especially those involving a coverage question or suspected insurance fraud, the insured's statement is an essential part of the investigation.

The statement's purposes are to establish the property's ownership, the cause of loss and facts surrounding the loss, and the extent of loss, and also to determine for subrogation purposes whether any third party is responsible for the loss. Statements can either be written or recorded. The statement usually follows this format:

1. The identity of the insured
2. The ownership of, or interest in, the property
3. The existence of other insurance
4. The existence of mortgages or encumbrances

5. The facts and cause of the loss, including the insured's location at the time, the presence of any witnesses, and the involvement of the police or the fire department
6. A description of the damaged property, including the nature and extent of the loss or damage to personal and real property, plus information regarding other losses that the policy might cover, such as loss of rent or business income loss
7. The establishment of a basis for subrogation, including identifying individuals or organizations who might be responsible for the damage

Some property loss adjusters use statement outlines, which can be useful guides, but they should not be the sole source of questions. They can be too restrictive to resolve a particular claim's problems. Additionally, a statement outline can cause the adjuster to fail to ask appropriate follow-up questions to an unusual or a curious statement. The adjuster must review the initial report and analyze all of the information at hand, including the policy, and should formulate areas of investigation or specific questions that fit the particular claim.

In some states or jurisdictions, obtaining a statement might waive the insurer's rights to an examination of the insured under oath; it might also waive the required filing by the insured of a sworn statement in a proof of loss. This waiver is based on the theory that the insurer has been fully informed of all the information that would normally be supplied by compliance with these conditions. A nonwaiver agreement avoids the problem of waiving any conditions. The adjuster should incorporate into the insured's statement the insured's understanding that the insurer will or might require the insured's full compliance with the policy conditions.

The adjuster needs witness statements when gathering information regarding the cause of loss, especially if fraud is suspected. Statements also give the adjuster information regarding the potential for subrogation. Witnesses can be identified through official reports, information provided by the insured or the agent, and by a witness canvass. A witness canvass involves contacting residents of the neighborhood, people living around the insured's residence, or persons or businesses surrounding the loss location. In making such contacts, the adjuster must avoid any comments implying that the insured was responsible for the loss. The adjuster should fully identify him or herself, state that the purpose of the contact is to locate anyone with knowledge regarding the occurrence, and obtain a statement when appropriate. Whether or not the witness canvass is helpful should be recorded in the file to document the adjuster's activity and the insurer's good-faith investigation.

Documentation

Adjusters must document the extent of loss or damage for the following reasons:

1. To identify the property for coverage and possible coinsurance concerns
2. To inform the insurer of the magnitude of the loss so that proper case reserves can be established
3. To establish the cost of repairs or replacement for ultimate settlement

4. To avoid disputes with the insured as to the amount payable
5. To assist contractors in preparing bids for repair or reconstruction

Documenting a loss can involve gathering records, photographing and videotaping the loss site, drawing floor plans and diagrams, preparing scopes of the damage and estimates, preparing inventories, and reviewing financial records. The type of documentation required varies depending on the type of loss. Most insurers have claim-handling guidelines that outline the many possible ways to document a loss.

Records

Books and records are useful in documenting loss to stock, inventory, and personal property. In most cases, the insured does not have all the information that the adjuster needs at the first meeting. The insured must often organize and submit bills or invoices to substantiate purchases and values later. Complete loss inventories also take time. The adjuster can help the insured by explaining specifically what is needed. For example, in a theft from a residence, some of the documentation that the adjuster might request includes bills or purchase receipts for the claimed items. If these are not available, a credit card record or monthly statement can prove the existence and ownership of the property, its age, and its purchase price. Photo albums can also help. A photograph might show a stolen television set in the background. If jewelry is involved, an appraisal might be available. For higher-value items, obtaining a copy of the receipt from the retailer might be possible. If an appliance is missing, the instruction manual or warranty paperwork might be available.

Photography and Videotaping

During the initial property inspection, photos should be taken or videotapes should be made to document the type of property, the nature and extent of the damage, the presence or absence of damage to the structure and contents, and the types of construction material used, as well as the overall condition of the premises. The number of pictures that the adjuster takes depends on the size of the loss. More pictures probably need to be taken in a large loss.

As to the structure, the adjuster should start by taking pictures of the exterior of the building or residence, including the roof in appropriate cases, and by photographing all sides. The adjuster should then move to the interior, usually starting with the main entrance to the building or residence, and take enough photos in each room to document the damage.

The photos of the structure might include pictures of the contents, merchandise, and equipment. Close-ups of the damaged property might be necessary. Extremely close photography is sometimes needed to depict nameplates with an item's manufacturer's name, model, and serial number. Documenting the absence of damage is not always warranted unless the adjuster receives some indication from the insured that a dispute will arise or when the insured claims damage that appears to be the result of wear and tear, deterioration, or something other than the reported cause of loss.

With videotaping, the adjuster should document the same items and structures, moving in the same pattern as in photography, and add narration that includes the date, identifying information, and comments regarding the videotaped property.

> **Adjuster Tip**
>
> When photographing or videotaping a loss site, an adjuster should include a ruler or a yardstick in the shot to indicate property's size and scale.

Floor Plans and Diagrams

Diagrams and floor plans are helpful in depicting a structure's size, the areas affected by damage, and the extent of the damage. Diagrams enable the adjuster to calculate repair costs and inform the insurer of the extent of loss. In smaller losses, the entire structure is not normally diagrammed, but for larger losses, a complete floor plan is essential. An example of a floor plan prepared for a kitchen grease fire appears in Exhibit 5-2.

EXHIBIT 5-2

Example of a Floor Plan

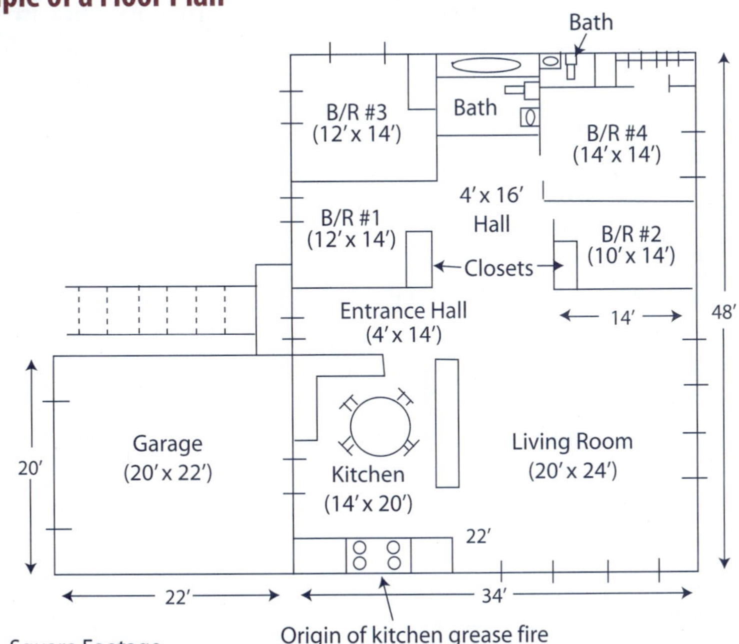

Square Footage
20′x 22′= 440 garage
34′x 48′= 1,632 house
2,072 total

Scale 1/4″= 2′

The adjuster typically starts by measuring and diagraming the structure's entire exterior perimeter. The adjuster then measures the interior rooms, usually noting the amount of damage on a scope sheet as well as each room's measurements. In addition to a floor plan diagram, side elevation diagrams are sometimes drawn to illustrate gable ends and unusual or oddly shaped structures so that repair costs can be estimated.

Scope and Estimate

Scope
A list of the areas damaged, which includes the type of damage, a description of the proposed type of repairs, and the measurements of those areas.

A **scope** or scope sheet is a list of the areas damaged, which includes the type of damage, a description of the proposed type of repairs, and the measurements of those areas. Exhibit 5-3 shows an example of a scope sheet for a kitchen grease fire.

A preliminary scope is normally provided to the insurer with initial reports, but it is also commonly provided to contractors who have been asked to submit repair or reconstruction bids. The preliminary scope allows the contractor to prepare a bid that covers the same items as the adjuster's scope.

Property loss adjusters can also use the scope to prepare an estimate that they can then use for proper reserving, to reach agreement directly with the insured when contractors' bids are not required, and to compare with contractors' bids when appropriate. In the last case, a line-by-line comparison of items can be made to ensure that the contractors have included all of the areas requiring repairs and to confirm that the contractor's cost of repair is fair and reasonable. If the contractor's repair costs appear to be too high or too low, the adjuster could discuss that particular item with the contractor and adjust the cost up or down. The goal is to achieve an agreement with the contractor or contractors so that settlement can be reached with the insured. Chapter 8 details the scope of a loss and the preparation of estimates.

Inventory

After the insured understands what information is required to support the claim and after a timetable has been set for submitting the evidence, the adjuster must examine the damaged property. An inventory should be taken and should include as much pertinent information about the property as is available. The property's manufacturer, serial and model numbers, size, color, age, and pre-loss condition are all helpful in determining value. The adjuster should note any property that might be obsolete or no longer available. To the insured, these items might have had some value, but they have relatively low actual cash value.

Use of Experts

Experts are commonly used to determine facts, to verify the extent of loss or damage, and to estimate the value of loss to real and personal property. The ultimate purpose of using experts is to assist the adjuster in determining

EXHIBIT 5-3

Example of a Scope Sheet

Property Loss Worksheet

Page No. 1

Preliminary Estimate 10/19/0X (Date)

Final Estimate ______ (Date)

M. Boyer (Adjuster)

Claim No. 524 BL 101

Insured J. Smith

Claimant Insured

1 Item	2 Description	3 Quantity	4 Units Age	5 Unit price Orig. cost	6 Cost Repl. cost	7 Deprec.	8 A.C.V.	9 Loss & Damage
1.	Permit (if required)							
2.	Demolition							
	Remove range hood							
	Remove cabinets (4 LF)							
	Remove drywall (above cabinet) (5' × 10' = 50 SF)							
	Remove Formica countertop (12 LF) (est. 2 men × 5 hrs. = 10 hrs.)							
3.	Cartage							
	1 pickup & driver (1.5 hrs.)							
	Dump fee ($10.00)							
4.	Clean range (est. 1.5 hrs.)							
5.	Install new range hood (Sears 30", est. 1 hr.)							
6.	Install upper cabinets Paint grade plywood of 4 LF × 3' tall (est. 1.5 hrs.)							
7.	New Formica countertop							

Continued on next page.

EXHIBIT 5-3

Example of a Scope Sheet

Property Loss Worksheet

Page No. 2

Preliminary Estimate 10/19/0X (Date)

Final Estimate ______ (Date)

M. Boyer (Adjuster)

Claim No. 524 BL 101

Insured J. Smith

Claimant Insured

1 Item	2 Description	3 Quantity	4 Units Age	5 Unit price Orig. cost	6 Cost Repl. cost	7 Deprec.	8 A.C.V.	9 Loss & Damage
8.	Drywall (above range) 5' × 10' = 50 sq. ft. Tape and texture (splatter finish)							
9.	Painting Kitchen — wash and paint (14' × 8') × 2 = 224 SF (20' × 8') × 2 = 320 SF 1 coat high gloss latex 2 coats on new cabinets Living Room — wash and paint 1 coat flat latex (20' × 8') × 2 = 320 SF (24' × 8') × 2 = 384 SF Entrance Hall (4' × 8') = 32 SF (14' × 8') × 2 = 224 SF							
10.	Shampoo carpets LR and halls (200 sq. yds.)							
11.	Clean vinyl tile in kitchen (280 SF)							
12.	Clean furniture (per estimate)							
13.	Contractor overhead & profit (OH/P 15% or 20%)							

whether and to what extent coverage should apply, that is, whether the claim is payable and how much should be paid. In subrogation cases, experts are consulted to ascertain and establish facts that would show whether the insurer has the right to seek reimbursement from a third party for the amount paid on the loss. Several types of experts can be used in connection with the adjustment of property losses. They include origin and cause experts, private investigators, accountants, restoration specialists, salvors, attorneys, engineers, architects, appraisers, and contractors. Any conflicts of interest among the adjuster, the insured, and any experts should be avoided.

Origin and Cause Experts

Origin and cause experts have an extensive background in fire science and arson investigation. They determine whether a fire was accidental or intentionally started and the identity of the person, organization, or entity that might have been responsible for the fire. The origin and cause expert's work includes investigating the scene at which the loss occurred and sometimes contacting witnesses. Private investigators and engineers can assist origin and cause experts when such expertise is required.

Origin and cause experts
Experts who independently determine how and where a fire began.

Private Investigators

Private investigators are typically employed when insurance fraud is suspected. They can also be used in connection with other intensive investigations. In most states, they must be licensed. They have the knowledge and skills required to obtain information for their clients from witnesses, public records, and law enforcement agencies. Insurers can use the information gathered by private investigators to reach coverage decisions, determine whether insurance fraud is being attempted, and document potential subrogation. Private investigators can work with origin and cause experts to establish facts that would determine whether an insured or someone at the insured's direction is guilty of arson. In personal property losses, private investigators can contact witnesses and retailers to confirm ownership. Generally, private investigators can be employed to ascertain the facts related to the insurance or the claim.

Accountants

Adjusters should have some knowledge of accounting, especially in connection with the handling of business losses. Nevertheless, accountants specializing in claims and legal matters are occasionally needed to resolve financial issues related to property claims. Claim accountants are often used to verify the extent of business merchandise or stock losses as well as business interruption losses. An accountant can help resolve cases in which the insured might have overstated or exaggerated the amount of a loss in the claim. Accountants can also determine the financial condition of the insured's business and whether the insured actually had the funds to purchase the property that was purportedly stolen or destroyed. For example, an insured might claim that a large amount of property was purchased within six months to a year before the date of loss. An accountant, using books and records and sometimes testimony obtained through an examination under oath (EUO), can determine whether the insured had the funds to purchase the items claimed to have been destroyed or stolen.

Restoration Specialists

Restoration specialists are firms specializing in cleaning structures, equipment, stock, merchandise, and personal property following a loss caused by fire, smoke, water, windstorm, or another peril. Property loss adjusters usually consult restoration specialists immediately after receiving the initial report so that steps can be taken to limit the amount of damage and protect the property from further damage. Household goods, personal property, merchandise, stock, and equipment are often moved to a restoration firm's plant or warehouse for further processing and cleaning. The removal of such items also facilitates the structure's cleaning, repair, and reconstruction. Restoration specialists can remove, clean, and dry carpets that have been damaged by smoke or water; they also clean and prepare interior walls and floors for painting and other repair work.

Salvors

Salvors
Specialists who separate damaged merchandise from undamaged merchandise, prepare inventories of damaged and destroyed property, and establish values of damaged or destroyed business property.

Salvors are mainly used in connection with business losses to separate damaged from undamaged merchandise, supplies, and equipment; to prepare inventories of damaged and destroyed property; and to establish values of damaged or destroyed business property. They can also inventory the entire stock of merchandise or supplies so that the insurer can determine whether a coinsurance penalty should apply or to confirm that the claimed amount of loss (by theft or burglary, for example) is accurate. Salvors are also employed to sell salvage or, by arrangement, to purchase salvage. Salvors are rarely used on homeowners claims except when the amount of loss is large.

Attorneys

Attorneys commonly provide advice and counsel to insurers on coverage issues and on investigations of complex claims. Insurers often retain attorneys to help direct investigations. They might conduct an investigation by formally requesting the insured's books and records and by conducting EUOs when (1) coverage might be in question, (2) the amount of loss payable is in dispute, or (3) insurance fraud is suspected. Attorneys provide accountants with copies of books and financial records as well as transcripts of testimony given during an EUO so that coverage and settlement disputes can be resolved. Attorneys also offer legal opinions and make recommendations to insurers regarding a claim's ultimate disposition. Of course, attorneys can also file suit on the behalf of the insurer to pursue subrogation, to resolve coverage disputes through declaratory relief actions, and to defend insurers against suits by insureds.

Engineers

Electrical engineers, mechanical engineers, and other engineers are occasionally needed to resolve issues related to the cause of loss. However, they are usually employed to document for subrogation purposes whether a third party or manufacturer is responsible for a fire or another cause of loss. An electrical engineer, for example, is sometimes used along with an origin and cause expert to establish whether a fire was accidental or whether it was caused by a defective or malfunctioning electrical device.

Architects

Architects are sometimes needed to draw plans and provide specifications for partial and complete reconstruction of structures. Plans are needed so that contractors can calculate accurate estimates or bids and can obtain remodeling or building permits. Architects can also be consulted to formulate engineering specifications for special equipment.

Appraisers

Appraisers are needed to establish the value of personal property, merchandise, equipment, and real property for settlement or for resolving disputes about the amount of loss. An appraiser can be anyone who has specialized knowledge of the kinds of property involved and their values. Some might be certified as appraisers in certain fields by professional organizations, such as the International Society of Appraisers. Others, such as real estate appraisers, are usually licensed by the state in which they do business. In connection with fire and windstorm claims, real estate appraisers can establish structures' actual cash value (usually the market value).

Contractors

Building contractors are often asked, sometimes on an emergency basis, to repair structures damaged by fire, water, windstorm, and other covered perils. However, in a dispute over the amount payable, building contractors can also act as appraisers.

Conflicts of Interest

Conflicts of interest can arise between an expert, an adjuster, and/or an insured whenever anyone receives gratuities or when a relationship is so close that there is an appearance of impropriety. When an appraiser (the expert) is needed to establish the amount recoverable in connection with a fire loss, that appraiser, whether a contractor or an antique dealer, should be impartial. The word "impartial" means that any appraiser must not be closely related to, a friend of, or economically dependent on, the insurer, insured, or adjuster. If the appraiser is not impartial and a conflict of interest exists, the appraisal award might not be binding and might be voided by either party unless the other party agrees to waive any objection before the proceedings. Therefore, the adjuster must choose experts carefully and keep the relationship on a professional level.

Subrogation

Subrogation
The process by which an insurer recovers payment from a negligent third party who caused a property or liability loss that the insurer has paid to, or on behalf of, an insured.

An insurer that pays a covered claim has the right, to the extent of the payment, to seek reimbursement and recover the amount paid from a third party who is legally liable for the loss or damage. This is called the right of **subrogation**. The insurer is said to be subrogated to the rights of the insured who is the party who would normally have the right to receive payment for damages. Subrogation is the substitution of one person or entity for another in a claim.

Subrogation rights are established by insurance policies and by law. Included in insurance policies are provisions regarding (1) the insured's role in the subrogation, (2) the waiver of subrogation, and (3) the subrogation's amount. The insurer's right to subrogation is established and expressed in the policy under a condition entitled "Transfer Of Rights Of Recovery Against Others To Us." This condition is often referred to as the subrogation clause. This clause or provision is listed in the conditions of all property insurance policies. For example, the transfer of rights of recovery clause of the ISO commercial property conditions reads as follows:

> If any person or organization to or for whom we make payment under this Coverage Part has rights to recover damages from another, those rights are transferred to us to the extent of our payment. That person or organization must do everything necessary to secure our rights and must do nothing after loss to impair them. But you may waive your rights against another party in writing:
>
> 1. Prior to a loss to your Covered Property or Covered Income.
> 2. After a loss to your Covered Property or Covered Income only if, at time of loss, that party is one of the following:
>   a. Someone insured by this insurance;
>   b. A business firm;
>   (1) Owned or controlled by you; or,
>   (2) That owns or controls you; or
>   c. Your tenant.
>
>   This will not restrict your insurance.[1]

Additionally, the insurer has a right of subrogation implied in law regardless of whether the policy expresses such a provision.

Insured's Role in Subrogation

Most subrogation clauses require the insured to cooperate with the insurer by executing assignment of rights to the insurer, also known as a subrogation agreement. The sworn statement in proof of loss often contains the subrogation agreement, or assignment. Additionally, the subrogation agreement typically requires the insured to give testimony and appear in court, when necessary, so that the insurer can establish the legal basis to recover.

An insured might breach the subrogation condition by impairing or interfering with the insurer's right of subrogation, by failing to cooperate in preserving evidence, by giving or failing to give testimony, or by releasing the responsible party from any liability following the loss. In case of a breach by the insured, the insurer would have a right to collect damages from the insured in the amount that would have been recoverable from the responsible third party.

Some policies permit the insured to waive rights of recovery *before a loss.* In those cases, the insurer waives its right of subrogation. Lease agreements between landlords and tenants typically contain waivers of liability or subrogation. Construction contracts often contain waivers of subrogation clauses in them. The insured might also release a third party before a loss in connection with bailment situations. For example, if the insured has placed personal property in the custody of other parties as a condition of the bailment, the insured might be required to waive the claim or release liability. If the insurer has not permitted a release of liability by the insured before a loss and the insured has executed a release or waiver before a loss, the insurer will not be liable for the loss claimed under the policy. It is very important for the adjuster to determine early in the loss adjustment process whether waivers of subrogation have been granted.

Amount of Subrogation

The insurer has the right to receive only the amount that it has paid. The insurer would have no right of recovery for losses that the insured absorbs because of lack of coverage, exclusions, or limitations of coverage under the policy. Thus, both the insurer and insured might have rights to recover damages against a responsible third party or parties. When insureds absorb only a deductible amount, insurers commonly pursue recovery of that deductible amount on their behalf.

The decision to pursue subrogation usually includes consideration of the cost involved and the likelihood of success. This is especially true if litigation is needed to pursue subrogation. Therefore, there may be times when the insurer decides that pursuing subrogation is not cost-effective. However, the insurer's decision does not preclude the insured from pursuing a third party for the unpaid portions of his or her claim.

Typical Claim Situations

Property loss adjusters encounter many situations in daily claim handling in which a third party is legally liable for damages, such as the following:

- Negligent operation or malfunctioning of equipment, such as automobiles, trucks, heavy equipment, and airplanes
- Fire, explosion, and water losses caused by the negligence of tenants occupying apartments or business complexes
- Fire, explosion, and water losses caused by construction workers at a building site or adjacent to a structure

- Losses resulting from poor workmanship of contractors or subcontractors that occur after work has been completed, such as malfunctioning sprinklers or alarms
- Losses caused by defective or poorly designed products such as electrical appliances
- Water and fire losses caused by owners or landlords failing to maintain plumbing and heating systems
- Losses caused by a government entity's failure to properly maintain public works, such as sewer and water systems
- Losses caused by a utility company's negligent installation of, or failure to maintain, gas and electrical lines

All of these situations have the potential for subrogation. The likelihood of success depends on the thoroughness of the claim investigation and the existence of contract provisions that might negate the pursuit of subrogation.

Preservation of Evidence

During the initial investigation into the cause of a loss, the adjuster should be mindful of potential avenues of subrogation. After a potentially responsible third party is identified, the adjuster should investigate this part of the loss at the same time that the insured's loss is being investigated. This ensures that evidence will not be discarded or destroyed.

Preserving evidence for use in subrogation proceedings and subsequent litigation is an important aspect of claim investigation. Without the physical evidence of the cause of the loss, the chances of successfully pursuing a subrogation claim against a third party are significantly diminished.[2] An insurer can be denied recovery if evidence is intentionally or negligently lost or destroyed. Similarly, an insurer defending a first-party coverage suit might be found liable if evidence is intentionally or negligently lost or destroyed. This is often referred to as spoliation of evidence. The property owner, the adjuster, and the origin and cause expert share the responsibility for preserving evidence.

Use of Experts and Attorneys in Subrogation

Property loss adjusters must recognize claims situations that have subrogation potential and must take steps to document the right to recovery through the use of experts, whenever warranted. Experts can be employed to gather and preserve evidence, to analyze and report on the cause of loss, and to testify in litigated cases. Any expert retained should have a set protocol for collecting and preserving evidence.

If an expert is not hired, then it will be the adjuster's responsibility to collect and preserve the evidence. It is advisable to get the property owner's permission in writing before taking any evidence from the scene. Photographs or a videotape should be taken of the evidence as it is found. This should document the surrounding area as well. Evidence collected should be clearly marked with the date and time of collection, where it was found, and by whom. Evidence should be stored in a clear container and kept in a locked storage area or compartment. Care should be taken if evidence must be refrigerated or heated. On some losses, many parties will be interested in the evidence. Whenever an adjuster takes possession or relinquishes possession of a piece of evidence, a written receipt should document the transfer of possession, and each party should retain a copy.[3]

After a coverage suit or subrogation action has ended, the evidence may be disposed of as long as no other litigation is pending. If the property owner's permission was given to take the evidence, the owner should be given notice that it will be destroyed. If other litigation is pending, then all interested parties should be advised that the evidence will be disposed of on a specific date and allowed the opportunity to take possession of the evidence. If an interested party requests that the evidence not be destroyed but does not wish to take possession of it, the insurer could recover reasonable storage fees.

In larger losses, attorneys might be enlisted from the start to help coordinate and direct the adjuster, investigators, and experts. After a loss is paid, an attorney can evaluate the evidence that has been gathered and give opinions on which party or parties should be pursued to recover the amount paid. The attorney can also handle the litigation. Many law firms specialize in subrogation; they typically handle cases on a contingent fee basis for a percentage of the recovery, plus expenses.

Intercompany Arbitration

When an individual or another responsible party has liability insurance, the first-party insurer who has paid a loss can present a subrogation claim for payment. In most cases, the liability insurer responds by paying the entire loss or by making an offer to compromise on the claim, depending on how the liability insurer assesses liability. When liability is questioned, arbitration can resolve disputes between the insurers.

Many insurers are members or signatories of the Property Subrogation Arbitration Agreement, which appears in Exhibit 5-4. This agreement was created by Arbitration Forums, Inc., so that insurers would have a means of resolving subrogation matters without resorting to litigation. A local office of Arbitration Forums, Inc., can advise an adjuster whether another company subscribes to this agreement. That agreement is a mandatory arbitration program for certain claims. Member insurers must use arbitration when liability or the amount payable is in dispute. It is not used to resolve coverage issues between insurers. The main benefits of the arbitration program are the savings in litigation expenses and the quick resolution of disputes.

Intercompany arbitration is accomplished by having the arbitrator(s) review the written submissions of the applicant (the party who applied for arbitration) and the respondent (the party who must respond to the applicant's allegations). Although it is possible to present the case in person, it does not often occur that way. Therefore, the claim material presented should be legible and in chronological order. The arbitration file

EXHIBIT 5-4

Property Subrogation Arbitration Rules and Agreement

WHEREAS, it is the object of companies which are now or may hereafter be signatories to arbitrate disputes among themselves, the undersigned hereby accepts and binds itself to the following Articles of Agreement for the arbitration of property damage claims arising from fire and losses other than automobile:

ARTICLE FIRST

Signatory companies are bound to forego litigation and in place thereof submit to arbitration any questions or disputes which may arise from:

(a) any fire subrogation or property damage claim not in excess of $100,000;

(b) any extended coverage subrogation or self-insured additional extended coverage claim not in excess of $100,000;

(c) any additional extended coverage subrogation or self-insured additional extended coverage claim not in excess of $100,000;

(d) any inland marine subrogation or self-insured inland marine claim not in excess of $100,000;

(e) any first party property subrogation or self-insured claim not in excess of $100,000 that is not within the compulsory provisions of other industry inter-company arbitration agreements, except for subrogation or self-insured claims arising from accidents on waters subject to the International Rules of the Road, the United States Inland Rules of the Road, or the Great Lakes and Western Rivers Rules of the Road, provided the accident occurs on a body of water within the geographic limits of one state.

This Article shall not apply to:

(a) any claim for the enforcement of which a lawsuit was instituted prior to, and is pending, at the time this Agreement is signed;

 1

(b) any claim as to which a company asserts a defense of lack of coverage on grounds other than

(1) delayed notice

(2) no notice

(3) noncooperation;

(c) subrogation claims involving policies written under Retrospective Rating Plans, Comprehensive Insurance Rating Plans, or War Risk Rating Plans unless prior written consent is obtained from the companies in interest.

ARTICLE SECOND

Any controversy, including policy coverage and interpretations, between or among signatory companies involving any claim or other matter relating thereto and not included in Article First hereof or which involves amounts in excess of those stated therein may also be submitted to arbitration under this Agreement with the prior consent of the parties.

For matters within Article First, if the law on the issue is in doubt and has not been interpreted by the courts of the jurisdiction, a party to the controversy may petition AF's Board of Directors to authorize the disputing party to proceed through litigation rather than arbitration. The Board's validation will be influenced by effect on the industry through litigation to clarify the law. The decision to waive the mandatory provisions of the Agreement and proceed through litigation will be at the sole discretion of the Board.

ARTICLE THIRD

Arbitration Forums Inc. representing signatory companies is authorized:

(a) to make appropriate rules and regulations for the presentation and determination of controversies under this Agreement;

(b) to select the places where arbitration facilities are to be available, and adopt a policy for the selection and appointment of arbitration panels;

2

Continued on next page.

(c) to prescribe territorial jurisdiction of arbitration panels;

(d) to make appropriate rules and regulations to apportion equitably among arbitrating companies the operating expenses of the arbitration program;

(e) to authorize and approve as signatories to this Agreement such insurance carriers, self-insurers or commercial insureds with large retentions as may be invited to participate in the arbitration program and also to compel the withdrawal of any signatory from the program for failure to conform with the Agreement or the rules and regulations issued thereunder.

ARTICLE FOURTH

Arbitration panels, appointed by AF from among full-time salaried representatives of signatory companies, shall function in the following manner:

(a) Arbitration panel members shall be selected on the basis of their experience and other qualifications. They shall serve without compensation;

(b) No panel member shall serve on a panel hearing a case in which his/her company is directly or indirectly interested, or in which he/she has an interest;

(c) the decision of the majority of an arbitration panel shall be final and binding upon the parties to the controversy without the right of rehearing or appeal.

ARTICLE FIFTH

Any signatory company may withdraw from this Agreement by notice in writing to Arbitration Forums Inc. Such withdrawal will become effective sixty (60) days after receipt of such notice except as to cases then pending before arbitration panels. The effective date of withdrawal as to such pending cases shall be upon final settlement.

Arbitration Forums Web site: http://www.arbfile.org/webapp/pgStatic/content/pgDownloadRules.jsp (15 July 2003).

should be self-explantory, but it is a good practice to highlight or tab specific documents for the arbitrator's benefit. A well-written arbitration statement, outlining the party's contentions, should accompany the file. Under the rules of intercompany arbitration, the decision of the arbitrator(s) is final and binding with no right of rehearing or appeal, except under very limited circumstances, such as lack of jurisdiction.

Reporting

Although property loss adjusters often make oral reports about a claim's status by telephone or in person at the office, most reports are written.

Following the reporting procedures within an adjuster's own organization is crucial. An insurer's reporting requirements, including form samples, format, content, and time for submission, are commonly detailed in the insurer's claim operating and procedures manuals made available to all adjusters. Such manuals establish the standards of performance for adjusters. Because reports are the product of the adjuster's work and are used by the adjuster's supervisor to measure job performance, adjusters must provide clear, concise, and timely reports.

Although reports primarily communicate to and document for the insurer what was done to investigate, adjust, settle, and otherwise resolve a claim, they also document for others, such as state insurance authorities or juries, an insurer's good-faith investigation. An insured's attorney can obtain files from the insurer through discovery in litigation that deals with allegations of improper claim handling or bad faith, so the files must reflect the following:

- Clear, concise, and accurate information
- Timely handling of the claim
- A fair and balanced investigation regarding the interests of the insured and insurer
- The absence of derogatory or inflammatory comments regarding the character of the insured or anyone connected with the claim
- A thorough good-faith investigation

Reports can be as brief as a handwritten memo or very detailed and lengthy, especially when written for larger, more complex claims. The three types of reports used in the investigation phase of the loss adjustment process are (1) preliminary, (2) status (or interim), and (3) summarized (or captioned) reports. These reports usually have attachments such as claim documents, official reports, diagrams, photos, statements, and correspondence.

1. *Preliminary Reports*. Preliminary reports are usually filed within the first twenty-four hours or up to seven days following assignment of the claim, depending on the insurer's reporting requirements. Many insurers provide preprinted, fill-in-the-blank-type forms or electronic templates that adjusters use to acknowledge receipt of the assignment, inform the

insurer about initial activity on the claim, suggest reserves on certain coverages, advise the insurer of coverage questions, and request assistance and guidance from file supervisors as to the handling of coverage questions or any aspect of the claim. Preliminary reports can also include a scope and preliminary estimate of damages. Additionally, the preliminary report can serve as a closing report when claims are small and uncomplicated and the loss has been adjusted and payment has been made.

2. *Status Reports*. Status, or interim, reports inform the insurer of a claim's progress and can be filed periodically, generally every fifteen to thirty days following assignment, depending on a particular insurer's reporting requirements. Their purpose is to keep the insurer advised of the status of an investigation or adjustment, to make reserve change recommendations, and to request assistance and settlement authority when the amount payable exceeds the adjuster's authority. Status reports also confirm that the adjuster is giving appropriate attention to the claim and that the work is progressing in a timely manner.
3. *Summarized Reports*. Summarized, or captioned, reports are typically very detailed narrative reports that follow an established format. They are usually filed within thirty days of the assignment's date. They are generally required whenever a claim must be reviewed by regional or home office claim personnel. Summarized reports might be required when the size of loss and settlement authority exceed the local office's authority. When coverage might be denied, many insurers require regional or home office review and approval. Some insurers require summarized reports on certain types of claims so that the regional or home office can keep abreast of what is happening in certain types of business. Claims involving suspected arson or insurance fraud are typically reported to regional and home office personnel because of their sensitive nature. Regional or home office claim personnel can respond by extending the authority to settle the loss, by giving authority to deny a claim, or by suggesting further investigation or documentation before a decision is made.

   Summarized reports have captioned headings, which usually specify the information indicated in Exhibit 5-5. Exhibit 5-6 shows another format, which is more concise and very effective.

Step 5: Determining Cause of Loss and Extent of Damage

After an adjuster has completed his or her investigation, a decision as to the cause of loss and extent of loss must be made. Using the investigation as a basis for an opinion, the adjuster must communicate to the insured whether the loss was caused by a covered cause of loss and, if it was, how much of the loss is recoverable. Negotiations as to the extent of the loss often occur at this time.

EXHIBIT 5-5

Summarized Claim Report

Insured: ____________________ Date of Report: ____________________

Policy No.: ____________________ Adjustment Firm: ____________________

Date of Loss: ____________________ Adjuster: ____________________

Producer: ____________________

---

1. Assignment Date

Give date notice of loss received and how.
Give date insured first contacted and how (phone or personal).

---

2. Enclosures

List items attached (photos, estimates, fire/police reports, etc.).

---

3. Activity Requested

List special request (expense payments, coverage questions, etc.).

---

4. Suggested Reserves

Suggested reserves should be shown net, by coverage, after any advances.

Show scheduled items separately.

Example:	Cov. A	$22,000
	Cov. C	10,000

---

5. Abstract of Coverage

Give forms applicable and amounts; state deductibles; identify other contributing insurance, if any; identify any limiting clauses.

---

6. Ownership/Encumbrances

List title holder, mortgagee, loss payees, additional named insureds, contract sellers, and liens. Indicate source of information. Also include opinion as to current solvency, cash flow, receipts.

---

7. Location and Cause of Loss

Give date-time-place of loss. State cause as determined by authorities. If an outside expert has been employed, identify that expert and give his or her findings. State the adjuster's opinion.

---

8. Insured/Employee Version of Loss

Give insured's version—indicate if statement was secured. Indicate manager, guards, and service personnel on premises at time of loss.

Continued on next page.

9. Witness's Version of Loss

Give witness's version—indicate if statement(s) secured. Indicate other parties present at time of loss.

10. Scope of Loss/Estimates of Damage

Describe property insured. Detail extent of damage. Cover any problems that might be encountered in reaching a settlement. List estimates received. Has an agreement been reached with the insured as to scope and procedures?

11. Salvage/Subrogation

Identify salvage, and give estimate of worth. Give details on your theory of subrogation and what steps have been taken to protect our interests.

12. Work To Be Done/Forecast of Closing

Itemize work to be done. Give your forecast of closing. Estimate hours needed for completion of each step.

13. Risk

Give your impression of the risk.

14. Remarks

Give comments on assistance of insured or insured's employees in completing investigation. Identify attorney or public adjuster if involved.

DATE OF NEXT REPORT

Step 6: Concluding the Loss Adjustment

When the adjuster has compiled the documentation and all of the adjuster's questions have been answered, the adjuster should assemble the claim and submit it to the insurer for review and for advice as to settlement authority. In many cases, the claim is submitted to the insurer in the form of a statement of loss. This statement is an accounting overview of the adjustment. It is generally a three-column listing that tells the value of the property, the amount of loss to the property, and the amount claimed under the policy. Exhibit 5-7 shows an example of a statement of loss. The statement should clearly indicate what the recommended payment is and why that figure is appropriate. The adjuster should also attach all supporting documents (so that the examiners can see where the figures came from) and should also outline the proposed adjustments in the closing report.

EXHIBIT 5-6

Investigation Report

INSURED:

COVERAGE:

FACTS OF LOSS:

ORIGIN AND CAUSE:

OFFICIAL REPORTS:

COINSURANCE:

EMERGENCY REPAIRS OR ADVANCES:

SCOPE OF LOSS OR EXTENT OF LOSS:

A. Structure

B. Contents, equipment, or merchandise

C. ALE or business income losses

SUGGESTED RESERVES:

RISK ADVICE:

FURTHER HANDLING/WORK TO BE DONE:

Attachments:

EXHIBIT 5-7

Statement of Loss

	Value	Loss	Claim
One-story bowling alley, masonry-constructed building			
Repairs to vandalism damage.			
Remove and replace solid core door w/three lights, framing, and paint to lounge.			
Remove and replace hollow core door and paint to liquor storage room.			
Remove and replace exterior metal double-door set and paint.			
Remove and replace door to manager's office.			
Repair door, frame, and paint to diner area.			
Repair door, frame, and paint to service area.			
Remove and replace door, frame, and paint to storage room.			
Emergency repairs by Argo locksmith			
Safe:			
Repair dial.			
Repair corner of safe.			
Repair cement pier.			
Total loss			
Deductible			
Net claim			
Value, Loss, and Claim			

Closing Reports

Closing, or final, reports are made whenever the adjuster has completed the assignment by claim settlement or denial or whenever the adjuster's claim handling has been discontinued or transferred to another adjuster. Some final reports use preprinted forms that can be simple memoranda. These reports might include recommendations regarding subrogation, advice to the underwriting department, and suggestions or requests for further administrative handling within the office.

Payments

After the claim has been concluded, the adjuster must issue the claim payment. Claim payments are made either by check, draft, or electronic transfer. A **draft** is distinguished from a check by the fact that when it is presented to a bank to be cashed, the bank must verify that it is authorized for payment by the issuing entity before disbursing any funds. A draft is not a problem if the payee is merely trying to deposit the draft. Usually, the funds will not be available immediately. It does cause a problem for a payee who does not have a bank account in which to deposit the draft, because the funds are not immediately available. The timing of claim payments is an important issue. Many states have regulations regarding the time period in which an insurer issues a claim payment. Additionally, the policies themselves have a time frame for payment in them. The BPP states that payment must be issued within thirty days of receipt of a valid proof of loss and agreement with the insured as to the amount or receipt of an appraisal award. The HO-3 has a sixty-day time frame.

Draft
An instrument that must be verified by the issuing entity before funds will be disbursed.

Property loss adjusters are often called on to make advance payments to an insured. These advance payments are usually issued to help the insured make repairs quickly or to resume business operations quickly. On large property losses, advance payments may go directly to a contractor or repair firm on the insured's behalf. When an advance payment is made, the insured should sign an **advance payment receipt** that acknowledges an understanding that the insured will have to pay the advance amount back if the loss is not a covered loss and that the payment is part of the overall loss.

Advance payment receipt
A document that helps keep track of payments made under certain coverages, helps comply with unfair claim practices laws, and clarifies to the insured that the advance payments will be applied against the final claim.

When making any payment, the adjuster must ensure that the proper parties are being paid. Because of the various parties who can have a financial interest in the property in addition to the insured, the adjuster must verify the payee before check issuance. A mortgage or finance company often has a financial interest in the property and appears as a payee in the policy. But not all potential payees are named in the policy. An adjuster must be aware that other parties not named in the policy may have an interest in the claim payment.

When the insured has assigned the policy proceeds to someone else, the adjuster must include that other party as a payee. One example of this is when the insured has retained a public adjuster or an attorney to represent the insured in the claim. The insured might also assign the claim's proceeds to a repair firm so that no delay occurs in the repair of the insured's vehicle or piece of equipment. When an assignment is made, the adjuster must be given notice of the assignment. This notice is usually in writing and supported by a copy of the contract between the parties.

Tax Liens

Before paying a large structural loss, a property loss adjuster must check whether any tax liens are on the property. Some states require that such checking be performed based on a dollar threshold, such as $5,000 for a homeowners loss and $25,000 for a commercial property loss. Also, many insurers' claim-handling guidelines require checking for liens. If an adjuster fails to check for tax liens and makes a payment to the insured, the insurer may be forced to pay the outstanding tax lien as well. This would amount to a duplicate loss payment. Checking for tax liens can usually be accomplished at the local municipal hall or at county offices.

Denial of a Claim

Not every claim is closed by payment. Adjusters are often called on to deny a claim because of lack of coverage or because of a breach of a policy condition. Many insurers have strict guidelines regarding claim denial, often requiring an underwriter and a claim manager to approve the issuance of a denial.

Before denying a claim, the adjuster must have thoroughly investigated the loss, carefully analyzed the coverage, and fairly and objectively evaluated the claim. The insured is usually given the benefit of any doubt or ambiguity in cases of questionable coverage. Internal guidelines for issuing a denial must be followed. If any of these criteria are missing, the adjuster may be found to have acted in bad faith.

Denial Letter's Contents

Upon receiving the authority to deny a claim, the property loss adjuster ensures that the denial letter is prepared on a timely basis. Denial letters are often drafted by attorneys to ensure compliance with that jurisdiction's legal requirements. Generally, a denial letter must state all the known reasons for the denial. Specific policy language should be quoted, and the location of the language in the policy should be cited, such as "p. 2 of 14 of the BPP, A. Coverage, 2. Property not covered, c. Automobiles held for sale." The policy provisions should then be related to the facts of the loss. Insureds who disagree with the denial should be invited to submit additional information that might cause the claim to be reevaluated. A general reservation of rights paragraph is also included in the letter.

Mailing Protocol

The denial letter should always be signed by the adjuster, even if an attorney drafts it. The adjuster who signs the letter is likely to be called as a witness in the event of a coverage lawsuit. Denial letters are usually sent by certified mail, return receipt requested, restricted to the addressee only. It is a good practice to also send the letter by regular mail, marked personal and confidential, in case the certified mail is not claimed. These procedures help ensure that the letter reaches the correct party. They also help insulate the adjuster from any allegation made by the insured that the letter is public defamation.

Reinsurance

Many property risks are subject to reinsurance. Reinsurers assume the financial consequences of a loss otherwise payable by the original insurer. Each insurer has its own reinsurance procedures, by which it flags a policy as being subject to reinsurance. Each insurer also sets a dollar threshold for the amount of the loss that will require notice to the reinsurer. The property loss adjuster needs to recognize when a policy is subject to reinsurance so that the proper notices and reports can be distributed.

Notice to the reinsurer can be given in several ways. Many insurers set a threshold of 50 percent of the retention as the point at which the reinsurer needs to be given notice of a potential claim. The issue of who actually puts the reinsurer on notice can be handled in several different ways. The handling adjuster can put the reinsurer on notice, but most insurers have a reinsurance accounting department that performs this function. Insurers may have a flag on the policy in their underwriting and claim processing systems, which automatically notifies the reinsurance accounting department when a claim over a specified amount is set up. The reinsurance accounting department would then provide notice to the reinsurer.

Reinsurers have the right to participate in a claim's investigation and settlement. The adjuster may have to work with the reinsurer, or the reinsurer may be satisfied with periodic updates from the adjuster. Claim payments and reserve changes often trigger a request for an update on a loss. Because a fiduciary relationship exists between the insurer and the reinsurer, the adjuster must be prepared to share relevant information with the reinsurer.

SUMMARY

The claim adjustment process begins when an insured, or his or her agent or broker, reports a loss to the insurer. The insurer acknowledges receipt of the loss and assigns an adjuster to it. The adjuster verifies coverage, reviews the policy, and contacts the insured to begin the investigation of the loss.

Coverage verification entails determining whether the effective dates of the policy cover the date of loss; determining who is insured under the policy; determining what is insured under the policy; determining what causes of loss are covered; determining what exclusions may apply to the loss; determining how the loss is to be valued; and, finally, determining what limits are contained in the policy.

The initial contact with the insured begins the investigation of the loss. The insured may be represented by a public adjuster. If that is the case, the public adjuster will do much of the work required to present the claim to the insurer. Public adjusters are usually paid a percentage of the amount of the claim settlement. This may lead some public adjusters to inflate the claim in an attempt to generate a higher fee. A property loss adjuster should handle a claim involving a public adjuster no differently than if the adjuster were dealing directly with the insured.

During the initial visit, the adjuster reviews the circumstances of the loss with the insured or the insured's representative and advises the insured of what steps will be necessary to investigate and document the loss. Following this initial contact, the adjuster investigates the loss in depth. The adjuster may take statements of the insured and witnesses, may examine books and records, may photograph or videotape the loss scene, may draw diagrams, and may create a scope of the loss. It may be necessary to call in experts to help determine the cause of the loss or to help quantify the extent of the loss.

During the investigation, the adjuster considers any potential source of subrogation against a third party. The adjuster will need to preserve evidence if it is determined that a responsible third party exists and it is cost-effective to attempt recovery.

During the course of the investigation, the adjuster prepares several reports. These reports serve to inform supervisors and managers about the loss. The preliminary report is usually prepared shortly after the receipt of the loss assignment. Status reports are required to provide updates on the course of the investigation. These status reports can be brief, or they can be detailed summary reports. Other reports may be required if reinsurance is covering the loss.

After the investigation is completed, the adjuster concludes the loss adjustment and issues a final report. The loss can be concluded by payment or by a denial of the claim.

Chapter 6 discusses various causes of loss and what types of investigations are associated with them. Coverage defenses and good-faith investigations are also discussed.

CHAPTER NOTES

1. Commercial Property Conditions, Form CP 00 90 07 88, Copyright, Insurance Services Office, Inc., 1987.
2. Brian Marx, "Preserve the Evidence," *Claims Quarterly*, 20, no. 1 (Feb. 2002), pp. 1–6.
3. E-mail of Michael P. Griffin, training specialist, Liberty Regional Agency Markets, Keene, N.H., November 2001.

Chapter 6

Direct Your Learning

Loss Investigations and Coverage Defenses

After learning the subject matter of this chapter, you should be able to:

- Describe the basic loss investigations for losses caused by:
    - Fire
    - Smoke
    - Lightning
    - Explosion
    - Theft
    - Water damage
- Explain the causes of mold claims and possible ways to handle these losses.
- Describe the physical environment and the loss adjustment environment created by a catastrophe.
- Describe pre- and post-loss adjustment procedures for a catastrophe.
- Explain the purpose and operation of the National Flood Insurance Program (NFIP).
- Explain what types of losses are covered under the NFIP policy.
- Explain loss adjustment procedures under the NFIP.
- Explain how waiver and estoppel can occur and how they can be avoided.
- Explain the bases for bad-faith claims and damages.
- Explain the purpose of an examination under oath (EUO).
- Explain how an EUO should be demanded and conducted.
- Explain how to resolve various problems that arise with an EUO.

OUTLINE

Develop Your Perspective

What are the main topics covered in the chapter?

This chapter discusses the basic investigations for various causes of loss. These discussions are a framework for the loss investigation. Each investigation dictates what actions are necessary to complete the investigation. This chapter also discusses coverage defenses and good-faith investigations, including the use of an examination under oath (EUO).

Examine a property claim in which the cause of loss is fire.

- What investigation was done?
- What experts were used?

Why is it important to know these topics?

Each claim dictates how much or how little investigation is necessary to make a decision on coverage and amount of the loss. Adjusters must perform these investigations in a good-faith manner. Having an outline to help guide an investigation will show that the adjuster has considered many possibilities in attempting to resolve the claim in good faith.

How can you use this information?

When adjusters handle a property loss, this information can suggest a course of action to take in an investigation. It can serve as a reminder of what a good-faith investigation entails. It can also promote discussion with defense counsel on coverage defenses and the use of an EUO.

Chapter 6

Loss Investigations and Coverage Defenses

Property loss adjusters encounter a wide variety of loss types in their work. Although every loss investigation follows the same basic steps, different types of losses require different types of investigation. This chapter provides guidance as to the areas of investigation that an adjuster can pursue. Specifically, the chapter discusses the basic investigations for cases involving fire, smoke, lightning, explosion, theft, water damage, and mold. Catastrophe loss adjusting and losses covered by the National Flood Insurance Program (NFIP) are also included. The chapter concludes with a discussion of coverage defenses and the use of an examination under oath (EUO) as an investigative aid.

FIRE LOSSES

Fire losses can be as simple as a small grease fire on a kitchen stove and as complex as a multi-alarm arson fire in a warehouse. Regardless of the extent of the loss, the adjuster must be able to articulate where the fire originated (origin) and what caused the fire (cause). The adjuster might need an origin and cause expert's services to determine the answers. Sometimes, witness statements suffice to determine origin and cause. Local fire officials issue origin and cause reports, and these might be sufficient. If it is suspected that accelerants were used, then obtaining the services of a chemical analysis expert may be necessary. If an appliance such as a coffee maker or toaster is identified as the source, the appliance should be sent to a testing lab. The adjuster must exercise good judgment as to how extensive (and costly) the origin and cause investigation must be to properly document the claim file. Exhibit 6-1 outlines the elements of an origin and cause report.

Fire losses can require photos, video, and diagrams. Good judgment will dictate the quantity and quality of such materials to support the claims. In property loss adjusting, a picture really can be more compelling than a thousand words.

Every fire loss requires a list of the damaged areas or scope. An adjuster can obtain a scope and estimate in several ways. The adjuster can go to the loss and prepare them. An independent adjuster can be dispatched to perform this task. For a simple homeowners claim, the insured might be permitted to supply the adjuster with estimates.

EXHIBIT 6-1

WHAT IS A GOOD ORIGIN AND CAUSE REPORT?

Taken from a presentation to the New Hampshire Adjusters Association by Stephen W. Houghton

While the focus of this presentation is on fire investigation reports, most of the principles stated here should apply in general to any report on cause.

GROUND RULE

Before beginning, it is necessary to review a basic ground rule that can get overlooked. This is an investigation being done for you so you are the "boss." Tell your expert what you want done and be sure he or she understands your needs. If you don't, you should not be surprised if you don't get what you expected. Most technical experts do not read minds. This is especially true if you have a budget in mind. It is extremely difficult to adhere to financial needs that are never stated. If the expert can't do the job for what you want to spend, you have two choices; find a new expert or change what you want him or her to accomplish. Remember the expert is working for you—you owe it to yourself and to the expert to establish your needs from the beginning.

WHO IS IT FOR?

As you read the report you should keep in mind whom the report is finally intended for. Who is the most important person who will read the report? The obvious answer is the potential members of the jury whether or not the file ends in litigation. If the report shows that the expert, and therefore your position, is ready for trial, the probability that you will end up there is diminished a great deal.

Expect that this report will have to stand up to scrutiny by opposing experts. It may also have to stand up to changes in testimony since fact witnesses' memories often play tricks as the years go by. There is also the possibility that some of the physical evidence gathered in support of the opinion in the report may be inadmissible in court. In short, the report should not hinge on any one element in the investigation but should be supported by all of the facts as they are known. That means you do not dismiss the observations of the fact witnesses simply because they don't fit your theory. If you do dismiss them, have good solid reasons for doing so or expect the opposing expert to throw them in your face.

FOUR ELEMENTS

Fire investigation reports should have four elements: 1) they should document the damage patterns; 2) they should reconstruct the scene; 3) they should eliminate all other sources of ignition; and 4) they should show the mechanism of ignition clearly.

DOCUMENT: This is usually done with photographs, videotape and a short narrative. One thing to check here is that the photographs match their captions and/or the descriptions in the narrative. Photographs should show conditions before the scene is disturbed as well as how the investigator put things together if they were able to put things together. There should also be references to any evidence taken from the scene.

RECONSTRUCT: Photographs and sketches are the most useful tools for preserving scene reconstructions. A narrative describing the scene before the fire accomplishes the same end. The important thing is that there is justification for identifying the area and point of origin and the probable cause of the fire.

ELIMINATE: This element is sometimes overlooked as unimportant. Our experience has shown that in origin and cause investigations, if other ignition sources are soundly and positively ruled out, the probability of an opposing opinion is reduced. It is difficult to dissent if there is no room for dissension.

DEMONSTRATE: One of the greatest keys to success is the clear demonstration of the mechanism of ignition. To demonstrate clearly requires an explanation of how the offending unit that caused the fire is supposed to work. It is then necessary to identify what the malfunction was and how that malfunction led to the fire. In other words, it is not enough to say "the compressor did it." An effort should be made to explain how the compressor normally works, then what part of the compressor failed and finally, how that failed part generated the heat that caused the fire. An explanation of how the fire spread from the unit to the surrounding area is also a part of this element.

KEEP IT SIMPLE

This is possibly the most important rule and it defines the adjuster's or attorney's most important role in assuring their company has a good report with which to work. Your ability to understand the reasoning in the report is critical. Your familiarity with the subject of the report is probably many times the understanding of the people who may be sitting on the jury. If you are confused by the report, won't they be also?

Often, an expert who is not sure of his or her opinion makes a report vague or complicates things with jargon and technical language. If you think you are getting the runaround, you may be right. Ask your expert to explain and, if necessary, to rewrite the report. It is your report, and you are paying for it.

Read the report, evaluate it, and be sure it meets your expectations. If it does not, find out why not. It may make the difference between recovery and simply adding expert fees to the loss.

Commercial fire losses provide certain challenges that homeowners fire losses do not. A commercial fire might produce hazardous material that requires the services of special containment companies to clean up. There may be stock that can be dried and cleaned (requiring a restoration company's expertise) and then sold as salvage (requiring a salvor's services). Repackaging and relabeling might be an issue. If a loss occurs to stock and inventory, it may be necessary to employ an accountant, who will review the business's books and records to verify the loss amount.

Businesses suffering a loss want to resume operations quickly, so the adjuster should be prepared to discuss options for relocating, retooling, and obtaining products from other sources to meet delivery deadlines.

Extensive fire losses may require the services of architects, engineers, general contractors, and many subcontractors if the building is to be repaired or replaced. Also, zoning issues, permit issues, tax issues, and increased costs stemming from ordinances or laws will arise.

A homeowners fire loss can be even more challenging to handle because of the complex and sensitive issues involved in the loss of a home and the insured's personal possessions. Collectibles, fine arts, and items with sentimental value can be difficult to adjust. It may be necessary for the adjuster to employ an appraiser to get appropriate values for some of these items. Moreover, specialists who restore artwork, photos, and oriental rugs can be used to restore property to pre-loss condition. If items cannot be restored, replacement services can assist the adjuster in replacing contents at a reasonable cost.

A family displaced from its home because of a fire needs temporary housing. The adjuster should know what is available and appropriate under the circumstances. Temporary housing services can assist the adjuster. Relocating dogs, cats, birds, and even horses as part of the loss might also be necessary. Understanding the family's lifestyle is key to managing this portion of the loss.

SMOKE LOSSES

In small fires, smoke can cause more damage than the fire itself. The type of smoke resulting from a fire depends on the fire's intensity, the material consumed in the fire, and the amount of oxygen consumed. Heavy smoke develops when burning material is shut off from an adequate supply of oxygen, thus preventing complete combustion.

Two types of smoke cause damage: (1) hot smoke and (2) cold smoke. Hot smoke is usually found closer to the fire's source and can penetrate the surfaces it contacts. Smoke cools as it moves away from the fire—this cold smoke rests upon, rather than penetrates, the surfaces it contacts. Hot smoke damage is more severe than cold smoke damage.

Hot smoke can deeply stain masonry. For example, ceramic tile has hairline cracks that are not readily visible but that appear when exposed to hot smoke. Once exposed to hot smoke, those cracks cannot usually be cleaned. An appearance allowance can be made when the tile or grout cannot be cleaned to the insured's satisfaction, or the tile might have to be replaced. Stonework, brick, and cement surfaces are also difficult to clean after exposure to hot smoke, but they can sometimes be cleaned with steam or boric acid.

Cold smoke is easier to remove from surfaces, but it can still extensively damage such items as wallpaper, drapes, and carpeting. Both cold and hot smoke residue should be removed from aluminum windows, metal fixtures, and ceramic kitchen and bathroom fixtures as soon as possible because the residue is usually acidic and can eat into these surfaces.

Metal and ceramic fixtures should be test-cleaned before the insurer and the insured reach an agreement for replacing all items in the smoke-damaged area. Cleaning alone might be sufficient. Cold smoke can travel some distance from the source of the fire before it reaches the surface on which it will settle, and this cold smoke comes to rest in the form of soot. Vacuuming, brushing, or washing the area can often remove it. Cold smoke does not usually leave a pungent odor, so the damaged area can be effectively cleaned.

Fire restoration companies specialize in working with insurance companies and adjusters to perform early cleaning and prevent further damage caused by hot and cold smoke. All fire loss adjusters should keep a list of fire restoration companies so that they can call such a company immediately after notification of a fire loss.

LIGHTNING LOSSES

A bolt of lightning is a release of electrical charges that have built up inside a cloud. A bolt of lightning is actually several strokes (from five to twenty-five) strung together. A lightning strike can carry the equivalent of 2.9 billion kilowatts of power (which is roughly six times the electrical generating capacity of the United States). Because of their height, the most frequent targets of lightning are roofs, chimneys, church steeples, power lines, antennas, and trees. Approximately 30,000 homes and buildings are struck every year in the United States.[1]

Direct strikes by lightning can have an explosive effect or start a fire. But direct strikes are not the only way that lightning can reach property and cause damage. If a lightning strike occurs near a utility line, an induced surge or spike of voltage will result. This surge can dissipate before it reaches a building, or it can be strong enough to overcome the safety devices on the power line and enter a building through the electric or phone service lines. The intense voltage can melt wiring and circuitry.[2]

The loss adjuster's challenge in handling a lightning loss is to determine that the damage was caused by lightning and not some other type of failure. The first step is to confirm that lightning occurred in the area at the time of the loss. The National Weather Service, lightning reporting services, local TV stations, and power companies are all good sources for this information.

Physically inspecting the damage is another means of verifying a lightning loss, but this is useful only up to a point. Certainly an adjuster can see damage on a building or to an appliance's exterior. Evidence of burning or scorching will appear on wood and siding. Block walls and chimneys can be split or shattered. Roof flashing, gutters, and siding may be twisted or melted. Roofing nails may have popped up. Stucco may explode. Light bulbs can shatter or burn out. Several fuses can blow or trip breakers. Wall switches and wall outlets will have evidence of arcing. If a ground surge occurs (when the lightning travels along the ground surface or just below it), a burrow will appear along the ground.

However, adjusters should not attempt inspections such as examining electrical products' internal workings. Such inspections should be left to competent repair people or consultants. Because repair personnel are aware that lightning is a covered cause of loss, they will often state lightning as the cause whether it is or not. One way to combat such a practice is to use an affidavit of lightning damage. This is a notarized statement from the repairperson. The fact that this statement is notarized helps to ensure the statement's veracity.

Because, at times, an affidavit is not enough, the adjuster should be aware that lightning destroys electrical equipment and its components in an expected order. It does not damage parts such as pipes or rotors. It damages more fragile parts before the more sturdy components. So if it is alleged that lightning damaged an electric dryer, for example, the repairer should state that there is damage to the timer (which has the smallest gauge wire) and not just damage to the heating coils (which have the heaviest). Similarly, the picture tube of a TV is one of its strongest components and is very far downstream in the TV set's electrical path. Therefore, if the picture tube is the only component damaged, it is unlikely that the cause is lightning.

Adjuster Tips

- Telephone systems are modular, so lightning damage is usually limited to the initial circuit board.
- Computer systems usually sustain damage only to the first and second components in the series. If the modem and the motherboard are damaged, the disc drive and monitor should be unaffected.
- Well water pumps are commonly claimed to be damaged by lightning. Barring a direct strike, the only damage to a pump should be the motor, not the entire pump.
- Air conditioning units, unless hit by a direct strike, usually suffer damage only to the condenser and minor electrical components.
- Burglar and fire alarm systems usually sustain damage only to a circuit board, not to the detectors, control boxes, and other parts.[3]

EXPLOSION LOSSES

Most explosion losses show evidence of shattered glass, broken or displaced masonry, splintered timbers, and widely scattered debris. However, an adjuster cannot always deduce from the evidence that an explosion has occurred. Such cases might raise the following questions:

1. Does evidence of sudden and rapid combustion or another similar process exist? (Not all instances of combustion by which other property is ignited are considered an explosion. The suddenness and rapidity of the process are important.)
2. Did a violent expansion of the air occur?
3. Was loud noise reported along with the occurrence?
4. Did a sudden and violent outbreak of physical forces occur?
5. Did a sudden or violent bursting or a breaking up from an internal force occur?

Determining the type and cause of an explosion can be difficult at times, and adjusters must often arrive at a logical conclusion by using the process of elimination. Adjusters should also consider several related questions: Were any explosive materials normally used or housed in the building? Where? In what kind of containers were they kept? What safety precautions were taken in using and storing these materials? What are the chances that the containers might have accidentally been broken and materials accidentally spilled or that fumes accidentally escaped?

Explosion Versus Cracking

Claims are often submitted under the explosion peril when construction activity is nearby and explosives are being used. Although the alleged blasting damage can include several items, the principal complaint is about cracked plastering.

When construction and blasting are performed near a residential area, the activity can annoy residents and become a topic of neighborhood conversation. Someone might suffer actual plaster damage as a result of the blasting, and word of it might spread. Then those living near the site of the damage might examine their plastered walls and ceilings, looking for cracks. Many of them are likely to find some plaster cracks because, regardless of nearby construction, few buildings are free of such cracks. However, many of those cracks result from normal shrinkage or expansion of building materials, completely unrelated to any blasting explosions.

Another source of plaster damage is the heavily loaded vehicles on a street or highway close to a building. Such trucks produce greater vibrations in the earth and shock waves to nearby houses than do blasting operations at reasonable distances from the house.

Adjusters must distinguish the results of explosion and cracking from other sources. Newly occurring cracks should look fresh and be free of dust and dirt. The adjuster investigating these claims should also check with the party conducting the blasting for seismic information. Those who do blasting work should know the likelihood of damage at various distances from a blast.

THEFT LOSSES

Theft is the taking of personal property from its rightful owner, without the owner's consent, with the intent to deprive the owner of its value. This broad definition encompasses burglary, robbery, fraud, and deception. Regardless of the type of theft, loss adjusters take certain actions to investigate a theft claim.

First, the adjuster ascertains whether theft is covered under the policy; then the adjuster determines whether any policy limitations apply. The adjuster confirms who owns the property and who has an insurable interest in the property. Depending upon his or her company's claim guidelines, the adjuster takes statements from the parties involved and from any witnesses. The adjuster obtains a police report of the incident. If the loss or security report concerns theft of an auto, a boat, or mobile equipment, the adjuster reports it to the appropriate index bureau, such as following:

- National Insurance Crime Bureau (NICB)
- Insurance Services Office, Inc., (ISO) Claim Search®, which encompasses the Marine Index Bureau (MIB), the Property Insurance Loss Register (PILR), and the Central Index Bureau (CIB) used for bodily injury claims.
- National Equipment Register (NER), for contractors' equipment
- Art Loss Register (ALR), for works of art

Theft claims often leave physical evidence to support them. The adjuster should confirm signs of forced entry, disabled or malfunctioning alarm systems, and—for example—even dust rings or scratch marks on the surface of the cabinet where a stolen TV once stood. If evidence of a malfunctioning or nonfunctioning alarm exists, the adjuster must investigate those circumstances. Did someone forget to set the alarm? Was the alarm broken, and if so, for how long? Did the alarm have a maintenance contract? Had the alarm been recently serviced? Was the alarm installed properly? Thinking along these lines will ensure that subrogation possibilities and potential fraud indicators are uncovered.

Documenting a Theft Claim

To document a theft loss as part of a claim investigation, an adjuster might request the insured to prepare an affidavit of theft, a proof of loss, or an inventory. Bills, receipts, credit card statements, warranties, instruction manuals, books and records, photos, or any other documents that tend to prove ownership and value should support the inventory. The best type of document is the original bill or receipt. The least credible is a photocopy of such a document. If the retailer makes up a duplicate receipt for the insured, a phone call to the retailer can verify the information supplied on the duplicate receipt.

Finally, with theft claims, there is always the possibility that the stolen property might be recovered. The adjuster should remember to place the investigating law enforcement agency on notice of the payment of the claim so that the insurer will be notified if recovery occurs. This notice will also be useful if an arrest and a conviction occur, because the court can order restitution as part of the penalty. It is also a good practice to remind the insured to contact the insurer if recovery occurs because the police might fail to do so. Also, the adjuster should recall that both homeowners forms and the Building and Personal Property Coverage Form (BPP) have provisions regarding recovered property.

One final word of caution regarding theft claims. They are, by far, the easiest to inflate or fabricate. So while the adjuster should be empathetic, he or she should also be skeptical when dealing with theft losses. For example, an adjuster should wonder whether all of the items that the insured claims were stolen from the trunk of his or her car could have actually fit in it. If the circumstances of the loss are questionable, the adjuster should investigate further and even enlist the assistance of the insurer's special investigations unit to confirm or deny suspicions.

WATER DAMAGE LOSSES

Regardless of water damage's cause, the key to successfully adjusting a covered water damage loss is speed. Whether it is a leaking shower pan in someone's home, a burst water pipe flooding a basement, sprinklers saturating the contents of a retail clothing store, or the roof torn off a warehouse during a hurricane, the faster the water is stopped from flowing and the earlier the drying process is begun, the better. So an adjuster should be familiar with what water damage is and is not covered under the policy. The adjuster must to be able to dispatch contractors and restoration companies to the scene of covered losses to mitigate the damages.

If a hurricane has torn a hole in a roof and rain is coming in, finding the source of the water is easy. Finding the source when a water stain is noticed in the middle of the living room ceiling, for example, is not as easy. Water does not necessarily travel in a straight line, so finding a leak within walls and ceilings can be difficult. Visual inspection will show only the result of a leak, be it a water stain, a puddle, or mold growth. It is usually necessary to do some tear-out before the source of the leak can be found. This is why both the HO-3 and BPP provide coverage for the cost of tearing out and replacing of a part of a building or structure when necessary to repair a leaking system or appliance.

MOLD LOSSES

Mold is one of the possible byproducts of water damage. The proper handling of, and communication about, mold damage claims are growing challenges that require property loss adjusters' special attention.

Despite the fact that most mold does not cause serious problems, mold claims are having a significant effect on the insurance industry. Both the volume of mold claims reported to insurers and the bad-faith verdicts for improperly adjusted water damage claims involving mold have significantly cost the insurance industry in both dollars and bad publicity. In 2001, a Texas jury leveled a $32.1 million bad-faith award (which was substantially reduced on appeal) against an insurer in a case that has come to be known as the "Ballard Case" (Ballard, et al., v. Fire Insurance Exchange, et al., No. 99-05252, 345th Judicial District Court, Travis County, Texas). The bad-faith lawsuit was brought against the insurer for the wrongful denial of the water damage claim and for failing to notify the Ballards that a form of toxic mold had been discovered in their house.

Not all molds are harmful. Some are actually useful, such as those in penicillin and blue cheese. Humans have coexisted with various types of mold for many years with little or no serious effects. Understanding what causes mold to grow, what damage mold can cause, and how to remediate or clean up mold helps a property loss adjuster to correctly handle losses involving mold.

What Causes Mold Growth?

Molds are a group of non-green plants that live by feeding on other organisms. They grow from spores and reproduce on a wide variety of natural and synthetic surfaces. Mold spores and particles continually drift through indoor and outdoor air. When the spores land on damp surfaces, they begin to grow by digesting the surface material, gradually destroying it. Mold spores can go dormant for many years until the conditions again support growth and reproduction.[4] While mold colonies can exist only on damp surfaces, they can extend a short distance through dry materials in search of moisture and digestible materials. When conditions are favorable, wet drywall can be covered with millions of spores per square inch within a week or two.

Clean water
Water that comes from pipes, sinks, or bathtubs, or that leaks through a broken window or roof.

Gray water
Water that comes from a dishwasher rinse cycle, a washing machine, a toilet, an aquarium, or a stagnant pool of seawater.

Black water
Water that is filled with bacteria; sources include sewage, seawater, and water that has flowed over organic materials.

Water is the essential ingredient needed to grow mold. There are three types of water found on residential and commercial properties: (1) clean, (2) gray, and (3) black. **Clean water** escapes from sources such as broken or leaking pipes, from an overflowing sink or tub, and from a leaky roof or window. Thoroughly drying these areas within forty-eight hours helps eliminate the risk of mold. Exhibit 6-2 offers specific cleaning recommendations for clean-water saturation as provided by the United States Environmental Protection Agency (EPA).

Gray water sources can include dishwasher, washing machine, or toilet overflow; broken aquariums; leaking waterbeds; and stagnant seawater. The gray color results from food, dirt, or other particles in the water. These particles contain high levels of bacteria that offer food for mold growth. Cleanup of gray water requires drying and the use of disinfectant cleaners to avoid mold growth. Gray water that sits for more than seventy-two hours can become black water. **Black water** sources include sewage, seawater, and water that has flowed over organic materials, where it collects numerous contaminants. Bacteria thrive in black water and can cause illness in people exposed to it.[5] Professional remediation is usually necessary for black water damage.

Physical Damage to Property

Property damage from mold claims can range from minor to extensive. Mold can collect on the surface of walls and look like an accumulation of black dirt. Such accumulation can usually be cleaned with disinfectant cleaner, but this will not remove the spores. This seemingly harmless condition could provide telltale signs of mold growth between the walls. Mold decay of a building's structural components can require that the building be condemned and demolished.

What Loss Exposures Can Result in Mold Damage?

Mold problems are common in areas where moisture manages to seep or run through building components. Mold accumulates around improperly fit windows and doors. Mold thrives where roofing is damaged and repairs have been postponed. Ice dams in gutters can cause moisture to leak into attics and can go undetected while mold and mildew flourish.

Other water damage that can cause mold growth include plumbing leaks, appliance failure (such as freezers, water softeners, or distillers), sewage intrusion, weather-related water intrusion (floods, windstorms, hurricanes), sprinkler leakage, and fire-suppression efforts.[6] Shoddy construction practices, such as failure to use flashing around windows; the misapplication of synthetic stucco exteriors or other materials; faulty heating, ventilating and air conditioning (HVAC) systems; and improper grading along foundation walls can also foster mold growth.[7]

EXHIBIT 6-2

Water Damage—Cleanup and Mold Prevention

Guidelines for Response to Clean Water Damage Within 24-48 Hours To Prevent Mold Growth*

Water-Damaged Material[†]	Actions
Books and papers	• For non-valuable items, discard books and papers. • Photocopy valuable/important items, discard originals. • Freeze (in frost-free freezer or meat locker) or freeze-dry.
Carpet and backing—dry within 24-48 hours[§]	• Remove water with water extraction vacuum. • Reduce ambient humidity levels with dehumidifier. • Accelerate drying process with fans.
Ceiling tiles	• Discard and replace.
Cellulose insulation	• Discard and replace.
Concrete or cinder block surfaces	• Remove water with water extraction vacuum. • Accelerate drying process with dehumidifiers, fans, and/or heaters.
Fiberglass insulation	• Discard and replace.
Hard surface, porous flooring[§] (Linoleum, ceramic tile, vinyl)	• Vacuum or damp wipe with water and mild detergent and allow to dry; scrub if necessary. • Check to make sure underflooring is dry; dry underflooring if necessary.
Non-porous, hard surfaces (Plastics, metals)	• Vacuum or damp wipe with water and mild detergent and allow to dry; scrub if necessary
Upholstered furniture	• Remove water with water extraction vacuum. • Accelerate drying process with dehumidifiers, fans, and/or heaters. • May be difficult to completely dry within 48 hours. If the piece is valuable, you may wish to consult a restoration/water damage professional who specializes in furniture.
Wallboard (Drywall and gypsum board)	• May be dried in place if there is no obvious swelling and the seams are intact. If not, remove, discard, and replace. • Ventilate the wall cavity, if possible.
Window drapes	• Follow laundering or cleaning instructions recommended by the manufacturer.
Wood surfaces	• Remove moisture immediately and use dehumidifiers, gentle heat, and fans for drying. (Use caution when applying heat to hardwood floors.) • Treated or finished wood surfaces may be cleaned with mild detergent and clean water and allowed to dry. • Wet paneling should be pried away from wall for drying.

* If mold growth has occurred or materials have been wet for more than 48 hours, consult Table 2 guidelines. Even if materials are dried within 48 hours, mold growth may have occurred. Items may be tested by professionals if there is doubt. Note that mold growth will not always occur after 48 hours; this is only a guideline.

These guidelines are for damage caused by clean water. If you know or suspect that the water source is contaminated with sewage, or chemical or biological pollutants, then Personal Protective Equipment and containment are required by OSHA. An experienced professional should be consulted if you and/or your remediators do not have expertise remediating in contaminated water situations. Do not use fans before determining that the water is clean or sanitary.

† If a particular item(s) has high monetary or sentimental value, you may wish to consult a restoration/water damage specialist.

§ The subfloor under the carpet or other flooring material must also be cleaned and dried. See the appropriate section of this table for recommended actions depending on the composition of the subfloor.

"Mold Remediation in Schools and Commercial Buildings." United States Environmental Protection Agency, February 20, 2002. World Wide Web: http://www.epa.gov/iaq/molds/intro.html (20 February 2002).

Mold growth resulting from covered water damage becomes part of that damage unless it is specifically excluded. Many personal and commercial policies exclude damage due to mold growth in clauses that are specifically aimed at avoiding coverage for deterioration of the property through natural causes or poor maintenance. However, these exclusions might not be applicable to all mold damage claims or upheld in every jurisdiction.

Investigating and Adjusting Mold Losses

Property loss adjusters should investigate potential mold losses as they would any other water damage loss. Timeliness is vital in investigating losses in which mold might be a factor. Carefully reading the policy and mold-related exclusions can avoid improper claim denial or settlement. When mold is identified, the choice of a remediation firm affects the final damages. (Selection of a remediation contractor will be discussed later.) Communication with building owners and inhabitants of dwellings with confirmed or suspected mold growth is crucial, regardless of whether coverage is provided for the claim. Mold can cause allergic reactions, so it is important to recognize it as a potential health hazard while investigating property damage.

Importance of Proactive Adjustment

Recognizing the potential for mold growth in water damage claims and promptly adjusting those claims is important to insurers for two reasons:

1. Early recognition and remediation of potential mold growth minimizes damage costs.
2. Prompt identification and communication of mold growth can minimize or avoid health risks for building occupants.

The following recommendations focus on proactive adjustment of potential mold claims:

- Recognize the types of losses that result in conditions supporting mold growth, and inspect them quickly.
- Use good photos and diagrams to document and identify locations of mold.
- Be alert for preexisting damage that could have supported mold growth. Uncorrected hurricane and flood damage are common culprits. Take statements to document any preexisting conditions that might have encouraged mold growth.
- Work with the insured to hire a well-trained remediator. Remediation of mold damage has become a thriving business for contractors willing to accept the risks. Issues peculiar to remediating mold damage make selecting a contractor a crucial decision for insureds.

Identification of Mold Hazard

Careful visual inspection is required to identify mold growth. Early mold growth can resemble dirt on the surface of walls, flooring, carpets, and other materials. Any telltale signs of mold require further inspection. Many times the problem is worse than it appears because mold can migrate through materials and affect both sides. The unexposed side of the material often reveals extensive mold growth and damage. Removal of a portion of the material for a visual inspection of the back might be appropriate. Ventilation systems should be visually inspected especially when damp filters are observed. A boroscope can be used to view spaces in ductwork and behind walls to check for mold growth. A moisture meter can be used to detect moisture in building materials. The meter can help identify hidden mold growth and aid in assessing the extent of water damage.[8] Property loss adjusters should continue inspection, even after a source of the water has been found. More often than not, multiple sources will be found.

Indications that mold likely exists in a water-damaged area include the following:

- Color changes in linoleum or wallpaper
- Discoloration, cupping, or warping of wood floors
- Discoloration of drywall or blotches on the surface
- Discoloration of fabrics, carpets, and draperies
- Earthy odors
- Noticeable humidity
- Rot on baseboards and carpet backing, and around windows and doors

Whether or not the visual inspection reveals mold, if the building's occupants report symptoms of a mold-related illness, further investigation is warranted. This could include air-quality testing and the retention of an expert. Exhibit 6-3 presents a mold-prevention flowchart that can be helpful to property loss adjusters investigating mold claims.

What Is the Effect of Preexisting Damage?

A challenge with mold claims is the difficulty in fully remediating the problem. Strong cleansers can sanitize a moldy surface, but unless every microscopic mold spore is removed, the spores go dormant and then flourish again when a new water source is presented. This creates problems for insurers who must determine the mold growth's cause. Suppose that mold damage existed previously, as from natural causes such as humidity in a basement. Then a covered cause of loss exacerbates the mold growth. How does a property loss adjuster properly assess the insurer's liability for the mold growth without risking a bad-faith suit? Careful investigation into preexisting conditions and knowledge of the law in the jurisdiction would help resolve this issue.

Remediation of Mold Damage

The New York City Guidelines (the full title is *New York City Department of Health, Bureau of Environmental and Occupational Disease Epidemiology's Guidelines on Assessment and Remediation of Fungi in Indoor Environments)* have been used by some states as a standard for remediating mold. This

EXHIBIT 6-3

Preventing Microbial Contamination

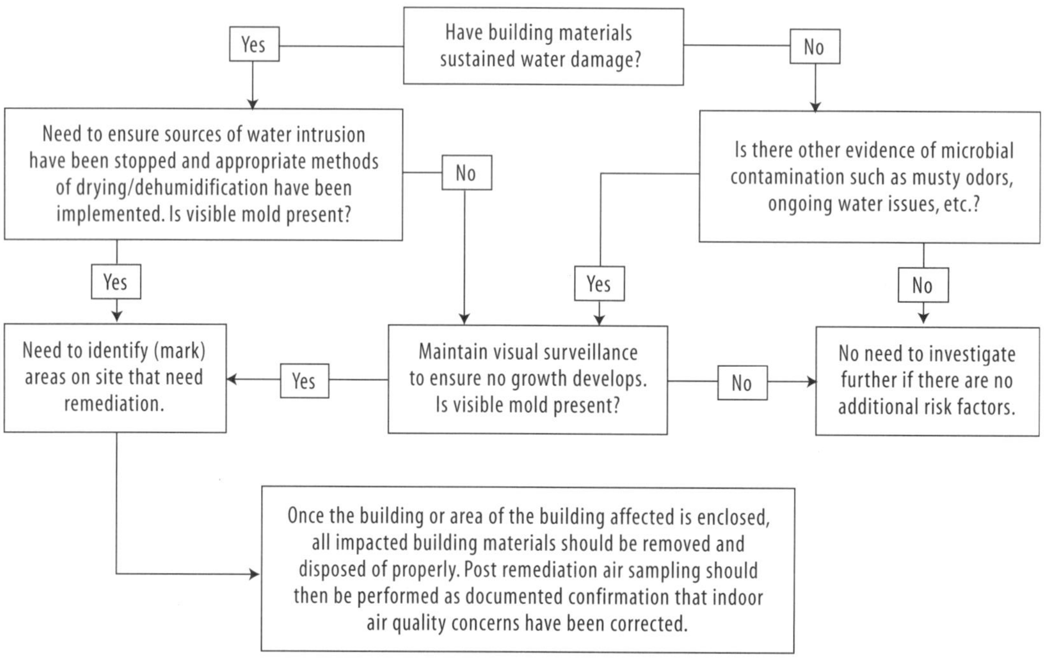

Russell S. Nassof, Environomics Southwest, LLC. "Preventing Microbial Contamination During New Construction." Phoenix, Arizona: Environomics Southwest, LLC, 2002.

document identifies five levels of mold damage and appropriate methods of remediation for each. Generally, the first step in remediating any mold damage is to immediately dry any moisture and correct the source of water infiltration. Repairs to buildings, pipes, or appliances will prevent recurrence of mold growth. Cleaning and drying the affected area, removing water-damaged materials, and maintaining humidity levels below 60 percent will prevent mold growth. Under the Guidelines, the scope of remediation escalates based on the square footage to be remediated.[9]

The EPA has also published recommendations for mold remediation in schools and commercial buildings. The "EPA Checklist for Mold Remediation" appears in Exhibit 6-4.

Selection of a properly trained, reputable remediation contractor is an important decision for the insured. Some opportunists have responded to the publicity associated with mold claims by offering mold remediation services without obtaining the necessary skills and equipment. If mold is not properly remediated, recurrence of the problem will be likely, and individuals who occupy affected buildings will be exposed to further health risks. Adjusters

EXHIBIT 6-4

EPA Checklist for Mold Remediation

Investigate and evaluate moisture and mold problems

- ❑ Assess size of moldy area (square feet)
- ❑ Consider the possibility of hidden mold
- ❑ Clean up small mold problems and fix moisture problems before they become large problems
- ❑ Select remediation manager for medium or large size mold problem
- ❑ Investigate areas associated with occupant complaints
- ❑ Identify source(s) or cause of water or moisture problem(s)
- ❑ Note type of water-damaged materials (wallboard, carpet, etc.)
- ❑ Check inside air ducts and air handling unit
- ❑ Throughout process, consult qualified professional if necessary or desired

Communicate with building occupants at all stages of process, as appropriate

- ❑ Designate contact person for questions and comments about medium or large scale remediation as needed

Plan Remediation

- ❑ Adapt or modify remediation guidelines to fit your situation; use professional judgment
- ❑ Plan to dry wet, non-moldy materials within 48 hours to prevent mold growth
- ❑ Select cleanup methods for moldy items
- ❑ Select Personal Protective Equipment—protect remediators
- ❑ Select containment equipment—protect building occupants
- ❑ Select remediation personnel who have the experience and training needed to implement the remediation plan and use Personal Protective Equipment and containment as appropriate

Remediate moisture and mold problems

- ❑ Fix moisture problem, implement repair plan and/or maintenance plan
- ❑ Dry wet, non-moldy materials within 48 hours to prevent mold growth
- ❑ Clean and dry moldy materials
- ❑ Discard moldy porous items that can't be cleaned

"Mold Remediation in Schools and Commercial Buildings." United States Environmental Protection Agency, February 20, 2002. World Wide Web: http://www.epa.gov/iaq/molds/intro.html (20 February 2002).

should use caution in recommending remediation contractors to the insured. Untrained remediation staff who fail to take the necessary precautions are also exposed to health hazards.

The lack of government regulation or guidelines for health risks and the remediation of mold cases make mold damage claims ripe for litigation. The New York City Guidelines have been adopted in some states, but they are only recommendations, not statutes. The United States EPA and the California Department of Health Services (DHS) have issued non-binding guidelines to homeowners and business owners to assist in evaluating mold existence, effects, prevention, and cleanup.[10] Research to determine mold's health effects continues. Regulation is difficult when research is not conclusive.

Fraud Potential

Mold claims have created an environment in which disreputable remediation contractors and dishonest insureds can flourish. Remediators can prolong the amount of work they do by dragging it out for months or doing their own testing, only to determine that the remediation is not complete and that the work must continue. Price gouging for materials is common, as are phantom charges such as the use of water extraction equipment that was not actually used.[11]

Insured's mold fraud scams entail buying a home, insuring it, furnishing it with cheap property, living in it, and then cracking the pipes or turning on a faucet to saturate the premises. The scam artists then turn on the heat and seal the doors and windows. The scammers then try to collect for the damage to the building, the replacement cost of the contents, and additional living expenses.

Insured's Duty To Protect the Property From Further Damage

Following any loss, an insured has a contractual duty to protect the property from further damage. In a water damage loss, the insured and the insurer must attempt to reach agreement on the steps to be taken to protect the property and preserve any evidence as to the cause of the loss. The insurer can protect itself from a breach of good claim-handling practices by advising the insured on the appropriate steps to protect the property from additional damage due to mold growth. Any verbal instructions given to the insured should be immediately followed in writing. The appropriate policy form numbers should be cited, along with quotations from the forms that describe the insured's duties after a loss. The letter should provide suggestions for preventing mold growth or accumulation. The letter should clearly state that the insured's failure to take actions to prevent mold growth could result in denial of coverage for further damages.

CATASTROPHES

Catastrophe
A single event that causes massive losses.

Catastrophes are single events that cause massive losses. Property Claim Services (PCS) of American Insurance Services Group officially recognizes and assigns a catastrophe serial number to any single event that causes more than $25 million in insured damage. Catastrophic events cause suffering to those who experience losses and place great strain on insurance adjusting resources. But insurers' financial support of covered losses and professional and compassionate treatment of insureds suffering losses in catastrophes demonstrate insurance's value and importance.

Many different types of events cause catastrophes. Each type presents special challenges, but catastrophes also share common characteristics, including geographic concentration, disruption of services, political sensitivity, and great emotional stress. Insurers have learned to respond to catastrophes by planning ahead and by adapting their standard loss adjusting procedures.

Types of Catastrophes

Hail, wind, and tornadoes are the most frequent causes of catastrophes. However, hurricanes, floods, and earthquakes cause more widespread damage. Fires and riots can also cause catastrophic losses. The nature of the losses and the demands on claim adjusters vary by type of catastrophe.

Hail

Hailstorms do not receive the same publicity in the national media as do other catastrophes, but every year they cause numerous catastrophes. Hailstorms can occur anywhere, but they are especially common in the Great Plains and Rocky Mountain states. The amount of damage caused by hail in 2000 was $446 million for property and $124.9 million for crops.[12] Adjusting hail losses is challenging, especially when the damage is minor to moderate. Severely damaged property can be repaired or replaced, just as when property is severely damaged by any peril. A claim for minor or moderate hail damage often raises two issues: (1) whether the property needs to be repaired at all and (2) whether the claimed damage existed before the hail.

Minor hail damage can include barely perceptible scratches and dings in siding and roofing. Such damage might be irreparable because of matching issues, and the property might need to be replaced. An insurance policy that measures loss as the cost to repair or replace might require the insurance company to pay for replacement. For example, the HO-3 measures loss to the building at the cost to repair (provided adequate limits of coverage exist and the insured actually makes repair). If an insured with an HO-3 suffers superficial scratching of the siding on his or her house, he or she will be entitled to the cost to repair or replace the property. Unless the repairs are satisfactory, the homeowner is entitled to the cost to replace. The cost of replacement can be extraordinary compared to any decrease in the market value of the home caused by the hail damage. Indeed, many homeowners in this situation prefer an actual cash value (ACV) settlement, an option that is always available and that does not require the insured to make repairs. In catastrophes, unfortunately, this dilemma occurs frequently.

An equally difficult problem with hail claims is the possibility of preexisting damage. Virtually all homes show some wear and tear. Scratches, chips, dings, and marks can come from innumerable sources. Following a hailstorm, homes typically have some new damage in addition to old damage. Moreover, some insureds might use the opportunity of a hailstorm to make a claim for old damage. Adjusters who handle hail claims regularly must become familiar with how normal wear on buildings and vehicles appears.

When settlements are made for ACV, distinguishing preexisting damage is crucial.

ADJUSTER TIP

When adjusters are doubtful about the circumstances of a hail-related loss, they should look for hail damage to exposed condenser coils of an HVAC (heating, ventilating, and air conditioning) unit because they are easily damaged by hail.

Wind and Tornadoes

Loss due to violent, severe winds and tornadoes can devastate a community. These losses usually occur in a specific geographic area. The extent of damage, injuries, and loss of life make adjusting such losses difficult. These losses share many of the characteristics of hurricane losses and are similarly handled.

Hurricanes

Hurricanes can arise in the tropical regions of the Atlantic Ocean and the Gulf of Mexico during summer and autumn. Once developed, hurricanes are hundreds of miles wide with sustained winds in excess of seventy-five miles per hour. They characteristically move westward and northward out of the Tropics. The Gulf and Southeastern states of the United States are especially vulnerable to hurricanes, but the Mid-Atlantic and New England states have also suffered hurricane damage. In addition to their powerful winds, hurricanes deliver enormous amounts of rain and cause tides to surge well beyond normal.

Most structures can withstand, with minor damage, a relatively low-velocity hurricane with winds between seventy-five and ninety miles per hour. However, as wind speeds increase, hurricane destruction becomes severe. In August 1992, Hurricane Andrew crossed southern Florida with sustained winds in excess of 130 miles per hour, obliterating homes and essentially causing the same damages as a thirty-mile wide tornado. Most hurricanes bring down trees and power lines and flood low-lying areas, making immediate travel dangerous.

Sustained rainy weather often follows a hurricane, when many homes have damaged roofs. Most homeowners are eager to comply with their insurance policy's requirement to mitigate damage after a loss, because they want to save their personal property. However, tarpaulins and repair materials are almost always in short supply following a hurricane. Insurers and adjusters should enforce the insured's duty to mitigate damage only to the extent that mitigating measures are feasible.

Property insurance policies cover damage from wind and wind-driven rain but generally do not cover damage from floods or tidal surge. Only flood insurance policies from the National Flood Insurance Program cover flood and tidal surge. Adjusters handling claims under ordinary property insurance policies must first determine whether wind or water caused the damage. Wind damage is covered, but water damage is covered only if it results from wind-driven rain. If the water that caused the damage rose up from the ground, then it was a flood, and the damage is not covered. If the water came from the sky, the resulting damage is covered.

Floods

Floods can result from melting snows, rising rivers and lakes, hurricanes, or heavy rains.

Except for certain specialized commercial policies, all flood insurance comes from the National Flood Insurance Program (NFIP). The NFIP has its own policy provisions and its own requirements for who can adjust flood claims. Flood insurance policies are relatively expensive, so many property owners choose to do without them. Thus, lack of insurance coverage is a serious problem in beachfront areas and in any area that suffers flood damage. Floods invariably result in a great amount of uninsured losses.

History of the National Flood Insurance Program

Because of the problems associated with flood insurance in the private market, the government has made flood insurance widely available through the **National Flood Insurance Program (NFIP).** Beginning in 1983, the Federal Insurance and Mitigation Administration (FIMA), of the Federal Emergency Management Agency (FEMA), invited private insurers to participate in a Write Your Own (WYO) program to increase the base and geographic distribution of flood insurance and to improve service and claim handling. A WYO company sells flood policies under its own name, collects premiums, services the insureds, adjusts the claims, and pays the losses. FEMA reinsures 100 percent of these losses. FEMA pays commissions on premiums and reimburses expenses and costs. If an insurer loses money on the program, FEMA makes up the difference. Any profits are returned to the government.

National Flood Insurance Program (NFIP)
A government-sponsored flood insurance program for communities in designated areas.

NFIP Coverage

The NFIP has three policy forms:

1. A dwelling form (DF) insures a one- to four-family residential dwelling or condominium unit and residential contents.
2. A general property form (GPF) insures other residential and nonresidential buildings and contents.
3. Another form insures residential condominium building associations (RCBAP).

Under the regular NFIP program, the insurance limits for property are as follows:

Building Coverage	
Single-family dwelling	$250,000
Two-to-four-family dwelling	$250,000
Other residential	$250,000
Non-residential	$250,000
Contents coverage	
Residential	$100,000
Non-residential	$500,000

Definition of Flood The NFIP policies cover the described property from direct loss by or from flood. Flood is defined in both policies as a *general* and *temporary* condition of partial or complete inundation by water of two or more acres of normally dry land or of two or more properties caused by any of the following:

a. The overflow of inland or tidal waters
b. The unusual and rapid accumulation or runoff of surface waters from any source
c. Mudflow, which is defined as a river of liquid and flowing mud on the surfaces of normally dry land, as when earth is carried by a current of water or collapse or subsidence of land along the shore of a lake or similar body of water as a result of erosion or undermining caused by waves, or currents of water exceeding anticipated cyclical levels that result in a flood, as defined above.[13]

Dwelling Form: Property Covered In this discussion of NFIP coverage, the text refers to the Dwelling Form. However, adjusters are reminded that other forms are available and that the coverages may differ. Building coverage (Coverage A) under the Dwelling Form is written similar to that under other property forms. Coverage is provided for the dwelling at the described location and the extensions and additions to the buildings, detached garages, building materials and supplies, and certain specifically described fixtures. Automatic coverage applies for a separate garage for up to 10 percent of the overall building coverage limit. If the detached building's value exceeds 10 percent, a separate policy should be obtained on that building. The 10 percent extension is not an additional amount of insurance, so using this coverage reduces the limit otherwise available for the dwelling. There is also an extensive list of items—such as built-in appliances, permanently installed bookcases, wallpaper, and paneling—that are considered to be part of the building. And there are limitations for items below the lowest elevated floor of the building or in a basement.

Contents coverage (Coverage B), if purchased, applies to direct physical loss by or from a flood to personal property inside a building at the described location, if owned by the insured or by household family members. Property must be contained in a fully enclosed building on the residence premises or secured against floating out of a partially enclosed building. The insured has the option to include the personal property of guests and servants. The policy also contains a list of items such as air conditioning units, carpeting, and grills that are deemed to be personal property.

Similar to the HO-3 policy, the Dwelling Form has a $2,500 limit for any one loss to high-value items such as artwork, jewelry, furs, and business personal property. It also has provisions for debris removal and loss-avoidance measures.

The policy also provides coverage for the cost of complying with a state or local floodplain management law or ordinance that affects the structure's repair or reconstruction. This coverage is called Increased Cost of Compliance (Coverage D). Activities such as elevation, floodproofing, relocation, and demolition are covered. The coverage applies to nonresidential structures and residential structures with basements that meet certain FEMA standards. The maximum amount payable is $20,000. This limit is in addition to the Coverage A limit; however, the combined total amount payable cannot exceed $250,000 for a dwelling or $500,000 for a commercial structure.

Property Not Covered The Dwelling Form lists the types of property not covered by the policy. Generally, property that is out in the open, such as trees, shrubs, decks, and fences, are excluded.

Exclusions Consequential or indirect loss is excluded. Loss of use, additional living expenses, and business income losses are indirect losses resulting from flood and are thus not covered. Increased costs of construction resulting from ordinance or law are not covered. A loss already in progress at the inception of the policy is not covered.

The policy also excludes the perils usually covered by a homeowners policy, such as fire or theft.

Several exclusions explain that a flood must be a general, not an individual, condition. Flood policies exclude water, moisture, mildew, or mold damage confined to the insured property, or any damage resulting from conditions within the insured's control. This exclusion applies to any design, structural, or mechanical defects, or any failures, stoppages, or breakage of water or sewer lines, drains, pumps, fixtures, or equipment. Any property or premises modifications by the insured that increase the hazard of flooding can exclude subsequent losses from coverage. Any intentional act by the insured is also excluded. Testing or monitoring of pollutants is not covered unless required by law. Finally, there is no coverage for loss to any building or personal property located on land leased from the federal government caused by a flood, where the lease holds the federal government harmless under flood insurance issued by a federal government program.

General Conditions Like other property policies, the dwelling form has a list of familiar conditions: a pairs and sets clause, a concealment or fraud clause, and an other insurance clause. The other insurance clause makes the NFIP policy primary over all other policies that state that they are excess. If the other policy does not specifically state that it is excess, then the NFIP policy is primary up to the other policy's deductible, and then the coverage becomes pro rata. After a loss, the insured must comply with requirements such as giving prompt notice of the loss, separating the damaged property from the undamaged property, making an inventory with backup documentation, submitting a proof of loss, cooperating with the investigation, allowing inspection of the damaged property, and submitting to an examination under oath if required. The insured cannot abandon property to the insurer. The amount of the loss can be reduced by salvage. Either party may demand an appraisal. Mortgagees' interests are protected.

The NFIP policy also has some unique conditions, such as a special condition for continuous lake flooding. If the structure has been flooded by lake water for ninety continuous days and it is reasonably certain that the structure will be a total loss, the insurer will make a settlement without waiting for further damage to occur. Naturally, there is a requirement for a release so that the insurer does not have to pay twice for the same property. There is a similar provision for flooding from a closed basin lake (a natural lake from which water leaves primarily by evaporation). However, this provision does not require ninety days of continuous flooding. Lastly, the NFIP policy does not allow a structure to be covered by more than one NFIP policy.

Loss Settlement Provisions Like all property policies, the Dwelling Form has a limit of liability and deductibles. Separate deductibles apply to the building coverage and the personal property coverage. The deductibles do not apply to loss avoidance measures, condominium loss assessments, or increased cost of compliance coverage.

Losses under the Dwelling Form can be settled in one of three ways: (1) replacement cost, (2) special loss settlement, and (3) actual cash value. Replacement cost and ACV are handled similar to the ISO HO-3. Special loss settlement involves the replacement cost to a manufactured (mobile) home or travel trailer.

Adjustment Procedures

The adjustment of flood losses involves numerous special procedures, most of which are dictated by NFIP requirements.

NFIP Authorization All independent adjusters must have NFIP authorization to handle losses, or they will not be paid for their work. NFIP sets standards for adjusters in five categories: (1) residential, (2) commercial, (3) large commercial, (4) manufactured and mobile homes, and (5) residential condominium building association (RCBA). The standards require an adjuster to have a number of years' experience and the ability to write estimates.

Loss Settlements, Denials, and Rejections Only NFIP personnel can accept or deny claims or reject proofs of loss, based on the investigating adjuster's recommendations. An NFIP proof of loss is required on every claim with payment recommended. On claims up to $7,500, the adjuster's final report will be accepted in lieu of a proof of loss. NFIP has its own forms for the purpose of loss settlement and reporting.

Earthquakes

California is known for its susceptibility to earthquakes, but other states are also at high risk, including Alaska, Hawaii, and Washington. Earthquakes strong enough to cause damage might occur in any state.

Earthquake damage is excluded from standard property insurance policies, but it is available by endorsement. Insureds in earthquake-prone areas are most likely to have such coverage. In California, homeowners insurers must offer earthquake coverage. Nevertheless, following an earthquake, most property owners are uninsured. Communities suffering earthquakes absorb much more of the financial loss than does the insurance industry.

Unless it strikes a rural area, an earthquake strong enough to cause damage can damage thousands or tens of thousands of properties at once. In this respect, earthquakes are similar to hurricanes. An entire community can be damaged and traumatized. In such an earthquake, thousands of people will need the same services at once. Immediately after an earthquake, highways, water pipelines, gas lines, and electric lines might be severed. Firefighters might be overwhelmed and lack adequate water. Fires might destroy buildings that survived the quake. Following a major quake, aftershocks continue for days or weeks, possibly inflicting significant damage on already weakened structures.

As with hail damage, the most challenging claims following an earthquake are for buildings with minor to moderate damage. Damage might be hidden inside walls and under floors. Separation of major structural elements might initially appear only as cracks in stucco or plaster. Even moderate earthquake damage to an ordinary house can cost $50,000 or more to repair. Unfortunately, relatively few people are qualified to assess earthquake damage properly. Only structural engineers or highly qualified contractors can determine the proper scope of repairs for the most difficult earthquake losses. After a serious earthquake, they will be in great demand. All of these issues may contribute to delays in closing files after an earthquake.

Fires

Fires are usually limited to one owner's property, but some are extensive enough to cause a catastrophe. In the United States, the West is much drier than the East and is consequently prone to fire following long droughts. Moreover, although cities throughout the United States have extensive and sophisticated firefighting forces, the concentration of properties clustered close together in cities can result in widespread conflagration.

Rural fires usually involve uninsured property, such as trees in national parks and forests or property that is self-insured by timber companies. Growing timber is not a type of property insured under most property insurance policies. Nevertheless, rural areas can contain significant insured property, both residential and commercial. Insurers might have difficulty providing prompt service to insureds in rural areas if they do not have preexisting relationships with independent adjusters and contractors in those areas.

A fire severe enough to cause a catastrophe will incinerate the property involved. Many homeowners who returned to their homes following the Oakland, Calif., fires of 1991 found nothing but the brick chimney still standing, surrounded by ashes. Under these circumstances, even the owner would have difficulty recreating the detailed plans of a home's construction. Nevertheless, insurance policies require the insured to prove the amount of any loss and to include all documentation specified in the proof of loss. Insurers differ in the type and extent of proof they require of insureds in these circumstances. Adjusters should not subject fire victims to an additional trauma, but they need to know the amount of every loss.

Riots

Riot losses include damage caused by fire, vandalism, and looting. Commercial structures and property are damaged disproportionately more than residential property by riots. Commercial insurance policies that otherwise limit coverage for theft losses often cover losses incident to a riot, even if the thief is not identified as a rioter. For example, the BPP with the Causes of Loss—Broad Form defines the peril of riot to include looting occurring at the time and place of a riot. The "time and place of a riot" are not specifically defined but would certainly include any place where riot activities required police intervention.

A riot in a declining urban area represents a perfect opportunity for a would-be arsonist. A commercial structure in such an area might be unsalable, and the owner might prefer an insurance settlement to the existing building. A property loss adjuster assigned a fire claim following a riot should investigate with neighbors to see whether anyone saw how the fire began. Neighbors are likely to be extra vigilant during a riot. They might be very cooperative with a claim investigation because they might be angry with the wrongdoers. However, unless an eyewitness is available, an arson investigation might be hopeless. In the context of a riot, proof of an incendiary fire does not necessarily implicate the insured. Even proof of a motive and an incendiary fire might not carry much weight.

The Catastrophe Environment

The environments of almost all catastrophes have certain common characteristics that are interrelated: the losses are geographically concentrated; necessary services are disrupted or in short supply; response to catastrophes is politically sensitive; and the claim adjusters who must operate in this environment and the people with whom they deal are under great stress.

Geographic Concentration

Catastrophes strike in one community or within a relatively limited geographic area. Even hurricanes, the geographically largest type of catastrophe, usually hit hard an area of just a few hundred square miles. After a catastrophe, thousands of people in a relatively small area need the same services. Existing services in that area, even if they survived the catastrophe, are inadequate to meet the sudden great need.

In particular, not enough property loss adjusters are in an area following a catastrophe. Most insurers set up catastrophe teams to augment the regular adjusting staff in a catastrophe area. The "Cat Team" adjusters and processors leave home for at least a few weeks to work fourteen-hour days out of cars and motel rooms. Many experienced personnel go from one catastrophe site to another with only brief periods of time off to return home. Unfortunately, this pattern of work exhausts all of the claim staff who participate in settling catastrophe claims. To keep errors to a minimum, the Cat Team is usually rotated out of the area after a few weeks or after having handled a specified number of claims.

Contractors are also in short supply following a catastrophe. The construction industry can have chronically high unemployment, so catastrophes attract contractors from out of state. This influx helps enormously in rebuilding a community, but it also raises potential problems. Unlicensed or incompetent contractors can take advantage of insureds who suddenly and simultaneously have large amounts of money and a significant need for contractors' help. An unscrupulous contractor might take an assignment of the insured's claim settlement, then disappear from the state. An incompetent contractor might be indifferent about correcting poor work because a great amount of other work is available. Legal remedies against contractors are of dubious value even under normal circumstances. Thus, property loss adjusters can provide valuable advice to insureds who are naive about their situation. Claim adjusters should advise insureds to select contractors carefully.

Interruption or Shortage of Services

In addition to claim adjusters and contractors, just about every other necessary service or supply is in shortage or unavailable following a catastrophe. Immediately after a catastrophe, essential utilities such as electricity, water, gas, and telephone might be disrupted. Such disruptions make an area unlivable and dangerous. Fortunately, public authorities usually have the most pressing and dangerous situations resolved in a few days.

Hotels and motels even a significant distance from the catastrophe area will be filled to capacity. Rental cars in the area will be quickly obtained. (However, cars can quickly be moved into a catastrophe area.) If the roads are blocked or severed, supplies of goods in supermarkets might run low.

Building supplies are often unavailable immediately following a catastrophe. Supplies usually become available within a few weeks, but prices are high and may remain so for months. Adjusters preparing estimates in catastrophe environments must be aware of prevailing prices. Estimating losses based on prices that prevail only during normal times is unrealistic.

Political Sensitivity

Public authorities and elected political officials face as much challenge from catastrophes as does the insurance industry. They are more responsible than the insurance industry for the immediate response, including control of threats to personal safety. Public authorities decide whether an area must be evacuated or kept off-limits until safe.

After the initial danger passes, public officials must process an enormous number of licenses and building permits stemming from repair work. As construction progresses, they must inspect and issue occupancy permits for a great number of properties. They also enforce building code provisions for new construction. Public authorities are not staffed to handle the unusual amount of work caused by catastrophes, which is an additional source of frustration and stress for insureds who have suffered a loss.

Most public officials recognize the importance of insurance settlement funds to rebuilding their community. They cooperate with property loss adjusters as much as possible. However, tensions can result when public officials involve themselves in the claim settlement process when they believe that their constituents are not being treated properly. After a catastrophe, community members, community leaders, and public officials may talk about perceived obstacles to insureds' recovery.

Nevertheless, public officials are usually not qualified to resolve specific differences that arise in claim settlements. Some public officials, who in their official capacity never thought about insurance, might make highly publicized pronouncements about how claims should be settled. These pronouncements are usually not legally binding and often are not even helpful. However, such adverse publicity following a catastrophe would not be surprising given the thousands of frustrated insureds concentrated in a single community.

State insurance department officials are more knowledgeable about insurance than are other public officials, but they are under just as much political pressure to show results. A catastrophe environment is an obvious opportunity to enforce an unfair claims practices act. Insurers with significant losses in a catastrophe often designate a liaison to the state insurance department to facilitate communication of complaints and concerns. After a catastrophe, state insurance department officials know which insurers performed well and which did not.

Emotional Stress

Virtually everyone involved with a catastrophe is subject to great emotional stress, including community members, public authorities, contractors, and property loss adjusters. Stress affects people differently. Some people become visibly agitated and unable to concentrate. Other people become vacant-looking and depressed. People subject to stress are less able to control their emotions or to communicate effectively.

Property loss adjusters who work in catastrophe environments are aware of the emotional climate. Nevertheless, because they are also subject to stress, property loss adjusters might sometimes be impatient, impersonal, distracted, or unreasonable. Monitoring staff morale is a key challenge for claim managers in catastrophe environments. Major catastrophes command the attention of senior claim officers, who realize that the insurer's reputation is at stake in a catastrophe situation. Claim officers and managers understand that the volume of work, emotional stress, and separation from home caused by a catastrophe require adjusters to be relieved on a regular basis.

Adjusters experienced with catastrophe environments know that listening to insureds is valuable. Insureds who have suffered great loss need an outlet for their feelings. Most experienced adjusters have encountered insureds who seem to need sympathy more than cash. Adjusters who regard catastrophe work as relieving human suffering are much more motivated, and often find more professional satisfaction, than adjusters who regard the work as primarily closing files.

Pre-Catastrophe Planning

Every major catastrophe teaches the insurance industry something new about the inadequacies of existing catastrophe plans. Property loss adjusters and managers must be prepared to improvise following any major disaster. Nevertheless, planning is essential to an effective catastrophe response. Insurers must have plans for providing the equipment, services, and staff necessary to adjust claims in catastrophe environments.

Equipment

A catastrophe requires that a huge number of adjusters and supplies be brought to the catastrophe area. Catastrophe planners must arrange for office supplies and major office equipment, such as furniture, copiers, files, manuals, and computers, to be available. Planning for computers is especially important because offices are increasingly automated and the types of computers needed in a catastrophe environment might not be the same as in normal circumstances. Adjusters might rely heavily on laptop computers because they are constantly in the field in places without electricity.

Communication equipment is important because normal communications in the catastrophe environment might be disrupted. Catastrophe planners must arrange for telephones, cellular telephones, pagers, and even satellite dishes. A catastrophe plan should also address an insurer's internal communications so that all company employees are clear about who should respond and within what time after a catastrophe.

Most insurers try to be fully operational within two or three days after a catastrophe. To do so, major insurers prepackage equipment on pallets for immediate airlift or trucking into the catastrophe site. They also package jackets, badges, and licenses or license information so that adjusters can be properly identified and authorized to work. Catastrophe kits usually include briefcases, cameras, film, batteries, flashlights, tape measures, and first-aid supplies.

Services

Catastrophe planners must prearrange various services. Property loss adjusters brought into a catastrophe area must have hotel or motel rooms, rental cars, office space, and telephones. Many major insurers have price arrangements with motel and car rental chains.

More important are the services necessary to adjust claims. Catastrophe planners prearrange prices and service with contractors, salvage companies, replacement services, engineering and architectural firms, and independent adjusters. When a catastrophe occurs, planners must be ready with detailed maps of the affected area. Insurers must also arrange reliable means for property loss adjusters to verify coverage. Agents' offices in the catastrophe area might be destroyed or nonfunctioning. Computerized coverage information is usually a listing of policy form numbers only, so adjusters must also have access to actual policy forms.

Staffing

Providing adequate staff is the most challenging aspect of a catastrophe. Unless an insurer is exceedingly overstaffed during normal times, it will have a shortage of qualified staff for a catastrophe. Major national insurers draw staff from around the country to work in a catastrophe, but doing so leaves the rest of the country with inadequate staff to handle normal claim volume. Leaving less-experienced staff to handle normal claim volume elsewhere in the country is not always satisfactory because normal claim volume includes major losses that inexperienced personnel cannot handle. Many insurers use retirees to cover normal claim volume in offices throughout the country.

Staff assigned to catastrophe duty must be rotated out after a certain time period or number of claims. Traditionally, insurers assigned "storm troopers" to a catastrophe for two to four weeks, then allowed them to return home. The effect of this practice was that insureds with major claims faced a parade of adjusters, each of whom had to become acquainted with that insured's claim. Those adjusters did not always deal consistently with the claim or the insured, resulting in the insured's dissatisfaction. Many insurers now assign an adjuster to a certain number of claims that the same adjuster handles to conclusion.

Independent adjusters are an essential resource for handling catastrophes. Independent adjusting firms have a great number of personnel experienced in the fieldwork integral to catastrophe claim adjusting. However, an insurer's staff cannot expect independent adjusters to give the insurer's needs in such cases top priority if the insurer never uses independent adjusters except for catastrophes. Independent adjusters give top priority to insurers that are regular customers.

An often overlooked aspect of catastrophe planning is the need for adequate support staff. Insurers do not usually move support staff from around the country to the same extent that they move adjusters. Nevertheless, catastrophe situations require support staff. Qualified adjusters should be focused on the adjusting work. Other staff should handle as much of the paperwork of a claim file as possible. Personnel from local agents' offices can answer phones and take loss reports. Help from temporary agencies can perform routine tasks. Although all insurers vie for temporary help after a catastrophe, insurers should also consider hiring additional workers for a specified time period. Such help might not be difficult to obtain because a portion of the local workforce might be looking for such employment or might be temporarily unemployed and available.

Catastrophe Loss Adjusting

Adjusting catastrophe claims is markedly different from adjusting typical claims. Aspects of claim adjusting handled differently in a catastrophe include the initial response and reserving practices, communications with insureds, price increases and settlement costs, and adjusting standards.

Initial Response and Reserving Practices

Immediately after a catastrophe, insurance companies typically send an initial survey team to the area to determine the geographic scope of the damage. A survey team can identify affected areas by ZIP Code. Computer searches can identify every insured in a given set of ZIP Codes. The initial survey should also identify the degree of damage typical of properties in the affected area. This information can help identify the level of expertise needed of catastrophe team adjusters and the extent to which the insurer can rely on telephone adjusters.

Information from the initial survey and from Property Claim Services (PCS) is used to set proper reserves for the catastrophe. PCS provides not only serial numbers for recognized catastrophes but also estimates of the total insured losses. PCS serial numbers and loss estimates are used to activate reinsurance treaties and to help primary insurers estimate their exposure in a catastrophe. Insurers typically set loss reserves for catastrophes in bulk. Bulk reserves are gross estimates of losses; individual loss reserves are determined claim by claim. An insurer's senior management must know that the catastrophe loss reserves are accurate. Without accurate reserves, senior officers are unaware of the insurer's true financial state and might make improper underwriting and reinsurance decisions. Senior officers do not appreciate surprises, such as loss reserves being continually revised upward for a year after a catastrophe occurs. Correct reserves also help claim department managers to determine proper staffing for a catastrophe.

Another important aspect of an insurer's initial response is hiring specialists to provide restoration services. Restoration companies perform a variety of tasks valuable to mitigating losses after a catastrophe, including drying, dehumidifying, decontaminating, cleaning, removing soot, inventorying, and packing away property. Restoration companies can work with salvage companies to save and recover as much of the damaged property's value as possible. Every year, the technology used by restoration companies improves. Property damage once deemed hopeless can now be repaired. Restoration work's success depends on timely retention of services. Insurers that wait until after disaster strikes to look for restoration contractors are unlikely to find any available.

Communications With Insureds

After a catastrophe, insureds are in shock. They need an outlet to express their loss and a source for specific advice about recovery. Claim adjusters should be both. Effective communications with insureds is as important to claim adjusting as is verifying coverage or preparing estimates. Nevertheless, several obstacles hinder good communications in a catastrophe environment.

Telephone service might be disrupted by a catastrophe or might be jammed immediately after a catastrophe. Agents' offices might be destroyed or overwhelmed with calls. Local claim offices might be shut down. Fortunately, most insurers can arrange with their telephone service to have calls redirected to an undamaged office. Insureds in the catastrophe area who can make an outgoing call should succeed in reaching their insurer. An insurer's catastrophe operation should inform affected insureds how to reach claim adjusters in the catastrophe area, providing insureds with all new or temporary telephone numbers that the local adjusters are using.

Insureds whose homes are unfit to live in can be hard to reach. They sometimes move elsewhere without leaving a new telephone number for their insurer. Such insureds eventually contact their insurer, but they should be told their duties following loss as soon after the loss as possible. Insurers operating in a catastrophe area have resorted to billboards, radio messages, and even banners towed by airplanes to let insurers know how to contact them.

Price Increases and Settlement Costs

Prices of many goods and services increase after a catastrophe, especially building supplies and contractor services. The local, regional, and national economies are organized to provide a flow of goods and services that meets a predictable, normal demand. Catastrophes result in unpredictable, abnormal demand. For example, the rebuilding after Hurricane Andrew in August 1992 caused high lumber prices throughout the country well into 1993. High prices can actually be beneficial to the extent that they encourage additional output that hastens recovery.

Claim adjusters can make two different mistakes when prices are high. The first is insisting that normal prices should prevail and refusing to settle claims for a higher amount. Normal prices are unlikely to return until most damaged properties have been repaired, but insureds should not wait that long to repair their property. The delay might also be irrational, from the insurer's point of view, if it causes increased living expense or business interruption claims.

The second mistake adjusters can make is paying any amount to close claims. Not every significantly damaged structure is a total loss or policy limits claim. Even in a catastrophe environment, adjusters must evaluate losses and pay an amount that indemnifies, not enriches, the insured. Adjusters need not pay exorbitant prices that appear because of acute shortages immediately after a catastrophe, nor must they accept at face value estimates from contractors so busy that they unapologetically quote clearly unreasonable prices.

Adjusting Standards

Adjusters face some tradeoffs among the cost of claim settlements, the speed of claim settlements, and the thoroughness of their adjusting work in catastrophes. Painstaking adjusting work is ideal for controlling the cost of claim settlements, but it is very slow. In a catastrophe environment, rapid, efficient work is essential. Thus, claim adjusters are likely to be less thorough in their adjusting procedures and more flexible about settlement cost. Adjusters' challenge in catastrophe environments is to be less thorough and more flexible in ways least likely to harm the insurer. For example, if adjusters do not require sworn proofs of loss, an alternative would be to require realistic estimates or damage inspections.

Some documentation or verification of the extent of loss is essential to know what settlement amount is appropriate and to discourage fraud. Insurers' special investigation units (SIUs) should have catastrophe capability so that catastrophes do not become an open invitation to fraud. However, property loss adjusters must recognize that severely damaged buildings are susceptible to fires and looting. Owners are required to protect their property from further damage, but adjusters can enforce this duty only to the extent feasible under the circumstances. Repair materials, generators, and pumps might not be available at any price shortly after a catastrophe, so the adjuster would not require them.

Adjusters may have to reopen numerous files from a catastrophe. They make many settlements at actual cash value, pending repair of the insured's property, and conclude the claim later with a replacement cost settlement. Reopening files might also occur because the initial adjusting work was too hasty or because hidden damage was not apparent until repairs began. Redoing adjusting work is inefficient, but it is predictable with certain catastrophes, such as earthquakes.

COVERAGE DEFENSES

A property loss adjuster performs an investigation to determine whether a loss should be paid and how much should be paid. Regardless of the type of coverage involved, insurers do not pay every claim presented by insureds. The adjuster's investigation may show that the insurance policy does not cover a claim. Claims can be denied because of the insured's improper behavior. Insurers can deny coverage in the event of the insured's fraud, but they can also do so for various reasons not involving any serious wrongdoing by the insured, including simple absence of coverage or the insured's failure to comply with a policy condition.

Insurer Not Obligated Under the Policy

The insurer may not be contractually obligated to pay a claim as a result of one or more of the following: (1) some change in conditions, ownership, or interest in the property before a loss that breaches an ongoing promise; (2) a cause of loss or type of property not covered or specifically excluded by the policy; or (3) the insured's breach of policy conditions following a loss.

Change in Property: Ongoing Promises

Promissory warranty
An agreement between the insurer and the insured that certain facts or conditions pertaining to the insured property will continue or will be done.

An ongoing promise, also known as a **promissory warranty**, is the insured's agreement made at the time of the application for insurance to do or refrain from doing certain things during the policy term. Under a property policy, such a promise might include the agreement to provide a burglar or fire alarm system, deadbolt locks, and fire extinguishers. In exchange for the insured's promise to provide these safeguards, the insurer usually provides a discount of the premium. For business property policies, such promises sometimes include the insured's agreement to provide guard services, burglar/fire alarm systems, sprinkler systems, and certain kinds of safes. A breach of a promissory warranty by the insured that causes a loss or increases the risk of loss might be a basis for the insurer to deny liability under the policy.

Excluded Causes of Loss or Property

A loss might not be covered because the cause of loss is not within the perils listed in the policy or is excluded in the policy. The policy might also specifically exclude coverage to certain kinds of property. Previous chapters discuss those possibilities. In such cases, the claim might be denied, or questions about coverage might be raised and need to be answered.

Policy Conditions Following Loss

All property policies include conditions requiring the insured to do certain things following a loss. In the HO-3 policy and the BPP, these requirements are listed under "Your Duties After Loss." Included is the insured's obligation to give prompt notice of the loss to the insurer; protect the property from further damage; file a sworn statement in proof of loss; provide an inventory of stolen, damaged, or destroyed personal property; submit books and records to document the facts and loss; and submit to one or more examinations under oath. The insured's failure or refusal to comply with these policy conditions is a breach of the policy and would preclude payment of the claim or a suit by the insured to enforce policy rights until the insured has complied.

Fraud, Concealment, and Misrepresentation

Although providing prompt claim service to insureds is a property loss adjuster's primary task, ensuring fair and equitable claim payments is equally important. Adjusters should pay no more than a fair and reasonable amount for covered claims while being vigilant for fraudulent activity. Unfortunately, insurance fraud is a reality that creates a special challenge for adjusters. The Insurance Information Institute estimates that property-casualty fraud costs insurers about $30 billion annually.[14] Yet it is almost impossible to determine the number of claims industry-wide that are fraudulent. Part of the difficulty comes from the lack of uniform definitions throughout the industry. Almost every claim may have an element that is termed a "fraud indicator," but that does not mean that the claim is fraudulent. Many claims that are fraudulent but not provable will be paid. Therefore, finding a uniform way to measure the number of fraudulent claims is difficult.

The opportunity for fraud can appear at many different places in the insurance process. The potential insured may misrepresent or conceal information during the application process. False information may be given to the underwriter about a risk's nature. Claims may be staged or exaggerated. Adjusters, attorneys, and insureds might conspire to obtain fraudulent claim payments. It is important to be aware of the opportunities but be mindful that most people do not accept the opportunity to commit fraud when presented with it.

Definitions

Although the terms "fraud," "concealment," and "misrepresentation" might seem to be synonymous, they are different and have distinct legal meanings.

Fraud
An intentional deception, by word, deed, or concealment, to cause another to part with something of value or to surrender a legal right.

Concealment
The withholding of information by one who knows that he or she has a duty to disclose it.

Misrepresentation
To make a false or misleading statement with the intent to deceive.

Fraud is a general term encompassing all types of acts by one or more persons intended to deceive another person. **Fraud** is an intentional deception, by word, deed, or concealment, to cause another to part with something of value or to surrender a legal right. For fraud to be actionable, the deceived party must suffer legal injury from having relied on the deception.

Concealment is the withholding of information by one who knows that he or she has a duty to disclose. Concealment in the application for insurance is the intentional withholding of any fact material to the risk, which the insured, in honesty and good faith, ought to communicate to the agent, underwriter, or insurer.

Misrepresentation is the statement of something as fact that is false. Misrepresentation includes statements that are only partially true. For example, an insured would misrepresent his or her loss history by revealing only one loss if several have occurred.

Policy Provisions

All property insurance policies provide that the policy will be void or that coverage will not be provided to an insured when the insured engages in fraud, concealment, or misrepresentation.

The HO-3 homeowners policy states the following in Section I—Conditions:

> Concealment or Fraud. We provide coverage to no "insureds" under this policy if, whether before or after a loss, an "insured" has:
>
> 1. Intentionally concealed or misrepresented any material fact or circumstance;
> 2. Engaged in fraudulent conduct; or
> 3. Made false statements;
>
> relating to this insurance.[15]

One purpose of the fraud and concealment condition in any policy is to prohibit payment of fraudulent claims. To pay such claims would be against public policy. The concealment or fraud condition applies to fraud in the application for insurance as well as to claim fraud.

Materiality and Intent

Misrepresentation in the application occurs when an insured has concealed or misrepresented some material fact that the insurer has relied on in issuing the policy. Common misrepresentations concern the insured's true loss or claim history, insurance history, interest in the property, and concealment of concurrent or duplicate coverage. In an insurance application, fraud, concealment, or misrepresentation is deemed material if knowledge of the facts would have influenced an underwriter in accepting a risk or charging a higher premium. In other words, if the insurer had known the truth about the insured's ownership, the insured's interest, encumbrances on real property, or the insured's actual insurance and loss history, the policy would not have been issued or would have been issued only at a higher price. In claims, a misrepresentation or concealment is material if the fact or matter misrepresented or concealed would have made a difference to the insurer in its investigation or in the amount paid under the policy.

To void the policy, the insurer must prove that the misrepresentation or concealment was willful. Concealment or misrepresentation is considered willful or intentional when the insured knows that his or her statements are false, swears falsely with reckless disregard of the truth, or swears to matters as true when he or she knows little or nothing about the facts. An intent to defraud can be inferred whenever the misrepresentation is both material and willful. In contrast, slight or trivial exaggerations, innocent or inadvertent mistakes in computation, or statements of opinion, made in good faith, regarding the property's value, do not provide the requisite intent to void the policy.

The burden of proving fraud and concealment for the purpose of voiding the policy is on the insurer. When an insurer documents fraud or concealment, the policy can be voided.

Fraudulent Claims

Adjusters assigned to investigate suspicious claims must do so responsibly. They must have an in-depth knowledge of the policy, proper investigative methods, and the law applicable to insurance fraud. Adjusters must also guard against being overzealous and must conduct the investigation fairly, being careful not to reach premature conclusions about a claim's legitimacy.

Fraudulent claims come in many forms. **Hard fraud** usually refers to staged or invented losses. **Soft fraud** is a fraud of opportunity such as padding or exaggerating an otherwise legitimate loss. Arson for profit is probably the best example of how insureds create losses. It is probably the most common and well-known type of property insurance fraud. However, dishonest insureds can create losses by explosion, water, or almost any other peril. Staged burglaries and thefts are also common—the insured merely creates circumstances indicating that a theft or burglary has occurred. The property supposedly stolen is simply stored off premises or hidden. In commercial losses, the allegedly stolen merchandise might have been sold before a purported burglary or might not have existed at all. Fake or altered receipts and other fraudulent documents might be submitted as proof of purchase. In some cases, dishonest insureds purchase duplicate insurance to increase the recovery amount. Such insureds conceal the existence of duplicate coverage from both insurers.

Hard fraud
Staged or invented losses.

Soft fraud
Padding or exaggerating a claim for a legitimate loss.

A legitimate loss can become the opportunity for soft fraud if the insured grossly exaggerates the extent of the loss. The insured might exaggerate the amount and value of personal property that was destroyed or stolen. Some insureds might claim loss of property that was not on the premises at the time of loss. Others might claim the destruction of property that was not owned or never existed. With building losses, some insureds misrepresent the type and value of building materials to increase their recovery.

GOOD-FAITH INVESTIGATIONS

Coverage issues must be resolved correctly and promptly to avoid waiver, estoppel, and bad faith. Many situations that present coverage questions require further investigation to determine whether the claim should be denied or paid. While attempting to resolve these coverage issues, adjusters must continue to look for facts that will confirm coverage as well as facts that will result in coverage denial. And adjusters must continue to quantify the loss so that payment will not be delayed, should coverage be confirmed. Until these matters are resolved, the adjuster and insurer must avoid any conduct that would lead the insured to believe that the claim will be paid. Otherwise, a waiver of coverage defenses and policy conditions may occur.

Waiver

Waiver is the voluntary and intentional relinquishment of a known and existing right. This surrender of a known right can be made expressly or by implication. It can be oral, written, or inferred through any conduct of the adjuster or insurer inconsistent with a particular right.

The circumstances under which a waiver can occur are varied. For example, whenever the adjuster or insurer makes an unconditional offer to pay a claim after becoming aware of a coverage defense or a basis for denying liability, the insurer waives its right to deny the claim. This is true regardless of whether the coverage defenses concern a right to rescind the policy because of misrepresentation in the insurance application, a cancellation of coverage before the loss, or the lack of coverage for the loss. Payment or an offer of settlement waives a defense based on fraud and concealment.

Waiver can also occur following a claim denial. The insured might allege that the insurer, upon denial of the claim, breached its obligations, thereby waiving the continued application of the policy conditions. The insured would therefore be relieved of any further obligation to comply with the conditions.

The adjuster or insurer can waive the insured's compliance by offering to pay the loss before the insured has complied with the conditions. In some jurisdictions, the insurer waives the proof of loss condition by failing to provide or request a proof of loss within the time limits established by the insurance code. In some jurisdictions, a claim investigation in which the adjuster obtains a detailed statement from the insured covering the facts and extent of loss waives the proof of loss and examination under oath conditions. The insurer is deemed to be fully informed of the information required to be produced by these conditions.

A waiver of the insurer's option to repair or replace the property can occur when the insurer elects to pay the claim in money or enters into a formal appraisal of the amount of the loss. Making payment or initiating appraisal also waives any coverage defenses unless the insurer expressly advises the insured that it is reserving its rights to investigate further and assert policy conditions.

Estoppel

An adjuster's or insurer's conduct might result in estoppel. For estoppel to occur, the insured must rely on the insurer's conduct. The insured might change his or her position about the policy, might incur some expense, or might be led into breaching a policy condition as a result of relying on the representations or conduct of the adjuster or insurer. This situation is called **detrimental reliance**. To permit an insurer to assert a coverage defense in such cases would be improper. Estoppel prevents an insurer from claiming its right, privilege, or defense if it would be inequitable to do so because of the insurer's conduct toward the insured.

Detrimental reliance
A situation in which an insured relies on the words or actions of an insurer and that reliance harms the insured's financial position.

For example, when an adjuster tells an insured to repair a structure or to replace or repair some personal property, causing the insured to incur expense, the insurer will be estopped from raising any coverage defense or exclusion. The insurer will be estopped from claiming a breach of the proof of loss condition when the adjuster has told the insured that the proof of loss need not be filed until settlement is agreed upon. The insurer waives its rights to have the insured show or exhibit the property or to take all or part of the damaged property as salvage if the adjuster has advised the insured to discard or sell the damaged property. In these circumstances, there have been a waiver and an estoppel; the insurer is estopped from asserting that the insured breached the policy because the insured relied on the insurer's direction. Anything said or done by an adjuster or insurer that causes the insured to conclude reasonably that coverage applies or that nothing more is required to collect under the policy can constitute a waiver and can estop the insurer from asserting coverage defenses or policy conditions.

All standard property insurance policies contain provisions (or general conditions) against a waiver or change of policy provision, unless the insurer consents to waive or change a provision in writing. However, the courts have consistently held that an adjuster, as the insurer's agent or apparent agent, can waive the policy conditions, either orally or through behavior.

Avoiding Waiver and Estoppel

Property loss adjusters can avoid waiver and estoppel with timely nonwaiver agreements or reservation of rights letters, followed by prompt investigation and, when appropriate, by a carefully considered denial of coverage or a retraction of the reservation of rights. Whenever an adjuster makes advance payments while a coverage issue is pending, he or she should include nonwaiver language in the advanced payments receipt. Because of jurisdictional differences, adjusters should check the law to determine the proper nonwaiver language.

Nonwaiver Agreements

Nonwaiver agreements and reservation of rights letters both serve the following general purposes:

1. To advise the insured that any action taken by the insurance company in investigating the cause of loss or in ascertaining the amount of loss is not intended to waive or invalidate any policy conditions
2. To clarify that the agreement's intent is to permit an investigation of the claim and that neither the insured nor the insurer will thereby waive any of its respective rights or obligations

The two types of nonwaiver agreements are general and specific. A general nonwaiver agreement includes the above two items. This type of agreement is commonly used in daily claim adjusting whenever the insurer is concerned about investigating a claim before the insured has substantially complied with the policy's duties after loss conditions. Exhibit 6-5 shows an example of a general nonwaiver agreement.

A specific nonwaiver is used whenever the insurer becomes aware of a specific coverage problem or defense. This might occur because of information provided in the initial report, during initial contact with the insured, or during an inspection of the damaged property. Exhibit 6-6 illustrates a specific nonwaiver agreement. It contains the same provisions as a general nonwaiver agreement, but it includes a blank space for the adjuster to enter the specific reasons for the coverage question after the words: "Specifically, your policy. . . . " The adjuster should fill in the specific policy provisions or exclusions that raise questions regarding coverage. The adjuster should then explain to the insured the reasons for requesting a nonwaiver agreement, request that he or she sign it, and provide the insured with a copy of the agreement.

Reservation of Rights Letters

Reservations of rights letters serve the same purpose as nonwaiver agreements, but they are in letter form. They contain the same general provisions and might include a more specific reason for the coverage question. Like a specific nonwaiver, a reservation of rights letter should list the specific coverage part, provision, or exclusion that applies to the situation in question. Some claim supervisors attach photocopies of the specific policy provisions at issue so that the insured understands the insurer's concerns. Reservation of rights letters also include wording through which the insurer reserves the right to raise other coverage issues later if they become known.

Reservation of rights letters are usually sent to all named insureds (sometimes with copies to loss payees) by certified mail and are return receipt requested. Some are hand-delivered so that the insurer has evidence of the insured's receipt of the letter. They are used whenever face-to-face contact cannot be

EXHIBIT 6-5

General Nonwaiver Agreement

NONWAIVER AGREEMENT—FIRE LINES

Insurance Company (hereinafter called the "Company") agrees with ______________________________
(hereinafter called the "insured") as follows:

1. The Company has heretofore issued to the insured policy No. ______________________________
2. The Insured has reported to the Company a loss said to have occurred as a result of ____________ on or about ____________ at ______________________________ by reason whereof the insured claims damage to the property insured by policy No. ____________
3. That any action taken by the Company in investigating the cause of loss, or investigating and ascertaining the amount of the actual cash value of the property or the amount of the loss and damage, shall not waive or invalidate any of the terms or conditions of the policy and shall not waive or invalidate any rights whatever of either of the parties to this Agreement.
4. Neither the examination of the insured or of any other person, the examination of the books of account, bills, invoices or other vouchers of the insured or of any other person, the request of any other information, or the furnishing thereof, or the incurring of any trouble or expense by the insured shall waive or invalidate any of the terms and conditions of the policy or policies, or any defense thereunder.
5. The intent of this Agreement is to preserve the rights of all parties hereto, and to permit an investigation of the cause of the loss, the investigation and ascertainment of the amount of actual cash value, or the amount of loss or damage, or any of them without regard to the liability of the Company.
6. Execution of this Agreement shall not be taken as a waiver or surrender by the insured of any claims or rights under said policy and no representations have been made by the Company to induce the insured to execute this Agreement, except as herein contained, and the insured affirms that he has read this Agreement and fully understands the terms and effect thereof.

Executed in triplicate this ________ day of ______________ 20 ____ .

Witnesses:	INSURANCE COMPANY
______________________________	By ______________________________
______________________________	Insured ______________________________

EXHIBIT 6-6

Specific Nonwaiver Agreement

NONWAIVER AGREEMENT

IT IS HEREBY UNDERSTOOD AND AGREED by and between the parties signing this agreement that any action taken by the hereinafter named Insurance Company or Companies in investigating the cause of loss, or investigating and ascertaining the amount of sound value, or the amount of loss and damage which occurred on ________________, 20 ______, shall not waive or invalidate any of the terms or conditions of any policy or policies, and shall not waive or invalidate any rights whatsoever of either of the parties to this agreement.

IT IS FURTHER UNDERSTOOD AND AGREED that neither the examination of the insured or of any other person, the examination of the books of account, bills, invoices, or other vouchers of the insured or any other person, the request of any other information, or the furnishing thereof, or the incurring of any trouble or expense by the insured shall waive or invalidate any of the terms and conditions of the policy or policies, or any defense thereunder.

Specifically, your policy ____

____

____

____

____

____

THE INTENT of this agreement is to preserve the rights of all parties hereto and to permit an investigation of the cause of loss, the investigation and ascertainment of the amount of sound value, or the amount of loss and damage, or any of them without regard to the liability of the named Insurance Company or Companies.

WITNESS our hands in duplicate this ________ day of ________________ 20 _____ .

______________________________	______________________________
	INSURANCE COMPANY
______________________________	BY: ______________________________
______________________________	______________________________

made to obtain a nonwaiver agreement or whenever the insured has refused to sign a nonwaiver agreement. A reservation of rights letter is as effective as a nonwaiver agreement as long as receipt by the insured can be shown. Some claim managers prefer to use both nonwaiver agreements and reservation of rights letters to ensure that notice to the insured of coverage questions is clearly documented.

Further Investigation

Once the insured has signed a nonwaiver or acknowledged receipt of a reservation of rights letter, the adjuster can investigate the cause and extent of the loss without concern about waiving either party's rights. The information obtained through the investigation can then be provided to claim management so that an informed decision can be made regarding coverage. Many adjusters treat nonwaiver agreements and reservation of rights letters as ends in themselves. This is a mistake. Both are tools that enable an adjuster to further investigate and evaluate a claim. The coverage issue must be resolved as quickly as possible, and the insured must be informed of the resolution.

Denial Procedures

Most insurers have established guidelines and strict procedures for the denial of claims not covered under the policy. The adjuster's supervisor or a file examiner might review smaller claims before the adjuster is authorized to deny them. Other claims, depending on the insurer's procedures, require review at the level of branch office claim manager. More serious claims and claims involving certain types of policies or types of business are typically referred to regional claim managers or are reported to home office claim staff.

To assist claim staff with difficult or questionable claims, many insurers have established claim committees within their branch, regional, and home offices. These committees are made up of personnel with extensive experience in claims, usually supervisors and claim managers. Adjusters handling doubtful claims present their claim at a committee meeting at which the claim file can be reviewed and discussed. If the claim committee thinks additional information is necessary to reach a decision regarding the claim, the adjuster will be given suggestions for further investigation. The claim committee might also require a legal opinion from an attorney before making a final recommendation.

The claim committee might decide that coverage is in order and that the claim should be paid. Or it may decide that denial is appropriate. The insurer then has two options: (1) the claim can be denied by letter, specifying the reasons for the denial and citing specific provisions of the policy, or (2) the insurer may file a declaratory judgment action. In a **declaratory judgment action**, the insurer requests a court to review the evidence and determine the parties' duties and obligations under the policy. Determining coverage through this type of legal action is usually done only when the law is unclear or undecided or when the exposure on the claim is high.

Declaratory judgment action
Legal action in which the plaintiff requests that the court review the evidence and determine the rights and duties of the parties to the dispute.

Advance Payment Receipts

Partial payments of claims are sometimes advanced to insureds when they demonstrate the need for, and request an immediate payment for, emergency reasons. In homeowners losses, insureds and their families might need temporary housing or money for food and clothing. In commercial property losses, insureds might need funds for emergency repairs to the structure or to replace destroyed or stolen equipment so that the business can operate and thereby minimize business income loss. Advance payments are usually made during the first few days after a loss before the insurer can fully investigate the cause of loss and before the insured has fully complied with policy conditions. Because the courts have held that payment waives coverage defenses, including the insured's failure to comply with policy conditions, the insurer must act to avoid a waiver. This is accomplished with an Advance Payment Receipt—Reservation of Rights Form. An example of such a receipt appears in Exhibit 6-7.

The receipt is essentially a nonwaiver agreement, but it also serves to advise the insured of the following:

1. The insurer has neither accepted nor denied the claim.
2. Payment is not an admission of liability.
3. Payment is made in response to the insured's good-faith representation regarding the loss and request for payment.
4. The insurer does not waive any conditions and expects full compliance under the policy.
5. If the claim is not covered or is invalid, the insured agrees to repay the insurer the amount advanced.
6. If the claim is valid, the advance will be deducted from or credited against any covered claims.

Advance payment receipts are routinely obtained even when the policy clearly covers the cause of loss and circumstances surrounding the loss. As a practical matter, they help to keep track of payments made under certain coverages, help comply with unfair claim practices acts, and clarify to the insured that the advance payments will be applied against the final claim. Such receipts are essential when handling losses involving suspected arson and insurance fraud; without them, payment of such claims would waive any defense against the insured's breach of conditions regarding false swearing, fraud, and concealment. Although advance payments demonstrate the insurer's good faith, they should not be made unless the property loss adjuster obtains a receipt.

Bad Faith

Many jurisdictions have enacted rules, regulations, and laws to control conduct involving claim handling and settlements. Adjusters' good-faith duties stem from three sources: (1) the policy or contract, (2) the law of bad

EXHIBIT 6-7

Advance Payment Receipt

Advance Payment Receipt and Reservation of Rights

I, the undersigned, hereby acknowledge the receipt of ________________ Dollars ($ ____________) in partial payment of the claim for insurance benefits which I have asserted in connection with a policy of insurance issued by ____________________________________ (herein the Company) and bearing Policy Number ________________. The claim I have made pertains to a __________________ loss which I reported as having occurred on or about the __________ day of ________________ , 20___.

I understand and acknowledge that the Company is continuing to investigate, in good faith, the claim I have made, that my claim has neither been accepted nor denied, that the advance payment is not an admission of liability whatsoever on the part of the Company, and that the payment should not be considered payment under the policy.

I further understand that the Company is making this advance payment in good-faith reliance upon the claim I have made, the representations I made to the Company in support of that claim, and my express request for an advance payment.

I further understand that the Company reserves its rights under the policy and will require full compliance with all the conditions of the policy including, but not limited to, my submission of a proper Sworn Statement in Proof of Loss, the submission of receipts, invoices, books and records, and that the Company may exercise its right to require me to take an examination under oath, if deemed necessary.

I further understand that if the policy or the claim is not valid and payment is not required by the Company, I will repay the advance to the company.

I further understand that if the policy and claim are deemed valid that the advance will be applied against any benefit due under the policy.

TO BE SIGNED BY ALL NAMED INSUREDS

______________________________________ Coverage paid under ________________________

Named Insured (specify)

____

Spouse or Partner

State of ________________________________

County of _______________________________

Subscribed and sworn to before me this ____________ day of ______________ , 20 ____ .

Notary Public for _________________________ My Commission Expires: ______________________

faith, and (3) unfair claim practices acts. A breach of these duties might be the basis for an insured's bad-faith lawsuit against the insurer. A bad-faith lawsuit seeks damages beyond those available in a breach of contract lawsuit. An insurer found to have committed bad faith might have to pay damages far beyond the claim amount. This payment would have to come from the insurer's own assets. Claim and corporate management are highly sensitive to any bad-faith suit because of the negative effect it can have on the insurer's reputation and financial status.

Contractual Duties

Insurance contracts contain conditions obligating each party to perform certain duties following the loss. The insured must report the claim promptly, file a sworn statement in a proof of loss, and do other things before the insurer is obligated to pay covered claims. The insurer must investigate the claim promptly and appraise and pay covered claims in a timely manner, either within the time limits specified in the policy or by the time limits set in the applicable unfair claim practices statutes. If an insurer fails to pay a covered claim or negligently denies liability under the policy, the insurer might be liable for breach of contract damages and/or extracontractual damages. Depending on the jurisdiction, contract damages might include prejudgment interest, court costs, other penalties prescribed by statute, and attorney fees, as well as the amount of the loss that should have been paid.

The Law of Bad Faith

In addition to a policy's contractual duties, the insurer has a duty implied by law to act in good faith. If the insurer has behaved otherwise, the insured may allege breach of the duties of good faith and fair dealing. In property claims, this is commonly called **first-party bad faith**. In most jurisdictions, the misconduct must go beyond ordinary negligence or breach of contract to be bad faith. The insured must usually plead and prove that the insurer *intentionally* breached its duty of good faith or was guilty of oppression, fraud, or malice. However, other states may have different standards. If the insured prevails in such cause of action, he or she might recover **extracontractual damages**. These are punitive damages and damages for things such as emotional distress, lost profits, or consequential damages awarded in addition to compensatory and statutory damages.

First-party bad faith
The insurer's mishandling of a first-party claim that can result in extracontractual damages.

Extracontractual damages
Damages that are beyond breach of contract damages.

An insurer's breach of its good-faith duties generally falls within one of five areas:

1. Inadequate investigation
2. Improper denial of coverage
3. Unreasonable delay in payment
4. Unreasonable compromise
5. Withholding payment of undisputed portion of the claim

An insurer cannot reasonably and in good faith deny payment to an insured without thoroughly investigating the facts of the case. This means that the adjuster and insurer must conduct a fair and unbiased investigation, giving as much consideration to the insured's rights under the policy as to their own. An insurer must also pay covered claims within a reasonable time after the insured has fully complied with policy conditions. An unreasonable delay in paying the claim can expose the insurer to extracontractual damages. Most policies and many state laws specify the time period in which the insurer must make payment or deny liability. Also, an insurer must not force an insured to accept a compromise settlement by alleging fraud or by threatening legal action or other consequences. The insurer may also pay that portion of the claim in which the coverage and amount of loss are undisputed, depending upon the jurisdiction. The insurer can then proceed to resolve disputes as to any remaining portion of the claim, such as by invoking the appraisal procedure.

Unfair Claim Practices Acts

Almost all states have enacted some form of unfair claim practices statutes. The acts are designed to prohibit certain unfair and deceptive claim practices. Some states have specific regulations that establish time limits (usually fifteen to thirty days) within which an insurer must pay, respond to, or deny claims following receipt of a proof of loss.

When an insurer has engaged in prohibited conduct with such frequency as to make the behavior a general business practice, the acts provide for fines or penalties, as well as administrative sanctions by the state insurance commissioner. In a few states, insureds may use violation of the act as a basis to sue the insurer and recover damages. However, in most states, only the department of insurance has the power to enforce the unfair claim practices act.

Most of the provisions in these acts deal with four major areas of unfair or deceptive claim practices:

1. Delays
2. Failures to act
3. Failures to communicate
4. Denials

Delays that are considered unfair and prohibited by law include delays in responding to claims or communications, delays in settling claims by requesting formal proof of loss, and delays in payment of claims when liability is reasonably clear. Failing to conduct a timely or an adequate investigation is considered an unfair claim practice by most acts. However, the acts usually have a mechanism by which an adjuster can obtain extensions of time to complete an ongoing investigation. Failing to communicate to the insured the specific coverage under which a payment was made is usually an unfair claim practice. Adjusters must also explain any denial or offer of a claim compromise with reference to the policy, the facts, and any applicable law. Unjustified denials, which include denying a claim without conducting a reasonable or an adequate investigation, are also considered an unfair claim practice.

EXAMINATIONS UNDER OATH

An examination under oath (EUO) can be a valuable tool for an insurer when a fraudulent claim is suspected. The EUO often clarifies issues sufficiently for the adjuster to recommend acceptance of the claim as submitted. The examination can provide new avenues of investigation for the adjuster to pursue. Or the EUO can reinforce the adjuster's suspicions regarding the fraudulent nature of the claim.

When To Use an Examination Under Oath

The adjuster should conduct an EUO as early as possible in the investigation if the claim's validity or value is in question or if the facts are unclear. The insurer can use the EUO to resolve serious questions about a claim, doubts about whether a loss actually occurred, or questions about who is covered under a policy.

Adequate Prior Investigation

Although the EUO should occur as early as possible in the investigation, the adjuster should have sufficient information for the examination to be useful. The adjuster should obtain statements of the parties involved and should receive, verify, and fully review bills, receipts, records, and other documentation *before* the EUO. The insurer's right to an EUO is not waived by the adjuster's taking informal statements from the insured, provided that the adjuster has issued a reservation of rights letter. Likewise, statements by the insured to fire marshals or other public officials do not eliminate the insurer's right to an EUO.

An effective examination also requires that whoever is conducting the examination has thoroughly established the questions that must be asked. Before the EUO, the adjuster and the insurer's attorney must review the entire claim file and agree on the areas of questioning as well as on the EUO's objectives.

Before or After Proof of Loss

Opinions vary about whether an EUO should be taken before or after a sworn statement if proof of loss is submitted. Although an EUO does not waive an insurer's right to a signed, sworn proof of loss, most adjusters prefer that a signed, sworn proof of loss be submitted before the EUO is scheduled. The rationale is that filing a proof of loss is a policy condition. The claim is considered submitted when the insurer receives the proof of loss. The insured is therefore committed to the facts sworn to in the proof of loss.

Demand for the Examination Under Oath

The examination is a condition of the policy and can be *demanded* at any time by the insurer. If an insurer decides that an EUO is necessary, the person to be examined must be told that it is a *demand* by the insurer, not a request.

Those Subject to Examination Under Oath

The insurer has the right to examine certain parties and can request an examination of others. The insured is required to give an EUO. Anyone claiming benefits under the policy is also subject to a demand for such an examination. This discussion concerns the ISO HO-3 policy, but some policies differ as to who is subject to an EUO, and the policy language also varies by state and insurer. Therefore, adjusters should examine the policy covering the person and property before arranging or demanding an examination.

In addition to those who are *required* to give an EUO, the insurer can request an EUO of anyone it chooses.

Date, Time, and Place

The insurer demanding the EUO must include a specific date, time, and place in a demand letter. Court cases have relieved an insured of the obligation to complete an EUO when the letter demanding an EUO did not state a definite date, time, and place and person before whom the insured should appear.[16]

The date, time, and place must be reasonable for the person being examined. An insurer cannot arbitrarily set a date and time that would make it impossible for the person to comply and cannot select a place that is an unreasonable distance from the examinee. The person being examined must also be given a reasonable amount of time to gather any documentation required for the examination.

Demand Letter

To be legally binding, a demand letter must contain the following elements:

- A demand clearly stating that the insurer is intent on conducting the EUO with the insured (or other examinee)
- A definite time and place for the examination as well as the name of the person who will be conducting the examination for the insurer
- The records or documents that the examinee must produce and bring to the examination
- The name, telephone number, and address of the person to contact if the examinee cannot, with good reason, be present for the examination

If the demand letter is not properly written, or if the time and place are unreasonable, the demand might not be enforceable. A second chance at obtaining the EUO might not be possible.

Procedures for Examinations Under Oath

The procedures for the EUO vary by area and company. Generally, the examination is conducted in an attorney's office. Although an adjuster can conduct the examination, insurers usually choose an attorney who is well trained in this area to conduct the examination.

Formalities

An insured required to give an EUO must appear in person and give oral testimony. Providing written answers to written questions is not sufficient. The insured need not submit to a polygraph (lie detector) test. The person examined under oath is sworn in by a court reporter that records every word said during the examination. The person examined might or might not be represented by an attorney.

Types of Questions

The insurer's attorney or the adjuster questions the person being examined. The examiner can ask anything relating to the loss. If an attorney is representing the examinee, the attorney can raise objections only to the materiality of a question. Questions are material if they might lead to information about the cause or amount of the loss, any possible contractual defense, or the insured's motives. Thus, questions about the insured's financial condition at the time of loss, the insured's whereabouts at the time of loss, the source of funds to buy the damaged property, or previous losses would all be material. The attorney cannot object to anything else and has no right to offer evidence or cross-examine the examinee. The person being examined must answer any question material to the loss and, for such a question, cannot invoke the Fifth Amendment right against self-incrimination.

Continuances

Every effort should be made to allow enough time to complete the examination in one sitting. When the examination is arranged, all parties should understand that the time allowed should be adequate for the entire examination to be completed, without having to continue or conclude prematurely. An EUO's results can change dramatically if the examination is continued.

If the EUO is not completed in one sitting, the record should state that the examination is incomplete and will be continued. The time and date for the continuance of the examination should be stated on the record. Although plausible reasons for continuances exist, they should be avoided whenever possible. A plausible reason for a continuance would be if the insured's story were much more involved and complicated than the initial evidence indicated. The attorney or another person conducting the examination should not neglect any relevant evidence just because the evidence is extensive or complex.

Signing and Swearing to Transcript

When the EUO is completed, the court reporter transcribes the statement. Next, the person who conducted the interview reviews it. The attorney or adjuster sends the document to the examinee to review and sign. Only then is the exam completed. The policy says that the examinee must "sign and swear" to his or her statements under oath.

Potential Problems With an Examination Under Oath

What happens if the examinee does not appear for the examination or appears without the demanded documents? What if more than one person must be examined? What if the insured faces criminal charges? These situations require the adjuster to proceed firmly but carefully.

Failure To Appear

When an examinee does not request that the examination be rescheduled and does not appear at the EUO's appointed date and time, the insurer has the following three options:

1. Do nothing further. In states in which an adjuster must respond to a proof of loss with a prescribed period, this is not an option if a proof has been filed.
2. Send a letter requesting that the examinee contact the adjuster to reschedule the examination.
3. Send a reservation of rights letter stating that because the examinee failed to appear, coverage for the loss may be denied.

Each insurer has different procedures for handling this situation. No further investigation with the insured should be conducted until management has been informed of the situation and has decided on a course of action.

Failure To Bring Documents

When an examinee appears for examination but does not have the demanded documentation, the insurer can (1) proceed with the examination without documentation and continue on a later date when the examinee must return with the documents or (2) record that the person appeared but did not bring the demanded documents and reschedule the EUO for another date and time.

In either case, exactly what occurred and exactly what documents were to have been and are to be produced must be recorded. The record must state the exact date, time, and place of the rescheduled examination. The meeting should not end without recording the rescheduled examination.

Separate Examinations

When more than one person is to be examined and the adjuster wants separate examinations, the attorney representing the parties might reject the demand and insist on the presence of all parties. Before demanding individual exams, the adjuster must check the law of the applicable state. Courts vary widely on this issue. Also, current ISO policies allow the adjuster to exclude any other "insured" from the examination. Thus, case law based on earlier policy forms should not determine this issue when a current ISO form applies.

Insured Facing Criminal Charges

An adjuster can demand an EUO from an insured who is being prosecuted or who is suspected of arson or fraud. If the insured refuses the EUO until after the fraud or arson charges have been decided and the insurer refuses to wait and denies the claim for violating the EUO condition, the insurer could become guilty of bad faith. Management must be involved in any decision to give an EUO under these circumstances. Although criminal charges against the insured do not eliminate the insured 's contractual obligation to appear for an EUO, it is better for the insurer to wait, if possible. Unless the adjuster's investigation will be prejudiced by delay, the claim investigation should be suspended until the insured can cooperate.

SUMMARY

Property losses vary by the type of peril that causes the loss and the type of building and contents involved in the loss. A fire loss often needs an origin and cause expert to determine where and how the fire started. If a piece of equipment or personal property is found to be the cause, the adjuster must undertake a subrogation investigation. This often requires the use of another expert to test the item alleged to be the cause of the fire.

Smoke damage can be a difficult loss to clean up. Successful restoration often requires specialists and depends on whether the smoke was hot or cold and what type of surface is involved.

Lightning is commonly alleged to be the cause of many losses, but sometimes lightning is not the real cause. Confirming the presence of lightning in the area of the loss is an important aspect of handling a lightning damage claim. Lightning often leaves distinctive damage on certain types of property. Inspection and testing can be performed to confirm that lightning caused damage.

Determining whether an explosion has occurred can be difficult because other sources of ignition can cause the same type of damage. Property loss adjusters often have to use a process of elimination to determine that an explosion is the cause of loss.

Additionally, claims for blasting damage, such as cracked plaster, are often submitted as explosion damage. Cracked plaster can result from various causes, so the property loss adjuster should thoroughly investigate the circumstances surrounding the loss before accepting the claim as damage from an explosion.

Theft claims can result from burglary, robbery, fraud, or deception. Property loss adjusters investigate the circumstances of the loss and determine coverage for the loss. Theft claims usually are reported to an index bureau containing a comprehensive database of stolen property, which can aid in detecting fraudulent claims.

Water can cause extensive damage in a short period of time. Often the source of the water is difficult to locate. And not all water damage is covered by insurance. Adjusters must always be on guard for maintenance issues when handling a water damage claim.

Mold can complicate water damage losses. Adjusters must be alert to the possibility of a mold claim in every water damage claim.

A single event that causes insured property damage in excess of $25 million is designated a catastrophe and assigned a serial number. For reinsurance purposes, all of the insured losses are aggregated at this serial number. Catastrophes present a challenge for adjusters. Large numbers of adjusters and support staff must be mobilized and sent to the area of the catastrophe. Essential services may not be functioning. Contractors and suppliers may be extremely busy and not easily available. Add to all of this the emotional stress being suffered by insureds, and the environment can be draining for all involved.

The National Flood Insurance Program (NFIP) was created to provide flood insurance to communities in flood-prone areas. The program covers residential and commercial buildings and contents. It can also insure residential condominium building associations. The NFIP has its own set of qualifications for an adjuster and its own set of claim-handling guidelines.

Despite the expansive property coverage available, not every claim is paid. Insurers can assert exclusions; changes in conditions, ownership or interest in the property; or breach of a policy condition to deny a claim. Fraud, concealment, and misrepresentation are grounds for denial of coverage. The fraud, concealment, or misrepresentation may occur during the application process, during the loss itself, or during the claim process. The adjuster must always be alert for the potential of fraud in a claim.

Every claim must be adjusted through a good-faith investigation. Adjusters must be careful not to waive any rights under the policy or engage in any conduct that would result in the insurer's being estopped from asserting its rights under the policy. One method used to avoid waiver and estoppel situations is a nonwaiver agreement. Nonwaiver agreements clarify the insurer's intent to investigate the claim without waiving any of its rights. A reservation of rights letter can also be used for this purpose. The distinction between the two is that the nonwaiver is submitted to the insured for his or her signature while a reservation of rights letter is not. Generally, each jurisdiction has case law regarding the construction of these documents and what details must be included in them.

In certain circumstances, the adjuster, in consultation with counsel, may decide that filing a declaratory judgment action is an alternative to denying a claim outright. In this lawsuit, the plaintiff (the insurer) requests that the court review the evidence and determine the parties' rights and duties under the contract. Before a declaratory judgment action is filed or a claim is denied, many insurers have the claim reviewed by a claim committee of more experienced claim handlers, to ensure that an appropriate course of action is chosen.

Many states have enacted rules and regulations regarding claim handling. The policy also establishes some requirements. And case law interprets the regulations and policy language. An insurer's breach of its good-faith duties usually occurs as a result of inadequate investigation, improper denial of coverage, unreasonable delay in settlement, unreasonable compromise, or withholding payment of the undisputed portion of the claim. If an insurer is found to have acted in bad faith, it can be subject to extracontractual damages.

One investigative tool that can aid in the resolution of a questionable coverage claim is the examination under oath (EUO). This tool should be used to verify the claim's validity. Many adjusters prefer to have a signed proof of loss before demanding the EUO. An attorney usually conducts the EUO. The insured is required by the policy to appear with requested documents and give sworn testimony. The EUO is recorded by a court reporter, and the typed transcript is later signed by the examinee.

Chapter 7 elaborates on fraud prevention, detection, and investigation. The chapter discusses various fraud schemes and arson. It also explains how special investigation units (SIUs) can be used in suspected fraud claims.

CHAPTER NOTES

1. Adapted from Dave Matana and Steve DiPilla, "Lightning Causes Electrifying Losses," *National Underwriter* (April 29, 1996), p. 9.
2. Adapted from Property Loss Research Bureau (PLRB), "Lightning and Electrical Losses, An Adjuster's Guide," 1994.
3. Adapted from Inland Marine Underwriting Association (IMUA) Loss Prevention and Control Committee, "Lightning Protection," 1996.
4. United States Environmental Protection Agency (EPA), "Mold Remediation in Schools and Commercial Buildings," World Wide Web: http://www.epa.gov/iaq/molds/intro.html (20 February 2002).
5. J. Brian Tuttle, "General Overview," *Toxic Mold: A Growing Risk,* seminar report, Guy Carpenter & Company, 2001, p. 6.
6. Cliff Zlotnik, presentation for Property Loss Research Bureau Claims Conference, February 14, 2001, p. 4
7. Patrick J. Wielinski, *Mold: Is There Coverage in Your CGL?* (Dallas: International Risk Management Institute, Inc., October 29, 2001), p. 23.
8. New York City Department of Health, Bureau of Environmental & Occupational Disease Epidemiology, "Guidelines on Assessment and Remediation of Fungi in Indoor Environments," World Wide Web: http://www.ci.nyc.ny.us/html/doh/html/epi/moldrpt1.html (20 February 2002).
9. New York City Department of Health and Mental Hygiene, "Guidelines on Assessment and Remediation of Fungi in Indoor Environments," World Wide Web: http://www.ci.nyc.ny.us/html/doh/html/epi/moldrpt1.html (20 February 2002).
10. California Department of Health Services, "Indoor Air Quality Info Sheet, Mold in My Home: What Do I Do?" World Wide Web: http://www.cal-iaq.org/mold0107.pdf (5 March 2002).

11. Adapted from Daniel Hays, "Mold Insurance Fraud Could Spread Nationwide," *National Underwriter* (September 9, 2002), pp. 28–29.
12. World Wide Web: http://www.nws.noaa.gov/om/severe_weather/sum.00.PDF.
13. Federal Emergency Management Agency, Federal Insurance Administration, Standard Flood Insurance Policy Dwelling Form, World Wide Web: http://www.appl.fema.gov/nfvp.
14. *III Fact Book 2002* (New York: Insurance Information Institute, 2002), p. 120.
15. Form HO 00 03 05 01, Copyright, Insurance Services Office, Inc., 2000.
16. Citizens Ins. Co. et al. v. Martin Herpolsheimer et al., 77 Neb 232, 10 NW 160.

Chapter 7

Direct Your Learning

Fraud Investigations

After learning the subject matter of this chapter, you should be able to:

- Describe the federal and state laws regarding fraud.
- Given a claim situation,
    - Identify indicators of fraud.
    - Identify industry resources and state and local resources used in fraud investigations.
- In an arson claim,
    - Explain under what circumstances an arson defense would be successful.
    - Identify the policy provisions used to support an arson defense.
    - Distinguish between the burden of proof in a civil lawsuit and a criminal lawsuit.
- Explain how a fire's origin and cause are determined.
- Explain the role of the members of an arson team.
- Explain how to evaluate suspicious burglaries and thefts.
- Explain the purpose of a special investigation unit (SIU) and the appropriate use of the SIU in a claim investigation.

OUTLINE

Develop Your Perspective

What are the main topics covered in the chapter?

The main subject of this chapter is insurance fraud in property claims. Several types of fraudulent property claims and suggested investigation activities are described.

Consider a suspicious claim that you are aware of and what techniques were used to investigate it.

Why is it important to know these topics?

Property loss adjusters are the first line of defense in fighting first-party insurance fraud. By recognizing potentially fraudulent claims, the adjuster can have a role in the insurer's financial success.

How can you use this information?

Apply the concepts learned in this chapter to every claim investigation to help prevent the payment of fraudulent claims.

Chapter 7
Fraud Investigations

Adjusters should be aware of opportunities to commit insurance fraud that stem from property losses. The fraudulent loss can be big or small, personal or commercial. Sometimes the fraud is perpetrated by a group of individuals, such as a car theft ring. Sometimes the fraud is caused by a single person, such as a husband arranging to have the house burned down, without his wife's knowledge. Whatever the situation, property loss adjusters must be vigilant for signs of fraud during the claim-adjustment process while at the same time conducting a good-faith investigation. This chapter discusses fraud prevention laws, fraud detection and investigation, arson, and special investigation units.

FRAUD PREVENTION LAWS

Insurance fraud not only costs insurers and insureds billions of dollars each year, but it is also a crime. Both the federal government and state governments have enacted laws regarding fraud. These laws can assist an adjuster who suspects that a claim is fraudulent. Additionally, various insurance industry organizations, such as the Coalition Against Insurance Fraud and the National Association of Insurance Commissioners, create model laws relating to insurance fraud and actively campaign for their enactment.

Violent Crime Control and Law Enforcement Act of 1994
A statute that makes insurance fraud a federal crime when it affects interstate commerce.

Federal Mail Fraud Statute
A statute that prohibits the use of the U.S. Postal Service for the purpose of defrauding or obtaining money or property by means of a false or fraudulent pretense, representation, or promise.

Racketeer Influenced and Corrupt Organization Act (RICO)
A statute that permits prosecution under federal law of two or more acts of racketeering activity, including arson, mail fraud, wire fraud, bank fraud, interstate transportation of stolen vehicles or property, and theft from interstate shipments.

Federal Laws

Various federal laws relate to fraud. The **Violent Crime Control and Law Enforcement Act of 1994**, 18 U.S.C. § 1033, makes insurance fraud a federal crime when it affects interstate commerce. (See the box that follows for tips on reading a legal citation.) The **Federal Mail Fraud Statute**, 18 U.S.C. § 1341, prohibits the use of the U.S. Postal Service for the purpose of defrauding or obtaining money or property by means of false or fraudulent pretenses, representations, or promises. The **Racketeer Influenced and Corrupt Organization Act**, 18 U.S.C. § 1961, is commonly referred to as the RICO statute. This law specifies the following as a racketeering activity: arson, theft from interstate shipments, mail fraud, wire fraud, bank fraud, and interstate transportation of stolen vehicles or property. Prosecution under the RICO statute requires at least two acts of racketeering activity.

Adjuster Tip

How To Read a Legal Citation

A legal citation begins with the name of the case (Smith v. Jones) or the name of the law (Racketeer Influenced and Corrupt Organization Act). The name is followed by the citation, which lists the volume of the series of books in which the case or law is found, the name of the series (called the reporter), and the page or section. An index of the reporter abbreviations usually appears at the beginning of any legal case reporter.

A citation looks like this:

Smith v. Jones,	575	P. 2d	672	(Alaska	1979)
↓	↓	↓	↓	↓	↓
Case Name	Volume	Reporter (Pacific 2d, in this case)	Page	State or Court	Year Decided

Note that the court's name and the year of the decision appear.

A citation to a law looks like this:

18	U.S.C.	§ 1961
↓	↓	↓
Volume	Reporter (United States Code, in this case)	Section

State Laws

Additionally, all fifty states and the District of Columbia have laws on various fraudulent activities. The states have reporting statutes and immunity statutes. Reporting statutes outline what types of activities must be reported to authorities and to whom the report must be made. The immunity statutes grant immunity to those who provide information to public authorities investigating a suspected fraud. In some states, immunity exists only when public authorities have initiated the request for information, but in most states, immunity also exists for those who initiate contact with the authorities. In most states, the immunity is limited in the sense that no immunity exists for malicious or fraudulent communications. Some states grant immunity from civil suits only, such as suits for defamation, false arrest, or infliction of mental distress. Most states grant both civil and criminal immunity. Adjusters must become familiar with the laws in the states in which they operate.

As an example, the reporting statute from the state of California says that an insurer that believes a claim is fraudulent shall report the claim within sixty days of such determination to the Bureau of Fraudulent Claims and that the insurer may also report the claim to law enforcement officials or licensing officials governed by the Business and Professionals Code. The California code grants immunity from civil lawsuits if the report is made without malice.[1]

California also has similar statutes concerning the reporting of fraudulent motor vehicle thefts, incendiary fires, and fraudulent workers compensation claims.

In many insurance companies, the special investigations unit (which is more fully discussed later in this chapter) does the actual reporting of suspected fraud, not the property loss adjuster. Even so, adjusters should be familiar with the reporting requirements and the immunity statutes in the states in which they adjust claims because they may specify the good-faith practices for claim handling in a particular situation.

FRAUD DETECTION AND INVESTIGATION

The adjuster is primarily responsible for detecting and investigating fraud. Therefore, the adjuster must be on the lookout for facts and circumstances that might signal a fraudulent claim. The adjuster should be familiar with fraudulent schemes that are common to insurance fraud but that could be carried out in different ways. Although part of the adjuster's job is to discover such schemes, the adjuster must investigate all claims fairly and thoroughly.

Fraudulent Schemes

Fraudulent schemes can be simple or complex. They can involve one person or many people. Adjusters who work in property claims become attuned to elements of a claim that might indicate a fraudulent scheme. Fraudulent schemes usually involve one or more elements. See the following box.

Typical Elements of Fraudulent Schemes

- Deliberately causing an accident or a loss
- Claiming that a loss or an event occurred when it did not
- Exaggerating the amount of a loss

Detection

When reviewing a claim, a property loss adjuster might notice one or two indicators of fraud that might or might not mean that the claim is fraudulent. The adjuster must use common sense: for example, how likely is it that a homeowner would have a receipt for every item claimed to have been stolen, or how likely is it that a business owner would not have any receipts or invoices to document his or her loss? The adjuster must consider all of the circumstances and then test any suspicions within that environment.

To be prepared to thoroughly investigate a claim, a property loss adjuster should be aware of some common fraud indicators. See Exhibit 7-1.

EXHIBIT 7-1

General Indicators of Property Insurance Fraud

Note: Adjusters should familiarize themselves with the following general indicators of insurance fraud which may apply to more than one type of fraud scheme. After review of the general indicators, the adjuster can then refer to the more specific fraud categories which follow. The following categories of fraud are separated merely to facilitate your understanding of that type of fraud. However, multiple forms of fraud may appear in a single claim.

- Insured is overly pushy for a quick settlement.
- Insured is unusually knowledgeable regarding insurance terminology and the claims settlement process.
- Insured handles all business in person, thus avoiding the use of the mail.
- Insured is willing to accept an inordinately small settlement rather than document all claims losses.
- Insured contacts agent to verify coverage or extent of coverage just prior to loss date.
- Insured is recently separated or divorced.
- Suspiciously coincidental absence of insured or family at the time of the incident.
- Losses occur just after coverage takes effect, just before it ceases, or just after it has been increased.
- Losses are incompatible with insured's residence, occupation and/or income.
- Losses include a large amount of cash.
- Commercial losses that primarily involve seasonal inventory or equipment, and that occur at the end of the selling season, e.g., a ski inventory loss in the spring or a farm machinery loss in the fall.

Reproduced by permission of the National Insurance Crime Bureau, copyright owner.

Some insurers are using technology to enhance the fraud-screening process. They are using software packages that screen claim data for specific indicators and then assign them a score or weight. A particular score or weight designates a claim as potentially fraudulent. These systems search the insurer's own claim data to find similar patterns. Links are possible to third-party databases, which increase the number of claims reviewed for potential matches.

Investigation

An adjuster has a good-faith obligation to conduct a fair and adequate investigation to determine whether a loss is legitimate and whether coverage exists for the loss. Likewise, an insured should expect to document his or her loss and that this documentation will then be verified. How far can an adjuster go in a fraud investigation without crossing over the line into invasion of privacy? Local law can vary, so an adjuster should consult with counsel to determine whether his or her investigative techniques are acceptable within the jurisdiction.

Once an adjuster has suspicions regarding a claim, it is best to involve the insurer's special investigation unit (SIU). Early involvement preserves the investigation's integrity and facilitates additional investigation. It also allows the adjuster to continue to work on the loss while the parallel SIU investigation is conducted. Industry and government resources can assist an adjuster in identifying and investigating potentially fraudulent claims.

Industry Resources

Industry resources that can assist in identifying and investigating potentially fraudulent claims include (1) index systems, (2) investigative support organizations, and (3) educational organizations. Various index systems are available to research individual claimants and specific properties that are involved in claims. These indexes are so important that they should be an integral part of every claim investigation, even for claims that do not initially appear to be suspicious. These systems can identify previously fraudulent claimants and can detect multiple claims for the same property.

Insurance Services Office, Inc., (ISO) provides an extensive database for its client companies. As of this writing, the ISO ClaimSearch® database contains information on 300 million claims and receives approximately 250,000 new claims each day.[2] Insurers, self-insurers, third-party administrators, and other participants submit claim reports on a daily basis. The database can match reports to other claims based on the same individuals or businesses, addresses, Social Security numbers, vehicle identification numbers, driver's license numbers, tax identification numbers, and parties to the loss. This database now includes information on bodily injury claims, property claims, and auto theft and physical damage claims. It allows for the search of public criminal and civil records by partnering with various federal, state, and local databases.

The Art Loss Register (ALR) can be found on the Internet at http://www.artloss.com. This is a private database of stolen artwork that can aid in its identification and recovery.

The National Equipment Register (NER) on the Internet at http://www.nerusa.com contains information on heavy equipment, construction equipment, and agricultural equipment. Insureds are encouraged to register their equipment at this site so that if a piece is stolen, the ownership can be traced. This site also provides for a used equipment search in case the adjuster is trying to find a replacement for a stolen or damaged piece of equipment. Both the ALR and NER are allied with ISO ClaimSearch®.

The National Insurance Crime Bureau (NICB) fights all types of insurance crime, including arson. The NICB's full-time field agents investigate potential criminal activity in insurance claims. The NICB sponsors a Special

Investigation Academy to educate claim personnel in all aspects of fighting fraudulent claims.

The Insurance Committee for Arson Control (ICAC) is composed of more than twenty of the leading insurers in the United States and includes participation from organizations such as the NICB and the Independent Insurance Agents and Brokers of America. ICAC is an educational and communication organization dedicated to fighting arson. It sponsors an annual National Arson Investigation Training Seminar, a training program for adjusters in the law, investigative techniques, and scientific principles of fighting arson. ICAC also sponsors an annual National Arson Forum, dedicated to coordinating the efforts of all parties interested in fighting arson, including the insurance industry, law enforcement authorities, public interest groups, and legislators.

The International Association of Arson Investigators grants the Certified Fire Investigator (C.F.I.) designation to those dedicated to investigating fire origin and cause and who meet education and experience requirements. It also publishes the quarterly *Fire & Arson Investigator*. This publication includes articles on the law and the investigation of arson as well as listings for educational programs on arson.

Various educational programs are specifically devoted to detecting and proving fraud, including arson. These include the Fraud Claim Law Associate (FCLA) program of the American Educational Institute and the fraud examiner program of the National Association of Certified Fraud Examiners.

Important resources for adjusters handling suspected fraud or arson are listed in the Appendix to this chapter.

Local and State Information

In addition to insurance industry resources, an adjuster can access information from many local and state government sources as well as the federal government. Some of these sources may require written authorization before releasing information. A special investigator or local counsel can help in determining what can and cannot be obtained without a written authorization.

Financial information may be obtained from the United States Federal Bankruptcy Court and from credit reporting agencies. Adjusters should be aware of what they can and cannot obtain under the Fair Credit Reporting Act and individual state acts. Because of the many privacy issues involved in obtaining financial information, adjusters should strictly adhere to their company's guidelines regarding the acquisition and use of such information. Some of these agencies may require written authorization before releasing any information. See the following box for other sources of information helpful to an adjuster.

Information Sources for Property Adjusters

- County registrar of deeds
- Local building permit department
- Local city recorder or clerk
- Local and county street department or department of public works
- Retailers
- State division of motor vehicles
- State division of vital statistics
- State and local tax assessor/collector
- State office of corporate registrations
- Telephone companies
- Utility companies

ARSON

Arson is one of the most significant types of fraud by insureds. **Arson** is deliberately setting fire to a building, car, boat, or other property for a fraudulent or malicious purpose. Arson is not only a property crime, but it also can involve fatalities of civilians, firefighters, and even the arsonist.[3]

Arson
The deliberate setting of fire to property for a fraudulent or malicious purpose.

Intent to defraud an insurer is not the leading cause of arson; vandalism is the leading cause. About one-quarter of arson fires are drug-related. Minors are responsible for almost half of the arson fires in the United States. The leading cause of church fires is arson, usually motivated by vandalism, revenge, or racial bias.[4]

The Arson Defense

The insurance industry pays most arson losses because (1) insureds do not commit many of the arsons and (2) proving insured involvement is often not possible. Generally, the insured is not the arsonist. Proving that the insured was involved in the conspiracy to start the fire is much more difficult than proving that the fire was intentionally started.

Arson is a defense to an insurance policy claim only if it is committed by the insured or at the insured's direction. Arson against an insured's property committed by someone else with whom the insured has not conspired is simply a covered fire. Thus, the insurance industry pays such arson losses. However, the industry also pays many claims when the insurer suspects that the insured committed arson but cannot prove those suspicions. The outcome of cases of suspected arson depends on the quality of the evidence. The quality of an arson investigation depends on the timeliness and alertness of the adjuster first assigned to the claim.

Policy Provisions

Property insurance policies have no specific arson exclusion or defense. The coverage defense for arson arises when an insured represents an arson fire as an accidental fire and seeks coverage for the loss. Such a representation violates the fraud or misrepresentation clauses that are part of every property insurance policy.

The HO-3 condition concerning concealment and fraud is discussed in Chapter 6. Neither it nor the Common Property Conditions attached to the BPP, quoted below, specifically mention arson. The Common Property Conditions state the following:

> This Coverage Part is void in any case of fraud by you as it relates to this Coverage Part at any time. It is also void if you or any other insured, at any time, intentionally conceal or misrepresent a material fact concerning:
>
> 1. This Coverage Part;
> 2. The Covered Property;
> 3. Your interest in the Covered Property; or
> 4. A claim under this Coverage Part.[5]

Representing an arson as an innocent or accidental fire violates these conditions. The true cause of a loss is certainly a material fact. Additionally, adjusters can use these conditions to void the insurance for material misrepresentations made before a loss or concerning the property in any way. Adjusters should remember the broad scope of these anti-fraud provisions when proving the cause of loss is difficult. Fraud of any type can be grounds for voiding the policy.

Other policy conditions might also be relevant to cases of suspected arson or fraud. Changes in the occupancy or use of a property are material and are usually addressed specifically in property insurance policies. For example, a substantial change in the risk covered by an HO-3 allows the insurer to cancel the policy. However, the policy remains in effect until canceled. Under the BPP, if the property is vacant for more than sixty consecutive days, the insurer need not pay at all for losses caused by vandalism, sprinkler leakage (if the insured has not protected against freezing), building glass breakage, water damage, theft, or attempted theft. The settlement amount for other losses will be reduced by 15 percent. Therefore, a fire loss would still be substantially covered.

Both the HO-3 and BPP provide that a mortgagee may submit a claim and be paid to the extent of its interest, even if the insured's claim can be denied. If a mortgagee is paid after an insured's claim has been denied, the insurer would be subrogated to the mortgagee's rights under the mortgage.

In such a situation, the insured/owner would be responsible to the insurer for the mortgage amount because, under most mortgages, the entire balance of the mortgage becomes due upon destruction of the premises.

Burden of Proof

With a specified-perils policy, the insured has the burden of proving that the cause of a loss is covered. If there is a covered cause of loss, such as fire, the insurer will then have the burden of proving any coverage exclusion, defense, or breach of policy conditions. For example, to succeed with an arson defense in denying coverage, the insurer must prove both that a fire was deliberately set and that it was set by, or at the direction of, the insured.

The arson defense is asserted in one of two contexts: (1) the insured sues the insurer for the amount allegedly due on the claim plus, usually, extra damages for bad faith, and the insurer defends on the grounds of arson; or (2) the insurer initiates a declaratory judgment action in which it asks the court to declare that the insurer has no liability under the insurance policy because of the insured's arson.

The legal standard of proof by which the insurer must prove its case is the preponderance of evidence. This is the same standard of proof applicable to any party with the burden of proof in a civil lawsuit. Preponderant evidence is the more believable evidence: it need only be slightly more believable than the evidence to the contrary. Believability is not the same as the greater quantity of evidence. Evidence in a case of suspected arson might include oral testimony, business records, tangible physical evidence, and expert analysis. The evidence might be circumstantial and might depend on inference for its meaning. In any case, properly preserved, legally admissible evidence is crucial. No amount of suspicion, conjecture, or conviction on the adjuster's part substitutes for evidence. Unless an adjuster can prove his or her suspicions with evidence, the claim is valid and should be paid.

The burden of proof in a civil suit between an insured and an insurer is easier than the burden of proof in a criminal case. Prosecutors must prove crimes beyond a reasonable doubt; a defendant should be acquitted whenever reasonable doubt exists. Unless the evidence is overwhelming, an insured might be acquitted of criminal charges of arson or might never be prosecuted. These circumstances do not prevent an insurer from asserting an arson defense to an insurance claim. A jury might believe an insured committed arson even if it is not convinced beyond a reasonable doubt. Nevertheless, an insurer considering an arson defense must recognize that some jurors will regard the insured's acquittal on criminal charges as favorable for the insured. In contrast, because of the higher standard of proof in criminal cases, an insured's conviction on criminal charges of arson is a conclusive defense to an insurance claim.

The Course of an Arson Investigation

A property loss adjuster's detection of a suspicious claim and the evidence gathered in the resulting investigation are crucial to fighting arson. An investigation into possible arson is time-sensitive and can have various outcomes. Upon initial assignment to the claim, an adjuster knows only that an insured has had a serious fire loss and expects to be paid. Adjusters must respond promptly and courteously to all initial reports of serious fire losses.

Adjusters usually become suspicious of a fire loss because of the fire's physical circumstances or because of the insured's behavior. Exhibit 7-2 lists some of the circumstances that the National Insurance Crime Bureau identifies as indicators of possible arson. However, these circumstances are only indicators and do not prove arson.

In any significant loss, especially one that might involve arson, the adjuster should obtain a nonwaiver agreement or issue a reservation of rights letter to preserve the insurer's rights while the investigation is conducted. The adjuster should preserve all of the insurer's rights, as soon as there is any indication of the existence of a coverage issue.

Upon obtaining a nonwaiver agreement or issuing a reservation of rights letter, the adjuster should immediately begin parallel investigations. The adjuster should simultaneously (1) involve all supervisors, experts, and other resources needed to prove an arson case and (2) devote an equal effort to proving the insured's innocence and determining the amount of the claim. Failing to pursue one or the other of these avenues might result in the claim being improperly resolved. If the claim does involve arson and the adjuster tries to handle it alone or with belated assistance, the important evidence could be lost, the claim could have to be paid, and the insurer could face a bad-faith lawsuit. However, developing evidence of the insured's innocence is an excellent outcome for an arson investigation. Unfortunately, some insurers have become so fixated on evidence of a deliberate fire that they have completely overlooked that the insured had no motive to commit arson and would suffer significant financial harm even with a full insurance settlement.

Exhibit 7-3 illustrates the importance of developing evidence carefully and not leaping to conclusions. Determining that a fire was deliberately set does not mean that the claim will not be paid, because the insured might not have set it. Determining that a fire was accidental does not end the need to preserve evidence because subrogation possibilities might exist. Many accidental fires and other losses result from some other party's negligence.

Arson investigations explore four areas: (1) proof of incendiary fire, (2) proof of opportunity, (3) proof of motive, and (4) other miscellaneous evidence.[6] An adjuster who becomes suspicious must act immediately. Because most adjusters do not conduct the actual fire-scene investigation, experts must be retained as soon as arson is suspected. Generally, a good practice is to hire an origin and

EXHIBIT 7-2

General Indicators of Arson-for-Profit or Fire-Related Fraud

Note: While arson-for-profit is unquestionably the most vicious and costly economic assault on the property insurance industry, claims personnel should also be alert to fraud which occurs when an insured takes criminal advantage of an accidental fire.

- Building and/or contents were up for sale at the time of the loss.
- Suspiciously coincidental absence of family pet at time of fire.
- Insured had a loss at the same site within the preceding year. The initial loss, though small, may have been a failed attempt to liquidate contents.
- Building and/or business was recently purchased.
- Commercial losses include old or nonsaleable inventory or illegal chemicals/materials.
- Insured or insured's business is experiencing financial difficulties, e.g. bankruptcy, foreclosure.
- Fire site is claimed by multiple mortgagees or chattel mortgagees.

Indicators at the Fire Scene

- Building is in deteriorating condition and/or located in a deteriorating neighborhood.
- Fire scene investigation suggests that property/contents were heavily over-insured.
- Fire scene investigation reveals absence of remains of noncombustible items of scheduled property or items covered by floaters, e.g. coin or gun collections or jewelry.
- Fire scene investigation reveals absence of remains of expensive items used to justify an increase over normal 50 percent contents coverage, e.g. antiques, piano, or expensive stereo/video equipment.
- Fire scene investigation reveals absence of items of sentimental value; e.g. family Bible, family photos, trophies.
- Fire scene investigation reveals absence of remains of items normally found in a home or business. The following is a sample listing of such items, most of which will be identifiable at fire scenes except in total burns. Kitchen: major appliances, minor appliances, normal food supply in refrigerator and cabinets. Living Room: television/stereo equipment, record/tape collections, organ or piano, furniture (springs will remain). Bedroom: guns, jewelry, clothing and toys. Basement/Garage: tools, lawn mower, bicycles, sporting equipment, e.g. golf clubs (especially note if putter is missing from otherwise complete set). Business/Office: office equipment and furniture, normal inventory, business records (which are normally housed in metal filing cabinets and should survive most fires).

Indicators Associated With the Loss Incident

- Fire occurs at night, especially after 11 P.M.
- Commercial fire occurs on holiday, weekend or when business is closed.
- Fire department reports fire cause is incendiary, suspicious or unknown.
- Fire alarm and/or sprinkler system failed to work at the time of the loss.

EXHIBIT 7-3

Course of a Fire Investigation

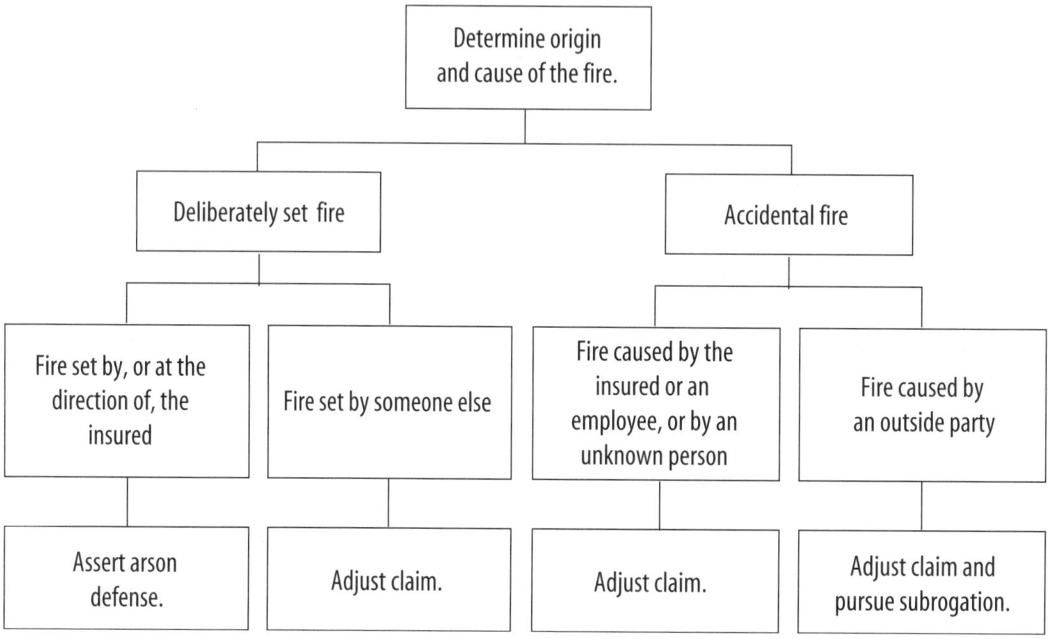

cause expert on any substantial fire loss. An origin and cause expert can assist in identifying subrogation possibilities. The experts whom an adjuster enlists in an arson investigation must also act promptly. Physical evidence from a fire-scene might be bulldozed and carted away in a matter of hours. The expert must ensure that his or her techniques for sampling, collecting, and testing will stand up to scrutiny at trial. After an insured has performed the duties following loss, he or she expects to be paid. In many states, an insurer has a certain number of days following receipt of a sworn proof of loss in which to pay a claim or to explain why it will not do so. Ideally, an insurer should have its arson investigation completed, or nearly completed, upon receipt of the sworn proof of loss. Submission of the proof of loss is likely to be only a month or two after the loss.

Duties Following Loss

The insured's duties following loss are crucial in cases of suspected arson. In a suspected arson, the adjuster must remind the insured that these duties are conditions to the policy and that the claim will not be adjusted unless these duties are performed. The adjuster should specify the need to perform these duties in the initial nonwaiver agreement or reservation of rights letter.

A proof of loss must be signed and sworn to and must state the cause of the loss. Thus, the proof of loss is a crucial document in a suspected arson. A false statement about the fire's cause is grounds to void the policy. The adjuster should also check the proof thoroughly for fraud with respect to any other matter included in the proof of loss, such as the nature of the insured's interest, the existence of other insurance, and the amount of the loss.

An insured will probably list the cause of a suspected arson as "fire." After reviewing the contents of an insured's proof of loss and supporting documentation, the adjuster should require the insured's examination under oath (EUO). If arson is suspected, an experienced examiner, perhaps an attorney who is experienced in arson investigations and arson trials, should conduct the EUO. An insured's failure to appear for an EUO, failure to bring requested documents, or refusal to answer questions is grounds to not adjust the claim any further until the insured complies. Most policies require the examinee to write his or her signature after providing answers to questions. The signature is a formality that the insurer should insist on so that a judge or jury eventually faced with the statement will have no doubt about its authenticity or materiality.

Was the Fire Incendiary?

An **incendiary fire** is an intentionally set fire. To prove that a fire was set intentionally, an investigator must determine where and how the fire began. These circumstances are known among fire investigators as the fire's origin and cause. Adjusters, or experts working for them, should determine the origin and cause of every fire, including fires that appear to be accidental. As mentioned previously, a fire might have subrogation possibilities. Fire investigators thoroughly explore the known accidental causes of fires either to rule out such causes or to verify that they played a role in the fire in question.

Incendiary fire
An intentionally set fire.

Origin and Cause of Suspicious Fires

In almost all cases, intentionally set fires do not begin or progress like accidental fires. Investigators can identify these fires as intentionally set by how they begin and progress. The **origin** of a fire is the place where it ignited. Whatever provided the heat and combustible material that led to ignition is the **cause** of a fire. Intentionally set fires usually present suspicious circumstances as to both the origin and cause. Nevertheless, a fire investigator must prove the origin and cause of any suspicious fire before an adjuster can assert an arson defense.

Origin
The location of a fire's ignition.

Cause
The mechanism or event that provided heat and fuel for a fire.

Arsonists usually intend to destroy the structure they target. To be successful, they cannot generally rely on matches and paper alone to start the fire. Small, relatively low-heat fires are easily contained and exterminated. Arsonists often use accelerants, such as gasoline or other highly flammable chemicals, to accelerate the heat and spread of the fire. A structure soaked with gasoline will be consumed in flames before firefighters arrive. Other signs that a fire was deliberately set include unusual ventilation, such as all windows open, or evidence that fire alarms and sprinklers were disabled.

A fire's origin is important. Accidental fires originate in typical places, such as electric wiring, kitchen appliances, and heating equipment. Intentionally set fires often have multiple points of origin. Multiple points of origin are powerful evidence of an incendiary fire. Accidental fires virtually never have more than one origin. Also, a fire that originates in the middle of a floor is odd and inexplicable. Such an origin likewise indicates an incendiary fire. Fires that begin around, but outside of, electrical appliances are also suspicious.

Tracing a Fire's Origin

Determining a fire's origin is not always easy or even possible. When a fire reduces everything within the four walls of a building to debris, the physical evidence from one part of the debris might be indistinguishable from another part. However, a fire that is thorough and intense is not typical, and determining the cause of such a fire might be sufficient evidence of an incendiary fire, even if the origin is never determined. Less-thorough fires leave evidence of their origin for an investigator to study.

All fires begin as a small flame. A small flame must grow and spread before it can destroy a structure. As a fire grows and spreads, the origin usually remains in the flame. Thus, a fire's point of origin usually burns longer and more intensely than does any other point. After a fire is extinguished, investigators trace the spread of a fire from its perimeter to its origin by examining burn patterns and by following basic principles of fire transmission.

Fires require combustible material to burn. After the combustible material is consumed, the fire will go out unless it has spread to, or been fed, additional combustible material. The structure itself might be a source of combustible material, but most structures do not burn readily, especially commercial structures of concrete, masonry block, and steel. Structures burn only after a hot fire has otherwise developed.

Fires spread upward much more readily than they spread horizontally. Firefighters characteristically open the roof of a burning building to relieve the built-up heat inside. Once the heat and flames can escape upward, the fire's intensity subsides considerably. A fire will not spread horizontally unless (1) it is trapped from moving upward by a ceiling or roof; (2) a great deal of combustible material, such as trash or inventory crowded closely together, is present; or (3) an accelerant is present.

Investigators looking for the origin of a fire with significant horizontal spread try to explain such spread in terms of the factors listed above. A fire trapped by a structure's ceiling or roof will burn the ceiling or roof intensely. Thus, a fire should not traverse the floor of a room unless the ceiling is severely burned. Inspection of the debris usually confirms the presence or absence of crowded combustible property, such as inventory. Lack of these factors suggests the presence of an accelerant.

Many types of witnesses can provide information regarding a fire. A complete fire investigation includes interviews with firefighters, police, the property's owners, the property's occupants, neighborhood witnesses, the caller who raised the alarm, and the person who discovered the fire. The adjuster should obtain the police report and the fire marshal's report regarding the loss. When interviewing any potential witness, the adjuster must not mention that arson is suspected or make any suggestion as to what he or she thinks caused the fire. Exhibit 7-4 lists important questions to ask witnesses. An investigator must compare the statements of witnesses to physical evidence for consistency.

EXHIBIT 7-4

Questions for Fire Witnesses

- Who discovered the fire?
- Who initiated the alarm?
- How did the witness happen to observe the fire?
- Where was the witness when he or she first observed the fire?
- Was the alarm given by an alarm or by telephone?
- Did the witness go near the building?
- Did the witness enter the building?
- What did the witness see?
- In what room or portion of the building was the fire burning when the witness first saw it?
- How large was the fire?
- What color were the flames?
- If the witness was close enough to observe, specifically what was burning?
- How rapidly did the fire spread to other portions of the building and the contents?
- Whom else did the witness observe around the building in the early stages of the fire?
- Was anyone observed in the building?
- Was anyone observed leaving the building, during or just before the fire was observed?

Identifying a Fire's Cause

Physical evidence of the cause of a fire can usually be found at its point of origin. Accidental causes of fires that begin in heating equipment, stoves, chimneys, or electric wiring can usually be identified. These devices are designed to handle fuel, heat, or electricity safely, but they can malfunction because of age, abuse, overuse, or poor maintenance. When a fire originates at one of these devices, an expert can examine the physical evidence and determine whether the fire began within the device or outside of it. A device burned from the inside shows different characteristics than one burned from the outside.

When an investigator cannot confidently identify the point of origin, the investigator must methodically examine all possible causes. In addition to examining all devices that handle heat, fuel, or electricity, the investigator should check for lightning, careless smoking, mischief by children, and vandalism. An adjuster should consider all possible innocent or accidental causes before concluding that the insured committed arson. Proving that a fire had an innocent cause is a favorable outcome of an arson investigation.

Detecting and Preserving Evidence of Accelerants

When the spread of a fire suggests the presence of accelerants or when all innocent explanations of a fire are disproved, an investigator must search for and preserve any evidence of accelerants. Fire consumes accelerants, but traces of unburned or partially burned accelerant usually survive the fire. Detection devices or trained dogs can locate accelerants in fire debris. Experts are needed to remove or document any surviving substances properly.

Sometimes, accelerants' presence can be proven indirectly. For example, if the depth of the charring on the floorboards is more than can be explained by the known heat of the fire, an accelerant was likely spread over that floor. Also, the burn pattern on the floor might show a telltale splashing pattern.

Investigators and adjusters should not leap to conclusions without adequate evidence. An insured might legitimately have gasoline, paint thinner, or similar substances stored on the premises that could catch fire. A wide variety of substances can serve as accelerants, and other materials, such as synthetic carpets, upholstery, and plastics, can have a chemical signature similar to accelerants. Thus, an expert's testimony must establish the exact nature of the substance in question and must show that the pervasiveness or pattern by which the substance was spread has no innocent explanation.

Did the Insured Cause the Incendiary Fire?

An incendiary fire is a covered loss unless it was committed by, or at the direction of, the insured. Proving the insured's involvement is an essential aspect of the arson defense. However, the insured's involvement is not necessarily likely just because an incendiary fire has occurred.

Sometimes, eyewitnesses see the insured start the fire, or the insured suffers burns while starting the fire. However, there is usually no direct evidence of who started the fire. An insured's involvement or noninvolvement in a fire is usually proven through circumstantial evidence. Some actions that the insured may have taken before, during, or after the loss can give rise to suspicion. These actions might include the following:

1. The insured is the only one at the property at the time of the loss or is the last person to be at the property before the fire.
2. In a residential loss, the insured and his or her family and pets are staying elsewhere for a short period of time.
3. The insured has a copy of the insurance policy and other records that would normally have been on the premises at the time of the fire.
4. The insured is having financial or marital difficulties.
5. The insured applies pressure for a quick settlement and is willing to take less than the policy limits so that he or she does not have to supply the adjuster with additional documentation.
6. The insured avoids using the U.S. Postal Service.

The Insured's Motive

The insured's motive for starting a fire is sometimes included as an essential element of the arson defense. Strictly speaking, the arson defense only requires proof that the insured deliberately caused the fire. Motive is not strictly necessary. However, in the absence of direct evidence of who set the fire, the insured's motive or lack of motive becomes the key circumstance. An adjuster should diligently investigate both an insured's motives to burn property and motives not to do so. Indeed, a conspicuous motive to commit arson might be the initial reason for thoroughly investigating origin and cause. Conversely, a conspicuous lack of motive is often a sufficient basis for an insurer to disregard an arson defense.

Financial need is the usual motive for an insured to commit arson. Property insurance policies are intended only to indemnify an insured for covered losses; that is, the loss settlement should return the insured to the same financial position that he or she was in before the loss. However, a loss settlement substitutes a liquid sum of cash for an illiquid, and sometimes unsalable, asset. An adjuster investigating an insured's financial motives to commit arson must examine whether the insured would be better off with cash than with the insured property. To do so, the adjuster must become familiar with the insured's financial condition. When the adjuster is investigating a fire at an insured's business site, expert accountants can inform the adjuster about the business's profitability, cash flow, and trends.

Financial motive to commit arson can arise when an asset is losing value, cannot be sold, or is overinsured. Out-of-season or obsolete merchandise is an example of property losing value. Certain other property might retain intrinsic value but be very hard to sell, such as a building in a glutted real estate market. Overinsuring property, unless done inadvertently, is suspicious. Insureds might be unaware of other insurance and other clauses of policies that prevent recovery for more than the property is worth. However, if aware of the significance of such policy clauses, an arsonist would not be likely to inform his or her insurer of other coverage.

Financial motives are not the only motives to commit arson. An incendiary fire committed by an insured is an arson even when the insured acts irrationally or harms himself or herself financially. An insured might act out of motives of revenge or hatred towards a spouse or business partner, especially during a difficult divorce or dissolution.

The Insured's Opportunity

Along with the motive to commit arson, the insured's opportunity to commit arson is powerful circumstantial evidence of involvement. The opportunity to commit arson can be demonstrated by the lack of an alibi, by behavior that enables another to commit arson, or by behavior demonstrating knowledge that arson was going to occur.

Alibi
An assertion that the party in question was elsewhere at the time the crime occurred.

An **alibi** is an assertion that the insured was elsewhere when the fire started. It is a strong defense if supported by unbiased witnesses. An adjuster should thoroughly explore an alleged alibi, including the relationships and motives of the insured's supporting witnesses. However, an insured can have a strong alibi even if he or she started the fire or enlisted someone else to start the fire. An apparent alibi can be meaningless if, for example, the remains of a timing device are found at the fire scene. A timing device can start a fire hours after being set. In such a situation, an insured with no verifiable alibi might be innocent, but that person would still have to be investigated as to having had the opportunity to commit the arson.

If, contrary to all previous practice, the premises where an arson occurred were apparently unlocked and burglar alarms were disabled, allowing access for the fire setter, an inference could be made that the insured was involved. Likewise, if an incendiary fire is set inside premises that are securely locked and have not suffered a break-in, an inference could be made that someone with keys to the premises started the fire. Proof of an incendiary fire in such circumstances is evidence supporting the allegation of the insured's involvement. However, following a major fire and firefighting activity, proving that a break-in did not occur is often impossible.

The insured's involvement can be inferred when the insured apparently knew that arson was about to occur. Following a fire, debris of personal property should be present throughout the premises. The debris should reflect the usual contents of similar premises. A business location should contain inventory, office equipment, and extensive business records. A residence should have the furniture, appliances, clothes, and other items typical to a home. The absence of a great deal of expected contents suggest these contents were removed before the fire, especially if the missing items are high-value or sentimental objects. If items seem to be missing, the adjuster should canvass neighbors for witnesses who saw their removal.

The Arson Team

An adjuster investigating and proving arson should not act alone. The adjuster should involve various experts as soon as he or she suspects arson. These experts include a professional investigator; an origin and cause expert; a forensic chemist; public authorities, such as the police, the fire marshal, and prosecutors; an attorney; and an accountant.

The Adjuster and Investigator

The adjuster or the supervisor, claim examiner, or claim manager directing the outside adjuster acts on the insurer's behalf. The insurer has promised to pay covered claims but is not obligated to pay intentionally caused losses. The adjuster must fulfill the insurer's promise but must protect the insurer's rights to deny fraudulent claims. Thus, the adjuster faces the fundamental issue in any arson investigation: Should the claim be paid or resisted? That decision has enormous consequences for both the insurer and the insured. The adjuster has an ethical obligation to deny claims that involve arson and pay claims that do not.

Adjusters must be familiar with the circumstances that might indicate arson. The adjuster's failure to recognize signs of arson could cause the insurer's rights to be waived. An adjuster who sees signs of a possible arson must know how his or her employer responds to suspected arsons and must involve the people and resources necessary to conduct a thorough and correct arson investigation.

The adjuster might serve as an investigator, or the insurer might hire an independent professional investigator. An insurer's adjuster can usually identify relevant sources of information and take statements from witnesses. Adjusters should also check industry resources for information on past claims. A professional investigator might be preferable for obtaining background information on the insured, such as financial, legal, and personal records.

The adjuster must coordinate the efforts of all others involved in the arson investigation, give clear instructions on the scope of an assignment, respond promptly to all inquiries and other issues that arise, and reserve for himself or herself the ultimate decision on the claim. An adjuster can make good decisions in cases of suspected arson by gaining experience and education in the elements of arson. Adjusters must develop a sophisticated sense of the credibility and persuasiveness of various types of evidence and should always approach an arson investigation with the attitude that proving an insured's innocence is preferable to proving arson.

Origin and Cause Expert and Forensic Chemist

Origin and cause experts are often former fire department investigators. They typically have much more experience studying fire scenes than even the most experienced adjusters do. Additionally, they usually have specific training and education in fire-scene analysis. An adjuster, even one with extensive experience, is not the best choice to determine origin and cause. Origin and cause experts must often testify in court. As the insurer's employee or agent, an adjuster would be seen as a biased witness. An origin and cause expert is crucial to proving that a fire was incendiary and thus essential to proving an arson.

To be an effective witness, the origin and cause expert must be able to demonstrate that his or her conclusions are based on specific scientific, technical, or specialized knowledge. Others must respect the methods and techniques used to support the expert's findings and conclusions in the field. An adjuster should select the origin and cause expert in consultation with senior claim staff and legal counsel so that the potential for a confrontation over the expert's methods and qualifications is minimized. Origin and cause experts should not rely solely on the fire marshal's investigation. An insurer that hires an origin and cause expert should expect an independent determination of how and where a fire began.

A forensic chemist plays a specific role in an arson investigation by detecting, identifying, and preserving chemical residue from a fire scene that is relevant to determining the cause of a fire. A forensic chemist must be trained in preserving evidence in a legally admissible manner. Also, the chemist is likely to have to testify in court and should be clear and well-spoken, especially when explaining scientific instruments and procedures. A forensic chemist might also serve as an origin and cause expert. However, the expertise of each job is distinct enough that insurers should get the best person for each element.

Public Authorities

A city or county fire marshal may investigate the fire. Some communities require all structural fires to be inspected. Others inspect only suspicious fires. The adjuster should ascertain the fire marshal's identity and scope of authority. When a fire is not investigated by a fire marshal, the adjuster must make his or her own determination as to the origin and cause, relying on the insurer's own expert.

A fire marshal has different goals than an adjuster has. The fire marshal's conclusions are used to prevent future fires, strengthen building codes with respect to fire protection, and identify suspects for criminal prosecution.

Adjusters are interested in criminal prosecutions, but they cannot defer their investigation on the assumption that the public authorities will investigate the cause of the fire and prosecute those involved. Public authorities might decline to prosecute because the evidence is insufficient for a criminal conviction or because no injuries or deaths resulted from the fire. Also, public authorities vary widely with respect to their ability, resources, and motivation to investigate and prosecute arson.

Adjusters should interview the firefighters who worked at the fire in question. These interviews should occur as soon as possible following the fire while the firefighters' memories are fresh and the public authorities are still organizing or conducting their own investigation. Property loss adjusters should determine what firefighters observed with respect to the fire's origin; whether the premises were locked and secured; whether fire alarms and sprinklers functioned; whether unusual smoke or odors were present; whether the owner appeared during the firefighting; and, if so, how the owner behaved. Firefighters might not have any special training in determining origin and cause, but their opinions about whether the fire seems suspicious are valuable. The adjuster should also interview the personnel in the fire department or fire marshal's office who are responsible for determining origin and cause.

When public authorities investigate a suspicious fire, they usually obtain a statement from the property owner. This statement should be available to the adjuster investigating the same fire. The owner's statement to the public authorities does not relieve the insured of the obligation to submit to an examination under oath. The examiner conducting the EUO should look for discrepancies between the EUO and the statement given to the public authorities.

Attorneys

A claim denied as arson is likely to result in a lawsuit. Adjusters must foresee having to prove their position to a judge or jury. Adjusters who handle suspected arsons must learn the rules of court evidence and develop their investigations accordingly. They might have to appear in court as witnesses. Attorneys experienced in arson cases help prepare adjusters for court and can answer legal questions.

Defending an arson claim has three key elements. First, a good investigation with proper documentation and qualified experts is essential. Second, the denial of the claim has to have been accomplished in a timely and effective manner. Third, a declaratory judgment action should be filed shortly after the denial is issued. Attorney involvement in all of these elements helps to ensure a successful defense.

Part of an adequate investigation is the examination under oath. An attorney usually conducts the EUO because experienced attorneys are familiar with the style and scope of questioning required in these examinations. Also, the adversarial nature of EUOs requires someone other than the adjuster to be the examiner because the adjuster must continue to communicate with the insured. An EUO is an excellent opportunity to see what kind of witness the insured will make. An arson defense's success or failure depends heavily on the insured's credibility. Adjusters should attend EUOs as often as possible.

Adjusters should also involve an experienced trial attorney in suspected arson cases as soon as possible. Attorneys with the right experience can advise adjusters about what evidence is essential, what evidence is persuasive, and what evidence is favorable to the insured. If they follow an experienced attorney's advice, adjusters should go to trial with an arson defense only with solid cases. A solid case is protection against bad-faith liability.

Accountants

Because one of the most common motives for arson is financial, involving an accountant in an arson investigation is important. By the time of an examination under oath, an adjuster should know as much about the insured's financial condition as the insured does. Few adjusters have sufficient training in accounting to do this by themselves. Upon first becoming suspicious of an arson, the adjuster should immediately request complete financial records from the insured. The BPP Duties In The Event Of Loss specifically provide, "As often as may be reasonably required, permit us to . . .examine your books and records. Also permit us to . . .make copies from your books and records."[7] An adjuster should request at least the insured's tax returns, records from suppliers, all evidence of indebtedness, all regularly prepared financial statements during the past year, and all bank statements from the past year. The adjuster should also consult with an expert accountant to determine what other records are important and likely to exist.

An accountant might want several years' worth of records to look for trends in the insured's business. The insured's business might have natural seasonal or annual trends. Apart from such natural trends, an accountant can discern the overall trend for the insured's company. Is the insured's business failing, or has it recently lost some revenue? Have the owners tried selling the business recently? An accountant can answer these questions and can spot other telltale signs of trouble. For example, a business that fails to pay the Internal Revenue Service (IRS) the withholdings from its employees' pay is in both legal and financial trouble. An accountant can address the ultimate question about the insured's financial motive: Would the insured be better off with an insurance settlement than with an intact building?

OTHER TYPES OF PROPERTY LOSS FRAUD

Arson is one of the most serious types of property loss fraud, but adjusters should be alert for other types of property loss fraud, including staged burglaries and thefts, padded claims, and claims under multiple policies. As with arson, the two keys to fighting any type of fraud are (1) detection and (2) proof. Adjusters must be alert for indicators of fraud and, once alerted, must diligently gather evidence that proves the fraud.

Staged Burglaries/Thefts

Following a burglary or theft, the insured property is gone and is rarely recovered. Thus, burglaries and thefts are easy to stage. An insured staging a burglary might break a door or window lock with a crowbar to simulate a burglar's break-in. A damaged lock can be included in the claim, but there need not be any physical evidence of the event. Most homeowners cannot document the vast majority of their personal property.

Exhibit 7-5 lists circumstances that the NICB has indicated would be suspicious in burglary or theft claims. Adjusters should remember these circumstances but must also remember that any of them can arise in legitimate losses. These circumstances are only indicators and not proof of fraud. An adjuster who is suspicious about the circumstances of any loss must gather solid evidence to prove fraud. As with arson investigations, adjusters must reserve the insurer's rights, must require the insured to perform all duties listed in the policy, and must move rapidly in the investigation.

Adjusters must exercise judgment with burglary and theft claims. Although most homeowners cannot document most of their personal property, they are more likely to have evidence of high-value items. They might have owners' manuals, checks, or receipts, or they might remember where they bought the items. Many stores have records of purchases that go back several years by individual customer name. If the property was alleged to have been a gift, the donor should be able to identify the store where it was purchased. Nevertheless, some homeowners who suffer genuine burglaries or thefts cannot produce documentation or remember how they obtained their property. Adjusters should be creative and reasonable regarding documentation. Photos, videos, boxtops, and labels can be useful in documenting ownership when the receipt is no longer available. However, just about anything can be created to document a fraudulent claim, so adjusters should scrutinize all information about the loss.

> **Adjuster Tip**
>
> The NICB has the technology to analyze receipts or documents to determine whether they are forgeries or whether alterations have been made to them.

Adjusters must evaluate the plausibility of every reported burglary or theft. Is the type and amount of property allegedly stolen consistent with the insured's standard of living? Does the claim include items such as artwork, antiques, jewelry, guns, or musical instruments that often have individual floater coverage and are individually underwritten? Were all items supposedly purchased recently? Does the claim include high-value items that burglars might not take because of their bulk or weight, such as large Oriental carpets or large power tools? Does the claim include items that burglars virtually never target, such as clothes, kitchen utensils, books, sofas, or washing machines?

Alleged burglaries to commercial insureds present different challenges than do homeowner claims. Commercial insureds should have complete records of their property, including types, amounts, quality, and sources and dates of purchase. Adjusters should be able to document the property's existence. With commercial insureds, a typical fraudulent burglary involves relocating the "stolen" property. Adjusters should canvass the neighborhood for witnesses of extensive moving operations, especially during irregular hours. The adjuster should try to interview employees, alone and separate from each

EXHIBIT 7-5

Indicators of Burglary/Theft Fraud

- Losses include total contents of business/home including items of little or no value.
- Losses are questionable, e.g. home stereo stolen out of car, fur coat stolen on trip to Hawaii.
- Losses include numerous family heirlooms.
- Losses include numerous appraised items and/or items of scheduled property.
- Extensive commercial losses occur at site where few or no security measures are in effect.
- No police report or an over-the-counter report in situations where police would normally investigate.

Indicators Associated With the Claims Process

- Insured over-documents losses with a receipt for every loss and/or receipts for older items of property.
- Insured's loss inventory differs significantly from police department's crime report.
- Insured cannot provide receipts, canceled checks or other proof of ownership for recently purchased items.
- Insured provides numerous receipts for inexpensive items, but no receipts for items of significant value.
- Insured provides receipt(s) with incorrect or no sales tax figures.
- Insured provides receipt(s) with no store logo (blank receipt).
- Loss inventory indicates unusually high number of recent purchases.
- Insured cannot recall place and/or date of purchase for newer items of significant value.
- Insured indicates distress over prospect of an examination under oath.
- Insured cannot provide bank or credit card records for recent purchases of significant value.
- Insured provides receipts/invoices from same supplier that are numbered in sequence.
- Insured provides receipts from same supplier with sequence numbers in reverse order of purchase date.
- Insured provides two different receipts with same handwriting or typeface.
- Insured provides single receipt with different handwriting or typefaces.
- Insured provides credit card receipts with incorrect or no approval code.

other, about the alleged event. As with arsons, adjusters need information about the financial condition of the insured's business. A successful business with good current inventory is much less likely to stage a burglary than is a failing business with unsalable inventory.

Adjusters should require all insureds to report all burglaries or thefts to the police. Among the duties after loss in the HO-3 is that the insured must notify the police in case of loss by theft. The BPP requires the insured to notify the police if a law may have been broken. Adjusters should require a signed, sworn proof of loss with every burglary or theft claim.

Padded Claims

A legitimate loss can be the occasion for an insured to inflate the claim by including items that were not part of the loss or by inflating the value of items that were. Insureds who engage in this behavior rationalize it in terms of recovering their deductible or premium payments. Some in the insurance industry even regard this "soft" fraud as less objectionable than the "hard" fraud of completely fabricated claims. Nevertheless, an insured who intentionally misrepresents a material fact commits fraud. Items that are the subject of a claim and their value are material facts to which the insured must swear in a proof of loss. The circumstances listed in Exhibit 7-5 might also be present when an insured pads a claim.

Requiring the insured to prove his or her claim is crucial to fighting padded claims. Adjusters should insist that insureds submit sworn proofs of loss and all required supporting documentation in all cases of suspected padding. As with suspicious burglaries, adjusters should consider the inherent plausibility or implausibility of the insured's claim. Unfortunately, padding can be difficult to detect.

Multiple Policies

An insured who has two or more policies covering the same loss and who does not disclose the multiple coverages to all insurers has almost certainly intended fraud from the outset. An insured might inadvertently have two or more policies in effect at once but should disclose these policies to all affected insurers when a loss occurs. The other insurance clauses of the various policies will then result in the insured's receiving only an amount that indemnifies the loss. An insured should not collect multiple recoveries for the same loss. However, if the various insurers do not know about the multiple policies' existence and if the insured has submitted a fraudulent proof of loss to each insurer, swearing in each that no other coverage exists, there is the potential for duplicate recovery.

An insured who submits the same claim to several insurers has probably staged the claim. Any indicators that a claim might have been staged should also alert the adjuster to the possibility of multiple insurance policies. By using one of the index systems, the adjuster can detect multiple claims from the same loss or multiple claims involving the same property. Adjusters should make a habit of submitting all claims to an index system, even those that seem completely legitimate.

SPECIAL INVESTIGATION UNITS (SIUs)

Special investigation unit (SIU)
A unit within an insurance company dedicated to investigating suspicious claims.

Insurers have established units specially dedicated to investigating suspicious claims and other possible frauds. These units are usually known as **special investigation units (SIUs)**. Personnel selected for SIU work are carefully trained. They perform investigations that are infeasible for claim representatives and property loss adjusters handling routine claims.

The Need for SIUs

Most claim departments are staffed on the assumption that all claims are routine. Such staffing makes devoting more time or effort to suspicious claims difficult. The appropriate investigation of suspicious claims, described earlier in this chapter, is time-consuming. Furthermore, since the 1970s, insurers have relied more on telephone contact than on in-person meetings to resolve claims.

State legislatures and insurance departments have been aware for years of fraud and its cost. Most states make insurance fraud a crime. Before the 1990s, only a few states had bureaus within the state government devoted to fighting insurance fraud. Today, forty-one states have some type of fraud bureau.[8] Additionally, several states require insurers to maintain SIUs. State requirements have increased the already existing incentive for insurers to create and operate SIUs.

The Mission of SIUs

SIUs do not exist simply to deny claims. Claim representatives could deny claims in much greater volume and at much less expense. Likewise, SIUs do not exist simply to prove fraud. SIU investigations often prove that a claim is legitimate and should be paid. SIUs exist to determine the facts about suspicious claims, to prove fraud when it can be proven, to avoid improper and unfounded accusations that can cause bad-faith problems, and to pay claims that the evidence supports.

SIUs investigate more than just first-party property claims. Suspicious circumstances might also exist in workers compensation cases, auto accidents, auto theft claims, and bodily injury claims. In addition to addressing individual claims, SIUs investigate organized rings of professional claimants and any doctors, lawyers, and body shops that assist such rings. When the evidence supports a finding of fraud, SIUs also try to obtain criminal prosecutions through the state attorney general, local prosecutors, or the United States Attorney, in cases of violations of federal law. Successful criminal prosecutions require expert collection and preservation of evidence. Therefore, many SIUs employ former police or other law enforcement authorities.

Some SIUs investigate types of fraud other than claim fraud. For example, SIUs might be assigned to investigate the following:

- Misrepresentations on policy applications, including identity and use of vehicles; exposure base and classification of workers compensation; the applicant's financial condition; and claims history
- Agents' wrongdoing, including the appropriation of trust funds, the issuance of phony bonds, and the failure to place coverage
- Internal fraud, including collusion by claim personnel with outsiders, embezzlement, and kickback schemes

SIU personnel who investigate white-collar wrongdoing in the insurance industry must have different skills than those required by typical criminal investigations, and they must have a thorough understanding of the legal, contractual, and business relations among insureds, applicants for coverage, agents, company personnel, and insurers.

Insurer Interest in SIUs

Insurers have a significant self-interest in fighting fraud. Payment of fraudulent claims is extremely expensive. Because of the nature of fraud and the difficulty of estimating exaggerated claims, the precise number of paid fraudulent claims is impossible to state. The annual cost of fraud is undoubtedly comparable to the cost of the worst natural disasters. Consequently, all property-casualty insurers fight fraud, and nearly all have a formal fraud-control program.

The insurance industry supports collective resources for fighting fraud, such as the NICB's Special Investigation Academy for training in fraud awareness and investigation. Also, the International Association of Special Investigation Units (IASIU) is a professional organization of SIU personnel. It has conducted an annual seminar on fraud awareness, investigation, and prosecution since 1986. Moreover, several insurers have joined the Coalition Against Insurance Fraud, a group of insurers, consumer organizations, and governmental bodies that tries to influence public policy through a united effort by the various organizations affected by fraud.

Anti-fraud programs' prevalence and size often depend on the insurer's size.[9] The lack of state requirements and specialization in types of insurance that are less prone to fraud are often reasons why a small-to-medium-sized insurer does not have a formal anti-fraud program.[10] The difficulty in performing a true cost-benefit analysis may be another reason. The costs of a formal anti-fraud program are usually quantifiable, but the benefits are far less easy to identify and quantify. Nevertheless, fighting fraud can result in the following benefits to an insurer:

- Successful denial of fraudulent claims that can be quantified (for example, arson of a known dollar amount)
- Successful denial of fraudulent claims that cannot be easily quantified (for example, phony injury claims whose dollar amount cannot be precisely known)

- Reduction of exaggerated claims
- Discouragement to those considering submitting fraudulent or exaggerated claims
- Increased public awareness that fraud can and should be fought

Although all of these benefits are real, only the first can be quantified. In contrast, the following are the costs of SIU operations:

- Direct salary, benefits, training costs, overhead, and support for the SIU. These costs are expended on a unit that is extremely inefficient in the sense of handling relatively few claims compared to ordinary claim operations.
- Increased legal expenses, even when the SIU is successful.
- Increased bad-faith lawsuits and legal expense to defend such suits, with occasional adverse results.

State Mandates

After hearing for years from insurers about the extent of insurance fraud, many state legislatures and insurance departments enacted laws making anti-fraud efforts mandatory. Although most states have anti-fraud bureaus within the insurance department or attorney general's office, a few states have gone further. A small but increasing number of states require anti-fraud plans from insurers, and a few require SIUs.

Exhibit 7-6 is an excerpt from the Pennsylvania law requiring anti-fraud plans of auto insurers. This law is typical of the requirements contained in mandatory anti-fraud laws. Additionally, the Pennsylvania Department of Insurance has enacted extensive and detailed regulations to enforce this excerpted provision. In states with mandatory anti-fraud laws, insurers must have specific procedures in place to fight fraud. As of February 2000, Arkansas, California, Colorado, the District of Columbia, Florida, Kentucky, Maryland, Minnesota, New Hampshire, New Jersey, New Mexico, New York, Ohio, Pennsylvania, Tennessee (for workers compensation only), and Washington had laws mandating anti-fraud plans, and Delaware required insurers to report all suspicious claims to the state bureau. Many of these states require SIUs as part of the plan. California has detailed requirements in its regulations as to the organization, staffing, education, and training for SIUs, and the detection, investigation, prosecution, recording, and reporting of fraudulent claims.

SIU Procedures

An SIU's chief purpose is to resolve claims correctly. In that respect, SIUs function like ordinary claim operations and perform many of the same tasks, such as building and maintaining claim files; communicating with insureds, claimants, and witnesses; and negotiating settlements. Nevertheless, the cases assigned to SIUs are suspicious ones that require much more investigation and

EXHIBIT 7-6

Content of Plans

The anti-fraud plans of each insurer shall establish specific procedures:

- To prevent insurance fraud, including internal fraud involving employees or company representatives; fraud resulting from misrepresentation on applications for insurance coverage; and claims fraud.
- To review claims to detect evidence of possible insurance fraud and to investigate claims where fraud is suspected.
- To report fraud to appropriate law enforcement agencies and to cooperate with such agencies in their prosecution of fraud cases.
- To undertake civil actions against persons who have engaged in fraudulent activities.
- To report fraud-related data to a comprehensive database system.
- To ensure that costs incurred as a result of insurance fraud are not included in any rate base affecting the premiums of motor vehicle insurance consumers.

Title 75, Pennsylvania Consolidated Statutes Annotated, § 1812.

scrutiny than the typical claim operation can perform. Most of the operating characteristics special to SIUs result from the nature of this work.

Staffing

Two backgrounds predominate among SIU personnel: prior claims work and law enforcement work. Both backgrounds provide valuable experience, but each must be supplemented with additional training.

Claim personnel selected for SIU work are usually among the best. They typically have several years of successful experience investigating and negotiating claims and have demonstrated the interest and energy necessary to take on special duties. Upon joining an SIU, claim personnel must acquire deeper expertise in investigating claims, collecting and preserving evidence in a legally admissible manner, and litigating policy defenses. They usually acquire expertise in particular areas, such as origin and cause analysis or examination of financial records.

Law enforcement personnel seeking career advancement and a stable work environment are often attracted to insurer SIUs. They might be police or fire marshal officers who have extensive training and experience in collecting and preserving evidence. However, not every former police officer is appropriate for SIU work. The orientation of claim work, even in SIUs, is to determine whether the insurance policy covers a given situation, while law enforcement authorities are interested in proving whether a person committed a crime. Although the coverage issue faced by SIUs is often whether an insured submitted a fraudulent claim, they should always try to resolve claims according to policy language. SIUs do not presume an adversarial attitude toward the subjects of their investigations. Once hired into an SIU, a former law enforcement officer must learn insurance policy coverages, insurance business relationships, and litigation in the civil courts.

Management of SIUs is usually directly under an insurer's senior claim officer, but, depending on an SIU's focus, it might be under other non-claims corporate officers or decentralized into regional or local offices. In any case, the person to whom the SIU reports must be understanding and supportive of the SIU's mission and must be able to command adequate resources for the SIU to perform properly.

Detection and Review

SIU personnel and claim personnel throughout an insurance company must recognize fraud indicators. They cannot defend claims as frauds unless they first recognize the possibility of fraud. Claim representatives should be familiar with the fraud indicators for the types of claims they handle, because the indicators differ by type of claim. For example, the indicators of workers compensation fraud are very different from those for auto theft fraud or arson.

SIU personnel must develop more sophistication about those indicators than the typical claim representative has. In a well-functioning claim operation, claim representatives refer files for review by the SIU when fraud indicators are present. The indicators alone prove nothing. SIU personnel must develop judgment concerning which specific cases referred to them are candidates for intensive investigation and scrutiny. Such judgment is based on combinations of circumstances or the recognition that a single circumstance in a given case is compelling. In well-functioning claim operations, more files are referred to the SIU than the SIU selects for investigation.

Investigation

All property loss adjusters investigate, but SIU personnel investigate more thoroughly. Their investigations often include steps that ordinary adjusters do not take. For example, SIU personnel must learn to preserve physical evidence to criminal case standards, which involves obtaining signed waivers from owners for removal of evidence and maintaining a log showing the chain of custody of that evidence.

SIU personnel usually investigate in person. Those who would commit fraud are especially uncomfortable with direct scrutiny. When taking statements from insureds, claimants, and witnesses, SIU personnel are more likely than ordinary adjusters to verify previous names, previous addresses, Social Security numbers, spouse identification, fictitious business names, date of birth, and any other information useful in establishing the complete history of a person or business. SIU personnel establish the insurance coverage history of any insured or claimant, especially the dates of coverage and the agents who placed the coverage.

SIU investigators try to obtain original documents rather than copies. To invoke the federal mail fraud laws, SIU personnel save envelopes when they receive items in the mail. They also obtain written or recorded statements from the person who supplied or can verify the documents. In first-party losses, SIUs require insureds to complete proofs of loss, including all supporting documentation.

Insureds seeking insurance policy benefits must provide financial and medical releases upon the insurer's request. SIU personnel use these releases to obtain complete histories of the claimant's financial or medical condition. Professional accounting or medical review might be necessary to clarify a claimant's situation.

Databases and online services have greatly increased SIU investigative power. All fifty states can be searched at once for information on a claimant.

Anti-fraud laws enacted in many states require insurers to share their investigations with law enforcement authorities when a claim is suspicious. SIU personnel are usually eager to do so because a criminal conviction would be conclusive as to an insurance claim. However, SIUs must not depend on law enforcement authorities. Criminal investigation or prosecution might not be pursued because the authorities do not have the staff, training, budget, or motivation to pursue the crime or because they determine that the evidence is insufficient for criminal charges.

Training

SIUs devote significant resources to training both SIU staff and other claim personnel. SIU staff receive training from more experienced members and from formal programs run by the IASIU and the NICB. The National Association of Certified Fraud Examiners and the American Educational Institute also have fraud education programs for SIU personnel.

Education of typical claim personnel is essential to any SIU's success. SIUs receive claims only by referral from other claim personnel. Claim personnel must be educated to recognize signs of possible fraud and must know how to make referrals to the SIU. SIU personnel can conduct regular seminars and meetings with claim staff to create awareness and remind everyone of the SIU's role. Company newsletters can feature SIU activities.

Paying or Denying Claims

An SIU's objective is to resolve claims correctly. Some SIU claims are paid, and some are denied. Claims are paid when the SIU investigation proves that the claim is legitimate, or when the SIU believes it cannot prove fraud, even though the claim still seems suspicious. From the point of view of the insured and society, paying claims is preferable unless fraud can be proven. Allegations of fraud are an extremely serious matter and can result in criminal charges. However, claim staff can become discouraged from making SIU referrals when suspicious claims end up being paid, especially if the claim staff did a great deal of the investigation required by the SIU. SIU staff should be sensitive to this reaction and should explain why fraud cannot be proven in a given case. Such explanations preserve the SIU's goodwill among the claim staff and will reinforce the claim staff's fraud education.

When claims are denied, the SIU must be prepared for lawsuits. SIUs should have extensive working relationships with attorneys and law firms experienced in insurance defense work, both first party and third party. SIU personnel should be sophisticated about insurance litigation, including the persuasiveness of various evidence, the value of proposed discovery, and the need to present scientific or financial information clearly. When a claim denial is successful, whether before or after civil litigation occurs, the SIU should consider asking the law enforcement authorities to prosecute. Some SIUs are satisfied to deny a fraudulent claim, but others believe criminal prosecution is important as a matter of principle and is the best deterrent to fraudulent behavior by others.

SUMMARY

The adjuster has the primary responsibility for detecting and investigating fraud. As such, the adjuster must always watch for facts and circumstances that might signal a fraudulent claim.

Arson is one of the most serious types of first-party property claim fraud. The arson defense arises when an insured submits a loss caused by arson but swears its cause was accidental. Adjusters should learn about and look for arson indicators. Arson is proven by showing that a fire was incendiary and was set by, or at the direction of, the insured. Both elements are crucial because juvenile vandals start many incendiary fires and because many insureds who have a motive for arson suffer an accidental fire. Proof of an incendiary fire is usually made through careful, scientific analysis of the fire scene. Proof of the insured's involvement is usually made through showing the insured's motive and opportunity to commit arson. The burden of proving arson is on the insurer, but it is an easier burden of proof than in criminal prosecutions. Many parties should be involved in arson detection and proof, including the adjuster, an investigator, an origin and cause expert, a forensic chemist, the fire marshal, public prosecutors, attorneys for the insurer, and accountants. The insurance industry supports numerous organizations, associations, and educational resources devoted to fighting fraud, including arson.

The most common first-party claim frauds, other than arson, are staged burglaries, padded claims, and duplicate claims under multiple policies. As with arson, the keys to defending such claims are detection and proof.

To fight both first-party and third-party claim fraud, most insurers have established special investigation units (SIUs). Insurers have an obvious interest in resisting fraudulent claims, but most ordinary claim units are staffed in a way that assumes almost all claims are routine. To have staff with the time and expertise to investigate suspicious claims, insurers created SIUs. Many state legislatures and insurance departments have required insurers to create detailed anti-fraud plans. Like other claim units, SIUs review, investigate, and settle claims. Their mission is not to deny claims, but to resolve them correctly. Because all of the claims that they handle are suspicious, SIU staff must be highly trained in proper investigation and legal procedures. SIU personnel also play a major educational role within insurance companies.

Chapter 8 introduces the basic concepts needed to prepare a structural damage estimate. The different types of building construction along with detection and suppression systems are discussed, as this information can be useful to the investigation of the cause of loss, potentially responsible third parties, and the extent of damage. The elements of a structure and basic estimating principles and methods are also explained.

CHAPTER NOTES

1. CA Insurance Code § 1872.5, 1872.5(a) and 1872.4(a).
2. Phone interview November 1, 2002, with Susan Black, assistant vice president, American Insurance Services Group (AISG).
3. Adapted from *Hot Topics & Insurance Issues*, "Arson," February 2003, Insurance Information Institute (III), World Wide Web: http://www.iii.org/media/hottopics/insurance/test1/content (August 1, 2003).
4. III, *Hot Topics & Insurance Issues*, "Arson."
5. Common Property Conditions, CP 00 90 07 88, Copyright, Insurance Services Office, Inc., 1983, 1987.
6. Arson Basics, www.interfire.org, "Motive, Means and Opportunity, a Guide to Fire Investigation," American Re-Ins. Co., 1996.
7. Building and Personal Property Coverage Form, CP 00 10 10 00, Copyright, Insurance Services Office, Inc., 1999.
8. The III *Insurance Fact Book 2002*, p. 121.
9. Insurance Research Council (IRC), *Fighting Insurance Fraud* (Malvern, Pa.: Insurance Research Council, 2001), p. 13.
10. IRC, *Fighting Insurance Fraud*, p. 14.

Appendix
Resources

The following resources are available for adjusters handling claims suspicious for fraud or arson:

Bureau of Alcohol, Tobacco, and Firearms, *ATF—Arson Investigative Guide*. World Wide Web: http://www.atf.treas.gov.

National Institute of Standards and Technology. World Wide Web: http://www.nist.gov.

International Association of Arson Investigators, *Book of Selected Articles for Arson Investigators*, 12770 Boenker Rd., St. Louis, Mo., 63044. World Wide Web://http://www.firearson.com.

John D. DeHaan, *Kirk's Fire Investigation*, 5th ed. (Old Tappan, N.J.: Prentice Hall, 2002).

Michael A. Boyer, *Personal Property Insurance Fraud Checklists* (Eagan, Minn.: West Group, 1991).

Chapter 8

Direct

Direct Your Learning

Fundamentals of Estimating

After learning the subject matter of this chapter, you should be able to:

- Describe the type of building construction, fire detection and suppression systems, and intruder alarm systems in a given claim situation.
- Identify and describe the parts of the basic building structure.
- Describe the elements of, and correct procedure for, taking a scope.
- Explain how to determine each of the following elements of cost contained in an estimate:
  - Materials
  - Labor and employer's burden
  - Tools and equipment
  - Overhead and profit
  - Direct costs
- Explain the labor and materials method of estimating and its application.
- Explain the unit cost method of estimating and its application.
- Describe the advantages and disadvantages of computerized estimating services.
- Explain how estimates are calculated in situations involving the following:
  - Demolition
  - Debris removal
  - Small losses
  - Large losses
- Explain two reasons for, and how to negotiate, differences in estimates with a contractor.
- Explain how various insurance policy provisions affect an estimate.
- Given a property damage claim, prepare the basic estimate.

OUTLINE

Develop Your Perspective

What are the main topics covered in the chapter?

This chapter describes the different types of building construction and the detection and suppression systems associated with various building uses or occupancy. It then describes the basic elements of a building structure and estimating fundamentals and methods.

Using a small building damage claim, prepare a scope of the loss.

Why is it important to know these topics?

The primary function of a property loss adjuster is to prepare a scope and estimate or to evaluate a scope and estimate prepared by someone else.

How can you use this information?

Basic estimating skills enable you to critically analyze estimates written by others, verify the costs on the estimate, and negotiate differences with confidence.

Chapter 8

Fundamentals of Estimating

This chapter explains the contents of an estimate and begins by introducing basic construction terminology. To estimate property damage, property loss adjusters should be familiar with different types of construction and the kinds of damage that the construction can be subject to. Knowing what type of building is involved in a loss helps an adjuster understand what is needed to repair or rebuild the building. It can also help with coverage analysis. The type of detection and suppression system installed in a building can also affect the loss.

If the damage presented by the loss is significantly different from the expected damage, the adjuster will have to ask more questions about the loss. This chapter explains how to scope a loss and how to cost out an estimate. The chapter includes a discussion of the basic arithmetic needed for these activities. It also mentions how insurance policy provisions affect estimates.

TYPES OF BUILDING CONSTRUCTION

Two versions of the classification of buildings by type of construction are available as resources that adjusters can use. One version is by Insurance Services Office, Inc., (ISO) and is used primarily by underwriters to determine a particular risk's damage potential. The second version is by the National Fire Protection Association (NFPA). It classifies building construction based on damageability from fire and on life safety issues. Adjusters should be aware that these two versions, while similar, are not the same, because they serve different purposes and consequently can use the same terms with different contexts and meanings. Also, these resources may use terms differently than how an adjuster might expect. For example, in both versions of the building classifications, there is no such thing as a fireproof building. Buildings are classified by their resistance to fire. A **fire resistance rating** is the resistance of a building to collapse or to total involvement in a fire.[1]

Fire resistance rating
A rating given to a building that indicates the resistance of the building to collapse or to total involvement in a fire.

The following discussion of construction types is based on the definitions used by ISO. Although primarily used to determine property insurance rates, these definitions provide an adjuster with basic knowledge of construction types.

Frame Construction

Frame construction
A type of construction in which the exterior load-bearing walls are constructed of wood.

A building made of **frame construction** is one in which the exterior load-bearing walls are constructed of wood. Wood can be combined with brick or stucco and still be considered frame construction. Because the structure is made up of wood, it is highly susceptible to fire damage. Exhibit 8-1 shows frame construction.

Adjuster Tip

A load-bearing wall is any wall that bears its own weight as well as other weight and the force of wind. Partition and panel walls are not usually load-bearing. The term "load-bearing wall" is often shortened to "bearing wall."

EXHIBIT 8-1

Frame Construction

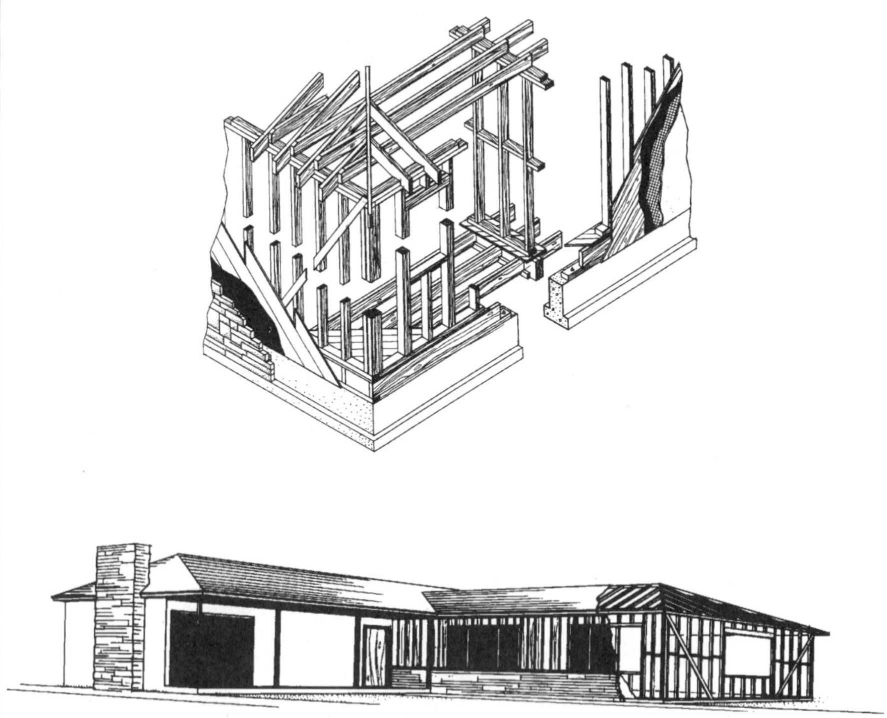

Joisted Masonry Construction

Joisted masonry construction has the exterior load-bearing walls constructed of brick, stone, and concrete, while the joists and beams that support the roof and floors are wood. In a fire, the interior will burn, leaving behind the masonry shell. If the fire is extremely intense, the masonry can be damaged also. Exhibit 8-2 shows joisted masonry construction.

Joisted masonry construction
A type of construction in which the exterior load-bearing walls are constructed of brick, stone, or concrete while the joists and beams that support the roof and floors are wood.

EXHIBIT 8-2

Interior Detail of Joisted Masonry Construction

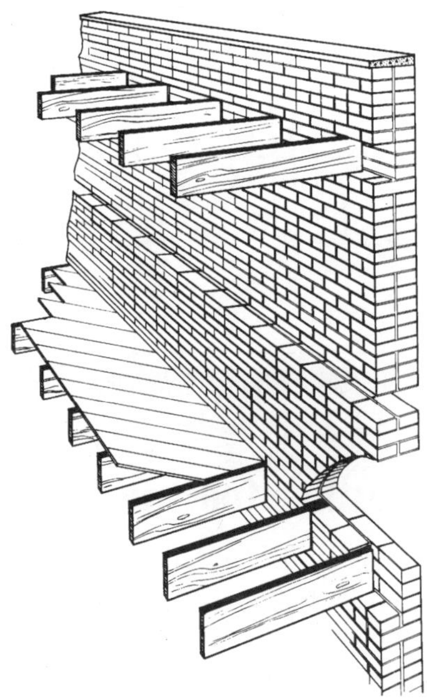

Noncombustible Construction

Exterior load-bearing walls, floors, and the roof in **noncombustible construction** are made of and/or supported by steel, metal, gypsum, or other noncombustible materials. Even though they do not contribute to the fuel for fire, they can be extensively damaged from the intense heat of a fire and generally lose their weight-bearing ability very quickly during a fire. All-metal construction is common. In a fire, the structural members can twist, crack, or expand to the point of collapse unless protected with fireproofing material or sheathing. Exhibit 8-3 shows noncombustible construction.

Noncombustible construction
A type of construction in which exterior load-bearing walls, floors, and roof are made of and /or supported by steel, metal, gypsum, or another noncombustible material.

EXHIBIT 8-3

Light Noncombustible Construction

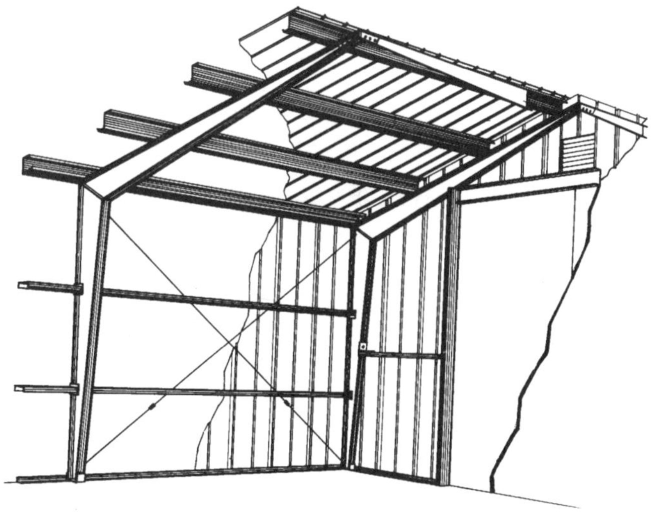

Masonry noncombustible construction
A type of construction in which the exterior bearing walls are constructed of self-supporting masonry and the floors and roof are steel or another noncombustible material.

Modified fire-resistive construction
A type of construction that has exterior bearing walls, floors, and roof made of masonry or fire-resistive material that has a fire resistance rating of one hour but less than two hours.

Fire-resistive construction
A type of construction in which the exterior bearing walls, floors, and roof are made of fire-resistive material such as masonry, reinforced concrete, or protected steel; has a fire resistance rating of not less than two hours.

Masonry Noncombustible Construction

In **masonry noncombustible construction,** the exterior bearing walls are constructed of self-supporting masonry. Floors and the roof are steel or another noncombustible material. Exhibit 8-4 shows masonry noncombustible construction. This type of building would supply little fuel for a fire, but the structural members would lose their weight-bearing ability during an intense fire.

Modified Fire-Resistive Construction

Modified fire-resistive construction has exterior bearing walls, floors, and roof made of masonry or fire-resistive material that has a fire resistance rating of one hour but less than two hours.

Fire-Resistive Construction

A building with **fire-resistive construction** is one in which the exterior bearing walls, floors, and roof are made of fire-resistive material such as masonry, reinforced concrete, or protected steel. It has a fire resistance rating of not less than two hours.

EXHIBIT 8-4

Masonry Noncombustible Construction

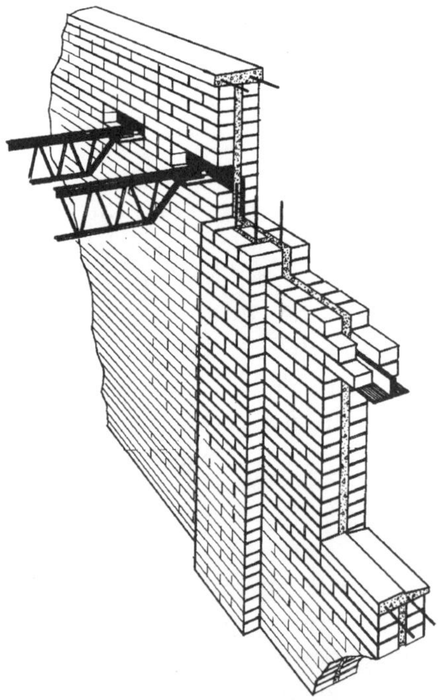

Although it is not essential that an adjuster know how a particular building is classified by the underwriter, it is valuable to know the various classes when evaluating the overall loss and considering use and occupancy issues as well as identifying potential avenues of subrogation.

DETECTION AND SUPPRESSION SYSTEMS

Detection and suppression systems encompass a wide variety of fire and smoke detectors, sprinklers, and intruder alarms. Commercial buildings often have complex devices that can detect and suppress fire, detect water leakage, or detect a break-in. Many homes have intruder alarms, and some have residential sprinkler protection.

Detection and suppression systems can affect a loss in many ways. Fire detection and suppression systems can mitigate the loss sustained as a result of fire. Intruder alarms, or burglar alarms, may scare off thieves. Quick police response may mean a significantly reduced loss or the potential of a recovery. Malfunctioning detection and suppression systems may even be a potential source of recovery through subrogation. The type of detection and suppression system used in a building is often dictated by the building's construction and use.

Fire Detection and Suppression Systems

Many types of fire detection systems are available. Most are tied into some type of fire suppression system as well as an alarm.

Wet Sprinkler Systems

Wet system
A sprinkler system that has water in the pipes at all times.

The most common type of sprinkler system is the **wet system**. It continuously has water in the pipes. Depending upon the type of sprinkler head installed, the system can be activated by heat, smoke, or flame. In a wet system designs, only the heads nearest the fire area will actuate. The sprinklers operate independently and do not actuate simultaneously unless a large area is involved in a fire. When a loss involves the actuation of a sprinkler, the adjuster asks questions concerning its installation and maintenance to determine if a malfunction caused the loss or made it worse.

Dry Pipe Systems

Dry pipe system
A sprinkler system in which the pipes remain dry until the sprinkler head is actuated.

Sprinkler systems can also be designed as **dry pipe systems**. This means that the pipes remain dry until a sprinkler head is actuated. A sprinkler that actuates from heat in a dry pipe system releases air pressure maintained in the piping network, eventually enabling a dry pipe valve to trip and allow water to enter the piping system. Like the wet pipe system, water is only distributed from sprinklers that have actuated from heat in the local fire area. Dry systems are used in locations that are prone to freezing temperatures, like an unheated warehouse.

Deluge Systems

Deluge system
A dry sprinkler system in which the heads are open all of the time; when the system is triggered, the deluge valve allows water to flow through the system.

A variation of the dry system design is the **deluge system.** It differs from the regular dry system because it has the sprinkler heads open continuously. When heat or smoke triggers the system (through combined detection of infrared and ultraviolet light), the deluge valve receives the signal and trips, allowing water into the entire piping system. As the sprinkler heads in a deluge system are all open, the water immediately discharges into the area from every sprinkler head in the system.

A hybrid of both the wet system and the deluge system is the pre-action system. In this design, a closed piping network uses a minimal amount of air under pressure. A deluge valve maintains the piping network in a dry state until receiving a signal from the actuating sprinklers or detectors. When it has received signals from two different sources, the deluge valve trips, allowing full water flow into the piping. Water is then distributed to the actuated sprinklers. This type of system is used in libraries and computer rooms, as it requires more than just sprinkler head activation to enable water flow to occur.

Foam and Chemical Systems

Other types of fire suppression systems include halogenated, dry chemical, foam, and carbon dioxide. The particular system used in a building depends on the building's use and occupancy. **Halogenated systems** are used in laboratories, art museums, and computer rooms because these buildings' contents should not be subjected to water. **Dry chemical systems** are often used in paint-spray booths, electric transformers, and in the deep fryer area of restaurants. These systems smother a fire rather than spread it around as water might. **Foam systems** have the same purpose as dry chemical systems and are used around flammable liquids and oil-storage facilities. Foam is used outside effectively because it will not blow around like dry chemical does. **Carbon dioxide systems** are used in dry cleaning plants, fur vaults, printing press rooms, and computer rooms. The carbon dioxide reduces the oxygen in the area to the point that combustion cannot be sustained.[2]

Halogenated system
A chemical system using halogen as a fire suppression material.

Dry chemical system
A chemical fire suppression system that smothers the fire by dropping a large amount of dry chemical on the fire.

Foam system
A chemical foam system that is used in outside areas to smother a fire.

Carbon dioxide system
A fire suppression system that uses carbon dioxide to reduce the oxygen in the area to the point that combustion cannot be sustained.

Intruder Detection Systems and Alarms

Many different types of intruder alarm systems exist. Both residential and commercial properties use them. The most familiar type of alarm is the sensor trigger alarm, whose circuit is normally closed. When the circuit is broken, the alarm is triggered. This type of alarm is recognizable by the strip appearing on the windows of the building. There is another type of sensor alarm in which the circuit is normally open. The trigger is usually a pressure mat. Once walked on, these mats close the circuit and trigger the alarm. There are also radio-controlled sensor alarms that can be mounted to doors and windows without wiring.

Alarms systems are usually tied into a police department or private security company. When investigating a loss involving a building that has alarm systems, the property adjuster obtains information regarding the alarm's installation and maintenance as well as how the alarm is set and by whom. Additionally, the alarm company or police department has vital information regarding the alarm's performance at the time of the loss.[3]

BASIC BUILDING STRUCTURE

A building has six essential parts:

1. Foundation
2. Framing
3. Windows and doors
4. Utilities (heating, cooling, plumbing, and electrical)
5. Interior finishes (trim, drywall, and plaster)
6. Exterior finishes (roofing and exterior wall coverings)

For the purposes of this chapter, a residential building is discussed in the examples.

EXHIBIT 8-5

Foundation

Photo courtesy of National Property & Casualty Claims Research Services, Inc. (NPCCRS).

Foundation

Houses sit on some form of foundation, such as a basement foundation, a slab, or a crawl space. Foundations can be made from concrete block or concrete poured into forms to create the walls or the slab. Poured concrete is often reinforced with reinforcing bars. See Exhibit 8-5. The shorthand term for these bars is "rebar." The amount of poured concrete to use is usually calculated by the cubic yard. Concrete blocks are calculated using the size of the block and the size of the desired foundation.

Adjuster Tip

An inadequate foundation can cause uneven settling of a house and cracking of the interior plaster, and ill-fitting doors and windows evidence this.

Framing

Framing is the term used to describe the structural members that form the skeleton of the building. Floors, walls, roofs, and ceilings are all framed out to construct the building. Framing begins with structural members that are attached to the foundation.

Framing
The structural members that form the skeleton of a building.

Floor Framing

After the concrete foundation has properly cured, wooden sills are attached to it. These provide the base for attaching the wood frame of the house to the foundation. See Exhibit 8-6.

EXHIBIT 8-6

Sill Plate Attached to Foundation

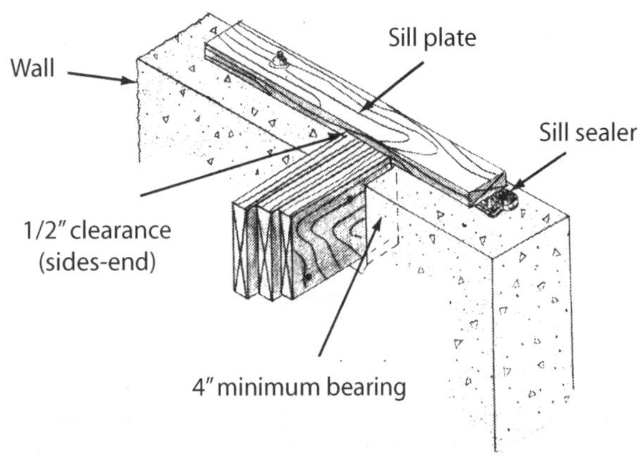

L. O. Anderson, *Wood-Frame House Construction* (Carlsbad, Calif.: Craftsman Book Company, July 1992), p. 34.

Floor joists are added next. The term **joist** is applied to a horizontal timber to which either the floor or ceiling is attached.

Floor joists are usually 2″ × 6″, 2″ × 8″, 2″ × 10″, or 2″ × 12″. The floor joists are installed so that the center of one floor joist is 16″ away from the center of the next floor joist. This is called on-center spacing. Note that the measurement is from the center of one joist to the center of another, not 16″ from the side of one to the side of the other. Floor joists extend the entire length of the house. If the length of a joist exceeds 8′, then bridging the joists will be necessary. **Bridging** means inserting a short piece of bracing (can be metal or wood) laterally between the joists. Exhibit 8-7 shows an example of bridging.

Joist
A horizontal timber to which either the floor or ceiling is attached.

Bridging
A short piece of bracing that is inserted laterally between joists.

After the floor joists are in place, a subfloor or rough floor is installed over them. This is the base for the finished floor. Subflooring is usually plywood sheets or particleboard. See Exhibit 8-7.

On top of the subfloor, following the outline of the foundation, soleplates are attached. These are pieces of lumber that anchor the wall studs to the floor. Soleplates are usually 2″ × 4″.

Wall Framing

Wall studs are nailed to the soleplates to form the frame of the walls. Studs are usually 2″ × 4″ in a two-story house. Wall studs are usually placed using 16″ on-center spacing. After the studs are all in place, a top plate is attached across the top of them to hold the studs and all the walls together. See Exhibit 8-8.

Studs are doubled around both sides of any window or door and tripled at the corners of the house. See Exhibit 8-9. Sheathing is installed on the exterior of the wall studs to enclose the structure. The exterior finish of the house will be attached to this sheathing.

> **ADJUSTER TIP**
>
> Framing lumber that has suffered fire damage does not always have to be replaced. If joists, rafters, and studs have suffered no structural damage, they can be scraped, sealed, and then covered.[4] Determining whether the joist is structurally sound may require the use of a contractor or an engineer. Another possible repair technique is called "sistering." This entails attaching a new section of joist, rafter, or stud, to the damaged section, overlapping the damaged section with a new section, thereby reinforcing the damaged section.

After the walls are up, the roof can be installed. Ceiling joists are installed, running in the same direction as the floor joists. They extend from the rafter plate to the top plate of the wall studding. See Exhibit 8-10.

EXHIBIT 8-7

Floor Framing

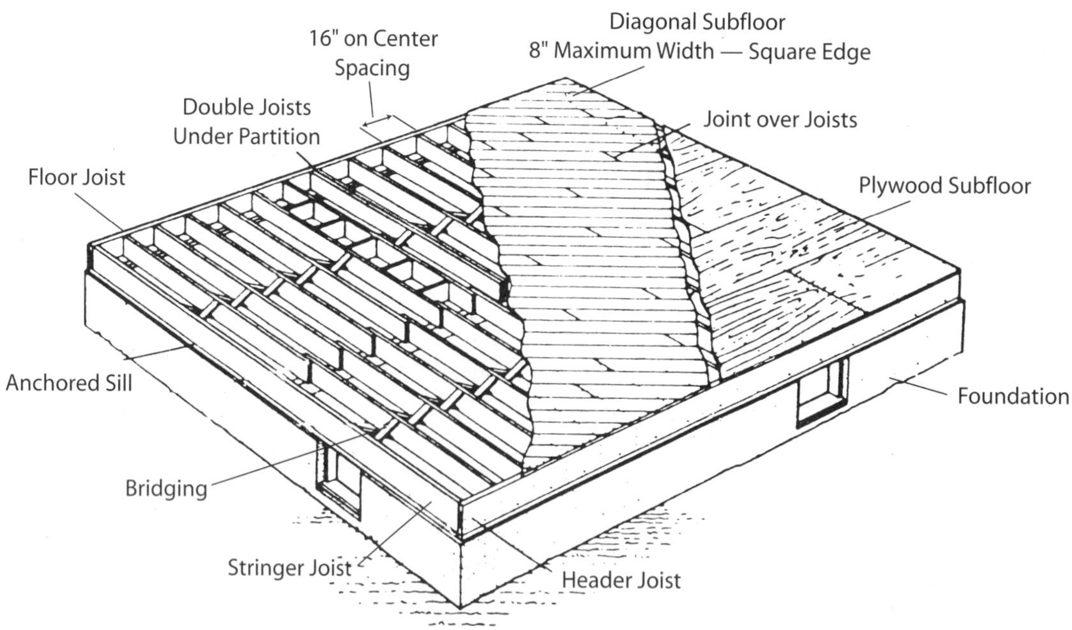

L. O. Anderson, *Wood-Frame House Construction*, U.S. Dept. of Agriculture Forest Service, Agricultural Handbook No. 73 (Washington, D.C.: U.S. Government Printing Office, July 1970), p. 27.

EXHIBIT 8-8

Vertical Application of Plywood or Structural Insulating Board Sheathing

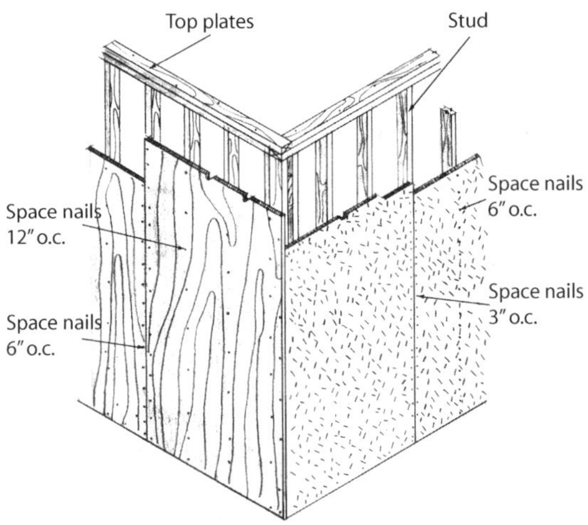

EXHIBIT 8-9

Headers for Windows and Door Openings

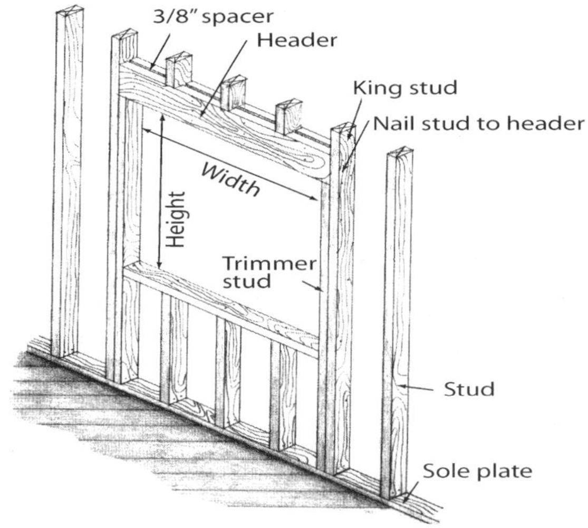

L. O. Anderson, *Wood-Frame House Construction* (Carlsbad, Calif.: Craftsman Book Company, July 1992), pp. 47, 71.

Roof Framing

Roof rafters are installed next. They run parallel to each other and can be 12 to 24 inches apart. The most common spacing is 16 inches. Rafters extend upward at an angle called a **pitch**. Roofs can be either flat or pitched. Flat roofs can have a slight slope in them to facilitate drainage. In a flat roof, the rafters serve as the ceiling joists. They attach at the top to a piece called the ridge board. See Exhibit 8-11a.

Pitch
The angle of the roof.

The ridge board runs the length of the roof, perpendicular to the rafters. After the rafters are in place, the roof sheathing is added to the exterior of the rafters. The sheathing serves as the base for the roof covering and adds strength to the roof frame. See Exhibit 8-11b.

ADJUSTER TIP

Using unseasoned wood as roof sheathing can cause buckling and lifting of shingles as the sheathing dries out.

Many roofs have dormers in them. A dormer is a gable in a pitched roof, usually containing a window. A gable is the triangular shape formed by the roofline of the dormer. See Exhibit 8-12.

EXHIBIT 8-10

Ceiling Joist Connections

At center partition with joists lapped or butted

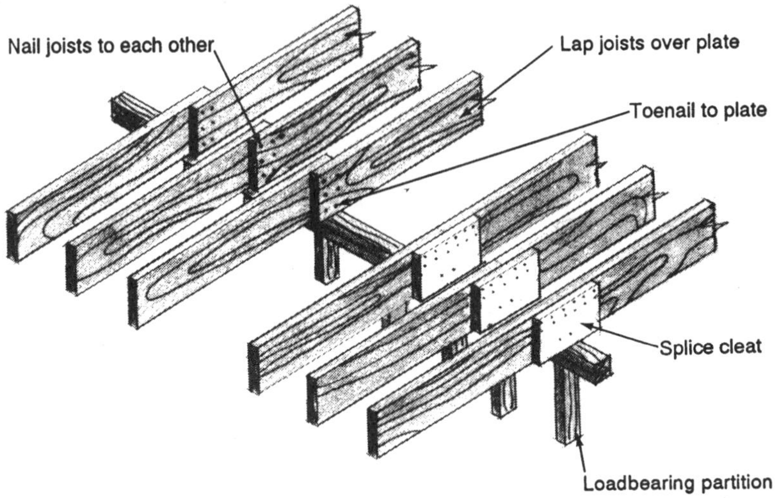

At outside wall

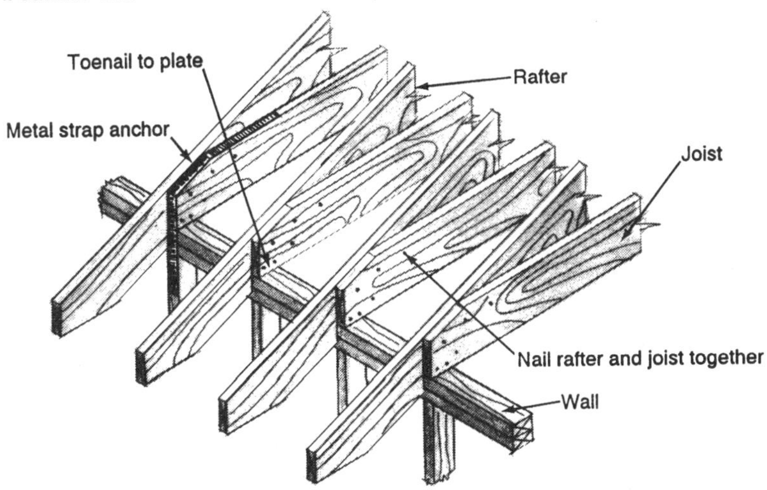

L. O. Anderson, *Wood-Frame House Construction* (Carlsbad, Calif.: Craftsman Book Company, July 1992), p. 54.

The intersection of the dormer roof and the main roof is called a valley. Valleys are formed whenever two sloping sides of a roof meet. Valleys have valley rafters and jack rafters as part of their structure to reinforce them. These are all basically the same piece of wood, usually a 2″ × 10″ or a 2″ × 12″, cut to different lengths and put to different uses in the structure. Their names derive from their use rather than from some significant difference in their composition. See Exhibit 8-13.

EXHIBIT 8-11a

Ceiling and Roof Framing

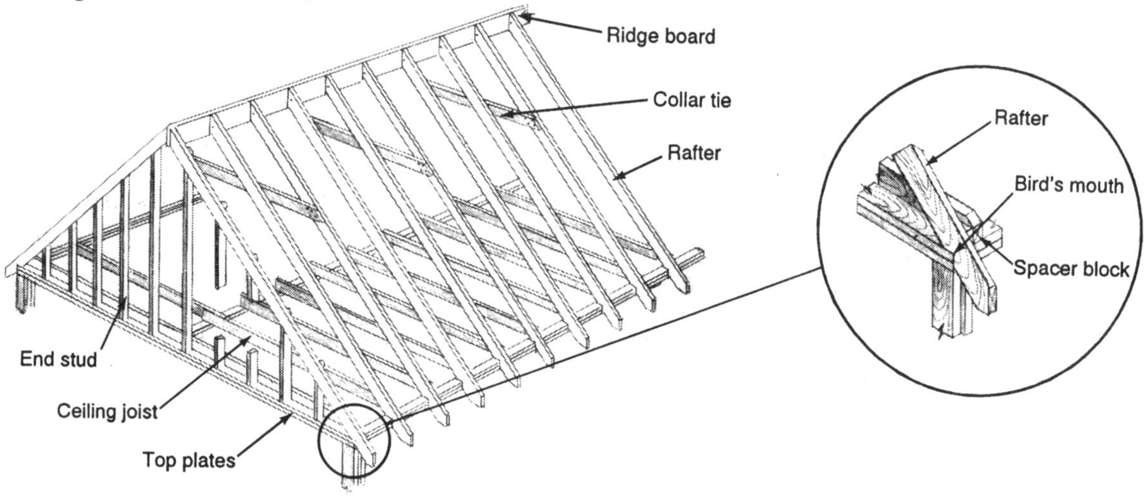

L. O. Anderson, *Wood-Frame House Construction* (Carlsbad, Calif.: Craftsman Book Company, July 1992), p. 60.

EXHIBIT 8-11b

Application of Plywood Roof Sheathing

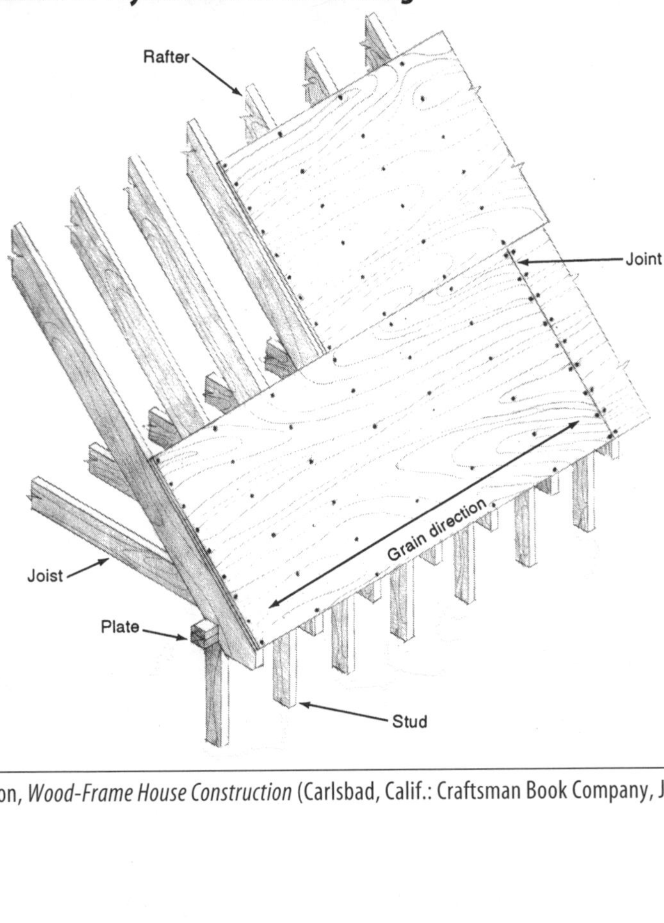

L. O. Anderson, *Wood-Frame House Construction* (Carlsbad, Calif.: Craftsman Book Company, July 1992), p. 79.

EXHIBIT 8-12

Dormer

Home Repair and Remodel: 2002 Cost Guide (Los Angeles: Marshall & Swift, L.P., 2002).

EXHIBIT 8-13

Framing at Valley

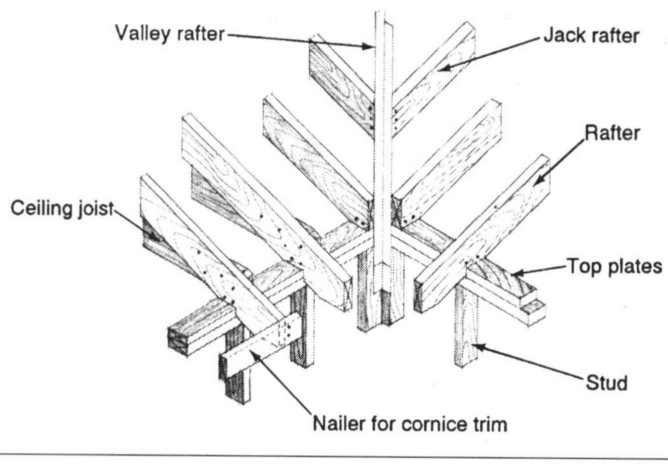

L. O. Anderson, *Wood-Frame House Construction* (Carlsbad, Calif.: Craftsman Book Company, July 1992), p. 61.

Interior Partitions

Load-bearing wall
A wall that runs at a right angle to the joists and bears the weight of the structure.

While the exterior walls and roof are being framed, interior partition walls are also erected. Interior partition walls can be **load-bearing** and non-load-bearing. Load-bearing walls run at right angles to the joists, and they help bear the weight of the above structure. Non-load-bearing walls merely define the room space. Doors and windows are framed out with studs, header beams, and sills.

Steel Framing

Framing can also be done in steel. Although steel framing is typically used for commercial buildings, some parts of the United States use steel as interior partition wall framing members for residential buildings and apartments. Steel framing is installed in much the same manner, and to the same specifications, as wood. Steel framing requires different insulation because of the ease in which heat is lost through steel framing. The most typical solution for this heat loss problem is to use full width batts of insulation (meaning that they cover the entire area in between the studs) or to use blown-in insulation. Steel can be an inexpensive, sturdy alternative to wood framing, but it does have its drawbacks. Steel is susceptible to rust at the points at which it has been cut and at which fasteners have penetrated the piece.[5]

Windows and Doors

Windows and doors are inserted into the framed openings. Windows and doors are constructed of many different structural pieces. Unless an estimate is being prepared to repair a part of a door or window, estimating these structural pieces individually is not necessary. Most doors and windows arrive from the manufacturer with all of the component pieces already installed.

Utilities

As the framing nears completion, the plumbers **rough in** the pipes. Roughing in is the installation of the pipes that will ultimately be concealed within the walls and ceiling. Roughing in does not include the attachment of the fixtures or appliances. See Exhibit 8-14. After the roof is on and the windows are in, the electricians usually do their roughing in of the wiring.

Rough in
To install the plumbing and electrical wiring that will ultimately be concealed within the walls and ceiling.

Interior Finishes

Following the rough in of the utilities, the insulation is put in and the walls are enclosed with drywall or plaster. Finished floors are installed, as are the fixtures and appliances. Installation of trim and molding usually completes the process.[6]

Exterior Finishes

After the wall sheathing and roof sheathing are completed, the exterior finish is installed. So many different types of exterior wall finishes and roof coverings are available that it is impossible for this text to fully discuss them all. Common exterior wall finishes are siding, shakes, stucco, and brick or another masonry product. Roofing material often is dictated by climate. For example, while asphalt shingles are used countrywide, Spanish tile is prevalent in the Southwest. Also, specialty buildings might have a slate or metal roof.

EXHIBIT 8-14

Roughing-in Pipes

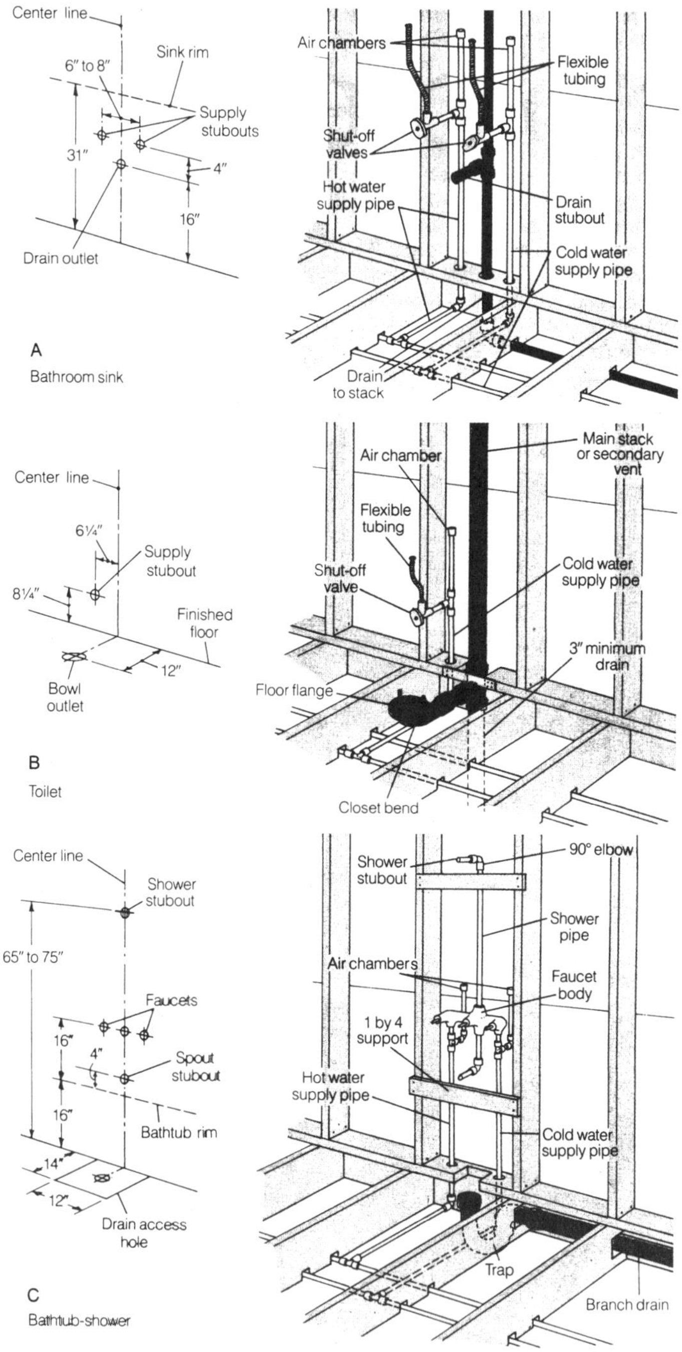

Basic Plumbing Illustrated (Menlo Park, Calif.: Sunset Publishing Group, 1985), p. 65.

> **Adjuster Tip**
>
> Examining items in a local lumber store or home improvement store can make the terms used in this text more meaningful after seeing the items close up.

In the course of building a small house, which is the example used in this discussion of basic building structure, carpenters, electricians, masons, and plumbers are involved. Other trade professionals who could be involved are tile setters; counter installers; heating, ventilation, and air conditioning (HVAC) installers; painters; wallpaper hangers; and landscapers. Trying to schedule all of these trades can be difficult because some may not be able to begin work until others are finished. For large jobs, a general contractor (G.C.) does this scheduling and supervision. By definition, a general contractor has a contract directly with the owner. On large projects, the general contractor arranges for all of the other trades to perform specific parts of the project. The G.C. may perform part of the actual construction in addition to supervising the work done by the other trades. These other trades are referred to as subcontractors. Their contract is with the general contractor, to perform some part of the general contractor's obligation to the owner. On small repair jobs, usually only one or two trades are needed. A G.C. is not needed on a small job. In such a case, each trade professional contracts directly with the owner.[7]

ESTIMATING BASICS

A property adjuster must know how to prepare an estimate as well as be able to evaluate an estimate prepared by someone else. Otherwise, it would be difficult to negotiate the extent of damage, the type of repair necessary, and the cost of labor and materials.

Estimate Essentials

Every estimate should contain the following information:

1. Specifications
2. Material
3. Labor
4. Overhead
5. Profit[8]

Specifications are the dimensions of the area that needs to be repaired, replaced, or built. The specifications also include special conditions like cramped workspace, the need for scaffolding, the weather, or the need to protect other areas from damage during the project.

Material specifies the quantity, quality, and size of the material needed to accomplish the work. Labor is the amount of time needed to complete each part of the job.

Overhead
The fixed costs to run a business.

Overhead encompasses the fixed costs for any business. Overhead has two varieties: (1) general and (2) specific. General overhead exists whether or not the contractor is working on a project. Some examples of general overhead items are the salaries of estimators, job supervisors, and office personnel; office rent; utilities; and business licenses. The contractor usually recovers these costs by charging a flat percentage on each estimate. Specific overhead is charged to a specific job. Examples of specific overhead are building permits, travel costs, equipment rental, and insurance. Depending on the location and type of job, the overhead can range from 5 percent to 20 percent. For example, if the fixed operating costs of the business are $100,000 per year and the contractor expects to do $1 million worth of work, then the contractor recovers the annual overhead by adding a 10 percent overhead charge to every job.

Profit is the amount over the costs of a job that the contractor expects to earn for his or her services. Profit varies depending on the job's size and complexity and how much competition there is for the job. Usually, the higher the estimate, the lower the percentage of profit charged. A large job or a competitively bid job can have a profit as low as 2 or 3 percent. Although the generally accepted amount is 10 percent, a small job consisting of only a few hundred dollars' worth of work can have a profit figure as high as 20 percent. If the insured elects to do the work himself or herself, profit is not usually included in the estimate.

When a general contractor is used to oversee the project, overhead and profit are included in the estimate. Note the distinction between "ten and ten," which is 10 percent overhead and 10 percent profit calculated off the total estimate, and the "ten on ten" method, which results in a total of 21 percent. The ten on ten method calculates the 10 percent overhead first, then adds it to the total estimate. Then the 10 percent profit is calculated using the new total. Exhibit 8-15 shows the difference in the final estimate using these two methods.

EXHIBIT 8-15

Examples of Overhead and Profit Calculations

	10 and 10 Method		10 on 10 Method
Estimate amount	$100,000		$100,000
10% overhead	10,000		10,000
		New total	$110,000
10% profit	10,000		11,000
Final estimate	$120,000		$121,000

In other areas, a flat 15 percent to cover both overhead and profit is common. Regardless of local practices, competitive pressures can dictate a different amount.

> **Adjuster Tip**
>
> The acceptable amount of overhead and profit can vary because of location, competitive bidding, and market conditions. Therefore, adjusters should verify what the acceptable amount of overhead and profit is for the loss location.

Local Practices

Estimates can vary among locations because of local practices. The terms used in the estimate can differ. Depending upon where the loss is, a wood sill can be called a sill, a soleplate, a shoe, or a mudsill. Roof sheathing might be called roof boards or roof decking.

Construction methods can also vary. Climate dictates what is the best local practice for a given trade. For example, if the loss is in the Southwest, stucco might be the preferred exterior finish and Spanish tile might be the preferred roofing material.

Estimating methods can also cause a difference in the bottom line. How waste is accounted for or whether the window and door openings are deducted from the measurements can affect an estimate's final cost. Market-driven conditions in an area might result in a local practice among tradesman so that they all charge the same labor rate.

Demolition

Demolition and removal can also vary from one estimate to another. Demolition is the tearing out of damaged components from their original place in the building. Demolition yields debris, which must be removed from the site (as explained in the following section). Demolition work is generally figured using a laborer's wage rate rather than a skilled worker's rate. The adjuster can estimate demolition on either a labor and materials basis (also called a time and materials basis) or a unit cost basis. The labor and materials method uses the cost of the labor (time) needed to complete the job and the cost of the materials. Unit cost is a way to streamline the estimating process. If the labor and materials rate has been calculated once, it can be divided by the unit of measure (such as square feet) to calculate the unit of measure cost otherwise known as unit cost. Calculating unit cost is explained in greater detail later in the chapter. Unit removal costs can be added to the unit item replacement cost to arrive at a remove and replace unit cost. Theoretically, the unit cost method should be as accurate as any other approach. Nevertheless, it can lead to serious overestimating, especially on larger losses, for the following reasons:

1. Some components are out of sight, requiring no tear-out.
2. Demolition of one component often includes demolition of another. To estimate both with a remove and replace cost duplicates the cost of the demolition.

3. The remove and replace cost tends to become the accepted norm and is often used when the repair option is more appropriate.
4. On larger losses, unit cost fails to recognize economies of scale. A few hours with heavy equipment can replace days of manual labor.
5. Many of the tear-out figures in the labor references are appropriate for careful remodeling demolition rather than for large-scale demolition involved in larger losses.

The labor and materials method is the best approach to use for demolition. If that method is used, the unit costs used in the rest of the estimate should not include removal.

Experience is necessary to estimate the number of work hours or days of demolition. The references contain enough information to get the adjuster started, but duplications are still possible. The tear-out time for the most significant item in a building assembly should be used. The labor factor usually includes secondary components. For instance, if 2.5 hours are allowed to tear out 100 square feet of partition wall, additional time to remove the drywall, wallpaper, switch plates, or heating vents should not be allowed.

One approach to checking the demolition portion of a contractor's estimate is dividing the amount by the local common labor rate. The result approximates the number of hours of demolition labor. If the hours seem excessive, negotiating time is usually easier than negotiating dollars.

Debris Removal

Debris removal cost is the labor and expense involved in removing debris from the site. The two types of debris are (1) the debris of the damaged property and (2) the waste produced by repairs. The demolition labor figures include the time needed to pile the debris on the premises. The debris removal cost represents the additional cost to remove the debris from the site and properly dispose of it.

The best approach to estimating the cost of debris removal is to estimate the number and size of boxes or trash bins needed to handle the debris and apply the fee quoted by a local waste disposal company. Disposal companies quote a single price to place the bin on the site and to pick it up when it is full. Trying to estimate debris removal costs by truckloads, hours of driving time, mileage allowances, and dump fees is not feasible. Demolition and removal usually is a lump sum in the estimate. It can also be called tear-out and cart, demo and trucking, debris removal, or drayage.

ADJUSTER TIP

Because demolition and removal is usually labor cost plus the cost of a dumpster and truck, contractors might inflate this item to cover other contingencies.

Temporary Repairs

A substantial loss in a residential or commercial property may necessitate temporary repairs. These repairs protect the property from further damage. These repairs can include closing up openings with boards or tarpaulins, providing temporary heat or light, and even draining the plumbing to prevent the pipes from freezing. It may be necessary to pump out water, dry out contents, or fence off an area to keep it secure. All of these temporary repairs can appear on an estimate.

Scope of a Building Loss

An adjuster inspecting a loss creates a scope of the loss. The scope is broader than the specifications already discussed. The scope is a list of the damaged areas, a description of the damage, a proposed method of repair, and the measurements of the damaged area. Exhibit 8-16 is a sample scope sheet.

The scope is used by the adjuster to create an estimate. The adjuster also uses the scope to reach an agreement with the contractor regarding the extent of the damage. How to scope a loss is discussed in greater detail later in this chapter.

Estimating is a two-step process. The first step is preparing the scope of damage at the loss scene. The adjuster itemizes the damage elements, or scopes the loss, to establish the extent of the insured's loss. The scope details the damage to each building component. (Some property adjusters substitute other terms for "scope." Common synonyms are "take-off," "survey," "specifications," or "field notes." Regardless of the name, the scope is the first and most crucial step in preparing a repair estimate.) The second step is pricing the work determined by the scope into a repair estimate. To properly price the estimate, the adjuster must know the quantity of material needed, the amount of labor that each task requires, what the overhead and profit margin will be, and what considerations must be taken into account.

For smaller losses, the adjuster prepares the scope and writes the estimate at the scene of the loss. For larger losses, trying to finish the estimate at the scene is impractical. Although completing the scope and estimate in a timely manner is important, the adjuster can use references to find labor and material usage rates and current prices.

Elements of a Proper Scope

The scope must contain enough detail to calculate loss restoration costs. For each damaged building component, the scope must describe the following three things:

1. Degree of damage, usually stated as a method of repair
2. Quality of the materials and workmanship of damaged property
3. Raw counts or measurements needed to calculate quantities

EXHIBIT 8-16

Scope Sheet

Property Loss Worksheet

Page No. 1

Preliminary Estimate 10/19/0X (Date)

Final Estimate ______ (Date)

M. Boyer (Adjuster)

Claim No. 524 BL 101

Insured J. Smith

Claimant Insured

1 Item	2 Description	3 Quantity	4 Units Age	5 Unit price Orig. cost	6 Cost Repl. cost	7 Deprec.	8 A.C.V.	9 Loss & Damage
1.	Permit (if required)							
2.	Demolition							
	Remove range hood							
	Remove cabinets (4 LF)							
	Remove drywall (above cabinet) (5' × 10' = 50 SF)							
	Remove Formica countertop (12 LF) (est. 2 men × 5 hrs. = 10 hrs.)							
3.	Cartage							
	1 pickup & driver (1.5 hrs.)							
	Dump fee ($10.00)							
4.	Clean range (est. 1.5 hrs.)							
5.	Install new range hood (Sears 30", est. 1 hr.)							
6.	Install upper cabinets Paint grade plywood of 4 LF × 3' tall (est. 1.5 hrs.)							

For example, assume that an interior water loss has occurred. The entire ceiling in a small bedroom is bowed, and the walls are stained. The scope entries for the damage in that room are as follows:

Bedroom: 9 feet × 10 feet × 8 feet.

Replace ⅝ inch ceiling drywall, complete.

Seal and paint walls and ceiling, flat latex.

The room's dimensions provide the raw measurements needed to calculate the surface areas that determine the amount of material needed. Replacing the drywall and sealing and painting the surfaces are the repair methods that indicate the damage degree. Finally, the thickness of the drywall and the type of paint describe the quality of the damaged component.

Contrast to Finished Estimate

The scope differs from the finished estimate in two ways. First, the scope does not necessarily list any prices, although prices can be used to describe quality. Second, the scope does not list the calculated quantities. It includes just the raw counts and measurements needed to calculate quantities for the estimate. Calculators are not needed to prepare a scope. The quantities should be calculated as the adjuster extends and prices the scope into a finished estimate.

Suggested Sequence for an Inspection and a Scope

Following a set sequence in inspecting the loss and preparing the scope is important. The sequence suggested here works well for larger fire losses, and it can be tailored to fit other types of losses. For smaller losses, some of the steps can be combined or eliminated. See the following box.

Inspection and Scope Steps

The steps in an inspection and a scope include the following:

Step 1—Conduct the initial survey.

Step 2—Prepare diagrams and sketches.

Step 3—Scope the damage.

Step 4—Consider coverage.

Step 5—Document with photographs.

Step 1: Conduct the Initial Survey

The adjuster inspects the building to get an idea of construction type, damaged areas, condition before the fire, and any building hazards. The adjuster should enter the building below the lowest damaged floor to check the condition of the floors above. On some losses, it may be necessary to have an origin and cause expert accompany the adjuster during this initial inspection. Partly as a result of the initial inspection, coverage issues that demand immediate attention might become apparent. Whenever possible, the adjuster should finish the scope during the initial inspection.

Step 2: Prepare Diagrams and Sketches

After preparing a perimeter diagram, the adjuster can draw in the interior walls. Starting with the perimeter helps ensure that the interior dimensions will all fit. Next, the adjuster should measure and sketch exterior elevations, trusses, cabinets, doors, and windows. Thoroughness makes the final detailed scope easier to prepare.

Step 3: Scope the Damage

Conducting an organized scope of the damage ensures that nothing is missed. See the following box. Whenever possible, the adjuster should complete the scope with the insured or with the insured's contractor. One of the purposes for preparing the scope is to agree on the extent of the damage. Insureds typically want to discuss every detail, so the insured and the adjuster should agree on anything that might become an issue. If the insured's contractor is present, he or she could be part of the agreement on the major unit costs and labor rates as well as on each repair item. Experts should resolve uncertainties or legitimate differences of opinion.

Scope the Damage

A scope of damage should include examining the following five categories in the following order. The adjuster should consider only one category at a time, necessitating five complete tours of the loss scene:

1. Structural components
2. Exterior, including insulation
3. Room by room (architectural items, finishes, fixtures, and components of building systems completely contained within the room)
   a. Floor
   b. Walls
   c. Trim, doors, and windows
   d. Ceiling
   e. Fixtures, appliances, built-ins, and cabinets
4. Building systems that cross room boundaries (plumbing, electrical, and heating and air conditioning)
5. General considerations (debris removal, permits, access, and equipment rental)

There are two reasons for beginning with the structural components. First, they are difficult to scope on a room-by-room basis. Second, structural component damage might require removing an undamaged component. Exterior items are next because they span room boundaries and cannot be seen from the inside. In the detailed scope of each damaged room, besides the finished ceiling, walls, and floors, the adjuster should also scope the fixtures, ducts, pipes, outlets, and wiring within the room. The next category, scoping the plumbing, electrical, and heating systems, is limited to the components that cross room boundaries. After these systems have been scoped, the adjuster should evaluate debris removal, permits, access items, and equipment rental.

For smaller or different losses, the individual situation often dictates a different sequence. For instance, if the insured reports a wind loss with interior water damage, starting on the inside to get an idea of where the roof is damaged is logical.

Common abbreviations found in a scope are as follows:

P&D	Paint and decorate	S&F	Sand and finish (usually floors and trim)
PL	Plaster		
R&R	Remove and replace	S&P	Seal and paint
REF	Refinish	T&C	Tear out and cart
REM	Remove	WW	Whitewash[9]
REP	Repair		

Step 4: Consider Coverage

The adjuster should consider code requirements, damage from excluded causes, and damage to excluded property. The adjuster should also gather enough information to calculate the building's value before the loss to establish that the insured has complied with the coinsurance or replacement cost requirements.

Step 5: Document With Photographs

The final step is to photograph the items important to the adjustment. A photograph of the overall premises is recommended for general descriptive purposes. Photos of the damaged area help preserve the scene and document the scene as found. Photos can also assist in identifying the quality or grade of items used in construction. Identifying marks on cabinets, siding, and appliances can be preserved in this manner. If the loss is sizable, documenting the loss with photos is essential for the benefit of others within the claim department who may be reviewing the file.

Pricing an Estimate

The second step in the estimating process is pricing out the scope into a final repair estimate. The adjuster estimates the loss restoration cost on the basis of the damage as itemized in the scope document. This section discusses construction costs and explains some specific estimating methods. Any construction operation involves the following types of costs:

1. Materials
2. Labor and employer's burden
3. Tools and equipment
4. Overhead and profit
5. Miscellaneous direct costs, such as permits and sales taxes

Materials

Establishing the cost of materials is also a two-part process. First, the adjuster must identify the materials, their quality, and the quantities needed to make the repair. Second, the adjuster must obtain current local prices for those materials.

Several sources can identify the items and quantities needed. *Home Repair and Remodel Cost Guide* by Marshall & Swift, L.P. and *Walker's Building Estimators Reference Book* by Frank R. Walker Company are two recognized sources that are updated annually. For each construction or repair operation, these references identify the materials needed and provide usage factors to convert the sale unit into the units used for estimating. For example, these books reveal that a gallon of latex wall paint covers 450 to 500 square feet of smooth walls. Estimating software packages also contain this same information.

Waste

Cutting and fitting waste
The amount of material that is left over after cutting and fitting to size for repair.

The material usage information is sometimes described as a "waste factor." There are two kinds of waste. The first is **cutting and fitting waste**, which can occur, for example, when installing a ceramic tile floor. The references indicate that an additional 5 to 10 percent of material should be added to the estimated quantity, allowing for breakage and cutting of tiles to fit the room. Cutting and fitting waste is also a factor in estimating required quantities of drywall, roofing, wallpaper, wood siding, paneling, and plywood.

Another way to handle cutting and fitting waste is to consider waste causes while determining the quantity needed. For example, some references state that the waste in drywall should be allowed by including door and window openings in the surface area measurements unless these spaces are larger than one full 4 ft. × 8 ft. sheet of drywall. If this method is used, adding a percentage of material might not be appropriate.

Milling waste
The difference between the actual size and the nominal size of a piece of material.

Nominal size
The size of a piece of lumber before it is surfaced or finished.

The second type of waste is more difficult to understand because it does not appear in the scrap pile. It is called **milling waste**. Milling waste is the difference between the actual size and the **nominal size** of a piece of material and is often associated with lumber. The nominal size of a piece of lumber is the size of the piece just after it was cut from the log. It then is dried out and planed to give it a more finished look. This causes it to lose some of its size. A piece of 1″ × 3″ oak flooring actually measures $^{25}/_{32}$″ thick by $2\frac{1}{4}$″

wide. The milling waste occurred because some of the board was removed when the tongue and groove were formed. The piece is called a 1 × 3, but it is actually smaller, which means that it will cover a smaller area. In this case, 33⅓ percent more material is needed to cover the nominal width of 3 inches with 2¼ inches of material. As a result, a 33 percent milling waste factor should be added to the actual floor area when determining the quantity of material required.

Lumber that is planed on all four sides, such as a softwood, is stamped "S4S." This stands for "surfaced 4 sides." Redwood is an exception to this rule. It can be sold rough or unsurfaced. Rough wood stays close to its nominal size. Because of the surfacing or planing, the actual size of a surfaced piece of lumber is something less than 2″ × 4″. It is actually 1½″ × 3½″. Exhibit 8-17 shows the nominal and actual size for common pieces of lumber.

Material Prices

The second part of estimating the cost of materials is to obtain local prices. Although reference sources exist, the best way to get current costs is to contact local suppliers. The adjuster should determine the contractor's price for the material delivered to the site. In many cases, this price is close to the price charged to the public without the delivery service. For small jobs, the contractor picks up the material at the lumberyard and pays the retail price.

Contractors who pay their bills on time might receive time payment discounts. On large jobs, a contractor receives an additional quantity discount. If a job requires a carload lot of one material type, there could be some discount. The type of material often dictates the discount. Construction materials range from commodity items such as lumber and nails to specialty items such as lighting fixtures and cabinets. Because of their generic nature, commodity items carry a relatively small markup, resulting in minimal discounts. However, specialty items often carry higher markups and, consequently, higher discounts. These discounts should be accounted for in the estimate.

Labor

Estimating labor costs consists of two steps similar to determining material costs: (1) determine the quantity of labor and (2) determine the price of labor. The quantity of labor is the number of hours needed to perform the operation. The price is the cost of work for each hour.

Quantity of Labor

The amount of labor required can be obtained from several reference sources. Some of the standard reference sources for estimating construction costs include *The Means Repair and Remodeling Estimator*, published by R. S. Means Company; the *Sweet's Repair and Remodel Cost Guide*, by Marshall & Swift Company; and *Walker's Building Estimators Reference Book* by Frank R. Walker Company. These sources give the amount of labor associated with

EXHIBIT 8-17

Standard Dimensions of Surfaced Lumber

Nominal Size	Actual Size
1 by 2	¾" by 1½"
1 by 4	¾" by 3½"
2 by 3	1½" by 2½"
2 by 4	1½" by 3½"
2 by 6	1½" by 5½"
2 by 8	1½" by 7¼"
2 by 10	1½" by 9¼"
2 by 12	1½" by 11¼"

any construction operation. For example, these references indicate that hanging, taping, and finishing 100 square feet of drywall require 2.5 hours. Estimating software packages also contain labor rates and location modifiers.

Published production rates reflect the average labor required for a usual quantity of new construction. If the job is very large or very small, the production rates can be adjusted accordingly. On small jobs, the adjuster adds the additional time needed for setup, preparation, and cleanup. On large jobs, the highest productivity figure given in ranges is usually appropriate.

Some repair operations require two or more skills. For example, a job might require the skills of a plumber and an assistant. The labor times quoted might refer to the crew. In this case, the crew is two workers. The adjuster might accidentally overestimate a plumbing loss if the plumber's rate is allowed when half of the hours should have been figured at the helper's rate. The standard references indicate whether the operation requires more than one labor type and more than one worker.

Employer's Burden

Employer's burden
The difference between the worker's wage and the contractor's hourly rate; includes costs such as taxable and nontaxable benefits, unemployment tax, Social Security tax, and insurance costs.

The contractor's price of a labor hour can be obtained from references or computed according to local rates. The most important part of accurately computing local labor costs is understanding and accounting for the difference between the worker's wage and the contractor's hourly price. This difference is a group of costs called **employer's burden**. The employer's burden costs are as follows:

1. Taxable fringe benefits, such as vacation and sick leave
2. Nontaxable fringe benefits, such as health insurance plans
3. State and federal unemployment tax
4. Employer's Social Security tax

5. Workers compensation costs
6. Liability insurance costs

To arrive at a local labor rate, add these costs to the base wage.

If a subcontractor is performing the work, the labor price might also be marked up to include the subcontractor's overhead and profit. The total costs to the general contractor produce the labor price to the public. The percentage of burden varies by trade and locale. An estimating reference book provides factors for each of these cost components.

Tools and Equipment; Overhead and Profit; Direct Costs

The cost of most tools and equipment is either borne by the worker or included in the contractor's overhead. However, some jobs require specialty equipment such as scaffolding, a floor sander, or heavy equipment such as a crane or a bulldozer. The best way to estimate the cost of specialty equipment is to allow a daily or hourly rental charge quoted by a local supplier. The labor associated with erecting scaffolding or using equipment comes from the same references as does any other labor factor. Overhead and profit and direct costs are then added to the estimate to complete it.

ESTIMATING METHODS

The same process of scoping the loss scene damage and pricing the estimate always applies, but preparing the estimate itself can involve different methods, depending on the nature and size of the loss. Although some estimates must be developed by using the labor and materials method, the unit cost method is more efficient in other situations. Estimates themselves might differ because of differences in the scope of the loss or differences in the price, and the adjuster must reconcile the differences. Insurance policy provisions also affect estimate preparation. Finally, the adjuster might be able to apply computerized tools as well as standard mathematical formulas to prepare estimates.

Adjusters use two primary methods to estimate the repair cost. They are not mutually exclusive; in fact, most estimates use both approaches depending on the item. Neither method is inherently more accurate than the other because both methods rely on the same data. They use the same labor and materials usage factors and the same local labor and materials prices. See the following box.

Estimating Methods

1. **Labor and materials method,** or **time and materials method.** Cost estimation with this method is based on the number of labor hours and the amount of material for each repair item. For instance, for a painting job, the estimate shows the number of hours and the gallons of paint required to paint each room. The labor and materials method is best for estimating the restoration cost of unique or unusual items such as elements of a house's frame, cabinets, fixtures, doors, and windows.

Continued on next page.

Labor and materials method
An estimating method based on the number of labor hours and the amount of material for each repair item.

Unit cost method
An estimating method based on a common unit of measure such as square feet, which combines the cost of the materials and the cost of the labor into one amount.

2. **Unit cost method.** A unit is the most common way of counting or measuring the quantity of material needed. Examples include square feet, cubic feet, or board feet. The unit cost shows the combined cost of material and labor needed to install one unit of material. For instance, for painting, the estimate shows the square footage of an area to be repainted and the cost to paint one square foot.

Application of Estimating Methods

The best way to describe the two methods is to estimate an item of repair both ways. Ceramic tile is a good example. Ceramic tile can be set in mortar or set directly on smooth plywood, drywall, or concrete by using an adhesive. The latter method is called "thin set." How much will replacing a thin set, ceramic tile floor in a room that is 8 feet × 10 feet cost? Assume that the local labor tile setter's rate is $20 per hour and that the local material cost is as follows:

1″ × 1″ white ceramic tile, 1 square foot paper-backed sheets: $1.75

Tile adhesive, 1 gallon: $10.00

Grout, 25 pounds: $11.00

How much of each material is necessary?

The Labor and Materials Method

First, the repair is estimated using the labor and materials method from the data found in an estimator's reference book.

Materials

The area of the 8′ × 10′ floor is 80 square feet. Add 10 percent cutting and fitting waste to arrive at a quantity of 88 square feet. Because the tile is sold in square-foot sheets, 88 sheets are needed. The cost for 88 sheets at $1.75 per sheet is $154. For the adhesive, the reference book says that a gallon covers 40 to 50 square feet. Two gallons are needed to cover the 80 square feet. The cost for 2 gallons at $10 per gallon is $20. For the grout, 1 pound is needed for 4 square feet of 1″ × 1″ tile. Dividing 4 into 80 square feet results in 20 pounds to grout 80 square feet. If 25 pounds costs $11, how much would 20 pounds cost? A simple formula that works when the quantity needed and the quantity of sale are stated in the same units of measure is as follows:

$$\text{Cost of quantity needed} = \frac{\text{Quantity needed}}{\text{Sale quantity}} \times \text{Sale price},$$

or, in this case,

$$\text{Cost} = \frac{20}{25} \times \$11 = \$8.80.$$

This example is for illustrative purposes only. Grout actually comes in five-, ten-, twenty-, and twenty-five-pound bags, so in reality the estimate would use the actual price for a twenty-pound bag and not go through this calculation.

Labor

For the labor in this job, the reference sources indicate that 8 hours of tile setter's labor are necessary to install 100 square feet of thin set ceramic tile. How many hours are needed for 80 square feet if 8 hours are needed to set 100 square feet? A version of the above formula can be used:

$$\text{Hours needed} = \frac{\text{Quantity needed}}{\text{Standard quantity}} \times \text{Hours required for standard quantity,}$$

or, in this case,

$$\text{Hours needed} = \frac{80}{100} \times 8 = 6.4 \text{ hours.}$$

The adjuster should allow for 6.4 hours at the tile setter's rate of $20. The labor cost to set 80 square feet is $128.

Final Estimate

The finished labor and materials estimate for this item is $310.80, as shown in Exhibit 8-18. Overhead and profit would then be added.

EXHIBIT 8-18

Labor and Materials Estimate

	Quantity	Materials	Labor	Total
Replace 1″ × 1″ Ceramic Tile	88 sq. ft. × $1.75	$154.00	6.4 hrs. @ $20 = $128.00	$282.00
Adhesive	2 gal. × $10.00	$20.00		20.00
Grout	20 lbs.	$8.80		8.80
Total				$310.80

The Unit Cost Method

If the adjuster must estimate the cost to repair or replace a ceramic tile floor a second time for another loss or in another room, he or she could repeat the labor and materials process or develop a unit cost to streamline the estimating process. From estimating the first job, the adjuster knows that replacing 80 square feet would cost $310.80. Dividing $310.80 by 80 provides the cost per square foot, $3.89. This is a unit cost that represents the labor and materials to replace one square foot of 1″ × 1″ white ceramic tile. The next time this tile is used in a repair, the adjuster can use the unit cost method. If the next room is 6 feet × 9 feet, the estimate would read:

Replace 54 square feet of 1″ × 1″ white ceramic tile @ $3.89 = $210.06.

The procedure used to estimate the floor repair can be used to estimate the cost of repairing base tiles around the perimeter of the room. Once the adjuster uses the labor and materials method, he or she can apply a unit cost for a linear foot of wall to determine the cost for that item.

Additional Items and Unit Cost

In estimating the cost to repair a bathroom floor, the adjuster must allow for access time—in this case, removing and resetting the toilet to replace the tile underneath it. The access time should be stated as a separate item using the labor and materials method. The references estimate that the work would take 1.0 hours and that the only material required is a wax ring at $1.

The estimate would therefore include the following:

> Remove and reset toilet, 1.0 hours at $20 + $1 material = $21.

The adjuster would not build that item into the unit cost for three reasons: (1) the access cost does not vary with the room size, (2) the cost might be used in rooms other than the bathroom, and (3) including access or preparation time in the unit cost can lead to counting the cost to gain access twice. The best approach is to keep unit costs as simple as possible. The adjuster should separately estimate and show extra labor and materials needed to gain access in a particular work area.

Choice of Estimating Methods

Which estimating method is better? Unit costs work well with common generic items such as paint, drywall, and floor coverings. Unit costs do not work as well with uncommon items because developing the unit cost takes as much time as using the labor and materials method. The time to develop a unit cost for common items is justified by the long-term time savings realized by applying that unit cost to similar items in that particular project or in subsequent projects, thus eliminating the time needed to recompute labor and materials. However, no timesaving can be realized in computing a unit cost for uncommon items such as the installation of a furnace, because differences in items make applying one item's unit cost to another item difficult. In this case, computing a unit cost simply adds to the time it takes to recompute labor and materials for each item.

For some components, such as framing, the labor and materials method is clearly more satisfactory. Although estimating a set of unit costs for different types of framing is possible, the unit costs do not help much because the labor factor depends on many variables. Rafters can help to illustrate the point. There are different factors for 2″ × 6″ rafters and 2″ × 8″ rafters. Installing rafters on hip roofs takes more time than installing them on gable roofs, which in turn takes more time than installing them on flat roofs. Depending on the design of the roof and the assessment of the job, some rafters are supported by collar beams. If the same variables were applied to the other framing components, the huge collage of unit costs would be more confusing than revealing. If the adjuster tried to simplify the unit costs for framing by developing an average cost, this average cost would be too much in some cases and too little in others. When properly used, the unit cost method is not an average cost method. Each unit cost should be tailored to a specific component, rather than to a class of similar components.

Unique items should also be estimated using the labor and materials method. Lighting fixtures, which come in various types and qualities, are a good example. However, the labor to install the fixtures is relatively constant. The most accurate way to estimate the cost to replace light fixtures is to price the fixture and add the labor to install it. The same holds true for cabinets, plumbing fixtures, and appliances.

The unit cost method should produce the same estimate as a pure labor and materials method, as shown in the tile calculation example. The only difference is that the adjuster does not spend the extra time calculating the number of gallons of paint or rolls of dry wall tape needed in each room. Unit cost estimating has fallen into disfavor with some insurers because some adjusters do not take the time to verify the unit cost quoted by a contractor. When presented with a unit cost estimate, the adjuster should determine if overhead and profit are included in the figure. The adjuster should also determine whether the figure has been rounded up. If it has, a substantial overpayment on a large loss could result.

Estimating Software Packages

Estimates are now done electronically with stand-alone software on laptops and personal digital assistants (PDAs) or through Web-based applications. An adjuster still scopes the loss at the scene but is able to enter the data directly into the estimating system, using codes for quality and grade. The system then calculates the time and material costs or the unit cost based on the information contained in its database.

The adjuster must have accurate measurements and descriptions when using one of these systems. The adjuster must also know when to override the system or to manually enter an item because of special circumstances.

Additionally, these systems also assist in preparing a personal property inventory and the cost estimate for restoration or replacement. They can also perform insurance to value calculations based on the data entered by the adjuster.

Cost Data

Most computer programs use unit cost data. Many create their unit costs from the labor and material costs method in much the same manner as the adjuster would do manually. In some systems, the adjuster uses location modifiers and does not research costs in every possible place. At the very least, a good system offers some breakdown, if not complete disclosure, of the prices and usage rates that make up the unit costs. Without this information, checking or negotiating individual items is difficult. Many systems use quality codes to indicate an item's relative cost and quality. However, more often than not, the adjuster must manually determine an unusual item's cost and then look for the quality code that produces that same cost. A more direct approach is to override the built-in costs for unusual items.

Estimators and those who review estimates must know what costs are included in the system's cost data. Does it remove door and window openings from the square foot calculation? What does the unit cost calculation include? Are overhead and profit included? If the adjuster does not know this information, a duplication in the estimate could occur.

Common Errors

Those who use estimating software programs must take some precautions in their use. The average unit cost in the system may not account for the conditions at a job site, such as adverse weather or limited road access. The unit cost may not take into account the productivity achieved because, for example, numerous rooms are having sheetrock applied. Some programs estimate removal or demolition by square feet or linear feet when the biggest cost is the hauling. Hauling cost varies by location, not by footage.[10]

Estimating systems may rely heavily on "remove and replace" rather than "repair or restore." They often fail to consider partial replacement as an alternative. It is also easy for an adjuster to allow for removal of sheetrock or drywall while at the same time removing wallpaper from the same wall. Keying errors can also occur, causing—for example—10 linear feet of cabinets to become 100 linear feet.[11]

Regardless of the estimating method used, the estimate should appear logical. Measurements must be accurate and correctly calculated. Material must be properly identified. There is an enormous difference in cost between manufactured stone and natural stone. The appropriate material grade must also be noted. The cost differential between stock cabinets and custom cabinets can add thousands of dollars to an estimate.

Other Features

One feature of a computerized system is the speed with which the adjuster is able to complete the scope and estimate. If the insured's contractor finishes his or her estimate first, the adjuster would need to negotiate from the contractor's figures. With an estimate in hand, the adjuster negotiates from his or her figures. In competitive bid situations, the system helps control the bids' form and format. Several programs print a scope that lists only the items and quantities, without pricing or extensions.

Another feature that helps negotiations is the automatic trade breakdown. Most programs print a trade estimate as well as a detailed room-by-room estimate. The trade estimate summarizes the detailed estimate by totaling the repairs for each trade. The trade estimate makes comparing the adjuster's estimate to a contractor's estimate that is itemized by trade easy.

Other Considerations in Preparing an Estimate

Often, the size of the loss dictates how the estimate is to be prepared. Estimates for small losses are usually done on a labor and materials basis. The economies of scale available on a large project do not exist in a small project.

Small Losses

The labor tables in most references allow time for normal setup, preparation, and cleanup. For small jobs, this allowance might be inadequate. Drywall repair is a good example. Even if the damage is less than one square foot and the actual repair time is less than one hour, completing the repair is more time-consuming because the drywall compound has to dry between coats. Even the smallest repair might require an additional trip or two, unless other work can be performed while the compound dries. On a large job, the worker would have other things to do while waiting for the compound to dry or could return to the job site later without the extra travel time significantly affecting the cost.

One approach to estimating a small job is to allow for driving time in addition to the time required to do the work. The more popular approach is to allow a minimum charge. The minimum charge quoted by a contractor usually represents two to four hours of labor and a small amount of material. Minimum charges are convenient but should be used with caution. The adjuster should consider whether separate trades are necessary when a small job involves minimum charges for several trades. If there are several small items for a single trade, a better approach is to estimate the damage using the labor and materials or unit cost method. When the estimate is completed, the adjuster checks to see whether the total for that trade exceeds the usual minimum charge.

Large Losses

An insurance adage states that the only difference between estimating a $10,000 loss and a $100,000 loss is one zero. Although those words might comfort a new adjuster, they are also misleading. Large jobs involve economies of scale. Subcontractors with specialized skills and equipment can produce significant savings. Material discounts for large quantities are possible. Finally, competition can play a greater role in larger losses.

The adjuster analyzes the unit costs and production rates used on smaller losses and adjusts as needed for large losses. If the loss involves painting the interior of an apartment building, the unit cost should be based on spray painting rather than brush or roller painting. Drywall specialists, who might be engaged for a large job, can work more efficiently than can the carpenter who only occasionally paints a room or two. Additionally, drywalling a large space is usually easier because it involves less cutting, fewer odd shapes, and more standard seams. The adjuster can check unit costs by talking with specialty subcontractors about pricing for the quantity of work involved. Finally, an adjuster might want to approach demolition as a single labor and materials item, avoiding the possibility of redundancy in remove and replace unit costs.

Negotiating Building Losses

Estimators looking at the same loss would develop two different repair figures for only two reasons. The first reason is scope differences, including measurement and quantity errors, as well as divergent opinions on the quality and the type of repair. The second reason is price.

Resolving Differences in the Scope

Estimating is not an exact science, and legitimate differences are common. Negotiating a repair figure begins with the first inspection. If the scope is agreed on early, the pricing issues are relatively easy to resolve through negotiation or competitive bidding. The easiest way to reach an agreement on a scope is for the adjuster to prepare it jointly with the insured or the insured's choice of contractor. An adjuster should find a way to resolve any differences in a scope before an estimate is written. See the following box.

Approaches to Resolving Scope-Related Issues

1. If the adjuster is scoping with a contractor, each should keep separate notes and diagrams, which help to identify differences more quickly, unless the contractor wants to work from the adjuster's notes.
2. The adjuster can resolve any question of hidden damage by arranging for some quick demolition or by doing a more complete inspection.
3. Some scope questions require an expert, such as a structural engineer. A common question is the degree of fire damage to concrete, masonry, or steel. Although building inspectors usually have an opinion, they might not have the training and resources to make an accurate decision.
4. Other differences in scope can be resolved by calling in a subcontractor. Most insurance repair contractors are general contractors who rely heavily on their subcontractors for technical expertise. Scope issues involving electrical, plumbing, and heating and air conditioning can be resolved by consulting a specialty subcontractor.
5. Test repairs can be made on a small area to determine whether a repair option would work.
6. Competitive bids can resolve scope problems in a few specific situations. If the insured has chosen a contractor who usually deals in remodeling or new construction, that contractor might want to tear out and replace everything. A more experienced contractor in damage restoration might be needed to identify more conservative yet equally effective alternatives.

Resolving Price Differences

Resolving price-related differences can begin only after the scope has been agreed on. Some contractors charge higher prices than others do. If a contractor with a reputation for quality work charges a higher price, the adjuster might decide to pay that price. Although no single price is correct, some ranges are acceptable. The following box lists general guidelines for negotiating price:

Price Negotiation Guidelines

1. Unit costs are difficult to negotiate. The adjuster can suggest the unit costs as the scope is prepared. Most contractors have a range of unit costs that they will accept. If the adjuster suggests a price on the lower side of the range, the contractor will be more likely to accept it during the scope phase than after the estimate is written. The same is true for labor rates. If the adjuster and contractor can agree on the price of labor in advance, they can then negotiate the labor production rates based on published sources.
2. If unit costs are not agreed to in advance, the labor and materials methods could be used to analyze and negotiate the unit cost. For larger losses, the standard labor production rates are usually on the high side, just as they are on the low side for small jobs.
3. For trades in which the involvement of a subcontractor is expected, the adjuster should ask the general contractor to confirm the price with the subcontractor. That gives the general contractor a chance to reduce the price without losing face. If the price still seems high to the adjuster, another subcontractor can be asked to bid on the repair. The difference might be an additional markup by the general contractor.
4. As a general rule, negotiating from a known quantity such as the adjuster's detailed estimate is more effective than negotiating without an agreed scope. Simply comparing estimates from contractors can cause errors if there is no established norm. The electrical portion of two general contractors' bids could have been prepared by the same subcontractor who accidentally hit the wrong key on the calculator. The two amounts will be similar, but both will be wrong. Bid comparisons are effective as long as everyone works from the same scope and presents the bid in about the same format. In each bid, some items will be higher, and some will be lower. The adjuster should address the bigger discrepancies. Trying to get a contractor to agree to the lowest price for every item is rarely successful.

Coverage Aspects of Estimating

Insurance policy provisions affect the preparation of estimates in several important ways.

Code Requirements

Without an endorsement, most policies exclude the additional repair costs needed to bring a damaged building up to current codes. These codes might require demolishing and replacing undamaged components, replacing obsolete components with new ones, or even adding new items. Determining the additional cost resulting from the codes involves determining the difference between the cost of replacing the damaged portion with items or material of like kind and quality and the cost of replacing with items or materials to meet the current code. In some situations, the amount is obvious. In others, it is not so clear. Because the insured will pay the extra cost, an expert opinion might be warranted.

Alternative Repairs

Generally, most adjusters estimate the cost of repairs using like kind and quality. Creative adjusters sometimes identify repair methods that add value to the insured yet cost less than the usual replacement with like kind and quality. Carpet damaged by a burning log rolling out of the fireplace is a good example. For wall-to-wall carpet, many companies pay to replace carpet in the damaged room and any area that cannot be closed from view. The insured, however, might choose to replace the burned area in front of the fireplace with quarry tile rather than replace several rooms of carpet. Installing drywall instead of plaster and using a butcher block to cover a small burned area on a countertop are other examples of alternative repairs. Although these approaches make sense, the usual policy language does not specifically address the issue of alternative repairs. The adjuster might suggest an alternative repair, but the insured must decide whether to accept that option. If necessary, the adjuster might rely on the policy provision of paying only the actual cash value until repairs are completed, which can prevent an overpayment.

Determining the Actual Cash Value of a Repair Estimate

Determining the actual cash value (ACV) of a repair estimate requires knowing the useful life of building components as well as the court decisions dealing with ACV in the jurisdiction. Determining ACV involves examining each item of repair and quantifying the extent of betterment. The item's age, condition, and expected use affect the amount of depreciation. If the paint in a family room was badly worn before a loss and the loss required that the room be repainted, it would be subject to greater depreciation than the paint in a guest room, which would show little or no evidence of wear. The process of making an objective judgment on depreciation follows no set rules, only general principles.

In determining the ACV of an item to be repaired, the adjuster must understand what causes building components to lose value. Following are some reasons:

1. Physical wear most frequently leads to loss in value. Paint, wall and floor coverings, roofing, and mechanical appliances wear out over time. The *Repair and Remodeling Quarterly* by Marshall and Swift contains a list of the expected life for some common building components. Another source of determining useful life is the manufacturer's warranty, although the useful life can be expected to be longer than the warranty period. These items are generally depreciated on a straight-line basis; therefore,

if a component has a useful life of ten years, it will depreciate in value 1/10th per year. Items that do not wear out are rarely subject to depreciation. However, exceptions occur. For example, evidence of rot or termite damage in framing would justify depreciation if the loss was caused by fire and damaged components were to be replaced with new ones.

2. Obsolescence also contributes to loss in value. As building materials and techniques change, older buildings' features lose value. An example is piping for gaslights in an old building. Although the lines might be functionally sound, they add no value to the building. However, obsolescence can be an elusive concept. The nine- and ten-foot ceilings that were becoming obsolete during the energy crisis of the 1970s are again considered a sign of superior construction as well as an aesthetic advantage.
3. Partial repairs usually do not improve the insured's financial position. As a result, they are rarely subject to depreciation. Replacing a few shingles causes no betterment, but replacing the entire roof usually does. Between the extremes of partial repair and total replacement, the adjuster must decide each case on its merits. Replacing only the damaged slope of a roof might not increase a house's value. However, it would reduce the ultimate cost of replacing the rest of the roof at a later date.
4. In large losses involving older buildings, the ACV of the entire building might be the measure of loss. The market eventually devalues building components that do not wear out. The old notion that the entire building's ACV should reflect the same reduction in value as the depreciated repair estimate is simply incorrect. The effective building age depends on factors beyond the simple deterioration of the components.

Estimating the Value at Risk

Confirming that a building meets coinsurance or replacement cost requirements involves a different sort of cost estimating. Most insurers use the Marshall & Swift/Boeckh (MSB) publications to verify the insured value. The simplest methods use square-foot costs for several classes and qualities of construction for each type of occupancy. The more complex methods come close to the detail of the stick-by-stick estimate. These publications can also be used to set reserves, settle total losses, and verify value.

The key to using these references is to identify the *class*, *quality*, and *occupancy* of the building correctly. The books define these three terms. Adjusters must study and apply these definitions rather than rely on what they think a term or terms might mean. For example, an office in a good quality warehouse is different from a good quality medical office. Another example of differences in definition is the case of an adjuster trying to determine whether the cost to replace a fitness club building includes the cost of a pool. The answer to this question depends largely on whether the publisher of the reference source defines a fitness club as including a pool. The adjuster must be sure to interpret this definition as the publisher intends.

Arithmetic for Estimating

This section summarizes the formulas needed to calculate quantities in estimating property losses. Such basic mathematics is of fundamental importance in preparing estimates.

Decimal Equivalents

Tape measures read feet and inches, but calculators use decimal equivalents. To develop speed in estimating, adjusters need to learn these decimal equivalents. If the table presented below is used often enough, it will be learned quickly. If adjusters try to shorten the process by rounding up to the next foot or half foot, however, estimates will be significantly higher when the loss involves many surface items such as paint and drywall.

Inches	Decimal Equivalent (in feet)	Inches	Decimal Equivalent (in feet)
1	0.08	7	0.58
2	0.17	8	0.67
3	0.25	9	0.75
4	0.33	10	0.83
5	0.42	11	0.92
6	0.50	12	1.00

The conversion calculation means simply remembering that one inch is $\frac{1}{12}$ of a foot. Dividing 1 by 12 results in 0.08.

Measurement Conversion

Being familiar with the units of measure that are most common in estimating is also helpful. It will often be necessary to convert inches to feet and feet to square feet. See the following box.

Conversion Table

HAVE	WANT	Multiply by	OR	Divide by
Inches	Feet	0.0833		12
Feet	Inches	12		0.0833
Square inches	Square feet	0.0069		144
Square feet	Square inches	144		0.0069
Square feet	Square yards	0.1111		9
Square yards	Square feet	9		0.1111
Cubic inches	Cubic feet	1/1728		1728
Cubic feet	Cubic inches	1728		1/1728
Cubic feet	Cubic yards	0.037		27
Cubic yards	Cubic feet	27		0.037

Surface Area

This section contains the basic formulas for calculating area. Subsequent chapters describe specific techniques applicable to different building components.

Parallelogram, Rectangle, and Square

Adjusters must know how to calculate the area of various shapes to perform estimating calculations for particular rooms and items. For example, a parallelogram is a four-sided plane figure whose opposite sides are parallel to each other. A rectangle is a type of parallelogram whose sides meet at a ninety-degree angle. A square is a type of rectangle with four sides of equal length. As Exhibit 8-19 illustrates, the area of these figures is found by multiplying the base by the height. For instance, the area of a 4′ × 8′ sheet of plywood is 32 square feet.

EXHIBIT 8-19

Area of a Parallelogram

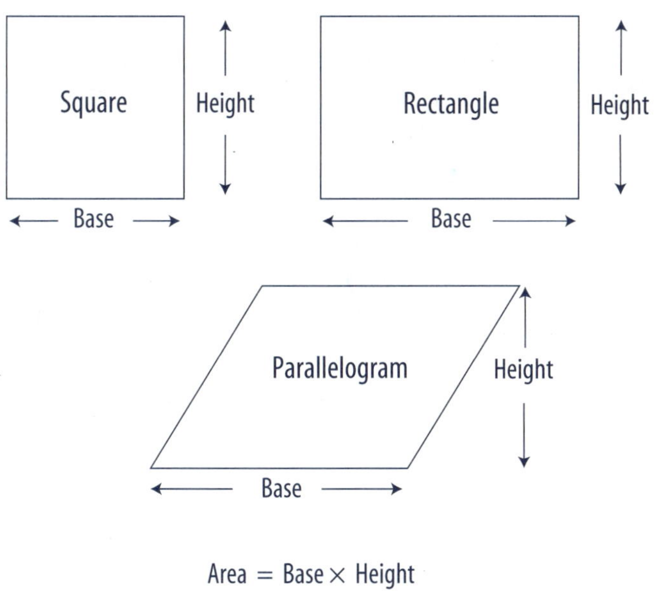

Trapezoid

A trapezoid is a four-sided plane figure with two parallel sides. The area of a trapezoid, shown in Exhibit 8-20, is one half of the sum of the parallel sides multiplied by the height.

EXHIBIT 8-20

Area of a Trapezoid

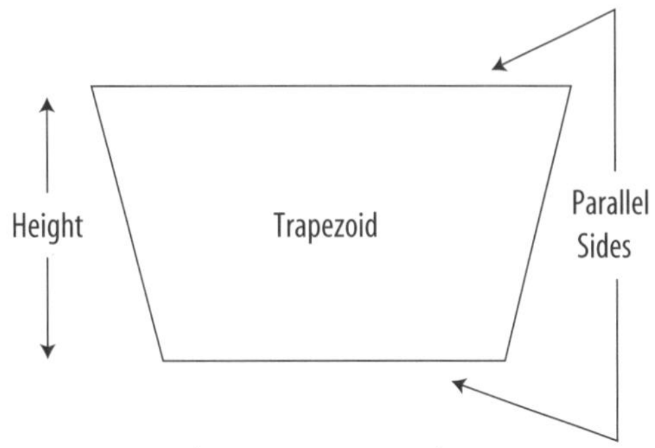

$$\text{Area} = \left(\frac{\text{Sum of Parallel Sides}}{2}\right) \times \text{Height}$$

EXHIBIT 8-21

Area of a Triangle

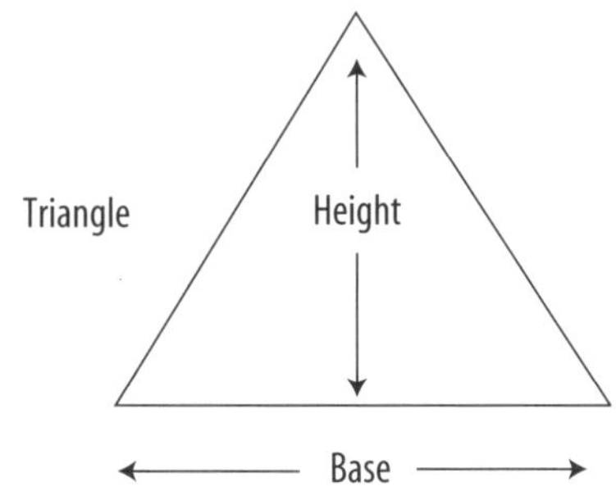

$$\text{Area} = \frac{\text{Base} \times \text{Height}}{2}$$

EXHIBIT 8-22

Area of a Circle

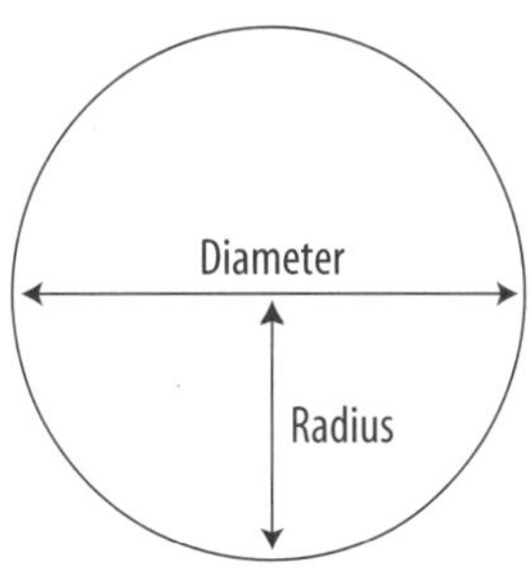

$$\text{Area} = \text{Radius}^2 \times 3.1416$$

Triangle

A triangle is a three-sided plane figure. As shown in Exhibit 8-21, the area of a triangle is one-half the base times the height.

Circle

A circle is a closed-plane curve in which every point is equidistant from a fixed point within the curve. To calculate the circumference (the perimeter), multiply the diameter by 3.1416. To find the area, multiply the square of the diameter by 0.7854. Here is an example:

The circle's diameter is 4 feet.

$$4^2 = 16.$$

$$16 \times 0.7854 = 12.56 \text{ sq. ft.}$$

The radius is half of the diameter. To obtain the area with just the radius, multiply the square of the radius by 3.1413. If the diameter in the prior example is 4 feet, the radius will be 2 feet.

$$2^2 = 4.$$

$$4 \times 3.1416 = 12.56 \text{ sq. ft.}$$

Exhibit 8-22 illustrates these concepts.

Square Feet Versus Square Yards

The area of a surface is expressed in square feet for the purpose of determining how much material is needed to restore that surface. However, some exceptions exist. The amount of surface area to be covered by carpet, plaster, and stucco, for example, is typically expressed in square yards. In some areas of the country, contractors also quote an amount of paint needed by the number of square yards it must cover. The number of square yards is obtained by dividing the area in square feet by 9.

For example, the area of a floor 10 feet × 12 feet is 120 square feet. Dividing 120 by 9 expresses the same area as 13⅓ square yards.

Volume

Volume calculations for loss or repair estimates are much less common, but they are necessary. For example, to know the amount of poured concrete needed to restore a patio, the adjuster determines the volume of the patio. Volume is calculated by multiplying the surface area of the patio (or other solid) by its depth or thickness. The units of measure should be consistent. For instance, in calculating the volume of a 10 feet × 12 feet patio that is 4 inches thick, the adjuster must convert the depth to feet. See Exhibit 8-23.

EXHIBIT 8-23

Illustration of Volume Calculation

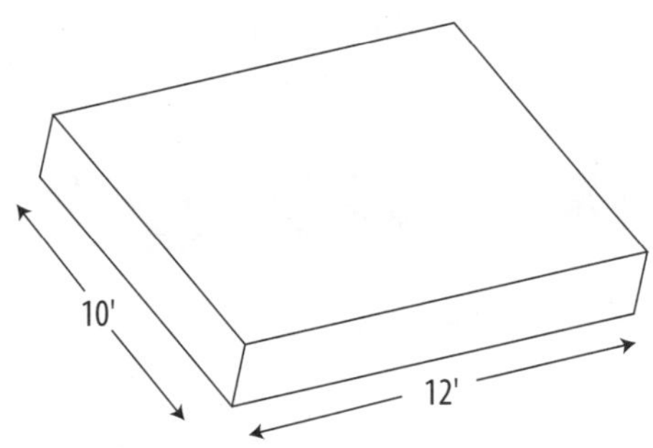

10 ft. × 12 ft. × 1/3 ft. = 40 cubic feet

Four inches is 4⁄12, or ⅓ of a foot. The volume of the patio is calculated as follows:

Surface area = 10′ × 12′ = 120 square feet.

Volume = 120′ × ⅓′ = 40 cubic feet.

Because concrete is quoted in cubic yards, the volume of this patio must be converted to cubic yards. Like a cubic foot, a cubic yard is a unit of measurement that expresses the volume of a solid. A cubic yard is 1 yard wide, 1 yard high, and 1 yard deep. Expressed in feet, a cubic yard is 3 feet wide, 3 feet high, and 3 feet deep. The volume of an object that is 1 yard wide, 1 yard high, and 1 yard deep is 1 cubic yard (1 × 1 × 1) or 27 cubic feet (3 × 3 × 3). To convert 40 cubic feet into cubic yards, 40 is divided by 27, which equals 1.48 cubic yards of concrete.

The units of measure for volume are as follows:

1,728 cubic inches = 1 cubic foot

27 cubic feet = 1 cubic yard

144 cubic inches = 1 Board Foot Measure (BFM)

128 cubic feet = 1 cord (cd)

Rafter Length

Rise of a roof
The vertical height from the supports of a roof to the ridge of the roof.

Run of a roof
The horizontal distance between the face of the walls and the ridge of the roof.

Span of a roof
The horizontal distance between the structural supports that form the roof.

A rafter's length can be determined in three ways. If the roof is accessible and sound, the best way is (1) to measure the rafter. If not, the adjuster can (2) look up rafter length in a rafter table or (3) calculate rafter length. Exhibit 8-24 shows the end of a plain gable roof. The rafter length is the hypotenuse of the right triangle formed by the **rise** and the **run**. The run of a roof should not be confused with the **span**. For clarity, both terms are shown in Exhibit 8-24, even though the span is not used to calculate the rafter length. The rise is the vertical height from the supports to the ridge of the roof. The run is the horizontal distance between the face of the walls and the ridge of the roof. The span is the clear horizontal distance between structural supports. The rafter length is equal to the square root of the sum of the squares of the rise and the run. The example is simple because the roof has no overhang. If the eaves extended beyond the exterior wall, the length of the overhang would be added to get the rafter's full length.

EXHIBIT 8-24

Rafter Length of a Gable Roof

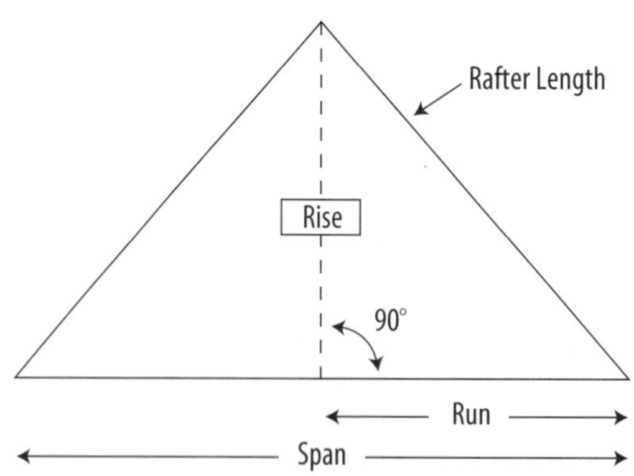

$$\text{Rafter Length} = \sqrt{\text{Rise}^2 + \text{Run}^2}$$

Board Feet

Many home centers sell lumber by the piece. A 2″ × 4″ that is 10 feet long might cost $2.10. A 2″ × 4″ that is 12 feet long might be priced at $2.52. Yet a lumberyard that deals with contractors might say that 2″ × 4″s, 8 to 14 feet long, cost $315.00 per thousand board feet. Lumber in bulk is not sold in the linear foot unit of measure. It is sold in board feet (BF) or board foot measure (BFM). (The traditional abbreviation for a board foot is FBM, but the abbreviation BF is becoming more common.)

These prices represent the same cost although they are stated in different units. Board foot terminology is becoming archaic in the retail lumber business, but it is still used in the estimating business because many labor tables quote labor requirements in hours per thousand board feet. The abbreviation MBF also appears in some labor tables. This abbreviation uses the Roman numeral for 1,000, M, to abbreviate 1,000, so MBF means 1,000 board feet.

Nominal Versus Actual Dimensions

As previously mentioned, a 2″ × 4″ is not actually 2 inches by 4 inches. Rather, 2″ × 4″ refers to the nominal size, meaning that is what this piece of lumber is called. Because of milling, it is actually ½ inch less on each dimension, or 1½ inches × 3½ inches. The lumber was a full 2 inches × 4 inches before it was planed at the mill. After it was smoothed or dressed, the piece lost ¼ inch on each side, or ½ inch on each dimension. The same holds true for any type of milled lumber. The actual measurements of wood paneling, siding, and flooring are less than the nominal size. In some older buildings, framing members are full size. They are called true dimension or full dimension lumber.

When estimating building losses, adjusters use the nominal dimensions rather than the actual measurement when calculating board feet. For example, a joist that measures 1½ inches × 9¼ inches, is a 2″ × 10″ for the purpose of calculating board feet.

A board foot is a measure of the volume of a piece of lumber, so a piece of wood 12 inches square and 1 inch thick is one board foot. A 1 inch × 12 inch piece that is 10 feet long is 10 board feet. A 2 inches × 12 inches piece of the same length is 20 board feet because it is twice as thick.

The Board Feet Formula

Board feet equal the number of pieces times the length of each piece times the nominal dimensions divided by 12:

$$\text{Board feet} = \frac{\text{Number of pieces} \times \text{Length of each piece} \times \text{Nominal dimensions}}{12}.$$

If the scope calls for replacing 20 rafters, each of which is 16 feet long, of 2 inches × 6 inches nominal lumber, the quantity can be converted to board feet as follows:

$$\frac{20 \times 16 \times 2 \times 6}{12} = 320 \text{ BF.}$$

Lumber is usually sold in even lengths. As far as waste is concerned, if the length of the piece required is not an even number, the adjuster should round up to the next even length before converting to board feet. If the example above involved 15-foot rafters, the adjuster would round to 16 feet and arrive at the same quantity requirement, 320 board feet of 16-foot 2″ × 6″s. Other than the rounding to even lengths, no other waste factor is used. Once the amount has been converted to board feet, looking up the labor required in a labor table is easy. If the table says that installing 2″ × 6″ rafters in a plain gable roof requires 30 hours per 1,000 board feet and that the job requires only 320 board feet, the adjuster should divide 320 by 1,000 and multiply by 30 hours:

$$\frac{320}{1{,}000} \times 30 \text{ hours} = 9.6 \text{ hours.}$$

SUMMARY

Knowing the type of building construction and the type of detection and suppression system (if any) involved in a loss gives a property loss adjuster an understanding of the type of damage to be expected in a loss and how best to repair or replace the damage.

Property loss adjusters must know how to estimate building damages. They should be able to identify the six essential parts of a building structure:

1. Foundation
2. Framing
3. Windows and doors
4. Utilities
5. Interior finishes
6. Exterior finishes

The two steps in the estimation process are (1) preparing the scope of damage at the loss scene and (2) pricing the work determined by the scope into a repair estimate.

A scope is a detailed list of damage to each building component. The scope consists of the raw counts of the materials necessary for the repairs, a description of the degree of damage to each component, and the quality of the materials of the damaged property. Unlike a finished estimate, a scope does not list any prices or the calculated quantities. This chapter described a recommended method for inspecting a loss site and preparing a scope.

Pricing an estimate involves estimating the loss restoration cost by using the itemized damage in the scope. Construction operations typically include costs for materials, labor and employer's burden, tools and equipment, overhead and profit, and other miscellaneous costs. Adjusters can use reference materials to identify the materials and quantities needed and to estimate other construction costs.

The process of scoping the loss scene and pricing the estimate is similar for most losses, but the process of preparing the actual estimate can differ depending on the nature and size of the loss. The two primary methods for estimating repair costs are (1) the labor and materials method (also called the time and materials method) and (2) the unit cost method.

The labor and materials method relies on data contained in various estimating reference books or software. These references list information such as the number of square feet that a gallon of paint will cover and how long a worker would need to paint a wall of a certain size. The unit cost method calculates the labor and materials necessary to repair one unit, such as installing one square foot of white ceramic tile. After the adjuster has determined the unit cost for a job, he or she can multiply that cost by the number of units that the job include. Depending on the circumstances of the job, either the labor and materials method or the unit cost method might be the more appropriate estimating choice. Unit cost estimating can be quicker if properly used, but adjusters must understand its limitations to apply it correctly.

Demolition, the removal of damaged components from their original place in the building, can lead to overestimating, so the labor and materials method is usually the best approach for estimating the cost of demolition.

One popular approach for estimating small losses is to allow a minimum charge that represents two to four hours of labor and a small amount of material, but adjusters can also use the labor and materials method or the unit cost method. For large losses, adjusters might be able to take advantage of discounts for the purchase of large quantities.

Estimators studying the same loss might develop different repair figures either because of scoping differences or because of different opinions on the quality and type of repairs. The best way for an adjuster to resolve scoping differences is to prepare the scope jointly with the insured or the insured's contractor. After the scope has been agreed to, the adjuster can resolve the difference in price by using the methods described in this chapter.

Policy provisions could affect the preparation of estimates. For example, most policies exclude the additional repair costs needed to bring a damaged building up to current codes. Additionally, an adjuster might be able to identify repair methods that add value but that cost less than the usual replacement with like kind and quality. Although the insurance industry has historically considered actual cash value, the basis of estimating repairs, to be equal to replacement cost less depreciation, the courts have used the broad evidence rule to include market value factors that can affect the amount of the cost to repair.

Adjusters can use computer estimating systems to prepare scopes. Those systems can produce easy-to-read printed estimates that are free of mathematical errors, but they cannot replace human judgment. Errors commonly occur in the use of these systems. The final section of this chapter summarized basic mathematical formulas that adjusters need to know to calculate quantities and estimate property losses. Chapter 9 applies some of those formulas to hypothetical losses.

Chapter 9 discusses the building of a wood-frame structure from the foundation up to the roof. It indicates how the estimate for repair or replacement can be calculated, using the estimating arithmetic learned in this chapter.

CHAPTER NOTES

1. Francis L. Brannigan, *Building Construction for the Fire Service* (Boston: National Fire Protection Association, 1971 and 1977), p. 8.
2. Sprinkler material adapted from Charles Bahme, "Fire Officer's Guide to Extinguishing Systems" (Boston: National Fire Protection Association, 1977).
3. Alarm information adapted from Vivian Cape, *Security Systems and Intruder Alarms* (Oxford: Newnes, 1999).
4. Paul I. Thomas, *How to Estimate Building Losses and Construction Costs*, 4th ed. (Englewood Cliffs, N.J.: Prentice-Hall, Inc., 1983).
5. "Using Steel for Optional Engineering of Framing Techniques," *Property Damage Report*, No. 501 (Newville, Pa.: National Property Casualty Claims Research Services, Inc., July 1994).
6. Adapted from Mutual Loss Research Bureau, 1969 Adjuster's Basic School Training Material.
7. Adapted from Paul I. Thomas, pp. 17–18
8. Adapted from Paul I. Thomas, pp. 18–50.
9. Adapted from Paul I. Thomas, p. 46.
10. Adapted from Curtis W. Driver, "Reality Estimating in the Property Insurance Industry," *Claims Magazine*, December 1999, pp. 60–66.
11. Adapted from "Estimating Errors," *Property Damage Report*, No. 532 (Newville, Pa.: National Property and Casualty Claims Research Services, Inc., September 1999).

Chapter 9

Direct Your Learning

Construction Fundamentals for Estimating

After learning the subject matter of this chapter, you should be able to:

- Create a residential construction estimate for each of the following:
  - Concrete and masonry
  - Frame carpentry
  - Drywall
  - Roofing
  - Painting and wallpaper
  - Siding
- Give examples of causes of damage, and explain the methods of repair and factors affecting repairs for each of the following:
  - Concrete and masonry
  - Frame carpentry
  - Drywall
  - Roofing
  - Painting and wallpaper
  - Siding
- Create a gross area and net area estimate for painting a room.
- Describe the elements of, and damage that can occur to, the following systems:
  - Electrical
  - Plumbing
  - Heating and cooling

OUTLINE

Develop Your Perspective

What are the main topics covered in the chapter?

This chapter examines how to prepare a building damage estimate from the ground up, using residential construction as an example.

Review an estimate that you have received on a claim.

- Do you understand the scope of the estimate and the recommended method of repair?
- Can you verify the cost calculations?

Why is it important to know these topics?

Whether you prepare the scope and estimate yourself or you are reviewing an estimate prepared by someone else, you need to understand how materials' cost and quantity are determined and how much labor is involved in the repair and cost of that labor.

How can you use this information?

When preparing or reviewing an estimate,

- Check the dimensions and calculations for accuracy.
- Verify that the correct labor rates are being used.
- Be prepared to discuss appropriate methods of repair and their related costs.

Chapter 9

Construction Fundamentals for Estimating

Understanding basic construction principles helps an adjuster to evaluate a loss, whether it is a field adjuster who goes out to loss sites and prepares estimates of damage or a liability adjuster who receives estimates to repair damage caused by insureds. This chapter follows a "ground up" approach to discussing construction, beginning with a building's foundation and ending with the exterior finish. Familiarity with such construction basics enables an adjuster to create, understand, and question construction estimates.

CONCRETE

Concrete is used as the foundation for most residences. It is used for patios, walkways, and driveways. Concrete is a fire-resistive material. Prolonged exposure to extreme heat causes concrete to lose its moisture. The surface then flakes off in thin pieces. This condition is called **spalling**. Spalling also results from repeated heating and cooling during firefighting activities. Concrete can also shrink as a result of fire, and that shrinkage causes cracks to form. Exhibit 9-1 depicts an example of spalling.

Spalling
The flaking of a concrete surface when exposed to prolonged extreme heat.

Fire-damaged concrete can be repaired by cutting out the damaged area and replacing it. Areas that have spalling can be scraped and resurfaced. Stained and smoke-damaged concrete can be cleaned with steam, sand, or chemicals. The concrete surface can also be painted to cover the stains.

Concrete comes in two forms: (1) ready mix and (2) mixed on site. Ready mix is delivered by large mixer trucks and is poured into waiting forms. Concrete mixed on site is prepared by stand-alone mixers and requires additional labor to mix it and haul it to the forms. Concrete also comes in various formulas to suit different purposes, although the essential ingredients are always cement, sand, and stone. There are concrete mixes for heavy-use locations, such as driveways and garage floors. There are also watertight mixes for foundations and pools. The cost varies depending on the mix.

EXHIBIT 9-1

Spalling

Photo courtesy of National Property & Casualty Claims Research Services, Inc. (NPCCRS).

Adjuster Tip

On smaller jobs using ready mix, there may be a minimum charge or a minimum amount, such as 5 cubic yards, that must be purchased.

Concrete is estimated by volume, and its unit of measure is cubic yards. Chapter 8 explains the calculation for volume of concrete.

Concrete form
A temporary mold to support the shape of concrete while it sets and cures.

Estimating concrete work entails more than just determining the quantity of material. Slabs, sidewalks, patios, floors, and foundations need to have forms built. A **concrete form** is a temporary mold to support the shape of the concrete while it sets and cures. The estimate must therefore include the quantity of lumber needed to build these forms. The forms are usually built by carpenters and torn down by laborers. Exhibit 9-2 shows an example of concrete forms.

Adjuster Tip

Some contractors reuse lumber from old forms, or they may have prefabricated forms that are reusable.

EXHIBIT 9-2

Concrete Forms

Photo courtesy of National Property & Casualty Claims Research Services, Inc. (NPCCRS).

The amount of lumber needed for forms is based on the square footage of the concrete surface. An average is between 2½ to 3 board feet per square foot of concrete.

MASONRY

Foundations can also be built from concrete block. Because concrete block, brick, and stone are similar in installation and estimation, this section discusses them together. A mason and helper usually install brick, concrete block, and stone. Brick is often the exterior finish to a house, but it can be used in a wall, in steps, in a walkway, in a patio, and in a fireplace. Concrete block is often used as a footing for another part of the structure. Stone has the same variety of uses as brick.

Masonry is most often installed using mortar to hold it in place. Mortar is a mix of cement, sand, water, and sometimes lime. Mortar is estimated on the basis of cubic feet or cubic yards needed. On average, 18 cubic feet or ⅔ cubic yards of mortar is used per 1,000 bricks. Forty cubic feet, or 1½ cubic yards, is used per 1,000 blocks. These numbers vary depending on the size of the brick or block used and how thickly the mortar is applied.[1]

Brick

A common brick is 4″ × 8″ × 2″. Its actual size is 3¾″ × 8″ × 2¼″. On average, there are 21 bricks to 1 cubic foot of masonry. One hundred bricks are called a strap, which is usually the minimum quantity available for purchase. A pallet is 500 bricks.

Many varieties of brick are available. Exhibit 9-3 illustrates various types of bricks. Intended use determines whether a specialty brick is needed, such as for a fireplace. Brick can discolor, crack, or spall. It can develop white surface deposits, which are salt crystals leeching out of the brick. These salt crystals can usually be removed with linseed oil. Brick can be cut out and replaced; however, matching its color might be difficult. When preparing an estimate for brick repair, the adjuster might have to include scaffolding or bracing needed to keep adjacent walls in place.[2]

Block

Concrete block is available in two weights and several sizes. Lightweight block (referred to as cinder block) is 8″ × 8″ × 16″ and weighs about 30 pounds. Its actual size is 7⅝″ × 7⅝″ × 15⅝″. Heavy block is also 8″ × 8″ × 16″, but it weighs about 45 pounds. Concrete block can also be found in smaller sizes.

Concrete block is susceptible to the same damage as is concrete. Although concrete block does not spall under extreme heat, it can crumble. Cracks usually result from fire, earth movement, blasting, and vibration. Damaged concrete block can be cut out and replaced. If this is done, adjacent walls may need to be braced during such repairs.

Estimating Brick and Block

To estimate the amount of 8″ × 8″ × 16″ concrete block needed, first calculate the square foot area of the wall and deduct all openings and corners. This is done by deducting the opening and by taking 8 inches off of 2 walls for a total of 16 inches when using 8″ × 8″ × 16″ blocks to deduct for corners. Multiply the square foot area by 1.125 to get the required number of blocks.

Brick walls pose a challenge for an adjuster because he or she must know how thick the wall will be. A one-brick-thick wall is a four-inch wall; two bricks thick is an eight-inch wall. The way to estimate the number of bricks needed is to find the gross wall area and deduct the openings. Then multiply the square feet by the number of bricks per square foot of the desired wall thickness. As an example, suppose that the wall is 8′ × 10′ and that it is going to be 8 inches thick. A table in an estimating reference book would show that 14 bricks make 1 square foot of an 8-inch wall. So 8′ × 10′ = 80 square feet × 14 bricks per square foot = 1,120 bricks. Exhibit 9-4 depicts a common brick wall.

EXHIBIT 9-3

Bricks

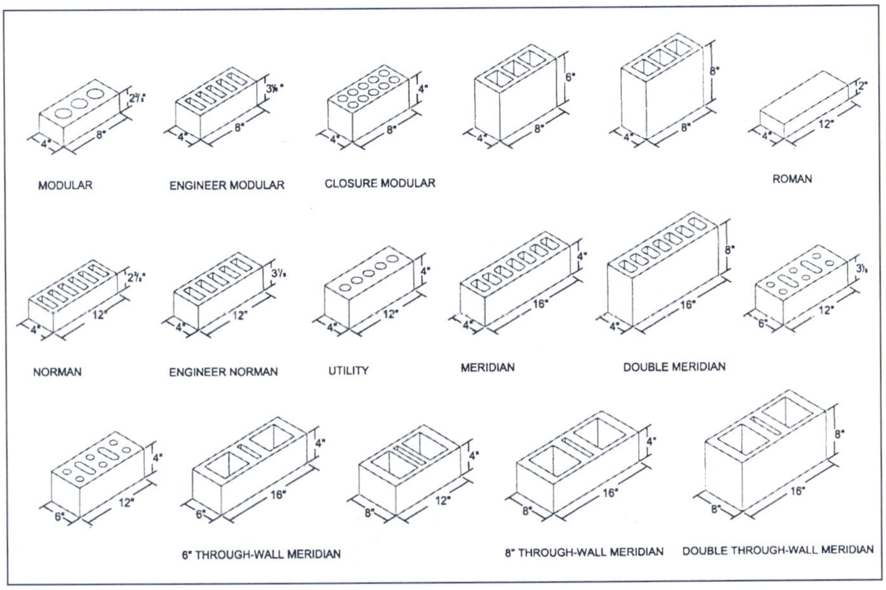

Modular Brick Sizes (Nominal Dimensions)

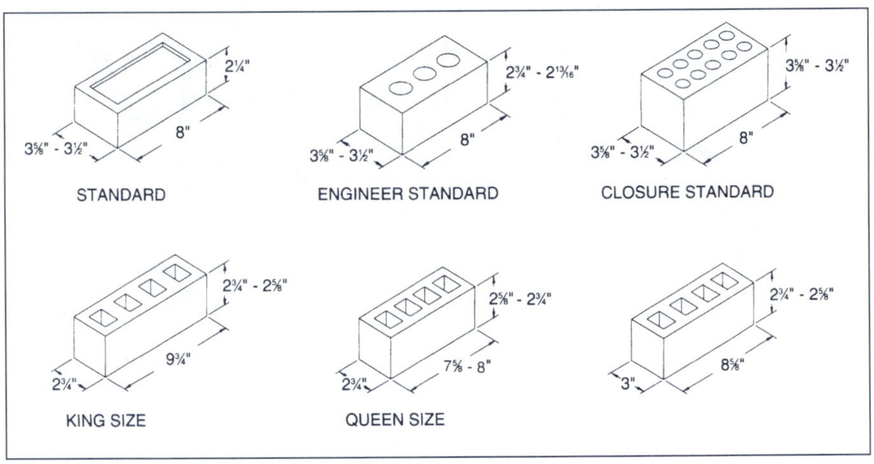

Non-Modular Brick Sizes (Specified Dimensions)

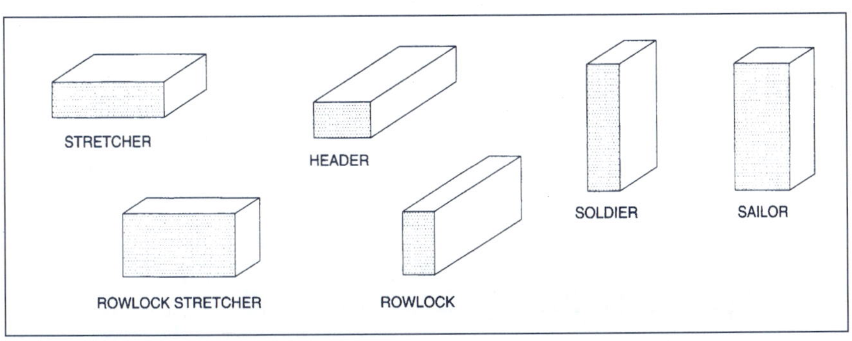

Brick Positions in a Wall

Used with permission of the Brick Industry Association.

EXHIBIT 9-4

Common Brick Wall With Block Backup

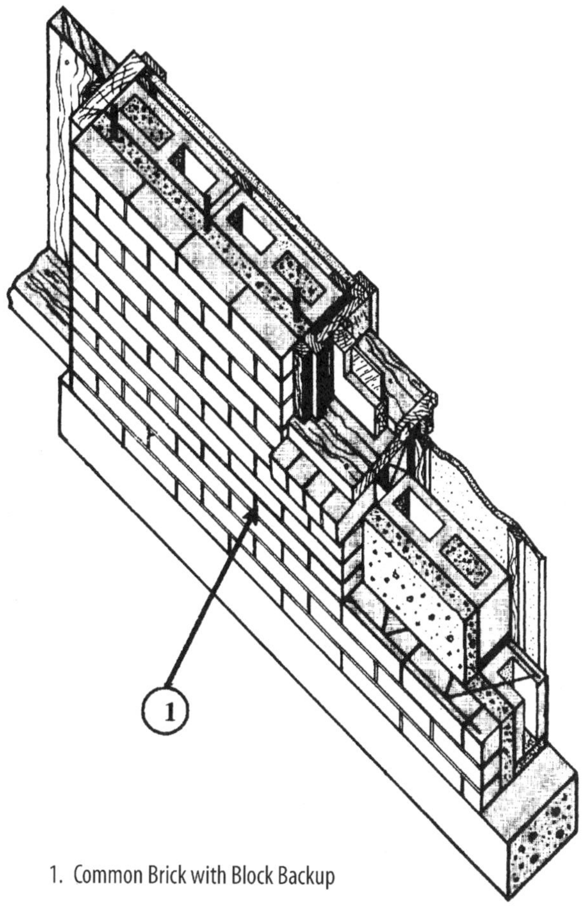

1. Common Brick with Block Backup

Home Repair and Remodel 2002 Cost Guide (Los Angeles: Marshall and Swift Publications Co., 2002), p. 410.

FRAME CARPENTRY

To properly complete a scope and an estimate for frame carpentry, an adjuster must identify the quantity and quality of the lumber needed. Correctly identifying the quantity and quality helps to ensure an accurate estimate.

Lumberyard Terminology

With so many different types of lumber available, an adjuster's job is easier if he or she understands the various types of lumber available and their uses. How lumber is sized and how it is sold directly affects the estimate's accuracy.

Varieties of Wood[3]

About 80 percent of building construction involves carpentry work. When wood is damaged, identifying its type and quality is essential. Wood is either hardwood or softwood. **Hardwood** comes from deciduous, broadleaf trees. **Softwood** comes from coniferous, evergreen trees. See the following box. The names are slightly deceiving because some hardwoods are actually softer in consistency than some softwoods. Generally, hardwoods are typically used in finish carpentry, and softwoods are used in framing.

Hardwood
Wood that comes from deciduous, broadleaf trees such as maple and oak.

Softwood
Wood that comes from coniferous, evergreen trees such as pine and cedar.

Types of Woods

Softwoods	Hardwoods	
Cedar	Ash	Gum
Cypress	Aspen	Mahogany
Fir	Basswood	Maple
Hemlock	Beech	Oak
Pine	Birch	Poplar
Redwood	Cherry	Sycamore
Spruce	Chestnut	Walnut
	Elm	Willow

Sizing

Softwood lumber usually comes in 6- to 20-foot lengths. It is sold only in two-foot increments, so an 18-foot length or a 20-foot length is available, but a 19-foot length is not available. Hardwood lumber is sold in random lengths based on availability. A strip is a small piece of lumber usually less than 1 inch thick and 3 inches wide. A board is normally 4 to 12 inches wide and less than 2 inches thick. Framing lumber ranges from 2 to 6 inches thick and is usually a minimum of 2 inches wide, so common sizes are 2″ × 4″, 2″ × 6″, or 4″ × 6″. Beams are 4 or more inches thick and are at least 2 inches wider than their thickness. Posts and timbers are usually 4 inches by 6 inches, and their width should not exceed the thickness by more than 2 inches.[4]

As Chapter 8 mentions, lumber is sold in two ways:

1. Linear foot is used for small quantities;
2. Board foot is used for large quantities.

The price for lumber is stated as the price per 1,000 board feet.

Frame Carpentry Damage and Repair

A house's frame can be damaged by various causes, including fire, smoke, windstorm, water, vandalism, earthquake, settlement, vehicle impact, and many other perils, some insured and others excluded. Serious losses might require replacing roof sections or completely reframing a room. Less severe losses might simply call for replacing a single rafter, stud, or floor joist.

Because framing members are the first elements to be constructed when a house is built, removing and replacing undamaged items are often necessary to repair damaged structural members, such as when an attic fire severely chars roof rafters. Even when only slightly damaged, the finished roof surface and roof sheathing must be removed and replaced to replace the rafters.

Exposure to extreme heat causes wood to lose moisture, so lumber might shrink, warp, or split. Exposure to excessive moisture causes wood to swell, and swelling will begin within hours of immersion. If left undisturbed, the swelling will stop within a few days.[5]

Splicing, sistering, or **scabbing**
A repair technique in which new framing members are placed alongside damaged members to reinforce them.

Damaged wood framing can be repaired by several methods. It can be replaced entirely, or it can be partially replaced, reinforced, concealed, or resurfaced. In some cases involving cracked, split, or charred framing members, the damaged parts do not need to be removed. Instead, they can be reinforced by **splicing** (also called **sistering** or **scabbing**) new framing members alongside them. Finished materials almost always cover framing members, so the change created by splicing has no cosmetic effect. Structural members that are only slightly charred or stained by smoke can be spray-sealed, painted, or covered by drywall. Most insureds simply want to be assured that the smell of smoke will not linger. Spray sealing is acceptable to most insureds and fire restoration contractors.

Frame Construction

The two basic types of residential frame construction are (1) platform (sometimes called "western") and (2) balloon. Platform construction, illustrated in Exhibit 9-5, is the common method employed today. Balloon construction, illustrated in Exhibit 9-6, is seldom used in new homes because of the cost of extra-long framing members. However, adjusters should be familiar with balloon construction because homes built before 1940 sometimes used this method of framing. These two types of frame construction are discussed below, followed by a description of the components that form the shell of a typical house.

Platform Construction

Platform construction
A method of construction in which each story of a house is built on a separate platform, like boxes stacked one on top of another.

In **platform construction,** each story of a house is built as a separate platform. Imagine each story as boxes stacked one on top of another. The wall framing in platform construction is built above the subfloor and extends to all edges of the building. A common method of building these walls is to prefabricate full sections of walls and tilt them up and into place. This method is not always possible if only sections of a wall damaged by loss are replaced.

EXHIBIT 9-5

Platform Frame Construction

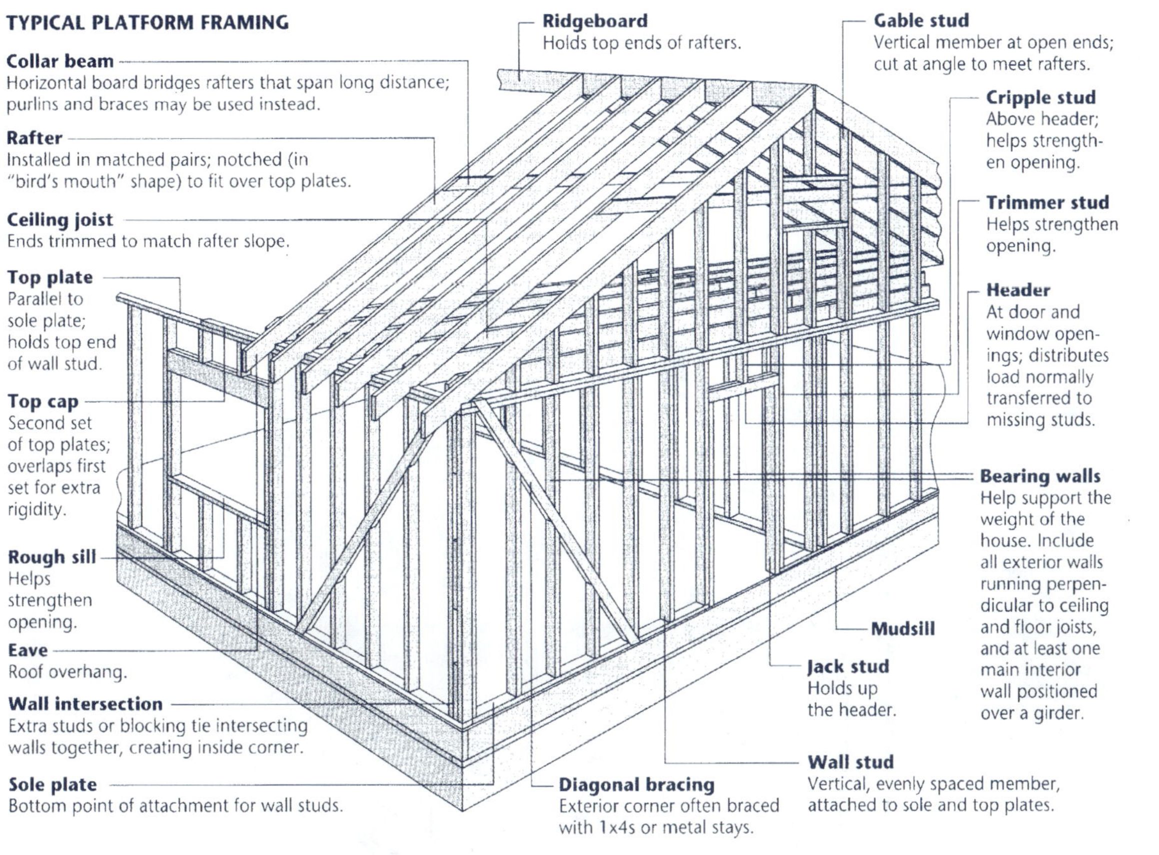

Basic Carpentry (Menlo Park, Calif.: Sunset Books, 1995), p. 52.

Balloon Construction

In **balloon construction,** the wall studs extend from the sill of the first floor to the top plate or end rafter of the second floor. In platform construction, the framed wall is complete for each floor. This is the major difference between balloon construction and platform construction. The construction of interior walls is the same for balloon framing as for platform framing.

Balloon construction
A method of construction that uses long wall studs that extend from the ground on up to the second floor.

Adjuster Tip

To tell what type of construction was used for a house, go into the basement or crawlspace and look for the mudsill on top of the foundation. If paired joists and studs are resting on the sill, the house was built using balloon construction. If only joists are visible below the subfloor, then the house was built with platform construction.[6]

EXHIBIT 9-6

Balloon Frame Construction

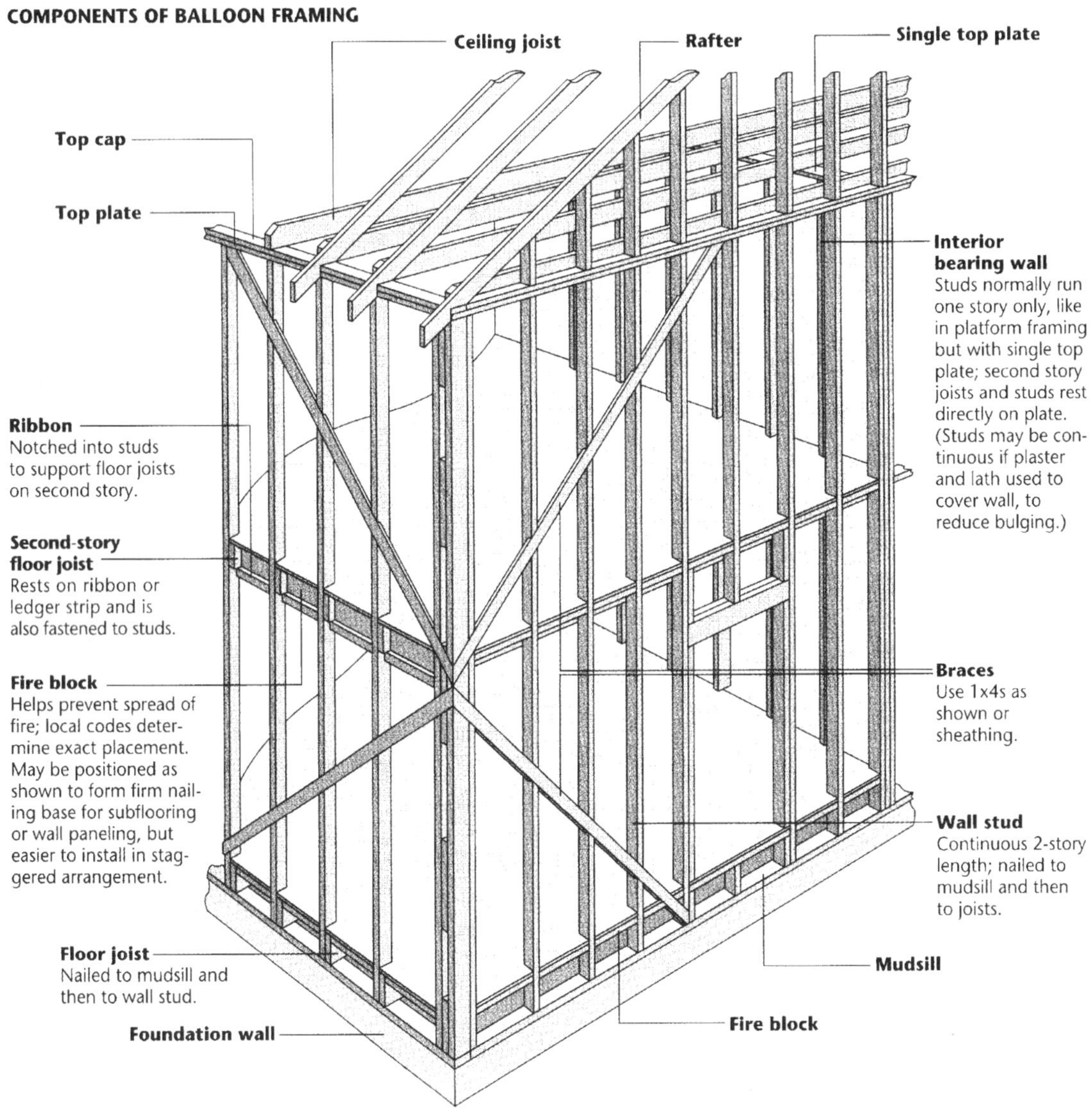

Basic Carpentry (Menlo Park, Calif.: Sunset Books, 1995), p. 53.

Elements of Frame Carpentry

Frame carpentry
The work done by carpenters to erect the basic skeleton of a house.

Frame carpentry, also called "rough carpentry," is the work done by a carpenter in erecting the basic shell of a house. Knowledge of frame carpentry is especially important because frame damage is not always visible after a loss. The easiest way to develop an understanding of frame carpentry is to study each of the basic elements of a house's shell separately. This section expands on the basic framing components that Chapter 8 discusses.

Floor Framing

The floor framing of a wood-frame house consists of the posts, beams, sill plates, joists, and subflooring. Together, these form the level platform for the rest of the house. The posts and center beams support the inside ends of the joists. Wood or steel posts are generally used to support wood girders or steel beams.

Posts and Girders

Wood and steel posts, girders, and beams are used in residential construction. The most common steel beam is the I-beam, which spans the full length of the house. When wood girders are used, they are generally built up, meaning that they are composed of two or more 2″ × 10″s or 2″ × 12″s nailed together. Some new homes are constructed with plywood I-beams, which provide great support and are lightweight.

Wood Sill

Exhibit 9-7 shows that platform construction uses a box sill consisting of a two-inch sill anchored to the foundation wall, which provides support and fastening for the joists and box header at the end of the joists.

EXHIBIT 9-7

Foundation Wall and Sill

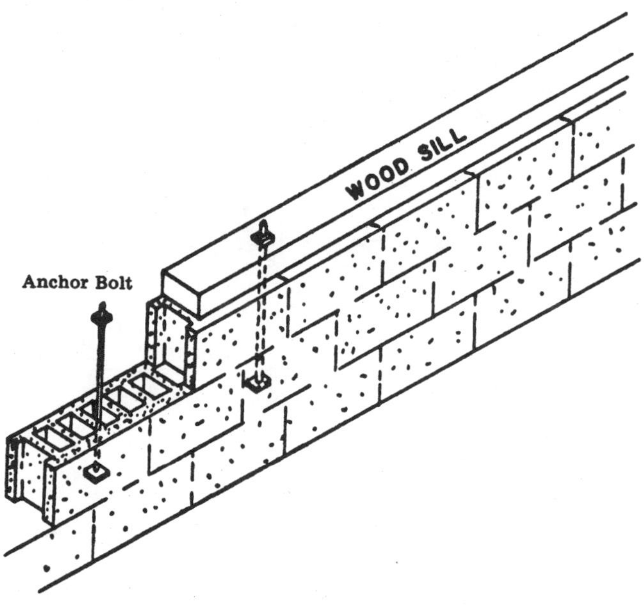

Adjuster Handbook (Denver: General Adjustment Bureau, Inc., 1972), p. 8.

> **Adjuster Tip**
>
> Sills cannot be replaced easily because of the amount of the building that they support. In a fire, usually only a sill's edges burn because they are the only surfaces exposed. Replace sills only if the bulk of the building on top of them is destroyed.

Floor Joists

Wood floor joists are generally 2″ × 8″s, 2″ × 10″s, or 2″ × 12″s. They run perpendicular to the center beam and usually sit directly on it, with their ends slightly overlapping (see Exhibit 9-8). They can also be attached directly to a wooden girder or steel beam by joist hangers or a supporting ledger strip. They are usually spaced sixteen-inch on center. Joists are attached to the sill, and the header joist is then attached to each stringer joist. Double joists are usually used under any area that will support additional weight, such as partition walls, bathtubs, fireplaces, or openings for stairways.

EXHIBIT 9-8

Floor Joists

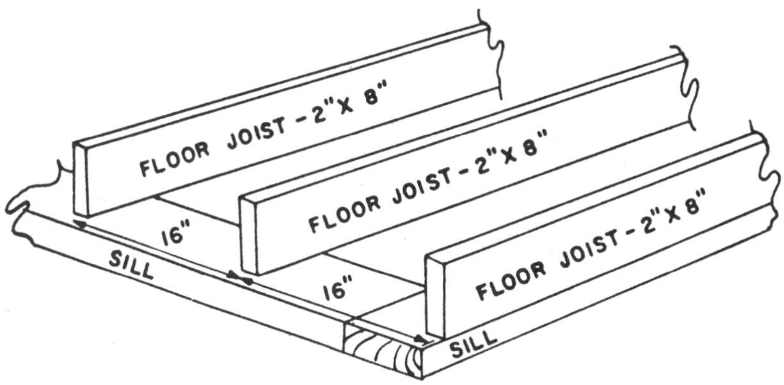

Adjuster Handbook (Denver: General Adjustment Bureau, Inc., 1972), p. 12.

Bridging

Cross bridging is placed between joists at various intervals to help transfer loads. Three types of bridging are commonly used in residential structures: (1) solid board, (2) wooden (usually using 1″ × 2″s or 1″ × 3″s), and (3) metal. Metal is rapidly becoming the most popular bridging material because it is strong, lightweight, and easy to install. Chapter 8 shows bridging examples.

Subflooring

Subflooring is used over the floor joists to provide a working platform and base for finish flooring. Exhibit 8-7 in Chapter 8 shows subflooring and floor framing. Plywood is by far the most common subflooring material. Plywood is graded by letter. "C" and "D" grade are typically used for sheathing. The sheets are usually 4′ × 8′ and cover 32 square feet. Depending on the strength needed, thicknesses from one-half inch to three-quarters of an inch are used. Plywood is installed with the grain direction running perpendicular to the joists and is staggered so that end joints in adjacent panels line up over different joists. To avoid squeaky floors, carpenters both glue and nail most plywood subflooring. This practice varies, however, depending on the quality of construction. Plywood is purchased in full sheets, so it is necessary to round up when estimating it. If the area is 100 square feet, divide by 32 square feet, which equals 3.125 sheets. Round up to 4 sheets for the estimate.

Subflooring
The working platform or layer that goes over the floor joists, providing a base for the finished floor.

Adjuster Tip

When subflooring is damaged, it is better to tear up and replace full sheets than to cut sheets to size unless it is necessary to cut because of a cabinet or another protrusion. Tearing up full sheets saves on labor because less cutting is involved.

Wall Framing

Wall framing includes the studs, sole plates, top plates, and window and door headers on interior and exterior walls. These walls support ceilings, upper floors, and the roof. The wall-framing members used in residential construction are generally 2″ × 4″ studs spaced sixteen inches on center. New construction often uses 2″ × 6″ studs spaced twenty-four inches on center to allow for thicker exterior wall insulation. Top plates and sole plates are also 2″ × 4″ or 2″ × 6″, depending on the studs used. Headers over doors and windows are doubled 2″ × 6″s or deeper members, depending on the opening's span. Double studding is used around window and door openings. See Exhibit 9-9.

Wall framing
The framing that provides the support for ceilings, upper floor, and roof; also provides the base to which wall sheathing is connected.

Window and Door Framing

Headers are the members used to span over windows and doors. Exhibit 9-10 illustrates a header supported at each end by the inner studs of a double stud joint at exterior walls and interior load-bearing walls.

Wall Sheathing

Wall sheathing is the outside covering installed over the studs, plates, and window and door headers. Various materials are used; half-inch plywood or chipboard is typically used in corners for reinforcement or when some form of continuous nailed exterior siding is planned. In some climates, plywood

Wall sheathing
The outside covering installed over the wall framing, usually made of plywood.

EXHIBIT 9-9

Studs

Sole Plate 127 FBM

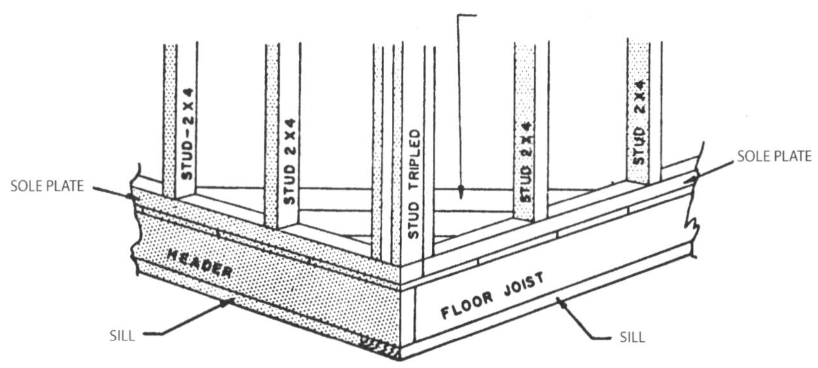

Adjuster Handbook (Denver: General Adjustment Bureau, Inc., 1972), p. 18.

EXHIBIT 9-10

Rough Framing for Wall Openings

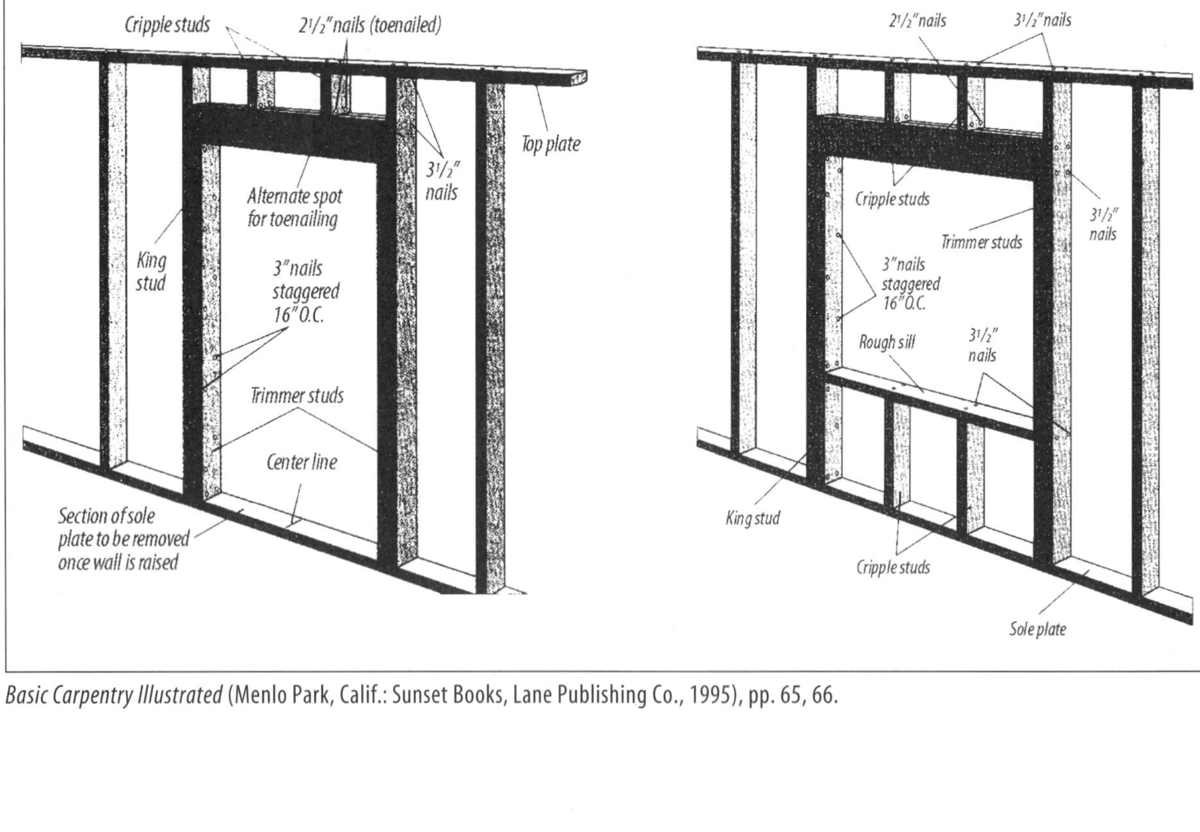

Basic Carpentry Illustrated (Menlo Park, Calif.: Sunset Books, Lane Publishing Co., 1995), pp. 65, 66.

siding serves as both the sheathing and the exterior finish. With plywood, adding corner bracing to the walls is unnecessary.

Insulated sheathing, sometimes referred to as "blackboard," is composed of ground wood fibers supplemented by asphalt or other water-resistant products. It is not as structurally strong as plywood or chipboard, but it is less expensive and provides better insulation.

More new construction uses a rigid foam sheathing that has excellent insulating properties. It is generally one-inch thick and comes in 4′ × 8′ sheets. Because the foam lacks strength, metal let-in braces, plywood, or chipboard is used to strengthen the exterior wall corners. Foam sheathing costs about the same as plywood and is preferable in climates requiring substantial insulation.

Ceiling Joists

After the exterior and interior walls have been constructed, ceiling joists can be nailed into place. Ceiling joists, illustrated in Exhibit 9-11, are normally placed across the width of a house. The joists' sizes depend on the span, the spacing between joists, and the load anticipated on the second floor or attic. Ceiling joists are used to attach the ceiling to the room below and act as floor joists for the floor above.

EXHIBIT 9-11

Ceiling Joists

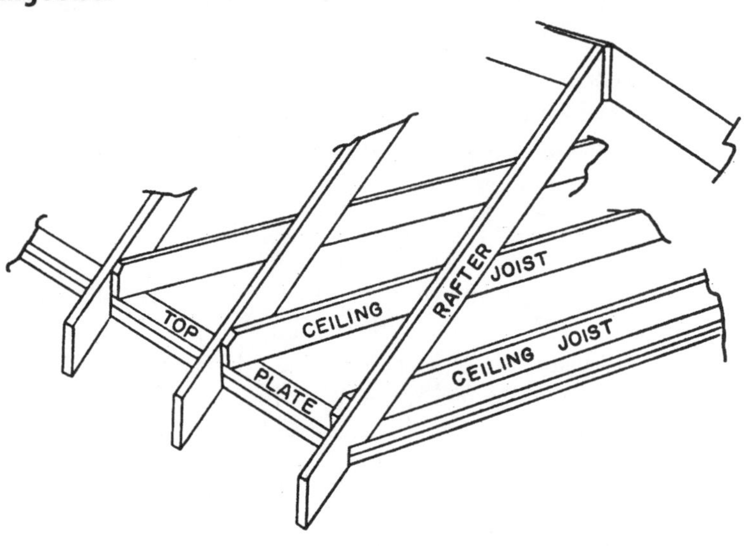

Adjuster Handbook (Denver: General Adjustment Bureau, Inc., 1972), p. 21.

Rafters and Ridge Board

The type of rafter used in residential construction varies depending on the style of roof. The various styles are discussed later in this chapter. In a gable roof, as shown in Exhibit 9-12, all rafters are the same length and run from a ridge board to the top plate of the exterior wall (or beyond, depending on the overhang). The ridge board is usually a 1″ × 8″ or a 2″ × 8″, which provides support and a nailing surface for the upper rafter ends. The rafters are notched out to fit snugly on the top plate.

> ### Adjuster Tip
>
> When estimating the number of rafters, use the entire roof length as the dimension, not the building's length. Using the roof's length includes the overhangs on a gable.

Trusses

Trusses
Pre-assembled roof framing.

Trusses are becoming very popular in the construction of new homes and are often recommended by contractors in the repair of existing homes whose roof-framing members have suffered significant damage. They take the place of the joists and rafters and are installed without a ridge board. Most trusses are pre-engineered and assembled by a truss-fabricating plant, then delivered to the job site, where they are installed quickly, generally with the aid of a crane. They are usually placed on twenty-four-inch centers. Exhibit 9-13 illustrates the three kinds of trusses used most often in residential construction: (1) the W-type, (2) the king-post, and (3) the scissors. However, many other types of trusses are available.

Individual members of a truss can be replaced without replacing the entire truss. Replacing one or more members often becomes necessary when a rafter (known as a "rafter-cord") breaks as a result of either the weight of ice and snow or the impact of a fallen tree limb.

Roof Sheathing

Roof sheathing is the covering over rafters or trusses and usually consists of either half-inch plywood or seven-sixteenth-inch chipboard. Refer to Exhibit 8-11b for an illustration of roof sheathing. Many roofs still have solid board sheathing, although its use in new construction is limited to homes that have wood shingles or shakes. Plywood is also an option for sheathing when wood shakes or shingles are to be installed.

Estimating Frame Construction

After the damaged area has been exposed and the demolition has been completed, estimating is similar to that for new construction. For example, if a tornado twists only the roof framing from a house, the adjuster needs to determine the cost to frame a new roof using materials and construction methods similar to those used for the previous roof.

EXHIBIT 9-12

Wood-Frame House Construction

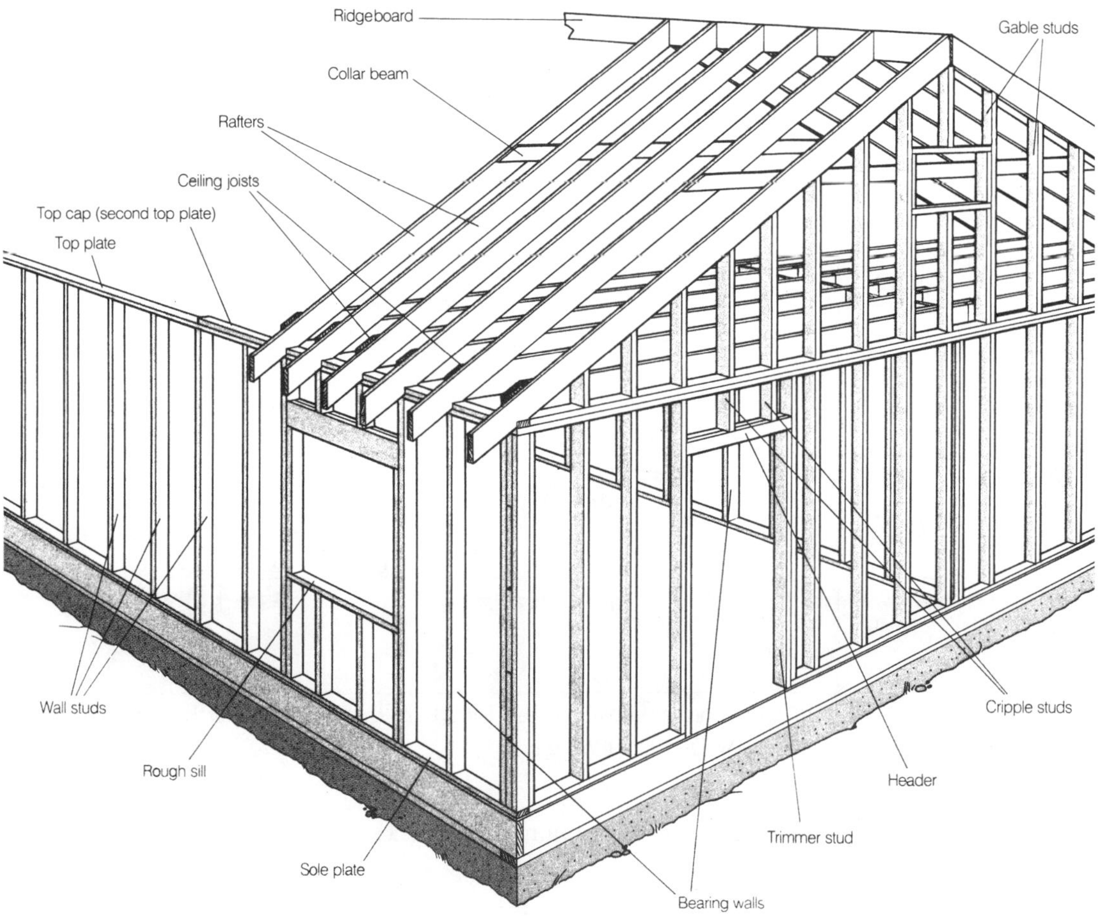

Stud walls, ceiling joists, and rafters complete the house skeleton. The walls are secured to the subfloor and to each other; ceiling joists rest on the top plates, and rafters run from top plates to the ridgeboard at the peak.

Basic Carpeting Illustrated (Menlo Park, Calif.: Lane Publishing Co./Sunset Publishing Group, 1984), p. 56.

Board Foot Calculations

Structural framing members such as joists, studs, rafters, headers, sills, and plates are sold by the board foot. Douglas fir is the most common material used for framing lumber, although Southern pine or larch is also used in some locations. Estimating the materials needed involves determining the number of pieces, their nominal dimensions, and their length. The following formula

EXHIBIT 9-13

Light Wood Trusses

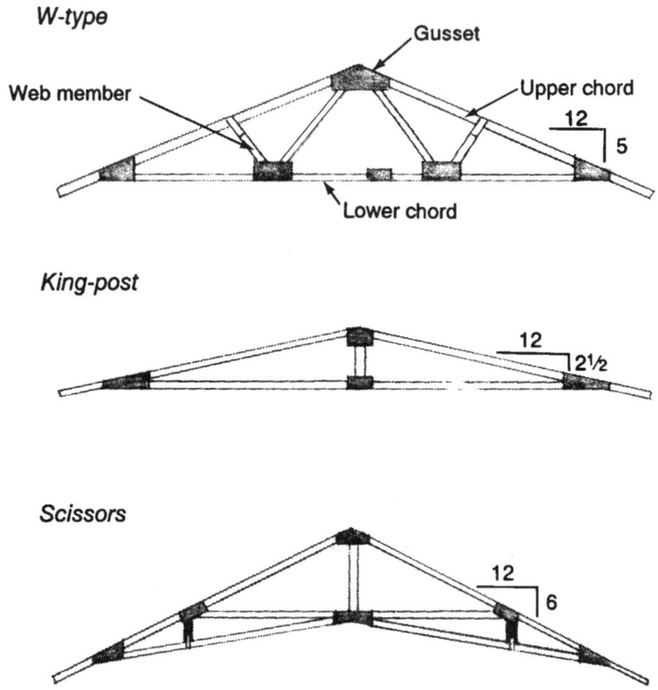

L. O. Anderson, revised by William Oberschulte, *Wood-Frame House Construction* (Carlsbad, Calif.: Craftsman Book Company, July 1992), p. 65.

is used to calculate the number of pieces (such as joists, rafters, or trusses) when counting the pieces is not possible:

$$\text{Number of pieces} = \frac{\text{Length of section (in feet)(measured perpendicular to framing pieces)} \times 12}{\text{On-center spacing (in inches)}} + 1.$$

For example, if a foundation measures 16′ × 24′, and the joists are spaced 16″ on center, the number of 16′ joists that are needed is calculated as follows:

$$\frac{24' \times 12}{16''} + 1 = 19 \text{ joists.}$$

The Board Foot Formula

The next step is to determine the number of board feet of joists. If 2″ × 10″s are used, the number of board feet would be found by using the formula presented in Chapter 8:

$$\text{Board feet} = \frac{\text{Number of pieces} \times \text{Length of each piece} \times \text{Nominal dimensions}}{12}.$$

$$\frac{19 \times 16' \times (2'' \times 10'')}{12} = 507 \text{ Board feet.}$$

Labor

Framing construction labor tables found in estimating reference books quote the number of man-hours necessary for a particular operation and the number of crew involved. In this example, 19 joists would be multipled by .020 man-hours to arrive at the number of hours needed to make the repair, or .38 hours. Exhibit 9-14 is a sample of a guide for estimating labor for frame construction.

EXHIBIT 9-14

Framing Lumber Time Estimates (in Hours)

Item Description		Installation Labor	No. of Crew
Studs	2′ × 4′ × 8 sq. ft.	.133	2
Joists	2′ × 8′, 800 sq. ft.	.020 manhours	2
Rafters	2′ × 12′, 896 sq. ft.	.018 manhours	2
Sheathing, floor	¾″ plywood	.013 manhours	2
Sheathing, roof	¼″ plywood	.015 manhours	2
Trusses	20′ to 24′ span	1.609 manhours	3

Adapted from *Sweets Repair & Remodel Cost Guide 2003* (New York: Marshall & Swift® McGraw Hill, 2003), p. 116–118).

Total Estimate

The cost of replacing the joists in this example can be calculated given the information that follows.

If 2″ × 10″s that are 16′ long cost $450 per 1,000 board feet, and the cost for labor is $1.57 per joist then:

Materials: $$507 \text{ board feet} \times \frac{\$450}{1{,}000 \text{ bd. ft.}} = \$228.15.$$

Labor: $$19 \text{ joists} \times .020 = .38 \text{ hours.}$$

$$19 \text{ joists} \times \$1.57 = \$29.83.$$

Total cost: $257.98

Profit and overhead should then be added.

INSULATION

Insulation is found in exterior walls, floors, and ceilings. It is designed to be a poor conductor of heat. It can also be used as a sound barrier, so it is used around family rooms and bathrooms.

Insulation is rated by its thermal resistance. This rating is called an R-value. The higher the value, the greater and the better the insulating properties. The insulation may have a moisture barrier on one side, or it may not, depending on its intended use. Insulation's type and size depend on where in the structure it will be used and what the climate is in that particular building location.

Insulation can be purchased in batts or blankets. Batts come in two widths, 15″ or 23″ wide, to fit between joists and studs. They are usually 48″ or 96″ long. Blankets can be 24 feet to 40 feet long. Both blankets and batts are used to insulate finished attic floors, attic rafters, the underside of floors, and open sidewalls. Foam insulation is used to insulate finished walls or places with limited access. Rigid board insulation is used to insulate exterior wall sheathing and basement masonry walls. There is also loose fill insulation, which can be blown in or poured in. Loose fill is usually used in finished attic floors and framed walls. See Exhibit 9-15.

Insulation can be made from many different materials. Fiberglass has been popular for many years and is now sold in an encapsulated form so that its fibers are prevented from becoming airborne.

Homes built before the 1960s usually contain mineral wool insulation. Mineral wool is made from natural stone or iron ore blast furnace slag. It is more water-resistant than fiberglass, provides better soundproofing, and can

EXHIBIT 9-15

Insulation

Insulation products come in several forms: blankets and batts are most popular; loose fill can be poured where access is limited; some rigid boards double as decorative ceiling panels.

Basic Carpentry Illustrated (Menlo Park, Calif.: Sunset Books, Lane Publishing Co., 1984), p. 53.

withstand higher temperatures. The disadvantage of mineral wool is that it uses density to boost its R-value; therefore, it is heavier than fiberglass and tends to be more expensive.

Rigid board insulation can be made from styrofoam or polystyrene. It is made in 4′ × 8′ sheets and is easy to install over interior walls or masonry surfaces. Rigid board is very susceptible to fire and can produce a toxic gas when burned.

Foam insulation is usually spray polyurethane. It can be obtained in aerosol cans that are good for sealing cracks around windows, doors, and fixtures. It is also blown in from trucks when large quantities are needed.

Insulation is susceptible to damage from fire, water, and smoke. Usually it cannot be dried or cleaned. Once it is damaged, it should be replaced.

Batt and blanket insulation are estimated using square footage of the area to be covered. It is pre-cut to fit inside wall studs and joists, so a carpenter can easily install it. Rigid board also uses square footage of the wall area and is easily installed by one person. A subcontractor usually handles foam and blown-in insulation. The material is estimated by the square foot of the area.[7]

DRYWALL

Common terms for **drywall** are "sheetrock," "wall board," "gypsum board," and "plaster board." It comes in 4-foot widths and 8- or 12-foot widths. Drywall is plaster material covered on both sides with a fiber paper bond. It has many advantages over plaster, a building material common in old structures but rarely used now. For example, the cost of drywall is relatively low compared to the cost of plaster. Drywall can also have a finished design face instead of its paper bonding. Its use is limited to interior walls and ceilings. Paint and wallpaper are the most common coverings for drywall. For kitchens and bathrooms, where moisture is present, a product called "green board" is often used. This product is similar to drywall, but it has one side coated with a green water-resistant material instead of fiberpaper board.

Drywall
A sheet of plaster material covered on both sides with a fiber paper bond; usually comes in 4-foot widths and 8- or 12-foot lengths.

Drywall Damage and Repair

Fire can consume drywall, and heat can scorch it, especially on ceilings and upper wall areas. In addition to direct fire and heat damage, vandalism or carelessness can puncture drywall. Opening a door forcibly can cause the doorknob to puncture or dent the wall surface. Small amounts of water generally do not affect drywall, but when drywall is exposed to water for a longer period, it tends to absorb the water like an ink blotter, resulting in brownish stains. If allowed to dry properly, it can be sealed and covered by paint or paper as long as the bonding of the exterior paper is not damaged.

Drywall is easily repairable. Even if punctured or pierced, drywall is repaired by spot patching another piece to the damaged area or by filling any area less than six inches with spackle or joint compound material.

> **Adjuster Tip**
>
> If water damage occurs, a portion of the drywall should be removed to permit the drying of the interior wall cavities. This would prevent mold and mildew from forming.

Drywall damage greater than six inches must be cut out. The drywall should be cut back with a utility knife to expose part of the vertical wall studs. Boards can be screwed to the vertical studs and the back of the existing drywall to provide a fastening surface for the new patch. After a patch of new drywall is screwed in place, it must be finished with drywall tape and joint compound.

Drywall Installation

Drywall can be nailed or screwed onto wall and ceiling studs, or screwed onto metal stud framing. Drywall can be installed with the long edges either parallel or perpendicular to the wall studs. The most common installation method is perpendicular. However, perpendicular installation is not used if the wall is higher than 8 feet because of the extra cutting and taping that would be involved. The ceilings should be done first so that the drywall that forms the walls butts under and supports the ceiling sheets. Nailing is recommended every six to eight inches vertically along the length of the stud on walls and every five to seven inches on ceiling sheets. The sides of the drywall are tapered to form a wide "V" shape where sheets butt together. This technique provides an area for joint compound and tape, which is used to smooth over and to create a continuous wall or ceiling surface.

Tape and joint compound are used for inside joints. On outside corners, that is, where two walls meet at a right angle, metal strips are nailed in place over the corner, then covered by joint compound. This technique protects the outside edges from damage. After carpenters install the drywall, finish subcontractors or drywall specialists commonly do the taping and apply joint compound. At least two and possibly three coats of joint compound are applied, with at least a day allowed for each previous coat to dry.

Estimating Drywall

Drywall can be estimated with a gross area method or a unit cost method. Chapter 8 discusses the unit cost method. The gross area method calculates the gross area of the room to estimate labor and materials needed.

Calculating Area

The gross area of the room can be used to estimate the amount of drywall needed. Only openings larger than fifty square feet should be excluded. Measuring in this way eliminates the need to apply a waste factor. Assume that a room measures 12′ × 12′. The wall height is 8′. It has a window (3′ × 4′) and a door (3′ × 7′) that are ignored because they are less than 50 sq. ft. in total area. This room has a gross wall area of 384 square feet [(12′ + 12′ + 12′ + 12′) × 8′].

Materials

The three basic thicknesses for drywall are ⅜″, ½″, and ⅝″. Prices vary by thickness. As mentioned, drywall comes in sheets 4-feet wide and 8- and 12-feet long. For this job, 4′ × 8′ sheets are used. To find the amount of drywall needed for this job, divide the total area of the room by the area of one sheet of drywall:

Ceiling	144	square feet
Walls	384	
Total area	528	square feet
Amount of drywall	528 ÷ 32 = 16.5, rounded to 17 sheets.	

The amount of nails or screws needed for installation depends on the on-center spacing. Assume that the studs are 16″ on center and that the nails will be placed 8″ apart. An average is 1,625 nails per 1,000 square feet. Nails are usually sold to contractors by the pound. Five pounds of 1½″ drywall nails installs 1,000 sq. ft. of drywall. For the purpose of this example, 5 pounds of 1½″ drywall nails cost $7.49.

Rather than price the materials for taping and applying joint compound individually, adjusters can use a unit cost per square foot of drywall in calculating the total materials cost:

17 sheets of drywall @ $8 per sheet	$136.00
Nails for 528 square feet	7.49
Tape and compound for 528 square feet @ $.07 per square foot	36.96
	$180.45

Labor

Labor is affected by the size of the job, by whether the drywall is installed horizontally or vertically, and by what will cover the drywall. Generally, the larger the job, the faster the rate of application. The common rate for installing drywall in a large area is 1.5 hours per 100 square feet; in a medium-size area (1 to 3 rooms), 2.5 hours per 100 square feet; and in a small area where accessibility is a problem, 3.5 hours per 100 square feet. Taping and applying joint compound require 1.2 hours per 100 square feet. If the drywall is to be painted or wallpapered, it must be taped, and joint compound must be applied. However, tape and compound are not required on walls that are to be paneled or otherwise covered by decorator wood materials.

Total Cost

The room in this example is a medium-sized area. The calculations for labor are shown below:

528 square feet × 2.5 hours per 100 square feet		
5.28 × 2.5 hours	13.2	hours
5.28 × 1.2 hours (tape and compound)	6.3	
Total labor time	19.5	hours
Labor: 19.5 hours @ $20 per hour	$390.00	
Materials	180.45	
Total estimated cost:	$570.45	

Unit Cost

Unit cost can be calculated by dividing the total cost by the area.

$$\frac{\$570.45}{507 \text{ square feet}} = \$1.12 \text{ per square foot}$$

The unit cost developed this way includes waste for openings. The example given did not state the size of any openings in the room, but it is assumed that there is at least a door. As an example, a 21 sq. ft. door would be subtracted from the area; otherwise, waste will be included in the cost twice.

WINDOWS

In the past, window building required the special skills of a master carpenter. Today, most windows are fully assembled at the factory and are shipped to the job site to be installed. They can be standard-size windows or custom-built windows. Although windows are factory-assembled, many manufacturers sell replacement parts, especially sashes that hold the glass.

Window Types

Proper estimating requires identifying the type of window. The most common styles are double hung, casement, sliding, fixed, and awning. Exhibit 9-16 depicts various window styles.

Double-hung windows are probably the most common. They consist of an upper sash and lower sash that slide up and down in separate grooves in the side jambs. Small wood members called muntins can divide the sashes into several different lights (pieces of window glass). The screens are located on the outside. The hardware for double-hung windows includes sash locks and sometimes sash lifts.

Replacement windows use the existing window jamb as the rough opening. The old pulley, chain, and sashes are removed and replaced with new mechanism, sashes, and glass.

EXHIBIT 9-16

Types of Windows

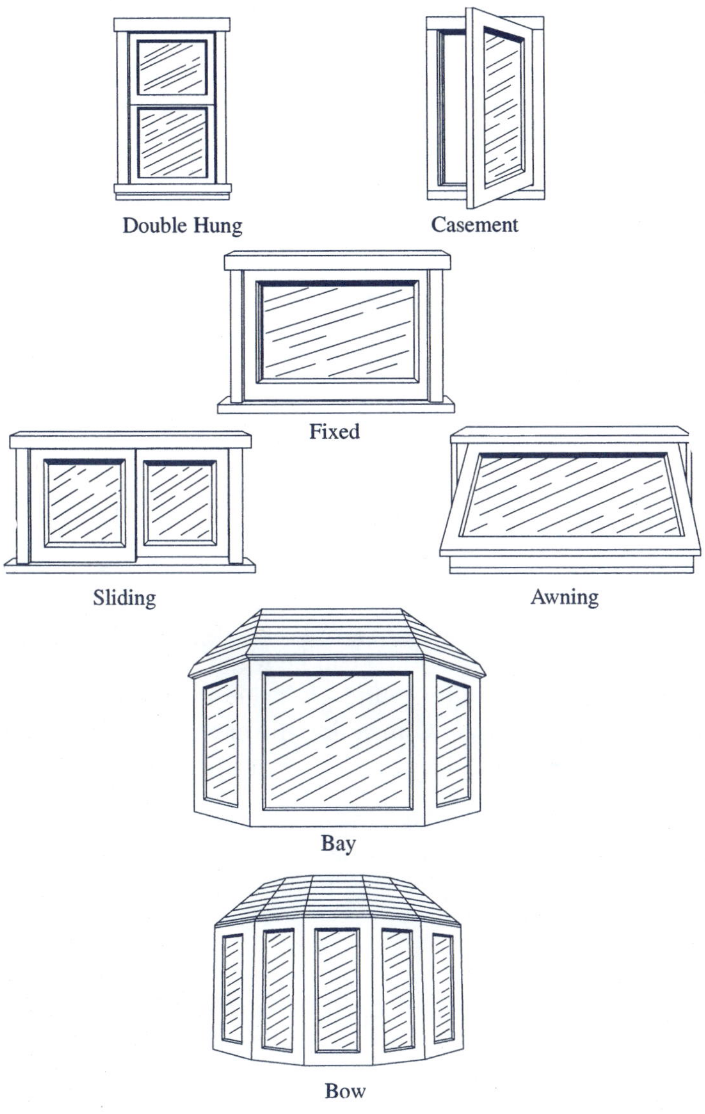

Home Repair and Remodel, 2002 Cost Guide (Los Angeles: Marshall and Swift Publications Co., 2002), p. 107.

Glazing Materials

At one time, a single pane of clear glass was sufficient for a window. But these windows were a source of serious heat loss. As the need for energy efficiency and ease of maintenance have become primary concerns, various types of glazing material have become popular.

Tempered glass is heat-treated to give it strength. It crumbles into small fragments when broken, rather than breaks up into sharp pieces.

Safety glass consists of two or more lights of glass with a layer of vinyl sandwiched in between. Pressure is applied to this glass "sandwich" to form a single unit. Safety glass can crack, but it does not break up into pieces.

Insulating glass is also made from two sheets of glass, but a space is maintained in between the panels. The air space helps decrease the amount of heat loss through the window as well as keeps condensation from forming. Some types of insulated glass have a gas such as argon fill the air space. Other types have the air from this space pumped out to create a vacuum.

Insulating glass is usually rated for its thermal conductivity. This is called the U-factor. For windows, a lower U-factor is better. The inverse of the U-factor is called the R-value. Good windows should have a high R-value.

Low E stands for low emittance. Low E glass allows short wavelength light to pass through it but reflects long-wavelength light back into a room. This means that natural light is allowed in while minimizing the damage to curtains, drapes, carpets, and furniture from ultraviolet light. Low E glass reflects heat back inside the home in the winter and reduces heat gain from the outside in the summer.

Estimating Windows

The key to estimating windows is to identify a window's type; size; and, if possible, the manufacturer. Windows can vary greatly in cost depending on the manufacturer and material, which can be wood, vinyl-clad wood, steel, or aluminum. The key to installing windows is taking proper measurements. The "rough" opening of a window (meaning the opening in the framing) is usually ½″ to ¼″ larger on all sides than the window unit itself.

After the material cost is established, the labor time for tear-out and replacement is generally standard. An estimating reference guide states the amount of time allowed for installation and demolition.

Doors

The two types of doors commonly found in residential construction are exterior and interior. The parts that make up a door are the jambs; the door; the doorstop; casings; and hardware, including hinges and locksets. The parts can be purchased separately, but many doors come as complete units. Most interior door units are pre-hung (assembled at the factory) and are easy to install. Exhibit 9-17 depicts a door's components.

Exterior doors are available in many types and styles. The panel type consists of stiles (solid vertical members), rails (solid cross members), and filler panels. Exterior flush doors are usually solid-core to provide more insulation and to prevent warping. Many new homes are built with decorative steel doors, which are foam-filled for even greater insulation. Most exterior doors also come complete and ready to install, except that they are not pre-drilled for the locksets.

EXHIBIT 9-17

Anatomy of a Door

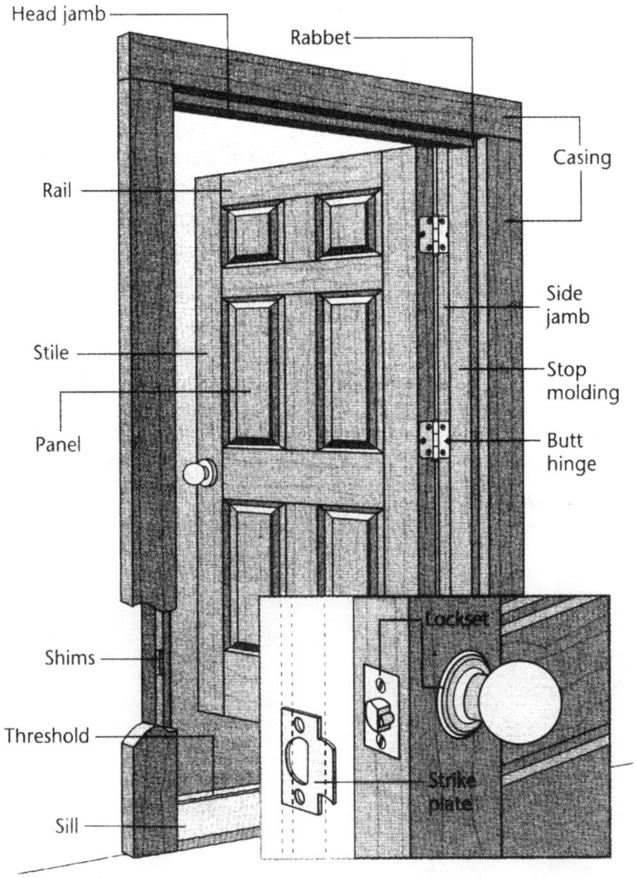

Basic Carpentry Illustrated (Menlo Park, Calif.: Sunset Books, Lane Publishing Co., 1995), p. 90.

Adjuster Tip

The local building code usually governs the type of exterior door used on a structure.

The two most common types of interior doors are flush and panel. Flush interior doors are usually made with a hollow-core framework of plywood, hardboard, or even cardboard. Flush interior doors are available in several different woods, including oak, birch, and mahogany. Closets often have wood or metal doors, which slide on tracks or are folding units.

Estimating Doors

Like windows, doors are available in various styles, so adjusters must be able to describe the manufacturer; the kind of material that the door is made of; and the door's size, style, thickness, and type of casings. The hardware varies depending on type, material, and manufacturer. Often, as in a burglary loss, only a part of the door unit must be replaced. At other times, the complete unit must be replaced. Estimating reference guides provide the average time needed to install and remove different kinds of doors.

Assume that a burglar, in an attempt to gain entry, damages a front door and frame beyond repair. The door is a pre-hung panel door. The door unit costs $640. The carpenter's labor rate is $20 per hour. The estimate for the job would be prepared as follows:

Demolition	1 hour × $20/hour (from estimating reference guide)	$ 20
Material cost	1 door unit, complete	640
Installation labor	3 hours × $20/hour (from estimating reference guide)	60
Reinstall lockset and deadbolt	.5 hour each × $20/hour	20
Total cost		$740

Profit and overhead should be added to this total.

ROOFING

One square
One hundred square feet of shingles.

The most common residential roofing material is asphalt composition three-tab shingle. Estimates for these types of shingles are calculated on the basis of units equal to **one square**, or 100 square feet. Each square has three bundles.

A bare roof consists of wooden boards, or decking, called sheathing, nailed onto roof rafters. Roofing felt paper is placed onto the roof sheathing and stapled, and shingles are then nailed over the roof felt paper. Shingles are usually installed with a five-inch exposure, and the remainder of the shingle is covered by the rows of shingles above it. In shingling a roof, a roofer starts at the bottom edge of the roof. The starter row is an "upside-down" row. Then the first row with the surface material showing is placed. This technique builds a slight incline that channels water into the gutter. It also prevents any leakage between the tabs of the first row of shingles. Subsequent rows of shingles are nailed in place, with each row overlapping about two-thirds of the previous row. Another double row is installed at the top (ridge), where shingles are cut and laid across the ridge joint to seal and join both sides of the roof surface at the top. Exhibit 9-18 shows how shingles are installed.

Wood shingles (which are sold four bundles to the square) are usually made from Western red cedar, but they can also be made of redwood and cypress. They are normally sixteen inches long, with a five-inch exposure. Thicker shingles may have a larger exposure. The roofing felt, which serves as a

EXHIBIT 9-18

Shingle Installation

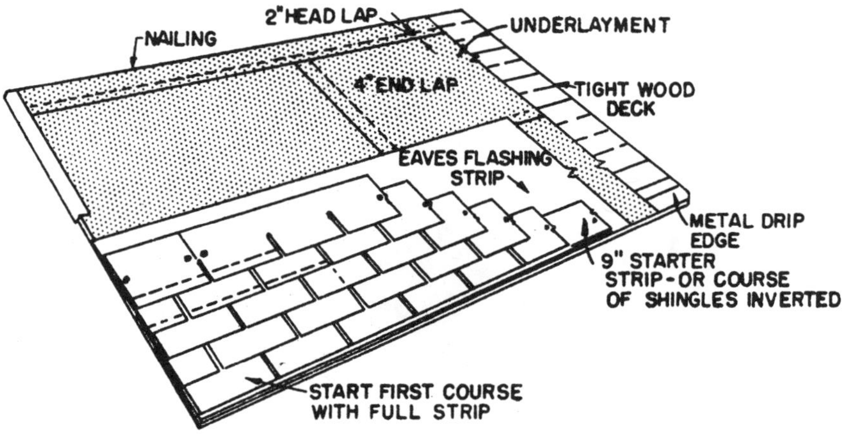

Adjuster Handbook (Denver: General Adjustment Bureau, Inc., 1972), p. 27.

moisture barrier, is not applied with wood shingles. Wood shingles must instead have ventilation from the underside to properly dry out and space on either side for expansion.

Slate and tiles are laid over thirty-pound felt and are never applied over existing roof materials.

Rolled roofing paper of ninety-pound weight covers 100 square feet of area and is usually double-covered in areas of heavy snow accumulation. It is the least expensive roof covering and is used on flatter surfaces where shingling is not adequate to protect the interior from moisture of melting snow or ice. See Exhibit 9-19.

Flashing is tin, aluminum, copper sheet, or rolled roofing material that covers any break on the roof surface. It is applied around chimneys and around plumbing vent pipes and can also be laid around the eave of the roof and where valleys are formed by intersecting roofs or dormers. Flashing is curled up along vertical surfaces and extends under the roof covering to seal any openings from moisture. Flashing on roofs extends up along the eave a distance of eighteen to twenty inches; when ice forms at the eave and then melts, the water does not run up under the shingle and damage the interior walls or ceilings.

Flashing
Tin, aluminum, or copper roofing material that covers any break on the roof surface.

Adjuster Tip

A common site for leaks is the flashing around vents, chimneys, valleys, and abutting walls.

EXHIBIT 9-19

Roofing Materials

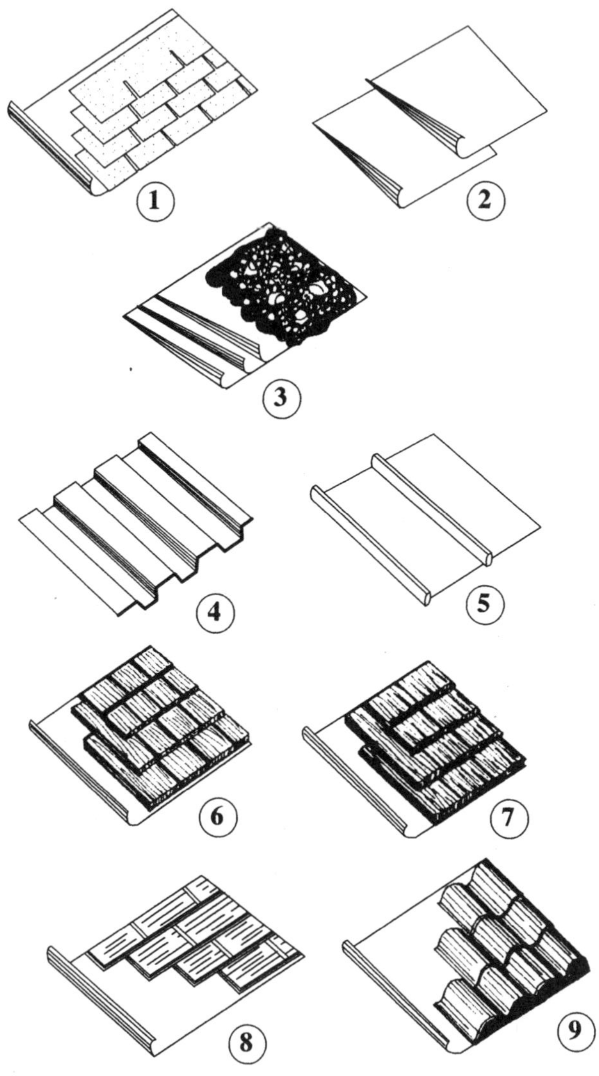

1. Asphalt Shingle (Low - $)
2. Roll (Low - $)
3. Built-up (Medium - $)
4. Preformed Metal (Low - $)
5. Standing Seam (Medium - $)
6. Wood Shingle (Medium - $)
7. Wood Shake (High - $)
8. Slate (High - $)
9. Spanish Tile (High - $)

Home Repair and Remodel, 2002 Cost Guide (Los Angeles: Marshall and Swift Publications Co., 2002), p. 410.

Built-up roofs are common on flat roof surfaces. Although much more common on commercial structures, they are also found on residences. In the installation of a built-up roof, the first step is to tack down a layer of red rosin sheeting over the roof board decking. This sheeting serves as a sealer or vapor barrier. A base covering of thirty-pound felt roofing paper is then applied and mopped with tar sealer. This process is repeated three times for a three-ply covering and five times for a five-ply roof. Crushed stone can then be put over the top layer. This type of roof is called a tar and gravel roof surface.

Roofing Damage and Repair

Strong winds (generally in excess of 40 miles per hour); hail; and falling objects such as tree limbs are the usual insured causes of loss to roofs. Steep pitched roofs are less likely to sustain wind damage from significant wind. Slate and tile roofs are unaffected by wind unless it is hurricane or tornado force.

Exposure to heat from the sun and normal wear and tear exact a heavy toll on common roof coverings. The average life of an asphalt composition shingle roof is fifteen to thirty years, depending on the roofing material's quality. Worn granular surfaces, curling of the shingle ends, and leaks into the interior are signs of age and damage that accumulates over time. Insurance does not cover wear and tear, but it might cover a new roofing job as part of an insurable loss to a home with replacement cost coverage. Because of their composition, asphalt roof shingles might sustain several slight incidents of damage that go unnoticed. The first indications of leakage usually signal the need for a new covering.

> **Adjuster Tip**
>
> South and west exposures deteriorate faster than north and east exposures. Also, steeper-sloped roofs last longer than flatter roofs.

A roof can sustain a great deal of damage from a hailstorm, depending on the roofing material and the size of the hail. Large hailstones can shatter Spanish tile and slate. Light gauge metal can be severely dented. Wood shingles can be dented or split. Even asphalt shingles can be dented by large hailstones.[8]

Inspection of Roofs

When inspecting damage to an asphalt roof, adjusters should, if possible, climb onto the roof. Wind might have broken the shingles, but unless the shingles are visibly torn, damage can be observed only by close inspection. Even if broken, the shingles will lie flat once the wind has subsided and will not appear to be damaged.

Roofs of slate, tile, fiber panels, or wood can be damaged if walked on. Adjusters can go up on a ladder to get a good vantage point for inspection and should take photos from the edge of the roof.

Most building codes allow only two layers of asphalt shingles on a roof. This amount is based on the roof structure's capacity to bear the cumulative weight of the material. Some adjusters believe that if the roof already has two layers, an allowance should be made to remove only the top damaged layer. The underlying layer, though, will almost certainly be damaged while the top layer is being removed, resulting in a need to replace parts of the underlying layer. The care needed to minimize underlying-layer damage can make the job take longer, increasing the labor cost. Whether both layers should be removed therefore becomes a matter of judgment.

Spot Repairs

Both asphalt composition shingles and built-up roofing can be repaired on a spot basis.

Individual shingles can be removed with a special tool. The nails of the next two layers are pulled up or cut off, exposing the entire shingle. The nails on the damaged shingle are then removed, and a new replacement shingle is inserted in place and nailed. The existing shingle or shingles above the new piece are renailed over that piece.

Shingles not only protect the interior, but they also contribute to the exterior appearance. Matching older shingles can be a problem. Reroofing an entire side might be necessary if damages appear so extensive as to warrant replacement of 50 to 60 percent of scattered, missing, and broken shingles. The labor involved in patching such a large area will exceed the cost of replacing one whole side. The best way to estimate individual spot-patch repairs is to use the labor and materials method. No unit price would accurately reflect such repairs. Built-up roofing is repairable by patching. Tar- and gravel-surfaced roof covering is usually affected little by hail or strong winds, but damage might occur nonetheless. The damaged area can be cut out, and the layers or plies can be removed down to the decking. Patches cut to the opening are put in with alternating tar, as when the roof was originally constructed. The top patch should overlap all sides by about two inches. It is nailed to the decking and then tarred over. Gravel stones can then be replaced on the patched area.

Roofing Estimates

The starting point for any roof estimate is determining the style of roof on the structure. Exhibit 9-20 shows some of the various styles. The roof's style directly affects the level of difficulty of the roofing job, thereby increasing labor. The style also affects the net area calculation. The more intricate the roof, the more calculations will have to be done. Estimating for roof damages is based on net area, to which a waste factor is applied. Measurements can be

EXHIBIT 9-20

Common Roof Styles

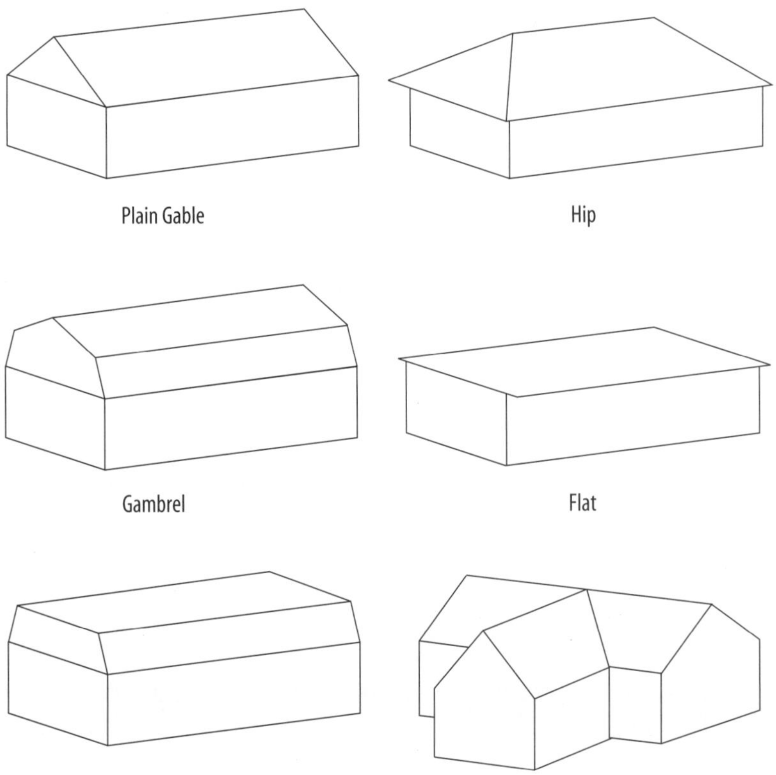

A variation of the plain gable is the intersection gable, which creates valleys at the intersections.

made directly by someone taking the measurements on the roof or by counting rows of exposed roof shingles. Measurements can also be made by mathematical computation. Measurements obtained directly should be accurate, but the roof must be sturdy enough for the adjuster to climb onto it. Counting rows of shingles is based on a standard exposure per row. For example, if each row is exposed five inches and thirty-six rows are showing, the distance from the eave of the roof to the ridge is 5 inches × 36 = 180 inches divided by 12 inches equals 15 feet. The same distance can be determined if the geometry and measurements of a gable end are known. The roof's pitch also affects roof estimates. A roof's pitch is the degree of its inclination. It is calculated as the relationship of the rise in height of the roof angle to the span. In Exhibit 9-21, the rise is 8 feet and the span is 26 feet. The pitch is 8/26. Expressed differently, it means that for every 13″ of span, the roof rises 4″. The lower the number that the pitch is, the flatter the roof angle.

EXHIBIT 9-21

Pitch

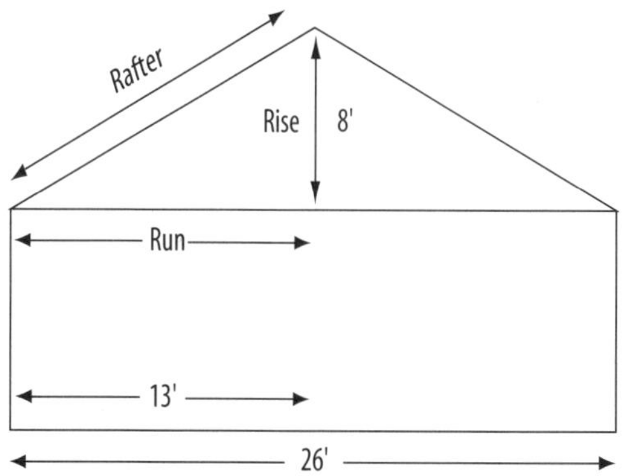

Roof Area

To calculate the area of a roof, the adjuster must know the rafter length. If the rafter cannot be measured, it is possible to calculate the length by using a formula, which the next section discusses.

Rafter Length

For this example, a gable roof is used. See Exhibit 9-22.

EXHIBIT 9-22

Rafter Length of a Gable Roof

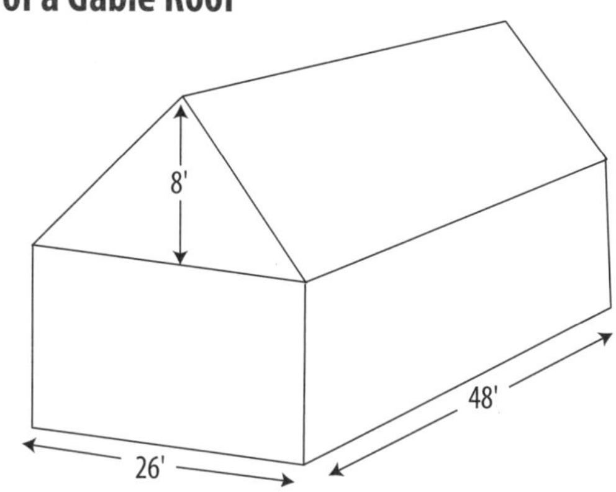

The rafter length for a gable end can be calculated by using the following formula:

$$\text{Rafter length} = \sqrt{(\text{Run})^2 + (\text{Rise})^2}.$$

This formula provides the length of the rafter in the example shown in Exhibit 9-22, as follows:

$$\begin{aligned}\text{Rafter length} &= \sqrt{13^2 + 8^2}\\ &= \sqrt{169 + 64}\\ &= \sqrt{233}\\ &= 15.26'.\end{aligned}$$

The roof in the illustration has no overhang. If it did, the overhang should be measured and added to 15.26′. The roof might also extend beyond the gable-end walls.

A calculated rafter length can be rounded to the next half foot. For the roof surface in Exhibit 9-22, a rafter length of 15′6″ can be used.

Total Area

The area of this roof, which has no overhang, would be as follows:

Rafter length of 15′6″	15.5 feet
Length of roof	48 feet
Area of one side	744 square feet (48′ × 15.5′)
Total area (both sides)	1,488 square feet (744 square feet × 2)

If the gable end overhangs, the extra length must be added to the overall length figure.

Material

In calculating the cost to remove damaged materials, adjusters should use the net area for removal labor. For calculating new felt and shingle materials, however, other factors might create a need for material beyond what the area alone indicates. For instance, in this case the eave edge is double-layered, and a cap layer is on the ridge to seal both sides of roofing. Waste would also result from fitting materials around roof openings, dormers, and valley areas. The most common way to account for waste is to use percentage allowances, such as those shown in Exhibit 9-23.

EXHIBIT 9-23

Approximate Percentage Allowances for Waste for Asphalt Shingles

Roof Shape	
Gable	10%
Hip	15
Hip with dormers	20

Walker's Building Estimator's Reference Book, 26th ed. (Lisle, Ill.: Frank R. Walker Company, 1999), p. 7.45.

For the example based on Exhibit 9-22 (total area of a roof), 10 percent waste would be appropriate:

1,488 square feet × 10% = 148.8, rounded to 149 sq. ft. for waste allowance.

1,488 + 149 = 1,637 square feet.

Shingles

Asphalt shingles are bought by the bundle, with three bundles per square. To determine the amount of material needed for the gable roof in Exhibit 9-22, divide the total area including waste by 100 square feet (because 1 square = 100 square feet), and then round up to the next ⅓ square:

$$\frac{1{,}637}{100} = 16.37 \text{ squares.}$$

Total shingles = 16⅔ squares = (16 × 3) + 2 = 50 bundles.

Felt

The underlying felt covers approximately 400 square feet per roll. It comes in a roll 3 feet wide and 144 feet long, or 432 square feet. The felt must overlap, so some waste is inevitable. An allowance for waste is already considered if a 432-square-foot roll is used to cover 400 square feet of roof area. If any more than one roll of felt is necessary, then another whole roll must be purchased. For the roof in this example, four rolls would be needed:

$$\frac{1{,}488 \text{ square feet}}{400 \text{ square feet per roll}} = 3.72, \text{ rounded to 4 rolls.}$$

Nails

A generally accepted allowance for roofing nails is two pounds per square.

Labor

The labor rate per hour reflects several considerations. Features that disrupt the surface such as dormers, several openings, and valleys with flashing slow productivity. Labor for roofing is also affected by the workers' experience, the roof's slope, the height of the area to be worked on, and workplace safety rules from the Occupational Safety and Health Administration (OSHA). If the roof is too steep to be easily worked on, roof scaffolding brackets can be fastened under the shingles, and boards can be put across triangular brackets to provide a level standing and working area. Access scaffolding might have to be erected for high areas. Materials might have to be hoisted to the roof area. An allowance for these additional labor expenses is appropriate.

Like materials, labor is based on a per-square measurement. As an example, the labor for the roof in Exhibit 9-22 would be the following:

Removal of 14.88 squares @ 1 hour per square	14.9 hours
Install 16.67 squares @ 2 hours per square	33.3
	48.2 hours
Labor @ $22 per hour	$1,060.40

The net area of the roof was used to determine the removal time because no waste removal is necessary. However, in the estimation of replacement time, a waste factor must be added because the roofer will handle all of the shingles, including the waste. Some estimators would not follow this practice but would estimate labor without consideration for waste. This approach would result in an estimate of 29.8 hours labor, which is 3.5 hours and $77 less.

Total Estimate

The total estimate for this job is shown below:

	Material	Labor
Removal is 14.9 hours @ $22 per hour	—	$ 327.80
Install 16.67 squares @ $35 per square	$583.45	
Labor is 33.3 hours @ $22 per hour		732.60
Nails for 16.67 squares × 2 pounds per square = 33.3 pounds @ $1 per pound	33.30	included
Felt paper for 1,488 square feet/400 square feet per roll = 3.72 = 4 rolls @ $15 each	60.00	included
Total materials and labor	$676.75	$1,060.40

Total cost (material + labor) = $1,737.15.

(Overhead and profit have not been included in this example.)

If the roof is cut up or if its height or access is a problem, the labor rate should be adjusted to allow more time per square. The labor to install individual shingles on several different areas of damaged roofing cuts productivity in half (four hours per square). Additional allowances for hauling debris, scaffolding, and a steep pitch might be necessary.

Unit Cost

The unit cost is determined by dividing the total cost of the job by the number of squares:

$$\frac{\$1{,}737.15}{14.88} = \$116.74.$$

The unit cost includes removal and felt paper because they were included in the estimate that resulted in the $1,737.15 figure.

Labor rates vary by area, and additional factors might cause a job to be more expensive than an average job, so adjusters should be wary about approaching every job on a unit cost basis. For an average residential roofing loss, a breakdown of labor and materials helps to resolve discrepancies between the adjuster's estimate and the contractor's estimate.

ELECTRICAL SYSTEMS

Although residential electrical systems might appear complicated, the methods used in wiring homes are generally straightforward and follow strict guidelines. The National Electrical Code establishes those methods, and most local codes and electrical contractors follow them.

Entrance of Electrical Service

The wires that transmit electricity from the power company to residences are either above or below ground. Most homes use a weatherhead, which receives the wires from the utility pole. Many newer homes have an underground cable running through a pipe called a "conduit." In both cases, the wiring passes through the electric meter before running into the service panel.

Service Panel

Circuit breaker, or **fuse box**
An electrical service panel that distributes electricity into several branches and acts as a safety device if an overload occurs.

After passing through the meter, the wires enter one of two types of service panels, a **circuit breaker** or a **fuse box**. The circuit-breaker panel and fuse box serve two purposes. First, they distribute electricity into several branch circuits. Second, they act as safety devices by breaking the circuit if an overload occurs, preventing the wiring from overheating and causing a fire.

These panels are rated by amperage. Adjusters need to identify the service panel rating when scoping the loss because it significantly affects the cost of the loss. The amperage of service is also often upgraded after a loss. The 60-amp fused service was standard before the invention and increased use of many modern electrical appliances. Today, new homes usually contain a 200-amp service using circuit breakers.

Branch Circuits

Branch circuits are made up of wires running from the service panel to the outlets, switches, and fixtures located throughout the house. They can generally supply different amounts of electricity, depending on their amperage, which varies by the wire's size.

With the exception of heavy-duty appliances, which should have their own circuits, most residential branch circuits serve eight to ten outlets each. The National Electrical Code recommends one 20-amp circuit for every 500 square feet of living area for lighting. Appliances such as air conditioners, electric ranges, electric water heaters, and electric dryers often have their own 220-volt circuit as opposed to the 110-volt circuits used for lighting and general usage.

Ground Fault Circuit Interrupters

Electrical shocks can be minor to fatal. The **ground fault circuit interrupter (GFCI)** was designed to protect people from fatal electrical shocks. The National Electrical Code requires GFCI outlets for bathrooms, kitchens, basements, garages, and outdoors. The GFCI monitors a current's flow through a circuit. When it senses a leak (ground fault), it shuts the power off to the circuit. If a person has become the ground for the leaking current, the person will still get a shock, but the GFCI will prevent that shock from being fatal.[9]

Ground fault circuit interrupter (GFCI)
A device that monitors the flow of current through a circuit; when it detects a leak (ground fault), it shuts the power off to the circuit.

Wiring Types and Methods

Wiring types and methods significantly affect the cost of materials and amount of labor required for repairs. Following are the most common types of wiring used in residential construction:

- Rigid conduit
- Thin-wall conduit
- Nonmetallic sheathed cable
- Armored cable

Wiring comes in two types: 2 wire and 3 wire. In a 2-wire strand, there is no ground wire. There is only a black wire that has current in it (referred to as the "hot" wire) and a white wire that is neutral. In a 3-wire strand, there is a green or bare copper wire in addition to the hot wire and the neutral wire. The green or copper wire is the ground wire.[10]

Rigid conduit is similar to water piping and is usually used outside or underground. It comes in ten-foot lengths and various inside diameters. The pipe is threaded for coupling and connecting to boxes. Conduit systems are installed before the wiring is threaded through them.

Thin-wall conduit is similar to rigid conduit in many ways. It is available in ten-foot lengths and the same inside diameters. However, because it can be easily cut and bent and because it has compression fittings rather than threaded ones, thin-wall conduit is far more popular than rigid conduit for residential electrical applications. Another name for thin-wall conduit is electrical metallic tubing (EMT). Thin-wall conduit can also be nonmetallic.

Nonmetallic sheathed cable is one of the most popular methods of electrical wiring. It is both less expensive than conduit and less time-consuming to install. Unlike the conduit systems, in which wires are run after the tubing has been installed, nonmetallic sheathed cable is made up of individual plastic-coated wires and a bare ground wire all wrapped in a flame-retardant, water-resistant plastic sheath. Connections must be made in metal or plastic junction boxes. Many local building codes prohibit the use of nonmetallic sheathed cable in some types of residential construction.

Armored cable is commonly called "BX cable." Armored cable is not used as often as it once was because of nonmetallic sheathed cable's popularity. Armored cable consists of two or more insulated wires encased in a spiral steel sheath. Like the other forms of wiring described, BX has special connectors and fittings.

Structured Wiring

Structured wiring, or infrastructure wiring
The wiring built into a building to accommodate audio, video, and data technology.

Most commercial buildings and many new homes are built with structured wiring to accommodate audio, video, and data technology. **Structured wiring** (also known as **infrastructure wiring)** consists of the wiring and components used for telephones, fax machines, computers, the Internet, audio equipment, security cameras, and video equipment such as cable or satellite TV. Commercial properties often use fiber-optic cables to transmit data. Some communities are installing fiber-optic cable so that residents can enjoy high-definition television.

Whatever type of wiring is used, structured wiring begins at a distribution box or panel, similar to the service panel found in most homes today. In addition to the electrical outlets are wall receptacles that contain jacks for telephones, fax machines, data lines, audio, and video. There may be control panels or keypads on walls to operate lighting, heating and air conditioning, and alarms. Repairs to structural wiring can be expensive because of the labor involved in "fishing" wire through enclosed walls.[11]

Damage

Residential electric systems can be damaged by various causes, but fire, lightning, and power surges are the most common. The extent of damage varies by the type of electrical wiring. Plastic sheathed cable can withstand less heat than can metal conduit. Building inspectors often require complete rewiring after a loss when it is not necessary. Adjusters should consider employing an electrical engineer or qualified contractor for an expert opinion, thus resolving disputes and satisfying the building inspector. Likewise, upgrades may be required by code. If this situation occurs, the adjuster must be aware of the potential coverage issue that it raises.

MECHANICAL SYSTEMS

Several building trades are more specialized than carpentry, including plumbing, heating, and cooling. The purpose of this section is not to teach the detailed methods of estimating claims involving mechanical systems, but rather to stress that adjusters should have a working knowledge of the vocabulary and elements of those systems and should be able to evaluate the estimates prepared by subcontractors specializing in those trades. Although estimates are not always easy to obtain, adjusters should insist that these estimates be broken down into specifications, labor, and materials so that an analysis is possible. The labor rates paid to these specialists are much higher than those for carpenters and other laborers. A rule of thumb for approaching costs in these trades is that rates can be expected to be one-and-a-half times the labor rate that carpenters charge.

Plumbing

The plumbing systems in residential construction use four distinct networks of pipes. The first two networks are made of the pipes that carry hot and cold water to faucets and appliances. The third network is the system of drainpipes that carry away wastewater through the main soil stack, and the fourth network is a vent stack that allows for the equalization of air pressure needed for the drain system to function properly. All plumbing systems work similarly, but materials can differ considerably among various systems.

Plumbing work consists of rough plumbing and finish plumbing. Rough plumbing involves placing pipes and drains within walls and under floors. Finish plumbing involves the installation and repair of fixtures.

Water Supply

Galvanized steel piping, rigid and flexible copper tubing, and polyvinyl chloride (PVC) piping are the most common materials in use. Galvanized steel piping comes in various inside diameters, but one-half inch and three-quarters of an inch are most common in houses. The ends are threaded, usually at the job site, so that the pipes can be joined to prevent leaks. Various elbows, tees, and angles are available to complete the system.

Copper tubing is the preferred and most common material used today. Joints are made through a process known as **sweating,** in which the point of connection between two pipes is heated and solder is applied and allowed to flow into the joint, thus sealing it. Because no threading is necessary, copper tubing is less time-consuming to install than is galvanized pipe. As with galvanized pipe, one-half inch and three-quarters of an inch are the most common sizes in residential plumbing.

Sweating a pipe
Sealing two pipes by heating and soldering the point of connection between them.

Although not allowed by many building codes, plastic piping is gaining popularity because it is less expensive and easier to install than either galvanized pipe or copper tubing. Plastic pipe is rigid and is joined by cement designed specifically for this purpose. It can be joined to existing galvanized or copper systems.

Drain/Waste/Vent Systems

In the past, cast iron was typically used for piping in these systems. The most common material used today is a plastic compound, acrilonitrile-butadiene-styrene (ABS). PVC might also be used in drain and waste systems.

Plumbing Fixtures

Hot tubs and whirlpools, in addition to great variety among the more common plumbing fixtures such as sinks, bathtubs, toilets, and faucets, have changed the task of estimating plumbing losses. Adjusters must identify the quality of plumbing fixtures involved in the loss because prices vary considerably depending on brand, material, finish, and installation.

Damage and Repair

The most common losses affecting plumbing are fire damage and water damage, primarily from leakage and freezing. Galvanized pipes can usually withstand considerable heat without being significantly damaged. Copper tubing can withstand less heat because the copper and especially the solder melt at lower temperatures. Plastic pipes also melt at relatively low temperatures. Smoke from a fire is usually acidic and can etch the finish on plumbing fixtures unless the fixtures are cleaned shortly after the fire. The porcelain finish on fixtures such as sinks and bathtubs is porous, and hot smoke can stain it permanently. Porcelain can be reapplied to bathtubs, but the cost of the procedure cannot usually be justified for sinks, which are far less expensive to replace.

Most residential insurance policies do not cover the cost to repair leaking pipes, although the resulting water damage is often covered, as is the cost to locate the leaks. Freezing damage, covered by most policies, is common in many climates. Both leakage and freezing losses can involve cutting into walls, floors, or ceilings to locate the damaged plumbing.

A qualified plumber should inspect most plumbing losses. A pressure test is usually performed on extensive losses to help pinpoint the damage. Appliances should also be inspected and tested to determine whether repair is feasible.

Heating and Cooling Systems

Each of the many available heating and cooling systems works according to similar principles. For example, with heating systems, each must transfer energy from a fuel source to either water or air; circulate the warm water or air throughout the house, allowing the heat to dissipate; and then return the water or air to the energy source to be reheated.

All heating systems have a thermostat that controls temperature. The thermostat sends an electric signal to the furnace, signaling the fuel valve to open up when the air temperature in the house falls to a certain point. Either an electric igniter similar to a spark plug or a pilot light ignites the fuel.

Adjusters must understand how the various types of heating systems work to analyze, evaluate, and negotiate losses involving these systems.

Warm-Air Heating

The most common systems for warm-air central heating are forced air and radiant systems. Each system uses a furnace fueled by oil, gas, or coal. Some systems allow wood to be used alone or in conjunction with other fuels.

Exhibit 9-24 illustrates a forced warm-air heating system. Forced warm-air systems have a blower at the cool-air entrance to the furnace to suck in the cool air while it blows out the warm air. The air flows through a system of warm-air ducts, and it exits through registers located in each room. Cool

EXHIBIT 9-24

Forced Warm-Air Heating System

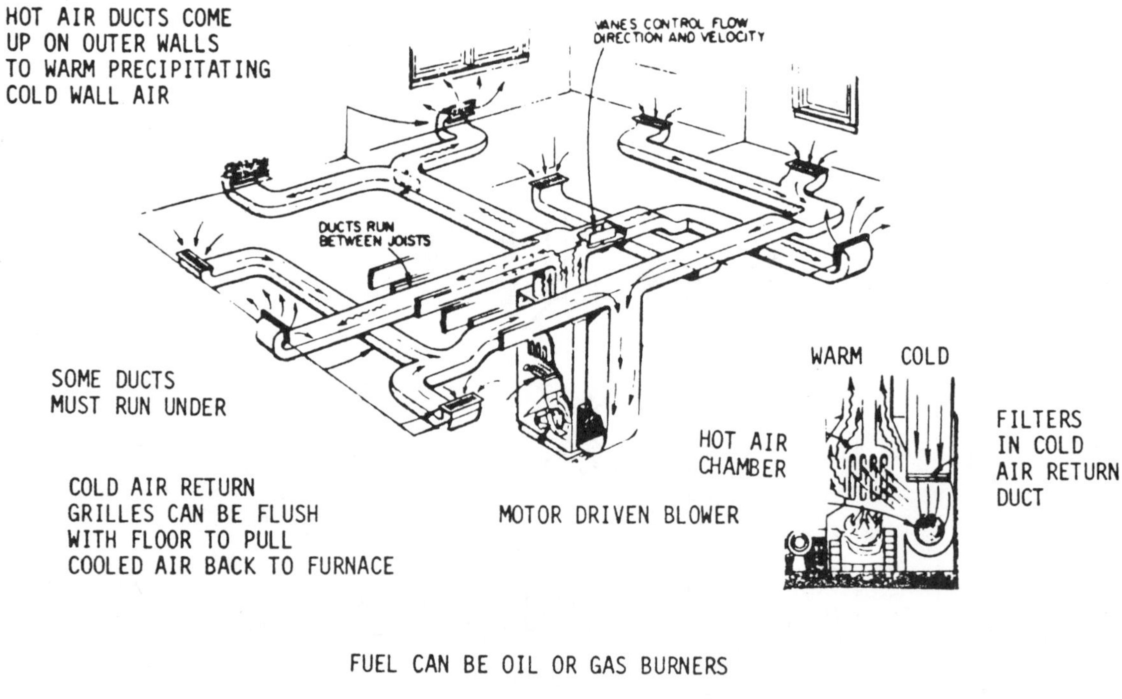

Used with permission of National Property & Casualty Claims Research Services (NPCCRS).

air is drawn through cold-air returns into ducts to be returned to the furnace. The cool air passes through a filter, which removes dust and other particles, and then flows through a heat exchanger that sits above the furnace's burners. Once heated, it enters the plenum, a chamber attached to the furnace where the duct runs begin.

Radiant heating systems have ducts or tubes, rather than registers, contained within the floors or ceilings. When heated by the ducts or tubes, these surfaces warm the air around them. The furnace and controls work like a forced warm-air system, although they are more difficult to access for repairs.

Steam and Hot-Water Heating Systems

Both steam and hot-water heating systems use a boiler rather than a furnace. Oil or gas usually fires the boiler. In a steam system, the water in the boiler is converted to steam and is circulated to radiators through pipes. The steam condenses in the radiators as it dissipates the heat and is then returned to the boiler either through the same pipes or in separate pipes connected to the opposite end of the radiators.

EXHIBIT 9-25

Hot-Water Heating System

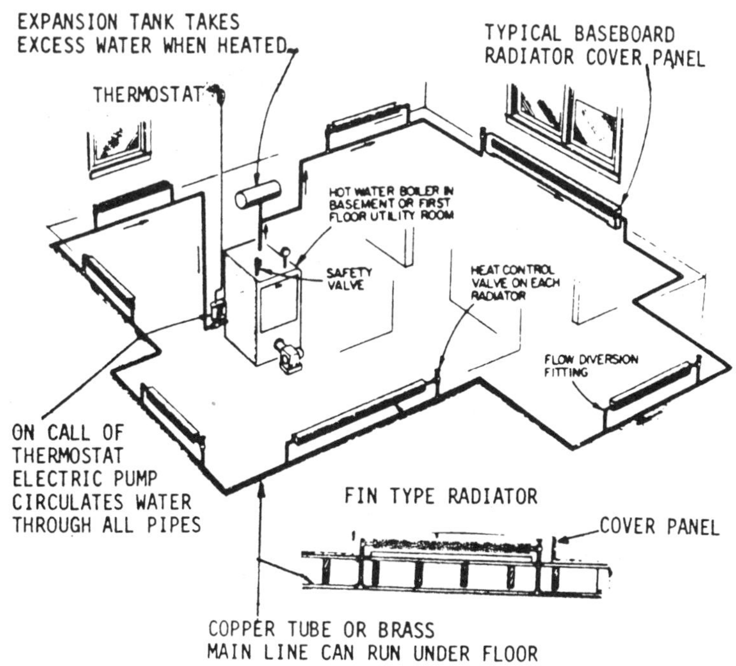

Used with permission of National Property & Casualty Claims Research Services (NPCCRS).

Exhibit 9-25 illustrates a hot-water heating system. Hot-water systems circulate heated water rather than steam; otherwise, they work in the same manner as do steam systems. Hot water can also be used with copper tubing in a radiant heating system.

Electric Heating

Electric heaters burn no fuel on site; require no vents; and are quiet, durable, and easy to maintain. The simplest and most common electric system is the baseboard heater, which is available in various sizes. It contains a series of fins, which are heated by electric coils. Warm air rises and gradually heats the air. One of the advantages of electric heat is that each baseboard heating unit can be controlled by a different thermostat, allowing each room to be heated to different temperatures and allowing individual units to be shut off.

Electric heaters can also be installed on walls or in ceilings. Some come with fans, which allow for greater air circulation. Electric heating units are generally installed by electrical contractors, rather than by contractors specializing in heating and air conditioning.

Air Conditioning

Residences are generally air-conditioned either by a central system or by room air conditioners installed in windows or in wall pockets. This section discusses only central air conditioning systems because losses involving room air conditioners are usually covered under the contents coverage section of a property policy. Exhibit 9-26 illustrates a central air conditioning system. A typical system includes a condensing unit located outside the house, evaporator coils placed within the furnace plenum, and refrigerant tubing connecting the two. For the purpose of circulating air, air conditioning systems are typically used in conjunction with a forced-air furnace, thereby using the furnace's blower and duct system.

EXHIBIT 9-26

Typical Central Air Conditioning System Installation

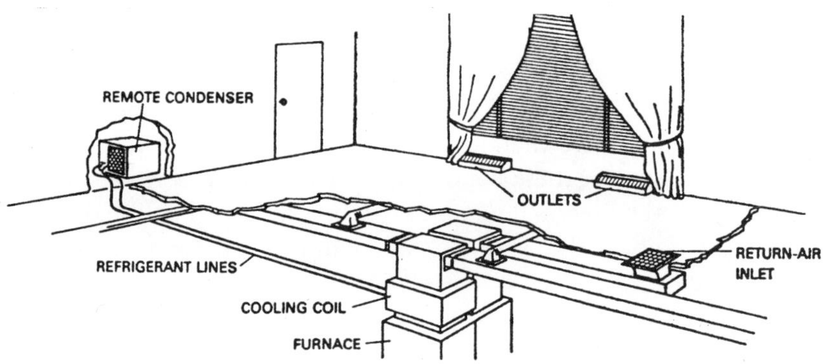

Used with permission of National Property & Casualty Claims Research Services (NPCCRS).

The furnace blower draws in warm air through the return ducts, filters it, and circulates it through the evaporator coils in the plenum to the supply ducts. Humidity removed in the cooling process runs down the coil and into a drain line running to a floor drain. A separate 240-volt circuit supplies the power that the compressor motor and fan in the condensing unit need. A thermostat controls the compressor and blower.

Miscellaneous Heating and Cooling Systems

Adjusters should be aware of several additional types of heating and cooling systems, including heat pumps and solar heating systems.

Heat pump
A unit that can act as an air conditioner and can reverse itself and draw heat from the outdoors to heat the inside of a house.

A **heat pump** is basically an air conditioner that not only draws heat from indoors and transfers it outdoors but also can reverse itself and draw heat from the outdoors to the interior of the house. Solar systems are used for a wide range of purposes, from preheating water for water heaters to heating swimming pools. In a typical solar system, water or another liquid is pumped through tubes to one or more solar collectors, where it is heated and returned to be circulated through copper coils. These copper coils might be located within a water heater or in a special solar tank. Because of the variety of solar collection systems, adjusters should consult with the original contractor or supplier when adjusting losses involving one of these systems.

Damage

Forced-air heating systems generally run for years with little trouble. Normal maintenance includes periodically changing the filters, lubricating the bearings, and cleaning. Fire is the most common cause of loss to these systems. When the smoke is heavy, the furnace often draws it in through the return ducts. Heat exchangers can crack when cold water is sprayed on them during firefighting activities.

Furnace puff-back
The sudden ignition of unconsumed fuel in the furnace, resulting in a heavy soot being spread throughout the building.

Furnace puff-back is caused by the sudden ignition of unconsumed fuel. As a result, heavy soot can be spread throughout the house, especially if the house contains an oil-fired furnace. A cracked heat exchanger can also cause soot deposits, but less gradually than a puff-back.

Steam and hot water systems are more likely to break down simply because they are more complicated than forced-air systems and have more parts. The most common claims for these heating systems are for freezing, which can crack radiators and boilers. These losses can be extensive because of the resulting water damage. Pressure tests are required to determine the extent of damage.

Claims for losses related to air conditioning are most often associated with the compressor, a hard-working unit subject to heavy wear. Lightning and power surge are the most typical causes of air conditioning failure. Adjusters should have experts check these units before committing to coverage.

KITCHEN CABINETS

In estimating the cost to repair or replace cabinets, adjusters should consider the cabinet type, quality, type of damage, and repair methods.

Cabinet Types

Kitchen cabinets can often account for a sizable portion of a claim. The key to estimating cabinets is identifying their quality. Cost usually depends on the quality of materials used for doors, drawer fronts, and hardware. There are three basic classifications of kitchen cabinets: (1) base, (2) wall, and (3) utility cabinets. Over the years, their sizes have become standardized.

Base cabinets rest on the floor and are covered with a countertop. They contain drawers and usually have shelves. They are generally twenty-four inches deep to allow for a twenty-five-inch countertop to overlap by one inch.

Wall cabinets are about half as deep as base cabinets and are attached to the wall above the countertop. They have shelves but no drawers.

Utility cabinets come in several sizes. One of the most common utility cabinets is the broom cabinet, which runs from the floor nearly to the ceiling.

Identifying Cabinet Quality

This section provides some guidelines for identifying the cabinets' quality by examining economy-quality, average-quality, and premium-quality cabinets.

Economy-quality cabinets often have a photographic wood grain veneered to particleboard or other composition material rather than consist of real wood for doors and drawer fronts. The doors are usually flush-mounted and lack a more appealing recessed edge. The shelves are usually particleboard or hardboard. The front frames are generally pine. Economy-quality cabinets sometimes have no back and are attached to the wall by a 1″ strip on the inside top and bottom. These cabinets only come in stock sizes. Drawer guides are usually plastic, and the drawers might not be removable.

Average-quality cabinets are the most common. The doors and drawer fronts are usually half-inch solid wood or raised panel. The front frames of cabinets are usually three-quarter-inch solid wood with a natural finish. The shelves and the rest of the cabinet are usually particleboard or plywood. The shelves are often fixed in place. Like economy-quality cabinets, these cabinets are available only in stock sizes. The drawer guides are metal with nylon rollers, and the drawers are usually removable.

Premium-quality cabinets are usually found in more expensive homes. They are often custom-made and can be ordered in special sizes. The doors are usually solid hardwood or raised panel. The front frames of cabinets are solid hardwood like birch, maple, or oak and are at least three-quarters of an inch thick. The shelves are usually plywood and adjustable on metal strips. Although very little particleboard is used in the construction of premium-quality cabinets, it is usually faced with some other material when it is used.

Damage and Repair

Fire, smoke, water, and vandalism are the most common perils causing cabinet damage. Kitchen grease fires might be the single most common cause of loss. Repair methods vary depending on the scope of damage, the cabinet's quality, and the insured's attitude. If all of an insured's cabinets are destroyed, the adjuster's job is simply to scope the damage to determine the replacement cost. However, if only one or two cabinets are involved in a loss, the adjuster would have several options, as in the following three examples.

First, if the cabinets are economy or average quality, the manufacturer might still make the same style, so exact replacements would be easy to obtain. Second, if the cabinets are custom-made, a cabinetmaker might be able to duplicate the cabinets, but stripping and refinishing all of the undamaged cabinets might be necessary to match the new ones. A third approach is to replace the damaged cabinets with new cabinets and only replace the doors and drawer fronts of the undamaged cabinets.

Because of the cabinetry's high cost, the repair options available to adjusters are numerous; the cost to replace more expensive items is usually much higher than the cost to repair them. Some imagination is often required to arrive at the best method for handling the loss. The final choice must be acceptable both to the insured and to the insurer.

Estimating Kitchen Cabinets

Cabinets are usually estimated on the basis of cost per linear foot. Because of the differences in cabinet quality, doors, drawer fronts, and hardware, adjusters should consult a lumberyard, supplier, or cabinetmaker to establish material costs. Generally, the cost quoted for base units differs from the cost quoted for wall units, and special cabinets might be individually priced. Cabinetmakers might quote the price installed. The adjuster should take a sample with permission from the insured, such as a drawer front, when seeking prices.

Regardless of cabinet quality, the labor to tear out and replace cabinets is usually standard. Most labor guides indicate 0.25 hours per linear foot for demolition and a range of between 0.25 and 0.5 hours per linear foot to install either base or wall cabinets.

Countertops

Base cabinets are generally covered with a countertop made from Formica, ceramic tile, stone, or a solid surface material such as Corian. Corian and Formica countertops can be assembled on site using flat stock; they also come preformed with rounded edges and a backsplash. They are usually laid over a three-quarter-inch-high density particleboard using contact cement. Ceramic tile is estimated and installed much like a tile floor. Stone such as granite or marble is cut and polished, then installed over the cabinets.

Countertops usually come in twenty-five-inch widths so that they overlap the base cabinets by one inch, giving a more finished appearance and protecting the cabinet surface from spills. They are usually priced on a cost-per-linear-foot basis. Granite, marble, and other stone surfaces have a higher labor rate than do other surfaces. There is extra cost because of the weight of the pieces. There are also costs for transporting, cutting, and finishing the stone countertops. Adjusters should inquire how these are handled if presented with a unit cost estimate from a contractor.

PAINTING

In adjusting losses involving damage to painted surfaces, adjusters determine how much area has been damaged and the cause of the damage (which often determines the type of necessary remedy). Then, an adjuster prepares an estimate for the painting by considering the preparation for painting, the type of surface to be painted, the materials necessary for the painting, and the labor. This section also discusses other considerations in adjusting painting losses: varnish, shellac, stains, and exterior painting.

Determining the Repair Method

Damage to painted surfaces can be repaired by cleaning, repainting, or sealing over and repainting. The degree of damage to interior finishes is closely related to their location relative to the cause of loss. Adjusters must be aware of this relationship when examining damages to interior painted surfaces. Water, heat, smoke, grease, soot, and fire can affect paint. In case of damage to interior paint surfaces, the cause of the damage, in many instances, determines the remedy.

Water Stains

Water stains to walls and ceilings are common. When water such as overspray from water hoses, fire extinguishers, or seepage of water from the outside damages painted surfaces, the result is generally a stain or multiple spots. Depending on the type of painted surface, the area might be cleaned with mild detergent. The adjuster should wipe the surface with a dampened cloth in an out-of-view area, a lower corner, or around a far window frame to determine whether the painted surface can be cleaned. With experience, adjusters will begin to recognize the relatively few times that such water stains or spots can be cleaned.

Water stains or spots on fiber material ceiling tiles such as acoustical tile have a brownish color. Most tiles discolored by water are not distorted or warped, but the stains cannot be removed. Covering the stained area with a sealer and painting the entire ceiling area can effectively hide the stains. A clear shellac or sealer additive in the paint prevents the stain from bleeding through the coat of paint. Unless such a sealer is used, the stain will continue to show no matter how many coats of paint are applied. As long as the tile itself is not bowed or warped, sealing and repainting the ceiling help to avoid extensive renovations.

Some areas are repeatedly affected by water seepage, such as from ice buildup along the eaves that forces water back into the interior or from rain driven under roof shingles by severe winds. In these cases, the tiles affected not only show several shades of brownish staining but also are probably bowed or warped. Replacement is the only appropriate solution for bowed or warped tiles.

Adjuster Tip

When confronted with what appears to be a repeated exposure to seepage or another water problem, adjusters should question the owner about previous occurrences. Insurance coverage excludes losses caused by repeated exposures.

Water Damage to Drywall

Unless continuously and repeatedly exposed to water or moisture, drywall ceilings and walls will dry and maintain their integrity. If the only damage is staining of the painted surface, sealing and painting the drywall can be effective. If an area of drywall must be replaced, the damaged area alone can be patch-repaired, smoothed, cleaned, and primer-sealed. The entire wall or ceiling area can then be painted to match the rest of the room.

Smoke Damage

In addition to damage by water, interior wall surfaces are subject to smoke damage. Smoke damage can occur from a fire, a furnace malfunction, or cooking grease fires. Smoke residue from sources other than grease fires or soot must be carefully examined and evaluated. Applying a light cleanser to an out-of-view area, such as over door trim, can determine whether the smoke residue can be removed. If the surface appears to clean readily, a cleaning allowance should be considered instead of repainting the surface. A professional cleaning service can provide an expert opinion when an interior cleaning appears possible. Generally, smoke from wood stoves and heating surfaces is cleanable. Because wood stoves and fireplaces are inherently dirty, their continued use deposits smoke on interior surfaces.

Soot

Greasy or oily soot deposits are generally not completely cleanable. Soot clings to drywall nailheads and settles in cracks and crevices and between ceiling tiles and paneling on the walls. Flat painted surfaces can be washed when rubbed briskly with detergents, but areas painted with semi-gloss paint and gloss paint are more resilient and might require industrial strength-detergent cleaning. Because over-wetted soot tends to smear and streak, the cleaning of soot is best left to professional cleaners. However, paneling, including marlite surfaces and ceramic tiles, can be cleaned easily.

Fire and Heat

Direct fire always severely damages painted surfaces, either by burning paint off or by blistering or scorching it. Damage from heat alone can also require repainting. Heat damage is most severe at the ceiling, on the upper walls, and especially around door and window openings. If the paint is bubbled or blistered, it must be completely removed, and the entire area must be thoroughly cleaned and then repainted.

Factors in Painting Estimates

The four important factors that adjusters must consider in preparing estimates for painting are (1) preparation before painting, (2) the type of surface to be painted, (3) materials, and (4) labor.

Preparation Before Painting

Examples of the types of preparation work and the estimated amount of work in square feet that can be done in an hour of labor are presented in Exhibit 9-27. Estimates of painting costs should show a separate breakdown for unusual amounts of preparation time, covering of walls, moving of furnishings, or cleaning.

Preparing Time Estimates

Paint should never be applied to any smoke- or soot-covered surface. The surface to be painted must be clean, dry, and smooth for best results. Nailheads should be spackled, and all drywall joints must be compounded and sanded. If new drywall has been applied, a sealer coat will be needed, followed by at least one and possibly two additional coats of paint. Cracked or peeling paint must be removed.

EXHIBIT 9-27

Painting Preparation Estimates

Approximate Number of Square Feet of Prepared Surfaces for Painting Completed Per Hour

Kinds of Work	Sq. Ft. Per Hour Per Coat
Sanding woodwork, preparatory	150–250
Sizing plastered walls	300–400

Paul I. Thomas, *How to Estimate Building Losses and Construction Costs*, 4th ed. (Englewood Cliffs, NJ.: Prentice-Hall, 1983), p. 327.

Type of Surface

Interior surfaces to be painted are usually plaster, drywall, wood trim, or ceiling tiles. Generally, surfaces not previously covered by paint absorb the first coat, and subsequent coats are needed to achieve a more finished and color-rich appearance. When estimating materials, adjusters must remember that completely new surfaces require more paint because of their tendency to absorb it. The additional cost created by the need for more materials is offset by the ease of applying those coats, thereby reducing the time and the cost of labor to apply the paint.

Masonry, or block walls, textured finishes, and metal ceilings are more difficult interior surfaces to paint. The rougher and more absorbent the surface is, the more labor and material are required. Some masonry materials contain water-soluble salts, which, if not washed down by muriatic acid or a similar product and rinsed thoroughly, can form white or powdery deposits on the surface. Masonry surfaces are best restored with epoxy paint. It forms a strong bond and is less susceptible to bubbling and peeling as a result of moisture penetration. Existing high-gloss surfaces of some masonry might have to be sanded lightly to ensure better adhesion.

Materials

Depending on the type of paint covering, the materials for any job might range in price from $10 to $30 a gallon. Sale prices of paint are not relevant in cost estimates because losses do not always coincide with sales. Interior paint is generally less expensive than exterior paint. Color and gloss are important factors. Although color is a matter of personal preference, gloss affects both appearance and wear. Adjusters can determine the average price range for paint in a locale and can usually use that price in their estimate.

Adjuster Tip

Adjuster should be aware that for large jobs, contractors buy paint in five-gallon buckets. An estimate for such work should reflect the contractor's price, not the retail price.

The most commonly used paints are latex, oil, and alkyd for interior and exterior finishes; rubber base and cement paints for masonry; and epoxy and urethane for those surfaces subjected to the toughest treatment and requiring the most protection from moisture, such as hardwood flooring.

One coat is generally enough to paint over a cleaned surface. If a sealer is used to cover a stain, one coat is also typically adequate. For heavily soot-damaged areas, two coats are usually needed despite the initial cleaning of the surface. This fact might justify reducing the cleaning allowance because the cleaning has not removed the need for two coats. If the soot is not as heavy, the cost of more extensive cleaning might be justified because either paint will not be needed at all or, more likely, only one coat will be needed because cleaning has effectively repaired the damage.

Primers are used for the first coat over new woodwork or new drywall. The new woodwork or drywall will absorb some of the primer, so each gallon of paint used on those surfaces will cover less square footage than normally.

Labor

Exhibit 9-28 presents the approximate number of square feet per hour for the application of paint or other materials to different surfaces. This exhibit is for

EXHIBIT 9-28

Painting Time Estimates

Approximate Number of Square Feet of Paint Application For Various Kinds of Work Completed Per Hour

Kinds of Work	Sq. Ft. Per Hour
Interior	
Painting primer on smooth walls	200–225
Painting, second coat	165–175
Painting wood floors, first coat	290–300
Exterior	
Painting primer on smooth walls	100–110
Painting smooth walls, second coat	115–125

Walker's Building Estimator's Reference Book, 26th ed. (Lisle, Ill.: Frank R. Walker Company, 1999), p. 9.176, 9.183.

illustrative purposes only. An estimating reference book would make the distinction between interior and exterior work, as well as the distinction between brushwork and the use of a roller or sprayer. There is also a difference in the labor rate for a primer coat and a finish coat. In the painting and decorating trades, labor represents approximately 70 percent of the total cost. One person can typically handle painting jobs, especially interior ones. In a given geographic area, wage rates are set by trade custom or by local economics. Wages per hour for a painter tend to be a few dollars less than for a roofer or general carpenter. In some areas of the country, union contracts might affect the number of workers hired for a job.

In most small residential losses, the time for preparation, set-up, cover-up, and other elements should be included in the estimate. Also included should be any unusual circumstances, such as extraordinary travel distance, very high or inaccessible areas, special types of surfaces, or material that would increase the time for the job. Working on ladders reduces mobility, thereby reducing the area painted per hour. If a room has no furnishings, a quicker pace is possible. Moving and covering furnishings and removing draperies and wall decorations all require extra time. A spray gun is faster than a brush or roller, but the time involved in properly covering and protecting areas not to be painted could offset the time saved by using such a device. Of course, the painter's experience also affects the rate of work.

Painting an area that is flat, smooth, and accessible requires less time than painting an area with windows, trim, cupboards, built-in shelving, and similar features. If the trim is a different color than the walls or needs to be covered with high-gloss paint as opposed to an alkyd or a latex paint, additional painting time is required. If an adjuster believes that a painting contractor's preliminary estimate figure is not justified, perhaps the adjuster has not fully considered the difficulties and limitations of the particular area involved.

Estimating Methods

This section explains three methods of measuring areas that need repainting. The first two, the gross area method and the net area method, are based on the labor and materials method that Chapter 8 describes. The third method, the unit cost method, is appropriate for larger jobs.

Gross Area Method

Exhibit 9-29 shows a room for which the gross area method can be used. The floor of the room in the exhibit is 28′ long × 15′ wide, and the ceiling is 10′ high. The door is 7′ high × 3′ feet wide. The room has three windows: two are 3′ high × 5′ wide, and the third is 3′ high × 6′ wide.

The gross area method does not deduct openings totaling less than 100 square feet from the room's total wall area. In effect, this method assumes that the door surface (21 square feet) and the three window areas (15 square feet, 15 square feet, and 18 square feet) are to be painted. This method therefore provides an allowance for the extra time needed to paint the trim around the windows and door, without requiring separate calculations.

The steps in calculating a painting estimate using the gross area of a room are as follows:

1. Calculate the surface area.
2. Deduct openings when the total area of all of the openings is 100 sq. ft. or more.
3. Estimate the materials.
4. Estimate the labor.
5. Total the estimate.

This section details each of those steps.

Step 1: Calculate the Surface Area

For the purposes of painting, the surface area in any room is the sum of the wall area and the ceiling area. The wall area equals the perimeter of the room, which is simply the sum of the lengths of the four walls multiplied by the room's height. In this case, the perimeter equals 86 linear feet (28 + 28 + 15 +15), so the wall area is 860 square feet (86 × 10).

The ceiling area equals the ceiling's length (28′) multiplied by the ceiling's width (15′), or 420 square feet. The total gross area is therefore the sum of 860 square feet and 420 square feet, or 1,280 square feet.

Adjusters must measure rooms precisely, and not simply pace them, guess, or even accept a homeowner's estimate. Even minor measurement errors can prove costly later. For example, an error of only two additional feet in this room's linear dimensions (30′ × 17′ room dimensions) would result in a wall area of 940 square feet and a ceiling area of 510 square feet, resulting in a gross

EXHIBIT 9-29

Example of Gross Area Method for Paint Estimates

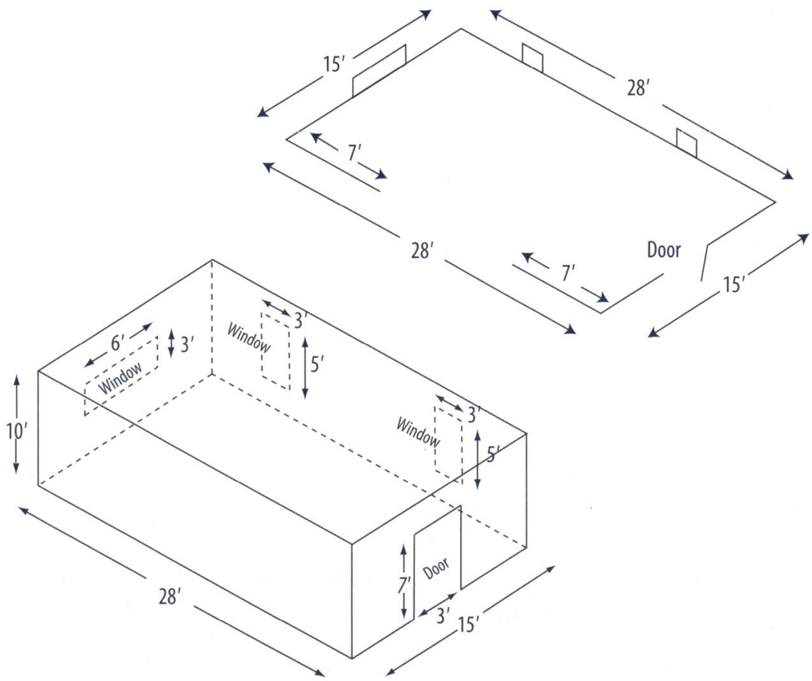

area of 1,450 square feet, which equals approximately 13 percent more area. If this miscalculation were multiplied by several rooms and multiple claim files, the potential for distortion would be enormous. Adjusters must also remember to deduct nonpainted surfaces (such as those that are paneled or papered) from the total gross area.

Step 2: Deduct Openings Totaling 100 Square Feet or More

In this example, there is no deduction for openings, because the total of the door and three windows is less than 100 square feet.

Step 3: Estimate the Materials

Labels on most paint cans estimate approximately 400 square feet of coverage per gallon. Paint is available in gallons or quarts. This text rounds up to the next gallon. Given that estimate, 3.2 gallons of paint (rounded to 4 gallons) are necessary to paint the room in this example (1,280 square feet divided by 400 square feet per gallon). If two coats are required, eight gallons of paint would be necessary (2 coats multiplied by 4 gallons per coat).

When several rooms will be painted the same color, a more accurate method for estimating the materials is to total the gross area of all of the rooms to be painted, divide by the number of square feet per gallon, then multiply by the number of coats before rounding up to the nearest gallon.

Step 4: Estimate the Labor

Exhibit 9-28 presents the approximate number of square feet of painting material that can be applied per hour to different surfaces. According to that schedule, 165 square feet of paint can be applied per hour to cover smooth walls with one coat of paint. Based on this rate, the labor for the sample room can be estimated at 7.75 hours (1,280 square feet gross area divided by 165 square feet per hour).

Included in the average rate is the time required for normal preparation such as dusting, sanding trim, and patching minor surface cracks. Not included, however, are any openings larger than 100 square feet and unusual items such as radiators and built-in bookshelves. Those items should be deducted from the gross area and considered as separate items. Also not included are preparatory tasks such as washing soot from walls and ceilings; removing furnishings such as draperies, light fixtures, and furniture; covering furnishings and wall-to-wall carpeting; and anything other than minor filling, sanding, and patching. Finally, ceilings and walls higher than nine feet might slow the rate of painting.

Step 5: Total the Estimate

The cost to apply one coat of paint to the room in the example is calculated as follows:

4 gallons of paint × \$18 per gallon	\$ 72
7.75 hours of labor × \$20 per hour	155
Remove/replace furnishings, cover floor, flooring, and fixtures as needed:	
1.2 hours × \$20 per hour	24
Gross area method total	\$251

For a small residential loss, the labor rate for the removal and replacement of furnishings will be the same as the painter's trade rate because the painter will be the only laborer on the job. For very large losses, those non-trade duties can be negotiated at a lower hourly rate.

Net Area Method

Most of the steps in the net area method of paint estimating are the same as the corresponding steps of the gross area method. The only difference between the two is that the net area method deducts the true size of all openings from the total actual area. The net area method uses the multiple system of measurement to calculate separately the size of all openings, and those areas are added to the adjusted area to estimate the materials. If a room has more than four windows and two doors, the net area method would probably be more appropriate than the gross area method.

Step 1: Calculate the Net Surface Area

The first step is to calculate the *net* wall and ceiling areas in the room. The room in this example is 28′ × 15′ × 10′. The gross area of the walls and ceiling is 1,280 square feet, but the room has four openings: a door and three windows. The door is 7′ × 3′, or 21 square feet. Two of the windows are 3′ × 5′, or 15 square feet apiece and 30 square feet combined. The third window is 3′ × 6′, or 18 square feet. Altogether, the openings represent 69 square feet of area. When that figure is subtracted from the 1,280 gross square feet of surface area, the result is 1,211 net square feet of area.

Step 2: Calculate the Openings

The multiple system of measurement adds a percentage or multiple of the actual size of a surface to the actual size to arrive at an effective size that reflects the time needed to paint such a surface. The adjustments to the actual openings can be considered a "difficulty factor." Exhibit 9-30 is an example of difficulty factors that affect the amount of labor needed for different jobs.

According to the multiple system of measurement, no opening should be calculated at less than 40 square feet. Therefore, the openings in the sample room would be calculated as follows (the numbers in the parentheses are the adjustments made based on the dimensions presented in Exhibit 9-29):

2 Windows	3′(+ 2′) × 5′(+ 2′) = 5′ × 7′ = 80 (40 minimum × 2)
1 Window	3′ (+ 2′) × 6′(+2′) = 5′ × 8′ = 40 square feet
Door	7′ (+ 1′) × 3′(+ 2′) = 8′ × 5′ = 40 square feet

Total effective area for calculating labor and time is 160 square feet.

Step 3: Estimate the Materials

The difficulty factors added through the multiple system of measurement only affect labor, so the actual square footage is used for determining materials.

The method for estimating the materials involves dividing the total number of square feet by the number of square feet that one gallon of paint can cover, rounding that number to the next half gallon, and multiplying that figure by the cost of a gallon of paint. In this example, one gallon of paint covers 400 square feet and costs $18, so the materials estimate is calculated as follows:

$$\frac{1{,}211\text{ square feet}}{400\text{ square feet}} = 3.03\text{ gallons, 4 when rounded to the next full gallon.}$$

Total materials = $72 (4 gallons × $18).

EXHIBIT 9-30

Painting Difficulty Factors

The factors are based on the time necessary to paint irregular surfaces compared to painting a simple wall or ceiling area. For example, the factor of 4 allowed for painting a picket fence indicates that four times as much time is necessary to paint a fence than is necessary to paint a wall area of the same dimensions.

All of these factors are for one coat of paint.

The actual measurements of the item should be shown in the Description column of the estimate. The Square Foot Equivalent should be shown in the quantity column of the estimate. For example, to paint a 50′ section of 3½′-high picket fence, $50 \times 3.5 \times 4 = 700$ square feet is necessary.

Item	Square Foot Equivalent
Cabinets with doors	L × H × 5
Bookcase, shelves, cupboards	L × H × 3
Drop or bevel siding less than 5″	L × W + 20%*
Drop or bevel siding 5″ or wider	L × W + 10%*
Eaves with open rafters	L × W × 3
Picket fence (both sides)	L × H × 4
Gratings/grille work	L × H × 4
Balustrade	L × H × 4
Stairs	No. of risers × W (in feet) × 8
Masonry or stucco	L × H + 30%
Windows	Add 2′ to both width and height of opening. Use 3′ × 6′ as minimum size window. Calculate all openings at a minimum of 40 sq. ft.

* Deduct for large openings greater than 100 SF (10′ × 10′)

Adapted from *Estimating Guide*, 14th ed. (Falls Church, Va.: Painting and Decorating Contractors of America), 1984, p. 15.

Adjuster Tip

A separate calculation must be done for each type of paint to be used in a room.

Step 4: Estimate the Labor

The hourly rate to paint smooth walls only with a coat of paint is 165 to 175 square feet per hour, according to Exhibit 9-28. The rate to paint windows, doors, and trim may only be 125 square feet per hour. Because the multiple system of measurement has already accounted for the difficulty of the trim, the rate for smooth walls can be used for the trim. Because the ceiling is higher than normal, the rate for smooth walls should be reduced to 150 square feet per hour. Based on these figures, the labor hours are estimated as follows:

Net area of walls: $\dfrac{\text{791 square feet}}{\text{165 square feet/hour}} = \text{4.79 hours.}$

Rate for windows, door (trim): $\dfrac{\text{69 square feet}}{\text{165 square feet/hour}} = \text{0.41 hours.}$

This comes from the multiple system of measurement calculation.

Ceiling: $\dfrac{\text{420 square feet}}{\text{150 square feet/hour}} = \text{2.8 hours.}$

Total labor: 8 hours × \$20/hour = \$160.

Step 5: Total the Estimate

The estimate for the whole job is the sum of the cost of the materials (\$72), the cost of the labor (8 hours at \$20 per hour = \$160), and the cost of removing and replacing the furnishings (1.2 hours at \$20 per hour = \$24). For this job, the estimate based on the net area method is \$256.

Unit Cost Method

The unit cost method is most appropriate when several areas of damage or large areas of damage must be repaired. Once the cost per square foot to paint one room has been determined, that unit cost can be applied to similar rooms. Only one additional step is needed to determine unit cost once the time and material figures have been calculated. That step is to divide the total cost by the total area:

Gross area method totals	\$266/1,280 square feet = \$0.20 per square foot.
Net area method totals	\$238/1,211 square feet = \$0.19 per square foot.

The unit cost method might not be accurate for smaller jobs (that is, those requiring fewer than three working days or twenty-four labor hours). Although less time is needed to complete smaller jobs, contractors have fixed overhead costs, so a five- or six-hour job might not be calculated at less than an eight-hour job.

Varnish, Shellac, and Stains

Clear finishes like varnish and shellac not only enhance wood's natural colorings, but they also provide needed protection. Stain enhances wood's grain by altering its color. The process of varnishing and refinishing solid wood surfaces is similar to painting, so the labor and material computations are identical to those used for painting.

Damage to Exterior Paint

Because exterior paint is exposed to weather, it can be damaged in ways that interior surfaces cannot be. Wind-driven rain, dust, and debris can chip or pit surface paint and can wear off its protective coating. Intense direct sunlight and heat and very cold temperatures and accumulations of ice and snow can peel and crack exterior paint and shorten its lifespan. Improper methods of construction, which prevent proper ventilation, can create a moisture build-up, causing wood siding to remain wet and paint to peel away from the surface. Problems such as these, caused by normal wear and tear, are not covered by insurance and are handled through regular maintenance.

The two basic adjusting considerations in handling damage to exterior paint are (1) distinguishing normal wear and tear and deterioration from insurable damages and (2) determining an allowance for appearance. Physical damage caused by fire or exposure to heat from fire at an adjoining property, hailstone damage, strong winds that propel objects into the exterior finish, and direct impact by vehicles are some of the causes of exterior paint damage that insurance might cover.

The complete exterior may be treated as one unit. Because paint can change color as it ages, new paint can rarely be perfectly matched to the old. Adjusters must carefully judge the situation after inspecting the property. Building interiors are segmented and are generally a variety of colors, but exteriors are usually one color and should present a consistent appearance. The adjuster must decide among painting only the damaged area, painting the entire side where the damage is present, or painting the entire building. Many states have claim practices regulations that dictate how this situation should be handled.

Factors in Exterior Paint Estimating

The main considerations in estimating exterior painting are the same as in interior painting: the initial preparation, the type of surface involved, and the amount and cost of materials and labor.

Preparation

Preparing exterior surfaces to be painted might include the removal and replacement of deteriorated wood siding. Adjusters should note areas that appear to be maintenance problems, take photographs to substantiate these findings, and communicate the problem to the insured and any contractor involved. No reputable contractor will paint a deteriorated exterior surface before replacing the rotted materials. Paint that is blistered, peeling, or cracked must be scraped, and the surface must be sanded and possibly filled with wood filler and then smoothed. Paint surfaces can be stripped to bare wood by heating the coating, but burning the paint might scorch the wood. Paint flakes off stucco or masonry for the same reasons that it peels from wood surfaces, but, in addition, masonry contains alkalis that affect the paint's ability to adhere to the surface. The damaged surface might have to be sandblasted or cleared by chemical strippers.

Staining can be a problem on exterior surfaces. Rust and stains must be covered or removed so that paint will properly adhere to the surface.

Type of Surface

For metal surfaces, paint adheres best to the bare metal. Painting over a previously painted metal surface is acceptable if the original coating is still firmly bonded. Both aluminum and steel should be prime-coated before a final coat of paint is applied. Masonite siding and clapboard sidings are the smoothest surfaces for paint coverage. Aluminum and masonry need more preparation and expertise in treatment. As with interior painting, the smoother the surface is, the better the result and the higher the productivity will be.

Materials

Materials for outside painting include alkyds, latex, epoxy, and oil. Because of weather exposures and the generally rougher surfaces to which exterior paints are applied, these paints contain additives that promote flexibility. Latex paint is the most versatile: it cleans in water, is the fastest drying, and allows water vapor to escape, reducing the chances of blistering. Latex might not, however, adhere over other types of paint. Although latex can be applied to masonry, an alkyd base or a rubber base coating is recommended for that type of surface. Oil-or alkyd-base metal paints are recommended for a direct application to metal siding.

Basic protection against moisture and expansion and flexibility characteristics needed for exterior finish materials are constantly being improved. An adjuster's knowledge of the proper use of these materials helps in assessing the reasons for preexisting conditions and enables the adjuster to make reasonable judgments regarding the distinction between direct physical damage and normal wear and tear.

Labor

The largest single factor to be considered in exterior paint estimating is the labor cost. Because of weather's effects and the special preparation for exterior surfaces, proper labor estimating requires that the surface be inspected. In estimating labor costs, an adjuster should list each distinct operation separately. Normal unit prices per square foot do not usually include preparation or scaffolding. Operations vary so much by job that a single unit cost is unlikely to apply to any particular job.

WALLPAPERING

Water, smoke, fire, or heat can damage wallpaper. Other types of losses to wallpaper are caused by vandalism, carelessness in moving furniture, or any striking or puncturing of the surface. Although these causes of loss affect wallpaper in different ways, the decision to repair a damaged section or to repaper a room is typically based on whether the existing paper can be matched. This section discusses the typical types of damage and repair options.

Water damage is the most common form of wallpaper damage. Water leakage from a shower, tub, or defective toilet seal in an upstairs bathroom can dilute the paste and cause the paper to loosen from the wall. In some cases, once the paper is dry, it can be carefully repasted with a small brush and laid back onto the wall. If the paper becomes stained or brittle, the only alternative is to replace the stained area. One advantage of papering is that it can often be repaired by applying a matching piece over the damaged area. The success of this approach depends on the paperhanger's experience, the type of paper and adhesive used, and the pattern design.

When confronted with stained wallpaper, an adjuster should ask the homeowner whether matching paper is available. Because people generally buy more paper than they need, if the paper was installed within the past several years, a roll might be stored in the attic or basement.

If there is no extra paper, a match might not be possible because wallpaper, although manufactured in long rolls, is often made in different dye lots. For this reason, even if a pattern is available that matches the damaged pattern, the colors might be different. If a match cannot be made, the paper must be completely replaced. Therefore, although some wallpaper losses are small, others are very large.

Wallpaper does not need to be *on* fire to be damaged *by* fire. A nearby fire can generate enough heat to scorch wallpaper. Smoke can be washed from some vinyl or fabric wallpaper. Untreated common vinyl-coated or cloth-backed papers can be washed. Professionals should handle these tasks, though, because pattern inks might run or the paper can tear if handled too roughly. Professional cleaning is also required for oily soot damage. If not properly treated, soot will streak wallpaper, as it does a painted surface. Foil, flocked, and felt coverings are not cleanable, so if they are damaged by soot, they must be replaced.

Factors Affecting the Costs of Wallpaper Losses

The main factors to consider in estimating wallpapering losses are (1) preparation, (2) the size and shape of the surface to be covered, (3) the quality of material to be replaced, and (4) labor.

Preparation

Like paint, wallpaper requires a smooth surface. The best surface on which to apply paper is a bare wall. Undercoats of paper, especially if the seams are overlapped rather than butted, result in a poor appearance. If the damaged layer is to be covered, any loose material must be removed before the new covering is applied. More than three layers of paper are not recommended because the weight of the newest layer and the moisture of its adhesive might loosen the layers beneath it. Additional time must be allowed to wet down, heat, or steam-remove underlayers; to patch the bare surface; and, in some instances, to properly size the bare wall area for adhesion. Sizing, the application of a thin coat of paste onto a bare surface, enables the paste or glue on the back of the wallpaper to adhere more securely.

Surface Features

As with painting, wallpapering can be accomplished most quickly over a flat, smooth, continuous surface. Door openings, built-in shelving, windows, and other features slow the process of application, especially for patterned wallpaper, for which the lengths of paper must be carefully aligned. That alignment might involve as much as 15 to 20 percent waste, even in average-sized rooms. Areas above and below large windows, where the pattern must be aligned both vertically and horizontally, create additional waste and delay.

Materials

Wallcovering materials include such items as cork, carpet-like deep-pile material, fabric-backed vinyl, felt, and grass cloth. Handprinted wallpaper, leather, and wood veneer laminates are also used. However, the most common covering is machine-printed paper, either plastic-surfaced or vinyl with paper backing. The variation in materials creates wide variations in costs. Consequently, adjusters must carefully identify the type of wallpaper to make an appropriate estimate. When possible, adjusters should take a sample from the damaged area and secure an opinion from a knowledgeable local supplier as to material cost.

Following are three common types of wallpaper:

1. *Vinyl.* Vinyl wallcovering is basically an elastic film on a backing of paper or fabric. Vinyl paper does not breathe, as most other wallcoverings do, so the proper anti-moisture adhesive must be used to prevent mildew. Because fabric-backed vinyls are washable and durable, they are commonly used in the kitchens, bathrooms, and hall areas. The thickness and weight of the vinyl wall covering determine its ability to withstand grease, smoke, and dirt from contact with people's hands. Categories of vinyl range from decorative to industrial.
2. *Fabric-backed foil.* Fabric-backed foils are installed in much the same way as vinyls, but more care is necessary to keep excess paste off the surface. If dried paste adheres to the foil facing, it can scratch it. Some foils have a plastic-coated covering that makes them more washable. Foils are difficult to work with, and their sheer surface magnifies any defects in the underlying wall surface. For this reason, lining paper is often used as a primer surface to reduce wall imperfections. Foil paper must be carefully applied so that the foil cover is not creased.
3. *Flocked coverings.* Flocked wallcovering has part or all of the design made from short textile ends that are bonded to the wallcovering material. The textile material stands on end.

Coverage

Standard double roll
Seventy-two square feet of wallpaper.

Wallcoverings are generally sold in a **standard double roll**, which measures 72 square feet, or in single rolls of 36 square feet. Similarly, a standard English bolt of wallpaper consists of 2 rolls and measures 72 square feet. A European bolt measures 57 square feet. Wallpaper designs include no pattern at all, random match patterns (which create an overall design effect, but which might not be the same design from roll to roll), straight-across matches, and drop matches. Drop is the length of movement needed to match a pattern. It is measured in inches. It literally means that the adjacent piece of wallpaper must be moved up or down by a certain number of inches to match the pattern. Determining the amount of coverage that a roll of wallpaper provides varies by manufacturer, by pattern, and by material. The only accurate way to estimate the area to be covered is to use the information given on the rolls themselves.

Waste

When estimating materials, adjusters can allow for the waste involved in a matching design by considering the area of coverage of a single roll to be 30 square feet and for a double roll to be 60 square feet. Use 46 square feet for a European bolt. This calculation is illustrated in the discussion of estimating below.

Labor

The paperhanger's experience is the most important factor in estimating labor costs. Paperhangers can generally work alone. Their rate is typically about the same as the rate for painters. When checking estimates, adjusters should determine the trade cost averages for the particular area. An allowance should be made for difficult materials or work circumstances. The more intricate the pattern is, the more expertise is required for applying the wallcovering.

As mentioned, wallcoverings should be applied to dry, flat, and clean surfaces. Removing existing paper that is plastic-coated, foil type, or not strippable requires that it be hand-sanded, then wetted and scraped off. Additional labor is needed if there are multiple layers of wallpaper. Spackling cracks and gouges create porous surfaces that must be primed or sealed. Drywall is very porous and does not allow the proper application of wallpaper, so new drywall surfaces must be primed. Additionally, the drywall would be damaged if the covering were ever stripped off. Sizing the surface to be covered creates a uniform and smooth surface to ensure good adhesion.

Estimating Wallpaper

Wallpaper estimates can be based on the net area method or unit cost method.

Net Area Method

Assume that a room to be papered is 18′ × 20′, has one door (3′ × 7′), one window (4′ × 5′), and a ceiling height of 8′. The wallpaper to be used is random match or small repeated pattern, so the anticipated average waste is between 15 and 20 percent.

Paper

If the amount of necessary materials is not estimated accurately, reordering at a later date might mean that the wallcovering is a different color or that the style is no longer available. Wallpaper comes in different widths, but each double roll always covers 72 square feet, and each single roll always covers 36 square feet. The most common width is 18 inches.

To determine the amount of materials necessary, the adjuster should measure the room's perimeter and multiply it by the height to determine the room's total wall area. This calculation includes two areas that will not be covered, a door and a window. Just as in the net area method for estimating paint jobs, the openings should be deducted to arrive at the net area to be covered. Those calculations are as follows:

Perimeter (20′ + 20′ + 18′ + 18′)	76	feet
Wall height	× 8	feet
Total wall area	608	square feet
Window (4′ × 5′)	20	square feet
Door (3′ × 7′)	+21	square feet
Total openings area	41	square feet
Total wall area less openings area	608	square feet
	− 41	square feet
Net wall area	567	square feet

Assume that a single roll, allowing for 15 to 20 percent waste, covers thirty square feet. This project requires 19 single rolls (567 ÷ 30 = 18.9, rounded to 19). If the wallpaper pattern is larger or less regular, more waste should be allowed, resulting in a need for additional material. However, a good average net area per single roll is 30 square feet; a good average for a double roll is 60 square feet.

Paste

To calculate the amount of paste needed, assume that 1 pound of paste is enough to apply 10 single rolls. Therefore, 2 pounds would be needed for 19 single rolls (19 ÷ 10 = 1.9, rounded up to 2). The sizing material is a gelatin sealer, which is already added to the paste compound and does not need to be calculated separately.

Labor

The labor is based on the number of rolls of wallpaper to be applied. Exhibit 9-31 shows average rates of application per hour. The rate to overlap paper is faster than when the edges are butted. Working with high-grade paper or wall coverings reduces the number of single rolls that can be applied per hour.

The room in this example requires 19 rolls for the walls. The average labor factor is 3 single rolls per hour for butt joint, average grade material. Dividing 3 into 19 rolls shows that 6.33 hours of labor are required to hang 19 single rolls.

If the previous layer and several other layers must be removed, the labor hours estimate will change. As Exhibit 9-31 shows, the rate to remove several layers of paper is 100 square feet per hour.

EXHIBIT 9-31

Wallpapering Time Estimates

Approximate Rate per Hour for Various Kinds of Paperhanging Work

Kind of Work	Quantity Per Hour
Remove wallpaper—single layer	150 sq. ft.
Remove wallpaper—several layers	100 sq. ft.
Hang wallpaper—butt joint—average grade	3 single rolls
Hang wallpaper—first grade	2 single rolls
Hanging borders	100 linear feet

Adapted from Paul I. Thomas, *How to Estimate Building Losses and Construction Costs*, 4th ed. (Englewood Cliffs, N.J.: Prentice-Hall, 1983), pp. 337–339, and *Walker's Building Estimator's Reference Book,* 26th ed. (Lisle, Ill.: Frank R. Walker Company, 1999), p. 9.210.

In the example, this rate adds 5.67 hours to the labor estimate. Total labor is then calculated as follows:

Removing paper	$\frac{567 \text{ sq. ft}}{100 \text{ sq. ft./hr.}} =$	5.67 hours.
Applying paper	$\frac{19 \text{ rolls}}{3 \text{ rolls per hour}} =$	6.33 hours.
Labor total		12 hours

These figures do not assume extensive preparation of the bare walls or sizing.

Total Cost

The following breakdown shows the total estimated cost to remove the old paper and to hang new paper on walls only (no ceiling) at the price of $10 per single roll with butted edges, no extreme pattern matching, and two openings:

Net area of walls: 567 square feet	
19 rolls @ $10 per single roll	$190
2 pounds paste @ $1 per pound	2
Labor to strip old and hang new paper	
12 hours @ $20 per hour	240
Total cost	$432

As with paint estimating, the labor factor should include access time and any above-normal preparation of the surface. These extra items can be listed separately on an estimate sheet. Each additional allowance should be explained.

Unit Cost Method

Because of the wide variation in the cost of materials, estimating a single unit cost for some jobs is difficult, but applying a unit cost to separate rooms in the same house is possible. As shown in Exhibit 9-31, even the labor hours differ with the grade of wallcovering being applied. The unit cost for the room in the example would be the total estimated cost for the job divided by the total net square feet, as calculated below:

$$\text{Unit cost} = \frac{\$432}{567\text{ sq. ft.}} = \$0.76\text{ per square foot.}$$

Any unusual preparation or accessibility problems should be figured separately and added to the unit cost estimate.

FINISH CARPENTRY

Finish carpentry is the work done by a carpenter to complete, or "finish off," a house's interior after the frame has been erected. It includes the installation of floors, windows, doors, cabinets, countertops, interior wood trim, stairs, and exterior wood trim.

Finish Wood Floors

The term "finish flooring" refers to the material used as a floor's top layer (subfloor for carpeting or tile) or final wearing surface. A wide selection of wood materials can be used for finished flooring. Hardwoods, softwoods, and laminated wood are available as strip flooring in various widths and thicknesses and as random-width planks and block flooring. Because each kind comes in different grades, adjusters should be certain of the kind, size, and quality of the flooring material.

If the final floor is going to be some surface other than finished wood, only a subfloor will be put down. Wall-to-wall carpeting, vinyl tile, linoleum, and ceramic tile can be installed directly over a subfloor. A subcontractor usually installs these floor surfaces.

An estimate for flooring is based on the floor's area. The price of materials and labor varies according to the type of flooring that will be installed.

Damage and Repair

Floors are susceptible to all sorts of damage. Fire and water can damage most types of flooring. Carpets are susceptible to damage from caustic chemicals, smoke, and soot. Ceramic tile can be broken. Vinyl often gets torn when a refrigerator gets moved.

Repairing damaged flooring can be a challenge. Similar to the problem of matching wallpaper, finding the exact flooring material with the same dye lot may be next to impossible. Even if the homeowner has material on hand, the existing floor may have been worn or faded to the point that it no longer matches the unused material. While there is some benefit to being creative in attempts to repair a floor, sometimes there is no option but to replace it.

Interior Trim

Interior trim consists principally of base moldings, baseboards, ceiling moldings, picture moldings, chair rails, and door and window trim. They add a decorative and finished appearance to interior walls, floors, and ceilings and are available in hardwoods, softwoods, and prefinished plastic. The hardwoods include birch, maple, and oak. The softwood is usually ponderosa pine and is sometimes available prefinished.

Base molding can be made of one, two, or three separate members. The main baseboard is between two and eight inches high and up to three-quarters of an inch thick. Large and ornate base molding is often constructed of hardwood in older houses. Exhibit 9-32 illustrates types of base molding and different molding patterns.

Ceiling moldings are usually of a cove or picture type and are almost always one member. Chair rails are one-, two-, or three-member moldings that are applied around the room's perimeter at chair-back height. Door and window trim (or "casings," as they are commonly known) is generally made of the same material and is usually included in the estimate along with the windows or doors. Exhibit 9-33 illustrates ceiling moldings.

Estimating Interior Trim

Interior trim is estimated by the linear foot. Adjusters must determine the style and type of wood as part of the scope. If the trim is popular, a lumberyard or supplier can give a material price per foot. Especially on older or more expensive houses, obtaining a bid to have the moldings specially milled to match the existing molding is sometimes necessary. A sample is needed for an accurate estimate. Tables are available to help adjusters calculate labor costs. These tables are usually based on hours per 100 linear feet.

EXTERIOR SIDING

The extent of, and potential for, damage to exterior siding are affected very much by the type of siding material. Wood shingles or shakes of redwood and Western red cedar normally have an excellent moisture-resistant composition. Nevertheless, weather-related losses are the main cause of damage to such shingles. Over time, wind-driven rains can seep behind siding and cause deterioration. Hail can split wood shingles and puncture or dent aluminum or vinyl siding. Hail can cause a range of damage, from minor cosmetic damage to moderate and severe losses. The same force of impact that would dent aluminum would cause little, if any, damage to more pliable vinyl or

EXHIBIT 9-32

Base moldings

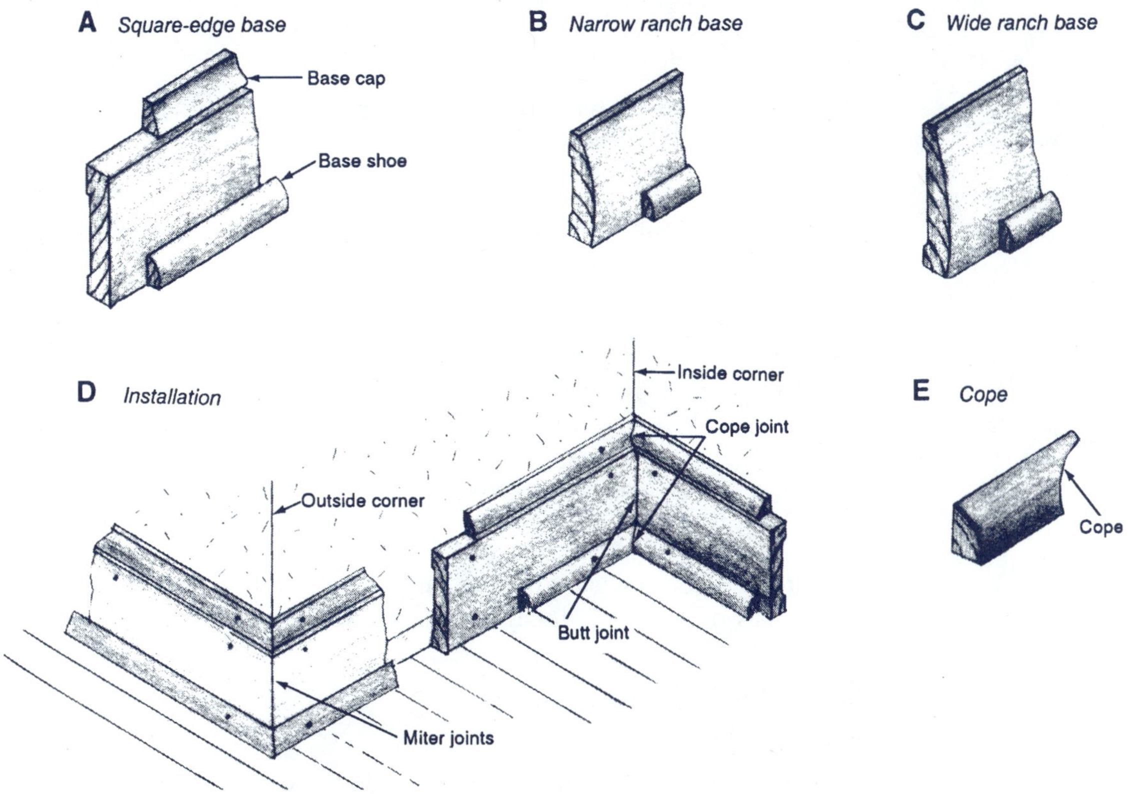

L. O. Anderson, revised by William Oberschulte, *Wood-Frame House Construction* (Carlsbad, Calif.: Craftsman Book Company, July 1992), p. 193.

EXHIBIT 9-33

Ceiling Moldings

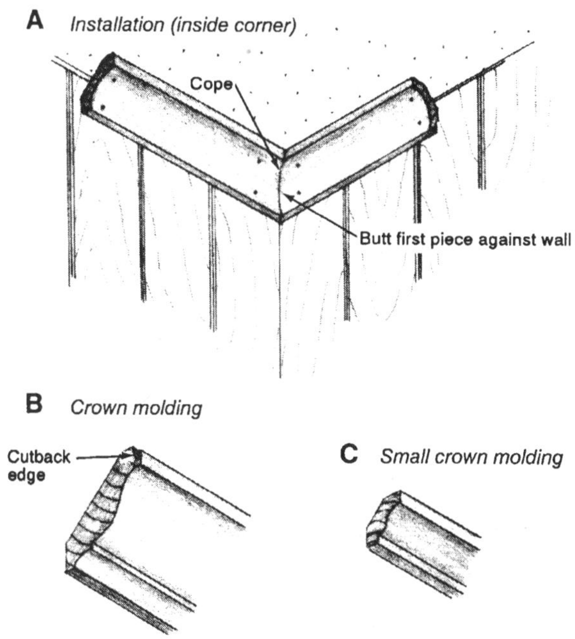

L. O. Anderson, revised by William Oberschulte, *Wood-Frame House Construction* (Carlsbad, Calif.: Craftsman Book Company, July 1992), p. 194.

even to wood clapboard surfaces. Siding losses related to vandalism involve spray paint damage or tearing of siding.

Although aluminum can be repainted, it will also need to be painted several years later. Even though it dulls over time, the original baked-on surface will not peel or crack, as will paint. Many siding losses, especially to aluminum siding, can be adjusted with an allowance for appearance. When in doubt, an adjuster should secure photographs of the damage, note the kind of siding involved, and try to arrange an inspection by an expert familiar with this kind of damage.

Spot repairs can be made to wood clapboard and vinyl/aluminum siding. Repair of wood siding is discussed in the next section.

Siding Materials

The major types of siding material are wood exterior panels such as wood shakes; hardboard; aluminum; vinyl; seamless steel; and fiber cement. Masonry, stucco finishes, and composition asphalt coverings are also used.

Wood Siding

The most common types of wood siding are bevel design and dropsiding. Examples of both are shown in Exhibit 9-34, along with other types of siding. Wood siding is usually white pine, redwood, Douglas fir, or red cedar. It is usually applied horizontally and readily accepts paint or stain. The corners can be finished with vertical trim boards or covered by metal corner caps. High-quality installations have mitered corners, which require more time.

Wood drop or bevel siding is applied over felt paper, which serves as a vapor barrier for the back of the siding. The siding is nailed directly onto the sheathing of the framed building. The siding material can range up to one inch thick and twelve inches wide and typically comes in lengths of eight to twenty feet.

Surface damage to wood siding can be filled and sanded, then painted. Broken boards, however, must be replaced. That replacement involves loosening the board strip above the damaged area, cutting the replacement boards to fit, and replacing all but the bottom board. The back lip of the bottom board must be cut away so that the board can be pressed against the siding and nailed in place. Wood siding can also be applied vertically.

EXHIBIT 9-34

Siding

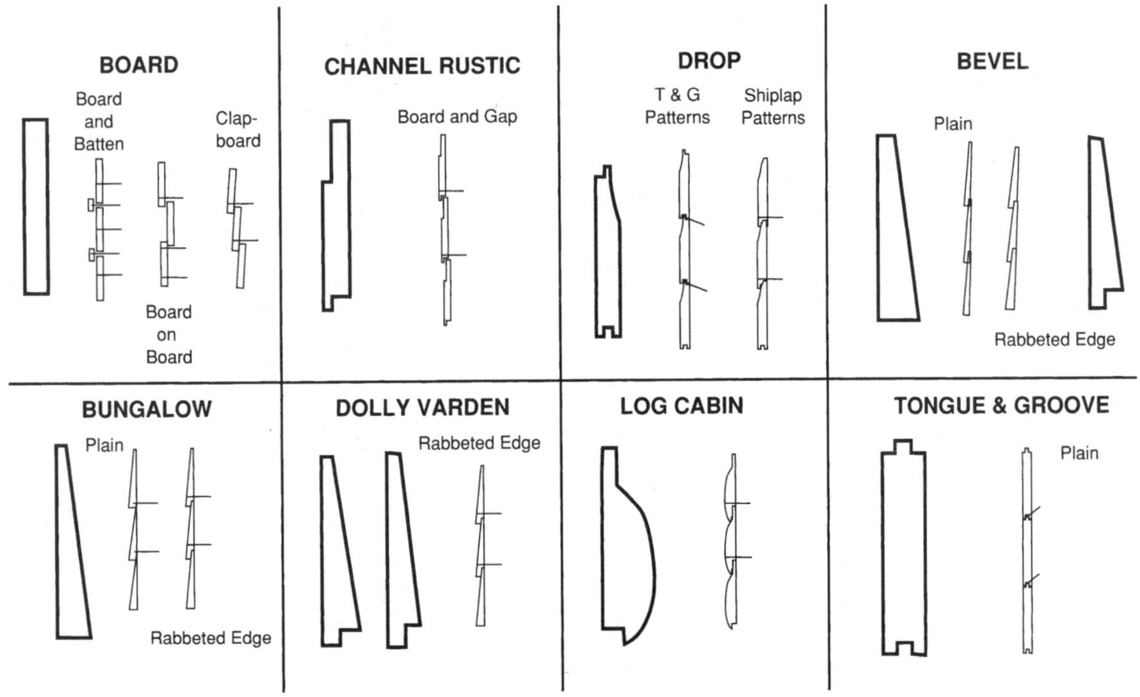

Adapted from "Wood and Composition Exterior Siding," *Property Damage Repair Reports,* No. 432 (Chambersburg, Pa.: National Property & Casualty Claims Research Service, Inc., formerly Vale Lab Research, January 1983), p. 1.

Sheet Materials

Exterior sheet materials generally come in 4′ × 8′ panels, various patterns, and several different colors. Exterior grades of particleboard and plywood can be used when quality is not the primary concern. These materials can be easily painted and should have a good vapor barrier behind them. Batten strips should be nailed where the edges butt against one another to prevent leaking at the seams.

Wood Shingles

Wood shingles come in lengths of 16, 18, and 24 inches. Shingles are sold by the square, with 4 bundles per square. Four bundles cover 100 square feet with an exposure of 5 inches. (The *exposure* of a shingle is the amount that is exposed to the weather.) With a smaller exposure, such as 4 inches, the shingles cover less area. Larger exposures, some up to 8 inches, are used depending on the size of the wood shingle.

Aluminum Siding

Aluminum siding is sold in cartons of twelve sheets, which cover 100 square feet of surface. They are interlocking and have an exposure of eight inches. For a slightly higher cost, they can be backed with insulating material.

Vinyl Siding

Vinyl siding might be an alternative to aluminum. Vinyl siding's color is part of the material and will not fade over time. It is pliable and not as prone to damage by hail or other minor impact. It can also be bought with or without insulation. Vinyl tends to stiffen in cold weather and can crack if bumped. Its surface is not adaptable to painting. Vinyl siding can be roll-formed at the work site so that it will be seamless when installed.

Seamless-Steel Siding

Seamless-steel siding is PVC-coated steel. It is manufactured on site, so it has no joints or endlap. It is a durable product that resists chipping and peeling.

Fiber Cement Siding

Fiber cement siding is cement and sand mixed with cellulose to form planks that look like wood siding. It holds paint much better than wood and has a very long usable life. Fiber cement siding's disadvantange is that is heavy and takes two professionals to install. It is also very hard on power tools and should be cut with a masonry or diamond-tipped blade.

Estimating Siding

In estimating the amount and cost of siding, adjusters must consider waste as well as materials and labor. Unit costs for siding can be calculated.

Waste

In estimating beveled siding, adjusters should use the net area method and add a percentage for mill waste, cutting, and overlap. An estimating reference book or an estimating software package will have the percentage of waste for the type of siding involved in the loss.

Calculating Area

Regardless of the type of material used, the structure's exterior must be measured, and the area of all openings must be deducted. To determine the exterior surface area of a house, multiply the perimeter measure by the height of the walls under the roofed eave, then calculate and add on the area of the gable ends.

Assume that a house is 40′ × 26′ and thus has a perimeter of 132′. The height of the walls under the roof eave is 8′, so the surface area is 1,056 square feet. The triangular area of each gable end is 104 square feet, (26′ × 8′) ÷ 2. To determine the total *net* surface area, the adjuster must deduct the area of the openings:

Total exterior surface area	1,056	square feet
Total gable end area (2 × 104′)	+208	square feet
Gross surface area	1,264	square feet
Door (3′ × 7′)	− 21	square feet
3 windows (4′ × 5′ each)	− 60	square feet
Net area	1,183	square feet

Materials

The house in this example has 1″ × 8″ bevel cedar siding that costs $1.25 per board foot. A 35 percent waste factor should be added for bevel siding of that size. Multiply the net area by 1.35 (1,183 × 1.35 = 1,597 BFM) to determine the amount of siding needed to cover the exterior walls and gable ends.

Before wood siding is installed, a vapor barrier is installed over the wood sheathing material. Each roll of the vapor barrier material covers approximately 500 square feet. There is no waste factor for vapor barriers.

Labor

Labor for installing siding is based on 1,000 BFM of material. The first step in estimating labor is to determine the time needed to do the job. Exhibit 9-35 indicates the labor hours per BFM for different types of siding and nominal material sizes. Because this job require 1,597 BFM of material, 57.5 hours of labor will be necessary:

$$1{,}597\text{ BFM} \times \frac{36\text{ hrs.}}{1{,}000\text{ BFM}} = 57.49\text{ hrs., rounded to }57.5.$$

The second step is to determine the labor rate per hour in the locality. At $20 per hour, the labor cost is $1,150 ($20 per hour × 57.5 hours).

EXHIBIT 9-35

Siding Installation Time Estimates

Hours of Labor Required to Install 1,000 BFM of Various Types of Wood Siding

Type of Siding	Size in Inches	Hours Labor per 1,000 BFM
Bevel siding—fitted ends	4	30.5
	6	23.0
Rustic and drop siding—fitted ends	6	21.4

Walker's Building Estimator's Reference Book, 26th ed. (Lisle, Ill.: Frank R. Walker Company, 1999), pp. 7.73, 7.75.

Total Cost

The total cost for material and labor to install 1″ × 8″ beveled siding is broken down as follows (the labor for the felt is included in the rate):

1,597 BFM @ $1.25 per BFM	$1,996.25
Vapor barrier: 3 rolls @ $16 per roll	48.00
Labor: 1,597 @ 36 hours per BFM 1,000 = 57.5 hours 57.5 hours @ $20 per hour	1,150.00
Total material and labor	$3,194.25

Additional factors that might need to be considered are removing damaged siding; erecting and disassembling scaffolding or staging; removing outside trim such as shutters, gutters, and headers; and applying stain, varnish, or paint.

Unit Cost

A unit cost per square foot is determined by dividing the total cost by the total board feet:

$$\text{Unit cost} = \frac{\$3{,}210.25}{1{,}597 \text{ sq. ft.}} = \$2.01 \text{ per square foot.}$$

This figure can be used as a basis for estimating the cost of other beveled wood 8″ siding installations. No one unit cost applies to patch repair jobs, however. In siding, as in other trades, smaller jobs make establishing a feasible unit cost more difficult.

SUMMARY

To adjust residential building losses, adjusters must have a working knowledge of concrete and masonry, frame carpentry, finish carpentry, interior and exterior finishes, and mechanical systems. This chapter provided construction basics along with estimating techniques for various types of losses affecting residences. Concrete foundations are the starting point for most residential construction. Frame carpentry is the work that a carpenter does in erecting the skeleton of the house. It includes the exterior and interior walls, the ceilings, the floors, and the roof. Various causes can damage the frame of a house, including fire, smoke, windstorm, water, vandalism, earthquake, and vehicle impact. Because framing members are the first elements to be constructed when a house is built, it is often necessary to remove undamaged portions of the house to repair damaged portions.

Finish carpentry describes the work done to install the top layer of the floor and the moldings around the rooms and openings. It also includes the installation of cabinets and countertops in the kitchen.

The amount of materials needed for a roof is estimated using the area of the roof. The area will differ depending on the roof's size and shape. The labor needed to install the roof can increase based on the roof's shape and pitch.

Electrical systems have become complicated and difficult to repair because of the wiring that is now needed to support the various technologies in many homes. The plumbing system is roughed-in during the framing of the house. Later, the fixtures and appliances are installed. The same is true for the cooling system.

Various interior finishes are found in homes. Painting and wallpapering both use the area of the walls and ceilings to estimate the amount of labor and materials needed for a job. Unit costs can be developed for these elements and are time saving on large jobs.

The mechanical systems discussed in this chapter include the electrical system, the plumbing system, and the heating and air conditioning systems.

The exterior finishes discussed in this chapter include the various types of siding and masonry products available to finish the walls of a home.

The past several chapters of this text have focused on physical damage to structures. Chapter 10 focuses on merchandise losses and how the property loss adjuster must use the insured's books and records to investigate and value the loss.

CHAPTER NOTES

1. Paul I. Thomas, *How to Estimate Building Losses and Construction Costs*, 4th ed. (Englewood Cliffs, N.J.: Prentice-Hall, Inc., 1983), pp. 134–155.
2. *Adjuster Handbook: Estimating Small Dwelling Losses* (Denver: General Adjustment Bureau, 1972).
3. "Wood Identification," *Property Damage Repair Report* (PDR), No. 524, (Chambersburg, Pa.: National Property & Casualty Research Services, Inc., May 1998).
4. *Basic Carpentry Illustrated* (Menlo Park, Calif.: Sunset Books, Lane Publishing Co., 1984), p. 35.
5. Paul I. Thomas, p. 234.
6. *Basic Carpentry Illustrated*, p. 59.
7. "Insulation and Moisture Control," *PDR*, No. 521 (Chambersburg, Pa.: National Property & Claims Research Services, Inc., Nov. 1997).
8. Paul I. Thomas, pp. 311–312.
9. "Ground Fault Interrupter," *PDR*, No. 467 (Chambersburg, Pa.: National Property & Claims Research Services, Inc., Nov. 1989).
10. "Wire, Wire Uses," *PDR*, No. 468 (Chambersburg, Pa.: National Property & Claims Research Services, Inc., Nov. 1989).
11. "Structured Wiring and Home Automation," *PDR*, No. 547 (Chambersburg, Pa.: National Property & Claims Research Services, Inc., March 2002).

Chapter 10

Direct Your Learning

Merchandise Losses

After learning the subject matter of this chapter, you should be able to:

- Distinguish between the coverage provided by the Building and Personal Property Coverage Form (BPP) and the Business Owners Policy (BOP) for merchandise and the insurable interest requirements of the BPP and the BOP for merchandise.
- Explain how replacement cost and actual cash value are determined for merchandise.
- Describe the information contained in a business's books and records and financial statements.
- Given a case, calculate the cost of goods sold by a business during a given time period.
- Given a case, calculate the book value of remaining inventory on a date of loss, using books and records.
- Describe a salvor's services, and explain the operation of salvage contracts.
- Given a case, calculate settlements involving salvage proceeds.
- Explain a reporting form policy's purpose and operation.
- Explain how reporting form policies treat underreporting and late reporting.
- Given a claim involving reporting form coverage, calculate a loss:
    - With proper reporting and no specific insurance
    - With proper reporting and specific insurance applicable
    - With underreported values and no specific insurance
    - With underreported values and specific insurance applicable
- Explain what procedures an adjuster should follow and what information the adjuster should gather in the adjustment of:
    - Loss to a large quantity of merchandise
    - Loss to a small quantity of merchandise
- Explain why percentage damage settlements of merchandise losses can be advantageous to both the insured and insurer.

OUTLINE

Develop Your Perspective

What are the main topics covered in the chapter?

This chapter discusses how losses to a business's stock or inventory are handled under the Building and Personal Property Coverage Form (BPP) and the Business Owners Policy (BOP). It also introduces reporting form policies and discusses how the reports affect loss calculations.

Not all insurance companies write commercial property policies. If your company does write commercial property, examine a retail store or manufacturer's loss. If your company does not write commercial property, try to recall a large fire or flood at a strip mall.

- What type of merchandise is present, and what type of damage did it suffer?
- How would the merchandise be valued?
- Would a salvor's services be helpful in the loss adjustment?

Why is it important to know these topics?

Merchandise losses require the property loss adjuster to use the insured's books and records to ascertain the merchandise's value. The use of a salvor may mitigate the extent of the loss. If the policy is a reporting form, reports' frequency and accuracy will be an issue in the loss adjustment.

How can you use this information?

This chapter provides an understanding of the valuation issues that can arise in a merchandise loss. It describes how to calculate losses with different variables under a reporting form policy.

Chapter 10

Merchandise Losses

Up to this point, the text has concentrated on the loss and damage that can occur to structures. This chapter discusses the nature of losses sustained by a business when its stock or inventory is damaged. These merchandise losses present adjusters with different policy terms, definitions, conditions, and limitations. This chapter explains the basic coverage, accounting procedures, methods of determining value and damage, and other typical adjustment practices involved in claims for merchandise.

Merchandise, also called "goods" or "stock," includes manufactured and processed goods as well as goods held by merchants for sale and is found in many different locations and conditions. Any piece of merchandise begins as raw material or a combination of raw materials in a manufacturing or processing plant, progresses through the manufacturing operation as goods in process and emerges as finished goods. The terms "raw materials," "work in process," and "finished goods" are found in various commercial policies.

Some finished goods become part of another manufacturing process. An example is in the garment industry. Ribbed knit cuffs are manufactured by a supplier then shipped to another manufacturer that stitches them onto a sweatshirt. Other finished goods are sent in transit to the premises of the manufacturer's customers, such as distributors or retailers. Separate policy provisions can cover merchandise in each stage: during manufacture, in transit, and at the retail level. This chapter addresses merchandise claims in this last stage. At the retail level, the adjuster determines the merchandise's insured value. This determination involves examining the insured's books and records. Merchandise losses frequently involve salvage. Reporting form coverage is common for merchandise, and adjusting merchandise losses requires unique considerations.

DAMAGEABILITY OF MERCHANDISE

In a retail establishment, merchandise is damaged most often by fire, smoke, water, firefighters' actions, flood, sprinkler leakage, leaking roofs, collapse, or windstorm. Merchandise can also be stolen. Damage to merchandise can be either total or partial. A total loss does not necessarily mean destruction. Merchandise can be damaged to the extent that it cannot be sold by the insured and is therefore treated as a total loss in the adjustment even though it has some remaining salvage value.

Hard goods
Merchandise made principally from glass, metal, and china, which can be cleaned after exposure to smoke or water.

Soft goods
Merchandise made principally from textile and fabric, which is not truly restored by cleaning.

Smoke, heat, water, or odor can inflict partial damage. Many items in a retail establishment are packaged in such a way that smoke or water does not penetrate to the merchandise itself. In this case, a cleaning allowance is an appropriate settlement of the claim. **Hard goods**, such as glass, metal, and china, can often be cleaned after exposure to smoke or water. **Soft goods**, such as apparel, linens, and other items made of fabric, however, are not truly restored by cleaning. Because the insured is in the business of selling new merchandise, not cleaned or laundered merchandise, adjusters must work with insureds to adjust losses involving goods that cannot be cleaned appropriately. In adjusting a merchandise loss, the adjuster considers coverage, insurable interest, and valuation issues.

COVERAGE FOR MERCHANDISE LOSSES

Adjusters encounter merchandise claims for retail goods under two general types of commercial property policies: (1) the Building and Personal Property Coverage Form (BPP) and (2) the Business Owners Policy (BOP).

The BPP

The BPP extends coverage for personal property to "furniture and fixtures; machinery and equipment; stock; meaning merchandise held in storage or for sale . . . and supplies used in packing or shipping."[1] Coverage is for direct physical loss unless excluded or on a specified-perils basis. Stock valuation is typically at actual cash value, but the policy can be modified to provide replacement cost coverage. For stock the merchant has sold but not delivered, the BPP provides reimbursement of "selling price less discounts and expenses you otherwise would have had."[2] Coverage on personal property of others is included, but with strict limitations. A coinsurance clause usually applies.

The BOP

Stock coverage under the BOP is similar to the coverage in the BPP. Although the BOP definition of "business personal property" is not as detailed as the BPP's definition, it extends to all likely exposures, including owned property, property of others, and improvements and betterments. Two kinds of BOPs are available. See the following box.

BOP Policies

1. Standard BOP: covers specified perils and values stock at replacement cost
2. Special BOP: provides coverage for direct physical loss unless excluded and also values stock at replacement cost

All BOPs incorporate a seasonal automatic increase clause, which automatically increases business personal property coverage by 25 percent, providing for seasonal variations. This seasonal increase is effective only if insureds carry insurance equal to at least 100 percent of their average monthly value during the twelve months preceding a loss. BOPs do not contain a coinsurance clause.

Coverage Review

On any mercantile claim, the adjuster must review the applicable policy thoroughly. The adjuster cannot rely on coverage information recalled from previous claims. Policies can differ in many ways, including such areas as a coinsurance clause, the coinsurance percentage, the deductible, and other differences. An adjuster handling numerous homeowners claims might eventually memorize general coverage provisions, but adjusters cannot memorize the many variations in commercial policies.

Insurable Interest

Commercial property policies' intent is to cover only the named insured's interest in the property. The BPP states that its coverage extends to "your business personal property."[3] The BOP covers business personal property owned by the insured. Both the BPP and the BOP contain identical language: "We will not pay you more than your financial interest in the Covered Property."[4]

Certain property not owned by the insured is automatically covered under commercial property policies. The BPP describes this property as personal property of others in the insured's care, custody, or control and located in or on the described building. The BOP is more explicit, describing the covered property of others as property held by the insured and belonging to others, but not exceeding the amount for which the insured is legally liable, including the labor value, materials, and charges furnished, performed, or incurred by the insured. The property coverage of others in the BPP differs from that in the BOP. Under the BPP, coverage exists regardless of the insured's legal liability for the damage. For example, if an event entirely out of the insured's control destroyed the insured's property as well as property of others, the insured would not be legally liable to the other owners, but the BPP would cover such losses. The BOP would not. Despite these policies' different wording, their coverage is similar with respect to the types of property to which coverage extends. Merchandise such as layaways and items in the insured's custody for alterations or repairs is covered.

In adjusting a retail store loss, the adjuster must separate the claim from any merchandise not owned by the insured, such as merchandise in leased departments. In larger stores, this merchandise usually includes jewelry, cameras, and shoes. In smaller stores, items such as sales displays of hosiery and watches are generally not the property of the insured merchant, although the insured might be responsible for them under contract. If the insured claims legal responsibility, the adjuster should examine the contract between the insured and the manufacturer or distributor.

Valuation

Commercial property policies normally insure retail merchandise for replacement cost or actual cash value (ACV). A policy might also base valuation on the selling price.

Replacement Cost

Replacement cost (for merchandise)
The insured's cost to buy stock from its suppliers less any trade discounts or allowances, plus incoming freight and the cost of receiving, opening, tagging, marking, and arranging.

Replacement cost for merchandise is the insured's cost to buy stock from its suppliers, less any trade discounts or allowances, plus incoming freight. It can also include the cost of receiving, opening, tagging, marking, and arranging the goods in the insured's premises by the supplier. These additional costs reflect the different (usually greater) value that the merchandise has on the merchant's premises ready for sale to the public as compared to the value it has in the supplier's warehouse or factory. Determining replacement cost is not difficult if the adjuster has access to the insured's books and to records such as invoices.

Freight

Incoming freight charges
The amount that the insured pays to have goods shipped to the insured's premises from a supplier.

Incoming freight charges are the amounts that insureds pay to have goods shipped to their premises from suppliers. Any freight paid by the insured's suppliers is not counted.

Trade Discounts and Allowances

Trade discounts and allowances
Reductions from the stated purchase price, given by the supplier, for such reasons as purchasing in bulk or paying in a timely manner.

Trade discounts and allowances are stated purchase price reductions that suppliers grant the insured for purchasing in volume or for paying in a timely manner. Discounts and allowances represent reductions in the effective price paid by the insured for its merchandise, and they reduce the cost value of the insured's inventory. For example, 2 percent may be deducted from the price if the invoice is paid within ten days.

Handling Costs

There are two types of handling costs: (1) internal, which are the costs of the insured's own employees handling the items and (2) external, which are the costs of a third party handling the item for the insured and adding a separate charge to the cost. Handling costs incurred on the insured's premises are not always accounted for in the value of merchandise, but they represent a real cost and real value. These costs reflect the difference in value to the insured between goods on a receiving dock and those ready for sale to the public. **Internal handling costs** are not added to the cost of goods sold. If external handling costs are identified in the insured's accounting records, they can be included for adjustment purposes in the value of goods. Insureds, however, do not always want these costs counted. These costs increase the insured's stock value for settlement purposes but also increase it for coinsurance purposes. Higher value does not necessarily translate into a higher settlement if a coinsurance penalty is incurred. Handling costs should be treated the same for loss settlement and coinsurance purposes.

Internal handling costs
The insured's cost to have its own employees handle stock, such as pricing and arranging.

Actual Cash Value

Calculating merchandise's actual cash value is more difficult than calculating its replacement cost because no policy defines the term "actual cash value." ACV can equal replacement cost when there is no depreciation, markdown, or other loss of value. If so, determining ACV requires examining the insured's purchase records item by item in the same way that replacement cost is determined.

Depreciation Causes

Any retail stock of merchandise can suffer a reduction in value and selling price because of depreciation, even if it never leaves the merchant's premises. The possible causes of depreciation are innumerable, but the principal causes are physical damage and obsolescence. Careless handling, dust, fading, moisture or humidity, missing parts, infestation, excessive heat, freezing, and thawing can cause physical damage. The adjuster must inspect the goods to determine whether any physical damage to merchandise existed before the loss. Obsolescence means that an item has lost value because it is out of fashion, past its marked shelf life, a fad, or a seasonal item; because it shows evidence of slow turnover; or because it was offered in an incomplete size, color, or pattern range.

Market Value

In California, courts have ruled that ACV equals market value. The market is where the insured merchant obtains its stocks of merchandise. The insured is a buyer in the wholesale market. The insured's costs reflect the value of goods in this market, including incoming freight and handling costs, less trade discounts. Unless unusual circumstances are present, the insured's costs can be interpreted as an accurate reflection of market value in a given wholesale market. Any loss of value to the merchandise once it is on the insured's premises is not easy to detect. Goods are seldom resold on the wholesale market. The adjuster must judge whether goods on the insured's premises would sell as prime merchandise on the wholesale market. If not, some reduction in actual cash value is appropriate. Markdowns at retail strongly suggest that goods have lost value to the merchant and would likewise have less value at the wholesale level.

Markdowns

Most retail accounting systems operate on the premise that when the merchant reduces the selling price of a piece of merchandise because the item is not moving, is approaching the end of its season, or has become shop-worn, the item's original cost value automatically drops by the same percentage by which the merchant has reduced the selling price. For example, if an item's retail price is reduced 40 percent, from $100 to $60, then its cost value must likewise be reduced by 40 percent. If the original cost value was $50, it would drop (for ACV purposes) to $30 (40 percent less). Examples of this phenomenon are calendars and date books. These items rapidly lose value after January of every year. A retailer who suffers a loss in March would certainly have reduced the retail price of its remaining calendars and date books by then. In determining the ACV of that loss, the adjuster would value any damaged date books and calendars not according to their cost value when purchased, but on the basis of the marked-down price. Because these items are nearly worthless to the merchant in March, regardless of what was paid for them, their ACV would be extremely low. It is also possible to have circumstances that cause the retail value to drop, yet the wholesale value remains the same.

Adjusters should use the accounting method for determining value that mirrors the insured's accounting system of valuation. If the adjuster can show that he or she is using the same method as the insured's own accounting system for valuing merchandise, the argument for using such value determination would be strengthened. All retail merchants mark down merchandise at some time. If the insured's inventory system reveals that end-of-year inventory values are always devalued, then the merchant clearly subscribes to the retail method of accounting and inventory valuation. The **retail method of accounting** assumes a consistent profit percentage, so that goods marked down at retail also lose value as assets on the business's books. This system should be included in ACV determination.

Retail method of accounting
An accounting procedure that assumes a consistent profit percentage so that goods marked down at retail also lose value as assets on the business's books.

An adjuster cannot automatically assume that all marked-down items have been reduced in price because of depreciation or obsolescence. Grocery markets commonly have weekly promotions during which certain popular items are marked down as loss leaders. At the end of the promotion, the unsold items are marked back up to their normal prices. This practice is also common in other retail establishments such as shoe stores, clothing stores, drugstores, and record stores. If a loss occurs during the promotion, the adjuster cannot realistically argue that an item only temporarily marked down for a sales promotion has actually been reduced in value and that its ACV should be reduced accordingly.

Selling Price

Adjusters sometimes encounter policies that give merchants selling price coverage on their merchandise. The selling price is the tagged price on the merchandise at the time of the loss, whether it is the originally marked selling price or a marked-down price. Almost all value calculations begin with the selling price marked on each piece of merchandise at the time of the loss.

Layaways

Layaways are treated differently from merchandise held for sale. A layaway should be valued at the selling price, whether it has been completely paid for or not. Layaways are valued on the assumption that once the item has been put aside for a customer, the sale has been made, and a profit has been realized. This standard for layaway values must be used whenever total valuation of the insured's stock of merchandise is relevant, such as when a coinsurance clause applies. The insured's inventory figure ordinarily does not include layaways because they are considered to have been sold.

Universal Pricing Code

The universal pricing code (UPC) is the small box of bars of various widths appearing on an item of merchandise. As the item is scanned at a checkout counter, the UPC registers an electronic entry in inventory records and prints a price on the register tape. This method of checking out merchandise eliminates the need for a price tag on each item. It complicates the process of determining retail inventory values, however, because the absence of a price on each item makes verifying the price on the date of loss more difficult. The approach used in conducting a partial or total physical inventory with the UPC system must be different from the one used when each item is tagged with a price. Fortunately, computerized inventory systems using UPCs usually have detailed histories of retail price changes and physical inventory counts.

BOOKS AND RECORDS

If merchandise has been partly or completely destroyed, its total value must be established. Merchandise has suffered a total loss if it has been destroyed, as by fire, or has been so badly damaged that the insured cannot be expected to try to sell it at a reduced price.

Merchandise damaged beyond recognition, called **out-of-sight merchandise**, poses a problem for adjusters because it cannot be inventoried or identified. One precaution that an adjuster should take when a loss involves out-of-sight merchandise is to determine by measurement that the quantity of merchandise claimed could have fit into the space in which it was supposed to have been stored or located. If a physical inventory is impractical because some merchandise has been destroyed or damaged beyond recognition, the only way to establish acceptable values is by using the insured's books and records.

Out-of-sight merchandise
Merchandise that has been damaged beyond recognition.

Types of Financial Records

The fundamental financial records of any business are its **income statement** and its **balance sheet.** See the following box.

Income statement (or **profit and loss statement; earnings statement)**
A financial summary of a business's operating activities during an accounting period; includes all revenue, expenses, and the resulting net income or loss.

Balance sheet
A financial statement that indicates an organization's assets, liabilities, and owner's equity at a particular point in time.

Income Statement and Balance Sheet

- The income statement is also called the *profit and loss statement* or *earnings statement*. It is an account of the operations of the business, from gross revenue to net profit before taxes, over a defined time period.

  At a minimum, an income statement is prepared at the end of the insured's fiscal year. Income statements are commonly prepared monthly so that merchants have the

Continued on next page.

opportunity to follow trends in the business. Year-end statements furnish adjusters with valuable reference material for handling property claims. They disclose the cost of goods sold and other merchandise-related costs that adjusters can use to value stock. They are also invaluable for handling attendant loss of earnings claims.

- A balance sheet provides values on a stated date of all assets, liabilities, and paid-in capital (also known as owner's equity). It is especially important for the property loss adjuster because it includes among the assets a physical inventory figure. A balance sheet is usually prepared only at the end of the fiscal year, and it furnishes an inventory figure for that date. This figure represents an actual physical inventory at values determined by the insured and the insured's accountant. To bring that inventory figure up to the date of loss, an adjuster must examine purchase and sales records since that physical inventory.

Determining Book Value

The value of an inventory that is lost out-of-sight can be determined by using the information contained in most businesses' books and records. The basic method is straightforward. The inventory was accurately known the last time a physical count was made, usually at the end of the year or at the end of the business's fiscal year. Since then, the business has added to its inventory by making purchases from its suppliers. Suppose that a retailer selling men's suits had 500 suits in inventory on December 31 and purchased 900 suits between December 31 and the date of loss. This retailer had a total of 1,400 (500 + 900) suits that it could have sold between December 31 and the date of loss.

The number of suits sold between December 31 and the date of loss is subtracted from the total number of suits that could have been sold. The remaining number is inventory unsold. In the example, suppose that 950 suits were sold between December 31 and the date of loss. The total remaining in inventory would be as follows:

1,400 (500 + 900)	(What could have been sold)
– 950	(What was sold)
450	(What remains in inventory)

This formula is useful when determining the amount of inventory that has been lost out-of-sight or damaged beyond recognition is necessary. The following summarizes the method for determining book value:

	Amount in last physical inventory
+	Amount added to inventory between last physical inventory and date of loss
=	Amount that could have been sold
–	Amount that was sold between last physical inventory and date of loss
=	Amount remaining in inventory on date of loss

The above method is presented in terms of the number of physical units. To determine inventory's true book value, dollar amounts must be used in the formula. All businesses maintain their accounting records in dollars; not all of them maintain records in physical units. The issue in a claim adjustment is the dollar value of lost inventory; an insurer would not be obligated to replace 450 suits, but the insured value of those suits. If the insured value of the suits is $100 per suit, the book value of inventory would be calculated as follows:

	$50,000	(500 suits × $100 each)	(Value of beginning inventory)
+	90,000	(900 suits × $100 each)	(Value of additions to inventory)
=	$140,000	(1,400 suits × $100 each)	(Value of amount that could have been sold)
–	95,000	(950 suits × $100 each)	(Value of amount that was sold)
=	$45,000	(450 suits × $100 each)	(Value of amount remaining in inventory on date of loss)

In the above analysis, the dollar figure for the amount of suits sold cannot be directly obtained from most businesses' records. Although all businesses can provide a dollar figure for the number of items sold, these sales figures are kept in terms of retail prices or values. To determine inventory's book value accurately, this amount must be reduced from the retail value to the business's cost of obtaining the suits. In the above analysis, $100 is the cost to the suit retailer of obtaining suits from its suppliers. This cost must be used for the following two reasons:

1. Sales figures and purchase figures are otherwise not comparable. Purchases to inventory worth $1,000 are not the same as retail sales of $1,000. Assume, for example, that the retail store actually sells the suits for $200. *Purchases* of $1,000 represents *ten suits*, but *sales* of $1,000 represents only *five suits*.
2. Generally, the insured value of stock with a business is the cost to the business of replacing the stock, not its selling price.

Determining Cost of Goods Sold

The historical relationship between the cost and the selling price of goods determines the **cost of goods sold**. This relationship is determined by examining a business's complete records for a year, or several years, in which no loss occurred.

Cost of goods sold
An expense incurred when goods are sold; represents the cost to the merchant to acquire the goods.

Cost of Goods Sold Formula

The cost of goods sold during a year is determined as follows:

	Beginning inventory
+	Additions to inventory
=	Amount that could have been sold during the year
–	End inventory (amount not sold during the year)
=	Cost of goods sold

In the above example, assume that in the year *before* the loss, the suit retailer began with an inventory of $52,500 and made purchases to inventory of $110,000. The cost of goods sold for this retailer was as follows:

	$52,500	(Beginning inventory)
+	110,000	(Additions to inventory)
=	162,500	(Amount available for sale)
–	50,000	(End inventory on 12/31)
=	$112,500	(Cost of goods sold)

The $112,500 can be compared to the retail sales figure to determine the historical relationship between these two figures. If retail sales were $225,000, then retail sales are twice the cost of goods sold, because $225,000 ÷ 112,500 = 2. This represents a 100 percent markup, as when a business buys a suit for $100 and sells it to the public for $200. Markups by retail businesses can be any percentage.

Cost-to-Sales Ratio

Cost-to-sales ratio
Cost of goods sold divided by retail sales.

In this example, the **cost-to-sales ratio** (cost of goods sold divided by retail sales) is one-half ($112,500 ÷ $225,000), or 50 percent. In the year of a loss, a business is not likely to have a figure for the cost of goods sold, and such a figure cannot be determined without an accurate ending inventory figure. When the inventory is lost out-of-sight, determining an accurate ending inventory figure is not possible. However, the business should know its historic cost-to-sales ratio and its retail sales figures for the year of the loss. The business should also know retail sales figures from the date of the last physical inventory to the date of loss. The cost-to-sales ratio multiplied by the retail sales figures is the cost of goods sold. For example, if retail sales were $84,000 and the cost-to-sales ratio is 50 percent, the cost of goods sold is $84,000 × 50 percent (or .50), which equals $42,000.

Summary of Book Value Method

After a loss occurs, a business can provide its sales figures since its last physical inventory. The adjuster or an accountant working for the adjuster can determine the cost-to-sales ratio from historical data. These two figures (the sales since the last inventory and the cost-to-sales ratio) determine the cost of goods sold during the year of the loss. This cost of goods sold figure can be inserted into the following formula:

	Beginning inventory
+	Additions to inventory
=	Amount that could have been sold
–	Cost of goods sold
=	Value of inventory remaining on date of loss

The inventory's value on the date of loss is the amount of the loss on which a settlement is based when the inventory is destroyed or lost out-of-sight. Exhibit 10-1 uses an income statement to show the calculation of the cost of goods sold and the value of inventory on the date of loss. Exhibit 10-2 is a more elaborate example of the calculation of book inventory.

Adjustment Difficulties With Book Inventory

The value of merchandise losses can in theory be determined from the insured's books and records, but practical difficulties can arise when adjusting a particular loss. These include the destruction of records, the phenomenon of shrinkage, and differences between perpetual and physical inventories.

Destruction of Records

The destruction of the insured's records at the time of the loss would make the adjuster's task difficult, but not impossible. If the insured has an outside accounting or bookkeeping service, year-end records will be available. If sales records have been destroyed, the adjuster could reconstruct sales history by referring to bank statements and to state sales-tax records. Purchase information can also be developed by referring to bank records and by requesting information from all known suppliers. Privacy laws may require the insured's permission to obtain this information. Tax returns are, in effect, profit and loss statements. They cover all salient points, including a total inventory figure. With the insured's permission, previous state and federal income tax returns can be obtained from the Internal Revenue Service (IRS) and the state tax department.

Shrinkage

The adjuster must also consider the phenomenon of **shrinkage**. All businesses suffer a reduction in stock on hand caused by petty theft, breakage, other mishaps, and unrecorded sales. This reduction, known as shrinkage, can be represented by a dollar figure. The total amount of shrinkage increases with the length of time that has passed since the last physical inventory. Shrinkage is not generally a large figure. Exhibit 10-2 shows shrinkage of about 1 percent. A deduction for estimated shrinkage could be included in the book value of inventory on hand, when it has been a regular pattern in past physical inventories.

Shrinkage
The reduction in stock on hand because of petty theft, breakage, unrecorded sales, and other mishaps.

Perpetual Inventories

Insureds often present a **perpetual inventory** record. The insured might tell the adjuster that the perpetual inventory eliminates the need for all the accounting work of producing a book inventory or the time and effort involved in a physical inventory. The insured might be completely sincere in believing that the perpetual inventory record is accurate, but that sincerity does not guarantee its accuracy.

Perpetual inventory
A method of continuously tracking inventory that may not have been reconciled to the actual physical inventory.

EXHIBIT 10-1

Income Statement for Period 1/1/X1 Through 12/31/X1

Good Times Merchandise Co., Inc.

Gross Sales		$240,000
Less:		
Returns and allowances	$ 2,500	
Discounts	2,800	
Bad debts	700	6,000
Net Sales		$234,000
Determination of Cost of Goods Sold		
Inventory 1/1/X1	$ 50,000	
Purchases	144,000	
Incoming freight	3,000	
	$197,000	
Less discounts received and returns	3,000	
Merchandise available for sale	$194,000	
Less ending inventory 12/31/X1	46,000	$148,000
Cost of Goods Sold	$148,000	
Gross Profit on Sales		
{36.75% of net sales, $234,000.00}	$ 86,000	$ 86,000
Expenses		
Payroll and taxes	$ 35,100	
Rent	18,000	
Advertising	2,000	
Utilities	6,000	
Supplies	2,000	
Telephone	1,000	
Depreciation	9,000	
Insurance	2,500	
Taxes and licenses	900	
Miscellaneous	500	$ 77,000
Net Income		$ 9,000

EXHIBIT 10-2

Calculation of Book Inventory

Good Times Merchandise Co., Inc., Total Fire—12/20/X2

Last Physical Inventory 12/31/X1 From Income Statement (Exhibit 10-1)		$ 46,000
Net Purchases		140,000
Available for Sale		$186,000
Less Cost of Goods Sold:		
Net sales, same period	$215,000	
Less gross profit % (36.75%) from income statement (Exhibit 10-1) or tax return	79,012	135,987
Indicated Inventory 12/20/X2		$ 50,013

Note: Insured's perpetual inventory records indicate stock on hand as of 12/20 to be $50,500. Shrinkage for 51 weeks could account for the difference. The book inventory figure should prevail.

A perpetual inventory's accuracy depends on the accuracy and adequacy of the method of entering information into the inventory. This information consists of a record of each purchase of merchandise and a record of each sale of merchandise, at cost. Over time, errors of omission and commission occur, and normal shrinkage might not have been deducted. By the end of a fiscal year, a perpetual inventory figure is almost never equivalent to the results of the physical inventory taken on that date.

For this reason, adjusters should not depend on the accuracy of a perpetual inventory figure because a computer printout is only as accurate as the method of entering data into the computer. People enter this information, and people can make mistakes. If it is necessary to use a computer printout in a book inventory calculation, a certified public accountant (CPA) should test the accuracy of the insured's data-entry method.

SALVAGE

Adjusters often use the services of an outside expert called a "salvor" on claims involving merchandise. Salvors are experts in preserving and realizing the value remaining in partially damaged merchandise. They are able to do this by preparing an inventory of the damaged items and then locating the best possible market for the goods.

Salvors' Services

If an adjuster anticipates that a salvage company will be needed, he or she should call the salvor in at the beginning of the adjustment process. A salvor can assist the adjuster in surveying the loss scene and can offer immediate advice on protecting remaining merchandise, minimizing further damage, and determining the feasibility of a physical inventory. A salvor can talk professionally with the insured about the insured's line of business. A salvor works with the insured's employees in separating damaged and undamaged goods, conducting a physical inventory, and checking invoices. A salvor can also offer the adjuster confidential and professional advice on merchandise's degree of damage.

Salvor's Role in Settlement

One of the most important decisions that an adjuster must make on a merchandise loss is the manner of settlement. The adjuster can choose to do any of the following:

1. Pay the insured the full value of the merchandise and take the salvage for the account of the insurer
2. Sell the salvage on the account of the insured and pay the insured the difference between the salvage proceeds and the merchandise's insured value
3. Agree with the insured on the merchandise's percentage of damage, paying the insured for that percentage of value and leaving the merchandise with the insured for disposal

The salvor can provide invaluable advice on the likely outcomes of these three choices. Even with the third option, in which the salvor does not sell the merchandise, the salvor's advice can be crucial.

Sale of Salvage

If the decision is made that the merchandise is salable, the salvor arranges a sale to dispose of the goods. This sale can occur at the insured's premises, or the salvor may take the goods to its own facility. The salvor can arrange for packing and shipping the merchandise or for an on-site, complete disposal of the merchandise in an "as-is, where-is" condition. A salvor knows the best people to contact if a sale is held and can ensure that the best possible price is obtained for the merchandise taken over by the insurer. The salvor is the adjuster's most important colleague in any sizable or complex merchandise claim adjustment.

In merchandise claims, certain types of damaged stock must be treated differently from ordinary stock. Examples are prescription drugs, for which there is practically no market, no matter how lightly they are damaged; alcoholic beverages, which can be disposed of only through licensed dealers; and highly perishable edibles, which should not be disposed of without the authority of local health and food inspectors. Salvors can assist adjusters in helping to realize some kind of return in disposing of these types of merchandise.

When necessary, the salvor must communicate with a health and food inspector. The salvor has the expertise to discuss in a professional manner the possible disposition of damaged edibles. For example, almost all granulated sugar can be re-refined at a reasonable cost, regardless of how it has been damaged. Contaminated salt and items not fit for human consumption but acceptable as animal feed also have markets. Salvors know of markets for merchandise of all kinds.

The Adjuster's Role

All insurers have a list of approved experts of all kinds, including salvors. An independent adjuster should not choose a salvor without first consulting the insurer, preferably by telephone. Staff adjusters should refer to their employer's list of recommended experts when choosing a salvor.

An adjuster who has engaged a salvor's services should not expect the salvor to substitute as an adjuster. The salvor should not argue any point with the insured. Professional salvors do not intercede in any dispute between the adjuster and the insured or the insured's representative. The adjuster must maintain control of the adjustment process and should not rely on others to negotiate with the insured.

Acting Without Salvor Assistance

Adjusters must be able to make on-the-spot field decisions during the adjustment of a merchandise loss. When certain types of merchandise become wet, they must be dried out to prevent mildew or staining damage. In such a case, an adjuster must work immediately with the insured to arrest the moisture damage. If an adjuster waits and submits a report asking for instructions, the merchandise affected by water might become worthless. Adjusters should realize when field decisions must be made and when the insurer must be consulted for instructions.

Salvage Contracts

Damaged merchandise is still owned by the insured and cannot be taken without permission. Salvors operate in a professional and legal manner and do not remove merchandise from an insured's premises until the insurer and the insured have signed a proper contract. An example of such a contract appears in Exhibit 10-3.

Salvage Fees

The salvor's fees and commissions come out of the sale proceeds. The settlement with the insured is based on *net* proceeds. The salvor's fees and commissions become part of the loss indemnified by the insurer.

EXHIBIT 10-3

Agreement for the Removal of Stock

XYZ COMPANY

AGREEMENT FOR THE REMOVAL OF STOCK
FOR BETTER PROTECTION AND DISPOSITION

Insured: ______________________ Stock: ______________________

Insurance Company: ______________________ Location of Stock: ______________________

______________________ ______________________

Date of Loss: ______________________ Stock No.: ______________________

BACKGROUND:

The Stock may have been damaged by fire, smoke, or other casualty, and it is to the benefit of all who may have an interest in the Stock that the Stock be handled with as little delay as possible and without waiting to determine the respective interests, rights, or liabilities under policies purporting to insure the Stock.

AGREEMENT:

1. XYZ Company ("XYZ") is hereby retained to take possession of the Stock and to place the Stock in the best possible order for sale and to sell the Stock in the interest of whom it may concern. The proceeds of any sale of the Stock, less XYZ's commissions and expenses, as set forth below, will be held by XYZ in trust until the loss is adjusted and will then be turned over to such party(ies) as may be entitled to receive those proceeds.
2. As compensation for its services, XYZ will receive an amount equal to (a)______% of the gross proceeds of any sale of the Stock, plus (b) all costs and expenses (including labor costs) incurred by XYZ in connection with the removal, handling, maintenance, and sale of the Stock. XYZ may retain such amount from the gross proceeds of any sale of the Stock.
3. If XYZ at any time determines that the cost of the removal, handling, and maintenance of the Stock exceeds the estimated salvage value of the Stock (less XYZ's expenses and commissions, as set forth above), the responsibility of XYZ for continued custody of the Stock may be terminated.
4. The Insurance Company and the Insured will hold XYZ harmless from and against any claim made by any person or entity, other than the Insurance Company or the Insured, who or which may claim an interest in the Stock.
5. This Agreement is the entire agreement between the parties hereto and may only be changed in writing.

Date: ________________, 20XX

XYZ COMPANY

By: ______________________

Its: ______________________

INSURANCE COMPANY

By: ______________________

Its: ______________________

INSURED

By: ______________________

Its: ______________________

Insured's Liability to Salvor

The insured is never directly liable for the salvor's fees, except possibly in one circumstance. The insured might want to use the salvor to separate, inventory, and protect the merchandise even though the insured ultimately retains the goods. This might happen when the insured's premises are in a physical condition that threatens the merchandise. Ordinarily, in this situation the policy covers the reasonable cost of removal for protection. An adjuster might disagree with the need for removal and might resist approving the expense. Because the insured owns the property, the insured is free to contract directly with the salvor. Although the insured would undoubtedly submit the salvage fees as part of its claim, the insured would bear the initial liability to the salvor. This situation is undesirable and should be avoided if possible. The salvor's expert advice should be sought to resolve any dispute between the adjuster and the insured over whether property should be removed. If the salvor believes it should be removed, the adjuster should approve the expense. If the salvor thinks that the property is safe on the insured's premises, the insurer bears the risk of the salvor's being wrong.

Sale Before Settlement

When goods must be sold quickly, as in the case of perishables, the adjuster and the insured do not have to settle the claim before the salvor can take over the goods. As long as the adjuster and insured agree that the goods must be sold, they can execute a contract to that effect with the salvor. The salvor will sell the goods on account of whom it may concern.

Salvage Proceeds

Various ways of accounting for salvage proceeds are described below. The adjuster should be familiar with the law in the jurisdiction of the claim because the insured may be entitled to first-dollar recovery on salvage regardless of coinsurance.

1. *Sale on Account of Insurer*. The adjuster and insured agree on the merchandise's full insured value. The insurer pays the insured this full amount and takes the salvage for its own account:

Agreed full value of stock	$100,000
Insurer pays insured	$100,000
Net proceeds from salvage sale paid to insurer	$35,000
Insurer's net payment	$65,000

2. *Sale on Account of Insured*. The salvage sale is used to determine amount of loss:

Agreed full value of stock	$100,000
Net proceeds from salvage sale paid to insured	$35,000
Therefore, insurer pays insured	$65,000
Total payments to insured from salvage and insurance	$100,000

3. *Sale on Account of Whom It May Concern*. The salvage sale is made before agreement on value of stock:

Net proceeds from salvage sale held by salvor pending agreement	$35,000
Agreed full value of stock	$100,000
Net proceeds paid to insured	$35,000
Insurer pays insured	$65,000

4. *Sale in Which Insured Coinsures*. If the insured has inadequate limits of coverage and is required to bear a coinsurance penalty, the insured will share in the net proceeds of the salvage sale in the same percentage as the loss. Assume a 25 percent coinsurance penalty:

Agreed full value of stock	$100,000
In light of coinsurance, insurer would pay no more than	$75,000
In light of coinsurance, insured might have to bear up to	$25,000
Net proceeds of salvage sale	$35,000
Shared 75 percent with insurer	$26,250
Shared 25 percent with insured	$8,750
Insurer's net payment ($75,000 – $26,250)	$48,750
Insured's net loss ($25,000 – $8,750)	$16,250

However, some jurisdictions mandate that the insured be made whole irrespective of the coinsurance provision.

REPORTING FORM POLICIES

Reporting form
A form to periodically report fluctuating property values to an insurer.

A **reporting form** is a type of coverage for merchandise associated with risks in which the value of covered merchandise fluctuates by season or by month. A reporting form is used for such risks because it is designed to respond to what can be extreme fluctuations in merchandise's value. Reporting form coverage is offered as an endorsement to a commercial policy. It affects the policy only by the method of determining compliance with policy conditions, such as the coinsurance clause. The ISO Value Reporting Form is an example of a reporting form coverage. A reporting form can cover one or many locations and even covers property at newly acquired and incidental locations. The form incorporates a declarations page, which describes all locations at which coverage is to be provided and also establishes different limits at different locations.

A reporting form is designed to provide maximum dollar coverage when it is needed. For a merchant with a seasonal business, carrying commercial insurance throughout the year with a coinsurance clause based on the maximum possible value on hand at peak season would be very expensive. With reporting form insurance, merchants can obtain coverage equal to full value, or the face amount of the policy, no matter how much the inventory fluctuates.

Operation of Reporting Forms

Reporting form coverage has certain conditions. First, a provisional amount of insurance is designated when the policy is written. This provisional amount becomes the maximum limit of liability and is also used for initial premium calculations. When reporting form insurance is in effect, the insured must report total values on hand at each of the designated reporting times during the policy's term. The insured must report the property as it is to be valued in the policy: selling price, replacement cost, or actual cash value. The reporting period is usually on a monthly basis, but it can be on a quarterly or semiannual basis. The value report must be submitted to the company through the producer within thirty days of the end of any designated reporting period. Any submitted report is binding upon the insured and cannot be changed or corrected after a loss has occurred.

Reporting Full Values

The reporting form accomplishes its purpose by replacing the coinsurance clause with what is called a **full reporting clause**. Although the intent of reporting form coverage is for an insured to report full value at every insured location within thirty days of the designated reporting date, the form does not explicitly require the full value to be reported. Instead, the full reporting clause allows the insured to coinsure the losses when values have been underreported. The full reporting clause replaces the coinsurance clause with the following:

Full reporting clause
A clause that states that if the last report of values is less than the full value of the covered property at the time of the loss, then the insured participates in the loss in much the same manner as in coinsurance.

COINSURANCE

a. If your report of values for a location where loss or damage occurs for the last "reporting period" before loss or damage, shows less than the full value of the Covered Property at that location on the report dates, we will pay only a proportion of loss. The proportion of loss payable, prior to application of the deductible, will not be greater than the proportion determined by:
   (1) The values you reported for the location where the loss or damage occurred, divided by
   (2) The value of the Covered Property at that location on the report dates.[5]

An adjuster should not regard an insured who has underreported values as willfully dishonest. Some insureds deliberately underreport by a certain amount, acknowledging that they will be in the position of a coinsurer in the event of a loss. The insured's premiums are reduced, and if no loss occurs during the policy term, a savings is realized.

Timeliness of Reports

Other restrictive conditions in the value reporting form address the insured's failure to submit reports on time. If an insured fails to make a report on a stipulated reporting date, thirty days after the end of the designated reporting period, the coverage at any insured location is limited to the amount of the last report made for that location, no matter how long before the date of loss it was made. If the insured is late in making a first report of value and a loss occurs before any report has been made, the coverage at any given location is limited to 75 percent of the amount that the insurer would have otherwise paid. That is not 75 percent of the amount of insurance shown for that location; it is 75 percent of what an adjusted claim would have been.

Specific Insurance

Specific insurance (reporting form)
The other insurance covering the same insured and the same property at the same location as the reporting form policy.

Another possible complication in adjusting a claim under a reporting form policy concerns the existence of what is referred to in the reporting form as **specific insurance**. Specific insurance is other insurance covering the same insured and at least some of the same property that the reporting form covers at the described location. The claim payable under the specific insurance, whether collectible or not, and after the deductible has been applied, must be calculated according to the terms of the specific insurance. The reporting form coverage applies to the balance of the claim. Specific insurance should be reported to the reporting form insurer along with each value report. This is often not done, so the adjuster must determine the existence of any specific insurance.

Checking Reported Values

In adjusting a claim under reporting form coverage, an adjuster must check and verify certain values. The value of all stock on the date of loss is not important except for a total loss. The value figure that must be verified is the value of the stock on the date of the insured's last report of values. Exhibit 10-4 illustrates this procedure. The adjuster should check these values against a copy of the last report received by the insurer or the producer.

The adjuster must determine book inventory, perhaps with an accountant's assistance. This calculation was demonstrated in Exhibit 10-2. Exhibit 10-4 also shows that a book inventory calculation can be worked either backward or forward. If establishing a precise total inventory value figure for the date of loss is possible, a reverse book inventory figure to a previous report date should be more accurate than one obtained by working forward from a past physical inventory figure, especially if the figure is from the distant past. The inventory's actual value on the date of the last report should be less than or equal to the value reported to avoid coinsurance. If the inventory's established value on the last report date exceeds the amount stated in the report, the insured must coinsure the loss.

Often the reported value does not include items such as incoming freight, the cost of handling and tagging merchandise after its receipt, and trade discounts. These items should be included when they are identifiable in the insured's accounting records. The adjuster must ascertain whether the value that he or she calculated, as of the date of the last received report, is determined on the same basis as the value that the insured used in making the report. The calculation of value for claim purposes must be made on the same basis.

EXHIBIT 10-4

Procedure for Determining Inventory Values for Last Report Date

Date of Loss 10/1
Demonstration of Value Calculation for Last Reported Date
Under Reporting Form Policy

Last report of value, for 7/1	$173,000	
Last physical inventory as of 1/1		$160,000
Add net purchases—1/1 to 7/1		70,000
Available for sale		$230,000
Deduct net sales, at cost, same period		60,000
Indicated inventory 7/1		$170,000

Variation
Reverse Book Inventory Calculation

Complete physical inventory for 10/1 (Date of Loss)	$150,000
Deduct net purchases 10/1 back to 7/1	8,000
	$142,000
Add net sales, at cost, same period	28,000
Indicated value as of 7/1	$170,000

Both methods indicate that the insured fully reported values for the last report date, 7/1. The reported amount, $173,000, exceeds the actual amount.

In calculating a book inventory figure, an adjuster must enter sales at *cost*, not at *selling price*. In some cases involving a claim under reporting form coverage, insureds have calculated value on hand on the date of each value report by taking the value figure from the previous report, adding purchases at cost, and subtracting sales at *selling price*. Because their policy had been in effect for several months, these insureds had been understating their values by an increasing amount with each report and would soon have been reporting no value at all had their mistake not been discovered.

Reporting forms might also cover furniture, fixtures, machines, and other personal property (even though their primary purpose is to cover stocks of merchandise). The reporting form is used to insure stock that might vary in total value each month. The insured is required to submit regular reports of values. The balance of non-stock items of personal property does not usually change much from month to month. Thus, the insured might overlook additions to personal property other than stock. The adjusters must carefully evaluate the non-stock portion of the values because new equipment purchased in the past few years might have been omitted from the monthly reports of values.

Value Reporting Form Examples

Exhibits 10-5 through 10-9 show solutions to various problems arising under claims involving reporting form coverage, with and without specific insurance, in which values were either properly reported or underreported. In these illustrations, assume under the reporting form that (1) the limit indicated is either the original provisional amount of insurance or the amount of the last report of value received by the insurer before the date of loss and (2) the insured is not delinquent in reporting.

EXHIBIT 10-5

Proper Reporting—No Specific Insurance

Bad Times Mercantile Co., Inc.
Date of Loss 10/1

Coverage: No specific insurance
$175,000—Stock reporting form limit (provisional)

Last report of value, for 7/31, new limit	$173,000
Actual value, 7/31	170,000
Agreed loss	26,000
Insured recovers entire loss subject to a deductible	$26,000

EXHIBIT 10-6

Proper Reporting—Specific Insurance Applicable

Bad Times Mercantile Co., Inc.
Date of Loss 10/1

Coverage: $25,000 —Specific insurance on stock, 80% coinsurance
$175,000 —Reporting form limit

Last report of value, for 7/31, to reporting form insurer

Total value, new limit	$173,000
Specific insurance	25,000
Actual value, 7/31	170,000
Actual value, 10/1	180,000
Agreed loss	26,000

Specific insurance pays:

$$\frac{\$25{,}000}{(80\% \times \$180{,}000)} \times \$26{,}000 \qquad \$\ 4{,}514$$

Reporting form insurance pays balance of loss	21,486
Insured collects entire loss subject to deductibles	$ 26,000

EXHIBIT 10-7

Values Underreported—No Specific Insurance

Bad Times Mercantile Co., Inc.
Date of Loss 10/1

Coverage: No specific insurance
$200,000—Reporting form limit

Last report of value, for 7/31	$150,000
Actual value, 7/31	170,000
Agreed loss	26,000
Deductible	250

Insurance pays:

$$\frac{\$150,000}{\$170,000} \times \$26,000 = \$\ 22,941$$

	−250	deductible
	$ 22,691	
Insured shares loss	$3,059	
	+250	deductible
	$ 3,309	

EXHIBIT 10-8

Values Properly Reported—Existing Specific Insurance Not Reported

Bad Times Mercantile Co., Inc.
Date of Loss 10/1

Coverage: $25,000 —Specific insurance on stock, 80% coinsurance
$175,000 —Reporting form limit

Last report of values, for 7/31, no report of specific insurance	$173,000
Actual value, 7/31	170,000
Actual value, 10/1	180,000
Agreed loss	26,000

Although not reported, the existence of specific insurance is developed.

Specific insurance pays, as in Exhibit 10-6	$ 4,514
Reporting form insurer pays	21,486
Insured collects entire loss subject to deductibles	$ 26,000

EXHIBIT 10-9

Values Underreported—Specific Insurance Applicable

Bad Times Mercantile Co., Inc.
Date of Loss 10/1

Coverage: $25,000 —Specific insurance on stock, 80% coinsurance
$175,000 —Reporting form limit

Last report of value, for 7/31	$150,000
Actual value, 7/31	170,000
Actual value, 10/1	180,000
Agreed loss	26,000
Specific insurance pays, as in Exhibit 10-6	$ 4,514

Reporting form insurer pays:

$\frac{\$150,000}{\$170,000} \times \$21,486$	18,958
Insured collects less the deductible	$ 23,472
Insured shares loss	$ 2,528

LOSS ADJUSTMENT

Adjusters should prepare a file and follow standard procedures for all large merchandise losses. Percentage damage settlements frequently arise with merchandise losses, and considerable negotiation might be required. Small losses do not require such elaborate procedures.

Preparation of File for Adjustment

To build an acceptable and reliable file, the adjuster must prepare to do everything in an orderly and complete manner. An adjuster should use a checklist, preferably a written one, beginning with the first visit to the insured's premises. Such a checklist includes at least the following steps, not necessarily in order of importance:

1. Introduce and establish a satisfactory relationship with the insured. Gain an understanding of how the insured business operates.
2. Inspect the entire premises, including merchandise that is not involved.
3. Decide whether to use a salvor. If a salvor is to be used, the insured should be told because the salvor will probably arrive while the adjuster is not present.
4. Take photographs.

5. Inquire about the existence and availability of books and records and other insurance. Explain to the insured how he or she will have to document his or her loss through the use of books and records.
6. Identify the insured's independent accounting firm or bookkeeping firm. Obtain authorization from the insured so that the accounting firm can release financial information.
7. Discuss with the insured immediate steps to minimize damage, including board-up and general security.
8. Obtain the insured's explanation of the origin and cause of the loss. Inquire about whether a fire department investigator has already been to the scene.
9. Provide the insured with a general description of the normal procedure to follow during the adjustment process. Be specific as to what the insured must do and what the adjuster will do.
10. Be prepared to answer the insured's questions in a professional and cautious manner. Anticipate many questions.
11. Investigate thoroughly any possibilities of subrogation upon arrival at the scene of the loss. In many claims, the adjuster discovers that the damage resulted from equipment malfunction or from some third party's negligence. Evidence in proof of subrogation possibilities can disappear rapidly, especially if the person who furnished or installed equipment or the person whose negligent act caused the damage realizes the exposure to a possible subrogation action. The adjuster must determine by questioning both the insured and any possible investigative authority whether subrogation possibilities exist.

Large Losses

When damage to merchandise is severe and widespread but not total, the first visit by the adjuster involves inspecting the premises, taking photos, and guiding the insured, who has probably suffered his or her first major insured loss. On this visit, the adjuster must establish a rapport with the insured and develop mutual trust and confidence.

Preliminary Survey

The adjuster's inspection of the premises and the damaged merchandise should reveal whether a complete physical inventory is practical or even possible. Even when an appreciable amount of merchandise has been damaged beyond identification, a physical inventory of remaining merchandise can help provide an estimate of the out-of-sight loss (by subtracting the inventory of remaining merchandise from book inventory) as well as help provide information on pre-loss obsolescence or other loss of value.

The adjuster should use the first visit to gain a preliminary idea of the scope of damage and of the total value involved (perhaps a statement from the insured will suffice) and to assure the insured that he or she will be treated fairly and reasonably throughout the adjustment.

Discussions With the Insured

During the first visit with the insured, the adjuster must establish general procedures that will be followed during the entire adjustment process. The adjuster must notify the insured of the insured's duties in the event of loss as outlined in the policy. The adjuster should not, on the first visit, try to describe to the insured every aspect of an adjustment. The adjuster should also refrain from confusing the insured, who is probably already upset, with discussions of the coinsurance clause or other complex matters that can best be discussed during subsequent visits.

Also important during the adjuster's first visit is a thorough but courteous questioning of the insured about the conduct of the business before the loss. The insured knows more about his or her business than does the adjuster. By questioning the insured about marketing and merchandising methods, the adjuster can gain insight into how this particular business operates and can develop some ideas of how to prepare the claim file. Most insureds are eager to answer such questions and to demonstrate their own expertise regarding the business's conduct.

If a great deal of lightly damaged merchandise remains on the premises, during the first visit the adjuster should determine the insured's attitude about a fire sale after the adjustment is complete. The insured's answer to a question about a fire sale will guide the adjuster in deciding whether a salvor's services are necessary.

The adjuster should be prepared to answer questions that the insured is likely to ask concerning board-up and protection of the premises, expenses that must be incurred immediately to minimize damage, and possibly the use of a public adjuster. In larger cities, public adjusters often contact insureds after a serious fire, even before the insurer's adjuster arrives on the scene. An insured that has never heard of public adjusters might be confused. The insurer's adjuster should be prepared to politely answer questions about public adjusters' activities and reassure the insured that the claim will be properly adjusted.

Nonwaiver of Rights

During the first visit, the adjuster should exercise the insurer's right of access to all books and records of the insured's business. If an outside accountant possesses the records, the adjuster should get permission to contact the accountant directly to obtain the necessary information.

The adjuster should be cautious during this first visit not to make any commitments, such as the following, that waive policy conditions:

1. Giving permission to move merchandise before it has been inventoried
2. Approving expenses that later prove not to be covered under the policy
3. Approving expenses that, although possibly covered, might not be justified by the circumstances

4. Making a decision on the property adjustment that might be prejudicial to adjusting the business income claim or that might inadvertently increase the business income claim

The insured's first impression of the adjuster is important. The adjuster should reflect an attitude of professionalism and competence and should proceed with authority and with prudence.

Percentage Damage Settlements

Merchandise damaged but still salable at the retail level is almost certainly worth more to the insured than to anyone else. If the insured is considering retaining the merchandise for a fire sale, the merchandise would only have to be moved within the store and repriced. Such expense would be much less than the cost of having an outside purchaser pack the merchandise, move it to another location possibly hundreds of miles away, unpack it, classify it, and reprice it. As an example, if a salvor estimates the net salvage return on merchandise after being taken over by the insurer to be 40 percent of cost, then the merchandise is likely to be worth more, perhaps between 50 and 60 percent of cost, to the merchant who retains it.

If, in the merchant's opinion, the stock has lost *at least* 40 percent of its value, the merchant could sell it for no more than 60 percent of its value. To the insurer, the stock has lost *no more* than 60 percent of its value. The insurer could reimburse the merchant 100 percent and take the stock for salvage. Because salvage is expected to yield 40 percent of value, it has suffered *no more* than a 60 percent loss. Settlement should be made at a loss figure between 40 percent (the least that the merchant would accept) and 60 percent (the most that the insurer would pay).

If both parties have accurately assessed the situation, any amount between 40 percent and 60 percent would be fair and advantageous to *both* parties. For example, assume a settlement at 50 percent. The insured receives 50 percent from the insurer and retains the stock, which the insured still believes has 60 percent of its value. The insurer would be satisfied to pay 50 percent because the only alternative would be to pay the insured 100 percent and take the stock as salvage, for a net loss of 60 percent. Sixty percent is the maximum, or break point, that an insurer should pay if the merchandise is left with the insured. Beyond 60 percent, the insurer would be better off paying the insured the merchandise's full value and taking the salvage for itself.

Use of Salvors in Percentage Damage Settlements

After a salvor is hired and has initially inspected the damaged merchandise, the adjuster and salvor meet. The salvor's advice should guide, but not control, the adjuster. The salvor offers opinions on the degree of damage and possible net salvage return and advises the adjuster on what the break point is likely to be.

If a large percentage of the insured's stock has been lightly or moderately damaged, the salvor might divide the stock into lots. The salvor can then assign a possible damage allowance percentage to each lot. Seldom is an entire stock subject to the same degree or percentage of damage.

Brands and Labels Clause

Certain policy conditions are sometimes added by endorsement, which makes merchandise's ultimate salvage value much less than might normally be expected. A brands and labels clause requires the manufacturer's label to be removed from all merchandise taken in salvage by the insurer. When the label is popular or prestigious, its removal certainly reduces the salvage's value to the insurer. The insured who keeps merchandise on a percentage-of-damage settlement need not remove labels. This increases the attraction of such settlements.

Negotiation

The adjuster's negotiation skills are especially important when adjusting serious merchandise damage claims. The adjuster's negotiating ability determines whether a satisfactory adjustment is possible. When the discussion focuses on damage allowances, the adjuster should inform the insured that a negotiated settlement of the damage allowance will be considered. During the process of negotiating an adjustment, the adjuster should maintain a confident but flexible attitude, depending on the insured's attitude. If the insured is inflexible about a percentage of damage allowance, the adjuster has the right to take over the damaged merchandise for salvage disposal. With the break point in mind, the adjuster will at some point realize that paying the insured the full insured value and taking the salvage for the insurer's account is less expensive than paying the percentage that the insured demands.

In negotiating a settlement for partial damage to merchandise, the adjuster is dealing in an area in which the insured is much more knowledgeable. The subject under discussion is the insured's own merchandise and the insured's ability as a merchandiser. The adjuster, in consultation with a salvor, should understand the goods' income potential if sold at a fire sale and should use this knowledge to bring the adjustment to a conclusion that is fair to both the insurer and the insured.

Small Losses

The preceding discussion outlined procedures and considerations for adjusters handling large, complicated merchandise claims. Most merchandise claims, however, are relatively small and uncomplicated. For such routine losses, following all of the preceding procedures can be contrary to the insured's and the insurer's interests. Adjusters should not overlook smaller merchandise claims. The adjuster should establish to the best of his or her ability, without bringing in outside salvors or accountants, the accurate measure of the insured's actual loss, and then apply policy conditions to readily conclude the matter.

Adjusters should handle every merchandise loss with at least one visit to the insured's premises. On merchandise losses, the adjuster should not leave the determination of loss and damage to the insured. The adjuster should work with the insured to establish the facts of the loss and fair and accurate figures.

SUMMARY

Merchandise includes goods or stock that is manufactured, processed, or held by a merchant for sale. A merchant's stock is insured under commercial property insurance policies whether the merchant owns the property or holds it on consignment. Merchandise can be valued at actual cash value or replacement cost. To determine value, adjusters must review records from the insured's suppliers and adjust the cost for freight, handling, and trade discounts. Settling losses to merchandise requires adjusters to follow procedures and make considerations not present in other claims.

An adjuster is not expected to have a professional accountant's expertise but must be able to follow financial records. Adjusters can use the information in the income statement and the balance sheet to reconstruct the value of an inventory destroyed or otherwise lost out-of-sight.

Merchandise losses are the most frequent circumstances in which adjusters use professional salvors. Salvors perform a variety of services, including protection, removal, inventory, and sale of merchandise involved in a loss. Most important, salvors provide invaluable advice to adjusters on how a loss can be settled to everyone's satisfaction. Adjusters must be familiar with salvage operations and salvage contract provisions and must be scrupulous in accounting for salvage sale proceeds.

Reporting form policies sometimes apply to merchandise losses. These policies were designed so that merchants could adequately insure inventories that fluctuate widely in value. They require the merchant periodically to submit reports of value to the insurer. A merchant who complies with this requirement should have adequate insurance coverage for any merchandise loss. When merchants are late with their reports or underreport inventory values, the merchant will coinsure the loss.

When negotiating merchandise losses, adjusters should have a clear understanding of (1) when to pay the insured a percentage of the inventory value for settlement and leave the damaged goods with the merchant for a fire sale and (2) when the insurer would be better off to pay the merchant full value and to take the remaining stock for salvage sale. Adjusters should also develop judgment about the degree of effort appropriate to settling small losses versus settling large losses.

CHAPTER NOTES

1. Building and Personal Property Coverage Form CP 00 10 04 02, Copyright, Insurance Services Office, Inc., 2001.
2. Building and Personal Property Coverage Form CP 00 10 04 02, Copyright, Insurance Services Office, Inc., 2001.
3. Building and Personal Property Coverage Form CP 00 10 04 02, Copyright, Insurance Services Office, Inc., 2001.
4. Building and Personal Property Coverage Form CP 00 10 04 02, Copyright, Insurance Services Office, Inc., 2001.
5. Value Reporting Form CP 13 10 04 02, Copyright, Insurance Services Office, Inc., 2001.

Chapter 11

Direct Your Learning

Business Income Losses

After learning the subject matter of this chapter, you should be able to:

- Explain the purpose of business income coverages.
- Explain the basics of accounting for organizations and how losses affect accounting statements.
- Explain the insuring agreement of the Business Income (and Extra Expense) Coverage Form (BIC).
- Explain the types of, and the extent of, extra expense coverage under the BIC policy.
- Given a loss, calculate the loss of business income.
- Explain how to determine the period of restoration.
- Explain the additional, optional, and extended coverages under the BIC.
- Explain the application of the coinsurance requirement or optional coverages instead of coinsurance for the BIC policy.

OUTLINE

Develop Your Perspective

What are the main topics covered in the chapter?

The adjustment of a business income loss is one of the property loss adjuster's most complicated tasks. This chapter discusses the coverage provided by the Business Income (And Extra Expense) Coverage Form (BIC). It also provides the basic tools for understanding financial statements and how these are used in the loss adjustment.

Why is it important to know these topics?

For a small business income loss, a property loss adjuster should be able to verify the amount claimed by the insured on his or her own. For larger, more complex losses, a property loss adjuster usually works with a forensic accountant to verify the amount claimed. Regardless of the loss's size, a property loss adjuster should be familiar enough with basic accounting principles to ask the right questions about the loss.

How can you use this information?

When faced with a business income loss, use this information to guide your investigation. Let it serve as a foundation for questions to ask the insured and the accountants working on the loss.

Chapter 11

Business Income Losses

With losses involving physical damage to, or destruction of, tangible property, adjusters normally indemnify insureds for the physical damage or destruction according to the terms of the insurance policy. Once the insured receives payment, he or she generally can repair or replace the property in question. Organizations, however, can suffer losses that go beyond tangible property's damage or destruction. For example, the damage or destruction of tangible property might interfere with an organization's operations. That interference could cause loss of revenue or increased expenses, both of which are harmful to organizations. Such losses of revenue or increased expenses, are called **business income losses** or **business interruption losses**. Property insurance policies did not originally cover these types of losses. However, coverage for loss of business income and increased expenses has become common in commercial policy forms. Loss of business income and increased expenses are also called **time element losses** because they occur over time. Because business income losses are purely financial losses, evaluating these losses involves examining business documents and financial records rather than inspecting tangible property.

Business income losses (business interruption losses)
The purely financial loss associated with damage to property, usually loss of revenue and increased expenses.

Time element losses
Loss of income and increased expenses because of a property damage loss.

This chapter discusses basic accounting concepts, the effects of a business income loss, evaluation of the loss amount, and available coverage. Any business can experience lost income or increased expenses as a result of property damage or destruction. The Business Income (and Extra Expense) Coverage Form (BIC) applies to a wide variety of business income losses.

BASIC ACCOUNTING FOR ORGANIZATIONS

To evaluate business income losses, property loss adjusters must understand basic accounting principles and the financial records of organizations that suffer direct physical losses. Adjusters should be comfortable analyzing sales and expense figures as well as inventory records, production records, budgets, orders or contracts for products, and tax records. Simple losses can be efficiently evaluated with a basic spreadsheet program, but more complex losses may require the assistance of a **forensic accountant** who is experienced in evaluating business income losses and business records for insurance claim purposes. However, even if the adjuster will primarily rely on forensic accountants, he or she must understand fundamental concepts related to business income losses.

Forensic accountant
An expert at evaluating business income losses.

The basic elements of accounting are essentially the same for all organizations, regardless of whether the organization is a for-profit business, a non-profit organization, a corporation, a partnership, a sole proprietorship, a large manufacturer, or a small retailer. The two basic financial statements for any organization are (1) the balance sheet and (2) the income statement.

Balance Sheet

Assets
The property (tangible and intangible) owned by an entity.

Liabilities
The financial obligations, or debts, owed to another entity.

Owners' equity or net worth
The difference between assets and liabilities.

An organization's balance sheet answers the question, "Where do we stand right now?" The balance sheet is a simultaneous listing of everything that the organization owns and everything that it owes at a particular moment in time. What it owns are called **assets,** and what it owes are called **liabilities.** Exhibit 11-1 shows a simple balance sheet.

The difference between assets and liabilities in a for-profit business is called **owners' equity** or **net worth.** Owners' equity is shown on the liabilities side of the balance sheet because a business does not own its net worth. It "owes" its net worth to its owners. Owners' equity (net worth) is *always* the difference between assets and liabilities. Owners' equity is therefore calculated as follows:

Assets
– Liabilities
Owners' equity (net worth)

EXHIBIT 11-1

A Simple Balance Sheet

ABC, Inc., Balance Sheet
December 31, XXX2

Assets		**Liabilities**	
Cash	$ 75,000	Accounts Payable	$ 50,000
Accounts Receivable	100,000	Bank Loan	150,000
Inventory	325,000	Mortgage	800,000
Plant and Equipment	1,500,000	Total	$1,000,000
Real Estate	1,000,000		
		Owners' Equity	$2,000,000
Total	$3,000,000		$3,000,000

For example, the owners' equity for ABC, Inc., shown in Exhibit 11-1, is calculated as assets minus liabilities equals owner's equity ($3,000,000 – $1,000,000 = $2,000,000). Owners' equity is negative whenever liabilities exceed assets. A business with negative owners' equity may be eligible for bankruptcy. Because of how owners' equity is calculated, the balance sheet always balances.

The Income Statement

An organization's income statement answers the question, "How did we do during a particular time period?" such as a year, month, or quarter. Whereas the balance sheet lists the organization's assets and liabilities at a given moment, the income statement describes the organization's experience over time. Exhibit 11-2 shows an income statement for ABC, Inc., for the year ending 12/31/XXX2.

Almost all organizations prepare annual income statements. Some organizations have a fiscal year different from the January-December calendar year. Their fiscal year is some other 365-day period of their choice. For example, a university or college might have a fiscal year of August 1 to July 31 that corresponds to the academic year.

EXHIBIT 11-2

A Simple Income Statement

ABC, Inc., Income Statement
January 1,XXX2 to December 31, XXX2

Revenue From Gross Sales	$1,500,000
Cost of Goods Sold	700,000
Gross Profit	$ 800,000
Operating Expenses	
Employee Wages	$300,000
Depreciation	100,000
Interest	100,000
Utilities	50,000
Total Operating Expenses	$550,000
Net Income	$250,000

This chapter is primarily concerned with a loss's financial consequences that affect the income statement. The important elements of the income statement are revenue and expenses. An organization's operations generate revenue, usually from sales, and incur expenses in creating such revenue. Normally revenue should exceed expenses. However, it is not unusual to find a business that shows minimal net profit annually. This is common in business structures that are closely held by an individual or a small group. The business may pay the owner a salary and may also pay operating expenses such as those for a company car, business travel expenses, and business entertainment expenses. Strictly speaking, if expenses consistently exceeded revenue, the organization would eventually run out of money and be forced to close. However, a business owner may continue and even support an operation that gathers minimal net income in some cases.

Revenue

The money generated by an organization's operations is its revenue. For a for-profit business, revenue usually comes from sales of its products or services. For a nonprofit organization, revenue might come from dues, memberships, contributions, or sales. A business's revenue depends on the number of sales it makes and the prices it can charge, both of which are affected by competitive pressures.

Only money generated by the organization's *operations* is counted as revenue. Operations do not include the purchase or sale of major assets, investment activities, or other unrelated receipts and expenditures. So, for example, if a manufacturing business sold a piece of real estate, the money it received would not be part of its revenue. The proceeds from the real estate sale would appear on the manufacturer's balance sheet, but not on its income statement. The asset "real estate" would decrease from the previous balance sheet, and the asset "cash" would increase. Likewise, when a business settles an insurance claim, the money it receives from the insurer is not revenue. For accounting purposes, settlement of an insurance claim substitutes one asset, cash, for another asset, insurance claim receivable, on the business's balance sheet. This transaction is explained further below.

Expenses

All organizations incur expenses in generating their revenue. The nature of these expenses depends on the organization's nature. For purposes of evaluating business income claims, every operating expense can be categorized either as a general operating expense or as an expense directly related to sales. An **expense directly related to sales** is one that increases or decreases in direct relationship to sales, such as the cost of goods sold, commissions, or the cost of the materials used to ship goods that have been sold. If there are no sales, these types of expenses are not incurred. A **general operating expense** is one that is necessary to run the business but bears no direct relationship to the volume of sales, such as a retail store's cost for heating or air conditioning. Whether sales are booming or nonexistent, the cost of heating or air conditioning is necessary each day. Understanding and recognizing this difference is important in evaluating coinsurance compliance and is useful in determining which expenses are likely to continue after a loss. These topics are discussed in greater detail later in this chapter.

Expense directly related to sales
An expense that increases or decreases in direct relationship to sales, such as cost of goods sold.

General operating expense
An expense that is necessary to run a business but bears no direct relationship to the volume of sales.

A key distinction among businesses is between those that sell services and those that sell goods. Professionals in service businesses, such as barbers, dry cleaners, insurance agents, physicians, and accountants, do not sell any significant tangible product. Thus, their businesses do not manufacture or purchase tangible goods for resale, and generally, their income statements do not show a specific cost of goods sold expense. But there are almost always some expenses directly related to sales even if they are not labeled as such (materials and supplies consumed, for example). Some businesses, such as auto repair shops, construction companies, and restaurants, sell significant goods in addition to services. These businesses incur some expense in acquiring the materials they resell. Other businesses, such as supermarkets, department stores, and manufacturers, are in business primarily to sell goods, and their income statements show a clear and substantial expense for cost of goods sold. These businesses have significant expenses for the cost to acquire or manufacture the goods that they sell.

Cost of Goods Sold

The cost of goods sold is an expense that deserves special note. Although the term "cost of goods sold" applies to any business, the type of business dictates the expenses that are included in it. In retail, the cost of goods sold is usually the business's cost to purchase its merchandise and shipping. In manufacturing, the cost of goods sold includes the cost of the materials to make the product, the labor involved, and the overhead to make the product. In a service business, the cost of goods sold is minimal because no physical product is being sold. Unlike most other operating expenses, the cost of goods sold corresponds directly to sales. Calculating cost of goods sold is an accounting method for appropriately recognizing as expense the cost of purchasing inventory. Inventory is an asset that appears on the balance sheet until it is sold. Directly showing the purchase of inventory as periodic lump sums to represent expense on the income statement would skew the income statement because the purchase of inventory and the resale of it are not perfectly timed. Businesses often stock up months in advance of a busy sales season and may not restock as their busy sales season nears an end. The cost of goods sold formula is a method of recognizing the expense of acquiring goods to sell and coordinating it directly with sales on the income statement. For this reason, the cost of goods sold expense that appears on the income statement is calculated according to the following formula:

Beginning inventory
+ Additions to inventory
= Amount that could have been sold
− Ending inventory
= Cost of goods sold

If there are no sales, the ending inventory is equal to the sum of the beginning inventory plus all additions to inventory. Notice that under this formula there can only be a cost of goods sold if there has been a sale that lowers the ending inventory from the amount that could have been sold. Once an item of inventory is sold, its cost appears as an expense on the income statement by operation of the cost of goods sold formula.

Some small or simple businesses may list merchandise purchased as a general operating expense even though doing so is not strictly in keeping with generally accepted accounting principles. If such a listing is found, the adjuster must account for the cost of goods sold according to the above formula to properly evaluate the loss.

The adjuster should pay close attention to the inventory numbers in the cost of goods sold formula. The most likely sources of error in computing cost of goods sold are the beginning and ending inventory figures. Valuing an inventory in which goods have been added and withdrawn at various times and at various prices is complex. Accounting rules recognize several valid methods for valuing inventories under these circumstances. These methods are beyond the scope of this text, but adjusters must be sure that the same method was used to evaluate the beginning inventory and the ending inventory.

Gross profit
The difference between revenue and cost of goods sold.

The difference between a business's revenue and its cost of goods sold is its **gross profit**. The income statement in Exhibit 11-2 shows gross sales of $1,500,000, gross profit of $800,000, and net income of $250,000. Although the cost of goods sold is an expense, it is separated from the other expenses. This placement on the income statement of the cost of goods sold expense to arrive at the gross profit is sometimes referred to as the trading section of the income statement. Any item deducted from revenue to arrive at gross profit is said to be included in the trading section. This section has a relationship to expenses that is sometimes referred to as being placed "above the line" to arrive at a gross earnings value in computing a business income loss. (See Exhibit 11-2.) This arrangement easily shows gross profit and is the starting point for the evaluation of continuing expenses and coinsurance.

Gross margin
Gross profit expressed as a percentage of gross sales.

Mark-up
Gross profit expressed as a percentage of cost of goods sold.

From gross profit, a business must cover all other operating expenses and try to earn net income. Gross profit expressed as a percentage of gross sales is sometimes called the **gross margin** ($800,000 ÷ $1,500,000 = 53%). Similarly, the gross profit expressed as a percentage of the cost of goods sold is sometimes called **mark-up** ($800,000 ÷ $700,000 = 114%). It could be said that the goods purchased by ABC, Inc., at wholesale are marked-up 114 percent for a retail price. It could also be said that 53 cents of every retail sales dollar is gross profit. Note, however, that the relationship between mark-up as calculated above and the actual percentage that a business marks-up its merchandise is not exact because the income statement figures reflect discounts, returns, allowances, and similar items.

Similar to the treatment of revenues, not all money spent by a business is counted as operating expenses. Expenses must be incurred in the business's *ordinary operations* to be recorded as operating expenses. For example, if a manufacturing business bought a piece of real estate, the money spent on the purchase would not be an expense item on the manufacturer's income statement. The purchase would appear only on the manufacturer's balance sheet, as a reduction of one asset, cash, and an increase in another asset, real estate. Exhibit 11-3 shows the effect on ABC's balance sheet of obtaining an additional mortgage to purchase a piece of real estate for $1 million (compare Exhibit 11-3 to Exhibit 11-1).

These large purchases of land, buildings, or equipment are called capital expenditures. These capital expenditures appear on the balance sheet but do not appear as one-time lump sums on the income statement. Although capital expenditures may seem to be simply very large operating expenses, showing

EXHIBIT 11-3

Effect of a $1 Million Mortgage Financed Real Estate Purchase on the Balance Sheet

ABC, Inc., Balance Sheet

After Receiving Mortgage but Before Real Estate Purchase

Assets		**Liabilities**	
Cash	$1,075,000	Accounts Payable	$ 50,000
Accounts Receivable	100,000	Bank Loan	150,000
Inventory	325,000	Mortgage	1,800,000
Plant and Equipment	1,500,000	Total	$2,000,000
Real Estate	1,000,000		
		Owners' Equity	$2,000,000
	$4,000,000		$4,000,000

ABC, Inc., Balance Sheet

After Real Estate Purchase

Assets		**Liabilities**	
Cash	$ 75,000	Accounts Payable	$ 50,000
Accounts Receivable	100,000	Bank Loan	150,000
Inventory	325,000	Mortgage	1,800,000
Plant and Equipment	1,500,000	Total	$2,000,000
Real Estate	2,000,000		
		Owners' Equity	$2,000,000
	$4,000,000		$4,000,000

such large expenditures as a one-time lump sum expense on an income statement would skew the income statement. Capital investments and expenditures are not operations. For this reason, capital expenditures appear on the income statement gradually over time, normally as a depreciation expense. A **depreciation expense** spreads out the expense of a large purchase over time and may be calculated based on the item's life expectancy or, more arbitrarily for accounting convenience, according to generally accepted accounting principles (GAAP). Depreciation is a common operating expense. As an operating expense, depreciation also lowers the business's net income for tax purposes. The question of whether depreciation expenses continue after a loss depends on the nature of the depreciated item, method of depreciation, extent of damage to the item being depreciated, and the facts of the particular loss. This issue is fact-sensitive and is often hotly debated.

Depreciation expense
An accounting method that spreads out the expense of a purchase over the life expectancy of the item.

Net Income

Net income
The difference between all operating revenue and all operating expenses.

The difference between all operating revenue and all operating expenses is called **net income**. Net income is often expressed as the following formula:

All operating revenue
– All operating expenses
= Net income

Therefore, in Exhibit 11-2, ABC's net income was computed as gross profit less total operating expenses ($800,000 – $550,000 = $250,000), which is all revenue less all expenses. The same result can be reached using the figures from Exhibit 11-2 and the above formula. $1,500,000 – $700,000 – $550,000 = $250,000. Net income is colloquially known as the "bottom line" because net income appears as the bottom item in a listing of revenue and expenses.

Net income can be negative whenever expenses exceed revenue. Negative net income is known as a net loss. Positive net income for a for-profit business is often called net profit. The ability to earn net income is essential to a business's continuation. Anything that decreases revenue or increases expenses threatens a business's profit and its future.

For nonprofit organizations, the difference between revenue and expenses might be called by a different name, such as "contribution to surplus" or "excess of revenue over expenses." Nevertheless, just like for-profit businesses, nonprofit organizations must have revenue greater than expenses.

Net income is the most precise term to use for the difference between all revenue and all expenses. The adjuster should be careful not to confuse net income (all operating revenue less all operating expenses) with gross profit (all operating revenue less cost of goods sold). This chapter uses net income to mean the difference between all revenue and all expenses for all organizations, whether for-profit or not-for-profit.

WHAT HAPPENS TO AN ORGANIZATION AFTER A LOSS?

All losses are troublesome, but some are so disruptive that they affect revenues, expenses, and net income. Therefore, organizations' risk managers recognize that insurance for direct physical losses alone might not be sufficient. Business income losses can threaten an organization's well-being as much as, or more than, direct physical losses. Adjusters who handle claims for business income losses must evaluate direct physical losses' effect on organizations' revenue, expenses, and net income.

Effects of Property Losses on the Balance Sheet

Direct damage to, or destruction of, physical property is the subject of most property insurance claims. For an organization, such losses affect the assets on the balance sheet.

An organization's typical assets include cash, inventory, machinery and equipment, and real estate and improvements. These are the items affected by insurance claims for direct losses. For example, suppose that an electronics merchant had $100,000 of electronic equipment stolen by burglars. Before the loss, the assets on the merchant's balance sheet included, "Inventory – $100,000." Immediately after the theft, the merchant's balance sheet would have to be adjusted to show "Inventory – $0," but it would include a new asset, "Insurance claim receivable – $100,000." Amounts that other persons or organizations owe to the merchant are *assets* to the merchant, including any amount that the merchant's insurer owes the merchant for a claim (this example ignores any deductible or possible problems with limits). After the claim is paid, the merchant's balance sheet would show "Insurance claim receivable – $0," but "cash" would increase by $100,000. Exhibit 11-4 shows these transactions.

An insured loss to a building would be accounted for in a similar way. Ignoring any possible coverage problems or limitations, insurance claims convert other types of assets on the balance sheet into cash. Thus, typical insurance claims for direct physical losses affect only an organization's balance sheet. However, physical damage or destruction of property can affect an organization's income statement if it disrupts the organization sufficiently to cause a decrease in revenue, an increase in expenses, or both. An adjuster can evaluate business income losses only by examining an organization's financial records.

Effects of Property Losses on the Income Statement

Because net income is the difference between revenue and expenses, either lower revenue or increased expenses can reduce net income. For example, when revenue goes down, most operating expenses do not automatically adjust downward in proportion, so net income is reduced. Likewise, after a property loss, a business might incur normal operating expenses at a higher rate that will lower net income or may incur expenses other than *normal* operating expenses just to continue operations.

Loss of net income would threaten any organization's survival. Insurance for business income loss responds to this exposure by covering an organization's loss of net income and continuing expenses during an interruption of operations. Business income insurance is meant to keep the organization in the same financial position as it would have been in had no loss occurred.

Effect of a Loss on Revenue

A direct physical loss will reduce revenue if it disrupts sales. Many types of direct physical losses can reduce sales, including loss of inventory, destruction of the organization's manufacturing plant, and destruction of its operating premises. The duration of any disruption of sales depends on how long it takes to repair or rebuild the physical damage and the extent to which customers have transferred their loyalties elsewhere during the repairs or rebuilding. An organization can continue to experience loss of income until (1) it has repaired any physical damage *and* (2) it has regained its old customers.

EXHIBIT 11-4

Loss Settlement for Theft of Merchandise

Loss Settlement for $100,000 Theft of Merchandise

Before Loss

Assets		Liabilities	
Cash	$ 50,000	Accounts Payable	$ 75,000
Accounts Receivable	50,000	Bank Loan	50,000
Inventory	100,000	Mortgage	200,000
Building	500,000	Total	$325,000
		Owners' Equity	$ 375,000
	$700,000		$700,000

Immediately After Loss

Assets		Liabilities	
Cash	$ 50,000	Accounts Payable	$ 75,000
Accounts Receivable	50,000	Bank Loan	50,000
Inventory	0	Mortgage	200,000
Insurance Claim Receivable	100,000	Total	$325,000
Building	500,000		
		Owners' Equity	$375,000
	$700,000		$700,000

Immediately After Claim Settlement

Assets		Liabilities	
Cash	$150,000	Accounts Payable	$ 75,000
Accounts Receivable	50,000	Bank Loan	50,000
Inventory	0	Mortgage	200,000
Insurance Claim Receivable	0	Total	$325,000
Building	500,000		
		Owners' Equity	$ 375,000
	$700,000		$700,000

After a loss, sales typically decrease or stop for a period of time, depending on the extent of damage and type of business. Some businesses cannot operate while repairs to damaged property are made, so sales will stop completely after the loss and resume completely after repairs are complete. Other businesses may be able to resume limited operations while repairs are being made and may make some limited amount of sales, which is referred to as partial sales.

Calculating loss of revenue is simple when a business's sales are level and do not fluctuate. However, most businesses are dynamic. Product lines come and go, as do competitors. Some businesses have seasonal fluctuation, some have annual fluctuation, and some have monthly fluctuation. Most businesses also show some overall trend of rising or falling sales in addition to their regular fluctuations. These fluctuations and trends in sales are easily observed by analysis of gross sales over a period of days, weeks, months, or years. An adjuster with basic spreadsheet proficiency can evaluate the fluctuations and trends, or the adjuster may choose to hire a forensic accountant to assist in the evaluation of gross sales trends and projections.

Effect of a Loss on Expenses

Direct physical losses can affect expenses in various ways. A business's normal operating expenses will either (1) stop, (2) continue at a decreased rate, (3) continue at the same rate, or (4) continue at a higher rate during the period of restoration. The normal operating expenses that continue during the period of restoration are covered at the rate at which they are incurred (subject to policy limits and terms) during the period of restoration as **continuing expenses.** Additionally, the business may have **extra expenses** that are an increase over the *normal* operating expenses to continue business operations during the period of restoration. For example, a business that is burned out of a building it owns may rent other space temporarily while the fire-damaged building is being repaired. Hospitals may not be able to relocate their patients while a loss is repaired. Risk managers for such organizations must plan to continue operations after a loss or disaster, even at greatly increased expense. However, extra expenses are covered only if the organization has purchased a policy with extra expense coverage.

Continuing expenses
Those operating expenses that continue during the period of restoration.

Extra expenses
The increase over the normal operating expenses incurred to continue business operations.

Adjuster Tip

Rental costs for premises may or may not continue after the loss. Check the terms of the lease for an abatement clause. Many leases allow for the abatement of rent following specified losses that damage a certain percentage of the premises.[1]

Some businesses are unable or unwilling to remain in operation after a loss. However, a business that shuts down temporarily is unlikely to eliminate its expenses completely, especially if the shutdown is expected to be brief. A business that expects to reopen soon is unlikely to lay off its workforce, because the cost of hiring and training new employees would exceed any savings from a layoff. Even a business that expects a prolonged shutdown usually retains its key employees on its payroll and incurs some amount of other expenses, such as those for utilities, professional services, and insurance.

Some expenses like the cost of goods sold and commissions are directly related to sales. Accordingly, these expenses will stop or continue at a rate directly related to sales. Expenses directly related to sales are not counted as continuing expenses. The cost of goods sold expense and expenses directly related to sales are sometimes referred to as "uninsurables" because there is no need for business income insurance to cover them. By their nature, these kinds of expenses cannot continue unless there is a sale, and if there is a sale, it pays for these kinds of expenses, so they cannot be claimed as part of the loss. The gross revenue from partial sales will pay for the cost of the uninsurable expenses incurred. Policy language addressing such uninsurable expenses is discussed later in this chapter.

The adjuster need only consider other normal operating expenses when evaluating the continuing expenses that are part of a business income claim. The adjuster must also be aware that an insured may present a claim for continuing expenses that actually includes items of extra expense, contents damage, building damage, or other items that are generally not expenses covered under the standard BIC form but may be covered elsewhere.

There is no definitive list of expenses that will or will not continue. Therefore, the adjuster must understand the insured's business to determine if an expense will likely continue or not. The adjuster will often have to examine the insured's business records to make this distinction. For example, a contract for advertising services may continue even though the business is closed. The only way to know is to examine the contract. Identifying expense fluctuations can often be done from a simple review of business records, but adjusters facing a large or complex loss may hire a forensic accountant. Exhibit 11-5 is an example of the components of a business income loss that was used in the adjustment of losses resulting from the Cerro Grande fire in New Mexico.

An adjuster must keep in mind that the replacement of damaged inventory (ending inventory) is covered under Business and Personal Property Coverage Form (BPP), not under the BIC form.

Adjuster Tip

Suppose that the insured purchases a large amount of office supplies to replace those destroyed in a fire. The expense of this purchase would be recorded, and upon examination of the records, this expense proves to be $5,000 more than normal. If the property insurer paid for these supplies as business personal property, then payment of the $5,000 as an extra expense would result in a duplicate payment to the insured. On large losses, in which this circumstance might occur, have the insured set up a special account designated for loss-related expenses. And if the property insurer is another company, check with it to see what was included in its settlement.[2]

EXHIBIT 11-5

Components of a Business Interruption Loss

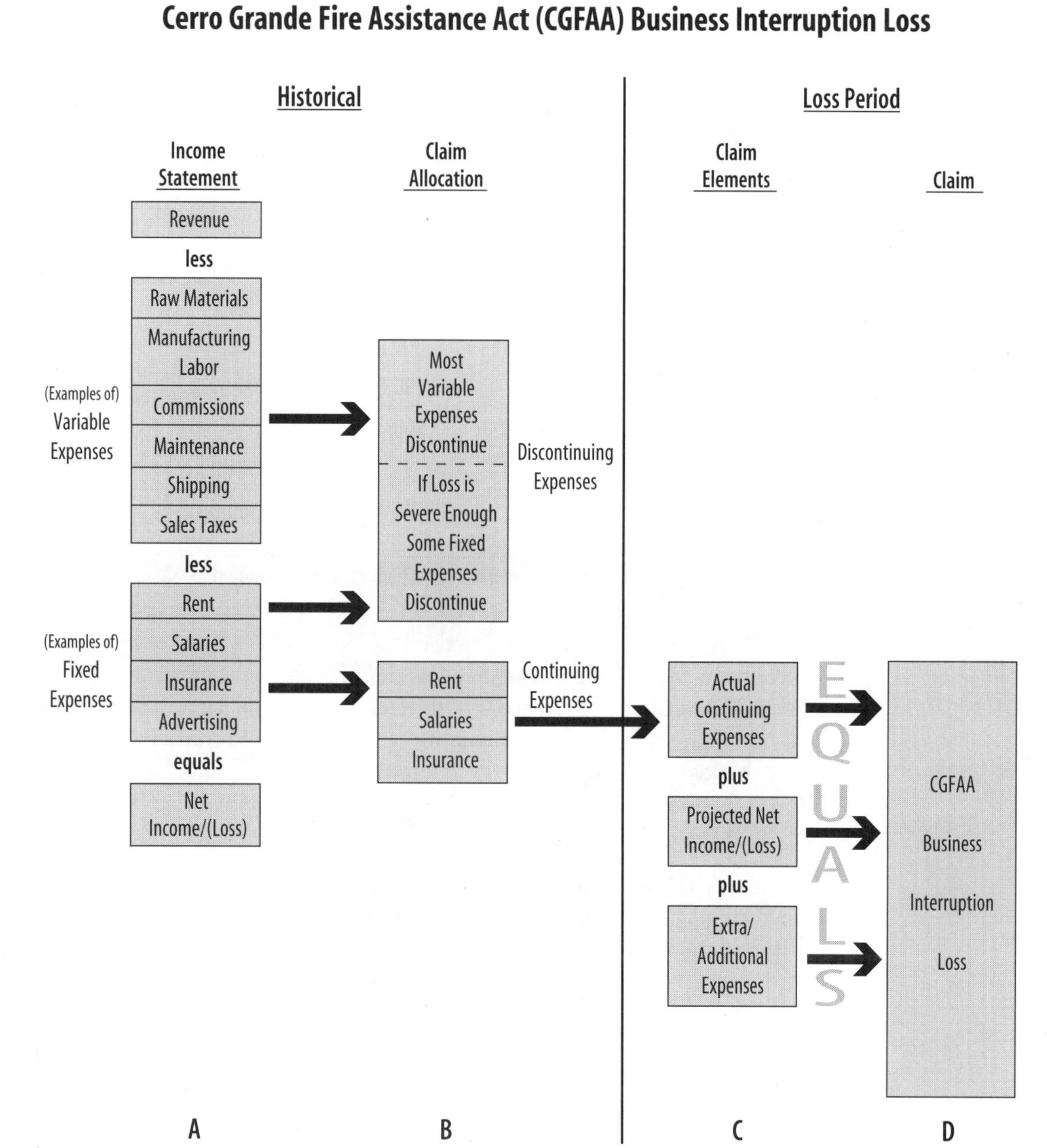

World Wide Web: http://www.fema.gov/pdf/cerrogrande/handbook022801.pdf (15 July 2003).

Possible Business Income Losses

The amount of a business income loss can be calculated using two different methods. First, start with gross revenues lost and subtract noncontinuing expenses. Alternatively, adding the continuing expenses plus the operating profit will equal the business income loss. Exhibit 11-6 provides examples of business income loss calculations for several companies.

EXHIBIT 11-6

Possible Business Income Losses

	Company A	Company B	Company C
Gross Revenues Lost	$3,100,000	$2,100,000	$ 300,000
Noncontinuing Expenses	600,000	600,000	600,000
Continuing Expenses	2,000,000	2,000,000	2,000,000
Operating Profit	500,000	0	0
Operating Loss	0	(500,000)	(2,300,000)
Business Income Pays	$2,500,000	$1,500,000	Nothing

R. Bryan Tilden, 2002 Commercial Property Policy Changes seminar handout, p. 60.

Based on information from the exhibit, Company A's gross revenue would have been $3,100,000 during the loss period. The noncontinuing expenses of $600,000 would be subtracted from the gross revenue for a net income of $2,500,000, which is the business income loss. An alternative way to calculate the loss would be to use the operating profit of $500,000 and add to that the continuing expense of $2,000,000 for a business income (BI) loss of $2,500,000.

Company B has no operating profit during the loss period. Instead, it has an operating loss of $500,000. Any interruption in its business because of a loss will only increase the amount of its operating loss. Gross revenue $2,100,000 minus noncontinuing expenses results in a BI loss of $1,500,000. The same result is obtained by taking the continuing expense of $2,000,000 and subtracting the $500,000 operating loss. This occurs because the insured can recover continuing operating expenses only to the extent that they are earned by the business's operations. If the business is losing money, it is not fully earning the funds to cover its expenses.

Company C is a start-up company. It is estimated that the gross revenue it would have earned during the loss period is $300,000. If the noncontinuing expenses of $600,000 are subtracted from the gross revenue of $300,000, the result is a net loss of $300,000, so there is no recovery. If the net income loss of $300,000 is added to the continuing expenses of $2,000,000, the operating loss is $2,300,000, so there is no business income recovery.

INSURANCE FOR LOSS OF BUSINESS INCOME AND EXTRA EXPENSE

The Insurance Services Office's Business Income Coverage (and Extra Expense) Form (BIC), CP 00 30 04 02, applies to a wide variety of organizations and to the business income losses that these organizations might suffer. ISO also offers a BIC without extra expense coverage and a form that covers extra expense only. Therefore, adjusters handling these losses must determine which coverage an insured has and must understand which losses are covered by each policy form.

Coverages

The policy statements of coverage for business income and extra expense are brief and relatively simple, but they must be read carefully. Adjusters handling losses under these coverages should understand both the policy language and basic accounting terminology.

Business Income

The insuring agreement of the BIC policy states the following:

> We will pay for the actual loss of Business Income you sustain due to the necessary "suspension" of your "operations" during the "period of restoration." The "suspension" must be caused by direct physical loss of or damage to property at premises which are described in the Declarations and for which a Business Income Limit of Insurance is shown in the Declarations. The loss or damage must be caused by or result from a Covered Cause of Loss. With respect to loss of or damage to personal property in the open or personal property in a vehicle, the described premises include the area within 100 feet of the site at which the described premises are located.[3]

The BIC form defines business income as follows:

> a. Net Income (Net Profit or Loss before income taxes) that would have been earned or incurred; and
>
> b. Continuing normal operating expenses incurred, including payroll.[4]

The references to operations, net income, and normal operating expenses clarify that this coverage is designed to protect insureds from losses resulting from interruption of normal operations. Business income losses are determined by examining operating income and operating expenses. Receipts and expenditures that do not appear on an organization's income statement would not be considered in the analysis of loss of business income.

The operation of the coverage and evaluation of claims is conceptually simple:

- The net income that would have been earned is the gross revenue that would have been earned minus the expenses that would have been incurred to do so had no loss occurred.

- Gross revenue that the business would have earned if no loss had occurred is projected from analysis of the business records of the pre-loss days, weeks, months, or years.
- Expenses that would have been incurred if no loss had occurred are projected from an analysis of the business records of pre-loss days, weeks, months, or years.
- The general operating expenses that continue while the business is shut down are projected or documented as they are incurred and are paid as the second part of the business income coverage provided.

Extra expenses that a business incurs to continue operations while repairs are underway are addressed by the policy separately under extra expense coverage as discussed in the next section of the chapter.

Extra Expenses

The most important additional coverage in the BIC policy is for extra expense. The BIC provides the following:

> Extra Expense means necessary expenses you incur during the "period of restoration" that you would not have incurred if there had been no direct physical loss or damage to property caused by or resulting from a Covered Cause of Loss.[5]

The coverage for extra expense is stated in three subsections. The first extra expense coverage is for continuing operations:

> We will pay Extra Expense (other than the expense to repair or replace property) to:
>
> (1) Avoid or minimize the suspension of business and to continue operations at the described premises or at replacement premises or temporary locations, including relocation expenses and costs to equip and operate the replacement location or temporary location.[6]

Subsection (1) above provides coverage if the insured tries to continue operations after a loss, but the expenses to do so are greater than those that the insured would have incurred through normal business operations. Expenses covered under this section would include, for example, the cost to rent a temporary selling location to maintain sales levels.

The second extra expense coverage is for the cost to minimize the suspension of business operations:

> We will pay any Extra Expense. . .(2) minimize the "suspension" of business if you cannot continue "operations".[7]

Subsection (2) responds to situations in which the insured cannot continue operations but incurs above-normal expenses to get back into business. A good example of this would be if the insured incurred travel expenses for extra buying trips needed to secure goods for sale.

Extra expense coverage also provides the following:

> We will also pay any Extra Expense to repair or replace any property, but only to the extent it reduces the amount of loss that otherwise would have been payable under this Coverage Form.[8]

Normally, the insured is limited to a reasonable value (either actual cash value or replacement cost, as applicable) for the repair or replacement of property. Subsection (3) allows the insured to incur any extra expense to repair or replace property *to the extent that it reduces the amount of the business income loss* such as the cost of overtime labor to expedite the repair or replacement of a damaged building.

> **Adjuster Tip**
>
> Another situation in which duplicate payments may occur is the insured's use of its employees to clean and make repairs. Usually these costs are paid for by the property damage insurers and would not be covered expenses on the business income claim.[9]

Subsection (3) may also apply to items of property that are not insured under the property coverages such as temporary repairs to the common area of a business condo to allow access to the insured's business.

Extra expense must reduce the amount of the suspension of business or eliminate the need for any suspension of business under Subsection (1) or reduce the amount of the suspension under Subsection (2), but it is payable under Subsection (3) only to the extent that it reduces the amount of loss that otherwise would have been payable under the coverage form. Only when dealing with the physical property's repair or replacement or records' restoration must the insured actually reduce the business income loss to at least the extent of the extra expense payment. Expenses that lessen the effect of the business income loss are fully recoverable under Subsection (1) and (2) even if the expenses exceed the reduction of business income loss.

Necessary Suspension of Operations

To recover a business income loss, the insured must show that an actual loss has been sustained or incurred as a direct result of a necessary suspension of operations, either partial or total, caused by direct physical damage to insured property. The BIC defines "operations" as "Your business activities occurring at the described premises. . . ."[10]

The manufacturing industry provides the best counter-example of a necessary suspension of operations. Manufacturing facilities typically have an annual scheduled shutdown of operations to perform maintenance on machinery and equipment. If an insured cause of loss resulted in damage to that machinery, the loss of use of the machinery during the shutdown would not be considered a necessary suspension of operations compensable by the BIC policy. In this case, because the insured had already scheduled a suspension of operations, the suspension was not made necessary *by the physical damage*. It was made necessary by the need for routine maintenance.

The requirement that a suspension be necessary is consistent with the insured's typical duty under property insurance policies to minimize loss. Insurance should not reimburse an unnecessary suspension of operations.

Covered Causes of Loss

The policy provides the following regarding the causes of loss:

> See applicable Causes of Loss Form as shown in the Declarations.[11]

The declarations page should show one of the causes of loss forms, Basic, Broad, or Special, applicable to the business income coverage. These are the same causes of loss forms used with the BPP.

The BIC form represents stand-alone coverage for loss of business income, just as the BPP represents stand-alone physical damage insurance. Neither form describes what perils are insured. A separate causes of loss form is used to specify whether coverage is to be on a named-perils basis or a special-form basis. This modular approach provides greater flexibility in designing coverages for a variety of risks. Although some type of property damage must occur for the loss of business income to be covered, the physical damage and loss of business income do not need to be covered for the same causes of loss. Although not common, different causes of loss forms can be used for physical damage and business income.

All of the causes of loss forms that might be attached to the BIC have special exclusions applicable to the BIC. These special exclusions are as follows:

- Loss caused directly or indirectly by a power failure or the failure of another utility service supplied to the described premises, regardless of cause, as long as the failure occurs outside of a covered building. If a covered cause of loss results from the failure of power or utility service, the loss resulting from a covered cause of loss will be covered.
- Loss caused by damaged or destroyed finished stock. Finished stock is defined in the BIC as stock that the insured has manufactured. Thus, this exclusion only applies to manufacturers. For manufacturers, the stock itself should be covered as direct physical damage. If a manufacturer suffers loss to its inventory of finished goods but not to its productive capacity, it may be able to work overtime to make up the lost inventory. This exclusion does not apply to extra expense.
- Loss caused by or resulting from damage to radio or television antennas (including satellite dishes) and their lead-in wiring, masts, or towers.
- Any *increase* of loss caused by or resulting from interference of strikers at the location where repairs or rebuilding is occurring, or caused by loss of

a contract, except to the extent that the loss of contract affects loss of business income during the period of restoration.

- Extra expense caused by or resulting from suspension, lapse, or cancellation of any license, lease, or contract, beyond the period of restoration.
- Any increase of loss caused by or resulting from delay in rebuilding, repairing, or replacing the property or resuming operations due to interference at the location of the rebuilding, repair, or replacement by strikers or other persons.
- Any other consequential loss.

Actual Loss

The term "actual loss sustained" is used to describe the extent of financial loss insured by the policy. The intent is to limit recovery to those losses that are real and direct, rather than speculative and remote. Losses must be real in the sense that not every property loss or interruption of operations results in loss of business income. For example, the owners of many small businesses are the chief salespersons. After a property loss, the owner might be occupied with the situation for a week or two, during which time no sales are made. Nevertheless, if the owner can make up sales after he or she returns to selling, it may turn out that no sales are actually lost. The capacity for make-up sales is common in service businesses and in some retail operations and must be considered carefully.

Difficulties might arise in the adjustment of business income losses concerning the degree of directness of the financial loss incurred by the insured. The last listed exclusion from a causes of loss form is for "Any other consequential loss." Business income losses are always consequential in relation to direct physical damage to property. The last listed exclusion simply eliminates consequential losses *other than* those described in the BIC form. One common other consequential loss is the long-term loss of customer loyalty or goodwill that could result from a business's extended shutdown.

The causes of loss forms also include an exclusion for a specific type of indirect loss, loss of contract. Direct physical damage can sometimes cause an insured to lose certain contracts. For example, an owner of a shopping mall might lose its tenant leases if the shopping mall is damaged by fire. After the shopping mall is repaired, the owner will continue to suffer loss because the leases terminated, allowing the tenants to depart. At this point, the losses are caused by the loss of contract, not by the physical damage. The causes of loss forms exclude both loss of business income and extra expense that occur after the period of restoration because of loss of contract.

Determining Loss of Business Income and Extra Expense

Loss of business income is the net income that would have been earned plus the continuing normal operating expenses. As stated previously, the coverage provided for loss of business income is conceptually simple. The net income loss is the gross revenue (or sales) that would have occurred minus the expenses that would have been incurred. These must be estimated from pre-loss business records allowing for overall trends in business and seasonal fluctuations. The continuing expenses are determined by a case-by-case analysis of which general operating expenses will continue and at what rate. Both net income and continuing expenses are limited by the time reasonably necessary to complete damaged property's repair or replacement. Extra expenses are also evaluated case-by-case if the insured's policy provides such coverage. Basic spreadsheet programs are used to create trend sheets and business income worksheets that are the tools used by adjusters to evaluate revenue and expenses. This chapter further discusses these tools in a following section.

The adjuster must evaluate the revenue and expenses so that the policy does for the business what it would have done for itself had no loss occurred; that is, normal operating expenses are paid and expected net income is received. Although this may not always be possible, given policy limits and other factors, it is the aim of the business income loss evaluation process. This evaluation will be difficult if the insured is in a dynamic business environment of growth, decline, new products, or new competitors. It should also be recognized that the loss settlement is based on the analysis, interpretation, and projection of historical business data. This process is not absolute or exact. The process requires communication and mutual compromise between the adjuster and the insured.

Loss of Business Income

The BIC form makes the following statement regarding loss determination:

> a. The amount of Business Income loss will be determined based on:
>
> (1) The Net Income of the business before the direct physical loss or damage occurred;
>
> (2) The likely Net Income of the business if no physical loss or damage had occurred, but not including any Net Income that would likely have been earned as a result of an increase in the volume of business due to favorable business conditions caused by the impact of the Covered Cause of Loss on customers or on other businesses;
>
> (3) The operating expenses, including payroll expenses, necessary to resume "operations" with the same quality of service that existed just before the direct physical loss or damage; and
>
> (4) Other relevant sources of information, including:
>
> (a) Your financial records and accounting procedures;
>
> (b) Bills, invoices and other vouchers; and
>
> (c) Deeds, liens or contracts.[12]

The above loss determination clause emphasizes that many factors can be considered in determining a business income loss. The qualification to the second listed item is included to avoid compensating insureds for loss of windfall business that would have existed only because of the covered loss. For example, an insured building supply company would expect windfall business following a hurricane. However, the BIC's intent is to place the insured in the same position as it would have been in had no loss occurred.

Normal operating expenses should be included in any determination of business income. The definition of business income clarifies that it intends to cover the insured's expected net income plus *normal* operating expenses that continue. In contrast, only extra expense insurance covers operating expenses above normal. For example, a fire-damaged business may rent storage trailers to hold inventory during reconstruction. The storage trailers' cost is not a normal operating expense. However, the storage trailers would be considered an extra expense.

Extra Expense Loss

Provision b. under Loss Determination in the BIC makes the following provision for extra expense:

> b. The amount of Extra Expense will be determined based on:
>
> (1) All expenses that exceed the normal operating expenses that would have been incurred by "operations" during the "period of restoration" if no direct physical loss or damage had occurred. We will deduct from the total of such expenses:
>
> (a) The salvage value that remains of any property bought for temporary use during the "period of restoration", once "operations" are resumed; and
>
> (b) Any Extra Expense that is paid for by other insurance, except for insurance that is written subject to the same plan, terms, conditions and provisions as this insurance; and
>
> (2) Necessary expenses that reduce the Business Income loss that otherwise would have been incurred.[13]

The evaluation of how much extra expense incurred by the insured is compensable by the BIC policy is a two-part process. Initially, the adjuster must determine if the expense is an extra expense, meaning that it exceeds the normal operating expenses that would have been incurred had no loss occurred. If it is not an extra expense, then the adjuster should determine whether it is a necessary expense that reduces the business income loss.

To determine whether the expense reduced the business income loss that would have been incurred had the additional money not been spent, the adjuster must understand the reasons why an expense is incurred. For example, if a damaged piece of machinery would take ten days to replace if shipped by truck, but it would take only two days if shipped by airfreight, the use of airfreight to expedite the repair of damaged machinery would reduce the loss of productive capacity from that machine, as shown below:

	Regular Freight	Airfreight	Difference
Freight in	$1,000	$1,500	$500
Income value of production per day ($500)			
Days saved by airfreight			8
Income value saved			$4,000
Difference between income saved and additional airfreight			$3,500

By spending $500 more on freight, the insured would be able to reduce the BIC loss by $3,500.

Evaluation of Revenue Trends

Trend sheets
Spreadsheets that show a business's historical gross revenue data in a series of days, weeks, months, quarters, or years.

Evaluation of revenue trends is essential in calculating a business income loss. **Trend sheets** are spreadsheets created by organizing a business's historical gross revenue data in a series of days, weeks, months, quarters, or years. The choice of what time period to use depends on the facts of the loss. For example, if a restaurant suffers a three-day loss that begins on Monday evening and ends on Wednesday evening, (ignoring for the moment, the seventy-two-hour deductible in the BIC form) a sequence of gross revenues on previous Monday to Wednesday evenings should give the most accurate picture of the loss period. This approach would certainly be more accurate than taking an average of all days because such an average would include weekend evenings that are typically higher in revenues. There may also be seasonal fluctuations to consider. A typical Monday to Wednesday evening for a beachside restaurant in the winter is likely to be lower in revenue than in the summer. The historical data that adjusters consider should reflect the loss period to achieve the most accurate projection of revenues.

Exhibit 11-7 shows a simple trend sheet for three years before the January 1, XXX3, date of loss for XYZ, Inc., a gift store that does its heaviest business during the last three months of the year.

The monthly revenue data is taken from the historical business records of XYZ, Inc. Simply arranging the data on a trend sheet provides much of the information about revenue trends. XYZ's busy season is clearly the last quarter of the year because the revenue is highest in October, November, and December and is otherwise flat. Comparing the annual figures from year to year shows steady growth of 5 percent from year to year.

$$\text{Percent Change} = \left[\left(\frac{693{,}000}{660{,}000}\right) - 1\right] \times 100$$

The same comparison applied month to month shows that the 5 percent growth is steady over the entire year. Exhibit 11-8 is a trend sheet with

EXHIBIT 11-7

Trend Sheet With Gross Revenue Data

XYZ, Inc. —Trend Sheet—Date of Loss 1/1/XXX3

	XXX0	XXX1	XXX2	XXX3
January	$ 50,000	$ 52,500	$ 55,125	
February	50,000	52,500	55,125	
March	50,000	52,500	55,125	
April	50,000	52,500	55,125	
May	50,000	52,500	55,125	
June	50,000	52,500	55,125	
July	50,000	52,500	55,125	
August	50,000	52,500	55,125	
September	50,000	52,500	55,125	
October	60,000	63,000	66,150	
November	70,000	73,500	77,175	
December	80,000	84,000	88,200	
Annual Gross Revenue	$660,000	$693,000	$727,650	

additional columns that show the annual percentage change from month to month. Adjusters often create spreadsheets with this type of detail to explain their evaluation to the insured.

If XYZ will be completely shut down from January 1, XXX3, until April 1, XXX3, the adjuster's first step in evaluating the business income loss is projecting the revenue for the loss period. The loss period is normally the time necessary to repair the physical damage or restore operations. The trend sheet analysis shows that revenue in January, February, and March of XXX3 would likely have been 5 percent higher than January, February, and March of XXX2 if no loss had occurred. XYZ would have earned $57,881 each month ($55,125 × 105% = $57,881) if no loss had occurred. The gross loss of revenue is projected to be $173,643 ($57,881 × 3 = $173,643).

The trend sheet analysis above is simplistic. Adjusters are cautioned to evaluate revenues carefully. Errors can occur easily in projecting revenue if the trend sheet analysis is not done properly and completely. Consider a claim for XYZ presented based on the previous three months of October, November, and December; or a flat monthly average based on the XXX2 annual figure; or an erroneous allegation by XYZ that it is growing at a rate of 14 percent based on a comparison of the last two full months of November and December.

EXHIBIT 11-8

Trend Sheet With Gross Revenue Data and Percentage of Change Over Time

XYZ, Inc.—Trend Sheet—Date of Loss 1/1/XXX3

	XXX0	XXX1	Percent Change	XXX2	Percent Change	XXX3
January	$ 50,000	$ 52,500	5%	$ 55,125	5%	
February	50,000	52,500	5	55,125	5	
March	50,000	52,500	5	55,125	5	
April	50,000	52,500	5	55,125	5	
May	50,000	52,500	5	55,125	5	
June	50,000	52,500	5	55,125	5	
July	50,000	52,500	5	55,125	5	
August	50,000	52,500	5	55,125	5	
September	50,000	52,500	5	55,125	5	
October	60,000	63,000	5	66,150	5	
November	70,000	73,500	5	77,175	5	
December	80,000	84,000	5	88,200	5	
Annual Gross Revenue	$660,000	$693,000	5%	$727,650	5%	

After the loss of gross revenue has been projected, the business's historical expenses must be analyzed to determine the net income and continuing expenses. Income statement worksheets are used to analyze expenses.

Evaluating Expenses

To project or estimate the expense for the BI loss, trend sheets should be created for the various expenses. If expenses are flat throughout the year, this exercise is relatively easy. As an example, if rental expense is $5,000 per month for twelve months, then it is easy to project that a three-month loss will be $15,000. But other expenses may vary each month. Utilities may be based on actual consumption. If the loss occurs in the summer and the doors and windows are open to facilitate repairs, the electric use may increase because of an increased demand on air conditioning. Other factors such as a rate increase can cause utility costs to change from one month to another. Projecting expenses is often quite a complicated process, and a thorough explanation of the process is beyond the scope of this text. Most adjusters rely on accountants to review the insured's books and records to make these projections. However, an adjuster should be able to ask specific questions as to what factors were considered when making the projections.

After the expenses have been projected, the adjuster can begin the loss adjustment. Two methods are commonly used by adjusters and accountants to determine the value of *net income plus continuing expenses* that is owed under the BIC form:

1. Net income plus continuing expense method
2. Gross profit less noncontinuing expense method

The best method for a particular loss depends on the size, complexity, and duration of the loss and related circumstances, but adjusters and accountants use any one or a combination of methods.

Net Income Plus Continuing Expense Method and Gross Profit Less Noncontinuing Expense Method

The net income plus continuing expense method most closely matches the policy language and is arguably the easiest method to reconcile with actual incurred expense figures once they are available. Exhibit 11-9 demonstrates both the net income plus continuing expense method and the gross profit less noncontinuing expense method. The adjuster must decide which expenses will continue and which will not. For the purposes of this illustration, assume that all expenses are evenly prorated throughout the year and that they did not increase over year XXX2. Wages, insurance, and interest will continue at 100 percent; depreciation will continue at 50 percent. Rent and expenses for utilities will not continue at all.

Exhibit 11-9 shows that the continuing expenses will amount to $68,725 and that the net income lost is $19,111. Note that 50 percent of the depreciation expense is continuing and that 50 percent is noncontinuing. Accordingly, the net income plus continuing expense loss amounts to $87,836. The gross profit less noncontinuing expense method also shows a loss amount of $87,836 ($104,186 – $16,350). Note that the $87,836 result is the same under both methods. However, legitimate and substantial deviations in final evaluation amounts are common. It is important to recognize that decimal rounding affects calculations and can be a factor when comparing manual calculations to more precise computer evaluations. Other methods of arriving at loss period expense amounts include turning the annual operating expense figures into daily figures (dividing by 365 days) and then multiplying by the number of days in the loss period. This, too, will create variations in final evaluation amounts.

Expenses may be paid daily, weekly, monthly, yearly, or at irregular intervals. However, note that the expenses are generally analyzed and negotiated from an annual figure. Determining which expenses will continue or discontinue and which methods to use in calculating loss period figures are key negotiating points in business income claims.

After XYZ, Inc.'s ninety-day loss period has passed, the insured may find that it did use some utilities or that not all wages continued as expected. The continuing expense figures can be easily adjusted to reflect actual incurred expenses. The process of reviewing actual incurred expenses against the projections done before the end of the loss period is called reconciliation. Reconciliation is almost always done on larger, more complex losses but may be mutually waived on smaller, simpler losses.

Reconciliation: Evaluation of Actual Incurred Continuing Expenses and Partial Sales

Reconciliation
The process of matching the net income and continuing expenses projections with the actual sales made and expenses incurred during the loss period.

Reconciliation is the process of matching the net income and continuing expense projections with the actual sales made and expenses incurred during the loss period. Often, a business maintains partial operations during the loss period. The less-than-normal sales are called partial sales. These partial sales are easily reconciled by deducting the gross amount of partial sales from the gross loss period sales projections before the application of the gross profit percentage or business income percentage described above. Consider the example of XYZ, Inc. Exhibit 11-9 shows a projected gross loss of revenue of $173,643. If XYZ, Inc. had been open for partial operations during the loss period and made partial sales of $20,000, the projected gross sales loss would be $153,643 ($173,643 – $20,000), as shown in Exhibit 11-10. The net income loss would be $7,110. Note that the cost of goods sold has changed to reflect the partial sales and that the net income lost has changed as well. Note also that the difference between the outcomes shown in Exhibit 11-9 and Exhibit 11-10 is $12,000, the amount of gross profit on $20,000 of sales. This occurs in this example because all of the expenses stayed the same in the two exhibits.

Because of disparity between when bills are paid as a matter of cash flow and when expenses are incurred for purposes of the income statement, adjusters or the accountants working for them might have to reconcile expenses. Business income insurance covers expenses as incurred on the income statement, not on the basis of bills paid.

For example, insurance premiums are often paid as a lump-sum amount at the beginning of the policy period. This payment does not result in an expense item on the income statement for the entire amount paid. Instead, insurance expense is recognized gradually throughout the year during the policy period. Therefore, under this payment scheme, it would not matter that the date for paying an annual insurance premium happened to fall within the period of the business income loss or outside of it. Insurance expense would be recognized as the pro rata amount of the annual premium represented by the period of shutdown. Real estate taxes are similarly paid as a lump sum but recognized gradually as an expense.

Other expenses might be incurred first and paid later, such as on a quarterly basis. For example, building maintenance expenses or professional fees, such

EXHIBIT 11-9

Income Statement Worksheet for XYZ, Inc., Showing Projected Lost Net Income Plus Expenses

Assumes that expenses did not increase over the prior year and that the expenses are prorated evenly throughout the year.

					Percent of Gross Sales
Revenue from Gross Sales	$173,643				100.0%
Cost of Goods Sold	69,458				40.0
Gross Profit	$104,185				60.0
Operating Expenses		**Continuing**	**Noncontinuing**	**Percent Continuing**	
Wages	$62,500	$ 62,500	—	100%	36.0
Rent	9,000	—	$ 9,000	0	5.2
Depreciation	2,700	1,350	1,350	50	1.6
Insurance	1,875	1,875	—	100	1.1
Interest	3,000	3,000	—	100	1.7
Utilities	6,000	—	6,000	0	3.5
Total Operating Expenses	$85,075				49.0
Projected Lost Net Income	$19,110				11.0
Total Continuing Expenses		$68,725			39.6
Total Noncontinuing Expenses			$16,350		9.4
Net Income PLUS Continuing Expenses		$87,836			50.6
Gross Profit LESS Noncontinuing Expenses			$87,836		50.6%

as for attorneys, are generally incurred as expenses first then billed and paid later. Heating oil expense is incurred in the winter but might be billed evenly throughout the year.

Most routine expenses are incurred as income statement expenses and are paid in cash in a consistent, congruent manner. However, failure to distinguish between when an expense is incurred and when it is paid can lead to improper calculation of covered expense, especially with relatively short periods of business interruption.

The reconciliation of expenses must be done on a case-by-case basis with careful attention to a fair evaluation of the insured's loss. Generally, business income coverage should do what the business would have done for itself had no loss occurred. Large losses with a long period of restoration can be reconciled several times, such as at the end of each month. However, on small

EXHIBIT 11-10

Income Statement Worksheet for XYZ, Inc., Showing Projected Lost Net Income Plus Expenses

Assumes partial sales of $20,000 and that expenses remain flat throughout the year.

					Percent of Gross Sales
Revenue from Gross Sales	$153,643 ($173,643 – $20,000)				100.0%
Cost of Goods Sold	61,458				40.0
Gross Profit	$ 92,185				60.0
Operating Expenses		**Continuing**	**Noncontinuing**	**Percent Continuing**	
Wages	$ 62,500	$62,500	—	100%	40.7
Rent	9,000	—	$ 9,000	0	5.9
Depreciation	2,700	1,350	1,350	50	1.8
Insurance	1,875	1,875	—	100	1.2
Interest	3,000	3,000	—	100	2.0
Utilities	6,000	—	6,000	0	3.9
Total Operating Expenses	$ 85,075				55.4
Projected Lost Net Income	$ 7,110				4.6
Total Continuing Expenses		$68,725			44.7
Total Noncontinuing Expenses			$16,350		10.6
Net Income PLUS Continuing Expenses		$75,836			49.4
Gross Profit LESS Noncontinuing Expenses			$75,836		49.4

simple losses, the reconciliation process may be mutually waived because the effect of reconciliation would be minimal.

Determining the Period of Restoration

Recovery for loss of business income and extra expense is limited to the period of restoration. The period of restoration is distinguished from the loss period. The loss period includes the seventy-two-hour deductible and may include extended business income loss after operations are resumed. Determining the period of restoration can present some complex adjusting issues. This section includes the policy definition of this period and explains the insured's typical duty to mitigate loss.

Definition

The BIC Form covers losses of business income and extra expense that occur during the period of restoration. This period is defined in the policy as follows:

> "Period of Restoration" means the period of time that:
>
> a. Begins:
>
> (1) 72 hours after the time of direct physical loss or damage for Business Income coverage; or
>
> (2) Immediately after the time of direct physical loss or damage for Extra Expense coverage;
>
> caused by or resulting from any Covered Cause of Loss at the described premises; and
>
> b. Ends on the earlier of:
>
> (1) The date when the property at the described premises should be repaired, rebuilt or replaced with reasonable speed and similar quality; or
>
> (2) The date when business is resumed at a new permanent location.[14]

The beginning date for the period of restoration creates a three-day (seventy-two-hour) deductible for loss of business income. However, extra expense is covered beginning immediately after a loss. In most cases, for the sake of determining the period of restoration, the date of loss is not at issue. However, the parties to the adjustment process might have to make a considerable effort to determine when the restoration period should end. The actual time period in which repairs to the insured property *are* made is not necessarily the time period in which such repairs *should* be made.

Due Diligence Requirement

The BIC policy definition of the period of restoration requires the insured to repair or replace the property with that of similar quality as quickly as possible.

The BIC form further includes the following loss conditions:

> 3. c. Resumption Of Operations
>
> We will reduce the amount of your:
>
> (1) Business Income loss, other than Extra Expense, to the extent you can resume your "operations"; in whole or in part, by using damaged or undamaged property (including merchandise or stock) at the described premises or elsewhere.
>
> (2) Extra Expense loss to the extent you can return "operations" to normal and discontinue such Extra Expense.[15]

The "as quickly as possible" standard, which applies to all business income loss evaluations, is important. For example, if a manufacturer could reduce the amount of his or her business income loss by using a competitor's facilities but would, as a result, reveal to a competitor a trade secret manufacturing process, the insurer would not be entitled to require such action because it would be unreasonable for the insurer to require the insured to give up a trade secret. Likewise, even if a retailer could arrange for delivery of merchandise to a nearby competitor's location, requiring the insured to direct customers to the competitor to continue to sell merchandise would be unreasonable. An insurer cannot ask the insured to sacrifice customers to reduce a business income loss. Nevertheless, an insured cannot remain idle and allow business income losses to accumulate. The insured's duty to mitigate the loss is inherent in all first-party insurance contracts and is especially important in a business income loss. Although an insurer can assist an insured in the repair or replacement of physically damaged property, the insurer cannot step in and run the insured's business.

Time Needed To Repair or Replace

Because the time element portion of an insured loss is measured by the time necessary to repair or replace the damaged property, the adjuster must determine the extent of the physical damage loss. To make an accurate determination, early in the adjustment process the adjuster must speak with the people involved in assessing and/or restoring the damage. Discussions with the insured and his or her representatives, including architects, engineers, contractors, and other consultants, are required as soon as possible to gain an early understanding of the probable duration of the financial loss.

The methods used to repair the damaged property directly affect the extent of the financial loss. For example, overtime labor can shorten the reconstruction period, as can other forms of fast-track construction techniques. The BIC form anticipates this possibility in its treatment of expediting expenses as covered extra expenses.

Obviously, not every possible type of loss and method of repair can be anticipated. Circumstances of the reconstruction, such as delays in the adjustment process itself, weather conditions, availability of materials, labor, alternative sites, and governmental restrictions, all affect the actual time needed for repairs.

Time in Which Repairs Should Be Complete

Because of the circumstances that affect actual repair time, a reasonably projected expected time for repairs, rather than an actual one, is often preferred in determining the extent of a business loss. A reasonable time period is the time in which restoration *should* be completed, as opposed to the time in which it is completed.

Depending on the circumstances of a given loss, all parties might benefit from the use of a reasonably expected time standard. This is true because (1) the physical damage is sometimes never repaired, or it is repaired in such a fashion that it bears no relationship to the originally damaged property; (2) certain extraneous circumstances not contemplated by the parties might affect the restoration period; and (3) loss adjustments can be made prospectively, that is, before the period of restoration is complete.

The fact that the insured, for whatever reason, chooses not to repair or replace the insured property does not prevent it from recovering a business income loss. In such a case, the parties must agree on what time should have reasonably been necessary to accomplish whatever repairs were insured by the property damage coverage. Experts can establish that time frame, depending on the degree of difficulty of the repair work.

Prospective settlement has some disadvantages as well. A reasonably expected time element estimate might be longer than the actual time needed to repair the physical damage, which would be a disadvantage for the insurer. Alternatively, the insured might fear that its actual loss will be greater than anticipated by any projection and that it will therefore be underpaid. Unforeseen events can also arise, such as a delay in the replacement of an essential component, which would lengthen the suspension period beyond the projection, creating a disadvantage for the insured. Any lengthening of the actual time period would be uncompensated, but the insured would still have received a certain sum well before property damage repairs were completed and would have the freedom to use the BIC loss proceeds as he or she sees fit. In each claim, the insurer and insured must carefully weigh the advantages and disadvantages of a prospective approach to the adjustment process.

Additional Coverage and Limitation: Interruption of Computer Operations

Prior editions of the BIC had a limitation of a business income loss caused by the destruction or corruption of electronic data. In the ISO BIC form (2001 edition), the limitation on electronic media and data has been removed. The Additional Coverage Interruption of Computer Operations and the Additional Limitation—Interruption of Computer Operations have been added. The limitation is meant to help clarify those situations in which coverage applies. It contains a lengthy description of what electronic data means in the policy. The additional coverage provides $2,500 of coverage for all business income extra expense due to a suspension of operations resulting from an interruption of computer operations caused by the destruction or corruption of electronic data by a covered cause of loss. The $2,500 is an aggregate limit for all losses sustained in any one policy year.

Delays Caused by Strikers

All of the causes of loss forms that might be attached to the BIC include a special exclusion that states the following:

> We will not pay for:
>
> (4) Any increase of loss caused by or resulting from:

> (a) Delay in rebuilding, repairing or replacing the property or resuming "operations", due to interference at the location of the rebuilding, repair or replacement by strikers or other persons. . . .[16]

This limitation applies only to striker interference at the insured premises. It does not apply to strike activities elsewhere. The last three words quoted could be construed to mean that any delay caused by any person is not covered. However, the sense of this entire clause is to exclude delays caused by strike activities, not every delay. The broad wording of the last three words is necessary because identifying perpetrators during strike activities is not always possible.

Additional, Optional, and Extended Coverages Under the BIC

The BIC provides valuable additional, optional, and extended coverage for interruptions caused by civil authorities, alterations and new buildings, business income losses that extend beyond the period of restoration for a short period of time, and business income losses that extend beyond the period of restoration for a long period of time. There is also a coverage extension for newly acquired locations.

Civil Authority

The BIC provides the following additional coverage for interruption caused by action of civil authorities:

> We will pay for the actual loss of Business Income you sustain and necessary Extra Expense caused by action of civil authority that prohibits access to the described premises due to direct physical loss of or damage to property, other than at the described premises, caused by or resulting from any Covered Cause of loss.
>
> The coverage for Business Income will begin 72 hours after the time of that action and will apply for a period of up to three consecutive weeks after coverage begins.
>
> The coverage for Extra Expense will begin immediately after the time of that action and will end:
>
> (1) 3 consecutive weeks after the time of that action; or
>
> (2) When your Business Income coverage ends;
>
> whichever is later.[17]

This coverage applies in the event of damage to property away from the described premises. The intent is to insure the loss of income that results from, for example, cordoning off an entire city block by civil authorities. This additional coverage is limited to three weeks.

Alterations and New Buildings

Another additional coverage provided by the BIC is for alterations and new buildings. The policy provides the following:

> We will pay for the actual loss of Business Income you sustain and necessary Extra Expense you incur due to direct physical loss or damage at the described premises caused by or resulting from any Covered Cause of Loss to:
>
> (1) New buildings or structures, whether complete or under construction;
>
> (2) Alterations or additions to existing buildings or structures; and
>
> (3) Machinery, equipment, supplies or building materials located on or within 100 feet of the described premises and:
>
> (a) Used in the construction, alterations or additions; or
>
> (b) Incidental to the occupancy of new buildings.
>
> If such direct physical loss or damage delays the start of "operations," the "period of restoration" for Business Income Coverage will begin on the date "operations" would have begun if the direct physical loss or damage had not occurred.[18]

The Alterations and New Buildings coverage parallels the extension of property damage coverage under the BPP policy for the same items. If the adjuster determines that the damaged property is covered, the resulting loss of use of that property is also insured. The BIC policy anticipates that property insured under this section might not yet be income-producing at the time of the loss. In that case, the time element is measured from when the property was to begin generating income to when the property actually does generate income after being repaired or replaced.

Extended Business Income

The additional coverage for extended business income (other than rental value) provides the following:

> ...we will pay for the actual loss of Business Income you incur during the period that:
>
> (a) Begins on the date property (except "finished stock") is actually repaired, rebuilt or replaced and "operations" are resumed; and
>
> (b) Ends on the earlier of:
>
> (i) The date you could restore your "operations" with reasonable speed, to the level which would generate the business income amount that would have existed if no direct physical loss or damage occurred; or
>
> (ii) 30 consecutive days after the date determined in (1)(a) above.
>
> However, Extended Business Income does not apply to loss of Business Income incurred as a result of unfavorable business conditions caused by the impact of the Covered Cause of Loss in the area where the described premises are located.

> Loss of Business Income must be caused by direct physical loss or damage at the described premises caused by or resulting from any Covered Cause of Loss.[19]

This feature of the BIC policy provides up to an additional thirty days after the restoration of the property within which the insured can regain whatever business was lost because of the interruption. This extended business income coverage does not increase the amount of coverage beyond what appears on the declarations page. For example, a retail store whose business is interrupted by a covered cause of loss often continues to lose sales income even after the shelves are restocked and the store has reopened. Once consumers discover alternative stores to shop in, insured storeowners may need to take extra steps to recapture customers. To that end, an insured might offer a grand reopening sale, which would be unnecessary if no loss had occurred. The extent to which the sale negatively affects the income that would have been anticipated for the additional thirty-day period had no loss occurred would be insured under this extension of coverage. Nevertheless, the additional coverage for extended business income does not include loss of income caused by unfavorable business conditions caused by the covered cause of loss. For example, after a catastrophe such as a hurricane, the economy in an entire area might be depressed. Losses caused by such a general business depression are not covered.

Interruption of Computer Operations

This provision allows the insured to extend the Business Income and Extra Expense coverage to a loss caused by an interruption in computer operations caused by the destruction or corruption of electronic data from a covered cause of loss. However, the provision limits the covered cause of loss.

Optional Coverage: Extended Period of Indemnity

This provision allows an insured to select a longer period of indemnity beyond the automatic thirty days granted under extended business income in the BIC form. The extension of the period of indemnity does not increase the amount of coverage beyond what appears on the declarations page. This extension usually applies to businesses with a marked seasonal selling period. For example, a retailer selling Christmas ornaments might have a peak season of approximately sixty days before Christmas. If the normal period of restoration and the normal thirty-day extended period ended shortly before the insured's peak season, an additional amount of time would be required for the insured to regain its share of the seasonal market.

Newly Acquired Locations Coverage Extension

The BIC provides extended coverage, beyond the stated limits, for newly acquired locations (other than fairs or exhibitions) for up to $100,000.

The intent of this coverage is to parallel the property coverages for locations acquired during the policy term. This coverage is limited in dollar amount and in duration, but it is additional to the Limits of Insurance. If an insured acquires a new location, it should report its value to the agent as soon as possible to obtain appropriate coverage.

Limits of Insurance for Additional Coverages

The Limits of Insurance section of the BIC form provides that the most that can be paid for any one loss is the limit of insurance shown on the declarations page. This clause also *restricts* recovery to the stated limit for the following additional coverages: (1) Alterations and New Buildings, (2) Civil Authority, (3) Extra Expense, and (4) Extended Business Income.

Coinsurance

Coinsurance requires the insured to carry a specific limit of insurance that is a percentage of the amount of potential loss "at risk." Under building or contents coverage forms, the amount at risk is the total value of the building or contents. Under business income coverage, the amount at risk is the projected annual net income and operating expenses from the date the policy was written or renewed. This section details how coinsurance compliance is determined under the BIC form. This section also discusses several optional coverages that substitute for coinsurance and explains why coinsurance is not a problem under the Businessowners Policy (BOP).

Coinsurance Policy Language

The BIC specifies the coinsurance requirement as an additional condition:

> If a Coinsurance percentage is shown in the Declarations, the following condition applies in addition to the Common Policy Conditions and the Commercial Property Conditions.
>
> We will not pay the full amount of any Business Income loss if the Limit of Insurance for Business Income is less than:
>
> a. The Coinsurance percentage shown for Business Income in the Declarations; times
>
> b. The sum of:
>
> (1) The Net Income (Net Profit or Loss before income taxes), and
>
> (2) Operating expenses, including payroll expenses,
>
> that would have been earned or incurred (had no loss occurred) by your "operations" at the described premises for the 12 months following the inception, or last previous anniversary date, of this policy (whichever is later).[20]

The policy language above is followed by a description of the coinsurance calculation and by a list of expenses that are deducted from all operating expenses for purposes of determining coinsurance compliance. The list generally includes those expenses that are directly related to sales such as returns and allowances, discounts, and bad debts. Adjusters should be familiar with this list. These uninsurable expenses are not, and cannot be, "at risk" and should not be included in required limits of business income coverage.

Evaluating Coinsurance Compliance

To evaluate coinsurance compliance, refer to Exhibit 11-11 and assume that the policy inception date was 1/1/XXX3. The annual net income and operating expenses for the previous year total $436,590 ($96,290 + $340,300 = $436,590). Note that this is also the amount of the gross profit that appears on the same exhibit. More importantly, note that the gross profit is 60 percent of gross sales. Now refer back to Exhibit 11-8. Note that sales are steadily increasing at a rate of 5 percent. Since the annual sales for XXX2 were $727,650, the annual sales from the policy inception date of 1/1/XXX3 are projected to be $764,032 ($727,650 × 105% = $764,032). With a gross profit percentage of 60 percent, the amount of net income and operating expenses "at risk" are $458,419 (764,032 × 60% = $458,419. If the BIC policy form carries an 80 percent coinsurance requirement, the insured must carry business income limits of $366,735 ($458,419 × 80% = $366,735). This calculation is also explained in the calculation below.

Annual gross revenues XXX2	$727,650
Sales trend projections	× 105%
Projected annual gross revenues XXX3 (policy inception 1/1/XXX3)	$764,032
Gross profit percentage	× 60%
Net income and operating expenses at risk	$458,419
Coinsurance requirement from policy	× 80%
Amount of business income coverage required by policy	$366,735

EXHIBIT 11-11

Annual Income Statement Received From Insured

XYZ, Inc.—Income Statement 1/1/XXX2 to 12/31/XXX2

Revenue From Gross Sales	$ 727,650
Cost of Goods Sold	291,060
Gross Profit	$436,590
Operating Expenses	
Wages	$250,000
Rent	36,000
Depreciation	10,800
Insurance	7,500
Interest	12,000
Utilities	24,000
Total Operating Expenses	$340,300
Net Income	$96,290

Using consistent sales projections is important. An insured may argue that sales are increasing when discussing the amount of claim payment and then argue that sales are flat or declining while discussing coinsurance compliance. Remember also that under the policy, the amount at risk is the projected annual net income and operating expenses *from the date the policy was written or renewed.* Often, a loss occurs many months after policy inception or renewal. This means that the evaluation will include some actual sales and expense data and some projected sales and expense data.

All expenses directly related to sales and excluded expenses listed in the policy are deducted from this calculation. Suppose that the adjuster learns from the insured that the "wages" listed on XYZ's business records includes commissions of 10 percent of gross sales. Commissions are normally listed as a separate expense item, but it is possible to find deviations from generally accepted accounting principles. Commissions are an expense directly related to sales. Accordingly, the adjuster or accountant evaluating coinsurance compliance would move the commissions expense "above the line," and Exhibit 11-11 would be modified as shown below in Exhibit 11-12.

EXHIBIT 11-12

Income Statement Worksheet for XYZ, Inc., Showing Commissions Above the Line

XYZ, Inc.—Income Statement Worksheet 1/1/XXX2 to 12/31/XXX2

		Percent of Gross Sales
Revenue From Gross Sales	$727,650	100.0%
Cost of Goods Sold	291,060	40.0%
Wages (10% Commissions)	72,765	10.0%
Modified Gross Profit	$363,825	50.0%
Operating Expenses		
Wages (Salaries Only)	$177,235	24.4%
Rent	36,000	4.9%
Depreciation	10,800	1.5%
Insurance	7,500	1.0%
Interest	12,000	1.6%
Utilities	24,000	3.3%
Total Operating Expenses	$267,535	36.8%
Net Income	$ 96,290	13.2%

Note that this does not change the net income amount. But it does show a modified gross profit amount and the modified gross profit percentage. With a modified gross profit percentage of only 50 percent and a coinsurance requirement of 80 percent, XYZ requires business income coverage of only $305,613 (see calculation below).

Annual gross revenues XXX2	$727,650
Sales trend projections	× 105%
Projected annual gross revenues XXX3 (policy inception 1/1/XXX3)	$764,032
Modified gross profit percentage	× 50%
Net income and operating expenses at risk	$382,016
Coinsurance requirement from policy	× 80%
Amount of business income coverage required by policy	$305,613

Implications of Being Underinsured

The implications of being underinsured are the same for all property coverages. If the limits are less than required, the loss payment owed is proportionately reduced. The amount of loss reduction is called the coinsurance percentage of loss and is calculated by the "Did Over Should" formula. For simplicity, refer to the first coinsurance calculation above showing a required coverage limit of $366,735, and assume that the business income coverage limits carried were only $325,000. Using the "Did Over Should" formula shows that the coinsurance percentage of loss is 88 percent ($325,000 ÷ $366,735 = 88%).

$$\text{Coinsurance percentage of loss} = \frac{\text{Limit Insured Did Carry}}{\text{Limit Insured Should Carry}} = \frac{325{,}000}{366{,}735} = 88\%$$

Applying this coinsurance percentage to the loss evaluation shown in Exhibit 11-9 results in a payable loss of $77,296 ($87,836 × 88% = $77,296).

Extra Expense and Coinsurance Calculations

The amount of extra expenses needed to reduce a given business income loss cannot be easily forecast and therefore cannot be included in the insurable values upon which coinsurance is based. The BIC policy follows this reasoning by excluding amounts insured under extra expense from the coinsurance condition.

Optional Coverages Instead of Coinsurance

The BIC policy contains three optional coverages that are available to the insured when certain conditions are met regarding either additional premium or reporting requirements. Each allows the coinsurance clause to be suspended.

Maximum Period of Indemnity

This optional coverage allows the insured to limit the period of restoration to 120 days. After that time period, the requirements of the coinsurance section of the policy are suspended, allowing the insured to purchase less insurance than would otherwise be required. This option is useful for insureds that do not expect an interruption to last long.

Monthly Period of Indemnity

This optional coverage allows the insured to limit coverage to a specific fraction of the total limit for each thirty-consecutive-day period after the beginning of the period of restoration. For example, a business income limit of $200,000 with a ¼ monthly limit of indemnity would provide up to $50,000 of business income coverage each month. *This does not limit the period of indemnity;* it only limits the amount that can be paid each month. In this example, the insured could also receive $20,000 per month for ten months, $25,000 for eight months, or any other combination that does not exceed $50,000 in any thirty-day period. As with the first option, the coinsurance provisions of the policy are suspended.

Business Income Agreed Value

This option suspends the operation of the coinsurance provisions of the policy when the insured reports business income values before the policy's inception date. However, the Agreed Value coverage operates like a new coinsurance requirement. The insured can pre-select the amount of coverage it must maintain, but Section d. of the Agreed Value coverage applies a factor to any loss settlement determined by the proportion of the actual limit to the values agreed at the policy's inception. In the example given in the policy, recovery is reduced by 50 percent because the business income limit of insurance is half of the agreed value reported at the policy inception date. Therefore, for the insured to recover, it must purchase 100 percent of any insured business income loss, and it must purchase 100 percent of the agreed value as the business income limit of insurance.

Limits Under Businessowners Policies

The ISO Businessowners Policy (BOP) provides package property coverages including coverage for loss of business income and extra expense. This coverage is substantially identical to the BIC coverage, except that the BOP has *no* dollar limit of insurance or coinsurance clause for business income loss. Instead, the BOP limits both the loss of business income and extra expense to twelve consecutive months after the date of loss.

Negotiating Business Income Claims

It is important to understand that evaluating business income claims is *not* a math problem with an exact answer; rather, it is an adjusting process. Adjusters should be comfortable developing a *range of reasonable settlement possibilities*.

Business income evaluations are a combination of interpretations and projections from available pre-loss data. Any figure subject to data availability, interpretation, and projection cannot be exact. The final outcome can be affected by factors as small as the number of decimal points used in a particular calculation. Accordingly, adjusters must make great efforts to ensure that their evaluations are well-reasoned and clearly documented. Some of the variables involved include the period of restoration, gross sales projections, methods of calculation, make-up sales, partial sales, which expenses will continue, coinsurance compliance, and reconciliation, as well as other issues that may arise in the adjustment process. Adjusters handling business income claims directly or indirectly with accountant's assistance should be comfortable with these concepts.

A business income loss could be considered a specialty loss because not all property loss adjusters handle this type of claim. Inland marine losses such as transportation losses, and other property losses such as condominium losses, are also considered specialty losses. These specialty losses and others are discussed in Chapter 12.

SUMMARY

Physical damage of property often results in a shutdown of business operations and loss of business income. Losses can include loss of income, increased expenses, or both. Insurance settlements for such losses are measured over the time necessary to repair or replace the damaged or destroyed property, so such claims are called time element losses.

Claim adjusters handling business income losses should understand basic accounting for organizations. The two principal accounting statements for organizations are the balance sheet and the income statement. The balance sheet lists an organization's assets and its liabilities. The difference between assets and liabilities is the organization's net worth. An organization's income statement lists the revenue and expenses for the organization for a given period of time. The difference between revenue and expenses is net income. Damage or destruction of property appears on an organization's balance sheet. However, if such damage or destruction results in loss of income or increased expenses, those effects appear on the income statement. Adjusters should be comfortable analyzing sales and expense figures because these are the building blocks of business income loss evaluations.

The Business Income (and Extra Expense) Coverage Form (BIC) covers an organization's loss of net income, its continuing expenses, and its extra expenses that result from a suspension of its operations. Property loss adjusters must be careful when determining losses and evaluating claims because claims are often made for items that are covered under building or contents coverages. In all cases, property loss adjusters must be able to evaluate the separate effects of and coverage for reduced revenue and increased expenses. The BIC covers losses occurring during the period of restoration, defined to end when repairs should be completed. This definition allows adjusters and insureds to settle claims prospectively, before restoration is completed, while allowing for reconciliation of actual sales and expenses after restoration is complete.

CHAPTER NOTES

1. Pat Magarich and Ken Brownlee, *Casualty, Fire & Marine Investigation Checklists*, 5th ed. (New York: Clark Boardman Callaghan, 1997), p. 493.
2. Property Loss Research Bureau, *Duplication of Claims*, 2002 Pasadena, Calif., conference.
3. Business Income Coverage (and Extra Expense) Form, CP 00 30 04 02, Copyright, Insurance Services Office, Inc., 2001.
4. Business Income Coverage (and Extra Expense) Form, CP 00 30 04 02, Copyright, Insurance Services Office, Inc., 2001.
5. Business Income Coverage (and Extra Expense) Form, CP 00 30 04 02, Copyright, Insurance Services Office, Inc., 2001.
6. Business Income Coverage (and Extra Expense) Form, CP 00 30 04 02, Copyright, Insurance Services Office, Inc., 2001.
7. Business Income Coverage (and Extra Expense) Form, CP 00 30 04 02, Copyright, Insurance Services Office, Inc., 2001.
8. Business Income Coverage (and Extra Expense) Form, CP 00 30 04 02, Copyright, Insurance Services Office, Inc., 2001.
9. Property Loss Research Bureau, *Duplication of Claims*, 2002 Pasadena, Calif., conference.
10. Business Income Coverage (and Extra Expense) Form, CP 00 30 04 02, Copyright, Insurance Services Office, Inc., 2001.
11. Business Income Coverage (and Extra Expense) Form, CP 00 30 04 02, Copyright, Insurance Services Office, Inc., 2001.
12. Business Income Coverage (and Extra Expense) Form, CP 00 30 04 02, Copyright, Insurance Services Office, Inc., 2001.
13. Business Income Coverage (and Extra Expense) Form, CP 00 30 04 02, Copyright, Insurance Services Office, Inc., 2001.
14. Business Income Coverage (and Extra Expense) Form, CP 00 30 04 02, Copyright, Insurance Services Office, Inc., 2001.
15. Business Income Coverage (and Extra Expense) Form, CP 00 30 04 02, Copyright, Insurance Services Office, Inc., 2001.
16. Causes of Loss—Basic Form, CP 10 10 04 02, Copyright, Insurance Services Office, Inc., 2001.
17. Business Income Coverage (and Extra Expense) Form, CP 00 30 04 02, Copyright, Insurance Services Office, Inc., 2001.
18. Business Income Coverage (and Extra Expense) Form, CP 00 30 04 02, Copyright, Insurance Services Office, Inc., 2001.

19. Business Income Coverage (and Extra Expense) Form, CP 00 30 04 02, Copyright, Insurance Services Office, Inc., 2001.
20. Business Income Coverage (and Extra Expense) Form, CP 00 30 04 02, Copyright, Insurance Services Office, Inc., 2001.

Chapter 12

Direct Your Learning

Specialty Losses

After learning the subject matter of this chapter, you should be able to:

- Explain the coverage provided and the adjusting considerations for transportation and motor truck losses.
- Explain the coverage provided and the adjusting considerations for bailee and warehouse legal liability losses.
- Explain the interests of the unit owners and the condominium association in the individual units and the common elements.
- Given a claim situation, adjust a loss under the condominium association coverage form and the unit owner's coverage form.
- Adjust a loss under builders' risk policies.
- Explain how subrogation, termination of coverage, and loss adjustment are handled under builders' risk policies.
- Describe the extent and limitations of coverage for crime losses under the Building and Personal Property Coverage Form (BPP) and the ISO Commercial Crime Coverage Form.
- Given a loss, outline the loss adjustment procedures for computer and computer-related losses.
- Describe legal liability for pollution under the Superfund law.
- Explain to what extent property insurance policies provide coverage for cleanup of pollution and how they exclude coverage.

OUTLINE

Develop Your Perspective

What are the main topics covered in the chapter?

Property loss adjusters may be asked to handle losses under various coverages. This chapter discusses transportation losses; bailee losses, including warehouse legal liability; condominium losses; builders' risk losses; equipment breakdown losses; computer losses; and contamination claims.

Why is it important to know these topics?

Whether or not your company writes these specialty coverages, it is important that a property loss adjuster be aware of these coverages and how losses are adjusted under them. Suppose that you are handling a homeowners loss under personal insurance coverage. You must determine what portion of the condominium is covered by your policy and what is covered by the condominium association's policy. Or suppose that the homeowner has personal property in storage in a warehouse that is destroyed by a fire. Understanding the warehouse legal liability coverage can help with subrogation.

How can you use this information?

Although all of these different types of losses involve damage to property, some of them are third-party claims that are handled as if they are first-party claims. Determining legal liability is necessary to adjust these types of losses, which is a new concept for many property loss adjusters.

Chapter 12

Specialty Losses

This chapter discusses several specialty losses that are less common than most property losses or require some specialized knowledge to analyze and adjust. The discussion covers inland marine losses involving transportation losses, bailees' losses, and warehouse legal liability losses. Although contractor's equipment losses are a type of inland marine losses, they are discussed in Chapter 13. This chapter also discusses property losses under condominium policies, builders' risk policies, crime policies, equipment breakdown policies, and computer equipment policies. The chapter concludes with a discussion of contamination claims brought under first-party coverage.

INLAND MARINE INSURANCE

Inland marine insurance includes a variety of insurance coverages. These coverages are grouped together as much because of their history as because of any logical relationship. Nevertheless, inland marine coverages share certain characteristics that adjusters must recognize and understand.

The categories of inland marine coverages are defined in the **Nationwide Marine Definition**, summarized in Exhibit 12-1. The definition was created to delineate the scope of inland marine underwriting. Although modern property-casualty insurers have full legal power to write all types of property insurance, the Nationwide Marine Definition remains important because inland marine business is less regulated and less standardized.

Nationwide Marine Definition
Categories of inland marine coverages created to delineate the scope of inland marine underwriting.

Common Characteristics of Inland Marine Insurance

Generally, an inland marine risk must be in transit (such as cargo) or bear some relation to transportation (bridge and tunnels) or communication (radio and TV transmission towers). Inland marine insurance can cover personal property such as cameras, golf equipment, and jewelry or commercial property such as signs, film, photographic equipment, and physicians' equipment. Inland marine insurance usually covers risks of direct physical loss.

Named-Perils or Special-Form Coverage

Many inland marine policies are written on a named-perils basis, but the special-form approach is the norm. However, an adjuster cannot assume that

EXHIBIT 12-1

Summary of the Nationwide Marine Definition

- *Transportation*, covering the shipper or owner's goods, or the interests of the common carrier
- *Bridges, Tunnels, Instrumentalities of Transportation or Communication*
  - Piers, dry docks
  - Pipelines
  - Telephone and telegraph property, including transmission lines and generating equipment
  - Radio and television communication equipment, including towers and antennas and electrical apparatus
  - Cranes and equipment to load and unload
- *Bailee—Bailor*
  - Garment contractors' floater
  - Bailee liability policy
  - Bailees' customers policy
  - Bailor policy
  - Warehouse legal liability policy
  - Furrier's customer policy
- *Floater policies (personal)*
  - Personal effects
  - Furs
  - Jewelry
  - Silverware
  - Fine arts
  - Stamps and coins
  - Musical instrument
- *Floater policies (commercial)*
  - Physicians' and surgeons' instruments
  - Patterns and dies
  - Theatrical
  - Live animals
  - Salespersons' samples
  - Exhibitions
- *Installment sales, covering the vendor or purchaser of property*
- *Contractors' equipment*
- *Builders' risk*
- *Dealers' policies (floor plan)*
- *Miscellaneous policies*
  - Jewelers' block
  - Valuable papers
  - Accounts receivable
  - Fine arts
  - Difference in conditions
  - Electronic data processing

inland marine special-form coverage is equivalent to the perils of the BPP with the Causes of Loss—Special Form or to any other familiar standard. Because inland marine policies were developed to meet specialized needs, the coverages are often distinctive. An inland marine policy's special-form coverage might be broader than that of other special-form policies. For example, it might extend to earthquake or flood. Conversely, it might be narrower because of exclusions unique to certain types of property.

Inland marine policies' additional coverages are often broader than those of conventional property insurance policies. For example, many policies include loss of use coverage. Other inland marine policies have attractive extra features, such as coverage for additional expenses and expanded coverage for property of others.

Adjusters must be aware of the nonstandard nature of many inland marine policies. Policy clauses or conditions that an adjuster might take for granted in other policies might not even exist, or they might be substantially different, in inland marine policies. Therefore, adjusters must read each policy related to a loss.

Multiple Parties

Inland marine losses often include transportation, custody, or use of property by someone who is not the owner. The losses often involve more than one party, even when only one named insured is on a given policy. The involvement of more than one party can result in multiple insurance policies applicable to a given loss. These policies might cover only the respective interests of the various parties in the property, or they might cover the same interest. An adjuster must be alert to these possibilities and must resolve overlapping coverage and loss-sharing problems when they arise.

Need To Consult Contracts and Documents

Because several parties can be involved in inland marine losses, adjusters must often consult contracts or documents to determine interests or property values. These contracts and documents include bills of lading, consignment contracts, warehouse receipts, equipment leases, construction contracts, and sales invoices. These documents might specify or determine who has an interest in property and who must insure the property. Adjusters must also become familiar with various industries' business practices and jargon.

Transportation Losses

Transportation coverages were the historic origin of the inland marine business and still account for a significant amount of the business. Most businesses have some transit loss exposure. Manufacturers receive and ship goods. Wholesalers and retailers receive and ship goods. Any organization that moves from one location to another is shipping goods. These exposures require adjusters to determine legal interests and responsibilities for the damaged property. Because various laws define the responsibilities of rail, air, and ocean carriers, this section deals only with motor carriers, as this is the type of transportation loss that most adjusters encounter.

Parties in Transportation Losses

Transportation losses sometimes involve one party, if the property is being transported by its owner on the owner's trucks to the owner's locations. Usually, however, transportation losses involve three parties.

Consignor
The party who is shipping goods.

The shipper, or **consignor,** is the party with whom transportation of property begins. The shipper of property is usually a seller sending property to a buyer. Because the shipper is usually in some business other than carrying goods, it usually hires a carrier to transport goods.

The consignee is the party to whom goods are to be delivered. The consignee is usually a buyer and, depending on the terms of sale, might also own the goods throughout the course of transit.

Carrier
The party in the business of transporting goods of others.

Carriers transport goods. They can operate by truck, railroad, aircraft, barge, or ship. Transportation of a shipment by two or more different modes of transportation is referred to as intermodal transportation. Rail, air, and ship carriers are subject to different laws of liability than are truck carriers, which are often regulated by federal statute. Even truck carriers face different liabilities depending on whether they are common carriers or contract carriers, as explained below.

Free on board (FOB) point of origin
A shipping condition in which ownership passes to the buyer as soon as the carrier picks up the goods from the seller's premises.

Free on board (FOB) destination
A shipping condition in which ownership passes from the seller to the buyer when the carrier delivers the goods to the buyer's premises.

Free along side (FAS)
A shipping condition in which ownership passes from the seller to the buyer when the seller delivers the goods alongside a vessel for loading onto that vessel.

Cost, insurance, and freight (CIF)
A shipping condition by which the seller is obligated to pay for the insurance and freight charges for delivery to the buyer.

Cost and freight (CF or C&F)
A shipping condition similar to cost, insurance, and freight (CIF), except that the seller is not obligated to provide insurance coverage and is obligated to provide freight charges.

Responsibility for Loss

Responsibility for loss to goods in transit depends on the answers to several questions. Who owns the goods? Who agreed to insure them? Was the carrier liable? Did any party limit its liability?

Who owns goods depends on the terms of sale. The seller and buyer can agree to any one of a number of sales terms, as shown in Exhibit 12-2. Ownership might transfer to the buyer at any point from the seller's warehouse to the buyer's receiving dock. So an adjuster must check the terms of sale to see who owns goods at the time of a loss.

EXHIBIT 12-2

Terms of Sale

FOB (free on board) point of origin—Ownership passes from the seller to the buyer as soon as the carrier picks up the goods from the seller's premises. The point of origin might be named.

FOB destination—Ownership passes from the seller to the buyer when the carrier delivers the goods to the buyer's premises. The destination might be named.

FAS (free along side) vessel at a named port—Ownership passes from the seller to the buyer when the seller delivers the goods alongside a vessel for loading onto that vessel.

C.I.F. (cost, insurance, and freight)—The seller is obligated to pay for the insurance and freight charges for delivery to the buyer. However, ownership passes when the seller has delivered the goods to the carrier. The insurance and freight charges become part of the goods' insured value.

C.F., or C. & F.—The same as C.I.F., except the seller is not obligated to provide insurance coverage and is obligated to provide freight charges.

No agreed terms—If the agreement requires or authorizes the seller to ship by carrier, the risk of loss is like FOB point of origin. If the agreement is silent about shipping terms, the seller bears the risk of loss until the goods are delivered to the buyer.

Typically, the goods' owner would have the greatest incentive to insure them, but when goods are being transported, the parties involved can agree on any arrangement. The adjuster must check the sales invoice and the bill of lading to see who has agreed to insure the goods. A **bill of lading** is both a contract of carriage between the carrier and the shipper and a receipt for the goods. Although an agreement to insure property does not automatically create insurance coverage, an adjuster who sees an agreement by a party other than the insured to insure the goods should investigate that party's coverage.

Bill of lading
The contract of carriage between the carrier and the shipper, as well as a receipt for the goods; it states the terms of the carriage and the carrier's liability for loss or damage.

Adjuster Tip

The sale document or shipping document provides information on ownership and terms of sale. The document may use the shorthand term "Ex works" or "Ex Factory." "Ex" is Latin for the word "from." So if the adjuster sees the term "Ex factory," he or she will know that the goods were shipped from the shipper's factory.

A carrier is usually legally liable for loss or damage to goods in its custody. A common carrier offers its services to the general public and is liable in all cases, except for losses caused by acts of God, acts of a public enemy, exercise of public authority, shipper's neglect, or inherent vice of the goods. A contract carrier operates under contract with a shipper. Its liability depends on the contract's terms. Its liability might be as strict as a common carrier's or less strict. For example, a contract carrier might be responsible only for losses caused by its negligence.

Carriers often limit their liability by the terms of a bill of lading. Particularly, they often limit their liability to a specified dollar amount. Adjusters should not conclude that a carrier would cover a loss without first checking for such a limitation. The buyer and seller might also limit their liability for loss, although liability between these parties usually depends entirely on ownership. The owner of goods at the time of loss bears the loss.

Transit Policies

Shippers and consignees can insure goods in transit with transit insurance. Transit policies can be annual transit policies (covering all of the goods shipped that year) or trip transit (which covers only one specific shipment). Coverage under transit insurance does not depend on ownership. It certainly covers owned property, but it might also cover property for which the insured is liable or has agreed to insure, or for which the insured is the consignee. Transit insurance applies only while goods are in transit. For an owner carrying its own goods, transit begins when the goods leave the starting point on their way to the destination. When a carrier for hire is transporting goods, transit begins when the goods have been placed in the carrier's custody, ready for shipment.

Transit claims' adjusting challenge concerns the issue of when the transportation actually ends. Minor deviations and customary stops usually do not signal the end of "due course of transit." However, if the stop is lengthy or the deviation is not work-related, issues could arise as to whether the transit has ceased. Temporary storage for the convenience of the shipper, carrier, or consignee is not an interruption of transit. Generally, transit ceases when the property is delivered to its final destination. But disputes often arise as to what constitutes delivery. Sometimes the truck arrives at its destination too late, and the goods cannot be unloaded. Sometimes the truck arrives on time, and the consignee is not ready for the goods. Sometimes the consignee refuses the delivery entirely. An adjuster must thoroughly research each of these scenarios in the jurisdiction of the loss before payment of a claim.

The shipper's/consignee's transit policy usually covers property while in the custody of a carrier for hire or on owned/operated vehicles. It generally excludes contraband or property that is illegal to transport. Some policies are written to exclude high-value items such as money, jewelry, precious metals, and furs.

These policies also cover goods in temporary storage, before delivery to their final destination. The policy does not define temporary. Although the policy is not intended to cover long-term storage, what constitutes temporary is open to judicial interpretation.

Covered Causes of Loss

Transit policies can be written on a special-form basis with few exclusions or on a named-perils basis. Both forms usually contain exclusions for loss caused by governmental action, nuclear hazard, and war.

Theft coverage gets special attention in transit policies. The policies might include an exclusion for the dishonest acts of the insured's employees. They might also include exclusions for voluntary parting, unauthorized instructions, unexplained disappearance, and inventory shortage. These policies often contain an exclusion for theft of property from an unattended vehicle unless the vehicle is locked and has visible signs of forced entry.

Most transit policies exclude breakdown of refrigeration equipment, but such an exclusion applies only to vehicles owned or operated by the insured. If the insured has this exposure, the policy can be endorsed to cover spoilage resulting from refrigeration equipment's breakdown.

Valuation

Transit policies typically use the invoice price as the basis for valuing shipments. This is the good's selling price as shown in the sales invoice. Shipments of goods other than those made between a buyer and a seller are usually valued at actual cash value or the least of the following:

1. The property's actual cost
2. The cost to restore the property
3. The cost to replace the property

Subrogation

When a carrier for hire moves goods, that carrier may be legally liable for loss or damage to the goods. The extent of the carrier's liability is governed by the bill of lading. The bill of lading contains a section called "Limitation of Carriers Liability." Unless a greater dollar value is declared by the shipper and stated in the bill of lading, the carrier's liability is limited to the amount stated in the limitation provision. This is commonly referred to as a "released bill of lading." For household goods movers, this limitation is expressed as XX amount of cents per pound. For other types of carriers, it is expressed as XX amount of dollars per package.

Adjusting Transit Losses

It is essential for any adjuster to begin a transit loss adjustment with the terms of the policy because they might be unique to the insured. The adjuster must gather all of the facts concerning the loss. The shipping documents, such as the bill of lading and the sales invoice, are necessary. If the goods have sustained damage, the adjuster should have the goods and the shipping container or packaging inspected. Prompt inspection also facilitates salvage.

Salvage is an important option in transit losses. If the goods are perishable, they must be moved quickly to maximize salvage recovery. If the bill of lading is released at only a fraction of the actual value of the damaged goods, salvage may be the only way to recoup some of the loss payment.

Motor Truck Cargo Liability Insurance

To protect a carrier for hire's exposure for loss or damage to cargo, the Motor Truck Cargo (MTC) Liability Policy was developed. Despite the fact that it is a liability policy, a property loss adjuster usually handles the claims because, under such a policy, the loss is to property, not to people.

Liability For Cargo

Section 14706 of Title 49, United State Code, describes motor carriers' cargo liability. It applies to any motor carrier, except for agricultural carriers, household goods carriers, express and package carriers, motor carriage incidental to air carriage, and contract carriage in which the contract's terms allow for specific conditions. Under Section 14706, a motor carrier's liability is strict liability subject to certain defenses and subject to limits agreed on in the bill of lading.

The defenses available to a motor carrier are the following:

1. Acts of God
2. Acts of a public enemy
3. Acts of public authorities
4. Fault or neglect by the shipper
5. Inherent vice or nature of the property

Act of God
An event that occurs without human intervention, or an act that cannot be prevented by the exercise of human care.

An **act of God** is defined as an event that occurs without human intervention or an act that cannot be prevented by the exercise of human care. Tornadoes, floods, and earthquakes are all classified as acts of God. However, if a carrier ignores a flood warning concerning travel on a particular road and the cargo suffers flood damage, it would be unlikely that the carrier would escape liability for the damage.

Public enemy
A nation or government at war with the nation in which the carrier is domiciled.

A **public enemy** is a nation or government at war with the nation in which the motor carrier is domiciled. It does not refer to an individual criminal or to groups of criminals. It is unclear what the status of a terrorist or terrorist organization might have under the exclusion.

Acts of public authorities refers to any act taken by a public official acting within the scope of his or her authority. If a U.S. Customs agent damages cargo while searching for illegal drugs, the carrier would not be held liable unless the carrier could reasonably have foreseen and prevented the damage.

A carrier may avoid liability if the loss is caused by the shipper's fault or negligence. However, the carrier must prove that the shipper's act was the sole cause of the loss and that the carrier did not contribute to the loss in any way. If the carrier is aware that the packaging or loading is improper and it accepts the shipment anyway, the carrier will be held liable for the loss.

Inherent vice
A condition that can cause property to deteriorate or destroy itself.

Inherent vice is a condition that can cause property to deteriorate or destroy itself. This condition can be a defect, disease, decay, or condition that will cause deterioration. For example, wood warps if subject to humidity for a period of time, and fruit decays after several days, especially without refrigeration.

Motor Truck Cargo Liability Policy Provisions

The MTC liability policy covers property in carriers' care, custody, and control, or when loaded or unloaded at a terminal for up to seventy-two hours, excluding Sundays and holidays. The property must be accepted under the terms of a bill of lading or shipping receipt.

The MTC liability policy excludes contraband and high-value items such as money, jewelry, and furs. Live animals are also usually excluded. Breakdown of refrigeration equipment is usually excluded but can be added back by endorsement.

BMC 32
An endorsement found on motor truck cargo liability policies that satisfies the federal regulation requiring a motor carrier to show evidence of financial responsibility for up to $5,000 for loss or damage to the contents of any one vehicle and $10,000 for aggregate losses at any one time or place with respect to any one shipper or consignee.

The **BMC 32** endorsement can be found on most motor truck cargo liability policies. The U.S. Code, 49 USC 13906, requires motor carriers operating within federal jurisdiction to show evidence of financial responsibility up to a minimum limit of $5,000 for loss or damage to the contents of any one vehicle and $10,000 for aggregate losses at any one time and place with respect to any one shipper or consignee. The insurer files a form with the Federal Motor Carrier Safety Administration, Licensing and Insurance Division, advising that the obligation is met. The BMC 32 endorsement states that the insurer will pay for loss or damage for which the motor carrier can be found legally liable for having caused. Under the terms of the endorsement, the insurer must pay the claim, subject to the limits, regardless of any exclusions or conditions contained in the policy. An example would be loss caused by the theft of goods by a carrier's employee. Although this is not a covered loss, the insurer would pay the claim subject to the limits in the BMC 32 endorsement and then attempt to recover the payment from the insured.

> **Adjuster Tip**
>
> The BMC 32 endorsement is valid until it is canceled by a proper filing made at the policy's expiration or cancellation. Cancellation or expiration of the policy without the proper filing is not sufficient to void the BMC 32.

Handling MTC Liability Claims

MTC liability coverage is a third-party coverage that most insurers treat as a first-party coverage. Because the loss is to property, insurers assign these claims to property loss adjusters. These adjusters must determine liability as well as coverage. The investigation must reveal the insured to be legally liable for the damage before the policy will respond.

Coverage verification is the starting point of any claim investigation, and the MTC liability claim is no exception. In fact, it can present new issues to the adjuster. MTC liability is written either on a scheduled-vehicle basis or a blanket/gross-receipts basis. If the coverage is on a scheduled-vehicle basis, then the unit involved in the loss must be listed on the policy. Because of the nature of the trucking industry, the identity of the named insured may also be an issue. There are many types of ownership, trip-lease, and owner-operator agreements used within the trucking industry, so it is important to verify that the legally responsible party is in fact insured under the policy.

The property loss adjuster must determine the facts of the loss, obtain all of the shipping documents, and inspect the loss. Salvage potential is just as important in the MTC liability claim as it is in a merchandise claim.

Bailee Losses

A **bailment** is the transfer of possession of property from one person to another for a specified purpose. Giving cargo to a carrier to transport is a bailment. But many other types of businesses are involved in bailments. They range from warehouses to repair shops, jewelry stores, or consignees of property on consignment. In these situations, title to the property remains with the owner, the **bailor**, and the property is expected to be returned to the bailor once the specific purpose has ended. The person entrusted with the property is the bailee and is responsible for the property while it is in his or her control.

Bailment
The transfer of possession of property from one person to another for a specified purpose.

Bailor
The owner of the property who delivers it to another for a specified purpose.

A bailment differs from both a lease or an agency situation. In a lease, the lessee has full rights during the lease to use the property *in any way*, even to the exclusion of the owner. In a bailment, the bailee's use of the property is limited to a specific purpose. If an agent or employee holds property, the law considers that condition as equivalent to possession by the principal/owner.

Liability in Bailment Situations

Bailment for the benefit of the bailor
A bailment in which the bailee owes only a slight duty of care to safeguard the bailed property from loss or damage.

Bailment for the benefit of the bailee
A bailment in which the bailee owes a high duty of care to safeguard the bailed property from loss or damage.

Bailment for the mutual benefit of bailee and bailor (mutual benefit bailment)
A bailment in which the bailee owes a duty of ordinary care to safeguard the bailed property from loss or damage.

There are three types of bailment situations. First is a **bailment for the benefit of the bailor** only, such as when one neighbor agrees to take care of a vacationing neighbor's plants. The property owner enjoys the sole benefit. In such a bailment, the bailee owes only a slight duty of care and would probably be liable to the owner only for intentional wrongdoing and gross recklessness.

The second type is a **bailment for the benefit of the bailee** only, such as when one neighbor borrows another's lawn mower. In this situation, the bailee owes a high duty of care and is presumably liable for any damage.

The third type is a **bailment for the mutual benefit of bailee and bailor (mutual benefit bailment)**. For example, a dry cleaner/bailee receives payment for the service of laundering, and the customer/bailor receives clean clothing in return for his or her payment. This situation is also known as a commercial bailment. The bailee owes a duty of ordinary care for the property in his or her possession.

Bailee Coverages

Coverage purchased by bailees typically falls into two broad categories: (1) the bailee liability policy and (2) the bailees' customers policy. The bailee liability policy covers the insured for sums that he or she becomes legally obligated to pay as a result of loss caused by a covered peril. As the name implies, this is liability coverage, and the insured would have to be legally liable for the loss for the policy to respond. Under the bailees' customers policy, coverage is provided for property in the bailee's custody with no need to prove the insured's liability or negligence. The coverage is often invoked when bailees want to maintain customer goodwill by replacing the customer's damaged property, even when the bailee has not been at fault. Bailees' customers policies always involve dual interests: both the bailee and the customer have interests in the property and in the claim settlement proceeds.

Bailor Coverages

Bailors do not necessarily rely on the bailees' coverage. Often, when a bailment is created, either the bailee provides no coverage or the bailee's coverage will not respond, such as when the bailee is found not to be legally liable for the loss. Sometimes, bailors insure an exposure despite coverage available from the bailee. Perhaps the property involved is of particularly high value or is hard to replace, or perhaps its loss would interfere with the bailor's regular business.

Most bailors seeking coverage for their property when it is off-premises first check the built-in extensions contained in their own homeowners or commercial property forms. The homeowners policy covers personal property while it is anywhere in the world. The BPP provides tightly limited off-premises coverage. Coinsurance requirements must be met, and the loss must occur at a place that the insured does not own, lease, or operate. Additionally, the covered property cannot be in or on a vehicle; in a salesperson's care, custody, or control; or at a fair or an exhibition. The limit for this extension is $5,000.

Because the built-in off-premises coverages are limited and might not be adequate for losses, several types of bailor policies are available. In personal insurance coverages, various endorsements can be added to cover specific property such as jewelry, cameras, and fine arts. These endorsements (often called floaters) cover more than just a bailment situation, but they do apply to losses occurring to property in a bailee's possession. Commercial bailors can also use numerous inland marine floaters and endorsements to provide off-premises coverage. A processing floater, used by businesses that send their goods to other businesses for processing, is an example.

Adjustment of Bailment Losses

Because of the many coverage possibilities, as well as the possibility of overlapping or joint coverage, a bailment loss requires special handling. Adjusters must determine all parties to the bailment and the nature and extent of their specific interest in the property damaged. Adjusters must also examine all documents related to the bailment to determine the parties' contractual rights and whether either party has waived any rights before the loss. For example, the contract might contain a hold-harmless agreement or might require a specific party to insure the property.

Adjusters must also be familiar with industry practices concerning specific types of property. For example, in the jewelry business, retailers typically hold property of others on a consignment basis. While the property is in the retailer's possession, he or she must usually provide insurance.

Adjusters should also be aware of differences in valuation clauses between policies. For example, under a bailee liability policy, the insurer would be liable to cover property on an actual cash value (ACV) basis; under a homeowners form, the coverage could be written either on an ACV or a replacement cost basis.

If a bailees' customers policy insures a laundry or dry cleaner and the loss involves virtually all of the bailor's property in the store, the adjuster could set up a claim operation on the premises. The policy usually covers the ACV of the customer's property. The adjuster might be dealing with 300 or more customers, so a standard procedure would be necessary. The adjuster might require each claimant to complete a claim form, then negotiate the claim and issue a check on site. The adjuster would handle claims involving a few shirts or a pair of slacks in this manner, but if a large value is involved, the adjuster might go to the claimant's home to settle the loss. Alternatively, the adjuster might simply have the insured distribute claim forms to its customers to be completed and then sent to the adjuster's office, after which negotiations are handled by phone.

In some cases, insurers allow the businessowners to settle losses up to a certain dollar amount with their customers, for example, up to $100 or $250. The insurer might believe that the insured knows the customer and the garments and is therefore better able to negotiate a reasonable actual cash value. This method, of course, has its drawbacks. The insured might be only interested in keeping its customers happy and might not subject their claims to adequate scrutiny. Another settlement method is to settle directly with the insured with a policy release, which allows the insured to handle the customers' claims.

Warehouse Legal Liability

Another type of bailment that is significantly involved in the transportation industry is the storage of goods in a warehouse. A warehouse is in the business of receiving and storing others' goods for a price. The Uniform Commercial Code (U.C.C.) regulates the business of warehousing. The U.C.C. is a body of rules that regulate all commercial transactions. Warehouses may be public, private, or bonded. A public warehouse is one that accepts goods for storage from anyone, for a price. A private warehouse is usually controlled by a large retailer or manufacturer for the storage of its own goods. A bonded warehouse is one in which goods are stored awaiting the payment of import duty. For the purposes of this text, the discussion focuses on public warehouses.

Warehouse legal liability policies cover the warehouse's legal liability for physical loss or damage to property of customers at specified locations. It, too, is a third-party liability policy handled as a first-party policy.

The warehouse legal liability coverage can be named-perils or special-form coverage. It excludes the same types of causes of loss as the motor truck cargo liability policy. It also excludes loss resulting from processing and war risks.

Generally a warehouse is not under a duty to insure stored property for the benefit of the owner or depositor. However, state statutes, the depositor's instructions, custom and practice, or a contract may require the warehouse to have insurance for the benefit of the depositor. The U.C.C. Article 7, Section 204, makes a warehouse liable if the loss or damage is caused by its failure to exercise reasonable care.

Investigating a Warehouse Legal Liability Claim

Warehouse legal liability claims present many levels of adjusting challenges. They can be some of the most complex and interesting claims to work on because a warehouse loss rarely involves only one depositor. When a warehouse is damaged by fire, water, smoke, wind, or any other possible cause of loss, the property of many different depositors is often affected. Large quantities of property for each depositor may be involved. Each depositor will require his or her own inventory. The adjuster may have to use different methods of restoration, salvage, and valuation to properly adjust these losses. The terms of each depositor's warehouse receipt or contract may be different, so the adjuster reviews every contract for its terms. The cause of loss investigation may be hampered by vast quantities of debris, uncooperative witnesses, and bad weather. The cause of loss investigation may lead to the discovery of information that affects coverage, such as the discovery that the insured was storing chemicals on the premises when the policy was written for a general merchandise exposure.

Initial Response to Loss

It is not uncommon for the warehouse legal liability policy to be placed with a different insurer than the insurer handling the building's property coverage. The warehouse may simply be a tenant in the building. If the building coverage is with another carrier, it is a good idea to work with the building carrier's property adjuster to secure the premises and share related expenses. Keep in mind that the warehouse legal liability interest and the building interests may ultimately be adverse to one another. For example, the building owner may blame the warehouse for causing a fire that guts the building. The warehouse may blame the owner for the fire based on the owner's failure to maintain the building. Nevertheless, until it is established that a conflict exists, it is best to try to work together to secure the site and protect all of the property from further damage.

Analysis of Storage Documents

The storage receipts of each depositor must be reviewed to determine the nature of the relationship between the depositor and the insured. It is possible for the relationship to be that of bailee-bailor, landlord-tenant, or carrier-shipper. Only the storage documents clarify the relationship. The storage documents also define the parties' obligations to each other. It is also a good idea to review correspondence, brochures, and advertisements to determine whether they affect the parties' obligations. This is especially true for losses resulting from extremes in temperature and humidity when the warehouse advertises itself to be climate-controlled.

Limitation of Liability

The warehouse receipt or other storage receipt includes a limitation of liability provision. The U.C.C. allows a warehouse to limit its liability under certain circumstances. To be an enforceable limitation, the terms must specify liability per article or item or a value per unit or weight. The warehouse must give the depositor the opportunity to increase the valuation.

Storage Arrangements

One of the key elements in determining the warehouse's liability and the potential for subrogation against another party is understanding the storage arrangement used by the warehouse. Warehouses generally use the following types of storage arrangements, alone or in combination:

1. Bulk storage
2. Solid piling storage
3. Palletized storage
4. Rack storage

The commodity can dictate what method of storage is used, and that method affects fire behavior, fire control, and the goods' susceptibility to water damage.

Bulk storage
Storage of loose granules, powder, or pellets in silos, bins, or tanks, or in piles on the floor.

Solid piling storage
A pallet, at floor level, piled high with cartons, boxes, bales, or bags, all in direct contact with one another.

Pallet unit
A wooden base stacked with smaller packages up to a height of 3 or 4 feet, which are usually banded or shrink-wrapped to keep the packages in place.

Rack storage
Steel shelving of any height, on which goods are stored.

Bulk storage refers to loose granules, powder, or pellets stored in silos, bins, or tanks, or in piles on the floor. Conveyors are usually in the building to help move the material. Automatic sprinklers are essential for this arrangement. Heat sensors are also a good idea because certain types of commodities can ignite while in a pile and the ignition might be difficult to locate deep inside a pile. **Solid piling storage** consists of one pallet, at floor level, piled high with cartons, boxes, bales or bags, all in direct contact with one another. Stacking is usually done by hand or with lift trucks. Piling in excess of fifteen feet can be difficult to protect with sprinklers.

A **pallet unit** is usually three or four feet in height and consists of many smaller packages stacked on top of one another. The pallet can be banded or shrink-wrapped to keep the packages in place on the pallet. Pallets are easy to move with a forklift, so they can be stacked very high. Because of the stacking, it is difficult for sprinklers to be effective against a fire occurring within the stack.

A steel shelf unit in one's garage or basement is an example of **rack storage**. Commercial rack storage is made of steel frames. The racks' height is only limited by the vertical reach of the handling equipment. Some rack-storage facilities are highly automated, using computers to track locations and inventory and control the material-handling equipment. Rack storage can have narrow aisles, allowing fire to jump easily from one rack to another. Conventional ceiling sprinklers are not very effective in a rack storage facility. In-rack sprinkler systems provide the best protection.

Liability Assessment

The type of storage arrangement and the sprinkler system within the building can affect the liability assessment. If a warehouse manager knowingly accepts goods for storage that are incompatible with his or her storage system and sprinkler system, then the warehouse's liability may be increased.

Adjuster Tip

Not all warehouses are sprinklered. Check local ordinances to determine whether the warehouse complies with fire regulations and building codes.

A warehouse may unknowingly accept goods that are dangerous. Because the standard of care depends on " reasonableness," the adjuster must investigate what a reasonable warehouse would have done under similar circumstances to determine the goods' exact nature. This becomes particularly important in chemicals' storage. When a chemical is stored in a warehouse, a **Material Safety Data Sheet (MSDS)** should be obtained from the depositor. The chemical manufacturer writes the MSDS. It describes what the chemical is; who makes it; what ingredients are in it; and how it reacts to heat, cold, and water. It describes the potential for fire and explosion and recommends the method for extinguishing a fire. It also describes how stable the product is, whether it will react to other chemicals stored around it, and whether there are any special handling instructions for it.

Material Safety Data Sheet (MSDS)
A document required by the Occupational Safety and Health Administration (OSHA) that describes a property's hazardous chemicals and how they must be handled.

Burden of Proof

In the event of a contested claim, the adjuster must ascertain which party has the burden of proof regarding the warehouse's negligence. Unfortunately, there is no uniformity among the states, so it will be necessary to consult with local counsel to learn who has the burden of proof. In states that favor the warehouse, the depositor must show that the warehouse was negligent by a preponderance of the evidence. In states that favor the depositor, the warehouse must show that the loss was not its fault and could not have been prevented by any reasonable action on its part.

OTHER PROPERTY LOSSES

Many different kinds of property policies are used for specialized risk exposures. This text highlights several of them to introduce the adjuster to the various risks insurable under property policies and the claim adjustment issues that ensue.

Condominium Losses

Condominiums are a special form of property ownership that present several unique legal, coverage, and adjusting issues. A **condominium** is one of the units in a multiple-unit structure, each of which is separately owned. These units can be dwelling or business-type units. Each unit owner receives a deed of record independent of any other unit owner. A single unit often consists of nothing more than a cubicle, or "box of air," of one or more levels of space within the structure's unfinished surfaces of walls, floors, or ceilings. After a developer has sold a certain percentage of the units, it relinquishes authority to the condominium association. A condominium should not be confused

Condominium
One of multiple units in a structure, each unit being separately owned.

Cooperative (co-op)
A nonprofit corporation that owns the housing units and the associated property.

with a cooperative. A **cooperative** or **co-op** is a nonprofit corporation that owns the units and the associated property. A tenant buys stock in the cooperative that entitles the tenant to lease a unit.

Common Elements

Condominium association
An organization that controls management of a condominium complex and is responsible for the upkeep of the common elements.

Common elements
Areas of a condominium that are jointly owned by all unit owners, including the land on which the buildings are located.

A **condominium association** manages the condominium complex and is responsible for the **common elements**. The association does not own the property. The common elements, or areas, are jointly owned by all unit owners and include the land on which the building is located as well as other real property, consisting of foundations; roofs; main support walls; halls; stairways; entrances and exits; lobbies; yards; gardens; parking areas; power; light; gas; plumbing; heating and air conditioning systems; elevators; pumps; duct work; storage areas or basements; and pools, playgrounds, and other recreation facilities on the grounds.

Because of the complexity of the relationship between unit owners and the association, condominiums are created and defined by legislation in most jurisdictions. These statutes also address insurance requirements. Most states require the association to provide insurance to cover loss or damage to the common elements. A unit owner must insure his or her contents and interest in his or her own unit. Some statutes state that improvements and betterments are to be covered under the unit owner's insurance because the improvements increase the value of the unit itself. Other statutes require improvements and betterments, whether to the individual units or to common areas, to be insured under the association's policy.

Master Deed and Bylaws

Master deed
A document that defines a condominium and specifies the relationship between the unit owners and the association.

To determine who is responsible for specific property, adjusters must check not only state statutes but also the **master deed** and the unit deeds of the condominium. The master deed might also be called the "declarations of the condominium association" or the "condominium association agreement." The condominium's developer or builder usually draws up the deed or declarations.

Barewalls concept
Term used to describe a unit owner's property that consists only of what is within the bare walls, including paint, wallpaper, carpet or flooring, appliances, and fixtures.

Either the master deed or separate bylaws describe the relationship between the unit owners, the duties of the association, maintenance fees, how assessments are to be made, and insurance requirements. The deed or bylaws also describe the transference of properties, how the association is to be governed, and requirements for any modifications or amendments to the bylaws.

Nature of the Unit Owner's Interest

All-encompassing concept
A condo association's interest when it owns and is responsible for all interior and exterior items within the individual condo unit at the time of the original purchase by the unit owner.

After reviewing a copy of the master deed and bylaws, adjusters can determine insurable interests and which policy is to provide coverage for damaged items. Condominium deeds outline the insurable interests in two possible ways: (1) the **barewalls concept** and (2) the **all-encompassing concept.** See the following box.

The Barewalls Concept

Under the barewalls concept, a unit owner's property consists only of what is within the bare walls, including paint, wallpaper, carpet or flooring, appliances, fixtures (electrical or plumbing), and interior walls. A claim adjustment under an association's policy would not cover these items. Conversely, the unit owner's policy would not provide coverage in the event of a loss for damage to drywall that forms an exterior, or load-bearing, wall; floor decking; joists; studs; rafters; foundations; or roofing.

For a loss adjustment based on the barewalls concept, the adjuster for the association and the adjuster for the unit owner must decide which policy provides coverage for which items. This issue should be decided before repairs are made so that no misunderstanding occurs during the final settlement or payment of the claim. When the structural damage is serious, a unit owner's insurer often allows the condominium association insurer to cover all repairs and reimburses it for the portion of the damages covered by the unit owner's policy.

The All-Encompassing Concept

Under the all-encompassing concept (also known as the "air space concept" or the "single entity concept"), the condominium association owns and is responsible for all exterior and interior items within the unit at the time of its original purchase by the unit owner. When the unit is sold with appliances, flooring, and fixtures already installed, the association is responsible for insuring these items. The purchase contract describes these items.

For a loss adjustment based on the all-encompassing concept, the condominium association insurer repairs or replaces all original installations. The unit owner's insurer covers damage to improvements and betterments and any personal property involved in the loss and installed by the unit owner.

Coverage Forms

Insurance Services Office, Inc., (ISO) provides a separate, simplified commercial property insurance program for condominium associations. Unit owners are protected by a special type of homeowners form or a commercial unit owner's form.

Condominium Association Coverage Form

The condominium association coverage form is used in conjunction with the common declarations, common and commercial property conditions, causes of loss forms, and other assorted forms. The condominium association form is similar to the Building and Personal Property Coverage Form (BPP) and contains the same coverages, additional coverages, extension of coverage, optional coverages, and property not covered. The condominium association coverage form provides coverage for the building. It also covers certain types of property within a unit, such as fixtures, improvements, and appliances, if the condominium master deed or bylaws require the association to insure such property. This coverage applies whether or not the unit owner owns these items. Under the unit owner's insurance provision, the insurance for the association is primary. It is not contributory with any insurance carried by the unit owner covering the same property.

Business personal property is covered if it is owned by the association or indivisibly by all unit owners. It is not covered if owned solely by a unit owner. Property under this coverage could include clubroom furnishings, deck or lawn chairs, lobby or hall decorations, and recreational equipment. The condominium association coverage form, like the BPP, provides coverage for personal property of others if shown in the declarations. This coverage includes unit owners' property.

Associations commonly appoint an insurance trustee to act on the unit owners' behalf. The insurance trustee is responsible for decisions regarding the placement of coverage and the settlement of claims. The condominium association coverage form has added a provision under loss payment to state that the insurer may adjust the loss with the association but pay the insurance to a trustee if one has been appointed. Any payment made to the trustee satisfies the claims of all unit owners.

The association is made up of individual unit owners. Accordingly, the right of subrogation by the insurer against individual unit owners has been waived in the waiver of rights of recovery provision.

Unit Owner's Coverage Form

Two types of unit owner's coverage are available: (1) coverage for commercial unit owners and (2) coverage for residential unit owners.

1. *Commercial unit owners.* Commercial unit owner's coverage complements the association policy and has many of the same provisions of the other commercial property coverages. It includes no building coverage because the building is insured under the association policy.

   It does include coverage for building fixtures, improvements, and alterations owned by the unit owner and not insured by the association. Any settlement on these items is subject to the policy's coinsurance provision. If the same property is covered under both the unit owner's policy and the association policy, the unit owner's coverage is excess over the association coverage. The condominium commercial unit owner's coverage has two optional coverages: (1) loss assessment coverage and (2) miscellaneous real property coverage.

   A **loss assessment** is a charge by the condominium association against the unit owners. The association has the right to make such charges, under certain circumstances, as described in the master deed or bylaws. Loss assessment coverage is limited to liability for assessments resulting from direct physical loss or damage by a covered peril to common property

Loss assessment
A charge by the condominium association against the unit owners for the cost of uninsured losses.

in which all unit owners have an interest. The unit owner purchases loss assessment coverage for protection in case the association's insurance is not sufficient to cover a loss. Loss assessment coverage can be purchased for multiples of $1,000, with a $250 deductible. If the assessment is made to cover a large deductible in the association's coverage, the limit of liability is $1,000 regardless of the amount purchased by the unit owner.

Miscellaneous real property coverage is provided under a separate limit of insurance. This class of real property includes property owned by the condominium unit insured only or required by the association agreement to be insured by the unit owner. An example is a storage structure located in the common areas and used solely by a unit owner.

2. *Residential unit owners*. Residential unit owner's coverage is provided by a homeowner's unit owner's form (HO-6). The policy insures against all broad-form perils, including fire; lightning; windstorm; hail; explosion; riot; civil commotion; aircraft; vehicles; smoke; vandalism; malicious mischief; theft; falling objects; weight of ice, snow, or sleet; accidental discharge of water or steam; tearing, cracking, burning, or bulging of a steam or hot water system; freezing; artificially generated electrical current; and volcanic eruption.

   Coverage against these named perils is important for the insured's personal property, but it also applies to building improvements and betterments and other building items owned by the unit owner and not insured under the association agreement. It also applies to other structures owned solely by the unit owner (other than the residence premises) and located on the residence premises. If a loss occurs, insurance provided under this form is excess to the association's policy covering the same property.

   Loss assessment coverage is an additional coverage under the HO-6 form. When an assessment is made as a result of direct loss to property owned collectively by all unit members and caused by a peril insured against, the insurer will pay up to $1,000.

Adjuster Tip

Do not assume that the occupier of the unit is the unit's owner. Tenants can occupy a condominium unit, and they would have renter's insurance for their personal property. Therefore, determining who all of the parties are when investigating the loss is very important.

Builders' Risk Losses

Property under construction has special loss exposures. Builders' risk coverage responds to these exposures. This coverage differs from standard commercial property insurance. Loss adjustment of builders' risk claims can be accomplished in several ways.

Builders' Risk Exposures

When a contractor or builder is prepared to begin construction of a new building, it faces the difficult situation of insuring a structure whose value and condition are constantly changing. Initially, machinery, equipment, tools and supplies, building materials, scaffolding, fencing, temporary buildings, and sheds might be on the site. Therefore, if the contractor were to secure ordinary commercial property insurance to cover the structure's completed value, it would pay excessive premiums while the building was under construction. As the construction nears completion, the contractor might be underinsured because of increased construction costs.

The contractor might be required to protect not only its own interests in the building but also the interests of the owners and the mortgagees as well as the subcontractors that work on the structure. The contractor might even be required to protect its suppliers' interests. The contractor's obligation to protect these other interests comes from the construction contracts. Although the contractor might not bear each of the preceding obligations, rarely is a contractor obligated to protect only its own interest.

The building also faces special hazards while the building is under construction. Building materials are difficult to protect while on a construction site. They are subject to theft and severe damage by windstorms and by fire. While under construction, the building itself is also exposed to these types of losses and to vandalism or collapse. Protecting the building from loss is difficult because it lacks safeguards such as sprinkler systems or even adequate access to water.

Coverage Forms

The builders' risk form was devised to address the special problem of changing values and the unique exposures to loss of a building under construction. The policy is written for one year but normally terminates when the building has been completed or occupied. A builders' risk policy can be written for basic, broad, or "direct physical loss unless excluded" coverage.

The policy can be written on a builders' risk form, or it can be a manuscript policy.

Commercial Property

A builders' risk form is attached to a commercial property policy and becomes subject to the common declarations and conditions, as well as the commercial property declarations and conditions and the causes of loss form that make up the policy.

Commercial property builders' risk forms do not cover collapse during construction unless it is added back by an endorsement that covers collapse caused by faulty design, plans, or workmanship. Nor do they cover theft of building materials not attached to a building under any causes of loss form. Even the Causes of Loss—Special Form eliminates theft coverage for building materials and supplies and also eliminates any coverage for machinery, tools, and equipment owned by, or in the care, custody, or control of, the insured.

Manuscript Forms

The policy can be written in a manuscript form to cover uncertain or uncommon exposures. The construction might take several years, or the project may be an unusually large and complex structure that requires more coverage than that provided by the standard commercial form. Manuscript forms may also cover the testing and commissioning of equipment installed in the building as part of the project.

Inland Marine Policies

Builders' risk coverage is also provided as an inland marine coverage under a builders' risk policy or an installation floater, usually on an "all-risks" basis. Inland marine builders' risk policies usually have broader coverage than commercial property policies do because they can cover property in transit and at other job sites, they cover collapse and theft, and they can be endorsed to cover earthquake and flood. Most important, inland marine policies may cover increased **soft costs**. Soft costs, such as interest, real estate taxes, advertising, architects' and engineers' fees, legal and accounting fees, and insurance, are incurred when there is a delay in the completion of the project. Adjusters may need professional assistance to identify and evaluate increased soft costs.

Soft costs
Various incidental expenses that may result from physical loss or from a delay in completion of a construction project, such as interest, real estate tax, advertising, architects and engineers fees, and legal and accounting fees.

Property Covered

Builders' risk policies provide coverage for buildings or structures in the course of construction on the described premises, including foundations and materials used for construction. It extends coverage to fixtures, machinery, and equipment that service the building. Inland marine forms cover building materials and supplies owned by the insured; building materials and supplies of others in the insured's care, custody, or control; and temporary structures, including scaffolding, cribbing, and construction forms.

As in most coverage forms, there is no coverage for land, water, or certain outdoor property such as lawns, trees, shrubs, plants, radio or television antennas or towers, and detached signs. Builders' risk coverage forms might also exclude the preexisting part of a building to which alterations, additions, repairs, or renovations are being made.

Handling Changing Values

The builders' risk policy is written on a completed value approach or a reporting form. Insurance is usually written for the completed value of the building or structure. The premium charged is reduced because the policy limits exceed the value at risk to the insurer until the building is completed. The completed value form includes a condition called "need for adequate insurance" that is effectively a 100 percent coinsurance clause. The policy limit must equal the expected completed value, or a penalty is imposed.

The reporting form requires the insured to make monthly reports of value. The initial premium is generally determined by computing the actual cash value of the property brought onto the insured premises at the start of construction. As the monthly reports are filed, the limits of liability are increased accordingly, and additional premium is computed. If the reports are late or undervalued, the insured can face severe penalties if a covered loss occurs. Because the coinsurance clause in a full reporting form is 100 percent, failure to report limits the insurer's liability to the actual cash value at the inception of the policy. Failure to report on time can limit the insurer's liability to the last reported value.

Subrogation

Because of the various interests covered by the policy and the relationship between these parties, adjusters should check both the policy and the contracts between the parties to determine whether subrogation is possible. Determining who is an insured, the extent of the interest insured, and whether subrogation has been waived in writing by agreement before an actual loss is important.

Many commercial property builders' risk forms require an insured to obtain the insurer's written permission to waive any rights to recovery before a loss occurs. The inland marine version of the builders' risk form may limit this provision to architects or engineers, thus permitting waiver of subrogation against other contractors or subcontractors. These provisions are especially important because many form contracts in the construction business, such as those provided by the American Institute of Architects, require waiver of actions by the parties. Such waivers might threaten a contractor's insurance coverage unless the insurer approves them.

Coverage Termination

The coverage of the builders' risk form ends when *any* one of the five following conditions is met:

1. The policy is canceled, the policy expires, or ninety days have passed since the completion of the project.
2. The owner or purchaser accepts the property. This acceptance, of course, should mean that other specific insurance on the completed building is in place.
3. The insured no longer has any interest in the property; therefore, the insured cannot suffer a loss if the property is damaged.
4. The construction is abandoned, and the insured has no intention of completing the building and has given up his or her right or interest in the building.
5. Sixty days after the building has been wholly or partially occupied or put to its intended use, or leased to others.

Loss Adjustment

The investigation of a builders' risk loss usually begins with an inspection of the construction site and the damaged property. Taking a statement from the site superintendent or clerk of the works can help the property loss adjuster obtain and understand the facts of the loss, the parties involved, and the extent of the damage.

An important part of a claim investigation involves gathering all contracts relevant to the claim-handling process. Relevant contracts include the construction contract between the general contractor and the owner, as well as those between the general contractor and the subcontractors.

Construction contracts often require one party to purchase insurance for the benefit of the other party. If this is the case, the adjuster should obtain certificates of insurance verifying that insurance was obtained as required. Additionally, reviewing contracts may help the adjuster determine whether they contain hold-harmless or indemnity agreements that might waive the insurer's subrogation rights against an at-fault party. For example, a hold-harmless agreement between the general contractor and a subcontractor may prevent the general contractor's builders' risk insurer from subrogating against a subcontractor who caused the loss. Several other documents may directly affect the amount of loss recoverable. In the case of physical loss, the receipts, subcontracts, and records of interim payments made by the owner to the contractor can give the adjuster a good idea of the amount of work actually completed at the site before the loss. This information can help to determine the amount of loss payable for a claim.

When handling a claim that includes soft costs, the adjuster obtains critical-path charts, minutes of site meetings, and other documents that help to establish the project's status at the time of loss and the loss's effect on the project's completion date. A critical-path chart is a schedule of the construction project that highlights the steps and stages that are vital to the project's completion. It is used to track job progress and completion. Reviewing the critical-path document enables the adjuster to determine whether the project was on schedule and whether the loss will result in a delay of the project's completion. If a delay will result and the policy covers loss of rental or business income, the adjuster will need to obtain an estimate of the revenue that the completed building would generate. To determine the amount of a soft-costs loss, it is usually necessary for an insured to produce a great deal of financial documentation, including the specifics of the project's financing package, contracts, and income projections presented to lenders when the project was proposed. Sometimes repairs can be accomplished without affecting the project schedule, thereby incurring no soft costs or delayed opening claim.

Determination of the amount payable in a builders' risk claim often requires the use of experts. When adjusting large losses, the insurer normally hires a construction consultant. The construction consultant is frequently an engineer or a general contractor skilled in commercial construction.

The consultant helps establish a reasonable amount of loss as well as the length of the delay that will result from the loss. If the claim involves soft costs, the adjuster may also need to hire an accountant. The accountant's role is to analyze the financial documentation and revenue projections and to apply them to the delay estimate prepared by the construction consultant.

In a large builders' risk loss, a significant portion of the adjuster's duties centers on managing the experts and integrating the various opinions and data into a fair valuation of the insured's claim.

Crime Losses

Crime losses are among the most challenging that an adjuster can face. An adjuster must verify coverage thoroughly and must understand the coverage applicable to a given loss. Crime coverage varies considerably from personal insurance to commercial insurance and from one commercial insured to another. Investigation of crime losses is difficult and sensitive. For example, the perpetrator would have tried to prevent discovery, an insured might have staged a loss, or an insider might be involved.

Burglary
The entry into a building with the intent to commit a crime.

Robbery
The act of taking property from a person by threatening or using violence.

Common law and modern criminal statutes define various crimes. Theft is the broadest category of illegally taking property with the intent to deprive the owner of the property. **Burglary** is entry into a building with the intent to commit a crime, usually theft. **Robbery** is the act of taking property from a person, or taking it in the presence of that person, by threatening the person with violence. Burglary and robbery are forms of theft. Insurance policy definitions might not be identical to common-law or crime statute definitions. For example, insurance policies usually define burglary as having "marks of forcible entry or exit," a characteristic that might be absent from crime codes.

Property thefts often occur in office, residential, retail, or warehouse-type occupancies where a quick, secretive act can go unnoticed. Personal property often disappears under a coat, in a shopping bag, or even in an employee's toolbox. Property can be easily disposed of in a pawnshop or kept for the thief's use.

Burglaries account for the largest dollar loss amounts among all thefts. The secrecy with which burglary is accomplished gives a perpetrator ample time to carry off large quantities of merchandise without detection. Notwithstanding burglar alarms, watchdogs, security guards, and other security measures, burglary is easier for criminals to commit than is robbery.

Robberies often occur in establishments that hold cash and have only one or two attendants, such as convenience stores, dry cleaners, and gas stations. Couriers for banks or high-volume retail stores are particularly susceptible to attack. Trucking companies are likely targets for robbery or theft of merchandise because the driver is usually alone. Criminals target high-value stock that is easily disposed of, such as liquor, cigarettes, and appliances.

Crime Coverages in Personal Insurance

Crime coverage is a standard part of all homeowners policies and is essential to a well-constructed personal insurance package. Crime against a private citizen can take many forms and can cause loss to both personal and real property. When copper was expensive, many homes were stripped of copper gutters and downspouts, which were then sold for scrap. Stained glass windows are also theft targets. Even woodwork, trim, or plumbing fixtures can be taken by thieves. Building materials awaiting installation are favorite and easy targets.

Standard homeowners policies cover an insured's real and personal property against theft losses, but the policies limit classes of property that have an extremely high loss potential, such as firearms, gems, gold, jewelry, furs, and other expensive articles. (Chapter 3 details the HO-3's special limits of liability.) However, these articles can be scheduled on an endorsement to the policy for an agreed value and for an additional premium. When these articles are listed in the policy, they are said to be **scheduled articles**. They are covered against a broader range of perils and for a wider geographical scope.

Scheduled articles
Personal property specifically listed on a homeowner's policy that is typically covered against a broader range of perils, for a wider geographic scope, and/or at an agreed value.

Crime coverage limited to the home would not completely cover an insured's entire exposure. At times, all insureds leave their residence and travel, often with substantial valuables on their person or in their baggage. For many reasons, the exposure to loss increases substantially when the owner leaves home. Articles are lost or misplaced and believed to have been stolen. Luggage is lost and believed stolen. Articles are left unattended. Travelers often innocently stray into high-risk areas. Insurers recognize this off-premises exposure and provide coverage for the insured's protection. In most policies, coverage extends to losses to personal property anywhere in the world. Coverage is for the named insured and other household members.

Theft of personal property at other locations owned by, rented to, or occupied by an insured is covered only while the insured is temporarily living there. For example, theft from a summer home while an insured is living there would be covered. The status of a student insured is slightly different. The student only needs to establish that he or she was at the temporary residence where theft occurred within forty-five days before the theft. The student's property is thus protected over long holiday periods, but not for a full summer. Theft coverage away from the residence premises does not apply to watercraft, their furnishings or equipment, outboard motors, or trailers or campers.

Homeowners policies usually have an Additional Coverage for losses caused by unauthorized use of a credit card, check forgery, or loss by receipt of counterfeit money. No deductible applies to any loss under this coverage. This coverage does not apply to losses arising out of business use or out of an insured's dishonesty. In the Additional Coverage, the insurer also agrees to settle or defend actions against an insured arising out of fraudulent fund transfer or credit card use. The insurer bears the cost of such a defense, which is not deducted from the available loss coverage. Defense costs are in addition to the policy coverage limit.

Crime Coverages in the BPP

Unlike the homeowners policy, which is a package, commercial insurance coverages are offered separately. Insureds choose the coverages they want. Exposures vary so widely by business that a package approach would not be an efficient way of meeting business insurance needs. A policy is built by selecting various forms that meet a customer's needs.

Nevertheless, the Building and Personal Property Coverage Form (BPP) provides certain limited crime coverages. They are so limited or restricted that a business with any significant crime exposure must consider purchasing crime insurance, such as ISO Commercial Crime Coverage, explained below.

The BPP with the Causes of Loss—Basic Form and the Causes of Loss—Broad Form include crime coverage only for vandalism and looting accompanying a riot. They cover only the damage to the building caused by the vandals' breaking in or exiting. This is the extent of the crime coverage provided under the Basic and Broad Forms.

The BPP with the Causes of Loss—Special Form is written to cover all losses that it does not specifically exclude or limit. This form includes crime coverage except to the extent that it is excluded or limited. This form specifically excludes losses caused by a dishonest or criminal act of the insured or employees or by voluntary parting of property caused by a fraudulent scheme, trick, device, or false pretense. The following limitations also apply to theft claims:

> We will not pay for loss of or damage to: . . .
>
> d. Building materials and supplies not attached as part of the building or structure caused by or resulting from theft. . . .
>
> e. Property that is missing, where the only evidence of the loss or damage is a shortage disclosed on taking inventory, or other instances where there is no physical evidence to show what happened to the property.
>
> f. Property that has been transferred to a person or to a place outside the described premises on the basis of unauthorized instructions.[1]

The following sublimits apply to covered theft losses:

> For loss or damage by theft, the following types of property are covered only up to the limits shown:
>
> a. $2,500 for furs, fur garments and garments trimmed with fur.
>
> b. $2,500 for jewelry, watches, watch movements, jewels, pearls, precious and semiprecious stones, bullion, gold, silver, platinum, and other precious alloys or metals. This limit does not apply to jewelry and watches worth $100 or less per item.
>
> c. $2,500 for patterns, dies, molds, and forms.
>
> d. $250 for stamps, tickets, and letters of credit.[2]

The ISO Crime Program

The crime coverage provided by the BPP and the standard causes of loss forms are inadequate for many businesses. To meet the need for expanded crime coverage, ISO has developed a commercial crime coverage form. The form's crime coverage options can be added to a package policy or written as a stand-alone policy.

Eight options for crime coverage are available under the ISO Commercial Crime Coverage Form. The declarations page indicates which of the eight possible insuring agreements have been selected, along with the limit of insurance and the deductible that will apply.

The eight coverage options are as follows:

1. *Employee Theft*. The definition of "employee" found in the policy is important to this coverage. An **employee** can be only a natural person, not a corporate entity. Temporary workers are considered employees, but leased workers are not. Terminated workers are considered employees for up to thirty days after their termination date.
2. *Forgery or Alteration*. This coverage protects the insured if he or she accepts a bad negotiable instrument or commercial paper or if the insured tenders a forged or altered negotiable instrument or commercial paper. It reimburses legal costs, in addition to the policy limit. The deductible does not apply to the legal costs. It covers anywhere in the world.
3. *Inside the Premises—Theft of Money and Securities*. Coverage is provided for theft, destruction, or unidentified disappearance but does not cover accounting or arithmetical errors. Theft by the named insured or partner is excluded.
4. *Inside the Premises—Robbery or Safe Burglary of Other Property*. This agreement provides coverage for other tangible property such as a watch that has been taken in to the insured for repair work and is then stolen from the premises.
5. *Outside the Premises*. This provides coverage for theft, disappearance, or destruction of money, securities, and other tangible property from a messenger or armored car. "Messenger" is defined as the insured, the insured's relatives, partners, members, or any employee while having custody outside the premises. The coverage for other tangible property is limited to loss from an actual or attempted robbery.
6. *Computer Fraud*. This provides coverage for loss to money, securities, and other property that results from the use of a computer to fraudulently transfer property from the insured's premises or bank to someone outside these premises.
7. *Funds Transfer Fraud*. If a fraudulent instruction to a financial institution to transfer funds results in a loss, there will be coverage under this option.
8. *Money Orders and Counterfeit Paper Currency*. If the insured accepts a counterfeit money order or paper currency, the loss will be covered.

Employee (for crime coverage)
A natural person employed by the insured, including temporary workers and terminated workers for up to thirty days after their termination date.

Occurrence (for crime coverage) Loss caused by one or more employees in a single act or through several acts.

Another important definition is "occurrence." For employee theft coverage, an **occurrence** encompasses loss caused by one or more employees in a single act or through several acts. The forgery and alteration coverage also has its own definition of "occurrence." It is all losses caused by any person regardless of the number of instruments involved. For all of the other insuring agreements, an occurrence is an act or series of related acts involving one or more persons or an act or event or series of related acts or events not involving any person.

Exclusions

Acts committed by the insured and acts committed by the insured's employees are excluded unless the employee theft option is selected. Legal expenses are excluded unless the forgery or alteration option is selected. There are the standard exclusions for government action, nuclear reaction and contamination, and war. Indirect losses are also excluded. An example of an indirect loss is the loss of a contract or sale as a result of a covered cause of loss. There is also an exclusion for the cost of proving that a loss has occurred, such as the cost of hiring an accountant.

Also, some exclusions apply to a specific insuring agreement. The employee theft agreement has an exclusion whereby it will not cover any employee who has been previously excluded from coverage because of a prior theft. It also excludes inventory shortage. The inside and outside coverage agreements all exclude loss as a result of accounting or arithmetical errors or loss as a result of the insured's making a mistake about an item's value. Loss by fire is also excluded unless the fire damages the vault or the safe that the goods are stored in.

The computer fraud option has a specific exclusion that states that the insured cannot use an inventory or profit and loss statement to prove that a loss has occurred.

Conditions

The policy's Conditions section is very important because it indicates whether the policy is a Discovery Form Policy or a Loss Sustained Form Policy. The Discovery Form conditions state that the policy applies to loss due to acts or events that occur at any time but are discovered during the policy period. The Loss Sustained Form applies to loss due to acts or events that occur during the policy period and are discovered during the policy period.

Both forms have an Extended Period to Discover Loss Condition. The Discovery Form allows an additional sixty days from the date of termination or cancellation to discover the loss. The Loss Sustained Form allows up to one year from termination or cancellation to discover the loss. Both forms state that the loss must be sustained before the cancellation or termination date. Should the insured replace the coverage with another policy, these extended periods of discovery end on the date of the new coverage.

Additional conditions apply to all of the insuring agreements. One is the condition that cancels coverage for an employee upon discovery that he or she is involved in the theft. However, the policy does not define discovery. This can be a major issue with ongoing theft. Is the discovery the date when the employee is first suspected, or is it the date when the employee is confronted or arrested or convicted? Case law can help provide an answer.

A suit clause in the Conditions states that suit cannot be brought until ninety days after the insured files a proof of loss and it must be within two years of the date of discovery of the loss. An individual state's laws can override this provision.

Loss Sustained Conditions

The Loss Sustained Conditions Form has some additional conditions. There is a condition that states that the insurer will pay the larger of the amounts covered by this policy or the prior policy for any loss covered partly by this policy and partly by the prior policy. However, this applies only if the prior policy was with the same insurer or an affiliate. There is a condition that if a loss is sustained during a prior policy and the insured did not collect on that loss because the time to discover the loss had expired, then this policy will cover the loss if two conditions are met: (1) the loss would have been covered under the prior policy and is covered under this policy, and (2) this policy became effective upon the prior policy's termination. There is also a clause that if two or more coverages of this policy cover a loss, then the insurer will pay the actual amount of the loss or the sum of the limits applicable to the coverages involved.

Lastly, the Loss Sustained Conditions has an Other Insurance Clause that is distinctive from the standard clause found in property policies. It states that the policy does not apply to loss recoverable or recovered under any other insurance. However, if the amount of the other insurance is insufficient to cover the entire amount of the loss, then this policy will apply to the unreimbursed part of the loss, subject to this policy's deductible and limits.

Valuation—Settlement

Under the crime coverages, a loss to money is paid at face value. Securities are valued as of the close of business on the day the loss is discovered. Other property is valued at replacement cost if the item is repaired or replaced. If not, then it is valued at ACV.

For Inside the Premises—Robbery or Safe Burglary and for Outside the Premises coverages, the policy will only pay for the loss that the insured cannot recover from the insurer of the armored car company. There is also a $5,000 limit, in any one occurrence, for loss to precious metals, precious or semiprecious stones, pearls, furs, or articles containing these items. Manuscripts, drawings, records, and the cost to restore them are also subject to this limit.

Investigation and Adjustment of Crime Losses

As in most investigations, the adjuster should tour the insured premises, survey the physical conditions of the property to see where the premises were entered and where the property was located, and get a general overview of the circumstances related to the loss. The adjuster should then investigate with the insured or anyone else who knows the most about the circumstances of the loss and the property itself. For commercial losses, the adjuster should obtain tape-recorded or written statements regarding the type of business; how it operates; how long it has been at the location; its loss history; its financial data, including inventory records, cost of goods, and mark-ups; its customer relationships; and other details of the loss. For homeowners losses, the adjuster should obtain documentation concerning purchase dates, invoices, and the condition of the property. The adjuster must know as much as possible about the property, the insured, and the circumstances of the loss.

Verification of the Event

Under any of the crime coverages, the adjuster's primary goal, after determining that coverage applies for the type of loss and property involved, is to establish that a loss has actually occurred. Staged crime losses are among the easiest types of frauds to accomplish. Unlike other perils, which show evidence of having occurred, a theft might leave no overt sign at all. Even if a fire might be arson, the adjuster would know that a fire occurred. But with a staged burglary or other theft, the insured could move or sell the property to create the appearance that a crime has occurred.

Because suspicion is a natural response to crime losses, adjusters need to be trained to interview insureds and others without offending them and creating an impression of bad faith. Interviews with employees, neighbors, or police might also be appropriate. In staged crime losses, neighbors often inform adjusters that they witnessed the insured carrying large amounts of property from the premises shortly before the alleged loss.

The insured might try to prove a loss by indicating, for example, the absence of three pallets or two shelves of merchandise. The decision to accept that a loss has occurred rests partly on the adjuster's assessment of the insured's integrity and partly on proof. For instance, an adjuster would have little reason to doubt the integrity of three teachers who attest to the theft loss of gym equipment from a high school because they probably would not have a personal interest at stake. In that case, the teachers' statements could be enough proof. Still, each case must be weighed on its merits, and the degree of proof required should be assessed accordingly. Significant dollar losses call for significant investigation. Many crime claims, especially under homeowners policies, are small and can be handled by telephone or inside adjusters. Though ostensibly cost-effective, such investigations are often not as thorough as an on-the-scene investigation and might be confined to securing a police report.

Fraud Indicators

Although some losses are undoubtedly totally fraudulent, fraud usually occurs when a legitimate loss occurs and the insured uses the opportunity of filing a claim to exploit the loss, claiming many times the amount actually stolen. Chapter 7 discusses the indicators of a fraudulent or exaggerated claim. Any of these indicators might also be present on legitimate claims, so the adjuster must interpret them carefully.

Insured's Statement

In most circumstances, adjusters are required to take a signed or recorded statement from the insured or other individuals. When a theft, burglary, or robbery occurs, a statement is almost mandatory except when the claim's value is small. The statement should record facts that are fresh in the insured's or witness's mind. It should also serve as an inventory of what was taken. If the adjuster asks questions logically and chronologically, a statement could evoke other thoughts and facts that might have been overlooked. Taking a statement puts the adjustment process into a more formal atmosphere and might deter an insured from some intended dishonest act. Statements might also be used to identify property or to recall facts years later during litigation. Examinations under oath can also be used to obtain the necessary information. Chapter 6 discusses the details of the EUO process.

Employee Involvement

In a commercial setting, after determining that a commercial covered crime loss has actually occurred and that the insured is not involved, the adjuster must then ascertain whether an employee is involved. All policies exclude losses caused by employees, except those specifically written for employee dishonesty or fidelity losses. Unless such coverage is purchased, the exclusions under all other crime coverages will bar recovery for theft by an employee. Employees, by definition, must be employed when the loss occurs. Independent contractors and other associates are not considered employees.

Determining an employee's involvement is often difficult, and the evidence is often circumstantial. If the only way that a loss could conceivably have occurred is through a specific employee's participation, such evidence should be enough to deny a claim. Whether the employee dishonesty coverage (which is often purchased separately from a different insurer) or the crime coverage should pay the loss is often a question. Certainly the insured should not suffer as the two insurers try to discover which is responsible. Complete payment to the insured should be made under an agreement between the insurers to arbitrate their differences. The insurers should agree that any payments made to the insured would not prejudice the insurers' rights at arbitration.

Amount of Loss

After being satisfied that a covered loss has occurred and that neither the insured nor an employee is involved, the adjuster must measure the loss. For many commercial crime losses, salvors and accountants can assist the adjuster in this effort. First to be determined is the type and amount of property that was at the insured's premises just before the loss. Salvors might be needed to count what remains after a loss to tangible property. An accountant can work backward with records of purchases and sales and with previous physical inventory to prove what existed just before the loss or to show how much money was on hand. Properly kept books and records are helpful. An insured with poor records causes much inaccuracy in this procedure. In fact, the adjuster might encounter a wide variety of accounting records—anything from a shoebox full of receipts to a certified public accountant's formal journals. Nevertheless, the adjuster must deal with whatever records are available. The policy requires that the insured divulge all records, regardless of their nature and quality.

Recovery of Property

Because of the nature of crime coverage, the adjuster is likely to communicate with police about the loss. It is expected that a report of the loss will be made to the police. Often, the police arrest and convict the responsible party. It is important that the adjuster notify the police of the insurer's loss payment to the insured because if an arrest and a conviction occur, the court may order restitution of the funds or property taken. Although this can be an involved process, it can be worth the effort.

Equipment Breakdown Coverage

Equipment breakdown coverage, often referred to as boiler and machinery (B&M) coverage, is very specialized. Only a small group of adjusters who regularly handle equipment breakdown claims fully understand the coverage and what is required in the investigation and adjustment of the losses.

Equipment breakdown insurance pays for a loss that results from the accidental breakdown of equipment that operates under pressure or that controls, transmits, transforms, or uses mechanical or electrical power.

Steamboilers, electrical generators, pumps, engines, air conditioning systems, production equipment, and even computers and copiers can be insured under an equipment breakdown policy. The BPP only covers this equipment for the perils enumerated in the causes of loss forms. Electrical or mechanical breakdown and steam boiler explosion are excluded. Equipment breakdown insurance provides coverage for these causes of loss as well. It also covers other property damaged by the breakdown as well as the attendant business income and extra expense loss.

Because the handling of equipment breakdown claims requires specialized knowledge, these claims are usually assigned to specific adjustment companies with the required engineering expertise.

Computer Losses

Handling computer losses is one of the fastest changing areas in loss adjusting. Most people are generally acquainted with various computer types and sizes, but the field is broadening daily. Present computer technology includes, in addition to computers, portable handheld personal digital assistant (PDA) devices, machine control systems, building mechanical control systems, communications relay systems, medical diagnostic tools, and technical test equipment. Telephone and intercom systems are often computer-driven. Almost all of these systems can be insured. Claims for repair or replacement of these items are surfacing with greater frequency.

The following is a review of some terms used in insurance policies and in the computer trade.

- **Data** include any information used in or with a computer. They are recorded in a magnetic code that is usable by a computer. Data include programs (software), raw information that has been placed in the system, calculations, and memory system content. Sometimes the term is used more restrictively, to mean only the stored user information, whether input or output.
- **Hardware** includes the physical machine and all of its component parts as well as connecting cables.
- **Media** are any computer-readable devices that can hold information. They include magnetic tapes, optical disks, compact discs (CDs), digital video discs (DVDs), and magnetic disks (hard or floppy) and their carriers. Media are tangible and serve only as vehicles to carry or store information. Some insurance policies define media to include data and programs.
- **Programs** (or software) are a series of logically connected steps that are loaded into the computer, allowing it to perform any given function when directed by an operator. They are carried on a disk or tape. Programs can be proprietary (fully owned and protected by copyright), licensed, or in the public domain. Some are general purpose and sold widely in the market, but others are so specialized that they have no value outside a particular application.

Data
Information recorded in a magnetic code that is used in or with a computer.

Hardware
A physical machine and all of its component parts and cables.

Media
Any computer-readable device that can hold information.

Programs or software
A series of logically connected steps that are loaded into a computer, allowing it to perform a given function.

Causes of Loss

Following are several causes of loss that can do the most damage to computers:

- Heat damage (with or without fire)
- Water damage/humidity
- Smoke
- Contamination
- Impact or crushing
- Voltage variation
- Magnetic field intrusion

Heat

A computer is built with many heat-sensitive materials. Plastics distort or degrade at relatively low temperatures. Tolerances change as materials expand. Heat damage might be produced internally because of cooling system failure, or externally, such as when a room heats up unexpectedly. A system's conductivity changes, and some cosmetic discoloration is likely to occur in the system or at the console. Heat caused by fire raises additional concerns about contamination.

Water/Humidity

Water falling into a computer or rising around it is extremely destructive. Excessive humidity can have the same effect. Water cross-conducts between pin connectors and may deposit chemicals whose corrosive action erodes and destroys connectors and circuit boards.

Repairing a water-damaged computer is best left to an expert. The *machine should be shut down* until it has been cleaned and decontaminated. Any effort to turn it on to determine whether it will work might do new and irreparable damage. If restoration personnel are not available for several hours or days, the cabinet should be opened, and warm air should be blown gently across the wet areas, concentrated particularly on cable plugs and connectors. A dehumidifier should be used to reduce the humidity in the area where the computer is located. These actions will mitigate the loss to the equipment. Exhibit 12-3 is a first-aid chart for computers and high-tech equipment.

Smoke

Smoke is made up of carbon and other chemicals that can destroy a computer. When smoke invades a computer and settles onto its connections and circuit boards, the result can be disastrous. Losses include internal and external discoloration, electrical failure through carbon chains, arcing, contact point failure, and varnish deposits.

As with water damage, the system should be turned off and protected against further invasion of smoke. It can be wrapped in plastic. Professionals should be called to dismantle and clean it. The smoke residue must be tested to identify the chemicals it carries and to enable the restorer to select a detergent that will remove those chemicals. Acids in the smoke can etch metal and even cut the trace lines on a circuit board. After twenty-four hours, rapid degradation of the affected areas or systems is likely.

Repairing the damage from smoke contamination is a job for a professional. Fans can eliminate smoke. Protective covers can be arranged. The entire unit might need to be dismantled so that it can be hand-washed with suitable solvents. In any case, the system should not be turned on until a competent restorer has checked it and approved it for use.

EXHIBIT 12-3

High-Tech First Aid

FIRST AID

WHEN DISASTER STRIKES YOUR HIGH-TECH EQUIPMENT

DO	**Disconnect All Equipment From Power Source**
DO NOT	**Start Up Equipment, Not Even For Testing**

FIRE

- Disconnect equipment from ALL power sources, including backup batteries and uninterruptible power supplies (UPS). At power panels, remove fuses and place tape over circuit breakers to keep them in the "OFF" position.
- Open windows and use fans to remove smoke.
- Remove portable equipment to dry, clean area.
- Where building repairs are underway, protect the equipment with plastic drop-cloths and run dehumidifiers beneath the shelter.
- Prevent further spread of smoke, soot and/or water contamination from the fire source to other areas.

WATER

- Immediately disconnect equipment from ALL power sources, including backup batteries and UPS. At power panels, remove fuses and place tape over circuit breakers to keep them in the "OFF" position.
- If water enters through the ceiling, protect the equipment with plastic drop-cloths and run dehumidifiers beneath the shelter.
- Vacuum and wipe water from walls, floors, subfloors, heating ducts, etc.
- Turn on the heating system and/or dehumidifiers to speed drying.
- Critical metallic surfaces or machinery and work-in-progress should be temporarily protected with water-displacement oil.

INDUSTRIAL DUST AND FIRE-EXTINGUISHING POWDER

- Disconnect all dust-sensitive equipment from power sources.
- Do not operate any dust-contaminated equipment.
- Seal off the area from further dust infiltration and eliminate the dust source.
- Change the air filters on any equipment that must continue to operate before decontamination.
- Keep equipment dry wherever fire extinguishing powder is present.
- Fire extinguishing agents are very abrasive and when they mix with moisture in the ambient air will lead to corrosion. Professionally decontaminate as soon as possible.

OES Technical Restoration Toll Free (866) 637-8324

OES Technical Restoration, Kansas City, Kans.

Contamination

Contamination includes water, smoke, and other airborne particles. The major concerns are dust and dirt, but oil, oil vapor, and other airborne fumes or contaminants can damage a computer.

In any loss by contamination, the machine should *not* be turned on. Attempts to do so to test its operation can be very costly. The best solution is to have the unit opened by a competent restoration service person and checked for foreign matter. If a contaminant is gaseous, the clean-up routine suggested for smoke should be followed. If the material is solid or fluid, the suggested recovery from water loss should be followed.

Impact or Crushing

Although computers are generally sturdy machines, if a cabinet is struck and bent by a lift truck or other heavy equipment, wires could be pinched, or connections could be stressed or broken. Sealed areas within the computer may be compromised.

Special preparations, as outlined by the manufacturer, should be made before a computer is shipped. Damage to a computer or one of its components can occur during shipping. Most freight carriers recognize the units as special-handling cargo. Even so, units get dropped, overturned, rained on, and otherwise abused along the way. Most physical damage from impact or crushing occurs while the units are in transit.

Voltage Variation

Voltage is the pressure exerted by electricity. If the voltage along a wire is doubled, twice as much electricity will flow through the wire. However, wire has a limit as to how much current it can safely carry. When the voltage increases and causes the current to surpass the wire's capacity, the wire heats up and melts—just like a fuse. Upon melting, the wire cannot carry current. Whatever appliance was receiving current at the output end of the wire would be deprived of power, and the system would be disabled.

This condition occurs when lightning strikes a power line and momentarily increases the voltage on that line. That increased pressure could travel down the line to a computer. The voltage at the wall plug could increase momentarily from 115 volts to 170 volts or to 500 volts, which is one type of line surge. Tiny wires in the computer, some thinner than a human hair, would become overstressed and melt, disabling the computer.

Adjuster Tip

If examination by an expert reveals that the only damage sustained is to the computer's internal modem, the cause is usually lightning. The only connection that the modem has to the outside world is the telephone or communication line and the computer's main board. If the computer is connected to a surge protector, a utility surge would damage something other than the internal modem.[3]

Many computers are fitted with voltage regulators to smooth out line surge. They should also have special grounding to intercept any lightning surges that come in on the power line. If a computer is fitted with these attachments, machine failure caused by lightning will be unlikely. In examining the circumstances surrounding a computer loss allegedly caused by lightning, the adjuster should check the local weather records for the time when the computer failed. Many power companies keep detailed records of their line voltages and lightning strikes to their lines, which are often available to an adjuster.

Magnetic Field Intrusion

Computer data are recorded in magnetic spots on a disk or tape that has an iron oxide face. These disks and tapes could be erased by simply passing them through a magnetic field that would rearrange the electrons in a uniform direction. In such a case, the intelligence encoded on the disk would be lost. The same effect would be produced by bringing a magnetic field near a computer. The magnetic field would also rearrange the electrons in the computer, on disks or on tape, and the intelligence stored in the computer would be lost.

Certain welding equipment generates a magnetic field. Induction heating coils operate through the use of magnetic fields, as do some other systems. Anything with an electromagnet has a magnetic field. Office workers often have magnets or magnetized objects on their desks. These objects can destroy computer disks. If the computer and its media are not shielded from magnetic fields, the data and programs on the disks could be accidentally erased.

Movement of recorded data through a magnetic field and vice versa can be equally damaging. Whenever data are missing or scrambled, the adjuster must consider the possibility that data were exposed to a magnetic field of enough strength to wipe it clean.

Coverage

Generalizing about computer coverages is difficult. This section presents some of the most important features of such coverage. An insured computer owner could suffer various kinds of loss, including the following:

- Physical loss to equipment or media
- Costs to replace data or programs
- Extra expense to continue computer operations
- Loss of business income

In working with any computer loss, an adjuster must be aware that these systems can be expensive and complicated and also that they might be the center for many other operations of the business. As a result, continuous disablement can have far-reaching effects.

Computer Coverage in the Homeowners Policy

The HO-3 or standard homeowners policies do not specifically deal with computer hardware or software. Computer equipment is considered personal property. Loss to computers would be handled similarly to any other piece of personal property. The issue that arises concerns items' valuation. ACV or replacement-cost basis may be difficult to calculate because of the insured computer's technological obsolescence. Even attempting to settle based on like kind and quality may mean that the insured nevertheless gets a better computer than what he or she had originally because of changes in technology that have occurred since the original purchase.

Computer Coverage in the BPP

The BPP provides valuable coverage for computer losses, but with significant limitations. Coverage for business personal property extends to equipment and all other personal property owned by the insured and used in the insured's business. Nothing in this language would exclude computer equipment and media. Additionally, the BPP provides a $2,500 coverage extension for the cost to research, restore, and replace valuable records, including those on electronic media. The BPP does not cover certain types of property, including accounts, bills, evidences of debt, and other specifically described property that other policies cover. The exclusion of the last type of property is significant because computer data can be covered specifically under inland marine forms.

The BPP causes of loss forms contain exclusions for power failure and for artificially generated electrical current that disturbs electrical devices, appliances, or wires, as well as for mechanical breakdown and changes in temperature or humidity. Thus, some of the most significant computer loss exposures are not covered. Also, the enumerated covered causes of loss in the Basic and Broad forms might not adequately address computer equipment exposures.

Electronic Data Processing and Electronic Commerce Coverage

For those businesses with a substantial loss exposure to computer hardware, software, data, and loss of business, more specific coverage is available.

Electronic Data Processing (EDP) Coverage is often added to commercial property packages to provide special coverage for hardware, software, and data. It also provides coverage for business income loss that results from direct loss to the equipment. This coverage is usually written as direct physical loss caused by a covered peril to covered property while on the premises described on the declarations, subject to a list of exclusions.

The E-Commerce endorsement is designed to cover loss arising from e-commerce activity conducted on the Internet or another computer network. It provides coverage for electronic data owned, licensed, or leased to the insured that originates and resides in computers located within the United States, its territories, possessions, Puerto Rico, and Canada.

Under this coverage, the insurer agrees to pay for the cost to replace or restore electronic data that has sustained damage from a covered cause of loss. The endorsement also provides business income and extra expense coverage.

The covered causes of loss are modified by adding back coverage for interruption of utility service, for loss caused by artificially generated electrical current, and for mechanical breakdown.

Several exclusions unique to e-commerce activity are added. These include loss or damage caused by a virus, by unauthorized use, errors in programming, faulty design or installation of the system, system or network overload, or failure of the Internet.

Computer Loss Adjusting

Losses to computer equipment, media, and data present the adjuster with unique loss mitigation and settlement challenges and opportunities. This section presents several of them.

Initial Assessment and Response

The adjuster's first obligation at the site of a computer loss is to be sure that the entire system is shut down and that it stays shut down until a full analysis of the loss is made and a qualified repair person is on site to monitor and initiate any restart. The adjuster must talk to whoever was present when the incident occurred to identify what systems were running at the time of the loss and the specific cause of loss. Examining the equipment and the loss site often reveals evidence that identifies the reason for failure. Adjusters are not expected to analyze the system's internal failures, but they should take charge, advise the insured of the duty to mitigate the loss, and help the insured to obtain the services of a competent repair technician.

Detailed Identification of Equipment

A precise identification of all of the components and peripherals that are damaged is essential to handling computer losses. The identification should include the make, model, and upgrades to the unit. This information will help the restorer as well as be useful in the determination of ACV or replacement cost.

Backup of Data

In most well-run computer operations, the data in the system are copied at specific intervals. The copy is stored as a backup in anticipation of a malfunction or damage to the computer system. An adjuster should ask the insured whether such a procedure is used, at what intervals the data are copied, and how the backup data are preserved. Are they retained on site? Are they sent to a secure off-site storage and, if so, where? How often? For an insured that relies on its computers for business, it is possible that the insured has made arrangements with another facility to run its operations temporarily.

The backup data could then be transferred to this facility, and the insured could be back in business with a minimum of downtime.

Settlement Options

An important factor in computer settlements is obsolescence, which results from the speed with which computer technology evolves. As a new model reaches the market, the related older models sharply lose value even if they are unsold. When these units become technically obsolete, they lose their salability. With small units, such as personal computers, new but obsolete models go on sale, and the inventory is quickly absorbed at reduced prices. However, larger obsolete components might remain in warehouses for months or years waiting to be sold. There is also a regular market trading in used equipment from major manufacturers. This inventory can be the adjuster's salvation. Finding and obtaining just the right replacement unit to fit into an existing system take patience but can result in dramatic savings.

Computers often contain a set or group of related items. Even a personal computer is usually made up of three or more components, each of which can be replaced separately. Replacing a single element without replacing an entire system might be possible and economical.

During repair evaluation, the adjuster often discovers that repairs, though possible, might take several weeks because of a delay in obtaining parts. At this point, the insured and the adjuster must decide how to proceed. The options are as follows:

1. Wait for the repairs to be complete.
2. Purchase a new unit.
3. Purchase a used unit.
4. Rent a temporary unit.

The analysis of how to make this decision is beyond the scope of this text. However, if the insured has business income loss coverage, the insurer providing such coverage would play a major role in the physical damage settlement. Extra expense coverage pays for the necessary extra expenses incurred to resume or continue operations as nearly as practicable. The adjuster must agree with the insured on a course that will best serve all concerned.

Insureds often lease computer equipment. An adjuster who identifies equipment as leased must review the written lease. Usually, the lessee is required to insure the equipment; however, this is not always the case. Sometimes a lease expires upon the equipment's destruction. In any case, the lessor is usually not named on a lessee's policy, so an adjuster can make settlement directly with the lessee. Software is licensed. By reviewing the licensing agreement, the adjuster can determine whether the insured is entitled to replacement software.

Computer Consultants

Although an adjuster may be able to handle a home computer loss, a commercial loss may require a consultant's services. Computer consultants have access to various sources for units. It is possible to get new units or refurbished units that are warranted to be as good as new. Obtaining a replacement unit can save other components of the overall system. This option might solve the problem of an insured who sees the need for an entirely new system. The *Orion Blue Book* is a good source of information on computers for valuation purposes.

Computer consultants have at their disposal several references on the value of used units and components. This valuation is not an exact science, and market conditions must be considered. Valuation is probably best determined by someone who is familiar with the industry, changes that are occurring, the history of any problems, the number of sales made, and the current quantity of unsold merchandise.

Most experienced adjusters can determine the value of a personal computer with an original cost under $3,000. Enough of a market exists in most communities to create a mutually acceptable value. By contrast, valuation of a $200,000 mainframe requires research on a national scale. No one locality will have a sufficiently large market to guide the adjuster. Using a paid consultant is advisable in such a case.

Service Contract

Service contracts protect owners of many computers. Through those contracts, service agencies maintain and repair the units during the life of the agreements. These agreements are generally void in the event of certain casualty losses to the unit. Thus, loss to a computer by fire would likely void the service contract protection.

Contamination Claims[4]

A great number of pollution/contamination claims are presented under property policies and other first-party coverages. These claims include a claim for damages from leaking or overflowed oil tanks, well water contamination, asbestos and lead abatement, herbicides and pesticides in the soil and groundwater, sewer backup, toxic smoke and fumes, mold, mercury, radon, and so on.

Other contamination sources arise from the third-party exposures resulting from the use, transportation, storage, disposal, release, or discharge of chemicals and other hazardous substances into the environment. Any hazardous substance in transit is especially vulnerable to vehicle accidents. Hazardous substances can be transported over water or land in barges, ships, trains, or trucks. Even when these materials are in storage, they can present a contamination threat to the environment. Many are explosive or combustible in nature and produce gases, creating pressure within the containment vessels, which then have the propensity to explode. The container or drum itself might spill, leak, or be damaged, enabling the solvents to seep into soil and groundwater and then leach across or down grades onto other properties, creating both first-party damage and a potential third-party liability situation.

This section briefly introduces first-party property insurance coverage and the principles of law, as they related to pollution and contamination cleanup claims.

Superfund

Both state and federal law may affect the legal rights and responsibilities of both the insured and the insurer concerning any claim for contamination cleanup damages under a first-party property coverage. The most important of these laws is the federal Superfund law.

Superfund law
Federal legislation that gave the Environmental Protection Agency (EPA) the authority to identify, investigate, and remediate hazardous sites.

The Comprehensive Environmental Response, Compensation, and Liability Act (CERCLA), known as the **Superfund** law, was enacted in 1980. It was not the first major federal environmental law, but it has had the greatest effect on the insurance industry regarding both first-party and third-party claims for damages. Under this law, the Environmental Protection Agency (EPA) is required to identify, investigate, and remediate hazardous sites. The EPA must consider whether a site has shown evidence of a release of a hazardous substance, or whether a potential release appears to be an imminent threat to the public. The EPA is required to create a list of hazardous sites that need attention in order of priority. This list of sites is referred to as the National Priority List (NPL). The EPA is also authorized to pursue and order Potentially Responsible Parties (PRPs) to eliminate the contaminants and to clean up the sites. If these parties fail to respond, the EPA is authorized to take the necessary remedial measures to protect public health and welfare and to pay for the cleanup efforts out of Superfund money. The EPA then proceeds to take legal action against the PRPs for reimbursement.

CERCLA imposes strict, joint and several, and retroactive liability for the costs of response, removal, and remediation of hazardous sites. The law allows the EPA to impose liability and to pursue those who deposited hazardous substances before the statute became law in 1980. Because of the magnitude of the number of hazardous sites and the huge estimated costs to cleanup the NPL sites and other areas across the country, there has been, and will continue to be, great emphasis on pursuing the recovery of costs from the responsible parties. The state and federal EPA agencies also work with and encourage the PRPs to enter into formal agreements to voluntarily cleanup their owned properties without litigation.

The EPA can seek recovery of its costs from the following potentially responsible parties:

1. The current property owner
2. The past property owner of the facility/property at the time that the hazardous substance was released, or the property operator who may have caused the contamination

3. Any person who contracted for, or arranged for, the disposal of the hazardous waste, referred to as the generator
4. Any person who accepted the hazardous waste for transportation or disposal, referred to as the hauler

The facility's past owners and operators can be held liable if hazardous substances were released on the property during their ownership. Current property owners become liable for all existing and retroactive contamination as soon as they take title to the land. The statute does not require that the PRP be negligent in disposing of its hazardous substances; rather, the statute has deemed this to be an absolute liability standard, or strict liability.

Only a few defenses can be effective against the strict liability standard. An act of war or act of God may be valid defenses if appropriate. Likewise, the act or omission by an unrelated third party could serve as a defense, provided that the defendant could not foresee that third party's negligence. Additionally, the parties can have no contractual relationship, not even by deed. Although the statutory defenses to liability are limited, the insured ultimately might avoid liability if the EPA cannot prove its case. The EPA's inability to prove a defendant's nexus as a PRP can limit or eliminate CERCLA liability.

The 1986 amendments to the Superfund law created an **innocent landowner defense**. This applies to an owner who may have purchased a contaminated site without knowledge of the problem even though he or she had conducted the required site investigation into its prior use. Most states now require an environmental property assessment be completed before any commercial property can be sold.

Innocent landowner defense
A possible defense to Superfund liability; used when a party purchases a contaminated site without knowledge of the problem, despite having conducted the required site investigation before purchase.

Coverage Issues in First-Party Property Insurance

The most significant effect of the Superfund law on first-party insurance is making the owner responsible for past and present contamination on his or her owned property. Because the owner's property is alleged to be damaged or defective from contamination, many owners have sought recovery from their first-party insurance. (Most of the insurance litigation arising out of environmental claims concerns third-party liability coverage; however, this text discusses only the problems of environmental claims under first-party coverages.)

Coverage for pollution/contamination claims depends on the facts and circumstances of the loss, the specific policy's language, and the law in the applicable state. The more important coverage issues in first-party property contamination claims surround "all-risks" policies, debris removal coverage, and suit limitation.

"All-Risks" Coverage

Since 1983, the phrase "all-risks" has been deleted from most property policies, and the phrase "risk of direct physical loss" has been substituted. Even with this policy language change, any loss still must be fortuitous for coverage to apply. Pollution or contamination can involve loss that is "direct" and "physical." The only remaining issues are whether the loss is to covered property and whether pollution/contamination or its cause is covered or not. The most significant type of property *not* covered in a pollution claim is land itself. Exclusions for pollution/contamination are also common.

Since 1987, ISO policies have been drafted to exclude loss by contamination unless that event is preceded by a covered loss. That is, pollution/contamination is now covered only as a consequence of a prior covered loss, and then only within narrow limits of coverage. Some losses (to land, for instance) are typically excluded. The BPP excludes pollution unless it is caused by a peril specifically named in a causes of loss form.

The Causes of Loss—Special Form, because of its use of the "risk of direct physical loss unless excluded" language, has a long list of excluded risks, including the following pollution/contamination exclusion stating that the policy does not apply to:

> l. Discharge, dispersal, seepage, migration, release or escape of "pollutants" unless the discharge, dispersal, seepage, migration, release, or escape is itself caused by any of the "specified causes of loss." But if the discharge, dispersal, seepage, migration, release or escape of "pollutants" results in a "specified cause of loss" we will pay for the loss or damage caused by the "specified cause of loss."[5]

The term "specified causes of loss" means fire; lightning; explosion; windstorm or hail; smoke; aircraft or vehicles; riot or civil commotion; vandalism; leakage from fire extinguishing equipment; sinkhole collapse; volcanic action; falling objects; weight of snow, ice, or sleet; and water damage. Water damage means accidental discharge or leakage of water or steam as the direct result of the breaking or cracking of any part of a system or appliance containing water or steam, on the described premises.

Debris Removal

Insureds have also sought coverage for pollution cleanup under debris removal coverage. They typically assert that the polluting material itself became debris after it had contaminated the insured property, or that the contaminated property itself constituted debris. The merit of this argument depends on the wording of the applicable debris removal clause. The ISO forms have been modified to prevent coverage for pollution cleanup under the debris removal clause. This property coverage issue continues to be frequently litigated in many states.

The additional coverage for debris removal includes the expense to remove debris of covered property that results from a covered cause of loss occurring during the policy period. These expenses must be reported to the insurer within 180 days of the date of loss.

Note that coverage extends only to removal of debris of *covered property* caused by a *covered cause of loss*. Any debris that does not satisfy both of these conditions is not included under this additional coverage. Furthermore, the clause specifically excludes pollution cleanup, such as the cost to extract pollutants from land or water.

The BPP specifically states that it will *not* respond to pollution claims under the Debris Removal Additional Coverages section. Instead, another type of additional coverage is specifically designed for pollution cleanup:

> d. Pollutant Clean Up and Removal
>
> We will pay your expense to extract "pollutants" from land or water at the described premises if the discharge, dispersal, seepage, migration, release, or escape of the "pollutants" is caused by or results from a Covered Cause of Loss that occurs during the policy period . . . .[6]

Here, the policy affirms its intent to pay for pollution that is a consequence of a covered loss that occurs during the policy period. The BPP has an annual aggregate limit of $10,000. Higher limits are available.

Suit Limitation Clause Another important property policy provision that affects a first-party claim for pollution/contamination damage or cleanup is the Suit Limitation Clause. This is one of the most significant differences between a third-party and a first-party policy as this Suit Limitation Clause is only found with first-party property coverages. In third-party claims or suits, insureds have been able to pursue coverage on policies that are decades old. First-party policies require that the loss occur during the policy period and that suit commence within one year after the date of loss. Generally, there is no problem with complying with this condition when a loss is easily detected. However, with pollution/contamination claims that lie dormant for long periods of time, the suit limitation period can become an issue and bar coverage on expired policies. This coverage provision has also been litigated frequently in the courts, and generally it is determined that because a first-party claim is brought by the insured, and the insured is generally aware of all the details surrounding the claim on the insured's property, the courts hold the insured to compliance with the policy condition and bar coverage. However, some jurisdictions have adopted rules that the time limit does not begin until the insured has become aware of the loss or has sufficient knowledge that the insured should have been aware of the loss. Other jurisdictions have ruled that the suit limitation period does not begin until the insurer has actually denied coverage.

SUMMARY

Specialty losses differ from typical property losses in that they are less frequently seen by the adjuster and they often require special knowledge or expertise in the adjustment process. For example, companies that write a significant amount of boiler and machinery coverage rely on adjusters who are experienced in that special field for loss adjustments and inspections.

The Nationwide Marine Definition lists a variety of items that can be insured by inland marine policies. The coverage categories include transportation insurance; coverage for bridges, tunnels and instrumentalities of transportation and communication; bailee-bailor policies; both personal and commercial property floaters; coverage for contractors' equipment; and builders' risk policies. Inland marine policies can be manuscripted by the underwriter to meet the insured's needs. Therefore, the adjuster must review the policy for every loss.

Transportation policies provide coverage for the shipper and the consignee of the goods as well as the carrier who transports the goods. The adjuster must ascertain who has the responsibility for loss to the goods. The shipping documents indicate when title to the goods passes. The contract between the shipper and the carrier, called a bill of lading, indicates any limitations to the carrier's liability for loss or damage. The BMC 32 endorsement included in most motor truck liability policies responds to a federal law requiring carriers to show evidence of financial responsibility up to $5,000 for loss or damage to goods on any one vehicle. The BMC 32 requires the insurer to pay any cargo claim for which the carrier is liable, whether covered by the policy or not. If the loss is not covered by the policy, the insurer would have the right to collect reimbursement from the insured for the loss payment.

Losses involving bailments are insured under bailee/bailor policies. Repair shops, jewelry stores, and dry cleaners all need this type of coverage. The bailee liability policy covers insureds for losses that they are legally liable for and that result from a covered peril. A bailees' customers policy provides that same type of coverage without the requirement of legal liability. Bailors who do not wish to rely on the bailee's coverage purchase bailor coverage. This covers their goods off their premises. Businesses that send their goods to other businesses for processing use this coverage to protect their property while it is being worked on off their premises.

Warehouse legal liability is another form of bailee insurance. The warehouse legal liability policy covers the warehouse's legal liability for loss or damage to a customer's property. Similar to a transportation claim, the warehouse receipt indicates the owner of the property, the condition it was received in, the terms of the storage, and any limitations on the warehouse's liability.

Condominiums are a special form of property ownership. Losses involving a condominium require review of the property deeds to determine ownership. Condominiums have areas called common elements owned by all of the members of the condominium association. The master deed of the condominium association describes what property belongs to the association and what property belongs to the unit owner. The barewalls concept means that the unit owner is responsible from the bare walls in. Under the all-encompassing concept, the condominium association is responsible for all exterior and interior items that the unit contains at the time of sale to a unit owner.

Builders' risk has special loss exposures. Because the structure is under construction, opportunities for theft and vandalism exist in addition to added exposure to windstorm and collapse. Various insurable interests may exist as well. The owner, the mortgagees, and the contractors that are working on the structure all have some interest in the structure. The builders' risk policy covers the structure during the course of construction as well as material, supplies, and temporary structures such as scaffolding. Often, the challenge in a builders' risk loss is determining the amount of the loss. Builders' risk policies may cover soft costs and business income loss. The adjuster must become heavily involved in the construction schedule to see whether the loss will affect the project's completion date.

Because the BPP offers limited coverage for crime losses, many commercial insureds purchase separate crime coverage to insure their exposures. Eight options for crime coverage give insureds the ability to tailor coverage to their specific needs. Investigation of crime losses requires the adjuster to have a high degree of tact and sensitivity. Interviews with employees, neighbors, and police are often required. The adjuster must also review the insured's financial statements and inventory records to verify the loss.

Equipment breakdown coverage, also called boiler and machinery coverage, is a highly specialized type of insurance. Only a small group of adjusters are qualified to handle these losses. Because of the expertise needed to handle boiler and machinery losses, insurers use an expert in the field to handle these losses.

Just about every business has a computer system. Individuals have home computers and handheld devices. Special policies have been developed to cover hardware, software, data, and media. Many of the computer coverages insure loss to hardware, software, and data. Computer equipment needs special handling in the event of a loss. Restoration and computer experts need to evaluate the damage and make recommendations on repairs. Adjusters often have to deal with the issue of obsolescence when handling computer losses. Adjusters can use computer consultants to find cost-effective replacement units.

Pollution and contamination of property claims have become more common in first-party policies. Most states require an environmental assessment when commercial property is sold. CERCLA of 1980 empowered the EPA to identify, investigate, and remediate hazardous sites. A property owner can be responsible for the property's past and present contamination. Insureds have attempted to find coverage for the contamination through their property insurance. Coverage depends on the facts and circumstances of the loss, the policy language, and the applicable state law. The BPP offers a $10,000 annual aggregate limit for pollution cleanup and removal, if caused by a covered loss.

Chapter 13 continues the discussion of specialty losses by focusing on two distinct types of property losses: auto physical damage and contractors' equipment. The adjustment of these types of losses usually requires specialized training. Chapter 13 introduces this highly specialized loss adjustment process.

CHAPTER NOTES

1. Causes of Loss—Special Form, CP 10 30 04 02, Copyright, Insurance Services Office, Inc., 2001.
2. Causes of Loss—Special Form, CP 10 30 04 02, Copyright, Insurance Services Office, Inc., 2001.
3. Robert Karbin, "Adjusting Power-Surge Damages," *Claims Magazine*, July 2002, p. 56.
4. Material contributed by Marcia Sweeney, Senior Consultant, The Hartford.
5. Causes of Loss—Special Form, CP 10 30 04 02, Copyright, Insurance Services Office, Inc., 2001.
6. Building and Personal Property Coverage Form, CP 00 10 04 02, Copyright, Insurance Services Office, Inc., 2001.

Chapter 13

Direct Your Learning

Auto Physical Damage and Contractors' Equipment

After learning the subject matter of this chapter, you should be able to:

- Describe the different types of auto physical damage coverages in the Personal Auto Policy.
- Explain how an auto physical damage claim is handled.
  - Identify vehicle frame types.
  - Identify structural components.
  - Properly use auto repair terminology.
  - Identify common estimating errors.
  - Describe the investigation of an auto theft claim.
  - Describe the loss adjustment process for a total loss of an auto.
- Describe the different types of contractors' equipment and their uses.
- Explain the causes of loss, the exclusions, and the coverage extensions commonly found in contractors' equipment policies.
- Explain the valuation of a total loss claim for a piece of contractors' equipment and the valuation for a business income loss that may also result.

OUTLINE

Develop Your Perspective

What are the main topics covered in the chapter?

This chapter focuses on how to handle claims involving physical damage or theft of an auto or a piece of contractors' equipment. Coverage for physical damage and theft under the Personal Auto Policy and a contractors' equipment policy are discussed.

Using your own vehicle:

- Decode the vehicle identification number (VIN).
- Identify the basic parts of the vehicle.

Why is it important to know these topics?

Although not every property loss adjuster handles auto physical damage claims or contractors' equipment, it is worthwhile to understand the fundamentals of adjusting these claims in the event that they become part of a property loss.

Imagine a claim involving a car that strikes a building or a garage filled with contractors' equipment that burns to the ground.

- How would you go about adjusting these losses?

How can you use this information?

Knowing the fundamentals of adjusting auto physical damage claims and contractors' equipment claims will enable you to understand and question estimates prepared by auto appraisers or heavy-equipment appraisers.

Chapter 13

Auto Physical Damage and Contractors' Equipment

While auto physical damage coverage and contractors' equipment coverage are written on distinctly different types of insurance policies, the claim handling process involving these policies is similar. Auto physical damage adjusters and appraisers and contractors' equipment or "heavy-equipment" adjusters and appraisers tend to be a very specialized group. Unlike most property loss claims, in which adjusters create repair estimates, evaluate coverage, and conclude the claim, auto physical damage claims and contractors' equipment claims are usually inspected by an appraiser who writes the appraisal or damage estimate and then forwards that information to an adjuster who makes the coverage determination and concludes the loss.

Insurers may have appraisers on staff or may hire independent appraisers to handle damage inspections. Despite the fact that auto physical damage and contractors' equipment losses require both an appraiser and an adjuster, this arrangement proves to be cost-effective for insurers who have a substantial volume of these claims. Auto physical damage appraisers and contractors' equipment appraisers have specialized knowledge of auto repair and equipment repair. By relieving the appraisers of the responsibility of adjusting the loss, the appraisers can inspect several losses in a day, which is a more efficient use of their time and knowledge.

The first part of this chapter introduces auto physical damage coverage and terminology and outlines auto physical damage estimates and damage analysis. After learning the subject matter of this chapter, property loss adjusters should be comfortable asking questions about any estimate they receive. The second half of the chapter discusses contractors' equipment. The chapter uses the Insurance Services Office, Inc., (ISO) Personal Auto Policy and the ISO Contractors' Equipment Policy for the coverage discussion. However, both auto physical damage coverage and contractors' equipment coverage vary by company and by state.

PERSONAL AUTO POLICY

The Personal Auto Policy (PAP) covers individuals and the cars that they drive for personal use. Among other coverages, it protects the insured from financial loss as a result of physical damage to his or her vehicle. This coverage is found in Part D—Coverage for Damage to Your Auto. The declarations page provides information about the insured, the autos insured, and the amounts of coverage. Exhibit 13-1 is a sample declarations page.

Who Is Insured?

The declarations page lists the name and address of the named insured. The definitions section further refines the term "you" to mean the named insured and the spouse if a resident of the same household. Parts A, B, and C provide additional clarification as to who is an insured for each of those coverage parts. Physical damage concerns only Part D—Coverage for Damage to Your Auto, which does not have any additional descriptions of who is insured under the policy.

What Is Insured?

Vehicle identification number (VIN)
A number assigned to a vehicle by the manufacturer that describes the manufacturer, body style, engine type, model, and series; the sequence in which the vehicle came off the assembly line; and sometimes a plant or factory code.

The declarations page also lists the insured vehicles, the coverage selected, the limits for each coverage, the policy form, and any endorsements. It also lists the year, make, model, and **vehicle identification number (VIN)** for each insured vehicle. The deductibles for Part D coverages are shown as well. The policy definitions expand the definition of "owned" vehicle to include leased vehicles with a written lease for a continuous period of at least six months.

Decoding the VIN[1]

The VIN is a unique identifier, and its combination of numbers and letters represent various features of the auto. Decoding the VIN is important. An improper VIN is a flag for potential fraud. The VIN is also necessary to select the proper parts for repair, and it is essential in identifying stolen vehicles. The most accessible VIN is the metal tag visible through the windshield on the driver's side dashboard. The number is also located on various parts of the auto to help identify it if it is stolen and dismantled.

The National Insurance Crime Bureau (NICB) annually publishes a Passenger Vehicle Identification Manual. It contains VIN information for the three prior years for U.S. and Canadian passenger vehicles, as well as light-duty trucks and motorcycles. It provides general information on snowmobile serial numbers and hull identification on vessels. Using the manual or a software package containing the same information is necessary to decode a VIN.

The VIN is made up of seventeen numbers and letters. The following is an example:

7M9 H L32 Y 5 8 8 456789

The first three digits are the World Manufacturer Identifier, unless the manufacturer builds fewer than 500 vehicles per year. If the manufacturer builds fewer than 500 vehicles per year, the third digit is always a "9," and the digits

EXHIBIT 13-1

Sample PAP Declarations Page

Personal Auto Policy Declarations

POLICYHOLDER:
(Named Insured)

POLICY NUMBER:

POLICY PERIOD: FROM:
TO:

But only if the required premium for this period has been paid, and for six-month renewal periods if renewal premiums are paid as required. Each period begins and ends at 12:01 A.M. standard time at the address of the policyholder.

INSURED VEHICLES AND
SCHEDULE OF COVERAGES

VEHICLE	COVERAGES	LIMITS OF INSURANCE		PREMIUM
1				
	Coverage A—Liability	$	Each Occurrence	$
	Coverage B—Medical Payments	$	Each Person	$
	Coverage C—Uninsured Motorists	$	Each Occurrence	$
			TOTAL	$
2				
	Coverage A—Liability	$	Each Occurrence	$
	Coverage B—Medical Payments	$	Each Person	$
	Coverage C—Uninsured Motorists	$	Each Occurrence	$
	Coverage D—Other Than Collision	Actual Cash Value Less $		$
	—Collision	Actual Cash Value Less $		$
			TOTAL	$

POLICY FORM AND ENDORSEMENTS:

COUNTERSIGNATURE DATE:

AGENT:

in the twelfth, thirteenth, and fourteenth positions are used. They identify the country and the manufacturer.

Positions four through eight are the Vehicle Descriptor Section. They are used by the manufacturers to identify various vehicle attributes. The digits are code for body style, engine type, model, series, etc.

The ninth digit is an accuracy check digit that is created by a mathematical formula.

The last eight positions are the Vehicle Identifier Section, the last four positions of which are always numeric. These eight positions are the identifier for that specific vehicle. They indicate the sequence of the vehicle in production when it came off the assembly line.

If the vehicle manufacturer uses a year code, it will be in the tenth position. If the manufacturer uses a factory or plant code, it will be in the eleventh position.

Policy Definitions

Property damage
Physical injury to, destruction of, or loss of use of tangible property.

The PAP defines "**property damage**" to mean "physical injury to, destruction of, or loss of use of tangible property."[2] This definition is important in the claim process. For example, insureds in some states make diminished value claims after repair. A discussion of this issue appears later in this chapter.

"Newly acquired auto" receives extensive treatment in the Definitions section of the PAP. If there is collision coverage for at least one auto already on the policy, there will be collision coverage for the newly acquired auto on the date that the vehicle is purchased. However, for a vehicle that is in addition to those shown in the Declarations, the insured must request insurance within fourteen days of acquisition for this coverage to apply. If the policy does not have an auto already listed with collision coverage, the newly acquired auto will still be covered for collision as long as the collision coverage is applied for within four days of acquisition. If a loss occurs between day one and day four of ownership, the collision coverage will apply with a $500 deductible provided that the insured applies for insurance coverage by day four. These same conditions apply to other than collision coverage.

Insuring Agreement

In the insuring agreement, the insurer agrees to pay for direct and accidental loss to "your covered auto or any non-owned auto," including the auto's equipment, subject to any applicable deductible. The insurer agrees to pay for loss caused by collision and/or other than collision coverage according to what is shown on the declarations page. Loss to a non-owned auto is covered by the broadest coverage applicable to a covered auto, as shown on the declarations page.

Collision and Other Than Collision (OTC)

Collision is the upset of the covered auto or non-owned auto or the auto's impact with another vehicle or object.

Collision
The upset or impact of a vehicle with another vehicle or object.

Loss caused by the following are considered **other than collision (OTC):**

Other than collision (OTC)
Any cause of loss that is direct, accidental, not excluded, and not considered "collision."

- Missiles or falling objects
- Fire
- Theft or larceny
- Explosion or earthquake
- Windstorm
- Hail, water, or flood
- Riot or civil commotion
- Contact with bird or animal
- Breakage of glass

If glass is broken as a result of a collision, the insured can elect which coverage will be used to pay the loss. So an insured need not pay two deductibles if a collision causes glass breakage.

Note that, despite this listing, OTC is an open-perils type coverage and not a named-perils coverage. Any cause of loss that is direct and accidental and not considered collision and not excluded will be covered.

Non-Owned Auto

A non-owned auto is defined by the PAP as:

> 1. Any private passenger auto, pickup, van, or "trailer" not owned by or furnished or available for the regular use of you or any "family member" while in the custody of or being operated by you or any "family member"; or
> 2. Any auto or "trailer" you do not own while used as a temporary substitute for "your covered auto" which is out of normal use because of its:
>   a. Breakdown;
>   b. Repair;
>   c. Servicing;
>   d. Loss; or
>   e. Destruction.[3]

A non-owned auto is covered for physical damage while the vehicle is in the custody of or being operated by the named insured or any family members. If the insured borrows a neighbor's car, the insured's physical damage coverage would apply to the borrowed vehicle. However, the insured's policy would be excess over any physical damage coverage already in place on the borrowed vehicle. Temporary substitute vehicles are also covered. A loaner car from the repair shop would be covered by the insured's policy for physical damage.

Transportation Expenses

In addition to paying for the loss to the vehicle, the PAP covers transportation expenses, up to a maximum of $600, without the application of a deductible.

Temporary transportation expenses, beginning twenty-four hours after the covered auto is withdrawn from use, will be paid, to a maximum of $20 a day, if the loss to a covered auto is caused by collision or other than collision, as long as the covered auto has one of these coverages.

This section states that expenses for which the insured becomes legally responsible as a result of a loss to a non-owned auto are covered. The loss must be caused by collision or OTC, and one of these coverages must be designated for the covered auto. These expenses are also limited to $20 a day. The same twenty-four-hour waiting period applies.

The payment of these expenses is limited to a reasonable time to repair or replace the covered auto or non-owned auto.

In the event of a total theft, the only expenses that will be paid are those incurred during the time period beginning forty-eight hours after the theft and ending when the theft loss is paid or the vehicle is returned to use.

Exclusions

The policy does not cover loss or damage resulting from the following:

- Wear and tear
- Freezing
- Mechanical or electrical breakdown or failure
- Road damage to tires

These exclusions do not apply if the damage results from a total theft.

Additional exclusions include loss due to or as a consequence of the following:

- Radioactive contamination
- Discharge of any nuclear weapon (even if accidental)
- War
- Civil war
- Insurrection
- Rebellion or revolution

The PAP does not cover damage to the vehicle if it is being used as a public or livery conveyance. However, the policy makes an exception for share-the-expense car pools.

Other exclusions include the following:

1. *Electronic Equipment Exclusions*. Loss to any electronic equipment and accessories designed for sound reproduction is excluded unless the equipment is permanently installed in the vehicle. Coverage would apply if the equipment is removable from a housing that is permanently installed in the vehicle, if the equipment runs off the vehicle's electrical system, and if it was in or upon the vehicle at the time of the loss.

   Other electronic equipment is also excluded. Any electronic equipment that receives or transmits audio, visual, or data signals and any accessories are not covered unless the equipment is necessary for normally operating the vehicle or monitoring the vehicle's operating systems. An exception is made for a telephone and its accessories, if the phone is permanently installed and operates from the vehicle's electrical system.

   Tapes, records, discs, or media used with electronic equipment are also excluded, as is loss to equipment designed or used for detection or location of radar or laser.
2. *Government or Civil Authorities*. Loss due to destruction or confiscation by the government or by civil authorities is not covered. However, this exclusion does not apply to the interest of any loss payees. This exclusion generally refers to thc confiscation of a vehicle because of illegal activities.
3. *Trailers, Campers, and Motor Homes*. Any loss to a trailer, camper body, or motor home not listed on the declarations page is excluded. This includes loss to cooking, dining, plumbing or refrigeration facilities; awnings and cabanas; and other equipment. The exclusion does not apply to a non-owned trailer and its facilities and equipment. The exclusion does not apply to a newly acquired trailer, camper body, or facilities and equipment, if it is reported to the insurer within fourteen days of purchase.
4. *Non-Owned Auto*. The policy excludes loss to a non-owned auto used without a reasonable belief that the insured was entitled to do so. It also excludes loss to a non-owned auto that is being maintained or used by any person in the business of selling, repairing, servicing, storing, or parking vehicles.
5. *Racing*. The policy excludes loss to owned and non-owned autos used for competition or used in practice and preparation for a race or speed contest.
6. *Custom Furnishings*. The policy excludes loss to custom furnishings and equipment for pickups and vans such as murals and graphics, facilities for cooking and sleeping, or height-extending roofs. The exclusion does not apply to a cap, cover, or bedliner for a covered pickup. Coverage for custom furnishings and equipment can be added by endorsement.
7. *Rental Vehicle*. The policy excludes loss to a non-owned rental auto that is rented by the insured or a family member if the rental company is precluded from recovering from the insured or family member by the terms of the rental agreement or by state law. This same exclusion applies to loss of use as well.

Limit of Liability

The policy specifies that the limit of liability for loss will be the lesser of the following:

1. Actual cash value (ACV) of the stolen or damaged property; or
2. Amount necessary to repair or replace the property with other property of like kind and quality.

It also states that depreciation and physical condition will be considered in determining ACV if a total loss occurs. Additionally, if the repair or replacement results in betterment, the amount of betterment will not be paid for. Betterment is usually only taken on items subject to wear, such as tires, batteries, upholstery, and some mechanical parts.

Any non-owned trailer is subject to a $500 limit. Any loss to equipment designed to reproduce sound, including accessories, which is installed in a location other than the location used by the manufacturer for such equipment, is limited to $1,000.

Diminished Value

In the sections of the PAP dealing with physical damage, no policy provision deals with diminished value. The policy states only that it will pay for direct and accidental losses.

Diminished value
The actual or perceived loss in market value or resale value that results from a direct and accidental loss to a vehicle.

Diminished value is generally defined in an ISO endorsement as the actual or perceived loss in market or resale value that results from a direct and accidental loss. This endorsement specifically states that the insurer will not pay for any loss resulting from diminution in value. This endorsement has not been approved for use in all jurisdictions.

Many courts have heard cases regarding claims for diminished value. There is no consensus as to decisions. They differ from one state to another as to whether diminished value should be paid as part of a loss. There is also no consensus among repair firms as to whether a repaired vehicle loses some of its value after a quality repair has been made.

The payment of diminished value on first-party claims is a hotly contested topic. Legal counsel should be consulted for the current status of diminished value claims in a particular jurisdiction.

Payment of Loss

The policy allows the insurer to pay for a loss in money or by repairing or replacing damaged or stolen property. Recovered stolen property may be returned to the insured, or the insurer may retain it for an agreed-upon or appraised amount. Loss payments include applicable sales tax.

Other Sources of Recovery

The PAP contains a clause that is similar to the "other insurance" clauses found in property policies. If there are other sources of recovery, the PAP only pays its share of the loss. The PAP share is the proportion that the PAP limit of liability bears to the total of all limits. If any PAP coverage applies to a non-owned auto, the PAP coverage is excess over any other collectible source of recovery.

Appraisal

Like other first-party property damage policies, the PAP has an appraisal clause so that if the insured and insurer do not agree on the amount of loss, either party may demand an appraisal. Each party picks an appraiser, and the two appraisers pick an umpire. A decision agreed to by any two is binding upon the parties.

Duties After an Accident or Loss

The insured must promptly notify the insurer of a loss as well as cooperate with the investigation. The insured must take reasonable steps to protect the vehicle from additional damage. Expenses stemming from this protection are reimbursable. The insured must make the damaged vehicle available for inspection before repair or disposal. And the insured must notify the police if the vehicle is stolen.

General Provisions

The PAP contains a fraud clause, a suit clause, and a subrogation clause, similar to other property policies.

AUTOMOTIVE ESTIMATES

To evaluate an estimate or damage appraisal, an adjuster should be familiar with the two types of vehicle bodies currently in use, various types of available replacement parts that might affect repair costs, painting procedures that might affect repair costs, and the correct terminology for the various parts of the vehicle.

Vehicle Body Types[4]

There are two types of vehicle body: (1) conventional full frame and (2) unitized or unibody construction.

Conventional full frame is found on trucks and some large private passenger autos. It is characterized by a separate steel frame to which the vehicle's body is bolted. See Exhibit 13-2.

Most passenger vehicles today have **unitized,** or **unibody, construction.** The body is made by welding sheet metal panels together. The unibody design has "crush zones" located within its structure. These crush zones are

Conventional full frame
A type of auto body usually found on trucks and large passenger autos, characterized by a separate steel frame to which the body of the vehicle is bolted.

Unitized, or **unibody, construction**
Passenger vehicle design by which sheet metal panels are welded together so that the body is in one piece rather than two.

EXHIBIT 13-2

Conventional Frame

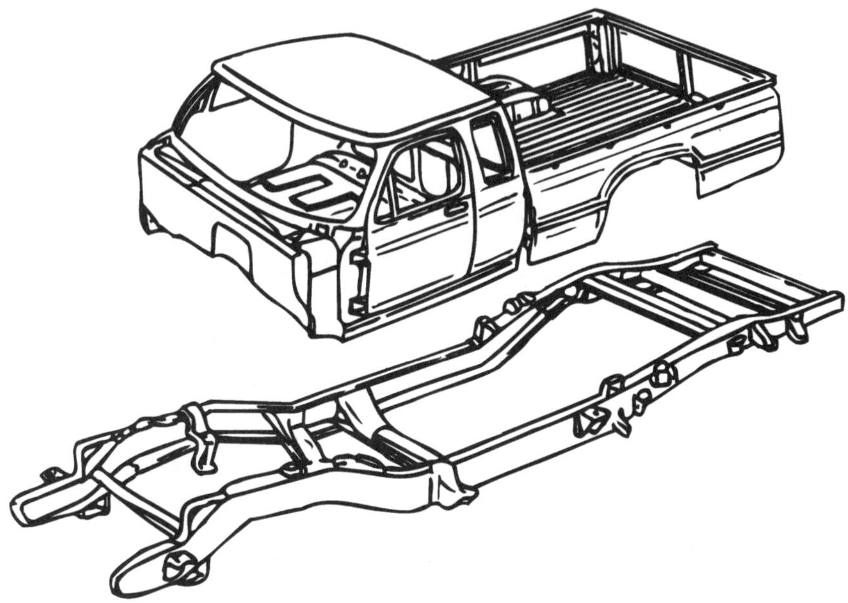

EXHIBIT 13-3

Unitized or Unibody Construction

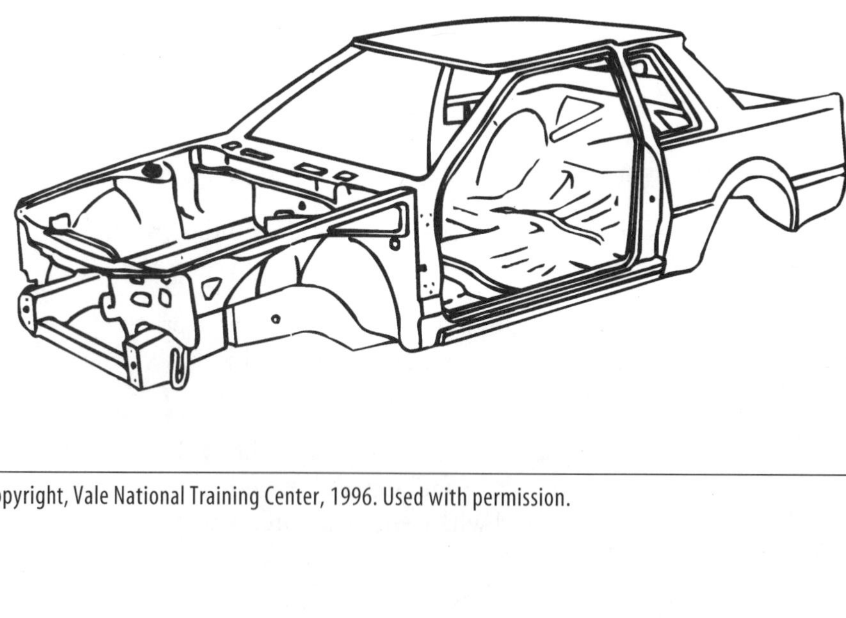

designed to absorb energy from an impact. As a result of an impact, the sheet metal that forms the unibody distorts, causing a misalignment of the unibody. See Exhibit 13-3.

Unibody construction anticipates the need for structural realignment by having control points designated with the unibody. A **control point** is a hole, bolt, or location that is used as the measure of the structural misalignment. The misaligned control points are realigned by using various types of pulling equipment. Exhibit 13-4 shows some of a car's control points.

Control point
A hole, bolt, or location on a vehicle body that is used as the measure of structural misalignment.

Replacement Parts

Various kinds of replacement parts are available to repair a vehicle. Recall that the PAP uses the phrase "like kind and quality" and betterment in the limit of liability provision. These terms become important because of the various types of parts available. An **original equipment manufacturer (OEM) part** is a new part made by the vehicle manufacturer. An **after-market (AM) part** is a new part made by someone other than the vehicle manufacturer. An after-market part may be certified by the Certified Automotive Parts Association, a nonprofit insurer-sponsored group. A **remanufactured (reman) part** is a used part that has been reconditioned. A **like kind and quality (LKQ) part** is a usable part found at a salvage yard.

Original equipment manufacturer (OEM) part
A part that is made by the manufacturer of the vehicle.

After-market (AM) part
A new part for a vehicle, made by someone other than the vehicle manufacturer.

Remanufactured (reman) part
A used part that has been reconditioned.

Like kind and quality (LKQ) part
A usable part found at a salvage yard.

When reviewing an estimate, the adjuster must understand the parts distinctions. Obviously, each of these types of parts have different costs. The insured would also be concerned about used parts' safety and reliability. Forty states have laws requiring the disclosure of the use of after-market parts in repairs. A few states even require the customer's consent to use such parts. Some insurers offer their insureds the option of endorsing the policy for OEM or after-market parts. Before reviewing an estimate, an adjuster should determine his or her company's policy regarding parts. Policies also might differ among states.

Painting

The repair process also includes painting, which includes cleaning, masking adjacent parts, application of primer and sealer, sanding (possibly a few times), applying the color, blending the color, and then applying a clear top coat. When a large area that encompasses two or more panels of the vehicle is painted, some of these steps are duplicated. For example, each panel might have a charge for masking the adjacent panels. But if two adjacent panels are damaged, then there should be only one masking charge because the two panels would be masked at the same time as a continuous process. This duplicated labor is referred to as "paint overlap" and is deducted from the estimate.

EXHIBIT 13-4

Control Points

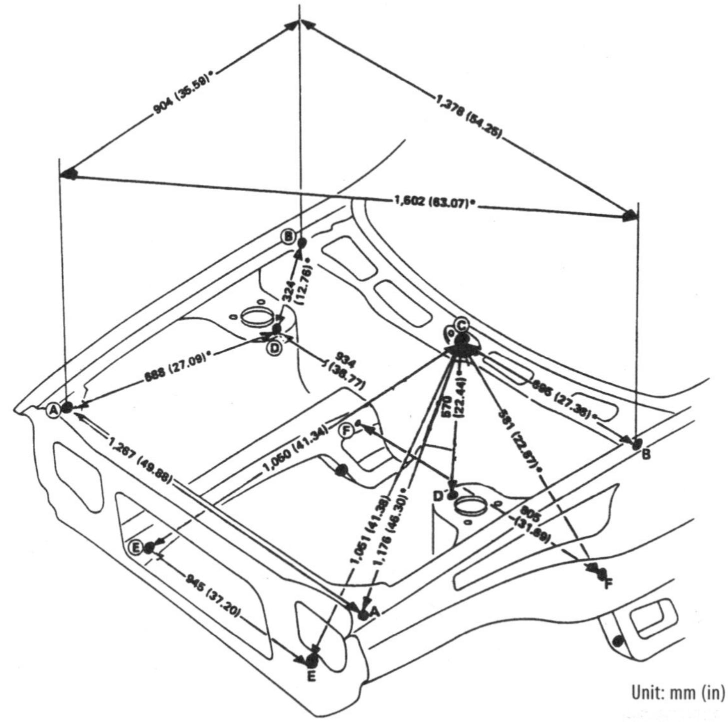

Typical Underhood Dimensions or Control Points

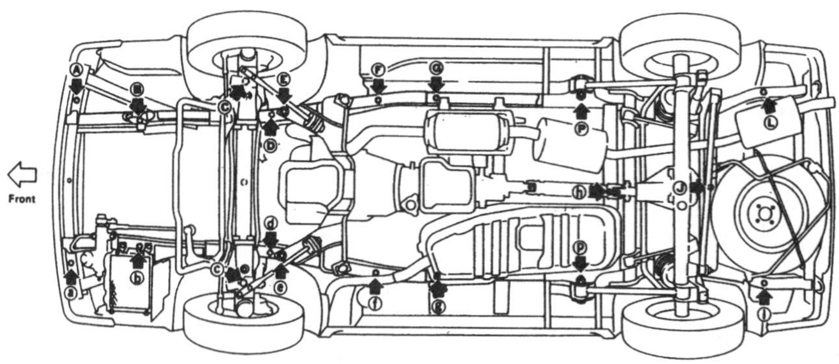

Typical Underbody Control Point Locations

Structural Components

The adjuster should be familiar with a car's components that are frequently damaged in collisions. Very often, the parts of a car combine to make up a unit referred to as an **assembly**. For example, the bumper is made up of many parts that combine to form the bumper assembly. This section of the chapter details the assembly level of car parts rather than enumerates every individual part of a car.

Assembly
A portion of a vehicle that is made up of several parts but when combined, the parts form a unit.

Front Outer Components

At the front end of the car, the front bumper assembly includes the impact absorbers, the bumper cover, the license plate bracket, and many smaller pieces. See Exhibits 13-5 and 13-6.

The front end contains a grille and various types of lamps. Often the lamps are referred to as an assembly.

The front end's exterior panels are the hood assembly and the left and right fender assembly.

The engine is located inside the front end for most, although not all, cars. In addition to the engine, the front end contains the radiator, the fan, the battery (not always), and the air conditioning unit. See Exhibit 13-7.

The wheel components for the front end may differ depending upon whether the vehicle is all-wheel drive, front-wheel drive, or rear-wheel drive. Rear-wheel drive vehicles have a suspension system and a drive axle. The steering system is located in the front end for all of the various types of vehicles.

Side Components

Both the front and rear windshields are considered side components, as is the roof panel. The side door panels, with all of their internal pieces, are also side components. See Exhibit 13-8.

Rear Components

The rear part of the car contains a bumper assembly similar to the front end and a wheel assembly that usually includes the transmission. The exhaust pipes and muffler are also located in the rear, although the exhaust pipes run all the way back up front to the engine. The gas tank is usually located in the rear of the car.

The body panels that make up the rear end include the trunk or deck lid, the liftgate (found only on hatch backs), the rear body panel, and the rear floor pan, which form the area commonly called the trunk. Additionally, the rear has a quarter panel (located behind the door and over the wheel) and both an inner and outer wheelhouse that are the sheet metal pieces covering the wheel and tire. Note that the rear end does not have fenders. Only the front end does. See Exhibit 13-9.

EXHIBIT 13-5

Front End—Bumper Assembly and Grille & Lamps

BUMPER ASSEMBLY

1. **FACE BAR** - IMPACT BAR - REINFORCEMENT: The main part of the bumper that provides strength and is not visible on models with a cover. The face bar is visible on models without a cover.
2. **ABSORBER CUSHION** - IMPACT ABSORBER: A foam or plastic part located between the facebar and cover to absorb impacts and support the cover, *on some models.*
3. **BUMPER COVER** - FACE BAR COVER - FASCIA: The outer appearance part that fits over the face bar and is usually made of flexible plastic, *on some models.*
4. **RETAINER** - SUPPORT - STAY: A metal or plastic strip that attaches the cover to other components.
5. **GUARDS:** (R & L) Vertical protrusions that protect the bumper from minor frontal impacts, *on some models.*

6. **LICENSE PLATE BRACKET:** A metal or plastic support that attaches a license plate to the bumper, *on some models.*
7. **FOG LAMP** - DRIVING LAMPS: (R & L) Lamps attached near the bottom of the bumper, *on some models.*
8. **PARK/SIGNAL LAMP:** (R & L) A dual purpose lamp consisting of a lens, bulb and housing that is commonly mounted within the bumper.
9. **IMPACT STRIP** - MOULDING - CUSHION - HORIZONTAL PAD - NERF STRIP: A single or multi-piece trim item that is attached to the front surface of the bumper extending from side to side, *on some models.*
10. **FILLER** - STONE DEFLECTOR: Cosmetic parts used to fill the space between the bumper and the body, *on some models.*
11. **BUMPER END** - END CAP - EXTENSION: (R & L) A plastic appearance part bolted to the ends of a visible face bar, *on some models.*
12. **VALANCE PANEL** - LOWER VALANCE: A plastic or metal panel located below the bumper, *on some models.*

GRILLE & LAMPS

13. **HEADER PANEL** - FRONT PANEL - GRILLE PANEL - NOSE PANEL: A plastic or metal part located above the bumper and in front of the hood, on some models. The header panel houses the grille and lamps.
14. **GRILLE:** A slotted appearance part usually plastic, which allows air flow to cool the radiator, *on some models.*
15. **EMBLEM:** A manufacturers symbol. **NAMEPLATE:** A make, model or trim package name with connected letters.
16. **COMPOSITE HEADLAMP** - REPLACEABLE BULB TYPE HEADLAMP: (R & L) This type of headlamp uses a removable "plug in" bulb.
17. **LENS** - LENS & HOUSING: (R & L) A clear lens attached to a plastic foil-lined enclosure that reflects light.
18. **BULB** & **SOCKET:** (R & L) The "plug in" halogen lamp used with composite headlamps.
19. **SEALED BEAM TYPE HEADLAMPS:** This type of headlamp uses a permanently sealed bulb, called a sealed beam.
20. **ADJUSTING RING** - MOUNTING RING - BUCKET - SEAT: (R & L) Supports the sealed beam and provides adjustment use of two adjusting screws.
21. **SEALED BEAM:** (R & L) A small bulb or filament permanently sealed within a larger glass or plastic lens assembly.
22. **RETAINING RING:** (R & L) A plastic or metal band that surrounds and holds the sealed beam in place.

    HEADLAMP CAPSULE: (R & L) An assembly consisting of multiple headlamp components.
23. **HEADLAMP BEZEL** - HEADLAMP DOOR: (R & L) A cosmetic outer trim item most commonly used with sealed beam type headlamps.

EXHIBIT 13-6

Front End—Hood Assembly and Fender Assembly

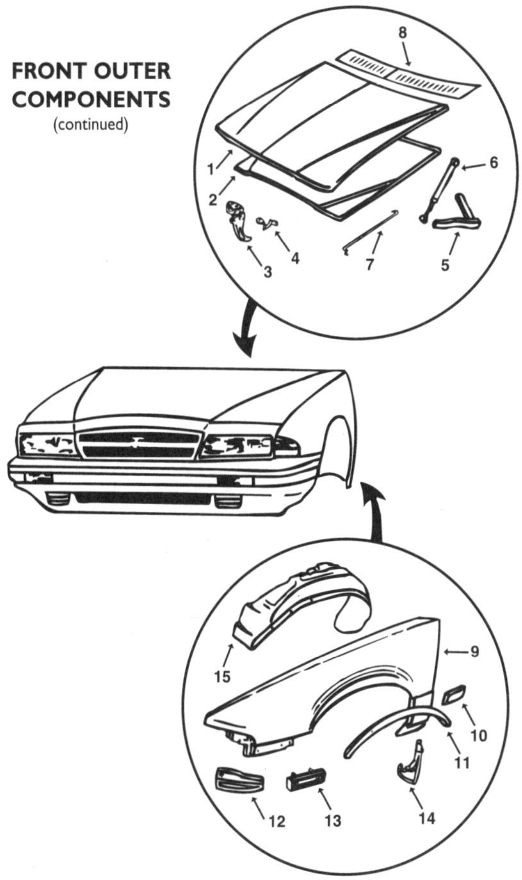

HOOD ASSEMBLY

1. **HOOD PANEL:** A large high appearance panel that covers the engine compartment and consists of an outer panel that is welded and/or bonded to an inner structure.
2. **INSULATOR PAD:** A fiber or foam blanket that may be attached to the underside of the hood to confine engine noise, on some models.

   HOOD LATCH (See radiator support/front inner structure)
3. **SAFETY CATCH:** A secondary latch that prevents the hood from opening if the primary latch is not secure.
4. **STRIKER** - LATCH BOLT: A device that enters the latch to secure the hood. May be bolted to or an integral part of the hood.
5. **HINGES:** (R & L) A pivoting device that allows the hood to open and close.
6. **SUPPORT STRUT** - ASSIST CYLINDER: A cartridge containing compressed gas that holds the hood in an upright position, on some models.
7. **PROP ROD** - SUPPORT ROD: A long thin manually operated metal brace that holds the hood in an upright position, on some models.
8. **COWL VENT PANEL** - COWL TOP PANEL - COWL VENT SCREEN: A slotted panel located behind the hood and in front of the windshield, *on some models.*

FENDER ASSEMBLY

9. **FENDER:** (R & L) An outer panel located over the front wheel that is usually bolted to the apron/wheelhouse.
10. **SIDE MOULDING** - SIDE PROTECT MOULDING - BODY SIDE MOULDING: (R & L) A horizontal trim item attached with clips or adhesive, designed to help protect the side panels from minor parking lot dents, *on some models.*
11. **WHEEL OPENING MOULDING:** (R & L) A trim item attached to the arched area of the fender, *on some models.*
12. **SIDE MARKER LAMP** -SIDE LAMP - (R & L) A lamp visible from the side using an amber lens that is illuminated along with the park lamps and/or the headlamps. On some models the side marker lamp and the park lamp may be combined into one unit, referred to as a combination lamp.
13. **CORNERING LAMPS:** (R & L) A lamp using a clear lens that is illuminated along with the turn signal lamps to provide the driver with better visibility while turning, *on some models.*
14. **MUDFLAP** - MUDGUARD - SPLASH GUARD: (R & L) A plastic, rubber or metal deflector mounted behind the tire to protect the fender and door from stone chips, *on some models.*
15. **LINER** - SPLASH SHIELD - SKIRT: (R & L) An arched, usually flexible plastic part attached to the fender and apron designed to protect those parts from road debris.

EXHIBIT 13-7

Engine

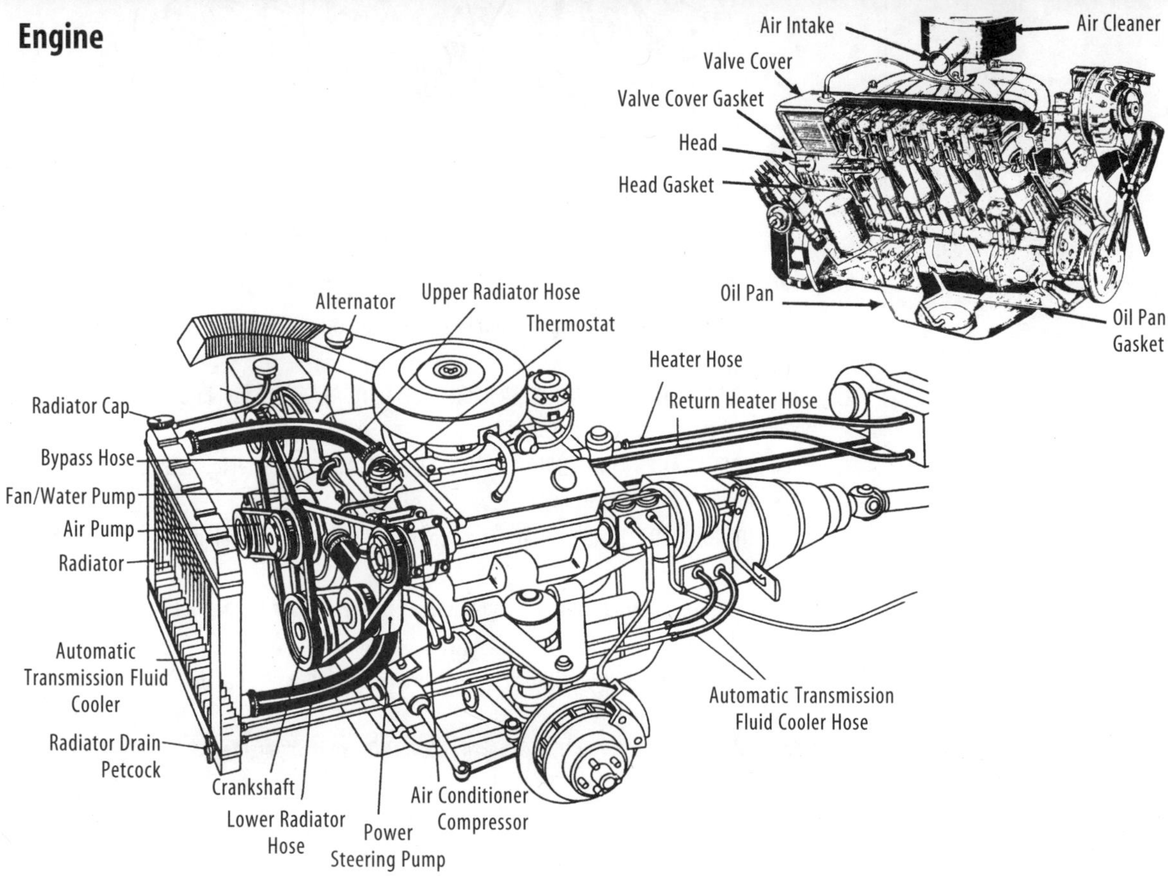

Courtesy of National Property & Casualty Claims Research Services, Inc.

EXHIBIT 13-8

Side Components

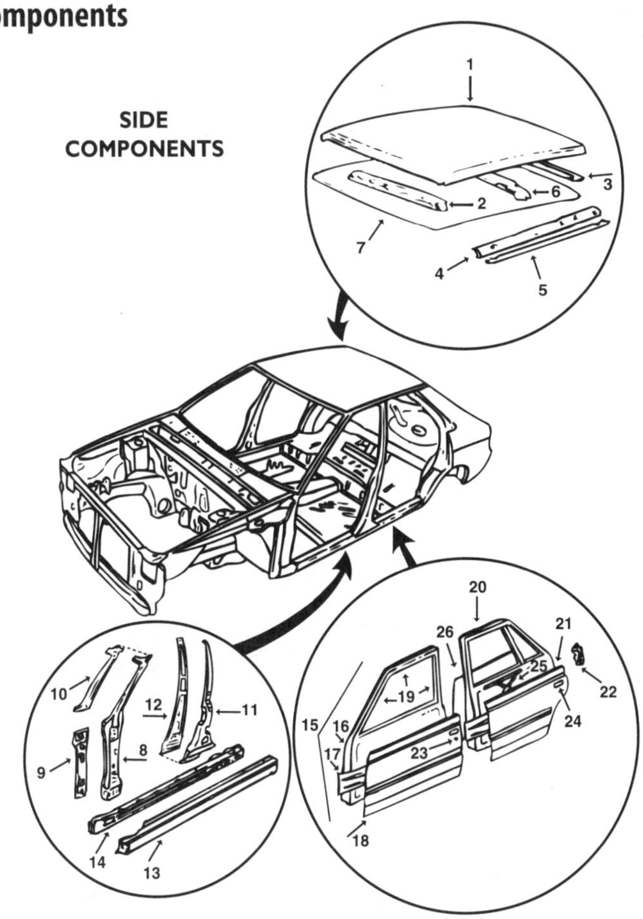

SIDE COMPONENTS

1. **ROOF OUTER PANEL:** A large sheet metal part covering the passenger compartment that is welded to inner panels.
2. **WINDSHIELD HEADER-** FRONT UPPER REINFORCEMENT: An inner panel located above the windshield extending from side to side.
3. **BACK GLASS HEADER -** REAR UPPER REINFORCEMENT: An inner panel located above the back glass extending from side to side.
4. **ROOF SIDE RAIL:** (R & L) An inner panel extending from front to rear along the outer edge of the roof.
5. **DRIP RAIL:** (R & L) A small gutter along the side of the roof used to channel water away from the door openings.
6. **ROOF BOWS:** Inner panels extending laterally from side rail to side rail that provide support for the roof outer panel.
7. **HEADLINER:** A large interior trim panel that covers the roof underside.

8. **HINGE/WINDSHIELD PILLAR** - "A" PILLAR: (S) (R & L) A sheet metal panel welded to the rocker panel extending vertically to the roof and is an attachment point for the front door and windshield. The beltline divides the hinge and windshield pillar.
9. **HINGE PILLAR REINFORCEMENT** - COWL SIDE PANEL: (R & L) A welded inner panel located below the beltline, used for additional strength.
10. **INNER WINDSHIELD PILLAR:** (R & L) A welded inner panel located above the beltline, used for additional strength.
11. **CENTER PILLAR** - "B" PILLAR: (S) (R & L) The center pillar is welded to the rocker panel extending upward to the roof. Found only on models with at least 4 doors, it is a latch point for the front door and a hinge point for the rear door.
12. **INNER CENTER PILLAR** - REINFORCEMENT: (R & L) A welded inner panel used for additional strength.
13. **ROCKER PANEL:** (S) (R & L) A welded sheet metal panel located below the doors to provide support for the floor.
14. **INNER ROCKER PANEL** - REINFORCEMENT: A welded inner panel used for additional strength.
15. **DOOR SHELL:** (R & L) A structure consisting only of the outer panel, door frame, guard beam and window frame.
16. **DOOR FRAME** - INNER STRUCTURE: (R & L) The sheet metal foundation used to attach most door related parts.
17. **GUARD BEAM** - REINFORCEMENT - INTRUSION BAR: (R & L) A high strength steel panel located inside the door extending from front to rear for side impact protection.
18. **DOOR OUTER PANEL**- REPAIR PANEL- DOOR SKIN: (R & L) The exterior sheet metal panel that is folded onto the frame around its outer edges and welded or bonded in place.
19. **WINDOW FRAME:** (R & L) A metal channel located around the edges of the door glass, on some models.
20. **WEATHER STRIP:** (R & L) A rubber strip attached to the door or the body to seal out wind and water.
21. **BELT MOULDING:** (R & L) A exterior trim item located at the beltline.
22. **LATCH - LOCK:** (R & L) A mechanical device that secures the door in a closed position.
23. **LOCK CYLINDER:** (R & L) Found on front doors this device uses a key to operate the locking mechanism.
24. **OUTSIDE HANDLE:** (R & L) An exterior lever or button that is used to open the door latch.
25. **REGULATOR:** (R & L) A mechanism that raises and lowers the glass.
26. **TRIM PANEL:** (R & L) The interior covering that is attached to the door frame.

EXHIBIT 13-9

Rear Components

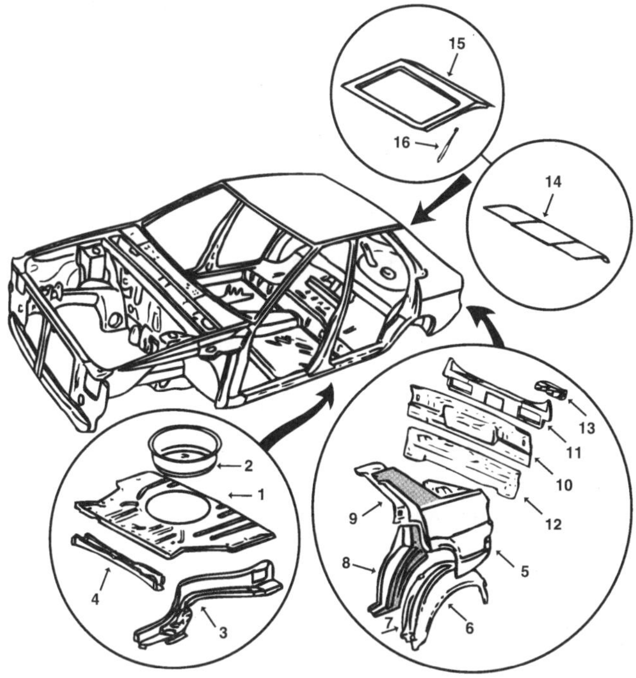

REAR COMPONENTS

1. **REAR FLOOR PAN -TRUNK FLOOR**: A flat sheet metal panel that forms the bottom surface of the luggage compartment.
2. **SPARE TIRE WELL:** A circular recessed compartment that houses the spare tire. A separate part on some models but usually part of the rear floor pan.
3. **REAR SIDE RAIL** - REAR RAIL - REAR SIDE MEMBER: (S) (R & L) A boxed sheet metal component welded to the underside of the rear floor pan for structural support.
4. **CROSSMEMBER** - X-MEMBER: (S) A boxed sheet metal component extending from side rail to side rail for lateral support.
5. **QUARTER PANEL** - 1/4 PANEL: (R & L) A large welded outer panel located behind the door(s) in the rear wheel area.

   SAIL PANEL - ROOF EXTENSION: (R & L) An area of the outer quarter panel located between the roof and the beltline. The beltline is an imaginary line located approximately halfway up the side of the vehicle at the base of the glass.

   DOG LEG: An area of the quarter panel located just below the arched area of the rear door and in front of the rear wheel and tire. Found only on 4-door models.

   REAR FLOOR EXTENSION - FILLER TO QUARTER: (R & L) A welded panel located behind the rear wheel that extends from the bottom edge of the outer quarter panel upward to the rear floor pan, *on some models.*

6. **OUTER WHEELHOUSE:** (R & L) The outer portion of rounded sheet metal that covers the wheel and tire. It is welded to the outer quarter panel and inner wheelhouse.
7. **INNER WHEELHOUSE:** (R & L) The inner portion of rounded sheet metal that covers the wheel and tire. It is welded to the outer wheelhouse and rear floor pan.
8. **LOCKPILLAR** - "B" PILLAR on a 2-door - "C"-PILLAR on a 4-door: (R & L) Located at the front edge of the quarter panel and is not visible when the door is closed. The lock pillar may be a separate part on some models or part of the outer quarter panel.
9. **INNER QUARTER PANEL:** (R & L) A welded sheet metal panel that is used for reinforcement and is usually covered by the interior trim.
10. **REAR BODY PANEL:** A single or multiple piece sheet metal panel that forms the rear wall of the luggage compartment. The rear body panel is welded to the rear floor pan and to the rear edge of both quarter panels.
11. **FINISH PANEL:** A bolt-on exterior part that covers the rear body panel, *on some models.*
12. **LOWER REAR PANEL** - REAR VALANCE PANEL: A separate part welded to the bottom edge of the rear body panel, on some models.
13. **TAIL LAMP ASSEMBLY** - T/L ASSY: (R & L) A combination lamp attached to the rear of the vehicle consisting of lenses, bulbs and a housing.
14. **DECKLID** - TRUNK LID - LUGGAGE LID: The outer panel located behind the rear glass that covers the luggage compartment, *on some models.* Constructed similar to a hood, but located in the rear.
15. **LIFTGATE** - HATCH LID: This part is found on hatch backs and contains the rear glass. It is attached to the rear of the roof and swings upward to provide a large entry to the rear storage area.
16. **SUPPORT STRUT** - ASSIST CYLINDER: (R & L) A cartridge containing compressed gas that holds the liftgate in an upright position.

DAMAGE ANALYSIS—ESTIMATING REPAIRS[5]

The appraiser who inspects the damaged vehicle decides whether to repair or replace a damaged part. Generally, a part should be replaced if repairs are not cost-effective or if repairing it will not return the vehicle to the condition it was in before the loss. The appraiser considers the extent of damage, the size of the damaged area, and the appearance. Usually, if the repair cost exceeds 75 percent of the cost to replace the part, replacement is appropriate.

Damage Estimate

Preparing a vehicle's damage estimate is similar to preparing a building's damage estimate, although the terminology differs somewhat. A vehicle appraiser determines the type, size, and extent of damage. He or she determines how the repairs can best be accomplished, what the parts will cost, and what the labor will cost. The estimator may use a computer-estimating package or may determine prices for parts and labor from estimating guide books. The appraiser can face the same issues as can a building damage estimator: preexisting damage, disagreement over extent of damage, and disagreement over how to repair the damage.

Terminology

Similar to the estimating process for a structure, vehicle damage appraisal has a set of standard terms. Some of the more frequently used are the following:

Remove and install (R&I)
The process of gaining access to damaged parts of a vehicle by removing undamaged parts.

Remove and replace (R&R)
The process of removing the assembly, putting in new parts, and then reinstalling and realigning the assembly.

Overhaul (OH)
A repair term for completely disassembling and reassembling a group of related parts, replacing the damaged parts in the process.

Included operation
Any labor operation completed in its entirety while another, concurrent operation is performed.

(R&I) **Remove and install**—Used to gain access to other parts—includes alignment back when reinstalling.

(R&R) **Remove and replace**—Remove the assembly, put in new parts, and reinstall and align.

(OH) **Overhaul**—To completely disassemble and reassemble an assembly, replacing the damaged parts in the process.[6]

Adjusters should be aware of included operations in an estimate or appraisal. An **included operation** is any labor operation completed in its entirety while another operation is performed. If a fender and side lamp are damaged, the "remove and replace" labor rate for the fender would include time to replace or transfer the side lamp, so there should not be a separate entry for labor to remove and replace the side lamp. The labor to do so would be included in the time needed to remove and replace the fender.[7]

Common Estimating Problems[8]

When reviewing an estimate, the adjuster should check the description column for incomplete labor/parts descriptions or inconsistent descriptions.

The adjuster should also check for duplication of smaller parts. Some computer estimating packages fail to guard against this type of duplication.

As with building damage adjusting, if a computer estimating system is used, the adjuster should know what the entries include. Some systems select parts based on the option package selected, so it is important that the correct option package is entered. The system may use the VIN to select parts, so the adjuster should verify that the VIN is correctly entered.

Direct Repair Programs

Direct repair program (DRP)
A program by which insurers provide a network of repair facilities that meet the insurer's criteria for quality work at cost-effective prices.

To try to control costs and increase customer satisfaction, many insurers have established direct repair programs. A **direct repair program (DRP)** is usually a network of repair facilities that have met an insurer's criteria for quality work at a cost-effective price. Very often, the DRP shop performs the appraisal and is able to transmit the information to the claim office via computer. The DRP shop may also be able to arrange to have a rental car available for the insured when the damaged vehicle is dropped off.

Anti-Steering Laws

Many states have laws that ensure the consumer's right to pick a repair shop to perform the repairs. Although these laws do not outlaw DRPs, they do put certain restrictions on what an insurer can request of an insured. Often these laws are phrased so as to prohibit the insured from having to travel an unreasonable distance for a repair. Others specifically prohibit an insurer from requiring that an insured go to a specific facility to obtain repairs.

Flood Damage[9]

The PAP specifically covers flood damage as an OTC loss. A flooded vehicle is not necessarily a total loss. The following are factors to consider:

1. Type of water—Salt water causes more corrosion damage than does fresh water.
2. Amount of time submerged—The longer the vehicle is underwater, the greater the potential damage.
3. Height of the flood—If the water only reached the bottom of the car door, there is a good chance that the engine is unaffected. If the water entered the engine and electrical system, the damage can be extensive.
4. How quickly can repairs begin—The sooner a vehicle is dried out, the less damage will occur.

Interior Restoration[10]

Generally, the most common interior problems are stains, odors, cuts, tears, and burns. Cleaning and deodorizing should be done by professionals. Repair of carpeting and upholstery that is cut or burned can often be accomplished without the need for complete replacement. A qualified repair facility should perform any type of repair to carpeting or upholstery. Recall that damage caused by wear and tear is not covered, so the cause of the problem must be verified—by the repairer, the insured, or an outside consultant— before such repair work is done.

Glass[11]

All of the glass used in an automobile is safety glass. However, there are two types of safety glass: (1) laminated and (2) tempered. Laminated glass consists of a sheet of polyvinyl film sandwiched between two layers of glass. Tempered glass is made by heating a single layer of glass to approximately 1,100 degrees Fahrenheit and then rapidly cooling it. This process causes the glass to be so strong that the glass cannot be cut or drilled. It can still be shattered, however, and for that reason it is not used in windshields.

Windshield glass can also have tinting or shading to reduce glare. Most cars also have rear window defrosters on the back windshield. Some cars have radio antennas in the windshield.

Windshields are installed either with an adhesive or, for older cars, with rubber gaskets. Windshields are considered a safety device. Federal standards regulate safety devices' installation and repair. Many manufacturers and repair shops insist that OEM windshields be used in replacements to meet the federal standards, and they specify the type of adhesive to be used.

Minor chips and breaks in a windshield can be repaired. The repairs are accomplished by injecting a resin into the damaged area. The resin is forced into all of the damaged area and then cured with an ultraviolet light.

Because of the safety issues involved with windshield repair and replacement, these types of repairs are usually handled by specialists who are trained to comply with federal safety regulations.

Fire Losses

Investigating a vehicle fire is similar to investigating a building fire. The adjuster should take statements; verify the vehicle's history; determine if there are any liens; determine its mileage, overall condition, and repair history; and determine the fire's origin and cause.

Taking the insured's statement will generate the basic information on the vehicle's history, repairs, overall condition, and whether there are any liens on it. The information gathered in the statement can then be verified by independent sources. NICB and ISO have a database that can give information about an insured's claim history, as well as information about the vehicle.

Almost every vehicle fire should be investigated by an origin and cause specialist, but that may not always be cost-effective. If the vehicle is worth more than $5,000, investigation would be prudent because the potential for arson and subrogation always exists.

Non-arson car fires usually are caused by one of the following:

1. A short in the electrical system
2. Ignition of fuel or oil
3. Malfunction in the exhaust system, usually the catalytic converter

Fires occurring under the hood of a car are usually a fuel fire or an oil fire that is ignited by a spark. If the hood is left closed, the fire could burn itself out from lack of oxygen. Likewise, a fire in a stationary vehicle is more likely to burn out, while a moving vehicle adds more oxygen to the fire.[12]

Interior fires usually start under the dashboard, primarily from an electrical short or from cigarettes. If the windows remain closed, the oxygen supply will be depleted quickly and the fire will be extinguished.

If only a car's exterior surfaces are burned, it would usually mean that the fuel for the fire and the ignition source came from outside the vehicle. Notice the burn pattern on the hood and roof of the car in Exhibit 13-10 and the lack of exterior burns on the hood of the car in Exhibit 13-11.

EXHIBIT 13-10

External Car Fire

Photo courtesy of National Property & Casualty Claims Research Services, Inc.

EXHIBIT 13-11

Internal Car Fire

Photo courtesy of National Property & Casualty Claims Research Services, Inc.

Total Theft Loss

Vehicle theft is a significant problem for insurers because it occurs frequently and presents the opportunity for fraud. When a vehicle is stolen, the claim can take one of four paths:

1. Not recovered
2. Recovered and repaired
3. Recovered and a total loss
4. Denied because of fraud or another coverage defense

Investigation

When receiving an auto theft claim, the adjuster should verify the vehicle's existence and the circumstances of the loss. It is possible for a car to be moved from its last known location and not to have been stolen. For example, the police may have impounded the vehicle, the bank may have repossessed the vehicle, a family member may have taken the car without permission, or an estranged spouse may have taken it. The adjuster should consider all potential scenarios when taking the insured's statement. Additionally, the statement should cover when and where the vehicle was acquired, the VIN, whether the car was financed, and whether it had recent repairs. A repair firm that recently worked on the vehicle can verify the VIN. The statement should also cover the vehicle's overall condition, its options, and its mileage.

Theft Report

If the vehicle is stolen, the insured must report the theft to the police. The police report is another tool in verifying how the loss occurred. The adjuster should report the theft to an index bureau as soon as possible. If the vehicle is recovered, this will aid in its return. This report can also provide the adjuster with feedback on other losses involving the vehicle and the insured.

Fraud Indicators

An adjuster should always be sensitive to the possibility of fraud in a claim. Although fraud has many indicators, the adjuster must view the totality of the circumstances and then make a judgment whether to refer the file to the SIU for further investigation. In auto theft, the following are some indicators:

- Domestic problems
- Duplicate title
- Heavy debt
- Incorrect VIN
- Leased vehicle with high mileage
- Major repair work needed
- New policy or newly added vehicle

- Prior losses
- Unemployment
- Unusual amount of personal property in vehicle

Stolen and Recovered

If the stolen vehicle is recovered, it will probably have suffered some damage in the process. Cars are stolen for many reasons, but the most likely ones are the following:

- Joy ride
- Transportation
- To be used in commission of a crime
- Parts
- Export

The first four on this list usually result in a recovered damaged vehicle.

Once the vehicle is recovered, it should be inspected promptly and a determination should be made whether to repair the vehicle or declare it a total loss.

Stolen and Not Recovered

Insurers often have claim guidelines regarding the time period that must pass before deciding that a vehicle is a total theft. Thirty days is common. The adjuster should also consult unfair claim settlement regulations because they may specify the time period in which to wait.

During this waiting period, the adjuster should conclude the investigation into the circumstances of the loss and work up the vehicle's actual cash value. The insured should have executed an affidavit of vehicle theft, an odometer statement, and a power of attorney. After the vehicle is declared a total theft, the claim should be paid and the title or bill of sale should be changed to a salvage title. This enables the vehicle to be processed as salvage if it is eventually found. Once payment is made, all of the law enforcement agencies involved should be advised so that their records can be updated.

Total Loss of Vehicle

The total loss to a vehicle can occur by theft or from damage. To determine whether a damaged vehicle is a total loss, the adjuster must obtain two values. One is the ACV at the time of the loss, and the other is the vehicle's salvage value, if any. A total loss because of damage occurs when the actual cost of repair exceeds the vehicle's ACV, less any salvage value. Actual cost of repairs should include repairs, loss of use, and betterment calculations. Some insurers set a threshold such as 75 or 85 percent, and if the cost to repair (including salvage value) exceeds 75 or 85 percent of the ACV, then the vehicle would be a total loss.[13]

Determining Vehicle's ACV

Several reference books are available for determining a car's pre-accident value, and most of them are available online. The *Kelley Blue Book*, the National Automotive Dealers Association (NADA) *Official Used Car Guide*, and other sources provide pre-accident values, as do many software packages. It is important to know how the values for each source are determined. Some states mandate how ACV is to be established, so it is important to know whether the value shown is the dealer's asking price or the lowest price for which the dealer will sell the car. Some states require ACV to be determined by a survey of local dealers. Regardless of the method used, the ACV calculation should factor in the vehicle's options package, mileage, use, and overall condition. The calculation should also include taxes and fees as required by the jurisdiction.

Common ACV Errors[14]

Whether done manually or by using a software package, one of the most common errors in calculating ACV is incorrectly identifying the vehicle's options package. One way to ensure against this error is to decode the VIN and confirm with the manufacturer what items were included in the option package coded into the VIN.

Other common errors include incorrectly assessing the vehicle's overall condition and failing to deduct for unrepaired prior damage.

Salvage[15]

A salvageable vehicle usually falls into one of three categories. It can be (1) rebuilt, (2) used for parts, or (3) used for scrap metal.

A rebuildable car is usually less than six years old, in better-than-average condition, with average or better mileage. The damage it has sustained is in an area that is conducive to repair, like in the rear or in the body panels.

A vehicle used for parts is usually less than ten years old with relatively little body damage and not much wear on the mechanical parts. The sheet metal and mechanical parts are scavenged for use in another vehicle.

A scrap vehicle is usually one that has been severely damaged with few usable parts.

Selling Salvage

As part of the adjustment process for a total loss, the adjuster must determine the vehicle's salvage value. How does an adjuster sell a vehicle as salvage? One method is to use a salvage pool. In a salvage pool, the cars are collected, stored, and then sold at a periodic auction, usually with a minimum bid set. This is usually an easy way of dealing with salvage.

Another way to handle salvage is through a bid process. The adjuster can get bids from salvage buyers directly (which is very time-consuming), or the adjuster can hire a salvage company, which will, for a fee, handle the bid process for the insurer.

The last option is owner retention of the damaged vehicle. This drastically reduces the amount of paperwork needed to resolve the claims because the owner retains the vehicle and has no need to transfer the title or to arrange for a salvor to take possession of the vehicle

The final salvage figure is the net amount received from the sale of the vehicle after deducting expenses such as towing and storage.

Total Loss Payment

When the waiting period for theft has expired or as soon as the damaged vehicle is declared a total loss, and all of the paperwork transferring ownership has been completed, the loss can be paid. The loss calculation would be as follows:

Claim Payment = ACV – Deductible.

If the insured chooses to retain the car, then the loss calculation would be as follows:

Claim Payment = ACV – Deductible – Salvage.

If the insured chooses to retain the vehicle, the adjuster must be prepared to explain how the salvage figure was calculated. Usually, a phone survey of reputable salvage dealers in the area of the loss for a salvage bid suffices. Many states have regulations that require this information to be given to the insured in writing, so adjusters should consult local statutes and unfair claim practices regulations for guidance.

CONTRACTORS' EQUIPMENT

This next section of the chapter discusses contractors' equipment. As Chapter 12 mentions, contractors' equipment coverage is an inland marine form of coverage. It is included in this chapter because the handling of a contractors' equipment claim more closely resembles an auto physical damage claim than it does a property damage claim involving a building.

Contractors' equipment can be defined as the tools and machinery used in projects involving construction, renovation, earth-moving, and many other activities. Contractors' equipment insurance protects the insured against direct physical loss to the covered property. Endorsements may be added to contractors' equipment policies to cover time element losses—either loss of income or extra expenses—resulting from physical loss to covered equipment. A contractors' equipment policy tailored to a contractor's unique needs can cover the cost to repair or replace the damaged piece of equipment.

Contractors' equipment
The tools and machinery used in projects involving construction, renovation, earth-moving, and other activities.

Adding rental reimbursement and business income coverage endorsements can then cover the costs of renting substitute equipment and the loss of income from interrupted operations.

The adjustment of a contractors' equipment loss follows the same pattern as an auto physical damage claim. The policy must be reviewed for coverage, the loss must be assessed, and the equipment must be either repaired or replaced.

Contractors' Equipment Policy Provisions

Contractors' equipment is a nonfiled class of insurance in most states, allowing inland marine underwriters to tailor policies to best fit each insured's operation. AAIS and ISO each offer a form for use, or the underwriter may chose to manuscript the policy completely. A contractors' equipment form can be a stand-alone policy or can be added by endorsement to a commercial package policy. Regardless of the form used, the basic policy provisions remain the same.

Declarations Page

The contractors' equipment policy declarations page lists the named insured on the policy. It also lists endorsements for loss payees, such as a financing company or a leasing company, on the covered property.

What Is Insured?

Contractors' equipment insurance covers the insured against loss or damage to mobile equipment, machinery, and tools used in the insured's business. Policy descriptions of covered property often have two components: (1) the applicable coverage basis (scheduled versus blanket) and (2) the policy definition of covered property.

Scheduled Versus Blanket Coverage

Scheduled basis
A basis for insuring each item of insured property by individually describing them in the policy declarations or schedule and assigning a coverage limit to each listed item.

Contractors' equipment insurance can be written on either a scheduled basis or a blanket basis. When written on a **scheduled basis,** each item of insured property is individually described in the policy declarations or schedule, and a limit is assigned to each listed item. A schedule of contractors' equipment also includes a full description of each item so that there is no question of identification or valuation. Information such as the manufacturer, model, model year, and serial number are included with the amount of insurance. The policy excerpt below shows an example of schedule language.

> Property Covered
>
> "We" cover the following property unless the property is otherwise covered, excluded, or subject to limitations.

1. Scheduled Equipment—When Scheduled Equipment is indicated on the "schedule of coverages", "we" cover direct physical loss caused by a covered peril to:
   a. "your" "contractor's equipment"; and
   b. "contractors' equipment" of others in "your" care, custody, or control;

   described on the "equipment schedule".[16]

When a contractors' equipment policy applies on a **blanket basis**, the policy is written for a single amount of insurance covering all items. Blanket insurance eliminates the need for a schedule of covered property, allowing insureds to cover all of their contractors' equipment without having to declare new pieces. Many insurers set a per item limit and a per occurrence limit in their blanket policies.

Blanket basis
A basis for insuring all items within a single amount of insurance without specifically identifying each item.

Many contractors' equipment policies offer both scheduled and blanket coverage. Individually listing and describing smaller items and hand tools can be impractical. Insurers, therefore, schedule higher-value items of equipment and establish a blanket amount of insurance for smaller items of lesser value.

Regardless of how the policy is written, be it scheduled, blanket, or a combination of the two, the policy should contain a list of the equipment associated with the policy. In a scheduled policy, the list is on the declarations page or attached to it. In a blanket policy or in a combined policy, the list of equipment that was used to determine the amount of coverage needed is usually in the underwriting file notes. For a blanket or a combined policy, this list provides some information but is not to be used as an agreed amount or as the item's ACV. The list provides background information and should include the make, model, and serial numbers of the equipment to be covered by the policy.

One of the problems associated with handling contractors' equipment losses is that—unlike autos, which have a standardized VIN—there is no standard form of identification for equipment. A serial number or a component part number can be located anywhere on the piece of equipment. Because there is no standard format for the number, it will not reveal any particular information about the piece of equipment as the VIN does for an auto. However, the number will be helpful if an adjuster must contact the manufacturer for information about the piece.

Covered Property

Insuring equipment on a scheduled or a blanket basis may not guarantee coverage for all property used by the insured. Many contractors that own equipment may also loan or borrow equipment for temporary use. Additionally, many contractors rent equipment from dealers for both short- and long-term use. Generally, the covered property in a scheduled or blanket policy includes property of others as covered property. However, property of others is not always included as covered property. Schedule requirements and differences in covered property provisions can create coverage gaps for newly acquired property, miscellaneous property items of lesser value, and property owned or used by a third party. Additional coverages and endorsements can amend such gaps.

Newly Acquired Property

In contractors' equipment policies written on a scheduled basis, newly purchased equipment is technically not covered. To remedy this, scheduled policies usually include a clause that automatically covers newly acquired property up to a specified amount, provided that the insured reports the new equipment within a stipulated number of days. This clause may be in the form of a coverage extension or an endorsement.

The clause for newly acquired property in scheduled policies generally covers the lesser of a specified dollar amount or a stipulated percentage of the total amount of insurance. For example, newly acquired equipment might be covered for no more than $50,000 or 25 percent of the total amount of the policy, whichever is less. Moreover, the clause may apply to accessories added or improvements made to equipment already scheduled. The piece of equipment is then covered for the scheduled limit plus the value of the improvement.

Property Leased, Rented, or Borrowed

Rental and leasing agreements obligate contractors to return equipment in as good a condition as it was—normal wear and tear excepted—when they took possession of it. A contractor that has leased or rented equipment can be held responsible for damage to the equipment that occurs during the rental period. A contractor will likely want its contractors' equipment policy to cover leased or rented property. Contractors' equipment policies may cover property leased, rented, or borrowed by the insured in any of the following ways: (1) by including property of others in the care or custody of the insured in the Covered Property Provision, (2) by including nonowned property in the Newly Acquired Equipment Clause, or (3) by including a coverage extension or endorsement for property leased, rented, or borrowed from others.

Contractors' equipment policies excluded property loaned, leased, or rented *to* others more often than they exclude property rented *from* others because greater hazards exist when property is removed from the insured's control. Many policies will cover property leased to others only if the insured provides a trained operator for the equipment.

Miscellaneous Property Items

Even when written on a scheduled basis, contractors' equipment policies often include blanket coverage on unscheduled miscellaneous items and hand tools owned, borrowed, or rented for use in the insured's business. A per item limit and a per occurrence limit typically apply to the coverage. Many contractors' equipment policies offer additional coverage for tools, clothing, and miscellaneous property items owned by the insured's employees, subject to limits separate from those for other unscheduled property.

Property Not Covered

Contractors' equipment policies contain various property exclusions. Many policies exclude (1) property in high-risk or uncontrolled working environments and (2) property more suitably covered by other types of insurance. Property exclusions can be modified depending on the insured's needs and the underwriter's assessment of the risk. The following sections describe the property exclusions commonly found in contractors' equipment policies.

Property in High-Risk Working Environments

The working environment of property directly affects its susceptibility to perils. For example, a loader used in underground mining faces perils, such as ceiling collapse, unlikely to occur if the loader were used in above-ground road building operations. That same loader in the custody of a party other than the insured may not be protected by the loss control practices—such as operator training and site security—that the insured would provide. Accordingly, contractors' equipment policies often exclude property located underground or underwater; property while waterborne or airborne; and property loaned, leased, or rented to others. Insurers may develop specific forms and endorsements designed to cover property in high-risk working environments. For instance, contractors that use equipment in water—such as a dredge used in quarry operations—may request that the underwriter delete the exclusion of waterborne property after a review of the risk. Therefore, the adjuster must review the policy and all endorsements carefully to determine what is and is not covered by it.

Property Covered by Other Insurance

Contractors' equipment policies generally exclude property more appropriately insured under other types of insurance policies. Coverage may be arranged for such property under additional coverage parts or policies. Contractors' equipment policies often exclude the following: aircraft and watercraft; money and securities; plans, blueprints, design specifications, and similar property; building materials and supplies; and property intended to become part of a permanent structure. Most contractors' equipment policies also exclude automobiles, motorcycles, motor trucks, trailers, and semitrailers; however, contractors' equipment additional coverages and endorsements exist for certain vehicles. An example of a coverage endorsement directly modifying the exclusion of trailers would indicate where the trailer would be covered, such as at a jobsite or in transit. It would also specify a limit of liability for the coverage.

Covered Causes of Loss

Contractors' equipment policies can be written on either a special-form basis or a named-perils basis. The special-form version typically insures against risks of direct physical loss or damage unless caused by a peril that is limited or excluded. Most contractors' equipment policies today provide special-form coverage.

Underwriters issue named-perils policies less frequently than they issue special-form policies, reserving named-perils policies for insureds desiring lower premiums or insureds posing special risks. Contractors' equipment policies issued on a named-perils basis can be tailored to include coverage for risks specific to the insured's operations. For instance, policies covering mining operations may add coverage for loss caused by slate fall, roof fall, cave-in, landslide, or squeeze.

Exclusions

Contractors' equipment policies usually contain exclusions for war, nuclear hazard, and governmental action but tend not to exclude earthquake and flood. These policies can also exclude mysterious disappearance, inventory shortage, voluntary parting, unauthorized instructions, and dishonest acts of the insured's employees or others to whom property is entrusted. In addition to the general exclusions discussed, a contractors' equipment policy may include some or all of the following exclusions, which may be subject to exceptions that allow coverage for the otherwise excluded exposure (under certain conditions).

1. *Artificially generated electrical currents*. Contractors' equipment can include complex electrical and computer systems that are sensitive to electrical disturbance. An artificially generated electrical current exclusion typically excludes damage caused by short circuits or electrical disturbances within the covered property. The exclusion often contains an exception stating that damage to covered property caused by fire or explosion ensuing from a surge or shortage is covered.
2. *Mechanical breakdown*. Most contractors' equipment policies contain a mechanical breakdown exclusion. The exclusion eliminates coverage for mechanical breakdown or failure—such as a blown head gasket or a broken axle. However, the exclusion typically does not apply to physical loss that *results* from mechanical breakdown provided that the resulting loss is caused by a covered peril. For example, the cost of repairing a fuel line that ruptures because of mechanical breakdown would be excluded. If this breakdown resulted in a fire, the resulting fire damage to the equipment would be covered.
3. *Work upon the property*. Contractors' equipment must be serviced and maintained, but repairs and adjustments may unintentionally damage equipment. Many contractors' equipment policies exclude coverage for work on the property. A "work upon the property" exclusion typically

excludes adjustments, servicing, and maintenance operations, unless fire or explosion ensues, and then only for loss caused by such ensuing fire or explosion.

Special Exclusions

Underwriters may attach exclusions for certain types of equipment, operations, or locations subject to unique perils. Crane operation provides examples of such exclusions.

Crane booms are very susceptible to loss, and operator error can easily damage them. Three types of exclusions apply to cranes and derrick booms: (1) weight-of-load exclusion, (2) tandem lift exclusion, and (3) boom operation exclusion.

A **weight-of-load exclusion** typically excludes loss caused by the weight of the load exceeding the manufacturer's rated capacity of the equipment. Claims involving a weight-of-load exclusion can be very complex to adjust. Should such a loss occur, the insurer would need to refer to manufacturer specifications and the equipment owner's manual, as well as obtain a detailed statement from the equipment operator.

Weight-of-load exclusion
An exclusion that typically does not allow coverage for loss caused by the weight of the load exceeding the manufacturer's rated capacity of the equipment

A **tandem lift exclusion** may be added to contractors' equipment policies to address situations in which two or more cranes are used together to perform a single lift. A tandem lift requires detailed coordination and must be engineered before the lift. Despite extensive pre-planning, tandem lifts performed by well-maintained equipment following specific operating instructions have a higher probability of causing loss or damage to lifting equipment. A tandem lift exclusion may be deleted for an additional premium if the underwriter reviews and accepts engineering plans.

Tandem lift exclusion
An exclusion that applies to losses occurring when two or more cranes are used together to perform a single lift.

If a contractors' equipment policy covering cranes does not contain a weight-of-load or a tandem lift exclusion, it may contain a **boom operation exclusion**. A boom operation exclusion deletes coverage for crane and derrick booms while being operated unless the loss is directly caused by specified perils, such as fire, lightning, hail, windstorm, explosion, riot, aircraft, vehicles, landslide, or overturning. The exclusion is commonly worded so as to prevent payment of claims resulting from such causes as metal fatigue, improper operation of the crane, and a load too heavy for the equipment. Some versions of the boom damage exclusion apply only to booms with a length exceeding a certain number of feet. Other versions preclude payment for a boom loss unless outriggers or stabilizers are extended to their full operating position at the time of loss.

Boom operation exclusion
An exclusion for losses to crane and derrick booms while being operated, unless the loss is directly caused by perils specified in the policy.

Coverage Extensions and Endorsements

Damage to covered property often results in expenses beyond the equipment's value. Many contractors' equipment policies contain coverage for rental reimbursement and business income and extra expense.

Rental Reimbursement Coverage

Rental reimbursement coverage Insurance that pays for expenses that the insured incurs to rent substitute equipment for covered equipment that has been damaged or destroyed by a covered peril.

Many insurers offer rental reimbursement coverage as an additional coverage or endorsement to contractors' equipment policies. **Rental reimbursement coverage** pays the expenses that the insured incurs to rent substitute equipment for covered equipment that has been damaged or destroyed by a covered peril. Because a loss to a piece of contractors' equipment rarely shuts down operations completely, most contractors can continue operations by renting substitute equipment until the damaged equipment can be repaired or replaced. Rental reimbursement coverage is thus a type of extra expense insurance.

Rental reimbursement coverage requires that the rented equipment be necessary to continue the insured's normal operations. Coverage would not apply if the insured has equivalent equipment that is lying idle. Rental reimbursement coverage is usually subject to a waiting period during which coverage does not apply. A typical waiting period is seventy-two hours following the time that the equipment is physically damaged. Rental reimbursement is usually subject to both a per day limit and an overall limit. Coverage ends when the damaged property has been repaired or replaced or the need for it no longer exists, whichever occurs first. The coverage typically requires the insured to exercise due diligence in having the covered property repaired or replaced. Sample rental reimbursement provisions are shown below.

Provisions

1. We will pay you the actual rental expenses up to the limits shown in the Schedule for renting equipment when all of the following apply:
   a. You have a loss to Covered Property;
   b. The equipment is necessary to continue as much as possible the normal operations or work in process;
   c. You do not have the equivalent, idle equipment available.
2. Payment is limited to expense incurred during the period starting 72 hours after the covered loss occurs and ending when the Covered Property has been:
   a. Replaced;
   b. Restored to service; or,
   c. Is no longer needed;

   whichever occurs first.

   Our payment will not be limited by the expiration date of this policy.
3. You and we agree that the Covered Property involved in the loss will be repaired promptly.[17]

Business Income and Extra Expense Coverage

In certain situations, physical loss to equipment can cause time element losses that cannot be adequately handled by rental reimbursement coverage. For example, one high-value, customized piece of equipment (such as a conveyor system in an underground coal mine or a special tower crane) may be an essential part of the insured's operations. If this piece of equipment is destroyed, operations may come to a halt until the equipment can be repaired or replaced. If the equipment's repair or replacement takes several months, the insured can lose several months of income. In such cases, the insured can purchase business income and extra expense coverage. Business income and extra expense coverage, usually added by endorsement, covers lost net income, operating expenses that continue during the business interruption, and extra expenses that the insured incurs to continue normal operations.

The extra expense component of the combined form of business income and extra expense coverage would cover the cost of renting substitute equipment, the cost of overtime labor to expedite repairs, and other reasonable expenses incurred to continue operations. Unlike rental reimbursement coverage, this type of extra expense insurance is not limited to paying the costs associated with renting substitute equipment.

Limits

The limits of insurance in contractors' equipment policies typically apply on a per item and per occurrence basis. Loss payments do not reduce the per item or per occurrence limits unless a total loss occurs to a scheduled item, in which case the item is no longer included in the schedule and any unearned premium on the item is returned to the insured.

Application of the per item and per occurrence limits varies between scheduled and blanket contractors' equipment policies. Scheduled policies establish a limit of insurance for each scheduled item. Policies with a large schedule of equipment may also contain a per occurrence limit, sometimes called a **catastrophe limit**. The catastrophe limit sets a maximum amount that the policy will pay for all property losses associated with a single occurrence. Catastrophe limits may be considerably less than the total of the scheduled limits because the likelihood of a loss to more than one piece of equipment is often minimal.

Catastrophe limit
A maximum amount that a policy will pay for all property losses associated with a single occurrence.

Blanket policies set an overall policy limit that applies to all covered equipment and machinery, often subject to a per item maximum limit. In both scheduled and blanket policies, limits for small tools and miscellaneous items, as well as for other coverages added by endorsement, are payable in addition to the per item and per occurrence limits for contractors' equipment.

Valuation

Most contractors' equipment policies cover on an ACV basis. ACV covers the cost to replace or repair damaged equipment and machinery less depreciation and obsolescence. Rather than depreciating based on the number of miles driven, contractors' equipment depreciates based on its age and its hours of use. Construction and contracting operations place a physical burden on the machinery they use, and wear and tear on contractors' equipment can be considerable. ACV valuation for contractors' equipment accounts for this physical depreciation and seeks to replace damaged equipment with equipment of the same physical condition and value.

Actual cash value can be difficult to assess on partial losses because of the wording of the pair or set language in the policy. Many contractors' equipment policies modify their ACV provisions to account for losses to a pair or set or a loss to equipment parts. For example, the boom of a truck-mounted mobile crane may be damaged by a collision with a nearby structure. Although the crane boom is completely destroyed, the truck to which it is mounted sustains no damage. A pair or set provision in a policy usually states that the loss should not be valued at the actual cash value of the entire truck-mounted mobile crane, but that it should be valued at the cost to repair or replace the crane portion of the equipment because a loss to a part of the unit is not considered a total loss of the pair or set.

Some contractors' equipment policies provide coverage extensions or endorsements that do not adjust losses for depreciation if the loss is less than a certain percentage of the equipment's scheduled value. A waiver of depreciation applies only to ACV policies and provides replacement cost coverage for some partial losses.

Full replacement cost coverage, which replaces lost or damaged equipment with new equipment of like kind and quality at current market prices, may be obtained for an entire schedule of equipment or for specified equipment. Some contractors' equipment policies also offer agreed value coverage by extension or endorsement for scheduled equipment. Agreed value usually applies in two ways: (1) total losses are covered for the amount stated in the equipment schedule, and (2) partial losses are covered for the lesser of the ACV of the property at the time of loss or the cost to repair or replace the damaged equipment with similar equipment.

Coinsurance

Contractors' equipment policies are generally written with an 80, a 90, or a 100 percent coinsurance clause that applies to each separate limit. The coinsurance calculation is as follows:

$$\frac{\text{Did}}{\text{Should}} \times \text{Loss}$$

Adjuster Tip

With a blanket policy, the ACV/RCV of all of the equipment is used in the calculation.

Insurance to Value

As a practical matter, the ACV of contractors' equipment is usually determined as the fair market value of equipment of the same make, age, and condition. Fair market value is "the price that a seller is willing to accept and a buyer is willing to pay on the open market."[18]

Adjusters can use several references to help determine whether the policy limits represent adequate values. The *Green Guide for Construction Equipment* lists current fair market values and specifications for construction equipment and optional attachments up to ten years old. The *Green Guide* also lists approximate resale and replacement cost values that can serve as a basis for determining insurance to value. Adjusters may also gather valuation information from other sources, including local equipment dealers and online equipment brokerage services. Print and electronic trade journals also advertise the prices of new and used construction equipment.

If a contractors' equipment policy requires 80 percent coinsurance, the insurance-to-value minimum for equipment valued for $100,000 at ACV would be $80,000. The replacement cost for the same equipment would be higher, and equipment valued for $120,000 at replacement cost would require a limit of at least $96,000 to meet 80 percent coinsurance requirements. Accurate establishment of insurance to value is important because overvaluing equipment may encourage a moral hazard, and undervaluing equipment can lead to inadequate limits and losses subject to coinsurance penalties.

Deductibles

A deductible may be represented as either a specific dollar amount or as a percentage of the value of the damaged item or scheduled amount. When a percentage deductible is used, minimum and maximum deductible amounts are typically indicated on the declarations page.

In addition to a deductible that applies to covered losses of scheduled equipment, separate deductibles for additional dollar amounts, sometimes called split deductibles, may apply to certain properties or perils. Coverage added by endorsement, such as that for waterborne equipment or employees' tools, may have a separate dollar or percentage deductible. Specific perils may also be subject to a separate deductible. For instance, a deductible provision can show a dollar deductible for all scheduled and blanketed equipment and a separate percentage deductible for losses incurred during boom operation.

Locations Covered

Contractors' equipment policies usually cover property wherever it is located, subject only to the policy's territorial limits. Territorial limits generally include Canada, Puerto Rico, and the continental United States, which includes Alaska. Some policies only cover the *contiguous* United States, which excludes both Hawaii and Alaska. Property located in those states can, at the underwriter's option, be covered by endorsement.

TYPES OF CONTRACTORS' EQUIPMENT

Contractors' equipment can be classified in various ways. The equipment can be self-propelled or in need of transport. If it has to be transported, it may be the type of equipment that can be hauled, such as an excavator, or the type of equipment that can be towed, such as an air compressor. If the equipment is self-propelled, it can be identified by method of travel. It either uses a crawler/track or tires/wheels. The equipment can also be identified by its attachment, such as a loader, backhoe, scraper, grader, or dozer. The proper identification of a piece of equipment usually has both the method of travel and the attachment in its title, such as crawler dozer or wheel loader.

> **Adjuster Tip**
>
> It is important to use the correct name for the piece of equipment. Otherwise, an adjuster's credibility with the insured or the repair facility may be diminished.

Equipment can also fall into categories based on function, such as earth-moving, site improvement, or material handling.

Earth-Moving Equipment

Earth-moving equipment
Equipment that clears job sites and moves, eliminates, or compresses large amounts of earth, rock, snow, debris, construction materials, and other materials.

Earth-moving equipment serves two basic functions necessary in almost every construction project. First, it provides the power to clear job sites and move, eliminate, or compress large amounts of earth, rock, snow, debris, and similar materials. Second, earth-moving equipment can be used to handle and move construction materials and components within the job site. Attachments can be added to further vary the functions of earth-moving equipment, allowing machinery to handle and place irregularly shaped materials, such as pipes. Exhibit 13-12 describes the most common types of earth-moving equipment, and Exhibit 13-13 shows their physical characteristics.

The earth-moving equipment described in Exhibit 13-12 is subject to several perils. Upset and overturn can occur because of rough working terrain, the equipment's large size, the equipment's weight distribution, and carried materials' weight. A high concentration of equipment on a job site can create traffic problems and increase the likelihood of fire and collision. Fire hazards develop from the variety of ignition sources and combustible materials found in equipment and on job sites. The most frequent cause of fire loss involves the breaking of hydraulic lines that operate shovels, buckets, and outriggers. The hydraulic fluid ignites when it is sprayed onto hot engine parts and burns combustible equipment, fuels, and debris allowed to accumulate in or under machinery. Flammable gasoline, oil, and lubricants in construction equipment and the fueling and building supplies stored near equipment increase the fire exposure.

Site-Improvement Equipment

Site-improvement equipment
Pieces of equipment that prepare and finish asphalt and concrete surfaces.

Contractors bring in **site-improvement equipment** after the area has been cleared and leveled by the earth-moving equipment. Primarily, site-improvement equipment prepares and finishes asphalt and concrete surfaces. Mixers

EXHIBIT 13-12

Types of Earth-Moving Equipment

	Uses	Attributes
Backhoe/Excavator	• Excavates below the level of own tracks or wheels for trenching, footing, basement excavation, and similar work. • Handles and places pipes, equipment, and other job site materials.	• Digs by extending hydraulic boom and bucket and then pulling bucket down and toward machine. • Available in different sizes, digging depths, and load capacities. • Attachments available for digging in hard earth, clearing debris from low areas, breaking and loosening rock, and lifting building materials. • Often combined with a front-end loader.
Dozer/Tractor	• Pushes and pulls materials to clear land and remove debris. • Fills in open pits and uneven surfaces. • Prepares ground for paving.	• Available in a number of sizes and horsepower ratings. • Blade attachments available for moving materials of differing weights and densities, ripping imbedded objects, maneuvering in small work areas, cutting trees and low growth, and carrying materials. • Serves as vehicle for attachable or towable equipment such as rollers, trenchers, and forklifts.
Power Shovel	• Excavates material at the face of hillsides or embankments. • Excavates roadbeds. • Loosens and loads material in quarry pits.	• Digs by moving bucket down and away from machine into material and then upward in a lifting motion. • Available in a number of sizes, digging depths, and load capacities.
Loader (Front End, Pay, Scoop, Bucket, Wheel, High Lift, Tractor Shovel)	• Loads and moves loose materials and construction supplies. • Excavates above wheel or track level from level or sloping surface.	• Available in a number of sizes and horsepower ratings. • Variety of bucket sizes and dumping angles. • Attachments available for lifting, debris cleanup, tearing packed materials, removing snow, lifting logs and pipes, etc.
Scraper/Grader	• Removes or relocates large volumes of earth during ground leveling or cut-and-fill operations. • Prepares surfaces for paving. • Scraper performs rough grading. • Grader performs final stage of fill and leveling.	• Scraping/grading device usually has its own towing unit but may be attached to or towed by a tractor. • Available in a number of sizes and horsepower ratings. • Graders may include laser detector and computer-leveling system.
Roller/Compactor	• Compacts earth or asphalt in preparation for laying asphalt or concrete. • Sheepsfoot roller (also called tamper) used for loose earth. • Static or drum roller used for finely granulated materials and smoother surfaces.	• May be self-propelled or attached to a tractor. • May have up to three compaction wheels. • Vibratory function to consolidate sand and soil available on most compaction equipment. • Attachments available to create different surface patterns and textures (such as "rumble strips").
Trencher	• Digs trenches for utility lines, drainage ditches, and similar underground structures.	• Uses a number of small buckets to continuously chew and remove material in the direction of travel. • May be self-propelled or attached to a tractor. • Available in different sizes, digging depths, and trench shapes. • Various models can dig in any type of material other than solid rock.

EXHIBIT 13-13

Earth-Moving Equipment

Dozer

Excavator

Front End Loader

and pavers are often large and difficult to move, making them less prone to theft but more prone to flood or earthquake damage. Additionally, upset, overturn, and vandalism can damage site-improvement equipment. Exhibit 13-14 describes the most common types of site-improvement equipment.

EXHIBIT 13-14

Site-Improvement Equipment

	Uses	Attributes
Batching and Mixing Plant	• Mixes components of paving materials. • Consolidates paving materials for installation.	• Includes automated measuring and mixing systems. • May be stationary or attached to pavers.
Paver	• Applies base, intermediate, and topcoats of asphalt or concrete. • Provides initial compaction of paving material.	• Allows for adjustable paving width and thickness. • Includes microcomputer leveling systems for precision alignment. • May be self-propelled or towed by tractors. • Concrete paver runs on track mountings. • Asphalt paver can be tire or track mounted. • Paver models available for special or smaller jobs such as shoulders, curbs, and sidewalks.
Pavement Planer	• Prepares existing pavement and similar surfaces for repaving. • Removes top layer of earth or pavement to specified depth and texture. • Removes and pulverizes materials for immediate recycling and reuse.	• Uses rotating cutting drum and conveyor to transport cut material for disposal or recycling. • Self-propelled on tracks or wheels. • Available in a variety of sizes from a small version used to create rumble strips to larger machines capable of grinding an entire highway lane.
Finisher	• Creates a smooth surface free from irregularities.	• Different size blades used to cut and scrape raised areas from paved surface. • May be self-propelled, handheld, or attached to a paving machine.

Material-Handling Equipment

To move large amounts of building materials and heavier objects within the site or into position within a structure, many contractors use **material-handling equipment**, typically lifts and cranes. Lifts raise, lower, and transport supplies and personnel within the job site. Cranes raise and move heavy materials. Cranes' lifting capacity varies according to the angle of the lift and the crane's size, strength, and stability. Tire-mounted truck cranes that can be easily moved from site to site may have a lifting capacity of a few tons, while tower cranes, because they are larger and used for a longer duration at one location, may be able to lift hundreds of tons. Crane services specializing in heavy lifts often use cranes that can lift thousands of tons. Exhibits 13-15 through 13-20 describe and illustrate some common types of lifts and cranes.

Material-handling equipment
Equipment that raises, lowers, and transports supplies and personnel within a job site.

EXHIBIT 13-15

Types of Material-Handling Equipment

	Uses	Attributes
Forklift	• Loads and unloads trucks, trailers, and similar vehicles. • Transports and raises building materials from ground level to elevated positions. • Handles heavy single units of packaged materials.	• Hydraulic and telescopic attachments allow for high-lift and forward-reach capabilities. • Attachments available for use in rough terrain, snow, mud, water, and other special conditions. • Attachments available for personnel baskets to permit working at elevations.
Hoist/Lift	• Raises personnel and smaller loads of materials above ground level on a platform. • Supplies materials to larger lifting equipment.	• May be mobile or fixed. • Hoist platform travels on extended mast. • Lift platform raises on scissor formation or telescopic boom. • Available in different heights and platform sizes. • Rough terrain models available.
Mobile Lift Crane (Mechanical and Hydraulic)	• Lifts, moves, and lowers materials. • Transports loads across job site.	• May be self-propelled or truck mounted. • Available in different lifting capacities and traveling speeds. • Lifting capacity and distance dependent on length of boom and mast and type of counterweight. • Attachments available to convert lift (hook) crane to an excavation machine include dragline, shovel, backhoe, and pile driver.
Tower Crane	• Lifts, moves, and places materials for high-rise construction or low-rise construction.	• Usually built on a fixed base, but truck-mounted tower cranes are available for short-duration, high-lift loads. • Freestanding or climbing base (raises and lowers height of mast).
Gantry Crane	• Lifts and moves materials within area spanned by the crane bridge. • Used in construction of precast concrete buildings or foundations in limited working spaces. • Used for dock and shipyard operations.	• Moves along rails mounted on an inverted U-shaped structure. • High-lift capacities available. • Can be designed and built to suit specific needs and operations.
Concrete Pump	• Carries concrete from ground to elevated level through a piping system within boom. • Used in larger projects requiring specific placement of concrete.	• May be mobile or fixed. • Available in different boom lengths and pumping capacities.

A crane is made up of five major components:

1. The base is that part of the crane that stays in contact with the ground during normal operation.
2. The cab sits on top of the base and contains the controls for the crane.
3. The boom is attached to the cab and is the arm that does the lifting.
4. The counterweights are at the rear of the cab and keep the crane from tipping over when it is moving a load.
5. The outriggers are hydraulic arms that extend down from the base. They, too, provide additional support and stability for the crane.[19]

Another important piece of a crane is the jib. This is a lattice-shaped extension that is attached to the boom. It may be set in line with the boom or at an angle to it. The jib allows the crane a greater range of motion than with just a boom. The crane in Exhibit 13-19 is an example of a jib crane. Inside the cab of the crane is an important piece of information called the load chart. This chart shows what the crane's maximum lifting capacity is in a given configuration and its boom extension. The crane's

EXHIBIT 13-16

Material-Handling Equipment

EXHIBIT 13-17

Lifting Crane, Fixed-Boom, Crawler Mounted

EXHIBIT 13-18

Lifting Crane, Fixed Boom, Rubber-Tired

EXHIBIT 13-19

Lifting Crane, Tower Boom, Rubber-Tired

EXHIBIT 13-20

Tower Crane

ability to lift heavy objects depends on the boom's length or extension and the angle that is created by this extension.

The cab also has many indicators in it. A very important one is the load moment indicator. This device warns an operator when a load exceeds a crane's limit.

> **Adjuster Tip**
>
> When investigating a loss involving boom damage that occurred during a lift, the adjuster interviews the operator and asks questions about the load and the load's movement, asks what was the calculated weight of the load, and asks whether it was within the load chart's limits. If the crane is rented, the adjuster determines whether the operator is an employee of the insured or of the rental company and how much experience the operator has.

There are two basic types of cranes: (1) a friction crane and (2) a hydraulic crane. A friction crane uses an open or lattice boom that is made up of several sections. The sections are usually trucked to the worksite and assembled there. Exhibits 13-17, 13-18 and 13-19 show friction cranes. A hydraulic crane

EXHIBIT 13-21

Hydraulic Crane

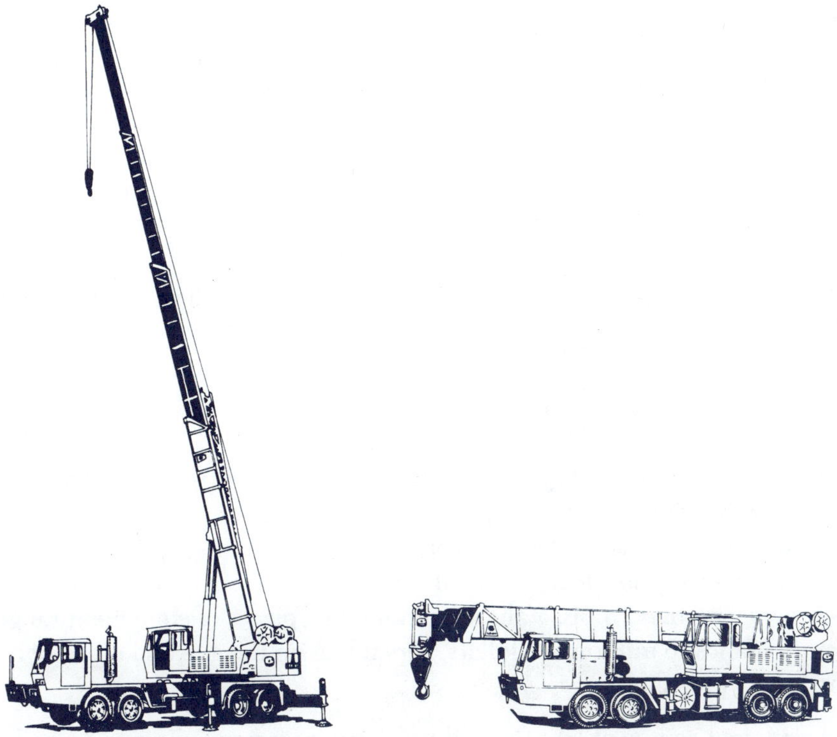

Reprinted with permission from Grove Manufacturing Co., Shady Grove, Pa.

has a telescoping boom that does not require assembly. See Exhibit 13-21. The crane is usually driven to the site, and then the boom is extended.

Booms represent a considerable portion of the crane's value, and collapsed booms generally result in a constructive or total loss. Long booms receive much handling because they are made in sections, erected at the job site, and dismantled when moved to another location. If any of the boom members bend during erection, dismantling, transit, or storage, the boom's structural integrity will be weakened, and it may collapse under a load that it could normally bear. Once a crane is erected, its height increases its exposure to loss by windstorm. Metal fatigue (a weakening in boom members) or weakened cables also contribute to boom collapse.

Booms often sustain damage during lifting operations. Lifting loads in excess of the equipment's lifting capacity or lifting loads in tandem with another crane can bend or twist the boom. Any sudden or uncontrolled movement of the crane, including bumping the boom against adjacent structures, allowing the load to swing into the boom, or releasing the load suddenly, may also cause damage. Upset may occur if crane outriggers or stabilizers are not in use under required conditions.

Other Types of Contractors' Equipment

Other types of contractors' equipment provide supplementary power and support functions to equipment and job sites. Nearly every type of contractor uses a generator, a pump, or an air compressor. In addition to facing loss by the principal perils of fire caused by refueling or poor maintenance, collision during transportation or operation, and flood damage when stored in low-lying areas, miscellaneous pieces of contractors' equipment are prone to theft. The small size, portability, and large market for compressors, generators, and pumps make them prime targets for theft.

TYPES OF OPERATIONS

One of the most familiar types of construction operation is that of a building contractor. Building contractors perform a wide range of specialized construction projects such as land clearing, concrete work, framing, and electrical work. The projects use many different types of mobile equipment, small machinery, and hand tools. Values for individual pieces of equipment range from thousands to millions of dollars, depending on the size and scope of a contractor's projects.

The principal causes of loss for building contractors are theft and vandalism. Contractors may leave equipment at unsecured job sites, allowing access by organized crime rings, disgruntled employees, and vandals. Other common perils include fire from poor equipment and site maintenance, overturn during excavation, and collision with other pieces of equipment or the structure being built. In building operations that use cranes, boom damage may occur as a result of overloading, improper operation, collision with nearby structures, upset from unstable footing, and windstorm.

Other types of operations that use contractors' equipment are road-building contractors, utility contractors, logging operations, mining operations, stevedoring operations, and agricultural operations. Each of these operations has exposures unique to its business, so the adjuster should understand what type of operation the insured is engaged in before going to the loss site or taking a statement.

Exposures and Investigation

Theft and vandalism of contractors' equipment account for the largest percentage of loss occurrences and loss dollars. Given the equipment's mobile nature and the ease of accessibility at job sites, this is not surprising. The investigation of an equipment loss is the same as the investigation for a stolen car, with minor alterations. It is a good practice to take the insured's statement and those of any witnesses who can describe the equipment and its last known location. The adjuster should obtain a police report. A report of the theft should be sent to an index bureau such as NICB, ISO ClaimSearch®, and the National Equipment Register. The National Equipment Register (NER) is a relatively new organization that asks equipment owners to register the piece before any loss. If a theft occurs, the equipment can be identified if recovered or if someone other than the owner attempts to sell the piece.

If the loss involves a rented or leased piece of equipment, the adjuster should obtain a copy of the lease/rental agreement. It may be necessary for the adjuster to contact the owner of the equipment to get the complete identification information and the maintenance history, to determine the equipment's actual condition at the time of loss.

Regardless of the type of loss, it is a good claim practice to obtain the maintenance log for the piece of equipment involved. This often helps in determining the cause of the loss in a fire. It also aids in evaluating the equipment's overall condition for ACV purposes.

Fire is a frequent cause of loss to contractors' equipment. Many fires result from poor maintenance. This is another reason why it is beneficial to obtain the maintenance logs for the piece of equipment involved. If a third party has done some repairs or maintenance immediately before the loss, there is a potential for subrogation.

In addition to boom collapse, overturn is a frequent cause of loss to cranes. An overturn can result from improper set up, exceeding the lift capacity, or soil collapse underneath the crane. If an overturn results from soil collapse, then it is important to determine whether a soil analysis had been done before the crane's use. The soil analysis would determine if the ground was sufficiently solid to support the weight of the crane under full load. It is common on large construction projects for an expert to perform the soil analysis for the general contractor.

The causes and coverages for boom collapse have been previously discussed. Because of the complexity of this type of failure, hiring a structural engineer or failure analysis engineer to determine the cause of loss is usually necessary. The manufacturer often makes repairs to a damaged boom because the crane must be certified as safe to use once the repairs are completed.

VALUATION

Contractors' equipment appraisers, like auto appraisers, are a highly specialized group. If an insurer writes many contractors' equipment policies, a heavy equipment appraiser will probably be on staff. These appraisers are usually certified by a training facility that specializes in heavy equipment. If an independent appraiser is used to inspect losses, the appraiser must be certified.

Total Loss

In the event of a total loss or a constructive total loss, the adjuster must determine ACV. The following factors affect ACV:

- Accessories
- Age
- Hours of use and type of use
- Local market demand
- Maintenance
- Manufacturer
- Prior unrepaired damage
- Salvage
- Type and size

Adjuster Tip

Pieces of contractors' equipment are rarely titled and registered with the state. If a total loss occurs, the adjuster must obtain a signed salvage receipt before taking the equipment.

Resources are available to assist in the calculation of the ACV for contractors' equipment. A canvass of local dealers and resellers will garner information on local values. Many Internet sites also provide global search capabilities for both valuation purposes and possible replacement of the equipment. The most relied-on source is the *Green Guide* that is available in print or online. A list of resources can be found in the course guide.

Business Income Loss

If a major piece of equipment sustains a loss, the equipment may have significant downtime while it awaits repair or replacement. If a piece of equipment is unusual or unique, there may be limited availability of repair parts or replacement equipment. The resulting downtime can result in a loss of revenue, contract penalties, and extra expenses. A contract penalty is an amount specified in the contract for failure to complete the project by a specified date. If the policy covers loss of use, then the adjuster will have to calculate the net income per day for the period of restoration, much like it is calculated for a building loss. The property loss adjuster must carefully review extra expenses in light of the policy terms to determine what may be covered.

SUMMARY

The claim-handling processes for auto physical damage and damage to contractors' equipment are similar. Auto physical damage appraisers and contractors' equipment appraisers have very specialized skills. They inspect and prepare estimates for repair or replacement of vehicles and equipment. They usually submit their estimate to another adjuster who will make a coverage determination and conclude the loss.

While the process may be similar, the coverages are not. The Personal Auto Policy covers individuals and their cars against direct physical loss caused by collision and other than collision. A contractors' equipment policy can cover the physical damage as well as business income loss, extra expense, and rental reimbursement.

Both vehicles and contractors' equipment are identified by a numbering system. The vehicle identification number (VIN) is a unique identifier for autos. It enables the adjuster to determine the manufacturer, the vehicle description, and the production sequence. Contractors' equipment does not have a standard form of identifier. Despite the lack of uniformity in contractors' equipment identifiers, both it and the VIN are valuable in identifying and recovering stolen vehicles and equipment.

The PAP pays the lesser of ACV or the amount necessary to repair or replace the property with other property of like kind and quality. A contractors' equipment policy may have a blanket limit of liability for all pieces of equipment, or the individual pieces may be listed on a schedule, each with their own limit of liability. Contractors' equipment may be written on an ACV or a replacement cost basis. The contractors' equipment policy has a coinsurance provision. The PAP does not have one.

The PAP only covers direct physical loss, but some courts have held that the repaired vehicle has diminished in value and that this amount should be recoverable as well. Diminished value claims are not usually a concern in contractors' equipment claims.

To properly evaluate an appraisal, the adjuster must be familiar with the basic parts of a vehicle and the basic types of equipment that contractors use today. Using the correct terminology helps establish the adjuster's credibility.

Repairs for an auto or a piece of contractors' equipment are established in much the same way. The estimate lists the item or work to be performed, the parts needed, and the labor involved to perform the repair. The prices for parts and labor are found in various estimating reference manuals and software packages.

If a total loss occurs, the adjuster must determine the ACV of the vehicle or equipment at the time of the loss. The salvage value must also be determined, should the item be recovered. Reference manuals and online guides such as the NADA book and the *Green Guide* establish ACV. Some states regulate the manner in which ACV is to be determined. Determining salvage value is usually done by contacting salvage dealers. Payment is then made based on the ACV of the vehicle or equipment, less the deductible and salvage if the insured retains the item. The contractors' equipment claim would also be subject to a coinsurance calculation.

TEXTBOOK SUMMARY

This textbook examined property loss adjusting by discussing coverage provided by the:

- HO-3
- Business and Personal Property Coverage Form (BPP) and its associated causes of loss forms
- National Flood Insurance Program (NFIP)
- Business Income Coverage Forms (BIC)
- Various inland marine and specialty property coverage forms
- Personal Auto Policy
- Contractors' Equipment Policy

The text focused on how to investigate and adjust property losses resulting from various causes of loss, such as fire, lightning, water, and theft. Fraud and arson investigations were discussed. Coverage defenses and the use of the examinations under oath (EUO) were also discussed.

The text detailed how to prepare a scope and estimate by using basic construction methods, terminology, and arithmetic.

It also examined how to adjust, and how to evaluate appraisals in, auto physical damage and contractors' equipment claims.

The framework for coverage analysis and investigation and the creation of a scope and estimate presented in this text can be applied to most property losses. Because each loss presents its own unique set of facts and issues, the property loss adjuster applies his or her expertise and knowledge to bring each loss to a timely, fair, and equitable conclusion.

CHAPTER NOTES

1. World Wide Web: http://www.NICB.org (15 July 2003).
2. Personal Auto Policy, PP 00 01 06 98, Copyright, Insurance Services Office, Inc., 1997.
3. Personal Auto Policy, PP 00 01 06 98, Copyright, Insurance Services Office, Inc., 1997.
4. This section is adapted from *Understanding the Basics of Automotive Estimatics* (Mechanicsburg, Pa.: Vale National Training Center, 1996).

5. Adapted from *Auto Damage Repair Reports*, No. 317 (Newville, Pa.: National Property & Casualty Research Services, Inc., October 1996).
6. "How to Prepare Complete and Accurate Estimates," *Auto Damage Repair Reports*, No. 318 (Newville, Pa.: National Property & Casualty Research Services, Inc., December 1996).
7. *Understanding the Basics of Automotive Estimatics* (Vale National Training Center, 1996), p. 33.
8. "Estimate Reviews," *Auto Damage Repair Reports*, No. 347 (Newville, Pa.: National Property & Casualty Research Services, Inc., October 2001).
9. "Auto Flood Damage Losses," *Auto Damage Repair Reports*, No. 231 (Newville, Pa.: National Property & Casualty Research Services, Inc., June 1982).
10. "Interiors, Cleaning and Restoration," *Auto Damage Repair Reports*, No. 257 (Newville, Pa.: National Property & Casualty Research Services, Inc., October 1986).
11. "Working With Today's Auto Glass," *Auto Damage Repair Reports*, No. 299 (Newville, Pa.: National Property & Casualty Research Services, Inc., October 1993).
12. "Auto Fire Losses," *Auto Damage Repair Reports*, No. 309 (Newville, Pa.: National Property & Casualty Research Services, Inc., June 1995).
13. "Total Losses and the Big Picture," *Auto Damage Repair Reports*, No. 329 (Newville, Pa.: National Property & Casualty Research Services, Inc., October 1998).
14. *Auto Damage Repair Reports*, No. 329.
15. "Maximizing Salvage Returns," *Auto Damage Repair Reports*, No. 330 (Newville, Pa.: National Property & Casualty Research Services, Inc., December 1998).
16. Form IM 7000 1201, Copyright, American Association of Insurance Services.
17. Rental Reimbursement Endorsement, Form IH 68 03 07 99, Copyright, Insurance Services Office, Inc., 1999.
18. *Black's Law Dictionary*, 7th ed. (St. Paul, Minn.: West Publishing Co., 1999).
19. *Cranes* (Greenfield, Mass.: Douglas G. Peterson and Associates, Inc., 2002).

Index

Page numbers in boldface refer to definitions of Key Words and Phrases.

A

B

C

D

E

F

G

H

I

N

O

P